Teacher Wraparound Edition

GLENCOE FRENCH 2

Bon voyage!

With features by
NATIONAL GEOGRAPHIC

Conrad J. Schmitt • Katia Brillié Lutz

 Glencoe

New York, New York   Columbus, Ohio   Chicago, Illinois   Peoria, Illinois   Woodland Hills, California

Copyright © 2005 by The McGraw-Hill Companies, Inc. All rights reserved. Except as permitted under the United States Copyright Act, no part of this publication may be reproduced or distributed in any form or by any means, or stored in a database or retrieval system, without the prior permission of the publisher.

Send all inquiries to:
Glencoe/McGraw-Hill
8787 Orion Place
Columbus, Ohio 43240-4027

ISBN 0-07-865660-5 *(Student Edition)*
ISBN 0-07-865661-3 *(Teacher Wraparound Edition)*

Printed in the United States of America.

3 4 5 6 7 8 9 10   055/058   10 09 08 07 06

From the Authors

Itinerary for Success
- ✓ Exposure to Francophone culture
- ✓ Clear expectations and goals
- ✓ Thematic, contextualized vocabulary
- ✓ Useful and thematically linked structure
- ✓ Progressive practice
- ✓ Real-life conversation
- ✓ Cultural readings in the target language
- ✓ Connections to other disciplines . . . in French!
- ✓ Recycling and review
- ✓ **National Geographic Society** panoramas of the Francophone world

Dear French Teacher,

Welcome to Glencoe's **Bon voyage!** French program. We hope you will find that the way in which we have organized the presentation of the French language and Francophone cultures will make the French language more teachable for you and more learnable for your students.

Upon completion of each chapter of **Bon voyage!** your students will be able to communicate in French in a real-life situation. The high-frequency, productive vocabulary presented at the beginning of the chapter focuses on a specific communicative topic and covers key situations where students would have to use French to survive. The structure point that follows the vocabulary presentation will enable students to put their new words together to communicate coherently.

After students acquire the essential vocabulary and structure needed to function in a given situation, we present a realistic conversation that uses natural, colloquial French and, most importantly, French that students can readily understand. To introduce students to the culture of the Francophone world, the chapter topic is subsequently presented in a cultural milieu in narrative form. The **Lectures culturelles** recombine known language and enable students to read and learn—in French—about the fascinating cultures of the people who speak French.

Any one of us who has taught French realizes the importance of giving students the opportunity to practice, a factor so often overlooked in many textbooks today. Throughout **Bon voyage!** we provide students with many opportunities to use their French in activities with interesting and varied, but realistic, formats. The activities within each chapter progress from simple, guided practice to more open-ended activities that may use all forms of the particular structure in question. Finally, activities that encourage completely free communication enable students to recall and reincorporate all the French they have learned up to that point.

We are aware that your students have varied learning styles and abilities. For this reason we have provided a great deal of optional material in **Bon voyage!** to permit you to pick and choose material appropriate for the needs of your classes. In this Teacher Wraparound Edition we have clearly outlined the material that is required, recommended, or optional in each chapter.

Many resources accompany **Bon voyage!** to help you vary and enliven your instruction. We hope you will find these materials not only useful but an integral part of the program. However, we trust you will agree that the Student Text is the lifeline of any program; the supporting materials can be used to reinforce and expand upon the themes of the main text.

Again, we hope that your yearlong journey with each of your classes will indeed be a **Bon voyage!**

Bien amicalement,
Conrad J. Schmitt • Katia Brillié Lutz

Table des matières

Teacher Edition

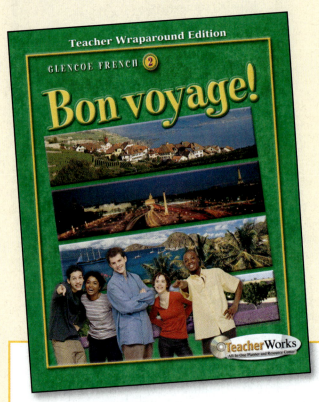

Scope and Sequence	T6
Pacing and Leveling	T19
Rubrics	T20
Web Strategies	T22
Special Needs	T24
Reading Strategies and Skills	T26
A Guided Tour of the Student Edition	T30
A Guided Tour of the Teacher Edition	T46
Bon voyage! Resources	T50
French Names	T54
Classroom Expressions	T55
Standards for Foreign Language Learning	T56

Student Edition
La francophonie

Révision
- **A** Les copains et l'école
- **B** La famille
- **C** Les courses
- **D** En voyage
- **E** Les sports
- **F** La routine quotidienne

Chapitre 1
Les loisirs culturels

Chapitre 2
La santé et la médecin

Chapitre 3
Les télécommunications

Chapitre 4
Des voyages intéressants

Révision Chapitres 1–4

NATIONAL GEOGRAPHIC Reflets de la France

LITERARY COMPANION

Littérature 1
Le Livre de mon père
Émile Henriot

Table des Matières

CHAPITRE 5
La banque et la poste

CHAPITRE 6
La gastronomie

CHAPITRE 7
La voiture et la route

> **Révision** Chapitres 5–7
> NATIONAL GEOGRAPHIC Reflets du Maghreb
> **LITERARY COMPANION**
> **Littérature 2**
> *Deux poèmes africains*

CHAPITRE 8
Un accident et l'hôpital

CHAPITRE 9
L'hôtel

CHAPITRE 10
Les transports en commun

CHAPITRE 11
À la ville et à la campagne

> **Révision** Chapitres 8–11
> NATIONAL GEOGRAPHIC Reflets des Caraïbes
> **LITERARY COMPANION**
> **Littérature 3**
> *Vol de nuit*
> Antoine de Saint-Exupéry

CHAPITRE 12
Les fêtes

CHAPITRE 13
Le savoir-vivre

CHAPITRE 14
Les professions et les métiers

> **Révision** Chapitres 12–14
> NATIONAL GEOGRAPHIC Reflets de l'Europe francophone
> **LITERARY COMPANION**
> **Littérature 4**
> *Le Malade imaginaire*
> Molière

HANDBOOK
InfoGap Activities
Study Tips
Verb Charts
French-English Dictionary
English-French Dictionary
Index

Scope and Sequence

Glencoe's **Bon voyage!** is a carefully articulated program written by experienced authors. The Scope and Sequence of **Bon voyage!** ensures that students are presented with material in a way that enables them to build the skills they need to become proficient in French. To allow you flexibility in moving through the program there is a review section at the beginning of **Bon voyage!** Level 2. In addition, Chapters 13 and 14 of Level 1 are repeated as Chapters 1 and 2 of Level 2. The subjunctive is presented in Chapter 12 of **Bon voyage!** Level 2 but is presented as brand new material in **Bon voyage!** Level 3.

LEVEL 1

■ Preliminary Lessons

Topics
- Greeting people
- Saying good-bye
- Finding out a person's name
- Ordering food
- The calendar
- Telling time

Functions
- How to greet people
- How to say good-bye to people
- How to ask people how they are
- How to ask and tell names
- How to express simple courtesies
- How to find out and tell the days of the week
- How to find out and tell the months of the year
- How to count from 1–30
- How to find out and tell the time

Chapitre 1

Topics
- Describing people
- Numbers 30–69

Culture
- Victor Gabriel Gilbert, *Enfants jouant au cerceau*
- French language in Africa
- Henri de Toulouse-Lautrec
- Connections—Geography of France

Functions
- How to ask or tell what someone is like
- How to ask or tell where someone is from
- How to ask or tell who someone is
- How to describe yourself or someone else

Structure
- Singular forms of definite and indefinite articles—**le, la, un, une**
- Agreement of adjectives
- Present singular forms of the verb **être**
- Making a sentence negative

Chapitre 2

Topics
- School
- Class subjects
- Numbers 70–100

Culture
- Pierre Bonnard, *Écriture de fille*
- French language in Haiti, Canada, Louisiana
- High school in France
- E-mail in French
- Connections—Biology, physics, and chemistry

Functions
- How to describe people and things
- How to talk about more than one person or thing
- How to tell what subjects you take in school and express some opinions about them
- How to speak to people formally and informally

Structure
- Plural forms of nouns, articles, and adjectives
- Present plural forms of **être**
- **Tu** and **vous**

Scope and Sequence

LEVEL 1

Chapitre 3

Topics
- The school day
- School supplies
- Numbers 100–1000

Culture
- Pierre Auguste Renoir, *La lecture*
- Jacqueline, a French student
- Antoine, a working Canadian student
- Popular French music: Manau
- Connections—Computers and technology

Functions
- How to talk about what you do in school
- How to talk about what you and your friends do after school
- How to identify and shop for school supplies
- How to talk about what you don't do
- How to tell what you and others like and don't like to do

Structure
- Present tense of **-er** verbs
- Negative indefinite articles

Chapitre 4

Topics
- Members of the family
- Birthdays
- Houses
- Apartments
- The rooms of a house

Culture
- Pierre Auguste Renoir, *Madame Charpentier et ses enfants*
- Housing in France
- Housing in French-speaking countries
- Origins of French names
- Connections—Art and history

Functions
- How to talk about your family
- How to describe your home and neighborhood
- How to tell your age and find out someone else's age
- How to tell what belongs to you and others
- How to describe more people and things

Structure
- Present tense of **avoir**
- Possessive adjectives
- Singular and plural adjectives

Chapitre 5

Topics
- Going to a café
- Names of food
- Eating utensils
- Going to a restaurant
- Meals

Culture
- Vincent Van Gogh, *Terrasse du café le soir*
- Three friends go to dinner at a restaurant in France
- Meals in France
- Popular foods in France
- Connections—Arithmetic

Functions
- How to order food or a beverage at a café or restaurant
- How to tell where you and others go
- How to tell what you and others are going to do
- How to give locations
- How to tell what belongs to you and others
- How to describe more activities

Structure
- Present tense of **aller**
- **Aller** + infinitive
- Contractions with **à** and **de**
- Present tense of **prendre**

Scope and Sequence

LEVEL 1

Chapitre 6

Topics
- Types of food
- Shopping for food
- Open-air market
- Supermarket

Culture
- Paul Cézanne, *Nature morte au panier*
- Shopping for food in small stores in Paris
- Shopping at the hypermarket in France
- Open-air markets in French-speaking countries
- Connections—Metric conversions

Functions
- How to identify more foods
- How to shop for food
- How to tell what you or others are doing
- How to ask for the quantity you want
- How to talk about what you or others don't have
- How to tell what you or others are able to do or want to do

Structure
- Present tense of **faire**
- The partitive and the definite article
- Negative form of the partitive
- Present tense of **pouvoir** and **vouloir**

Chapitre 7

Topics
- Clothing
- Shopping for clothes
- Sizes and colors

Culture
- **Un tissu de la Côte d'Ivoire**
- Shopping for clothes in Paris
- Shopping for clothes in Africa
- Differences between shoe and clothing sizes in the United States and in France
- Connections—Poetry

Functions
- How to identify and describe articles of clothing
- How to state color and size preferences
- How to shop for clothing
- How to describe people's activities
- How to compare people and things
- How to express opinions and make observations

Structure
- Present tense of **mettre**
- Comparative adjectives
- Present tense of **voir** and **croire**

Chapitre 8

Topics
- The airport
- On board an airplane

Culture
- René Magritte, *La grande famille*
- A trip to Paris
- International time zones
- Antoine de Saint-Exupéry
- Connections—Climate

Functions
- How to check in for a flight
- How to talk about some services aboard the plane
- How to talk about more activities
- How to ask more questions
- How to talk about people and things as a group

Structure
- Present tense of **-ir** verbs
- **Quel** and **tout**
- **Sortir, partir, dormir,** and **servir**

Scope and Sequence

LEVEL 1

Chapitre 9

Topics
- The train station
- On the train

Culture
- Claude Monet, *La locomotive*
- Train travel in French-speaking Africa
- Erica Saunders, an American student travels by train in France
- Connections—The 24-hour clock and the metric system

Functions
- How to purchase a train ticket and request information about arrival and departure
- How to use expressions related to train travel
- How to talk about people's activities
- How to point out people or things

Structure
- Present tense of **-re** verbs
- Demonstrative adjectives
- **Dire, écrire,** and **lire**

Chapitre 10

Topics
- Soccer
- Basketball
- Volleyball
- Bicycling
- Running

Culture
- Robert Delaunay, *Les coureurs*
- Hockey and basketball in French-speaking countries
- Le Tour de France
- Connections—Anatomy

Functions
- How to talk about team sports and other physical activities
- How to describe past actions and events
- How to ask people questions

Structure
- **Passé composé** of regular verbs
- **Qui, qu'est que, quoi**
- Present tense of **boire, devoir,** and **recevoir**

Chapitre 11

Topics
- Summer weather and activities
- Spring
- Winter weather and activities
- Autumn

Culture
- Maurice Utrillo, *Montmartre sous la neige*
- A trip through Quebec, Canada
- Some of the best places to vacation in France
- Carnival in Quebec
- Connections—French painters

Functions
- How to describe summer and winter weather
- How to talk about summer activities
- How to talk about winter sports
- How to discuss past actions and events
- How to make negative statements

Structure
- **Passé composé** of irregular verbs
- Negative statements
- **Passé composé** with **être**

Scope and Sequence

LEVEL 1

Chapitre 12

Topics
- Daily routine
- The kitchen
- Watching television

Culture
- Edgar Degas, *Toilette matinale*
- An Algerian family living outside of Paris
- Differences between breakfast foods in the United States and in French-speaking countries
- Connections—Ecology

Functions
- How to describe your personal grooming habits
- How to talk about your daily routine
- How to talk about your family life
- How to tell some things you do for yourself
- How to talk about daily activities in the past

Structure
- Reflexive verbs in the present
- Reflexive verbs in the **passé composé**

Chapitre 13

Topics
- Going to the movies
- Going to the theater
- Going to a museum

Culture
- Des statues béninoises de seizième siècle
- Cultural sites in France
- African music
- Connections—Music

Functions
- How to discuss movies, plays, and museums
- How to tell what you know and whom you know
- How to tell what happens to you or someone else
- How to refer to people and things already mentioned

Structure
- Present tense of **savoir** and **connaître**
- Indirect object pronouns
- Direct object pronouns

Chapitre 14

Topics
- Minor illness
- Parts of the body
- The doctor's office
- The pharmacy

Culture
- Édouard Vuillard, *Le docteur Viau dans son cabinet*
- Doctors making house calls in France
- Comparing the cultural view of health in the United States and in France
- Medical services in France
- Connections—Diet

Functions
- How to explain a minor illness to a doctor
- How to have a prescription filled at a pharmacy
- How to tell for whom something is done
- How to talk about some more activities
- How to give commands
- How to refer to people, places, and things

Structure
- Pronouns **lui, leur**
- Present tense of **souffrir** and **ouvrir**
- Commands
- The pronoun **en**

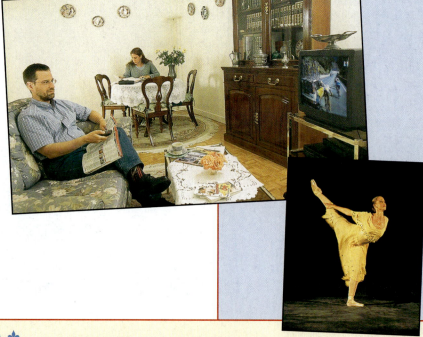

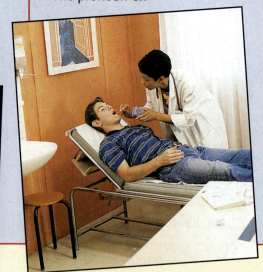

Scope and Sequence

LEVEL 2

Review Lessons

Topics
- Friends and school
- The family
- The home
- Birthdays
- Food shopping
- Clothes shopping
- Traveling by train
- Traveling by airplane
- Summer weather and activities
- Winter weather and activities
- Soccer
- Daily routine

Functions
- How to describe people
- How to describe a home
- How to describe a family
- How to talk about shopping for food and clothing
- How to discuss traveling by train and airplane
- How to describe the seasons and summer and winter activities
- How to tell about daily routines

Structure
- Agreement of adjectives
- Present tense of **être** and **aller**
- Contractions
- Regular **-er** verbs
- The partitive
- Present tense of **avoir** and **faire**
- Present tense of **vouloir** and **pouvoir**
- The infinitive
- Present tense of **prendre**
- **-ir** and **-re** verbs
- Present tense of **sortir, partir, dormir,** and **servir**
- **Passé composé** of regular verbs with **avoir**
- Irregular past participles
- Reflexive verbs in the present tense
- **Passé composé** with **être**
- Reflexive verbs in the **passé composé**

Chapitre 1

Topics
- Going to the movies
- Going to the theater
- Going to a museum

Culture
- **Des statues béninoises de seizième siècle**
- Cultural sites in France
- African music
- Connections—Music

Functions
- How to discuss movies, plays, and museums
- How to tell what you know and whom you know
- How to tell what happens to you or someone else
- How to refer to people and things already mentioned

Structure
- Present tense of **savoir** and **connaître**
- Indirect object pronouns
- Direct object pronouns

Chapitre 2

Topics
- Minor illness
- Parts of the body
- The doctor's office
- The pharmacy

Culture
- Édouard Vuillard, *Le docteur Viau dans son cabinet*
- Doctors making house calls in France
- Comparing the cultural view of health in the United States and in France
- Medical services in France
- Connections—Diet

Functions
- How to explain a minor illness to a doctor
- How to have a prescription filled at a pharmacy
- How to tell for whom something is done
- How to talk about some more activities
- How to give commands
- How to refer to people, places, and things

Structure
- Pronouns **lui, leur**
- Present tense of **souffrir** and **ouvrir**
- Commands
- The pronoun **en**

Scope and Sequence

LEVEL 2

Chapitre 3

Topics
- Computers
- Fax machines
- Telephones
- Making telephone calls

Culture
- Maurice de Vlaminck, *La route*
- Different kinds of telephones
- Telephone cards in French-speaking countries
- Communicating over distance before telephones
- Connections—History of the computer

Functions
- How to talk about computers, e-mail, the Internet, faxes, and telephones
- How to talk about habitual and continuous actions in the past
- How to narrate in the past

Structure
- Forming the imperfect
- Using the imperfect

Chapitre 4

Topics
- The train station
- Riding in a train
- The airport
- Flying in an airplane

Culture
- Claude Monet, *La gare Saint-Lazare*
- Trains of today and yesterday in France
- A trip to Switzerland
- A trip to Benin
- Connections—Archeology in the French-speaking world

Functions
- How to talk about train travel
- How to talk about air travel
- How to describe past events
- How to identify cities, countries, and continents

Structure
- The imperfect versus the **passé composé**
- Telling a story in the past tense
- Present tense of **venir**
- Prepositions with geographic names

Chapitre 5

Topics
- The bank
- Exchanging currency
- Managing money
- The post office
- Mailing letters

Culture
- Vincent Van Gogh, *Le facteur Joseph Roulin*
- Allowances in France
- Monetary units in the United States and in the French-speaking world
- The post office in the United States and in France
- Connections—Personal finance

Functions
- How to talk about using the services of the bank
- How to use words and expressions related to postal services
- How to give more information in one sentence
- How to refer to people and things already mentioned
- How to tell what you and others do for one another
- How to make negative statements

Structure
- Relative pronouns **qui** and **que**
- Past participle agreement
- Reciprocal actions
- Negative statements

Scope and Sequence

LEVEL 2

Chapitre 6

Topics
- The kitchen
- Types of food
- Recipes
- Preparing food

Culture
- Henri Matisse, *L'harmonie en rouge*
- Different cuisines across France
- Dinner with a Moroccan family
- A recipe in French
- Connections—François Rabelais

Functions
- How to talk about foods and food preparation
- How to describe future events
- How to refer to people and things already mentioned
- How to tell what you have others do

Structure
- Forming the future tense
- Two pronouns in the same sentence—**me, te, nous**
- **Faire** + infinitive

Chapitre 7

Topics
- Traveling by car
- Trucks and motorcycles
- Reading a map
- Driving on the highway

Culture
- Tamara de Lempicka, *Autoportrait*
- Driving in France
- Tunisia
- Connections—Ecology

Functions
- How to talk about cars and driving
- How to give directions on the road
- How to talk about what would happen under certain conditions
- How to describe future events
- How to refer to something already mentioned

Structure
- The conditional
- The future and conditional of irregular verbs
- **Si** clauses
- Two pronouns in the same sentence—**le, la, les**

Chapitre 8

Topics
- Accidents
- The emergency room
- Parts of the body
- The doctor's office
- Surgery

Culture
- Jean Geoffroy, *Le jour de la visite à l'hôpital*
- L'Hôtel-Dieu, a hospital in Paris
- Doctors Without Borders
- Connections—Louis Pasteur

Functions
- How to talk about accidents and medical problems
- How to talk about emergency room procedures
- How to ask different types of questions
- How to tell people what to do
- How to compare people and things

Structure
- Interrogative and relative pronouns
- Commands with pronouns
- The superlative of adjectives
- Expressing "better"

Scope and Sequence

LEVEL 2

Chapitre 9

Topics
- Checking into a hotel
- The hotel room
- The bathroom
- Checking out of a hotel

Culture
- Philippe Lebas, *Hôtel Negresco, Nice*
- A trip to Nice
- Youth Hostels in France
- Club Med in French-speaking countries
- Connections—Language, the word hôtel

Functions
- How to check into and out of a hotel
- How to ask for things you may need while at a hotel
- How to talk about past actions
- How to refer to previously mentioned places
- How to talk about people and things already mentioned
- How to describe how you do things

Structure
- **Passé composé** of **être** and **avoir**
- The pronoun **y**
- Pronoun + **en**
- Formation of adverbs

Chapitre 10

Topics
- The subway
- The bus

Culture
- G. E. Ducasse, *Quand les camionettes sont en marches à l'avenue J. J. Dessalines à Port-au-Prince*
- The metro and the bus in Paris
- Public transportation in the French-speaking world
- Connections—Literature

Functions
- How to talk about public transportation
- How to request information formally and informally
- How to tell what you and others have just done
- How to find out how long someone has been doing something

Structure
- Questions
- **Venir** + infinitive
- Expressing time

Chapitre 11

Topics
- The city
- Parking in the city
- The country
- Farm animals

Culture
- **Ornement traditionnel du Mali**
- A farming family in France
- Abidjan, Ivory Coast
- Montreal, Canada
- Connections—Sociology

Functions
- How to talk about life in the city and give directions
- How to talk about life in the country
- How to ask questions to distinguish between two or more people or things
- How to describe some more activities

Structure
- **Lequel** and **celui-là**
- Present tense of **suivre**, **conduire**, **vivre**
- Infinitive after prepositions

Scope and Sequence

LEVEL 2

Chapitre 12

Topics
- 14th of July
- Carnival
- Christmas
- Hanukah
- The New Year
- Marriage

Culture
- André Lhote, *Le 14 juillet 1931*
- Holidays in France
- Carnival in the French-Speaking world
- Connections—Henry Wadsworth Longfellow

Functions
- How to talk about holidays and celebrations
- How to talk about things that may or may not happen
- How to express what you wish, hope, or would like others to do

Structure
- The subjunctive
- The subjunctive with wishes and commands

Chapitre 13

Topics
- Parts of the body
- Manners
- Emotions
- Introductions

Culture
- Berthe Morisot, *Au Bal*
- Manners in the United States and in France
- **Tu** versus **vous**
- Greetings in French-speaking Africa
- Connections—Literature

Functions
- How to talk about social etiquette
- How to introduce people to each other
- How to describe some feelings
- How to express opinions
- How to talk about more things that may or may not happen
- How to express emotional reactions to what others do

Structure
- Expressing opinion with the subjunctive
- Irregularities in forming the subjunctive
- Expressing emotion with the subjunctive

Chapitre 14

Topics
- Professions
- Trades
- Finding a job
- The workplace

Culture
- Fernand Léger, *Les constructeurs*
- The career of an ambassador
- American corporations in France
- Classified ads in French
- Connections—Economy

Functions
- How to talk about professions
- How to apply for a job
- How to express doubt
- How to express wishes about yourself and others
- How to express certainty and uncertainty

Structure
- Expressing doubt with the subjunctive
- Infinitive versus subjunctive
- The subjunctive in relative clauses

Scope and Sequence

LEVEL 3

Chapitre 1

Topics
- Summer activities
- Winter activities
- Camping
- Taking vacations
- Travel by car, train, and airplane
- Weather

Culture
- Travel habits of the French
- Modes of transportation in France
- A weather report from a French newspaper
- A magazine advertisement for a hotel in Tunisia

Functions
- How to get the information you need in different travel situations
- How to describe past actions
- How to read and discuss newspaper and magazine articles
- How to talk about actions that may or may not take place
- How to express wishes, preferences, necessity, or possibility

Structure
- The **passé composé** with **avoir** and regular verbs
- The **passé composé** with **avoir** and irregular verbs
- The **passé composé** with **être**
- The **passé composé** with **avoir** versus **être**
- The subjunctive of regular verbs
- The subjunctive of irregular verbs
- Using the subjunctive to express necessity and possibility

Chapitre 2

Topics
- Everyday life of young people in France
- Shopping

Culture
- Language used by young people in France
- Equality between men and women in France

Functions
- How to ask questions formally and informally
- How to make sentences negative
- How to describe things in the past
- How to express wishes, preferences
- How to express actions that may or may not take place

Structure
- Formal and informal questions
- Negative sentences
- The imperfect
- Expressing wishes, preferences, and demands
- The subjunctive versus the infinitive
- Irregular forms in the subjunctive

Chapitre 3

Topics
- Leisure activities in French-speaking countries
- Cultural events in France
- Music

Culture
- Useful and inexpensive pastimes in French-speaking countries

Functions
- How to talk about actions in the past
- How to compare people and things
- How to express emotional reactions to others, uncertainty, and uniqueness
- How to express emotions or opinions about past events

Structure
- The **passé composé** versus the imperfect
- Comparative and superlative adjectives
- Expressing emotional reactions using the subjunctive
- Expressing uncertainty or uniqueness using the subjunctive
- The past subjunctive

Scope and Sequence

LEVEL 3

Chapitre 4

Topics
- North and West Africa

Culture
- Léopold Senghor
- The Touareg people

Functions
- How to use prepositions with geographical names
- How to refer to things already mentioned
- How to say what you and other people will do or might do
- How to express uncertainty and doubt
- How to use certain time expressions

Structure
- The imperfect versus the **passé composé**
- Telling a story in the past tense
- Prepositions with geographic names
- The pronoun **y**
- The future tense
- The conditional
- The subjunctive with expressions of doubt
- The present and the imperfect with **depuis**

Chapitre 5

Topics
- French media
- The police and firefighters
- Social problems and petty crime

Culture
- French newspapers
- French magazine articles

Functions
- How to tell what you do for others
- How to tell what others do for you
- How to refer to people and things already mentioned
- How to use the subjunctive after certain conjunctions

Structure
- Direct and indirect object pronouns
- Using two object pronouns in a sentence
- Object pronouns with commands
- Using the subjunctive after certain conjunctions

Chapitre 6

Topics
- French customs

Culture
- Day care for children in France
- Public notices in a French newspaper

Functions
- How to express some and any
- How to refer to things already mentioned
- How to express who, whom, which, and that
- How to express of which and whose
- How to talk about past actions that precede other past actions
- How to express what would have happened if certain conditions had prevailed
- How to express conditions

Structure
- Partitive articles with indefinite quantities
- The pronoun **en**
- Relative pronouns **qui** and **que**
- Relative pronoun **dont**
- The **plus-que-parfait**
- The past conditional
- Expressing conditions with **si**

Scope and Sequence

LEVEL 3

Chapitre 7

Topics
- Public health
- Exercise
- Going to the doctor's office
- Nutrition

Culture
- Articles about hearing loss, sound, and noise pollution
- Article about what time of day is best to play certain sports

Functions
- How to tell what people do or did for themselves and for others
- How to ask who, whom, and what
- How to express which one, this one, that one, these, and those
- How to tell what belongs to you and to others

Structure
- Reflexive verbs
- The **passé composé** of reflexive verbs
- Interrogative pronoun **qui**
- Interrogative pronouns **que** and **quoi**
- Interrogative and demonstrative pronouns
- Possessive pronouns

Chapitre 8

Topics
- French heritage

Culture
- The death of Napoleon
- Festivals in France

Functions
- How to tell what you and others have people do for you
- How to express actions that occurred prior to other actions
- How to form complex sentences
- How to tell what you and others will do before a future event
- How to talk about two related actions

Structure
- Causative constructions with **faire**
- Past infinitive
- Prepositions with relative pronouns
- The future perfect
- The present participle and the **gérondif**

Pacing and Leveling

Each chapter of **Bon voyage!** contains required, recommended, and optional material. **Vocabulaire, Structure,** and **Conversation** sections are always required. The recommended sections include the first cultural reading in **Lectures culturelles, C'est à vous,** and **Assessment. Lectures supplémentaires, Connexions,** and **On parle super bien!** are optional. The following chart provides you with a guide to the number of required, recommended, and optional pages in each of the fourteen chapters.

Chapter Planning in the Student Edition

	required number of pages	recommended number of pages	optional number of pages
Chapter 1	15	7	8
Chapter 2	15	7	8
Chapter 3	17	7	8
Chapter 4	19	7	8
Chapter 5	17	7	8
Chapter 6	17	7	8
Chapter 7	17	7	8
Chapter 8	17	7	8
Chapter 9	15	7	8
Chapter 10	15	7	8
Chapter 11	13	7	8
Chapter 12	15	7	8
Chapter 13	15	7	8
Chapter 14	15	7	8
Total:	222 required	98 recommended	112 optional

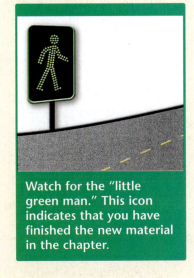

Watch for the "little green man." This icon indicates that you have finished the new material in the chapter.

LEVELING

The activities, conversations, and readings within each chapter are marked according to level of difficulty. **E** indicates easy. **A** indicates average. **C** indicates challenging. Some activities cover a range of difficulty. In some activities, for example, advanced students will be able to produce more extensive responses while students who learn at a different rate may give less detailed responses. The leveling indicators will help you individualize instruction to best meet your students' needs.

Note: Chapters 13 and 14 of **Bon voyage! Level 1** are repeated as Chapters 1 and 2 of **Bon voyage! Level 2** for additional flexibility.

Rubric for Speaking

Analytic Scoring Guide for Rating Speaking Products

VOCABULARY

4. Vocabulary is generally accurate and appropriate to the task; minor errors, hesitations, and circumlocutions may occur.

3. Vocabulary is usually accurate; errors, hesitations, and circumlocutions may be frequent.

2. Vocabulary is not extensive enough for the task; inaccuracies or repetition may be frequent; may use English words.

1. Vocabulary inadequate for most basic aspects of the task.

0. No response.

GRAMMAR

4. Grammar may contain some inaccuracies, but these do not negatively affect comprehensibility.

3. Some grammatical inaccuracies may affect comprehensibility; some control of major patterns.

2. Many grammatical inaccuracies may affect comprehensibility; little control of major patterns.

1. Almost all grammatical patterns inaccurate, except for a few memorized patterns.

0. No response.

PRONUNCIATION

4. Completely or almost completely comprehensible; pronunciation errors, rhythm and/or intonation problems do not create misunderstandings.

3. Generally comprehensible, but pronunciation errors, rhythm and/or intonation problems may create misunderstandings.

2. Difficult to comprehend because of numerous pronunciation errors, rhythm, and intonation problems.

1. Practically incomprehensible.

0. No response.

MESSAGE CONTENT

4. Relevant, informative response to the task. Adequate level of detail and creativity.

3. Response to the task is generally informative; may lack some detail and/or creativity.

2. Response incomplete; lacks some important information.

1. Response not informative; provides little or no information.

0. No response.

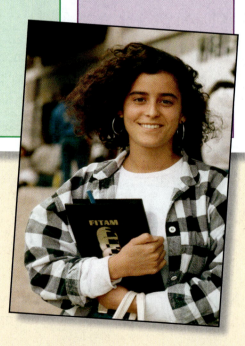

Rubric for Writing

Analytic Scoring Guide for Rating Writing Products

VOCABULARY

4. Vocabulary is generally accurate and appropriate to the task; minor errors may occur.

3. Vocabulary is usually accurate; occasional inaccuracies may occur.

2. Vocabulary is not extensive enough for the task; inaccuracies may be frequent; may use English words.

1. Vocabulary inadequate for most basic aspects of the task.

0. No response.

GRAMMAR

4. Grammar may contain some inaccuracies, but these do not negatively affect comprehensibility.

3. Some grammatical inaccuracies may affect comprehensibility; some control of major patterns.

2. Many grammatical inaccuracies may affect comprehensibility; little control of major patterns.

1. Almost all grammatical patterns inaccurate, except for a few memorized patterns.

0. No response.

SPELLING

4. Good control of the mechanics of French; may contain occasional errors in spelling, diacritics, or punctuation, but these do not affect comprehensibility.

3. Some control of the mechanics of French; contains errors in spelling, diacritics, or punctuation that sometimes affect comprehensibility.

2. Weak control of the mechanics of French; contains numerous errors in spelling, diacritics, or punctuation that seriously affect comprehensibility.

1. Almost no control of the mechanics of French.

0. No response.

MESSAGE CONTENT

4. Relevant, informative response to the task. Adequate level of detail and creativity.

3. Response to the task is generally informative; may lack some detail and/or creativity.

2. Response incomplete; lacks some important information.

1. Response not informative; provides little or no information.

0. No response.

Web Strategies

How Can I Use the Internet to Teach Foreign Language?

From the Internet to round-the-clock live newscasts, teachers and students have never before had so much information at their fingertips. Yet never before has it been so confusing to determine where to turn for reliable content and what to do with it once you have found it. In today's world, foreign language teachers must not only use the Internet as a source of up-to-the-minute information for students; they must teach students how to find and evaluate sources on their own.

What's available On the Internet?

✔ **Teacher-Focused Web Sites**
These Web sites provide teaching tips, detailed lesson plans, and links to other sites of interest to teachers and students.

✔ **Cultural Information**
Sites on the Web provide information to help students explore both "Big C" and "Little C" culture. Information about museums, stores, restaurants, schools, holiday celebrations, and customs can be found on Web sites that allow the student to virtually immerse into the culture.

✔ **Geographical Information**
The Web holds a variety of geographical resources, from historical, physical, and political maps; to interactive mapping programs; to information about people and places around the world.

✔ **Statistics**
Government Web sites are rich depositories for statistics of all kinds, including census data and information about climate, education, the economy, and political processes and patterns.

✔ **Reference Sources**
Students can access full-text versions of encyclopedias, dictionaries, atlases, and other reference books. Students have easy access to newspapers written in the target language.

✔ **News**
Traditional media sources, including television, radio, newspapers, and news magazines, sponsor Web sites that provide updates, as well as in-depth news coverage and analysis.

✔ **Topical Information**
Among the most numerous Web sites are those organized around a particular topic or issue. These Internet pages may contain essays, analyses, and other commentaries, as well as primary source documents, maps, photographs, video and audio clips, bibliographies, and links to related online resources.

✔ **Organizations**
Many organizations such as museums post Web pages that provide online exhibits, archives, and other information.

Glencoe Online

Glencoe provides engaging **Student Web Activities** plus **Self-Check Quizzes** for each chapter that let you and your students assess their knowledge. There are games in each chapter to afford students extra practice. You can also access additional resources,

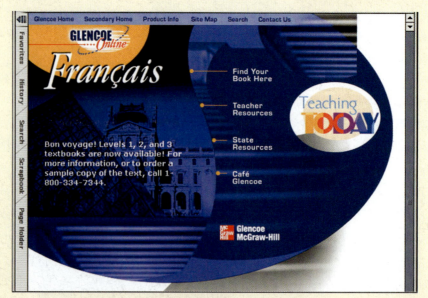

Web Strategies

including enrichment links.

Finding Things on the Internet

The greatest asset of the Internet—its vast array of materials—is also its greatest deterrent. Many excellent foreign language-specific sites provide links to relevant content. Using Internet search engines can also help you find what you need.

✔ A search engine is an Internet search tool. You type in a keyword, name, or phrase, and the search engine lists the URLs for Web sites that match your search. However, a search engine may find things that are not at all related or may miss sites that you would consider of interest. The key is to find ways to define your search.

✔ Not all search engines are the same. Each seeks out information a little bit differently. Different search engines use different criteria to determine what constitutes a "match" for your search topic. The Internet holds numerous articles that compare search engines and offer guidelines for choosing those that best meet your needs.

✔ An advanced search allows you to refine the search by using a phrase or a combination of words. The way to conduct an advanced search varies from search engine to search engine; check the search engine's *Help* feature for information. Encourage students to review this information regularly for each of the search engines they use.

How do I teach students to evaluate Web sites?

Anyone can put up a Web site. Web content is easy to change, too, so Webmasters constantly update their Web sites by adding, modifying, and removing content. These characteristics make evaluating Web sites both more challenging and more important than traditional print resources. Teach students to critically evaluate Web resources, using the questions and criteria below.

1. **Purpose:** What is the purpose of the Web site or Web page? Is it an informational Web page, a news site, a business site, an advocacy site, or a personal Web page? Many sites serve more than one purpose. For instance, a news site may provide current events accompanied by banner ads that market the products advertisers think readers might want.

2. **URL:** What is the URL, or Web address? Where does the site originate? That can sometimes tell you about the group or business behind the Web page. For example, URLs with .edu and .gov domain names indicate that the site is connected to an educational institution or a government agency, respectively. A .com suffix usually means that a commercial or business interest hosts the Web site, but may also indicate a personal Web page. A nonprofit organization's Web address may end with .org.

3. **Authority:** Who wrote the material or created the Web site? What qualifications does this person or group have? Who has ultimate responsibility for the site? If the site is sponsored by an organization, are the organization's goals clearly stated?

4. **Accuracy:** How reliable is the information? Are sources listed so that they can be verified? Is the Web page free from surface errors in spelling and grammar? How does it compare with other sources you've found on the Web and in print?

5. **Objectivity:** If the site presents itself as an informational site, is the material free from bias? If there is advertising, is it easy to tell the difference between the ads and other features? If the site mixes factual information with opinion, can you spot the difference between the ads and other features? If the site advocates an opinion or viewpoint, is the opinion clearly stated and logically defended?

6. **Currency:** When was the information first placed on the Web? Is the site updated on a regular basis? When was the last revision? If the information is time-sensitive, are the updates frequent enough?

7. **Coverage:** What topics are covered on the Web site? What is the depth of coverage? Are all sides of an issue presented? How does the coverage compare with other Web and print sources?

Special Students

Addressing the Needs of Special Students
How can I help ALL my students learn foreign language?

Today's classroom contains students from a variety of backgrounds and with a variety of learning styles, strengths, and challenges. With careful planning, you can address the needs of all students in the foreign language classroom. The following tips for instruction can assist your efforts to help all students reach their maximum potential.

- ✔ Survey students to discover their individual differences. Use interest inventories of their unique talents so you can encourage contributions in the classroom.
- ✔ Model respect of others. Adolescents crave social acceptance. The student with learning differences is especially sensitive to correction and criticism—particularly when it comes from a teacher. Your behavior will set the tone for how students treat one another.
- ✔ Expand opportunities for success. Provide a variety of instructional activities that reinforce skills and concepts.
- ✔ Establish measurable objectives and decide how you can best help students meet them.
- ✔ Celebrate successes and praise "work in progress".
- ✔ Keep it simple. Point out problem areas—if doing so can help a student affect change. Avoid overwhelming students with too many goals at one time.
- ✔ Assign cooperative group projects that challenge all students to contribute to solving a problem or creating a product.

How do I reach students with learning disabilities?
- ✔ Provide support and structure. Clearly specify rules, assignments, and responsibilities.
- ✔ Practice skills frequently. Use games and drills to help maintain student interest.
- ✔ Incorporate many modalities into the learning process. Provide opportunities to say, hear, write, read, and act out important concepts and information.
- ✔ Link new skills and concepts to those already mastered.
- ✔ Allow students to record answers on audiotape.
- ✔ Allow extra time to complete tests and assignments.
- ✔ Let students demonstrate proficiency with alternative presentations, including oral reports, role plays, art projects, and with music.
- ✔ Provide outlines, notes, or recordings of readings.
- ✔ Pair students with peer helpers, and provide class time for pair interaction.

How do I reach students with behavioral disorders?
- ✔ Provide a structured environment with clear-cut schedules, rules, seat assignments, and safety procedures.
- ✔ Reinforce appropriate behavior and model it for students.
- ✔ Cue distracted students back to the task through verbal signals and teacher proximity.
- ✔ Set very small goals that can be achieved in the short term. Work for long-term improvement in the big areas.

How do I reach students with physical challenges?
- ✔ Openly discuss with the student any uncertainties you have about when to offer aid.
- ✔ Ask parents or therapists and students what special devices or procedures are needed, and whether any special safety precautions need to be taken.
- ✔ Welcome students with physical challenges into all activities, including field trips, special events, and projects.
- ✔ Provide information to help able-bodied students and adults understand other students' physical challenges.

How do I reach students with visual impairments?
- ✔ Facilitate independence. Modify assignments as needed.
- ✔ Teach classmates how and when to serve as guides.
- ✔ Limit unnecessary noise in the classroom if it distracts the student with visual impairments.
- ✔ Provide tactile models whenever possible.
- ✔ Foster a spirit of inclusion.

Special Students

Describe people and events as they occur in the classroom. Remind classmates that the student with visual impairments cannot interpret gestures and other forms of nonverbal communication.
✔ Provide taped lectures and reading assignments.
✔ Team the student with a sighted peer for written work.

How do I reach students with hearing impairments?

✔ Seat students where they can see your lip movements easily and where they can avoid visual distractions.
✔ Avoid standing with your back to the window or light source.
✔ Use an overhead projector to maintain eye contact while writing.
✔ Seat students where they can see speakers.
✔ Write out all assignments on the board, or hand out written instructions.
✔ If the student has a manual interpreter, allow both student and interpreter to select the most favorable seating arrangements.
✔ Teach students to look directly at each other when they speak.

How do I reach English language learners?

✔ Remember, students' ability to speak English does not reflect their academic abilities.
✔ Try to incorporate the students' cultural experience into your instruction. The help of a bilingual aide may be effective.
✔ Avoid cultural stereotypes.
✔ Pre-teach important vocabulary and concepts.
✔ Be cognizant of difficulties that may arise from learning a new written notation.
✔ Encourage students to make comparisons between their heritage culture and language and the target culture and language.
✔ Encourage students to preview text before they begin reading, noting headings, graphic organizers, photographs, and maps.

How do I reach gifted students?

✔ Make arrangements for students to take selected subjects early and to work on independent projects.
✔ Ask "what if" questions to develop high-level thinking skills. Establish an environment safe for risk taking.
✔ Call on gifted students to provide more open-ended responses. Use the material as optional for enrichment.
✔ Emphasize concepts, theories, ideas, relationships, and generalizations.
✔ Promote interest in the past by inviting students to make connections to the present.
✔ Let students express themselves in alternate ways, such as creative writing, acting, debate, simulations, drawing, or music.
✔ Provide students with a catalog of helpful resources, listing such things as agencies that provide free and inexpensive materials, appropriate community services and programs.
✔ Assign extension projects that allow students to solve real-life problems related to their communities.

Hints for Inclusion Classes

Advice from Diane Russell
Delaware City Schools
Delaware, Ohio

In an inclusion setting, all students can respond to and get immediate feedback when using a set of dry-erase boards (cut at the local hardware store from a 4' by 8' laminated panel). For vocabulary review, students can write dictated words or sketch their meanings on the boards. Students can also be asked to draw what they hear from a story read aloud by the teacher to check listening comprehension. When students take turns illustrating different pages of a story, the pictures can be displayed on the chalk ledge as cues for retelling or writing a summary.

Reading Strategies and Skills

The What, Why, and How of Reading

Reading is a learned process. You have been reading in your first language for a long time and now your challenge is to transfer what you know to enable you to read fluently in French. Reading will help you improve your vocabulary, cultural knowledge, and productive skills in French. The strategies in the chart are reading strategies you are probably familiar with. Review them and apply them as you continue to improve your French reading skills.

Skill/Strategy

What is it?	Why It's Important	How To Do It
Preview Previewing is looking over a selection before you read.	Previewing lets you begin to see what you already know and what you'll need to know. It helps you set a purpose for reading.	Look at the title, illustrations, headings, captions, and graphics. Look at how ideas are organized. Ask questions about the text.
Skim Skimming is looking over an entire selection quickly to get a general idea of what the piece is about.	Skimming will tell you what a selection is about. If the selection you skim isn't what you're looking for, you won't need to read the entire piece.	Read the title of the selection and quickly look over the entire piece. Read headings and captions and maybe part of the first paragraph to get a general idea of the selection's content.
Scan Scanning is glancing quickly over a selection in order to find specific information.	Scanning helps you pinpoint information quickly. It saves you time when you have a number of selections to look at.	As you move your eyes quickly over the lines of text, look for key words or phrases that will help you locate the information you're looking for.
Predict Predicting is taking an educated guess about what will happen in a selection.	Predicting gives you a reason to read. You want to find out if your prediction and the selection events match, don't you? As you read, adjust or change your prediction if it doesn't fit what you learn.	Combine what you already know about an author or subject with what you learned in your preview to guess at what will be included in the text.
Summarize Summarizing is stating the main ideas of a selection in your own words and in a logical sequence.	Summarizing shows whether you've understood something. It teaches you to rethink what you've read and to separate main ideas from supporting information.	Ask yourself: What is this selection about? Answer who, what, where, when, why, and how? Put that information in a logical order.

Reading Strategies and Skills

What is it?	Why It's Important	How To Do It
Clarify Clarifying is looking at difficult sections of text in order to clear up what is confusing.	Authors will often build ideas one on another. If you don't clear up a confusing passage, you may not understand main ideas or information that comes later.	Go back and reread a confusing section more slowly. Look up words you don't know. Ask questions about what you don't understand. Sometimes you may want to read on to see if further information helps you.
Question Questioning is asking yourself whether information in a selection is important. Questioning is also regularly asking yourself whether you've understood what you've read.	When you ask questions as you read, you're reading strategically. As you answer your questions, you're making sure that you'll get the gist of a text.	Have a running conversation with yourself as you read. Keep asking yourself, Is this idea important? Why? Do I understand what this is about? Might this information be on a test later?
Visualize Visualizing is picturing a writer's ideas or descriptions in your mind's eye.	Visualizing is one of the best ways to understand and remember information in fiction, nonfiction, and informational text.	Carefully read how a writer describes a person, place, or thing. Then ask yourself, What would this look like? Can I see how the steps in this process would work?
Monitor Comprehension Monitoring your comprehension means thinking about whether you're understanding what you're reading.	The whole point of reading is to understand a piece of text. When you don't understand a selection, you're not really reading it.	Keep asking yourself questions about main ideas, characters, and events. When you can't answer a question, review, read more slowly, or ask someone to help you.

Reading Strategies and Skills

What is it?	Why It's Important	How To Do It
Identify Sequence Identifying sequence is finding the logical order of ideas or events.	In a work of fiction, events usually happen in chronological order. With nonfiction, understanding the logical sequence of ideas in a piece helps you follow a writer's train of thought. You'll remember ideas better when you know the logical order a writer uses.	Think about what the author is trying to do. Tell a story? Explain how something works? Present how something works? Present information? Look for clues or signal words that might point to time order, steps in a process, or order of importance.
Determine the Main Idea Determining an author's main idea is finding the most important thought in a paragraph or selection.	Finding main ideas gets you ready to summarize. You also discover an author's purpose for writing when you find the main ideas in a selection.	Think about what you know about the author and the topic. Look for how the author organizes ideas. Then look for the one idea that all of the sentences in a paragraph or all the paragraphs in a selection are about.
Respond Responding is telling what you like, dislike, find surprising or interesting in a selection.	When you react in a personal way to what you read, you'll enjoy a selection more and remember it better.	As you read, think about how you feel about story elements or ideas in a selection. What's your reaction to the characters in a story? What grabs your attention as you read?
Connect Connecting means linking what you read to events in your own life or to other selections you've read.	You'll "get into" your reading and recall information and ideas better by connecting events, emotions, and characters to your own life.	Ask yourself: Do I know someone like this? Have I ever felt this way? What else have I read that is like this selection?
Review Reviewing is going back over what you've read to remember what's important and to organize ideas so you'll recall them later.	Reviewing is especially important when you have new ideas and a lot of information to remember.	Filling in a graphic organizer, such as a chart or diagram, as you read helps you organize information. These study aids will help you review later.
Interpret Interpreting is using your own understanding of the world to decide what the events or ideas in a selection mean.	Every reader constructs meaning on the basis of what he or she understands about the world. Finding meaning as you read is all about interacting with the text.	Think about what you already know about yourself and the world. Ask yourself: What is the author really trying to say here? What larger idea might these events be about?

Reading Strategies and Skills

What is it?	Why It's Important	How To Do It
Infer Inferring is using your reason and experience to guess at what an author does not come right out and say.	Making inferences is a large part of finding meaning in a selection. Inferring helps you look more deeply at characters and points you toward the theme or message in a selection.	Look for clues the author provides. Notice descriptions, dialogue, events, and relationships that might tell you something the author wants you to know.
Draw Conclusions Drawing conclusions is using a number of pieces of information to make a general statement about people, places, events, and ideas.	Drawing conclusions helps you find connections between ideas and events. It's another tool to help you see the larger picture.	Notice details about characters, ideas, and events. Then make a general statement on the basis of these details. For example, a character's actions might lead you to conclude that he is kind.
Analyze Analyzing is looking at separate parts of a selection in order to understand the entire selection.	Analyzing helps you look critically at a piece of writing. When you analyze a selection, you'll discover its theme or message, and you'll learn the author's purpose for writing.	To analyze a story, think about what the author is saying through the characters, setting, and plot. To analyze nonfiction, look at the organization and main ideas. What do they suggest?
Synthesize Synthesizing is combining ideas to create something new. You may synthesize to reach a new understanding or you may actually create a new ending to a story.	Synthesizing helps you move to a higher level of thinking. Creating something new of your own goes beyond remembering what you learned from someone else.	Think about the ideas or information you've learned in a selection. Ask yourself: Do I understand something more than the main ideas here? Can I create something else from what I now know?
Evaluate Evaluating is making a judgment or forming an opinion about something you read. You can evaluate a character, an author's craft, or the value of the information in a text.	Evaluating helps you become a wise reader. For example, when you judge whether an author is qualified to speak about a topic or whether the author's points make sense, you can avoid being misled by what you read.	As you read, ask yourself questions such as: Is this character realistic and believable? Is this author qualified to write on this subject? Is this author biased? Does this author present opinions as facts?

A Guided Tour of the Student Edition

Expand your students' view of the Francophone world

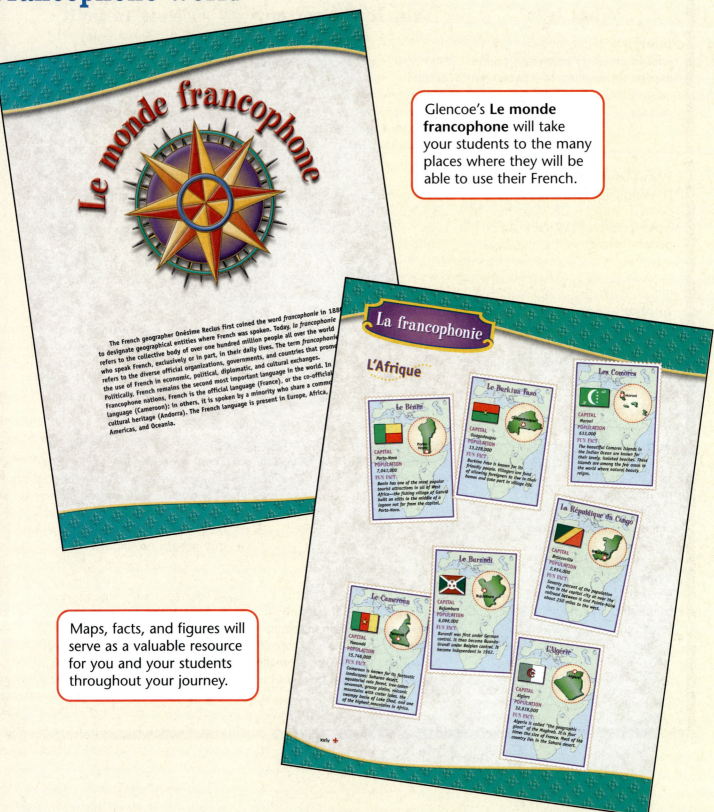

Glencoe's **Le monde francophone** will take your students to the many places where they will be able to use their French.

Maps, facts, and figures will serve as a valuable resource for you and your students throughout your journey.

Awaken your students' interest with an introduction to the chapter theme in a cultural context

Itinerary for Success
- ✓ Exposure to Francophone culture
- ✓ Clear expectations and goals
- ✓ Thematic, contextualized vocabulary
- ✓ Useful and thematically linked structure
- ✓ Progressive practice
- ✓ Real-life conversation
- ✓ Cultural readings in the target language
- ✓ Connections to other disciplines . . . in French!
- ✓ Recycling and review
- ✓ **National Geographic Society** panoramas of the Francophone world

Objectives let students know what they will be able to do at the end of the chapter.

CHAPITRE 6

La gastronomie

Objectifs
In this chapter you will learn to:
- ✓ talk about foods and food preparation
- ✓ describe future events
- ✓ refer to people and things already mentioned
- ✓ tell what you have others do
- ✓ discuss the cuisine of various French provinces

Henri Matisse *L'harmonie en rouge*

Fine Art related to the chapter enriches students' cultural knowledge and serves as a springboard for discussion.

Opening photo provides a cultural backdrop for the chapter.

A Guided Tour of the Student Edition

Give students something to talk about with thematic, contextualized vocabulary

Provide practice for the mastery of new vocabulary

Itinerary for Success
- ✓ Exposure to Francophone culture
- ✓ Clear expectations and goals
- ✓ Thematic, contextualized vocabulary
- ✓ Useful and thematically linked structure
- ✓ Progressive practice
- ✓ Real-life conversation
- ✓ Cultural readings in the target language
- ✓ Connections to other disciplines . . . in French!
- ✓ Recycling and review
- ✓ National Geographic Society panoramas of the Francophone world

Historiette enables students to tell and retell a story, using their new words.

Glencoe's Web site, **french.glencoe.com**, takes students on virtual field trips to learn more about the chapter theme.

Paired and small-group activities allow students to communicate about the chapter topic.

Continuous reentry occurs as the chapter vocabulary and topic are used to practice the new structure points.

A Guided Tour of the Student Edition

Build communicative competence with thematically linked structure

> Immediate reinforcement shows students how structure works to build meaning.

> Realia adds interest to the lesson. Students see language they are learning in real-life contexts.

> New structures are presented in simple terms with familiar vocabulary.

Structure

 **Le futur simple**
Expressing future events

Rappelez-vous que...
You already learned that the future can be expressed in French by using **aller** + infinitive.
Vendredi, je vais sortir avec Émilie.

1. To form the future tense in French, you add the future endings to the entire infinitive of verbs that end in **-er** or **-ir**. You drop the **e** before adding the endings to **-re** verbs. Study the following.

Infinitive	PARLER	FINIR	ATTENDRE
Stem	parler-	finir-	attendr-
	je parler**ai**	je finir**ai**	j' attendr**ai**
	tu parler**as**	tu finir**as**	tu attendr**as**
	il/elle/on parler**a**	il/elle/on finir**a**	il/elle/on attendr**a**
	nous parler**ons**	nous finir**ons**	nous attendr**ons**
	vous parler**ez**	vous finir**ez**	vous attendr**ez**
	ils/elles parler**ont**	ils/elles finir**ont**	ils/elles attendr**ont**

2. The verbs **être, faire, aller,** and **avoir** have an irregular stem in the future tense.

ÊTRE je serai, tu seras, il sera, nous serons, vous serez, ils seront
FAIRE je ferai, tu feras, il fera, nous ferons, vous ferez, ils feront
ALLER j'irai, tu iras, il ira, nous irons, vous irez, ils iront
AVOIR j'aurai, tu auras, il aura, nous aurons, vous aurez, ils auront

3. The future tense is not commonly used in spoken French. You use **aller** + the infinitive more often to express the future. However, you must use the future tense after **quand** when the main verb in the sentence is in the future tense.

*Je te ferai un bon repas quand tu **seras** à Paris.*
*Quand tout le monde **sera** là, je mettrai la viande...*

> Graphic organizers and clear examples aid comprehension.

182 ✦ cent quatre-vingt-deux

Comment dit-on?

11 Historiette *Un de ces jours...* Répondez que oui.
1. Un de ces jours, Sandra voyagera en France?
2. Elle prendra l'avion pour y aller?
3. Elle passera quelques semaines à Paris?
4. Elle visitera les monuments?
5. Elle s'amusera?
6. Sa copine Liz l'accompagnera?
7. Elles sortiront souvent?
8. Elles dîneront dans de bons restaurants?

PARIS

12 Historiette *Une bonne cuisinière*
Inventez des réponses.
1. Sandra ira dans une école culinaire quand elle sera à Paris?
2. Elle apprendra à faire des plats français quand elle sera à Paris?
3. Elle préparera des repas exquis quand elle rentrera aux États-Unis?
4. Elle invitera ses amis à dîner?
5. Elle leur fera de la cuisine française quand elle les invitera?

Une fondue au fromage

Un marché à Aix-en-Provence

13 *Une salade de fruits* Répondez que oui.
1. Tu feras une bonne salade de fruits?
2. Tu mettras des oranges, des pommes et du raisin?
3. Tu laveras les fruits?
4. Tu éplucheras les pommes?
5. Tu couperas les bananes en rondelles?
6. Tu ajouteras du sucre?
7. Tu serviras de petits gâteaux avec ta salade de fruits?

LA GASTRONOMIE cent quatre-vingt-trois ✦ 183

> Students build confidence as they complete activities that progress from easy to more challenging.

Strengthen proficiency with continuous reinforcement and reentry

Itinerary for Success
- ✓ Exposure to Francophone culture
- ✓ Clear expectations and goals
- ✓ Thematic, contextualized vocabulary
- ✓ Useful and thematically linked structure
- ✓ Progressive practice
- ✓ Real-life conversation
- ✓ Cultural readings in the target language
- ✓ Connections to other disciplines . . . in French!
- ✓ Recycling and review
- ✓ **National Geographic Society** panoramas of the Francophone world

> Models help students understand how to complete the activity.

Structure

14 Pour ton anniversaire Posez des questions à Laurent d'après le modèle.

donner une fête →
Laurent, tu donneras une fête?
1. inviter des amis
2. préparer des hors-d'œuvre
3. jouer de la guitare
4. chanter
5. mettre des CD
6. danser

15 Historiette Au restaurant Répondez d'après les indications.
1. Tu iras au restaurant à quelle heure demain soir? (à neuf heures)
2. C'est toi qui choisiras le restaurant? (oui)
3. Tu y dîneras seul? (non, avec Julie)
4. Vous prendrez une table avant l'arrivée de vos amis? (oui)
5. Vous demanderez la carte aussi? (non)
6. Vous attendrez vos amis? (absolument)

Le restaurant Julien à Paris

16 Un voyage à la Martinique Répondez que oui.
1. L'hiver prochain Émilie aura des vacances?
2. Elle fera un voyage?
3. Elle ira à la Martinique?
4. Elle fera le voyage en avion?
5. Elle sera fatiguée après le vol?
6. Tu feras ce voyage avec Émilie?
7. Vous irez ensemble à la Martinique?
8. Vous y ferez des excursions ensemble?
9. Vous irez à la plage?
10. Vous prendrez des bains de soleil?
11. Vous serez bronzé(e)s?

17 De bonnes résolutions Vous avez décidé de prendre de bonnes résolutions pour le nouvel an. Par exemple: **Je serai gentil(le) avec ma sœur.** Faites une liste et comparez-la avec la liste d'un(e) camarade. Quelles sont les résolutions qui sont les mêmes?

18 J'espère... Travaillez avec un(e) camarade. Dites ce que vous espérez pour l'avenir. Par exemple: **J'espère que je n'aurai plus de devoirs l'année prochaine.**

184 ✦ cent quatre-vingt-quatre   CHAPITRE 6

Structure

Deux pronoms dans la même phrase
Referring to people and things already mentioned

1. It is possible to use both a direct and an indirect object pronoun in the same sentence. Study the following sentences.

   Le serveur **me** donne **la carte.**   Il **me la** donne.
   Il **nous** sert **la soupe.**   Il **nous la** sert.

2. The pronouns me, te, nous, vous precede the pronouns le, la, les.

Elle me/te/nous/vous le/la/les donne.

3. The double object pronouns, the same as a single pronoun, come directly before the verbs they are linked to. Study the following sentences.

Affirmatif	Négatif
Il me le donne.	Il ne me le donne pas.
Il va me le donner.	Il ne va pas me le donner.
Il me l' a donné.	Il ne me l' a pas donné.

Rappelez-vous que...
In the **passé composé**, the past participle must agree with the preceding direct object.
Il t'a donné la recette?
Oui, il me l'a donnée.

LA GASTRONOMIE   cent quatre-vingt-cinq ✦ 185

> **Rappelez-vous que...** links what students already know to the new structure being presented.

A Guided Tour of the Student Edition

Engage students in real conversation

Students listen to speakers from diverse areas of the Francophone world to improve pronunciation.

Students can watch and participate in the interactive conversation on CD-ROM.

Use realia to expand acquired language skills.

Students apply newly learned vocabulary and structures to real-life situations.

Students have a sense of accomplishment when they are able to comprehend the conversation.

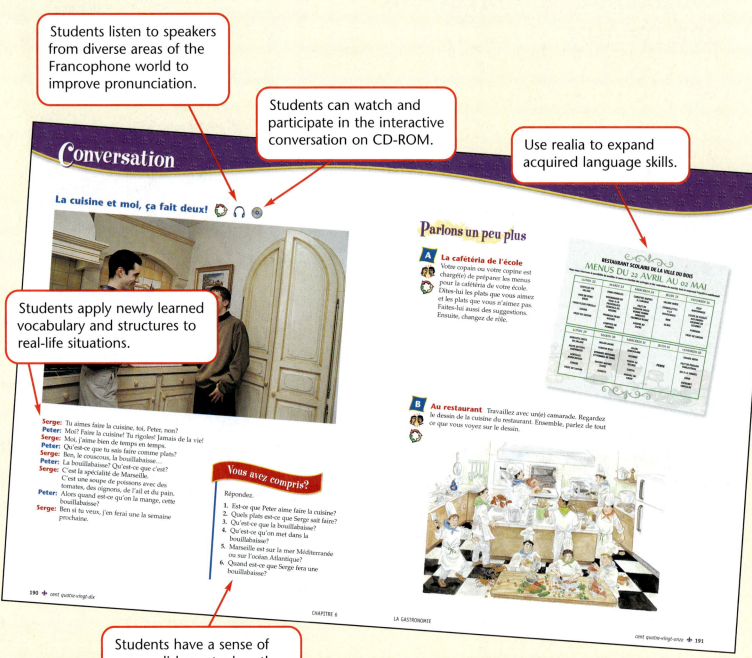

Heighten students' cultural awareness

Itinerary for Success
- ✓ Exposure to Francophone culture
- ✓ Clear expectations and goals
- ✓ Thematic, contextualized vocabulary
- ✓ Useful and thematically linked structure
- ✓ Progressive practice
- ✓ Real-life conversation
- ✓ Cultural readings in the target language
- ✓ Connections to other disciplines . . . in French!
- ✓ Recycling and review
- ✓ **National Geographic Society** panoramas of the Francophone world

Recorded reading on CD provides options for addressing various skills and learning styles.

Reading strategies help students develop reading skills.

Cultural reading uses learned language to reinforce chapter theme.

Many visuals help students comprehend what they read.

Activities reinforce vocabulary skills and comprehension.

Lectures culturelles

Un voyage gastronomique

Charles Smith est un étudiant américain à l'université du Michigan. Il fait du français parce qu'il s'intéresse au commerce international. Charles a toujours eu envie d'aller en France pour travailler son français. L'été prochain, il réalisera son rêve[1] quand il passera deux mois en France. Il voyagera dans toute la France.

Charles est un vrai gourmand, c'est-à-dire qu'il aime bien manger. Il sait que la France est connue dans le monde entier pour sa bonne cuisine. Chaque région a ses spécialités.

Alsace
Charles va commencer son voyage à Strasbourg, en Alsace, près de la frontière allemande. Là, il prendra sans doute une choucroute avec du jambon, des lardons[2] et des saucisses. La cuisine alsacienne ressemble à la cuisine allemande.

Provence
Ensuite, Charles ira dans le sud, en Provence. Quelle différence! En Provence on mange des pâtes et même de la pissaladière, un genre de pizza. Dans les plats provençaux, on utilise ce qu'on appelle les herbes de Provence: du thym, du laurier, du basilic, du romarin[3]. On utilise aussi des tomates, des oignons et de l'ail. La cuisine est toujours faite à l'huile d'olive. On n'utilise pas de beurre.

[1] rêve *dream*
[2] lardons *bacon bits*
[3] romarin *rosemary*

Bourgogne
Après huit jours en Provence, Charles visitera la Bourgogne. La Bourgogne est une région de vignobles[4]. Les vins de Bourgogne sont très appréciés et on les utilise beaucoup dans la cuisine bourguignonne. Bien sûr, Charles va manger un bœuf bourguignon—une des spécialités de la région. On prépare le bœuf bourguignon avec du bœuf, bien sûr, mais aussi avec du vin rouge, des oignons, du thym et du laurier. On le sert avec des pommes de terre cuites à l'eau ou à la vapeur[5]. Un vrai régal[6]!

Bretagne
Ensuite Charles ira en Bretagne, dans le nord-ouest. Il visitera de jolis villages de pêcheurs, comme Cancale, par exemple. Et qu'est-ce qu'il va manger en Bretagne? Il aura l'occasion de manger les meilleurs fruits de mer du monde—des huîtres, des moules et des coquilles Saint-Jacques[7].

Normandie
Avant de rentrer à Paris, Charles passera par la Normandie. Comme la Normandie est une région de pâturages, il y a beaucoup de vaches[8]. Pour cette raison, les Normands préparent leurs sauces avec de la crème et du beurre. Une escalope[9] à la normande est une escalope de veau avec une sauce à la crème et des champignons. C'est délicieux!

Quand notre gourmand sera en France, il apprendra sans doute que «la cuisine en France, c'est un art». Et quand il rentrera aux États-Unis, il aura certainement pris quelques kilos de plus.

[4] vignobles *vineyards*
[5] à la vapeur *steamed*
[6] régal *treat*
[7] coquilles Saint-Jacques *scallops*
[8] vaches *cows*
[9] escalope *cutlet*

Le port de Guilvinec en Bretagne

Vous avez compris?

A Le voyage de Charles Répondez.
1. Le français sera utile à Charles plus tard? Pourquoi?
2. Il ira en France quand?
3. Il visitera quelles régions?
4. Qu'est-ce qu'il apprendra quand il sera en France?

B Provinces et plats Donnez les informations suivantes.
1. le nom des provinces françaises que Charles visitera
2. un plat qu'il mangera dans chaque province

T37

Enrich students' cultural knowledge

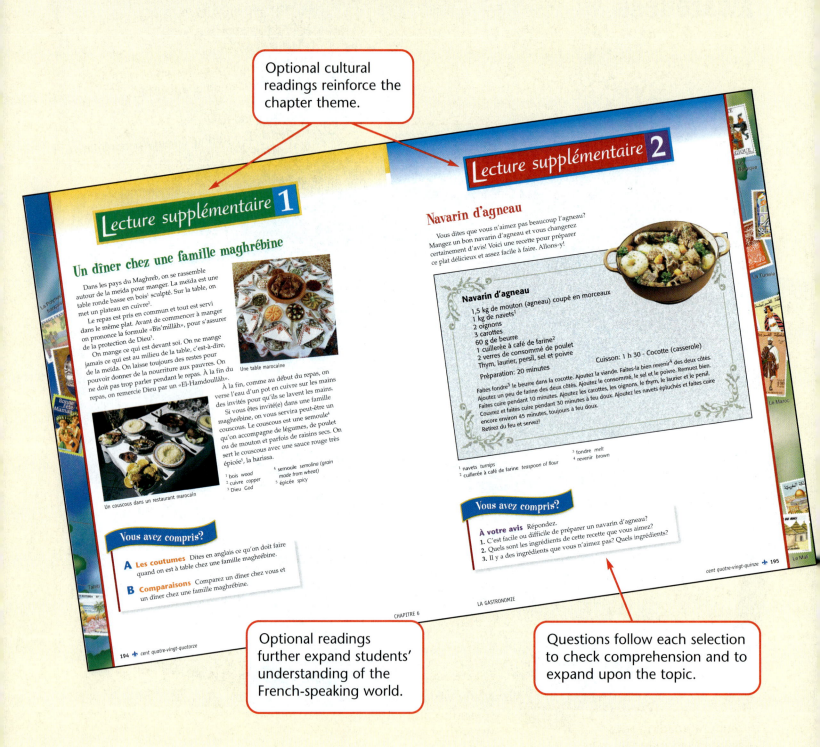

Optional cultural readings reinforce the chapter theme.

Optional readings further expand students' understanding of the French-speaking world.

Questions follow each selection to check comprehension and to expand upon the topic.

Connect with other disciplines

Itinerary for Success
- ✓ Exposure to Francophone culture
- ✓ Clear expectations and goals
- ✓ Thematic, contextualized vocabulary
- ✓ Useful and thematically linked structure
- ✓ Progressive practice
- ✓ Real-life conversation
- ✓ **Cultural readings in the target language**
- ✓ **Connections to other disciplines . . . in French!**
- ✓ Recycling and review
- ✓ **National Geographic Society** panoramas of the Francophone world

Introduction to the **Connexions** *provides the background for students to understand the reading.*

CONNEXIONS

La littérature

Gargantua de Rabelais

Have you ever heard the expression "gargantuan appetite" used to describe a person who eats a lot? The word "gargantuan" comes from the name of the main character in a book written by François Rabelais, a famous French author of the sixteenth century. An enlightened thinker of the Renaissance period, Rabelais challenged the constraints of medieval thought, particularly in the field of education. As we shall see, the character of Gargantua shows how education can transform an individual. Gargantua exhibits gross and animalistic behavior until he comes under the tutelage of a Renaissance humanist named Ponocrates.

François Rabelais, gravure d'un artiste inconnu

Gargantua

Gargantua est le fils de Grangousier et de Gargamelle. Tous deux sont des gros mangeurs et buveurs. Ils adorent manger et boire. Ce trait est transmis à leur fils. Dès l'instant¹ qu'il est né, il crie «À boire, à boire, à boire!» Son père l'entend et dit «Que grand tu as!»—et de là vient le nom de Gargantua. Le «petit» enfant a bu le lait de 17 913 vaches. Il s'est développé vite et il est devenu énorme—un véritable géant.

Quand il se réveillait, il sautait² dans son lit comme un mouton. Pour lui:

> peigner, laver et nettoyer³ était perdre son temps en ce monde. Puis rotait⁴, crachait⁵, toussait, éternuait, et déjeunait: belles tripes frites⁶, belles carbonnades [grillades], beaux jambons.

¹ Dès l'instant *From the moment*
² sautait *jumped up and down*
³ nettoyer *clean*
⁴ rotait *burped*
⁵ crachait *spit*
⁶ tripes frites *fried tripe*

Gargantua aime manger, mais il n'aime pas du tout faire de l'exercice. Quand on lui dit de faire de l'exercice, il répond:

> Quoi! n'ai-je fait suffisant exercice?
> Je me suis vautré⁷ six ou sept tours
> parmi le lit⁸ avant de me lever.
> N'est-ce assez?

La vie et le comportement de Gargantua changent complètement quand son père décide de confier son éducation au sage⁹ humaniste Ponocrates. Gargantua apprend alors à se laver, se peigner, s'habiller et se parfumer. Il assouplit¹⁰ son corps par toutes sortes d'exercices physiques. On stimule son esprit par des jeux. Il rend visite aux artisans et converse avec les savants.

⁷ Je me suis vautré *I rolled around*
⁸ tours parmi le lit *times in bed*
⁹ sage *wise*
¹⁰ assouplit *loosens up*

La Devinière, le village natal de Rabelais

Vous avez compris?

Gargantua Répondez.
1. Quel est un trait des parents de Gargantua?
2. Ce trait a été transmis à leur fils?
3. Quand Gargantua est né, qu'est-ce qu'il a crié?
4. On lui a donné quel nom?
5. Qu'est-ce qu'il a bu?
6. Qu'est-ce qu'il est devenu?
7. Qu'est-ce qu'il faisait quand il se réveillait?
8. Qu'est-ce qu'il mangeait?
9. Il aimait faire de l'exercice?
10. Quand est-ce que tout cela a changé?

Students further their knowledge of other disciplines—in French!

A Guided Tour of the Student Edition

Encourage students to apply what they have learned

Students use their newly acquired skills to communicate in meaningful, open-ended activities.

Writing Strategy gives students the tools they need to develop better writing skills.

Students practice what they have learned while improving their written French.

Check students' progress

Assessment activities give students a chance to evaluate what they have really learned.

"Sticky" notes direct students to the correct pages for review.

Itinerary for Success
- ✓ Exposure to Francophone culture
- ✓ Clear expectations and goals
- ✓ Thematic, contextualized vocabulary
- ✓ Useful and thematically linked structure
- ✓ Progressive practice
- ✓ Real-life conversation
- ✓ Cultural readings in the target language
- ✓ Connections to other disciplines . . . in French!
- ✓ Recycling and review
- ✓ **National Geographic Society** panoramas of the Francophone world

A Guided Tour of the Student Edition

Take students beyond the text to learn more about culture and language
Give students opportunities to review and use their vocabulary in creative ways

The illustration provided at the end of each chapter recombines material students have learned to remind them of what they know how to say in French. Use this illustration as a prompt to allow your students to demonstrate all they know how to say or write.

Vocabulary is categorized to help recall.

Students can use the list as a self-check at the end of the chapter.

Cultivate an appreciation of the diverse Francophone world with National Geographic Reflets

Itinerary for Success
- ✓ Exposure to Francophone culture
- ✓ Clear expectations and goals
- ✓ Thematic, contextualized vocabulary
- ✓ Useful and thematically linked structure
- ✓ Progressive practice
- ✓ Real-life conversation
- ✓ Cultural readings in the target language
- ✓ Connections to other disciplines . . . in French!
- ✓ Recycling and review
- ✓ **National Geographic Society** panoramas of the Francophone world

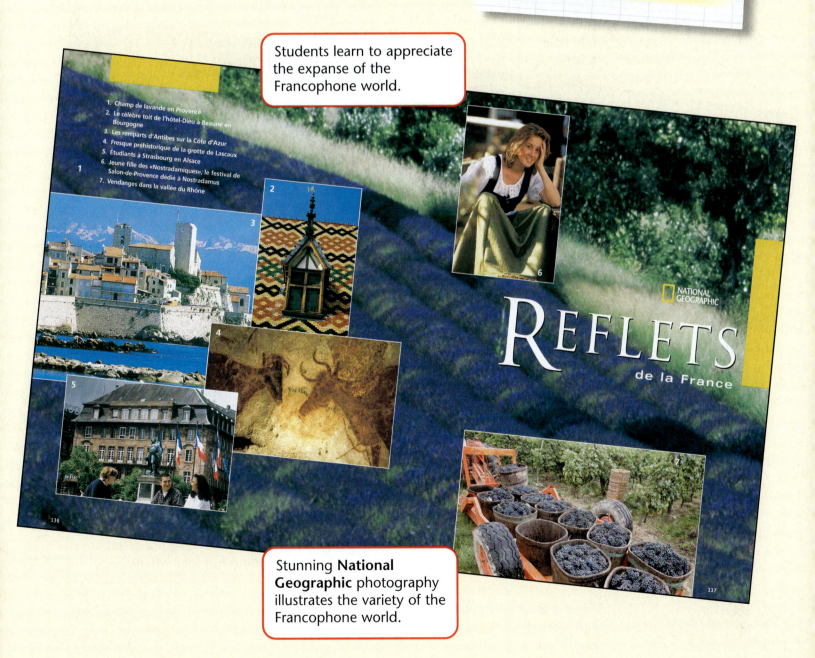

Students learn to appreciate the expanse of the Francophone world.

Stunning **National Geographic** photography illustrates the variety of the Francophone world.

A Guided Tour of the Student Edition

Enhance appreciation of literature and culture

Itinerary for Success
- ✓ Exposure to Francophone culture
- ✓ Clear expectations and goals
- ✓ Thematic, contextualized vocabulary
- ✓ Useful and thematically linked structure
- ✓ Progressive practice
- ✓ Real-life conversation
- ✓ Cultural readings in the target language
- ✓ Connections to other disciplines . . . in French!
- ✓ Recycling and review
- ✓ **National Geographic Society** panoramas of the French-speaking world

Literary Companion affords students yet another opportunity to apply their reading skills in French.

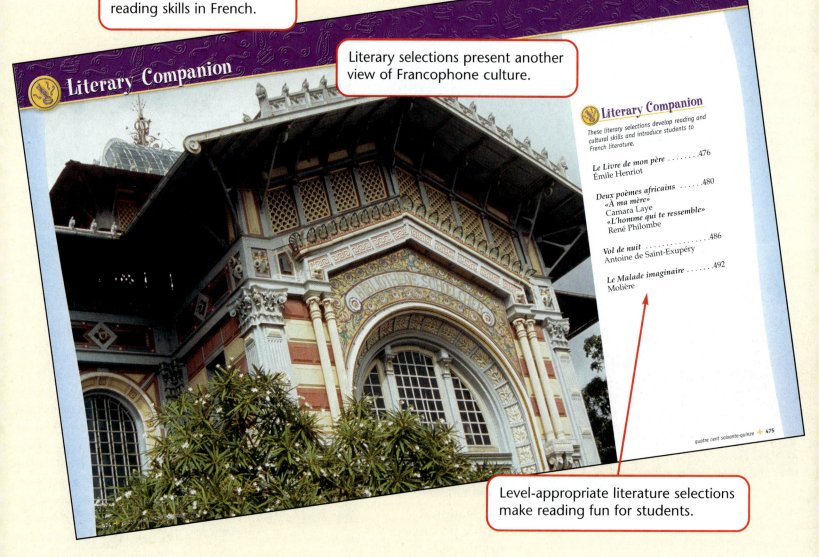

Literary selections present another view of Francophone culture.

Literary Companion

These literary selections develop reading and cultural skills and introduce students to French literature.

- *Le Livre de mon père* 476
  Émile Henriot
- *Deux poèmes africains* 480
  «À ma mère»
  Camara Laye
  «L'homme qui te ressemble»
  René Philombe
- *Vol de nuit* 486
  Antoine de Saint-Exupéry
- *Le Malade imaginaire* 492
  Molière

Level-appropriate literature selections make reading fun for students.

Take your students on a tour of the French-speaking world with the Bon voyage! Video Program

Itinerary for Success
- ✓ Exposure to Francophone culture
- ✓ Clear expectations and goals
- ✓ Thematic, contextualized vocabulary
- ✓ Useful and thematically linked structure
- ✓ Progressive practice
- ✓ Real-life conversation
- ✓ Cultural readings in the target language
- ✓ Connections to other disciplines . . . in French!
- ✓ Recycling and review
- ✓ **National Geographic Society** panoramas of the Francophone world.

The **Bon voyage!** Video Program, filmed in various Francophone countries, lets your students experience the diversity of the French-speaking world while reinforcing the language they have learned and improving their listening and viewing skills.

Your students will love seeing the adventures and mishaps of the **Bon voyage!** video characters.

Students will visit places where they will hear different accents, dialects, and languages spoken. The **Bon voyage!** Video Program will take you and your students on an exciting tour of the French-speaking world.

A Guided Tour of the Teacher Edition

Preview and objectives let you know what to plan for

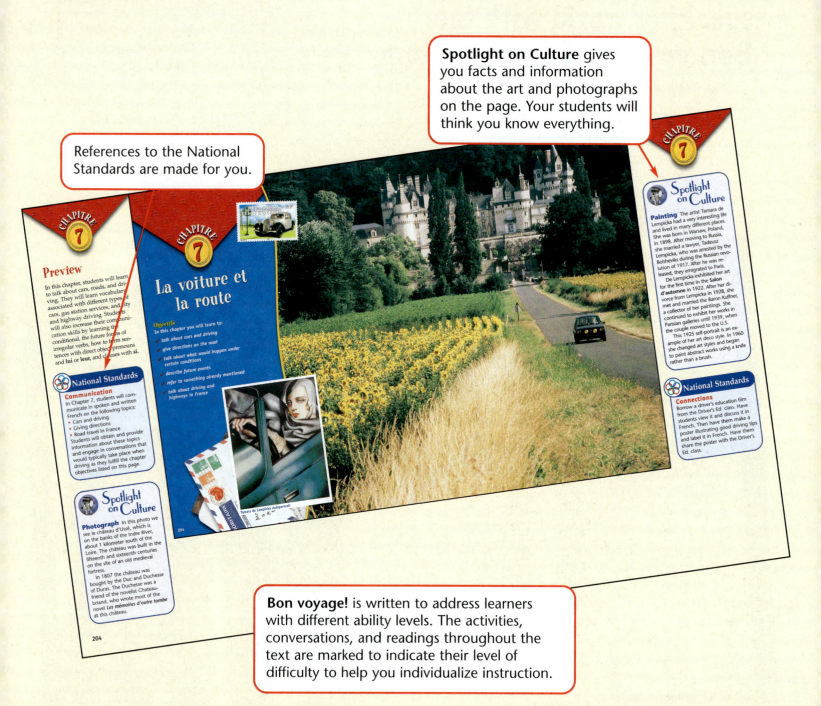

References to the National Standards are made for you.

Spotlight on Culture gives you facts and information about the art and photographs on the page. Your students will think you know everything.

Bon voyage! is written to address learners with different ability levels. The activities, conversations, and readings throughout the text are marked to indicate their level of difficulty to help you individualize instruction.

Step-by-step hints help you through the chapter

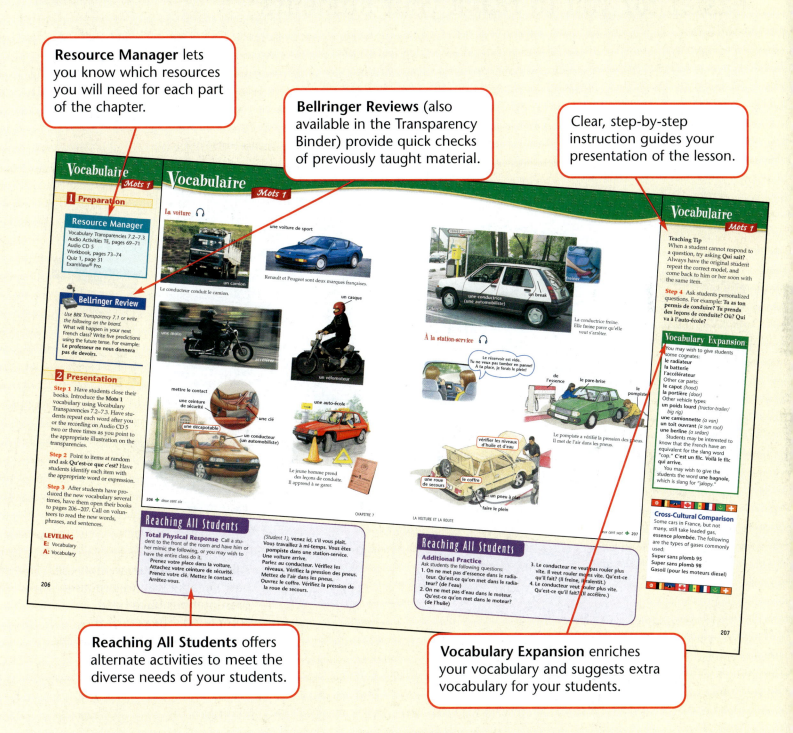

Resource Manager lets you know which resources you will need for each part of the chapter.

Bellringer Reviews (also available in the Transparency Binder) provide quick checks of previously taught material.

Clear, step-by-step instruction guides your presentation of the lesson.

Reaching All Students offers alternate activities to meet the diverse needs of your students.

Vocabulary Expansion enriches your vocabulary and suggests extra vocabulary for your students.

T47

A Guided Tour of the Teacher Edition

Painless presentation of structure makes it easier for you to reach your students

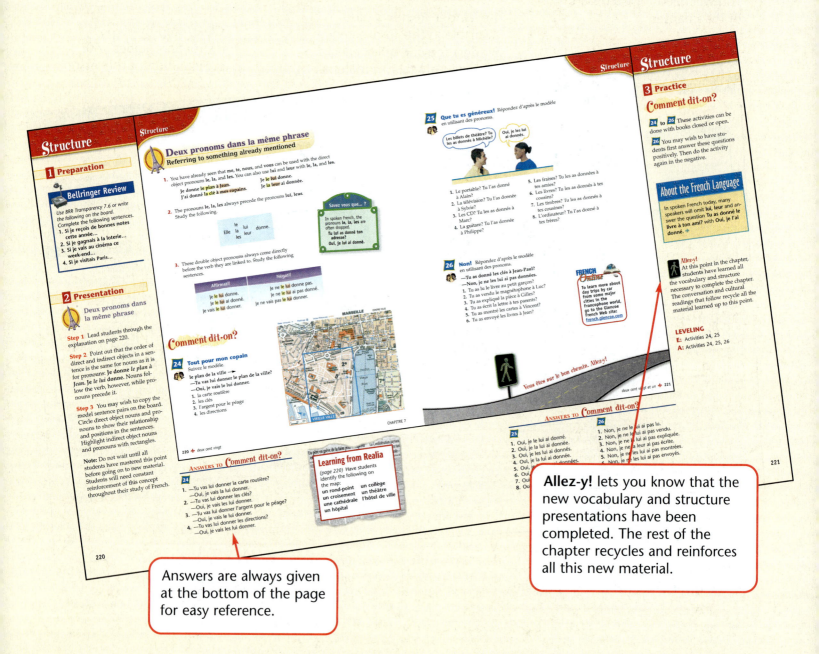

Help your students feel confident about their speaking skills

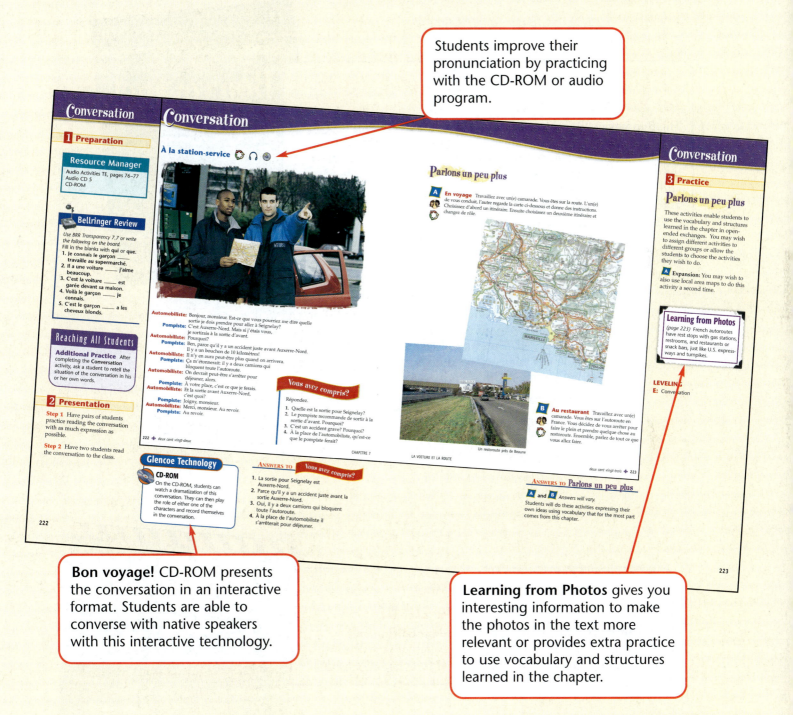

Students improve their pronunciation by practicing with the CD-ROM or audio program.

Bon voyage! CD-ROM presents the conversation in an interactive format. Students are able to converse with native speakers with this interactive technology.

Learning from Photos gives you interesting information to make the photos in the text more relevant or provides extra practice to use vocabulary and structures learned in the chapter.

Bon voyage! Resources

Build proficiency in all language skills

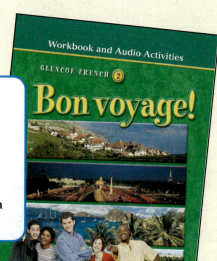

Provide Meaningful and Varied Practice for Your Students!

The **Bon voyage! Workbook** includes numerous activities to reinforce every concept presented in the Student Edition. Varied activities provide several ways for students to practice and apply the material you have presented in class. **Un peu plus** provides additional opportunity to have students practice with realia. **Mon autobiographie** provides a tool for portfolio assessment.

Improve Listening and Speaking Skills!

The **Audio CDs** provide recordings of the vocabulary words and some of the activities from the Student Edition as well as new activities to reinforce and expand upon what students have learned. The cultural readings are also recorded. Students may use the Audio Activities sheets to guide them through the **Audio Activities.**

StudentWorks Plus™ Helps Lighten the Load!

StudentWorks Plus™ include the **Student Edition** and **Workbook and Audio Activities.** This alternative to the textbook is available on CD or online at french.glencoe.com.

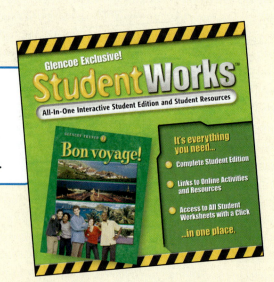

Have students learn by interacting in French!

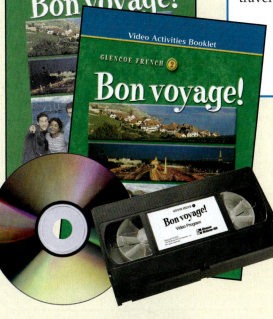

The Bon voyage! Video Program takes students on many adventures through the French-speaking world. Students become involved with the escapades of five teens and travel to different countries. Each episode is related to a chapter of the textbook by its theme. The language provides comprehensible input and gives the students opportunities to hear many regionalisms and dialects. **The Bon voyage! Video Program** is available on VHS and DVD.

With the **Interactive Conversations CD-ROM** students have an opportunity to interact with a native speaker by participating in the chapter conversation. Students first watch a video of the conversation. They then choose to play the role of one of the characters in the conversation, record their own voice into the conversation and compare their pronunciation and fluency to that of the native speaker.

The **MindJogger** is a video review game that saves teachers precious time and that students love to play. Each chapter of the text (Levels 1 and 2) has an accompanying MindJogger segment in which students are quizzed about the vocabulary, structure, and culture of the chapter. You may form teams and play MindJogger as a class activity or students may play the MindJogger DVD individually on a computer. MindJogger is available on VHS and DVD.

Glencoe French Online gives students many opportunities to review, practice, and explore. There are chapter-related activities, online quizzes, and many links to Web sites throughout the vast Francophone world. Go to <u>french.glencoe.com</u>.

Bon voyage! Resources

Save planning time with ancillaries organized and filed by chapter!

We make your life easier by organizing your written resources by chapter in convenient **FastFile Booklets**. The FastFile booklets include several essential resources.

- **Letter to Parents** Explains goals and suggests activities to do at home.
- **Workbook Teacher Edition** In your version of the student workbook answers are provided for all activities.
- **Audio Program Teacher Edition** The Audio Program TE includes the scripts to the audio activities and the answers to the students' activities. The audio activities found on these pages are recorded on the Bon voyage Audio Program CDs.
- **TPR Storytelling** We have written a story for each chapter and provided the illustrations to allow you to implement TPR Storytelling in your classroom. The stories are written using the vocabulary and structure for each chapter.
- **Situation Cards** Situation Cards provide your students with topics they can talk about. Several scenarios are provided for each chapter. There are blank cards provided as well should you or your students want to make up new situations.
- **Quizzes** Quizzes are provided to cover every concept taught in each chapter. These quizzes give you immediate feedback about your students' progress.
- **Tests** There are four kinds of tests with each chapter: Reading and Writing, Listening, Speaking, and Proficiency. The Listening Tests are available on CD. You can be sure that you are assessing your students' proficiency in each of the skill areas. In addition, the Reading and Writing Tests are leveled, meaning that there is a separate test for average students and another more challenging test for more able students.
- **Performance Assessment** The Performance Assessment Tasks allow your students to show you what they can do with their language skills at the end of each chapter. Rubrics are provided to help you evaluate your students' performances.

Multimedia resources help you diversify your instruction!

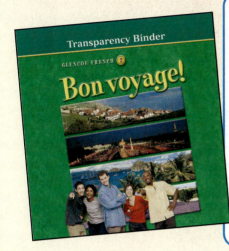

Enhance Your Lessons Visually!

The **Transparency Binder** gives you all the visual support you need to enhance your presentation.
- **Vocabulary** transparencies include the photos and art you see on the Student Edition pages, overlays with the French words, and French/English vocabulary lists for chapter vocabulary.
- **Maps** help you present the Francophone world.
- **Bellringer Review** transparencies provide a quick review activity to begin each class.
- **Pronunciation** transparencies provide a visual for pronunciation practice.
- **Communication** transparencies illustrate the chapter theme. These can be used for communicative practice or for assessment.
- **Assessment** transparencies replicate the Assessment pages of the student text. Assessment Answer transparencies allow you to easily review the answers with your students in class.

Fine Art transparencies are full-color reproductions of the fine art from the text. These transparencies can be used to reinforce the cultural topics introduced in the text and improve your students' awareness of French Fine Art.

The **Vocabulary PuzzleMaker** allows you to create four kinds of puzzles at the touch of a key. The Vocabulary PuzzleMaker includes all the vocabulary introduced in your **Bon voyage!** It is also easy to add your own words to the vocabulary banks.

The **Audio CDs** provide additional practice to reinforce the material presented in **Bon voyage!** Students benefit from hearing a variety of voices from around the entire French-speaking world.

The **Test Program CD** includes the recorded portion for the Listening Tests.

Interactive Chalkboard provides ready-made, customizable PowerPoint presentations with sound, interactive graphics, and video. This presentation tool will help you vary your lessons and reach all students in your classroom.

ExamView®Pro helps you make a test in a matter of minutes by choosing from existing banks of questions, editing them, or creating your own test questions. You can also print several versions of the same test. The clip art bank allows you to create a test using visuals from the text.

TeacherWorks is your all-in-one planner and resource center. This convenient tool will help you reduce the time you spend planning for classes. Simply populate your school year calendar with customizable lesson plans. TeacherWorks will also allow you to easily view your resources without carrying around a heavy bag of books. TeacherWorks provides correlations to standards.

 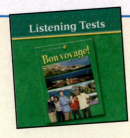 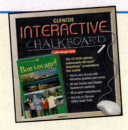  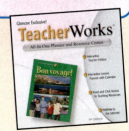

French Names

The following are some French boys' and girls' names that you may wish to give to your students.

Garçons

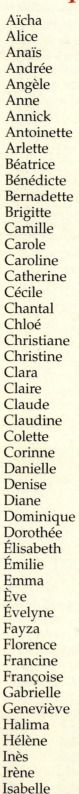

- Ahmed
- Alain
- Albert
- Alexandre
- Alexis
- Amin
- Amir
- André
- Antoine
- Arnaud
- Baptiste
- Benjamin
- Benoît
- Bernard
- Bertrand
- Bruno
- Cédric
- Charles
- Christian
- Christophe
- Claude
- Clément
- Daniel
- David
- Denis
- Didier
- Dominique
- Édouard
- Emmanuel
- Éric
- Étienne
- Fabrice
- Florian
- François
- Franck
- Frédéric
- Georges
- Gérard
- Gilbert
- Gilles
- Grégoire
- Guillaume
- Guy
- Henri
- Hervé
- Hugo
- Jacques
- Jamal
- Jean
- Jérôme
- Joseph
- Julien
- Khalil
- Laurent
- Loïc
- Louis
- Lucas
- Marc
- Marcel
- Martin
- Matthieu
- Maxime
- Michel
- Nicolas
- Olivier
- Pascal
- Patrice
- Patrick
- Paul
- Philippe
- Pierre
- Quentin
- Raoul
- Raphaël
- Raymond
- Rémi
- René
- Richard
- Robert
- Roger
- Roland
- Romain
- Sébastien
- Serge
- Shakir
- Stéphane
- Sylvain
- Théo
- Thierry
- Thomas
- Tristan
- Valentin
- Victor
- Vincent
- Xavier
- Yann
- Yves

Filles

- Aïcha
- Alice
- Anaïs
- Andrée
- Angèle
- Anne
- Annick
- Antoinette
- Arlette
- Béatrice
- Bénédicte
- Bernadette
- Brigitte
- Camille
- Carole
- Caroline
- Catherine
- Cécile
- Chantal
- Chloé
- Christiane
- Christine
- Clara
- Claire
- Claude
- Claudine
- Colette
- Corinne
- Danielle
- Denise
- Diane
- Dominique
- Dorothée
- Élisabeth
- Émilie
- Emma
- Ève
- Évelyne
- Fayza
- Florence
- Francine
- Françoise
- Gabrielle
- Geneviève
- Halima
- Hélène
- Inès
- Irène
- Isabelle
- Jacqueline
- Janine
- Jeanne
- Julie
- Juliette
- Justine
- Latifa
- Laura
- Laure
- Laurence
- Léa
- Liliane
- Lise
- Louise
- Lucie
- Madeleine
- Magali
- Manon
- Marguerite
- Marianne
- Marie
- Marine
- Martine
- Maryse
- Mathilde
- Michèle
- Mireille
- Monique
- Morgane
- Nadine
- Nathalie
- Nicole
- Océane
- Odile
- Pascale
- Patricia
- Pauline
- Renée
- Sabine
- Sandrine
- Sarah
- Simone
- Solange
- Sophie
- Stéphanie
- Suzanne
- Sylvie
- Thérèse
- Valérie
- Véronique
- Virginie
- Yasmin
- Zahra

Classroom Expressions

Below is a list of words and expressions frequently used when conducting a French class.

du papier	paper
une feuille de papier	sheet of paper
un cahier	notebook
un cahier d'exercices	workbook
un stylo	pen
un stylo-bille	ballpoint pen
un crayon	pencil
une gomme	(pencil) eraser
une craie	chalk
le tableau	chalkboard
une brosse	chalkboard eraser
la corbeille	wastebasket
un pupitre	desk
un rang	row
une chaise	chair
un écran	screen
un projecteur	projector
une cassette	cassette
un livre	book
une règle	ruler
un ordinateur	computer
une vidéo	video
un CD	CD
un DVD	DVD

Viens.	Venez.	Come.
Va.	Allez.	Go.
Entre.	Entrez.	Enter.
Sors.	Sortez.	Leave.
Attends.	Attendez.	Wait.
Mets.	Mettez.	Put.
Donne-moi.	Donnez-moi.	Give me.
Dis-moi.	Dites-moi.	Tell me.
Apporte-moi.	Apportez-moi.	Bring me.
Répète.	Répétez.	Repeat.
Pratique.	Pratiquez.	Practice.
Étudie.	Étudiez.	Study.
Réponds.	Répondez.	Answer.
Apprends.	Apprenez.	Learn.
Choisis.	Choisissez.	Choose.
Prépare.	Préparez.	Prepare.
Regarde.	Regardez.	Look at.
Décris.	Décrivez.	Describe.
Commence.	Commencez.	Begin.
Prononce.	Prononcez.	Pronounce.
Écoute.	Écoutez.	Listen.
Parle.	Parlez.	Speak.
Lis.	Lisez.	Read.
Écris.	Écrivez.	Write.
Demande.	Demandez.	Ask.
Suis le modèle.	Suivez le modèle.	Follow the model.
Joue le rôle de…	Jouez le rôle de…	Take the part of . . .
Prends.	Prenez.	Take.
Ouvre.	Ouvrez.	Open.
Ferme.	Fermez.	Close.
Tourne la page.	Tournez la page.	Turn the page.
Efface.	Effacez.	Erase.
Continue.	Continuez.	Continue.
Assieds-toi.	Asseyez-vous.	Sit down.
Lève-toi.	Levez-vous.	Get up.
Lève la main.	Levez la main.	Raise your hand.
Tais-toi.	Taisez-vous.	Be quiet.
Fais attention.	Faites attention.	Pay attenion.

Attention.	Attention.
Attention, s'il vous plaît.	Your attention please.
Silence.	Quiet.
Encore.	Again.
Encore une fois.	Once again.
Un à un.	One at a time.
Tous ensemble.	All together.
À haute voix.	Out loud.
Plus haut, s'il vous plaît.	Louder, please.
En français.	In French.
En anglais.	In English.

Standards for Foreign Language Learning

 Bon voyage! has been written to help you meet the Standards for Foreign Language Learning as set forth by ACTFL. The focus of the text is to provide students with the skills they need to create language for communication. Culture is integrated throughout the text, from the basic introduction of vocabulary to the photographic contributions of the National Geographic Society. Special attention has been given to meeting the standard of Connections with a reading in French in each chapter about another discipline. Linguistic and cultural comparisons are made throughout the text. Suggestions are made for activities that encourage students to use their language skills in their immediate community and more distant ones. Students who complete the **Bon voyage!** series are prepared to participate in the French-speaking world.

Specific correlations to each chapter are provided on the teacher pages preceeding each chapter.

Communication

Communicate in Languages Other than English

Standard 1.1	Students engage in conversations, provide and obtain information, express feelings and emotions, and exchange opinions.
Standard 1.2	Students understand and interpret written and spoken language on a variety of topics.
Standard 1.3	Students present information, concepts, and ideas to an audience of listeners or readers on a variety of topics.

Cultures

Gain Knowledge and Understanding of Other Cultures

Standard 2.1	Students demonstrate an understanding of the relationship between the practices and perspectives of the culture studied.
Standard 2.2	Students demonstrate an understanding of the relationship between the products and perspectives of the culture studied.

Connections

Connect with Other Disciplines and Acquire Information

Standard 3.1	Students reinforce and further their knowledge of other disciplines through the foreign language.
Standard 3.2	Students acquire information and recognize the distinctive viewpoints that are only available through the foreign language and its cultures.

Comparisons

Develop Insight into the Nature of Language and Culture

Standard 4.1	Students demonstrate understanding of the nature of language through comparisons of language studied and their own.
Standard 4.2	Students demonstrate understanding of the concept of culture through comparisons of the cultures studied and their own.

Communities

Participate in Multilingual Communities at Home and Around the World

Standard 5.1	Students use the language both within and beyond the school setting.
Standard 5.2	Students show evidence of becoming life-long learners by using the language for personal enjoyment and enrichment.

GLENCOE FRENCH 2

Bon voyage!

WITH FEATURES BY
NATIONAL GEOGRAPHIC

Conrad J. Schmitt • Katia Brillié Lutz

 **Glencoe**

New York, New York   Columbus, Ohio   Chicago, Illinois   Peoria, Illinois   Woodland Hills, California

About the Authors

Conrad J. Schmitt

Conrad J. Schmitt received his B.A. degree magna cum laude from Montclair State University. He received his M.A. from Middlebury College. He did additional graduate work at New York University.

Mr. Schmitt has taught Spanish and French at all levels—from elementary school to university graduate courses. He served as Coordinator of Foreign Languages for the Hackensack, New Jersey, public schools. He also taught Methods of Teaching a Foreign Language at the Graduate School of Education, Rutgers University. Mr. Schmitt was Editor-in-Chief of Foreign Languages and ESL/EFL materials for the School Division of McGraw-Hill and McGraw-Hill International Book Company.

Mr. Schmitt has authored or co-authored more than one hundred books, all published by Glencoe/McGraw-Hill or by McGraw-Hill. He has addressed teacher groups and given workshops in all states of the United States and has lectured and presented seminars throughout the Far East, Latin America, and Canada. In addition, Mr. Schmitt has traveled extensively throughout France, French-speaking Canada, North Africa, French-speaking West Africa, the French Antilles, and Haiti.

Katia Brillié Lutz

Katia Brillié Lutz has her **Baccalauréat** in Mathematics and Science from the Lycée Molière in Paris and her **Licence ès Lettres** in languages from the Sorbonne. She was a Fulbright scholar at Mount Holyoke College.

Ms. Lutz has taught French language at Yale University and French language and literature at Southern Connecticut State College. She also taught French at the United Nations in New York City.

Ms. Lutz was Executive Editor of French at Macmillan Publishing Company. She also served as Senior Editor at Harcourt Brace Jovanovich and Holt Rinehart and Winston. She was a news translator and announcer for the BBC Overseas Language Services in London.

Ms. Lutz is the author of many language textbooks at all levels of instruction.

Copyright © 2005 by The McGraw-Hill Companies, Inc. All rights reserved. Except as permitted under the United States Copyright Act, no part of this publication may be reproduced or distributed in any form or by any means, or stored in a database or retrieval system, without prior permission of the publisher.

The feature in this textbook entitled **Reflets** was designed and created by the National Geographic Society's School Publishing Division. Copyright 2005. National Geographic Society. All rights reserved.

The name "National Geographic" and the yellow border are registered trademarks of the National Geographic Society.

Send all inquiries to:
Glencoe/McGraw-Hill
8787 Orion Place
Columbus, OH 43240-4027

ISBN: 0-07-865660-5 (Student Edition)
ISBN: 0-07-865661-3 (Teacher Wraparound Edition)

Printed in the United States of America.

2 3 4 5 6 7 8 9 10 058/055 10 09 08 07 06 05 04

Teacher Reviewers

We wish to express our appreciation to the numerous individuals throughout the United States and the French-speaking world who have advised us in the development of these teaching materials. Special thanks are extended to the people whose names appear below.

Anne-Marie Baumis
Bayside, NY

Claude Benaiteau
Austin, TX

Sr. M. Elayne Bockey, SND
St. Wendelin High School
Fostoria, OH

Linda Burnette
Rockville Junior/Senior
  High School
Rockville, IN

Linda Butt
Loyola Blakefield
Towson, MD

Betty Clough
Austin, TX

Yolande Helm
Ohio University
Athens, OH

Jan Hofts
Northwest High School
Indianapolis, IN

Kathleen A. Houchens
The Ohio State University
Columbus, OH

Dominique Keith
Lake Forest, CA

Raelene Noll
Delmar, NY

Nancy Price
Fort Atkinson High School
Fort Atkinson, WI

Sally Price
Marysville-Pilchuck
  High School
Marysville, WA

Bonita Sanders
Eisenhower High School
New Berlin, WI

Deana Schiffer
Hewlett High School
Hewlett, NY

Julia Sheppard
Delaware City Schools
Delaware, OH

James Toolan
Tuxedo High School
Tuxedo, NY

Mary Webster
Romeo High School
Romeo, MI

Marian Welch
Austin ISD
Austin, TX

Richard Wixom
Miller Middle School
Lake Katrine, NY

Brian Zailian
Tamalpais High School
Mill Valley, CA

For the Parent or Guardian

We are excited that your child has decided to study French. Foreign language study provides many benefits for students in addition to the ability to communicate in another language. Students who study another language improve their first language skills. They become more aware of the world around them and they learn to appreciate diversity.

You can help your child be successful in his or her study of French even if you are not familiar with that language. Encourage your child to talk to you about the places where French is spoken. Engage in conversations about current events in those places. The section of their Glencoe French book called **Le monde francophone** on pages xxi–xxxv may serve as a reference for you and your child. In addition, you will find information about the geography of the French-speaking world and links to foreign newspapers at **french.glencoe.com**.

The methodology employed in the Glencoe French books is logical and leads students step by step through their study of the language. Consistent instruction and practice are essential for learning a foreign language. You can help by encouraging your child to review vocabulary each day. As he or she progresses through the text, you will to want to use the study tips on pages H22–H37 to help your child learn French. If you have Internet access, encourage your child to practice using the activities, games, and practice quizzes at **french.glencoe.com**.

Table des matières

La francophonie

Le monde francophone xxi
Le monde xxii
La francophonie xxiv
La France xxxi
Paris xxxii
Le métro xxxiii
Le Canada xxxiv
L'Afrique xxxv

Révision

A Les copains et l'école
Vocabulaire R2
Conversation R4
Structure
   L'accord des adjectifs R5
   Les verbes **être** et **aller** R6
   Les contractions R8

B La famille
Vocabulaire R12
Conversation R14
Structure
   Les verbes réguliers en **-er** R15
   Le partitif R16
   Les verbes **avoir** et **faire** R18

C Les courses
Vocabulaire R22
Conversation R24
Structure
   Les verbes **vouloir** et **pouvoir** R25
   L'infinitif R26
   Le verbe **prendre** R26

D En voyage
Vocabulaire R30
Conversation R32
Structure
   Les verbes en **-ir** et **-re** R33
   Les verbes **sortir, partir, dormir, servir** R34

E Les sports
Vocabulaire R38
Conversation R40
Structure
   Le passé composé des verbes réguliers avec **avoir** R41
   Les participes passés irréguliers R43

F La routine quotidienne
Vocabulaire R48
Conversation R50
Structure
   Les verbes réfléchis au présent R51
   Le passé composé avec **être** R53
   Les verbes réfléchis au passé composé R55

Table des matières

CHAPITRE 1 — Les loisirs culturels

Objectifs

In this chapter you will learn to:
- ✔ *discuss movies, plays, and museums*
- ✔ *tell what you know and whom you know*
- ✔ *tell what happens to you or someone else*
- ✔ *refer to people and things already mentioned*
- ✔ *talk about some cultural activities in Paris*

Vocabulaire
Mots 1 2
   Au cinéma 2
   Au théâtre 3
Mots 2 6
   Au musée 6

Structure
Les verbes **savoir** et **connaître** 10
Les pronoms **me, te, nous, vous** 12
Les pronoms **le, la, les** 14

Conversation
On va au cinéma? 18

Prononciation
Le son /ü/ 19

Lectures culturelles
Les loisirs culturels en France 20
La musique africaine 22

Connexions
La musique 24

C'est à vous 26
Assessment 28

Table des matières

CHAPITRE 2 La santé et la médecine

Objectifs

In this chapter you will learn to:

- ✔ explain a minor illness to a doctor
- ✔ have a prescription filled at a pharmacy
- ✔ tell for whom something is done
- ✔ talk about some more activities
- ✔ give commands
- ✔ refer to people, places, and things already mentioned
- ✔ discuss medical services in France

Vocabulaire
Mots 1 34
   On est malade. 34
Mots 2 38
   Chez le médecin. 38
   À la pharmacie 39

Structure
   Les pronoms **lui, leur**. 42
   Les verbes **souffrir** et **ouvrir** 44
   L'impératif. 45
   Le pronom **en** 48

Conversation
   Chez le médecin 50

Prononciation
   Les sons /u/ et /ü/ 51

Lectures culturelles
   Une consultation. 52
   Culture et santé. 54
   Les services médicaux en France 55

Connexions
   La diététique 56

C'est à vous 58

Assessment 60

Table des matières

CHAPITRE 3 Les télécommunications

Objectifs
In this chapter you will learn to:
- ✔ *talk about computers, e-mail, the Internet, faxes, and telephones*
- ✔ *talk about habitual and continuous actions in the past*
- ✔ *narrate in the past*
- ✔ *discuss today's telecommunications*

Vocabulaire
Mots 1 66
  L'ordinateur 66
  Le télécopieur, le fax. 67
Mots 2 70
  Le téléphone 70

Structure
L'imparfait. 74
Les emplois de l'imparfait 78

Conversation
Des devoirs difficiles 82

Lectures culturelles
Le téléphone d'hier et d'aujourd'hui 84
La télécarte 86
Les communications avant et maintenant 87

Connexions
L'ordinateur 88

C'est à vous 90

Assessment............................. 92

Table des matières

CHAPITRE Des voyages intéressants

Objectifs

In this chapter you will learn to:
- ✔ talk about train travel
- ✔ talk about air travel
- ✔ describe past events
- ✔ identify cities, countries, and continents
- ✔ discuss old and modern trains in France

Vocabulaire
Mots 1 98
   Les trains d'hier et d'aujourd'hui 98
Mots 2 102
   À l'aéroport 102
   À bord de l'avion 102
   À l'arrivée 103

Structure
   L'imparfait et le passé composé 106
   Raconter une histoire au passé 109
   Le verbe **venir** 112
   Les prépositions avec les noms
      géographiques 113

Conversation
   À l'aéroport 116

Lectures culturelles
   Les trains d'hier et d'aujourd'hui 118
   Un voyage en Suisse 120
   Un voyage au Bénin 121

Connexions
   L'archéologie 122

C'est à vous 124

Assessment 126

RÉVISION

Chapitres 1–4 130

Reflets de la France 136

LITTÉRATURE 1

Le Livre de mon père
Émile Henriot 476

Table des matières

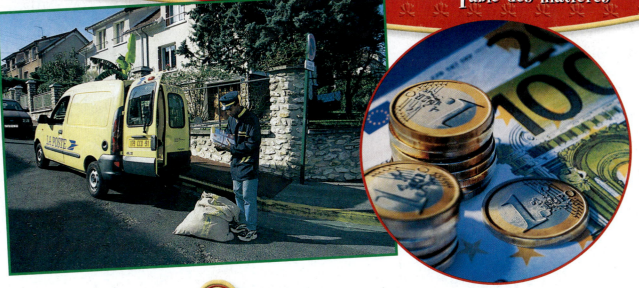

CHAPITRE 5 — La banque et la poste

Objectifs

In this chapter you will learn to:

- ✔ talk about using the services of the bank
- ✔ use words and expressions related to postal services
- ✔ give more information in one sentence
- ✔ refer to people and things already mentioned
- ✔ tell what you and others do for one another
- ✔ make negative statements
- ✔ talk about teen spending habits

Vocabulaire
Mots 1 142
   À la banque 142
   Au bureau de change 143
   Sandrine et Luc 143
Mots 2 146
   À la poste 146

Structure
Les pronoms relatifs **qui** et **que** 150
L'accord du participe passé 153
Les actions réciproques 155
Personne ne... et **rien ne...** 157

Conversation
Au bureau de change 158

Lectures culturelles
La semaine des jeunes Français 160
Les devises étrangères 162
La Poste 163

Connexions
Les finances 164

C'est à vous 166

Assessment 168

Table des matières

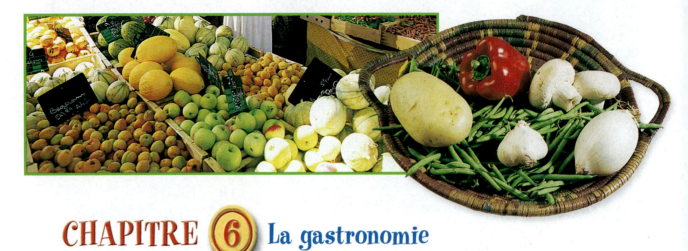

CHAPITRE 6 La gastronomie

Objectifs
In this chapter you will learn to:
- ✔ talk about foods and food preparation
- ✔ describe future events
- ✔ refer to people and things already mentioned
- ✔ tell what you have others do
- ✔ discuss the cuisine of various French provinces

Vocabulaire
Mots 1	174
Dans la cuisine	174
Des aliments	174
Mots 2	178
Faisons la cuisine!	178
D'autres aliments	179

Structure
Le futur simple	182
Deux pronoms dans la même phrase	185
Faire + infinitif	187

Conversation
La cuisine et moi, ça fait deux!	190

Lectures culturelles
Un voyage gastronomique	192
Un dîner chez une famille maghrébine	194
Navarin d'agneau	195

Connexions
Gargantua de Rabelaìs	196

C'est à vous 198

Assessment 200

CHAPITRE 7 La voiture et la route

Objectifs

In this chapter you will learn to:

✔ talk about cars and driving
✔ give directions on the road
✔ talk about what would happen under certain conditions
✔ describe future events
✔ refer to something already mentioned
✔ talk about driving and highways in France

Vocabulaire
Mots 1 206
   La voiture 206
   À la station-service 207
Mots 2 210
   En ville. 210
   Sur la route 211

Structure
Le conditionnel. 214
Le futur et le conditionnel des
   verbes irréguliers 216
Les propositions introduites par **si** 218
Deux pronoms dans la même phrase 220

Conversation
À la station-service. 222

Lectures culturelles
La conduite en France 224
Partez à l'aventure en Tunisie! 226

Connexions
L'écologie 228

C'est à vous 230

Assessment 232

RÉVISION	Chapitres 5–7 236
	Reflets du Maghreb. 242
LITTÉRATURE 2	Deux poèmes africains 480

Table des matières

CHAPITRE 8 Un accident et l'hôpital

Objectifs

In this chapter you will learn to:
- ✔ talk about accidents and medical problems
- ✔ talk about emergency room procedures
- ✔ ask different types of questions
- ✔ tell people what to do
- ✔ compare people and things
- ✔ talk about a medical emergency in France

Vocabulaire
Mots 1 248
    Un accident 248
    Au service des urgences 248
    Le corps 249
Mots 2 252
    À l'hôpital 252
    Une salle d'opération 253

Structure
    Les pronoms interrogatifs et relatifs 256
    Les pronoms et l'impératif 258
    Le superlatif des adjectifs 261
    Meilleur/mieux 262

Conversation
    Au service des urgences 264

Lectures culturelles
    À l'Hôtel-Dieu, à toute vitesse! 266
    Médecins Sans Frontières 268

Connexions
    Louis Pasteur et l'Institut Pasteur 270

C'est à vous 272

Assessment 274

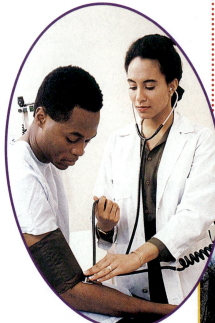

Table des matières

CHAPITRE 9 L'hôtel

Objectifs
In this chapter you will learn to:
- ✔ check into and out of a hotel
- ✔ ask for things you may need while at a hotel
- ✔ talk about past actions
- ✔ refer to previously mentioned places
- ✔ talk about people and things already mentioned
- ✔ describe how you do things
- ✔ talk about hotels in France

Vocabulaire
Mots 1 280
   L'arrivée à l'hôtel 280
Mots 2 284
   Dans la chambre d'hôtel 284
   Dans la salle de bains 284

Structure
   Le passé composé: **être** ou **avoir** 288
   Le pronom **y** 289
   Un pronom + **en** 291
   La formation des adverbes 292

Conversation
   À la réception de l'hôtel 294

Lectures culturelles
   L'Hôtel de la Gare 296
   Les auberges de jeunesse 298
   Le Club Med 299

Connexions
   Le langage 300

C'est à vous 302

Assessment 304

Table des matières

CHAPITRE 10 Les transports en commun

Objectifs
In this chapter you will learn to:

✔ talk about public transportation
✔ request information formally and informally
✔ tell what you and others have just done
✔ find out how long someone has been doing something
✔ talk about taking the bus and subway in Paris

Vocabulaire
Mots 1 310
    Le métro 310
Mots 2 314
    L'autobus 314

Structure
    Les questions 318
    Venir de + infinitif 321
    Les expressions de temps 323

Conversation
    Le métro 324

Lectures culturelles
    Les transports en commun à Paris 326
    Les transports en commun en Haïti
      et en Afrique 328

Connexions
    La littérature 330

C'est à vous 332

Assessment 334

CHAPITRE 11 À la ville et à la campagne

Objectifs

In this chapter you will learn to:

✔ talk about life in the city and give directions
✔ talk about life in the country
✔ ask questions to distinguish between two or more people or things
✔ describe some more activities
✔ talk about life on a farm in France

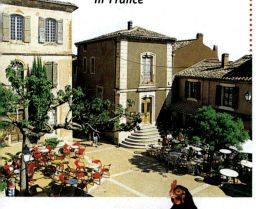

Vocabulaire
Mots 1 340
   La ville..................... 340
   Au centre-ville / En ville 340
Mots 2 344
   À la campagne 344
   Des animaux................ 345

Structure
   Lequel et **celui-là** 348
   Les verbes **suivre, conduire, vivre** 350
   L'infinitif après les prépositions 351

Conversation
   La ville ou la campagne................ 352

Lectures culturelles
   Une famille d'agriculteurs................ 354
   Abidjan 356
   Montréal 357

Connexions
   La démographie 358

C'est à vous 360

Assessment 362

RÉVISION   Chapitres 8–11 366

NATIONAL GEOGRAPHIC   Reflets des Caraïbes 370

LITTÉRATURE 3   *Vol de nuit*
Antoine de Saint-Exupéry 486

Table des matières

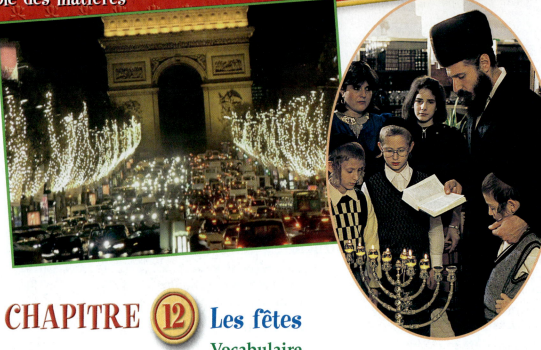

CHAPITRE 12 Les fêtes

Objectifs
In this chapter you will learn to:

✔ talk about holidays and celebrations
✔ talk about things that may or may not happen
✔ express what you wish, hope, or would like others to do
✔ discuss some family celebrations

Vocabulaire
Mots 1 376
   Le 14 juillet 376
   Le carnaval 377
Mots 2 380
   Noël 380
   Hanouka 381
   Le jour de l'An 381
   Le mariage. 381

Structure
Le subjonctif 384
Le subjonctif après les expressions
   de souhait ou de volonté. 388

Conversation
C'est bientôt le 14 juillet. 390

Lectures culturelles
Des fêtes en France. 392
Carnaval 394

Connexions
Histoire et Littérature. 396

C'est à vous 398

Assessment. 400

Table des matières

CHAPITRE Le savoir-vivre

Objectifs

In this chapter you will learn to:

- ✓ talk about social etiquette
- ✓ introduce people to each other
- ✓ describe some feelings
- ✓ express opinions
- ✓ talk about more things that may or may not happen
- ✓ express emotional reactions to what others do
- ✓ compare etiquette in France and the United States

Vocabulaire

Mots 1 406
   D'autres parties du corps 406
   Bien ou mal élevé(e)? 406
   Comment se tenir à table? 407

Mots 2 410
   Les émotions 410
   Les présentations 411

Structure

Le subjonctif après les expressions
   impersonnelles 414
D'autres verbes au présent du subjonctif 416
Le subjonctif après les expressions
   d'émotion 418

Conversation

Il faut qu'on s'habille. 420

Lectures culturelles

Le savoir-vivre en France. 422
Le tutoiement 424
Les salutations en Afrique occidentale 425

Connexions

Étiquette 426

C'est à vous 428

Assessment 430

Table des matières

CHAPITRE 14 — Les professions et les métiers

Objectifs

In this chapter you will learn to:
- ✔ talk about professions
- ✔ apply for a job
- ✔ express doubt
- ✔ express wishes about yourself and others
- ✔ express certainty and uncertainty
- ✔ discuss the advantages of learning French for future employment

Vocabulaire
Mots 1 436
   Un lieu de travail 436
   Des professions 436
   Des métiers 437
Mots 2 440
   Au bureau de placement 440
   On travaille 441

Structure
   Le subjonctif après les expressions de doute . . . 444
   L'infinitif ou le subjonctif 447
   Le subjonctif dans les propositions relatives . . . 448

Conversation
   Au bureau de placement 450

Lectures culturelles
   Un jeune homme appelé Bobby 452
   Le français et votre carrière 454
   Petites annonces 455

Connexions
   L'économie 456

C'est à vous 458

Assessment 460

RÉVISION   Chapitres 12–14 464

NATIONAL GEOGRAPHIC   Reflets de l'Europe francophone 470

LITTÉRATURE 4   *Le Malade imaginaire*
Molière 492

 Table des matières

Table des matières

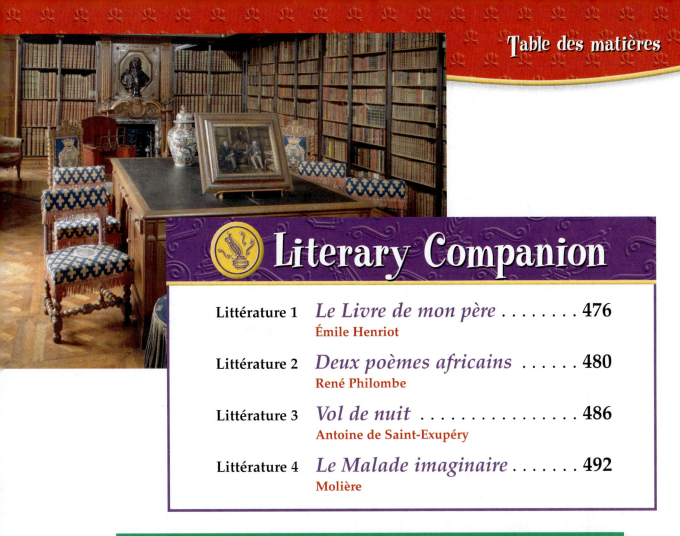

Literary Companion

Littérature 1	*Le Livre de mon père* .... 476 Émile Henriot	
Littérature 2	*Deux poèmes africains* ...... 480 René Philombe	
Littérature 3	*Vol de nuit* .... 486 Antoine de Saint-Exupéry	
Littérature 4	*Le Malade imaginaire* .... 492 Molière	

Video Companion

Using video in the classroom 498

Épisode 1 500	Épisode 8 507
Épisode 2 501	Épisode 9 508
Épisode 3 502	Épisode 10 509
Épisode 4 503	Épisode 11 510
Épisode 5 504	Épisode 12 511
Épisode 6 505	Épisode 13 512
Épisode 7 506	Épisode 14 513

Table des matières

Handbook

InfoGap Activities H2
Study Tips H22
Verb Charts H38
French-English Dictionary H49
English-French Dictionary H79
Index H109

Guide to Symbols

Throughout **Bon voyage!** you will see these symbols, or icons. They will tell you how to best use the particular part of the chapter or activity they accompany. Following is a key to help you understand these symbols.

 Audio Link This icon indicates conversations in the chapter that are recorded on compact disk.

 Recycling This icon indicates sections that review knowledge from previous chapters and reading sections.

 Paired Activity This icon indicates sections that you can read aloud and practice together in groups of two.

 Group Activity This icon indicates sections that you can read aloud and practice together in groups of three or more.

 Encore Plus This icon indicates additional practice activities that review knowledge from current chapters and reading sections.

 Allez-y! This icon indicates the end of new material in each section and the beginning of the recombination section at the end of the chapter.

 Literary Companion This icon appears in the review lessons to let you know that you are prepared to do the literature selection indicated if you wish.

 Interactive CD-ROM This icon indicates that the material is also on an Interactive CD-ROM.

Le monde francophone

The French geographer Onésime Reclus first coined the word *francophonie* in 1880 to designate geographical entities where French was spoken. Today, *la francophonie* refers to the collective body of over one hundred million people all over the world who speak French, exclusively or in part, in their daily lives. The term *francophonie* refers to the diverse official organizations, governments, and countries that promote the use of French in economic, political, diplomatic, and cultural exchanges. Politically, French remains the second most important language in the world. In some Francophone nations, French is the official language (France), or the co-official language (Cameroon); in others, it is spoken by a minority who share a common cultural heritage (Andorra). The French language is present in Europe, Africa, the Americas, and Oceania.

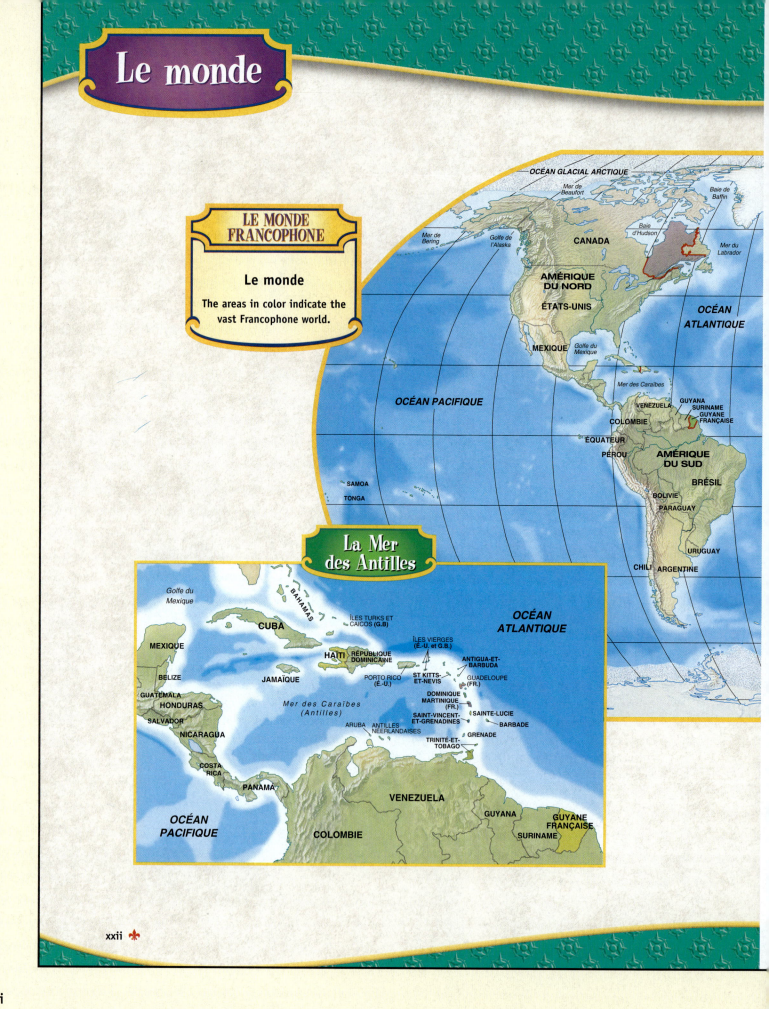

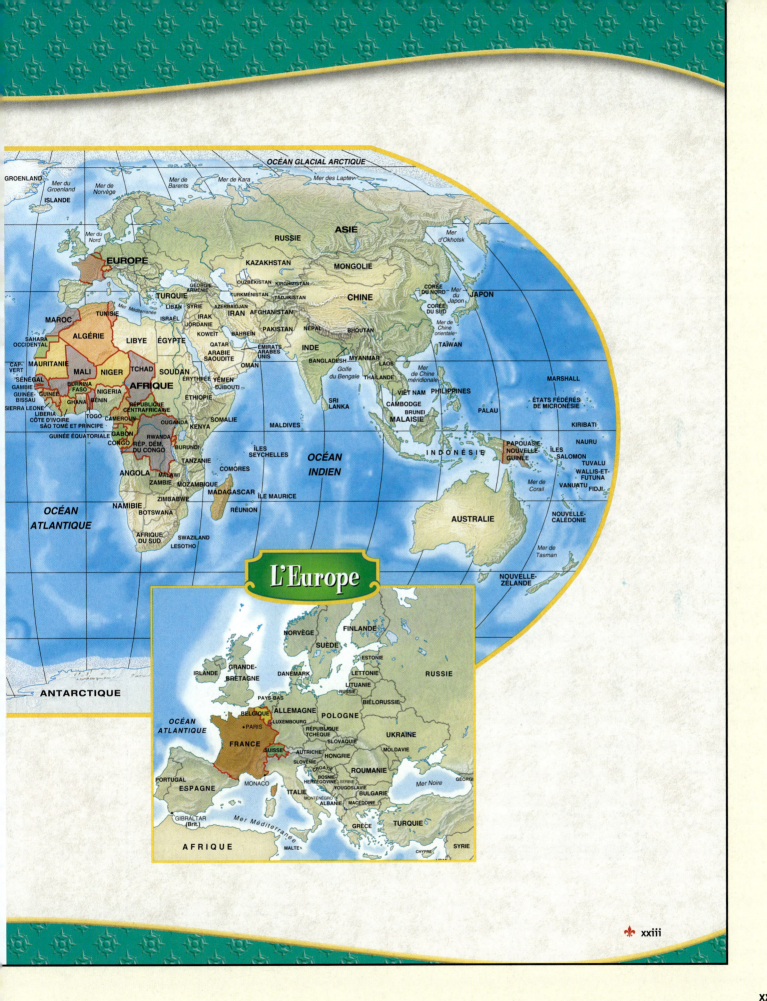

La francophonie

L'Afrique

Le Bénin
CAPITAL
Porto-Novo
POPULATION
7,041,000
FUN FACT
Benin has one of the most popular tourist attractions in all of West Africa—the fishing village of Ganvié built on stilts in the middle of a lagoon not far from the capital, Porto-Novo.

Le Burkina Faso
CAPITAL
Ouagadougou
POPULATION
13,228,000
FUN FACT
Burkina Faso is known for its friendly people. Villagers are fond of allowing foreigners to live in their homes and take part in village life.

Les Comores
CAPITAL
Moroni
POPULATION
633,000
FUN FACT
The beautiful Comores Islands in the Indian Ocean are known for their lovely, isolated beaches. These islands are among the few areas in the world where natural beauty reigns.

La République du Congo
CAPITAL
Brazzaville
POPULATION
2,954,000
FUN FACT
Seventy percent of the population lives in the capital city or near the railroad between it and Pointe-Noire about 250 miles to the west.

Le Burundi
CAPITAL
Bujumbura
POPULATION
6,096,000
FUN FACT
Burundi was first under German control. It then became Ruanda-Urundi under Belgian control. It became independent in 1962.

Le Cameroun
CAPITAL
Yaoundé
POPULATION
15,746,000
FUN FACT
Cameroon is known for its fantastic landscapes: Saharan desert, equatorial rain forest, tree-laden savannah, grassy plains, volcanic mountains with crater lakes, the swampy basin of Lake Chad, and one of the highest mountains in Africa.

L'Algérie
CAPITAL
Algiers
POPULATION
32,818,000
FUN FACT
Algeria is called "the geographic giant" of the Maghreb. It is four times the size of France. Most of the country lies in the Sahara desert.

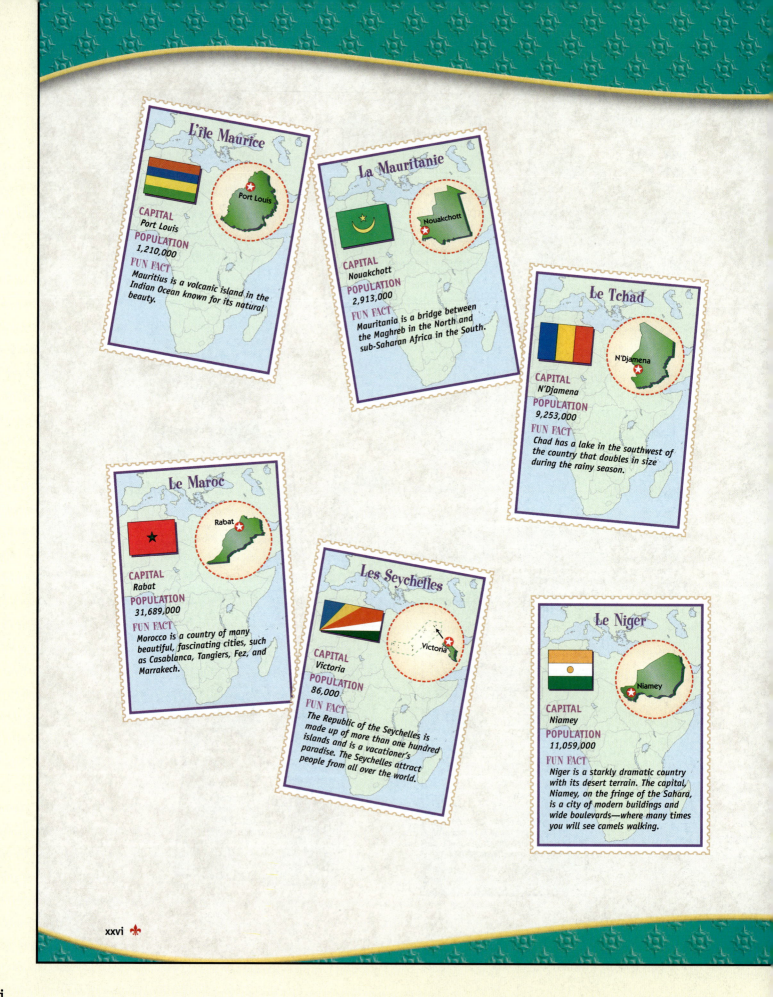

L'Amérique du Nord et du Sud

La Guadeloupe
PRÉFECTURE Basse-Terre
POPULATION 440,000
FUN FACT Guadeloupe, a French overseas department in the Caribbean, is made up of two major islands in addition to some smaller ones. It is known for its jungle highlands and beautiful seaside resorts.

La Guyane française
PRÉFECTURE Cayenne
POPULATION 187,000
FUN FACT French Guyana on the east coast of South America is an overseas French department. It is famous for its Devil's Island, which once served as a French penal colony.

Haïti
CAPITAL Port-au-Prince
POPULATION 7,528,000
FUN FACT Haiti shares the island of Hispaniola with the Dominican Republic. Its friendly people are known for their musical and artistic talents. Haitian art is sought after in art galleries around the world.

La province de Québec
CAPITAL Québec
POPULATION 7,040,000
FUN FACT Quebec is the oldest and largest of Canada's provinces. About 90 percent of Quebec's inhabitants are French-speaking.

La Martinique
PRÉFECTURE Fort-de-France
POPULATION 426,000
FUN FACT Martinique, like Guadeloupe, is a French overseas department in the Caribbean Sea. It is a highly developed island famous for its beautiful, exotic flowers—orchids, hibiscus, and flamingo flowers.

Saint-Pierre-et-Miquelon
PRÉFECTURE Saint-Pierre
POPULATION 7,000
FUN FACT Saint-Pierre and Miquelon are French-speaking islands in the Atlantic Ocean, south of Newfoundland. Many residents work in the cod-fishing industry.

L'Océanie

La Nouvelle-Calédonie

CAPITAL
Nouméa
POPULATION
211,000
FUN FACT
New Caledonia is a French overseas territory in the South Pacific. It is made up of one large island and numerous small, beautiful coral islands.

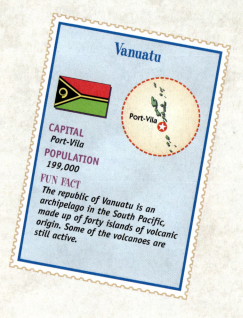

Vanuatu

CAPITAL
Port-Vila
POPULATION
199,000
FUN FACT
The republic of Vanuatu is an archipelago in the South Pacific, made up of forty islands of volcanic origin. Some of the volcanoes are still active.

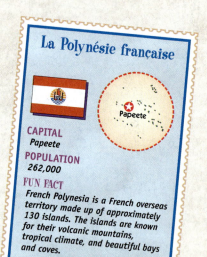

La Polynésie française

CAPITAL
Papeete
POPULATION
262,000
FUN FACT
French Polynesia is a French overseas territory made up of approximately 130 islands. The islands are known for their volcanic mountains, tropical climate, and beautiful bays and coves.

Wallis-et-Futuna

CAPITAL
Mata-Utu
POPULATION
16,000
FUN FACT
Wallis-et-Futuna is a French overseas territory in the South Pacific. The mountainous islands of the archipelago are surrounded by coral reefs.

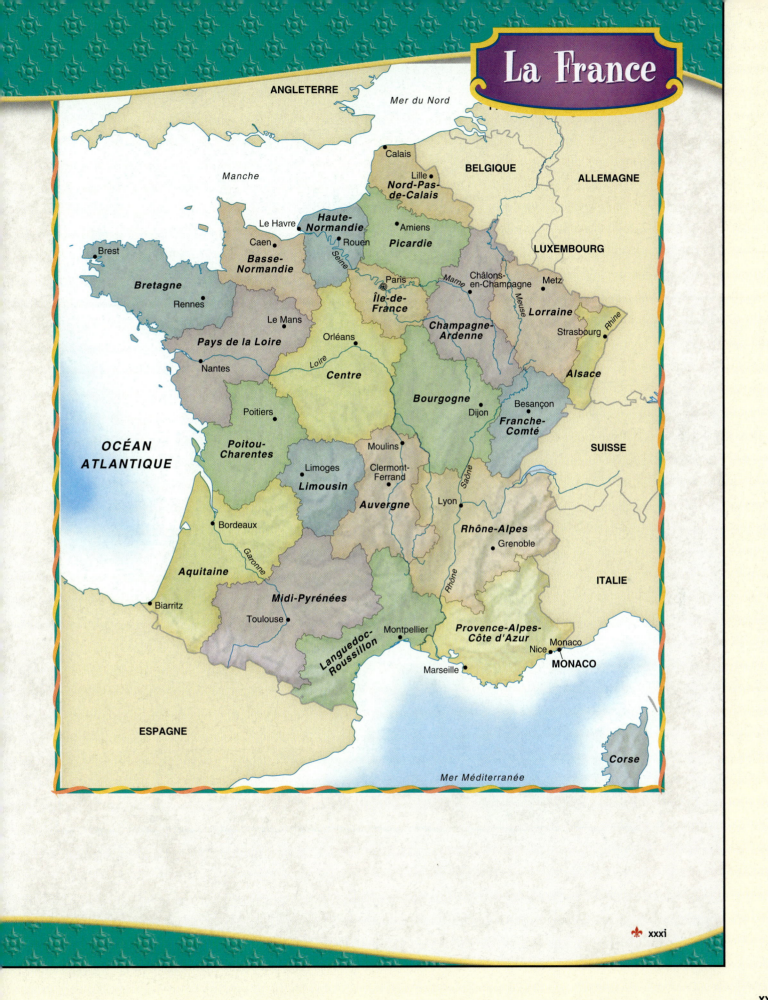

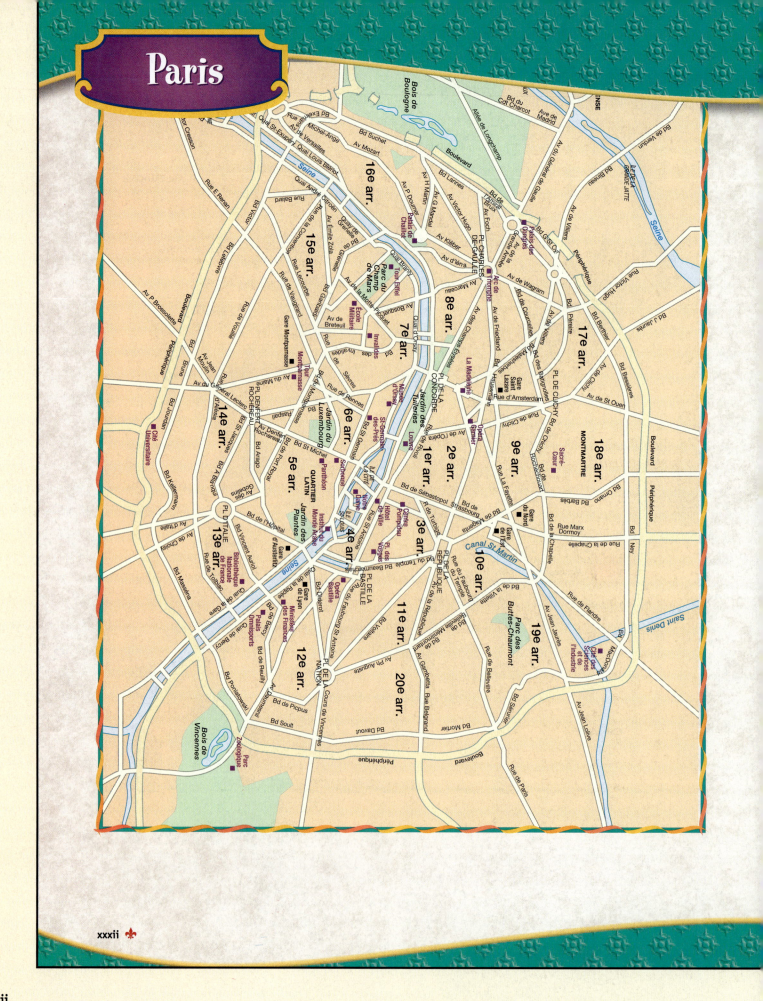

Métro

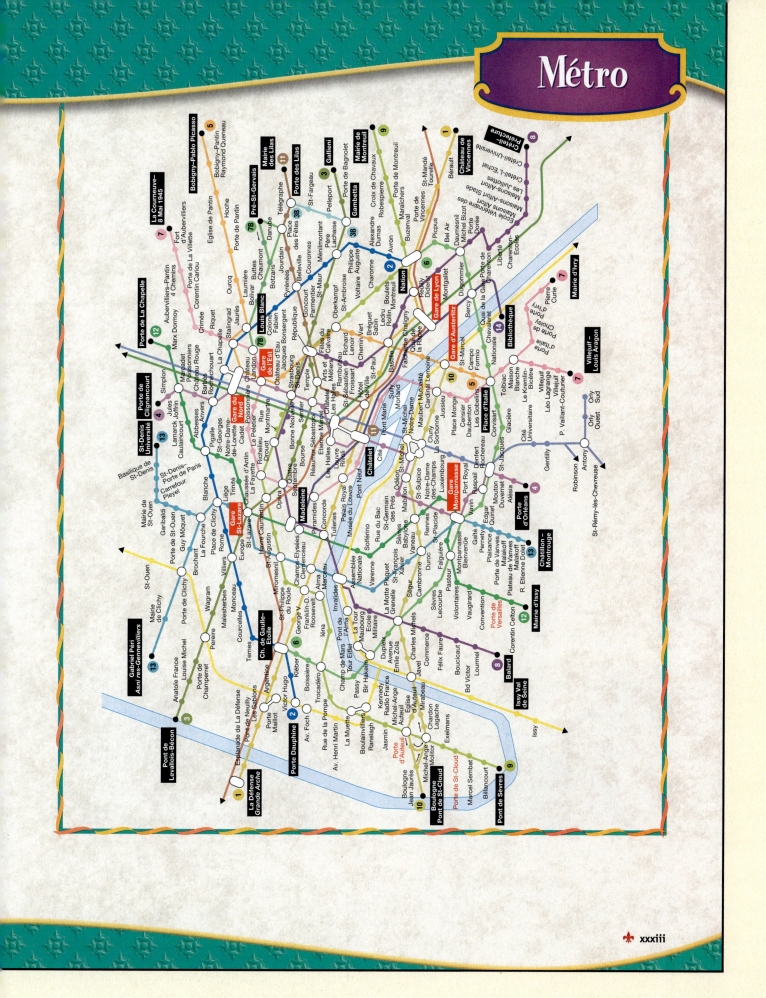

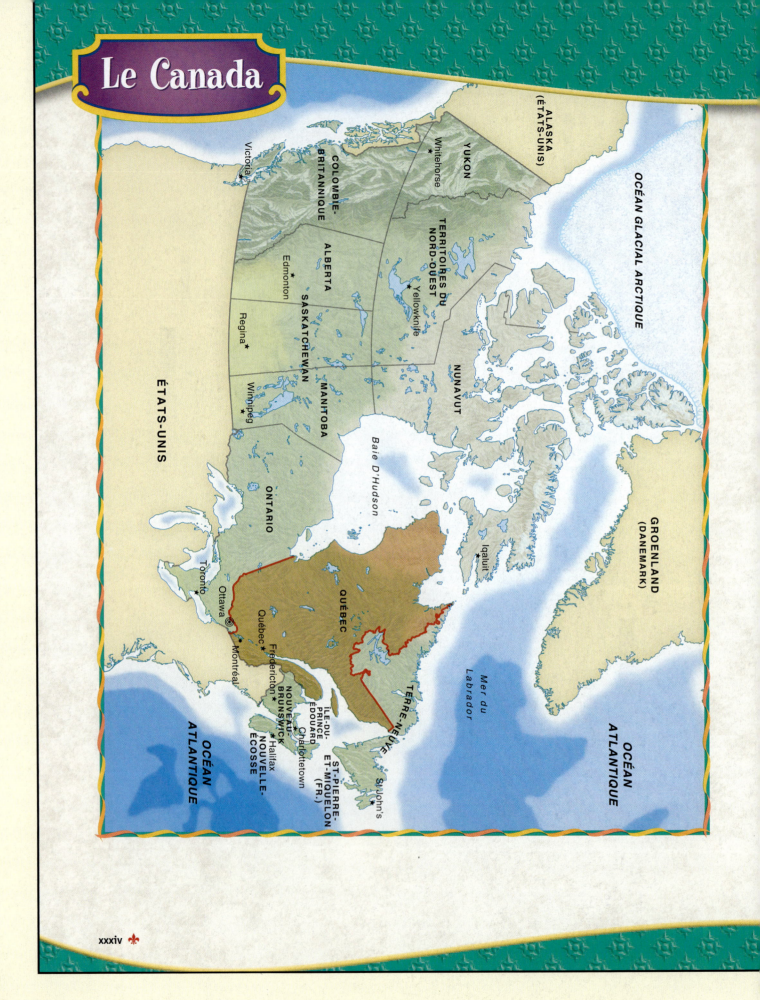

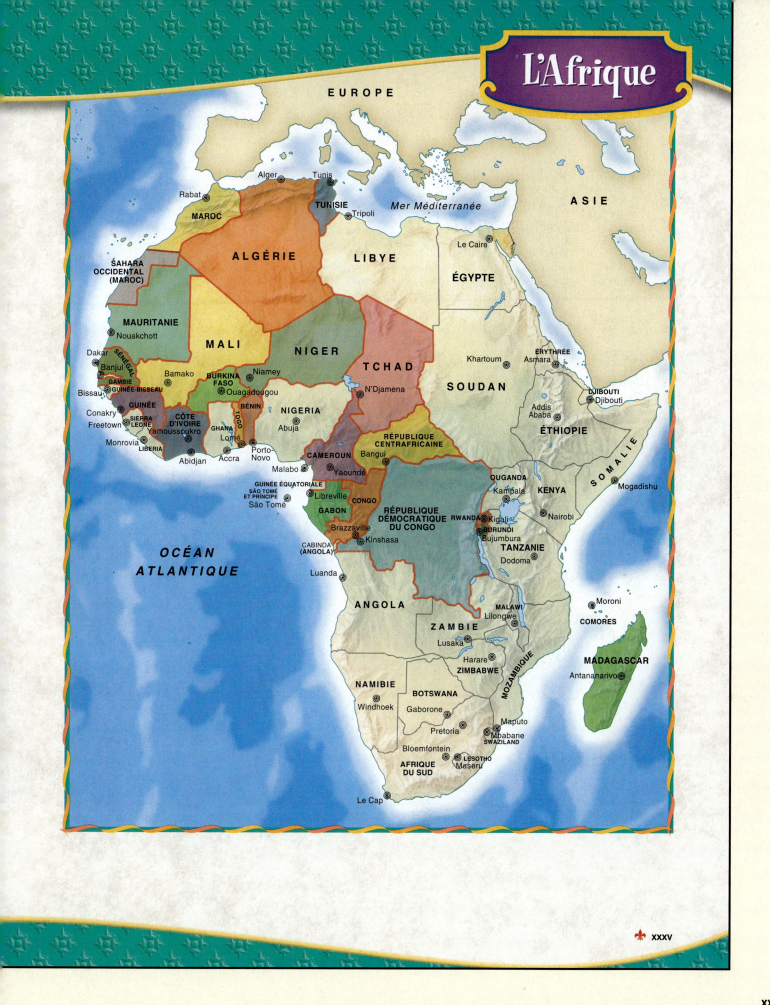

Révision A

Preview

This review covers vocabulary needed to describe people and school. These topics were first presented in **Bon voyage! Level 1.** The agreement of adjectives, the present tense of the verbs **être** and **aller,** and the contractions with **à** and **de** are also reviewed.

National Standards

Communication

In Review A, students will communicate in spoken and written French on the following topics:
- Describing people
- School activities

Students will also narrate present events. They will obtain and provide information and engage in conversations about people and school.

LEVELING

The activities, conversations, and readings within each chapter are marked according to level of difficulty. **E** indicates easy. **A** indicates average. **C** indicates challenging. Some activities cover a range of difficulty. In some activities, for example, advanced students will be able to produce more extensive responses while students who learn at a different rate may give less detailed responses. The leveling indicators will help you individualize instruction to best meet your students' needs.

The Review lessons are all **E**.

Révision A

Les copains et l'école

Révision A

 Spotlight on Culture

Photograph The Lycée Charlemagne is a typical Parisian lycée with a very good academic reputation.

Learning from Photos

(page R1) Have students describe as many students as they can in the photo.

Révision A

Resource Manager
Workbook, pages R1–R6
Tests, pages R1–R2, R15, R25
ExamView® Pro

Vocabulaire

Bellringer Review
Use BRR Transparency R.1 or write the following on the board.
Make a list of words that can be used to describe a person.

Presentation

Step 1 Have students open their books and repeat the sentences about Sandrine and Aurélien after you.

Step 2 Have students identify the descriptive words used in the sentences.

Attention!
When students are doing the activities, accept any answer that makes sense. The purpose of these activities is to have students use the vocabulary. They are not factual recall activities.

Révision A

Vocabulaire

Voilà Sandrine.
Sandrine est française. Elle n'est pas américaine.
Elle est très intelligente.
Elle est élève au lycée Louis-le-Grand à Paris.
Elle va au lycée Louis-le-Grand.

Aurélien et Sandrine sont copains.
Ils vont tous les deux au même lycée.
Aurélien et Sandrine sont très amusants.

Révision A

1 Historiette Une fille française Inventez des réponses.

1. Caroline est française?
2. Elle est de Paris, la capitale de la France?
3. Elle est élève au lycée Louis-le-Grand?
4. Elle va au lycée Louis-le-Grand?
5. Caroline est intelligente?
6. Les copains de Caroline sont intelligents aussi?
7. Ils sont amusants?
8. Ils vont tous au même lycée?

Des copains au lycée

2 Historiette Guillaume
Répondez d'après les indications.

1. Guillaume est de quelle nationalité? (américain)
2. Il est d'où? (de New York)
3. Qui est élève? (Guillaume)
4. Il est élève où? (dans une école secondaire à New York)
5. Il va à l'école à quelle heure le matin? (à sept heures et demie)
6. Comment est Guillaume? (intelligent et amusant)

Historiette Each time **Historiette** appears, it means that the answers to the activity form a short story. Encourage students to look at the title of the **Historiette**, since it can help them do the activity.

2 Expansion: Have students rewrite the questions in this activity in order to ask questions about a student in the class.

Writing Development
Have students write the answers to Activities 1 and 2 in paragraph form.

Learning from Photos
(pages R2–R3) Have students describe the students in the photos. Don't restrict them to adjectives; see if they can recall any clothing and colors, for example.

Reaching All Students

Additional Practice Have students make up questions about Sandrine or Sandrine and Aurélien to ask you or classmates.
  Have students make up false statements about Guillaume. Their classmates will correct these statements.

Answers to Révision

1 *Answers will vary but may include:*
1. Oui, Caroline est française.
2. Oui, elle est de Paris, la capitale de la France.
3. Oui, elle est élève au lycée Louis-le-Grand.
4. Oui, elle va au lycée Louis-le-Grand.
5. Oui, elle est intelligente.
6. Oui, ils sont intelligents aussi.
7. Oui, ils sont amusants.
8. Oui, ils vont tous au même lycée.

2
1. Guillaume est américain.
2. Il est de New York.
3. Guillaume est élève.
4. Il est élève dans une école secondaire à New York.
5. Il va à l'école à sept heures et demie.
6. Guillaume est intelligent et amusant.

Révision A

Conversation

Presentation

Step 1 Review the expressions used for greeting people. Have the class repeat the conversation after you.

Step 2 Call on two students to read the conversation to the class.

Révision A

Conversation

De bons copains

Marc: Salut!
Léa: Salut!
Marc: Tu es une amie de Carole Bertrand, non?
Léa: Oui, je suis une amie de Carole.
Marc: Je m'appelle Marc. Marc Legrand. Et toi?
Léa: Je m'appelle Léa. Léa David.
Marc: Tu es d'où?
Léa: De Rouen. Et toi, tu es de Versailles?
Marc: Oui, moi je suis d'ici comme Carole. Carole et moi, nous sommes bons copains aussi.

Vous avez compris?

Répondez.

1. Léa est une amie de qui?
2. Marc aussi est un ami de Carole?
3. Léa est d'où?
4. Et Marc et Carole, ils sont d'où?

ANSWERS TO Vous avez compris?

1. Léa est une amie de Carole Bertrand.
2. Oui, Marc aussi est un ami de Carole.
3. Léa est de Rouen.
4. Ils sont de Versailles.

Structure

L'accord des adjectifs

1. Adjectives must agree with the noun they describe or modify. Review the following.

	Féminin	Masculin
Singulier	une fille intelligente une amie timide	un garçon intelligent un ami timide
Pluriel	des filles intelligentes des amies timides	des garçons intelligents des amis timides

2. Note that adjectives such as **intelligent** that end in a consonant in the masculine form, change pronunciation in the feminine and have four written forms. Adjectives that end in **e**, such as **timide**, do not change pronunciation and have only two written forms.

Julie Décrivez Julie.

Les copains Décrivez les copains.

Julie Latour

Les copains

LES COPAINS ET L'ÉCOLE

R5

Note: Here is a list of some of the adjectives the students have learned through Chapter 7 of **Bon voyage! Level 1**: petit, grand, brun, blond, amusant, patient, intelligent, intéressant, sympathique, timide, énergique, égoïste, dynamique, sociable, enthousiaste, français, américain, difficile, facile, strict, fort, mauvais, beau, nouveau, vieux, large, serré, habillé, sport, joli, favori.

Révision A

Structure

Bellringer Review

Use BRR Transparency R.2 or write the following on the board. Describe the student sitting closest to you.

Presentation

L'accord des adjectifs

Step 1 Read Item 1 to the class.

Step 2 Write the adjectives in the chart on the board. Cross out the **e** at the end of **intelligente** and remind students that the pronunciation changes. Have them repeat **intelligente/intelligent** after you. Then ask them what the difference is in pronunciation.

Step 3 Explain to students that adjectives that end in a consonant have four forms and those that end in **e** have two forms.

3 and **4** Encourage students to say as much as they can when doing these activities. After students do them orally, you may wish to have them write out their answers.

ANSWERS TO Révision

3 *Answers will vary but may include:*
Julie est une fille intelligente. Elle est française. Elle n'est pas américaine. Elle est élève dans un lycée français. Elle est amusante.

4 *Answers will vary but may include:*
Les copains sont amusants. Ils sont élèves au lycée Louis-le-Grand. Ils sont français. Ils sont intelligents et ils sont sympas aussi.

R5

Révision A

Les verbes être et aller

1. Review the forms of the verbs **être** (to be) and **aller** (to go).

ÊTRE	
je suis	nous sommes
tu es	vous êtes
il/elle/on est	ils/elles sont

ALLER	
je vais	nous allons
tu vas	vous allez
il/elle/on va	ils/elles vont

2. To make a sentence negative, you put **ne (n')… pas** around the verb.

Je suis française.   Je **ne** suis **pas** américaine.
Fabien est amusant.   Il **n'**est **pas** timide.

5 **Paul est de Montréal.** Répétez la conversation.

Maude: Bonjour Paul, ça va?
Paul: Ça va. Et toi?
Maude: Ça va… Paul, tu es américain, non?
Paul: Non, je suis canadien.
Maude: Ah oui, tu es d'où?
Paul: De Montréal.
Maude: Et tu vas à l'université à Montréal?
Paul: Non, je suis toujours à l'école secondaire.

6 **Historiette** **Américain ou canadien?**
Répondez d'après la conversation.

1. Paul est américain?
2. Il est de quelle nationalité?
3. Il est de quelle ville?
4. Il va à l'université?

Un lycée à Montréal

7 Moi! Donnez des réponses personnelles.

1. Tu t'appelles comment?
2. Tu es d'où?
3. Tu es de quelle nationalité?
4. Tu vas à quelle école?
5. Tu vas à l'école avec des copains?
6. Tes copains et toi, vous allez à l'école à pied ou en car scolaire?
7. Où est votre école?
8. Comment sont les professeurs?

Des copains à Pointe-à-Pitre

8 Historiette Au restaurant
Complétez en utilisant le verbe **être** ou **aller**.

1. C'____ un petit restaurant. Il ____ vraiment bon.
2. Les serveurs ____ vietnamiens.
3. La cuisine vietnamienne ____ délicieuse.
4. Les copains de Mélanie ____ au restaurant.
5. Qui ____ demander l'addition au restaurant?
6. Qui ____ payer?
7. Vous ____ laisser un pourboire?

Un restaurant vietnamien à Paris

LES COPAINS ET L'ÉCOLE

R7

ANSWERS TO Révision

7 Answers will vary but may include:
1. Je m'appelle ____.
2. Je suis de ____.
3. Je suis américain(e).
4. Je vais à l'école ____.
5. Oui, je vais à l'école avec des copains.
6. Nous allons à l'école en car scolaire.
7. Notre école est dans la rue ____.
8. Les professeurs sont intelligents et sympas.

8
1. est, est
2. sont
3. est
4. vont
5. va
6. va
7. allez

Révision A

Les contractions

1. The preposition **à** can mean "in," "to," or "at." Remember that **à** contracts with the articles **le** and **les** to form **au** and **aux.**

à + la	= à la	Je parle à la fille.
à + l'	= à l'	Je parle à l'élève.
à + le	= au	Je parle au professeur.
à + les	= aux	Je parle aux élèves.

2. The preposition **de** can mean "of" or "from." **De** is also a part of longer prepositions such as **près de** and **loin de. De** contracts with **le** and **les** to form **du** and **des.**

de + la	= de la	Il habite près de la station de métro.
de + l'	= de l'	Il habite loin de l'université.
de + le	= du	Il habite près du collège.
de + les	= des	Il habite loin des magasins.

Le prof parle à un élève.

Une classe au lycée Janson de Sailly à Paris

9 **On y va ou on n'y va pas?**
Complétez.

Aujourd'hui on ne va pas __1__ parc; on ne va pas __2__ restaurant; on ne va pas __3__ maison; on ne va pas __4__ pâtisserie. Où est-ce qu'on va alors? On va __5__ école. On va __6__ cours de français. On va parler __7__ professeur et __8__ élèves.

10 **Tu habites où?** Donnez des réponses personnelles.
1. Tu habites près ou loin de l'école?
2. Tu vas à l'école à quelle heure?
3. Tu habites près ou loin des magasins?
4. Tu vas souvent aux magasins?
5. Tu es un copain ou une copine du frère de Nathalie?
6. Tu habites près du magasin des parents de Nathalie?

11 **À la Martinique** You are spending your spring vacation with a family in Martinique. Tell your "brother" or your "sister" (your partner) all you can about your French class and your French teacher. Answer any questions your partner asks. Then reverse roles.

12 **Les cours** You are speaking with an exchange student from France (your partner). You want to know all about his or her school, class schedule, and classes. Ask him or her all about school life in France.

La Martinique

Révision B

Preview

This review covers vocabulary needed to describe home and family. These topics were first presented in **Bon voyage! Level 1.** The structures reviewed are the present tense of **-er** verbs, **avoir, faire,** and the partitive.

National Standards

Communication

In Review B, students will communicate in spoken and written French on the following topics:
- Describing their family
- Describing their home
- Food

Students will also narrate present events. They will obtain and provide information and engage in conversations about home and family.

Révision B

La famille

Révision B

Resource Manager

Workbook, pages R7–R14
Tests, pages R3–R4, R16, R26
ExamView® Pro

Vocabulaire

Bellringer Review

Use BRR Transparency R.5 or write the following on the board. Sketch a family tree of your own family or of a family you create. Label the family members, indicating their relationships to each other.

Presentation

Step 1 Have students repeat the sentences after you. Intersperse your presentation with questions such as:
La famille Grandet a une jolie maison?
Les Grandet ont un chien?
Comment est leur chien?
Il a quel âge?
Il joue où?

Reaching All Students

For the Younger Students You may wish to have students create an invitation for the party in the photo on page R12. Have them include the occasion, time, and date for the party. Use the invitations to review time and dates.

Révision B

Vocabulaire

La famille Grandet a une jolie maison.

une salle de bains   les toilettes   une cuisine   une salle à manger

une chambre à coucher

La maison a cinq pièces.

une salle de séjour

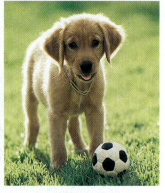

Les Grandet ont un chien.
Leur chien est adorable.
Il est très jeune. Il a six mois.
Il joue toujours dans le jardin.

C'est l'anniversaire de Jennifer.
Elle donne une fête.
Ses copines ont des cadeaux pour elle.

Reaching All Students

Additional Practice Ask students the following questions:
  Tu donnes souvent des fêtes?
  Tu invites qui?
  Ils arrivent à quelle heure?
  Qu'est-ce que vous faites dans une fête?
  Vous parlez? Vous écoutez des CD?

Ask students the following questions about the house on page R12.
  Comment est la maison de la famille Grandet?
  Il y a combien de pièces?
  On prépare le dîner où?
  On dîne où?
  Les enfants étudient où?

Révision B

1 **Historiette** **La famille Aragon**
Inventez une histoire.

Un dîner en famille

1. La famille Aragon est une grande famille?
2. M. et Mme Aragon ont combien d'enfants?
3. Ils ont une maison ou un appartement?
4. Ils habitent en ville ou en banlieue?
5. Leur maison ou leur appartement a combien de pièces sans compter la cuisine et la salle de bains?
6. Qui prépare le dîner?
7. Les Aragon dînent dans la salle à manger ou dans la cuisine?
8. Après le dîner, ils regardent la télévision? Dans quelle pièce?
9. Qui parle très souvent au téléphone?
10. Qui fait bien ses devoirs? Qui ne fait pas ses devoirs?

2 **Qu'est-ce qu'on fait?** Choisissez.

1. On ____ la télé dans la salle de séjour.
   a. regarde b. donne c. prépare
2. On ____ au téléphone.
   a. paie b. joue c. parle
3. On ____ à la cantine.
   a. joue b. déjeune c. étudie
4. On ____ un cahier dans une papeterie.
   a. coûte b. achète c. travaille
5. On ____ l'école à trois heures.
   a. arrive b. rentre c. quitte
6. On ____ après les cours.
   a. travaille b. déjeune c. demande

LA FAMILLE

R13

Révision B

Conversation

Presentation

Step 1 Have the class repeat the conversation after you.

Step 2 Call on two students to read the conversation to the class.

> **Learning from Photos**
>
> *(page R14)* The lycée Pierre Fermat is in Toulouse. Toulouse is an important city in the Midi-Pyrénées region. It has some very famous monuments, and it is the center of the French aerospace industry.

Révision B

Conversation

Le cours d'espagnol

Carl: Salut!
Hugo: Salut!
Carl: Tu fais de l'espagnol, non?
Hugo: Oui, je fais de l'espagnol.
Carl: Tu as qui comme prof?
Hugo: Mme Lesage.
Carl: Moi aussi. Elle est sympa, hein!
Hugo: Oui, je suis d'accord, elle est très sympa.
Carl: Justement j'ai cours avec elle aujourd'hui.
Hugo: Et moi, demain.

Vous avez compris?

Répondez.

1. Qui parle?
2. Qui fait de l'espagnol?
3. Comment s'appelle le professeur d'espagnol de Hugo?
4. Comment s'appelle le professeur d'espagnol de Carl?
5. D'après les deux garçons, comment est Mme Lesage?
6. Qui a cours avec elle aujourd'hui?
7. Qui a cours avec elle demain?

Answers to Vous avez compris?

1. Carl et Hugo parlent.
2. Hugo fait de l'espagnol.
3. Le professeur d'espagnol de Hugo s'appelle Mme Lesage.
4. Le professeur d'espagnol de Carl s'appelle Mme Lesage aussi.
5. Mme Lesage est sympa.
6. Carl a cours avec elle aujourd'hui.
7. Hugo a cours avec elle demain.

Structure

Les verbes réguliers en -er

The infinitive of many regular French verbs ends in **-er**. Review the present tense forms of regular **-er** verbs.

PARLER		AIMER	
je parle	nous parlons	j' aime	nous aimons
tu parles	vous parlez	tu aimes	vous aimez
il/elle/on parle	ils/elles parlent	il/elle/on aime	ils/elles aiment

3 **Moi!** Donnez des réponses personnelles.
1. Tu habites dans quelle ville?
2. Tu habites dans une petite ou une grande ville?
3. Tu arrives à l'école à quelle heure le matin?
4. Tu parles à tes copains?
5. Tes copains et toi, vous étudiez le français?
6. Vous aimez le cours de français?

Saint-Paul-de-Vence en Provence

4 **Historiette** On dîne au restaurant. Complétez.
1. Ce soir, Juliette ne ____ pas le dîner. (préparer)
2. Elle ____ à sa copine. (téléphoner)
3. Elle ____ sa copine au restaurant. (inviter)
4. Elles ____ dans un restaurant italien. (aller)
5. Les deux amies ____ au restaurant à sept heures. (arriver)
6. Le serveur ____ à leur table. (arriver)
7. Les deux amies ____ une pizza. (commander)
8. Juliette ____ l'addition. (demander)
9. Tu ____ la pizza? (aimer)
10. Quand tes copains et toi, vous ____ dans un restaurant italien, qu'est-ce que vous ____? (aller, commander)

LA FAMILLE R15

Révision B

Structure

Bellringer Review

Use BRR Transparency R.6 or write the following on the board. Make a list of all the activities you do on a regular basis.

Presentation

Les verbes réguliers en -er

Step 1 Write the forms of **parler** and **aimer** on the board and underline the endings.

Step 2 Have students read the forms aloud. Point to the ones that are pronounced the same even though they are written differently.

3 This activity can be done with books closed or open.

4 After completing this activity, call on a student to give the information in his or her own words.

Learning from Photos

(page R15) Saint-Paul-de-Vence is a beautiful town north of Nice.

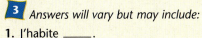

3 Answers will vary but may include:
1. J'habite ____.
2. J'habite dans une grande ville.
3. J'arrive à l'école à huit heures.
4. Oui, je parle à mes copains.
5. Oui, nous étudions le français. (Oui, on étudie le français.)
6. Oui, nous aimons le cours de français. (Oui, on aime le cours de français.)

4
1. prépare
2. téléphone
3. invite
4. vont
5. arrivent
6. arrive
7. commandent
8. demande
9. aimes
10. allez, commandez

Révision B

Bellringer Review

Use BRR Transparency R.7 or write the following on the board. Make a list of the words or expressions you would need for shopping for food at a market.

Presentation

Le partitif

Step 1 When going over Item 1, mention some other things people may like: **J'aime le lait. J'aime les légumes. J'aime les sports.**

Step 2 When going over Item 2, put some objects on a table and point to them from a distance. To demonstrate the use of the partitive say, for example: **Il y a des livres sur la table. Il y a des crayons sur la table. Il y a de l'argent.**

Step 3 Then take the items off the table to demonstrate the negative: **Il n'y a pas de livres sur la table. Il n'y a pas de crayons sur la table. Il n'y a pas d'argent.**

Révision B

5 Historiette Une fête Donnez des réponses personnelles.

1. Tu aimes donner des fêtes?
2. Tu donnes des fêtes?
3. Tu invites qui?
4. Tu téléphones à tes copains?
5. Ils acceptent toujours ton invitation?
6. Quel soir est-ce que tu donnes une fête?
7. Tes amis arrivent à quelle heure?

C'est l'anniversaire de Julie.

Le partitif

1. In French, you use the definite article when talking about something in a general sense.

   Le chocolat, c'est très bon.
   J'aime les fruits.

2. However, when you refer to only a part or a certain quantity of an item, the partitive construction is used. The partitive is expressed in French by **de** + the definite article.

de + le = du	Je voudrais du pain.
de + la = de la	Je voudrais de la viande.
de + l' = de l'	Je voudrais de l'eau.
de + les = des	Je voudrais des pommes.

3. When a partitive follows a negative word, all forms change to **de**.

   | Je voudrais | du pain. / de la viande. / de l'eau. / des pommes. | Je ne veux pas | de pain. / de viande. / d'eau. / de pommes. |

ANSWERS TO Révision

5 Answers will vary but may include:

1. Oui, j'aime donner des fêtes.
2. Oui, je donne des fêtes.
3. J'invite tous mes copains.
4. Oui, je téléphone à mes copains.
5. Non, ils n'acceptent pas toujours mon invitation.
6. Je donne une fête _____.
7. Ils arrivent à _____.

6 Le dîner en famille Répondez.

1. Tu dînes toujours en famille?
2. Tu manges souvent des légumes au dîner?
3. Tu aimes les légumes?
4. Tu manges aussi de la viande?
5. Tu manges du bœuf ou du porc?
6. Tu préfères le bœuf ou le porc?
7. Tu aimes boire de l'eau au dîner?
8. Après le dîner, tu aimes boire du café?

Un coq au vin, de la soupe à l'oignon et une tarte à l'orange

7 Ils vont où? Complétez.

1. Adrien et son frère n'ont pas ____ classeurs. Ils vont à la papeterie pour acheter ____ classeurs.
2. C'est l'anniversaire de Cédric. Tout le monde a ____ cadeaux pour Cédric. Cédric, il veut ____ argent!
3. Il n'y a pas ____ viande dans le frigo. Madame Delon va à la boucherie où elle achète ____ bœuf et ____ poulet. Tout le monde aime beaucoup ____ bœuf.

LA FAMILLE

Révision B

Les verbes avoir et faire

1. Review the forms of the irregular verbs **avoir** (to have) and **faire** (to do, to make).

AVOIR		FAIRE	
j' ai	nous avons	je fais	nous faisons
tu as	vous avez	tu fais	vous faites
il/elle/on a	ils/elles ont	il/elle/on fait	ils/elles font

2. You use the verb **avoir** to express age.
   —Tu as quel âge?
   —Moi? J'ai quatorze ans.

3. The verb faire is used in many expressions such as:
   faire du français, faire la cuisine, faire de la gymnastique, faire les courses.

Rappelez-vous que...

In negative sentences, **un, une, du, de la,** and **des** change to **de (d')**.
J'ai un frère.
Je n'ai pas de sœur.
Elle fait du sport.
Elle ne fait pas de danse.
Tu as des cahiers.
Tu n'as pas de classeurs.

8 Historiette Les Pelleray Complétez en utilisant le verbe **avoir**.

1. La famille Pelleray ____ un appartement à Paris.
2. L'appartement des Pelleray ____ cinq pièces.
3. M. et Mme Pelleray ____ deux enfants.
4. Jean-Claude ____ quatorze ans et Catherine ____ seize ans.
5. Les Pelleray ____ un chien.
6. Vous ____ un chien?
7. Non, nous n'____ pas de chien, mais nous ____ un chat.

Un quartier résidentiel à Paris

9 **Moi!** Donnez des réponses personnelles.

1. Tu as une grande famille?
2. Tu as combien de frères?
3. Tu as combien de sœurs?
4. Ta famille et toi, vous avez un chat ou un chien?
5. Tu as une voiture?

10 **Qu'est-ce qu'on fait?** Complétez en utilisant le verbe **faire**.

1. Tes copains et toi, vous ____ souvent de la cuisine?
2. Qui ____ du latin? Ta sœur ou ton frère?
3. Qu'est-ce qu'ils ____, tes parents? Ils travaillent où?
4. Madame Morin ____ ses courses le matin?
5. Tu ____ de la gymnastique?
6. Moi? Non. Je ne ____ pas de gymnastique.

11 **Quand?** Work with a classmate. He or she will suggest an activity. You will tell where and when your friends typically take part in this activity.

12 **Des appartements** Work with a classmate. Look at these plans of apartments. A different family lives in each one. Give each family a name. Then say as much about each family as you can. Don't forget to describe their apartment. Be as original as possible.

1.   2.   3.

13 **Au café** Work in groups of three or four. You are all friends from school. Since two of you are exchange students from Quebec, you speak French together. After school you go to a café where you talk about lots of things—school, teachers, friends, home, family. Have a conversation together.

Révision C

Preview

This review covers vocabulary needed to talk about shopping for food and clothing. These topics were first presented in **Bon voyage! Level 1.** The structures reviewed are the present tense of **vouloir, pouvoir, prendre,** and the infinitive.

National Standards

Communication
In Review C, students will communicate in spoken and written French on the following topics:
• Describing shopping for food
• Describing shopping for clothing
Students will also continue to narrate present events. They will obtain and provide information and engage in conversations about shopping for food and clothing.

Révision C
Les courses

Révision C

Photograph This photo is of a street in a small town in Brittany.

Learning from Photos
(page R21) Have students say what they would buy in the stores in the photo.

Révision C

Resource Manager
Workbook, pages R15–R20
Tests, pages R5–R6, R17, R27
ExamView® Pro

Vocabulaire

Bellringer Review
Use BRR Transparency R.9 or write the following on the board. Write down as many clothing items and related terms as you can think of.

Presentation

Step 1 Have students share the words they wrote down for the Bellringer Review.

Step 2 Have students repeat each word and sentence of the vocabulary presentation after you. Intersperse with questions such as:
   Qui fait les courses?
   Qu'est-ce qu'il veut acheter?
   Il va où pour acheter une baguette?

Attention!
When students are doing the activities, accept any answer that makes sense. The purpose of these activities is to have students use the vocabulary. They are not factual recall activities. If you wish, have students use the photos on this page as a stimulus, when possible.

Révision C

Vocabulaire

La nourriture

des fruits   des légumes   de la viande   des poissons   un jambon

Luc fait les courses.
Il veut acheter une baguette.
Il va à la boulangerie.

Chloé est à l'épicerie.
Elle va acheter une bouteille d'eau minérale.
Elle veut aussi six tranches de jambon.
Chloé va faire un pique-nique.

Les vêtements

Vous faites quelle taille?
Je fais du 39.
la manche

Romain est au rayon des vêtements pour hommes.
Il veut acheter une chemise à manches longues.

une chemise

la caisse

Madame Leclerc paie à la caisse.

Paired Activity
Have students work in pairs and make up a conversation about a visit to the market, supermarket, or a clothing store.

Révision C

1 Des aliments Identifiez.

1.   2.   3.   4.

5.   6.   7.   8.

2 Un fruit, un légume ou de la viande? Identifiez.

1. du bœuf
2. une orange
3. des haricots verts
4. des épinards
5. du porc
6. une pomme

3 Historiette Au grand magasin
Inventez une histoire.

1. Paul veut acheter des vêtements?
2. Il va aux Galeries Lafayette?
3. Il est au rayon des vêtements pour hommes?
4. Il va acheter une chemise?
5. Il veut une chemise à manches longues ou à manches courtes?
6. Il fait quelle taille?
7. Il achète une chemise?
8. Il paie où?

4 Sport ou habillé? Identifiez.

1. des baskets
2. un complet
3. un chemisier
4. un survêtement
5. une jupe plissée
6. une cravate
7. un polo à manches courtes
8. un anorak

Les Galeries Lafayette à Paris

LES COURSES

Révision C

Conversation

Un achat

Vendeuse: Bonjour, mademoiselle. Vous voulez voir quelque chose?
Christine: Bonjour. Oui, je voudrais un jean, s'il vous plaît.
Vendeuse: Vous faites quelle taille?
Christine: Du 36.
(Christine essaie le jean.)
Vendeuse: Ça va, la taille?
Christine: Je crois que c'est un peu petit.
Vendeuse: Vous voulez essayer la taille au-dessus?
Christine: Oui, s'il vous plaît.

Vous avez compris?

Répondez.

1. Christine est où?
2. Elle parle à qui?
3. Qu'est-ce qu'elle veut acheter?
4. Elle fait quelle taille?
5. Le jean est un peu petit?
6. Christine veut la taille au-dessus?

Structure

Les verbes *vouloir* et *pouvoir*

Review the verbs **vouloir** *(to want)* and **pouvoir** *(to be able)*.

VOULOIR	
je veux	nous voulons
tu veux	vous voulez
il/elle/on veut	ils/elles veulent

POUVOIR	
je peux	nous pouvons
tu peux	vous pouvez
il/elle/on peut	ils/elles peuvent

 5 **Je veux bien, mais je ne peux pas.**
Répondez d'après le modèle.

—Tu veux aller au restaurant?
—Je veux bien. Quand?
—Vendredi soir.
—Ah non, je ne peux pas.

1. Tu veux aller au café?
2. Tu veux dîner avec Caroline?
3. Tu veux travailler avec moi?
4. Ta sœur veut faire des courses avec nous?
5. Et vous deux, vous voulez aller au cinéma avec nous?

Un petit restaurant à Paris

 6 **Qui peut préparer le dîner?** Complétez.

Marie: Je voudrais bien faire le dîner ce soir, mais vraiment, je ne __1__ (pouvoir) pas.
Julien: Tu ne __2__ (pouvoir) pas? Pourquoi?
Marie: Je __3__ (être) très fatiguée! Je __4__ (être) vraiment crevée.
Julien: On __5__ (pouvoir) aller au restaurant, si tu __6__ (vouloir).
Marie: Oh, je ne __7__ (vouloir) pas aller au restaurant ce soir.
Julien: On __8__ (pouvoir) faire des sandwichs.
Marie: Oui, ou… toi, tu __9__ (pouvoir) faire le dîner.
Julien: Je __10__ (vouloir) bien, mais ce n' __11__ (être) pas une très bonne idée.
Marie: Pourquoi?
Julien: Parce que je __12__ (faire) très mal la cuisine!

LES COURSES   R25

Révision C

Structure

Bellringer Review

Use BRR Transparency R.10 or write the following on the board.
List five things you want to do this weekend.

Presentation

Les verbes *vouloir* et *pouvoir*

Step 1 Have students read the verb forms aloud.

Step 2 **Expansion:** Have students read the list they made for the Bellringer Review. Then have them say whether they can do each thing or not.

5 Have students practice in pairs, then call on some pairs to perform their dialogue for the class.

ANSWERS TO Révision

5
1. —Je veux bien. Quand?
   —Samedi soir.
   —Ah non, je ne peux pas.
2. —Je veux bien. Quand?
   —Vendredi soir.
   —Ah non, je ne peux pas.
3. —Je veux bien. Quand?
   —Mercredi.
   —Ah non, je ne peux pas.
4. —Elle veut bien. Quand?
   —Samedi matin.
   —Ah non, elle ne peut pas.
5. —Nous voulons bien. Quand?
   —Samedi soir.
   —Ah non, nous ne pouvons pas.

6
1. peux
2. peux
3. suis
4. suis
5. peut
6. veux
7. veux
8. peut
9. peux
10. veux
11. est
12. fais

R25

Révision C

L'infinitif

1. The infinitive form of the verb often follows verbs such as **aimer**, **détester**, **vouloir**, and **pouvoir**.

   J'**aime faire** les courses mais je **déteste faire** la cuisine.
   Il **veut dîner** mais il **ne peut pas aller** au restaurant ce soir.

2. You can use the infinitive after the verb **aller** to tell what you or others are going to do in the near future.

   Je **vais donner** une fête samedi soir.

7 Historiette Au magasin Répondez.

1. Tu vas aller au magasin Paramètre?
2. Tu veux acheter un cadeau?
3. Tu vas donner le cadeau à ta mère?
4. Tu aimes acheter des cadeaux pour ta mère?
5. Tu vas avoir assez d'argent pour payer?

Le verbe prendre

1. Review the forms of the verb **prendre** (to take).

PRENDRE			
je	prends	nous	prenons
tu	prends	vous	prenez
il/elle/on	prend	ils/elles	prennent

2. Remember that the verbs **apprendre** (to learn) and **comprendre** (to understand) are conjugated the same way as **prendre**.

   On apprend le français à l'école.
   Je comprends bien le français.

Le magasin Paramètre à Paris

Révision C

8 **Au pluriel** Mettez au pluriel.
1. *Je prends* le car scolaire pour aller à l'école.
2. *Je prends* l'ascenseur pour monter au 6ᵉ étage.
3. *Tu prends* le bus ou le métro pour aller en ville?
4. *Tu prends* beaucoup de notes en classe?
5. *L'élève apprend* beaucoup de choses.
6. *Elle comprend* le professeur.

Un marché à Saint-Rémy-de-Provence

9 **Ce que je prends** Donnez des réponses personnelles.
1. Qu'est-ce que tu prends quand tu as soif?
2. Qu'est-ce que tu prends quand tu as faim?

10 **Qu'est-ce qu'on veut acheter?**
You and your friend are in an open-air market in France. Make a list of the items you want to buy. Take turns being the vendor and the customer as you shop for the items on your list.

11 **Qu'est-ce qu'on va manger?** Work with a classmate. Prepare a menu in French for tomorrow's meals—**le petit déjeuner, le déjeuner et le dîner.** Based on your menus, prepare a shopping list. Be sure to include the quantities you need.

12 **C'est qui?** Work with a classmate. One of you describes what someone in the class is wearing and the other has to guess who it is. Take turns.

LES COURSES

Teacher's notes (Révision C sidebar)

10 You may wish to supply props for students to use for this activity.

12 Have students use their description from the Bellringer Review to begin this game.

ANSWERS TO Révision

8
1. Nous prenons
2. Nous prenons
3. Vous prenez
4. Vous prenez
5. Les élèves apprennent
6. Elles comprennent

9 Answers will vary but may include:
1. Quand j'ai soif, je prends de l'eau minérale.
2. Quand j'ai faim, je prends un sandwich au jambon.

10 Answers will vary depending upon what students want to buy. Some expressions that students know and can use are: un kilo de, une douzaine de, une boîte de, une bouteille de, ça fait combien, avec ça, c'est tout.

11 Answers will vary but students should use many of the foods they have already learned.

12 Answers will vary but may include:
—Il porte un jean et un polo rouge à manches courtes. Il porte des baskets.
—C'est Marc!

Révision D

Preview

This review covers vocabulary needed to describe traveling by train and plane. These topics were first presented in **Bon voyage! Level 1**. The present tense of **-ir** and **-re** verbs, and verbs like **partir** and **dormir,** are reviewed.

National Standards

Communication
In Review D, students will communicate in spoken and written French on the following topics:
• Traveling by train
• Traveling by plane
Students will also narrate present events. They will obtain and provide information and engage in conversations about travel.

Révision D

En voyage

Révision

Spotlight on Culture

Photograph This photograph shows the **TGV (le train à grande vitesse)** in the La Rochelle train station.

Révision D

Resource Manager

Workbook, pages R21–R26
Tests, pages R7–R8, R18, R28
ExamView® Pro

Vocabulaire

Bellringer Review

Use BRR Transparency R.12 or write the following on the board. Write down as many words and expressions as you can think of having to do with airports.

Presentation

Step 1 Have students share the words they wrote down for the Bellringer Review.

Step 2 Have students repeat the vocabulary words and sentences after you.

Vocabulaire

À la gare

un guichet

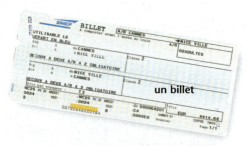
un billet

Les voyageurs n'attendent pas le train.
Ils descendent du train sur le quai.

Le train part à l'heure.
Il arrive à l'heure.
Il n'a pas de retard.

À l'aéroport

un aéroport
un avion
une carte d'embarquement

une valise

Marie sort son billet de son sac à dos.
Elle choisit sa place dans l'avion.
Elle veut une place côté couloir.

1 **Historiette À la gare** Inventez une histoire.
1. Il y a beaucoup de voyageurs dans la gare?
2. Il y a souvent une queue devant le guichet?
3. On vend des billets de train au guichet?
4. Les voyageurs entendent l'annonce du départ de leur train?
5. Le train arrive sur quelle voie?
6. Le train part à l'heure?

La gare de l'Est à Paris

Une hôtesse de l'air sert une collation.

2 **À l'aéroport** Vrai ou faux?
1. Un aéroport est toujours dans le centre d'une ville.
2. Les avions atterrissent sur une piste.
3. Les avions décollent d'une porte d'embarquement.
4. Les passagers ont une carte d'embarquement.
5. Les stewards et les hôtesses de l'air travaillent à l'aéroport.

EN VOYAGE

ANSWERS TO Révision

1 *Answers will vary but may include:*
1. Oui, il y a beaucoup de voyageurs dans la gare.
2. Oui, il y a souvent une queue devant le guichet.
3. Oui, on vend des billets de train au guichet.
4. Oui, les voyageurs entendent l'annonce du départ de leur train.
5. Le train arrive sur la voie numéro 5.
6. Oui, le train part à l'heure.

2
1. faux
2. vrai
3. faux
4. vrai
5. faux

Révision D

Attention!
When students are doing the activities, accept any answer that makes sense. The purpose of these activities is to have students use the vocabulary. They are not factual recall activities. If you wish, have students use the photos on this page as a stimulus, when possible.

Historiette Each time **Historiette** appears, it means that the answers to the activity form a short story. Encourage students to look at the title of the **Historiette**, since it can help them do the activity.

2 Have students correct any false statements.

Writing Development
Have students write the answers to Activity 1 in paragraph form.

Learning from Photos
(page R31 right) Paris has six train stations. The **gare de l'Est** serves destinations in the east of France, as well as cities in Germany, Switzerland, and Austria.

Paired Activity
Have students work in pairs and make up a conversation about a trip to a French-speaking destination that interests them. Then ask for volunteers to present their conversations to the class.

Révision D

Conversation

Presentation

Step 1 Have the class repeat the conversation after you.

Step 2 Call on two students to read the conversation to the class.

Geography Connection

🌐 Casablanca is the largest city in Morocco. The well-planned modern part of the city is crossed by attractive, wide, palm-lined avenues, which radiate from large central squares. Avenue Hassan II, shown in the photo on page R32, is the main inland artery (much of the city is very close to the coast). It skirts the large **parc de la Ligue Arabe**, which has a small stadium whose entrance is on Avenue Hassan II.

Révision D

Conversation

Tu vas à Casablanca?

L'avenue Hassan II à Casablanca au Maroc

Olivier: Tiens Anne! Mais qu'est-ce que tu fais là?
Anne: Salut! Ben, j'attends mon avion! Bizarre, hein?
Olivier: Toujours aussi sarcastique! Non, mais, tu vas au Maroc?
Anne: Oui, je vais à Casablanca.
Olivier: Moi aussi. C'est sympa d'être ensemble.
Anne: Oui. Tu as quelle place?
Olivier: 22A. Et toi?
Anne: 15B.
Olivier: Oh, on va pouvoir changer après le décollage.
Anne: Oui. C'est sûr. Mais il faut d'abord partir!

Vous avez compris?

Répondez.

1. Où sont Olivier et Anne?
2. Qu'est-ce qu'ils attendent?
3. Ils partent pour quel pays?
4. Anne a quelle place? Et Olivier?
5. Est-ce qu'ils veulent être ensemble dans l'avion?
6. Est-ce qu'ils vont pouvoir changer de place?
7. D'après vous, l'avion va partir à l'heure?

ANSWERS TO *Vous avez compris?*

1. Ils sont à l'aéroport.
2. Ils attendent leur avion.
3. Ils partent pour le Maroc.
4. Anne a la place 15B. Olivier a la place 22A.
5. Oui, ils veulent être ensemble dans l'avion.
6. Oui, ils vont pouvoir changer de place.
7. Oui, l'avion va partir à l'heure. (Non, l'avion ne va pas partir à l'heure).

Structure

Les verbes en -ir et -re

Review the following forms of regular **-ir** and **-re** verbs in French.

FINIR		ATTENDRE	
je finis	nous finissons	j' attends	nous attendons
tu finis	vous finissez	tu attends	vous attendez
il/elle/on finit	ils/elles finissent	il/elle/on attend	ils/elles attendent

3 **Un voyage en avion** Donnez des réponses personnelles.
1. Quand tu voyages en avion, tu choisis Air France comme compagnie?
2. Tu choisis une place côté couloir ou côté fenêtre?
3. En général, les passagers choisissent des places côté couloir?
4. Ta famille et toi, vous attendez longtemps à l'aéroport?
5. Vous remplissez vos cartes de débarquement avant l'arrivée?
6. Vous atterrissez en général à l'heure?

Un steward sert un café.

EN VOYAGE

Révision D

Bellringer Review

Use BRR Transparency R.14 or write the following on the board. Rewrite each sentence with the new subject.

1. Ils vont en France.
   Il _____.
2. Ils choisissent un vol Air France.
   Il _____.
3. Nous voulons prendre le même vol.
   Je _____.
4. Nous répondons aux questions de l'agent.
   Je _____.

Presentation

Les verbes sortir, partir, dormir, servir

Step 1 Have students repeat the verb forms after you. Remind students to drop the final sound of the **ils/elles** form to get the pronunciation for all singular forms.

5 and **6** Have students retell the stories in their own words.

Learning from Photos

(page R34) The **gare de Lyon** is one of the major train stations in Paris.

Révision D

4 À la gare Complétez.

1. À la gare, on _____ les billets de train au guichet et on _____ des magazines et des journaux au kiosque. (vendre)
2. Quelques voyageurs _____ dans la salle d'attente et d'autres voyageurs _____ sur le quai. (attendre)
3. Nous, nous _____ sur le quai. (attendre)
4. Et vous, vous _____ le train où? (attendre)
5. J'_____ l'annonce du départ de notre train. (entendre)

Un kiosque à la gare de Lyon à Paris

Les verbes sortir, partir, dormir, servir

Review the forms of the following **-ir** verbs.

SORTIR	PARTIR	DORMIR	SERVIR
je sors	je pars	je dors	je sers
tu sors	tu pars	tu dors	tu sers
il/elle/on sort	il/elle/on part	il/elle/on dort	il/elle/on sert
nous sortons	nous partons	nous dormons	nous servons
vous sortez	vous partez	vous dormez	vous servez
ils/elles sortent	ils/elles partent	ils/elles dorment	ils/elles servent

5 Historiette En voiture! Répondez d'après les indications.

1. Le train part de quelle voie? (numéro deux)
2. Il part à quelle heure? (18 h 16)
3. On sert des repas dans le train? (oui)
4. Qui sert les repas? (des serveurs)
5. Les voyageurs dorment? (oui)
6. Quand le contrôleur arrive, tu sors ton billet? (oui)

ANSWERS TO Révision

4
1. vend, vend
2. attendent, attendent
3. attendons
4. attendez
5. entends

5
1. Le train part de la voie numéro deux.
2. Le train part à 18 h 16.
3. Oui, on sert des repas dans le train.
4. Des serveurs servent les repas.
5. Oui, les voyageurs dorment.
6. Oui, quand le contrôleur arrive, je sors mon billet.

Révision D

6 Historiette Caroline fait un voyage. Complétez.

Caroline est à la gare. Où est-ce qu'on __1__ (vendre) les billets? Ah, voilà le guichet. Caroline achète son billet. Elle __2__ (sortir) de l'argent de son sac à dos et paie. Son train __3__ (partir) de la voie numéro quatre. Tous les trains __4__ (partir) à l'heure. Beaucoup de voyageurs __5__ (dormir) dans le train. Mais Caroline ne __6__ (dormir) pas. Elle aime bien voyager en train.

L'Eurostar fait Paris-Londres.

7 En avion Make a list of words associated with airline travel. Write a short paragraph using these words to describe a plane trip you'd like to take.

8 La gare Describe the illustration in your own words.

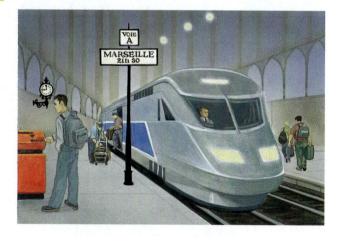

FUN FACTS

The Eurostar connects Paris and London by way of the new Eurotunnel between France and England. The trip takes a mere three hours.

Révision E

Preview

This review covers vocabulary related to seasons and a variety of sports. These topics were first presented in **Bon voyage! Level 1**. The **passé composé** of regular and irregular verbs is reviewed.

 National Standards

Communication

In Review E, students will communicate in spoken and written French on the following topics:
• Seasons
• Individual and team sports
Students will also narrate past events. They will obtain and provide information and engage in conversations about seasons and sports.

Révision E

Les sports

Révision E

Spotlight on Culture

Photograph This photo shows France and Brazil competing in a World Cup final.

Learning from Photos

(pages R36–R37) Ask students the following questions about the photo: **Il y a combien de joueurs sur la photo? Ils jouent au foot? Il y a combien d'équipes? Il y a des gradins?**

Révision E

Resource Manager
Workbook, pages R27–R32
Tests, pages R9–R10, R19, R29
ExamView® Pro

Vocabulaire

Bellringer Review
Use BRR Transparency R.15 or write the following on the board.
Write as many words as you can about the following sports.
le football
le basket-ball

Presentation

Step 1 Use gestures to reinforce the meaning of **nager, faire du ski nautique, prendre des bains de soleil, mettre de la crème solaire, faire du ski, faire du patin à glace, jouer au foot, donner un coup de pied dans le ballon.**

Step 2 Have students repeat the vocabulary words and sentences after you.

Paired Activity
Have students work in pairs and make up a conversation about a sport that interests them. Then ask for volunteers to present their conversations to the class.

Révision E

Vocabulaire

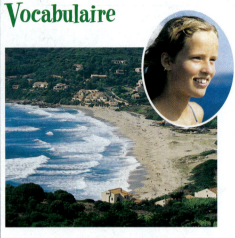

Julie a passé l'été dernier au bord de la mer.
Elle a pris des bains de soleil.
Elle a mis de la crème solaire.
Elle a bronzé.

L'hiver dernier Marc a appris à faire du ski.
Il a descendu la piste verte.

Samedi dernier, notre équipe a joué au foot.
Fabien a donné un coup de pied dans le ballon.
Il a marqué un but.
Notre équipe a gagné 6 à 4.
Nous avons joué contre Orsay.

Aimée a beaucoup nagé.

Lisette a fait du ski nautique.

Magali a fait du patin à glace.
Elle a eu un petit accident.

Geography Connection
The beach shown in the photo on page R38 is near the city of Ajaccio, on the island of Corsica **(la Corse).** Corsica, the third largest of the Mediterranean islands, is officially **un département** of France. It is a very popular vacation spot, particularly for families. Corsica is a very mountainous island with many forests and sprawling beaches along the coast.

Learning from Photos
(page R38 top right) The ski resort of Avoriaz in the Mont-Blanc region is known for its chic clientele. No automobiles are allowed, and it is reached by cable car from the resort town of Morzine.

1 Historiette Un voyage à la montagne
Répondez d'après les indications.

1. Quand est-ce que Nicole a fait un voyage à la montagne? (en février)
2. Qu'est-ce qu'elle a pris? (des leçons de ski)
3. Elle a eu un moniteur? (oui)
4. Elle a beaucoup appris? (oui)
5. Elle a descendu quelle piste? (la piste verte)
6. Elle a eu un accident? (non)
7. Où est-ce qu'elle a fait du patin? (à la patinoire)

Une leçon de ski

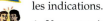
Courchevel, France

2 Un match de foot
Répondez d'après les indications.

1. Vous avez joué au foot hier? (oui)
2. Lafitte a passé le ballon? (oui)
3. Garros a bloqué le ballon? (non)
4. Lafitte a marqué un but? (oui)
5. Les spectateurs ont applaudi? (oui)
6. L'équipe de Lafitte a perdu le match? (non)

Un match de foot

LES SPORTS

Révision E

Conversation

Presentation

Step 1 Have the class repeat the conversation after you.

Step 2 Call on two students to read the conversation to the class.
Note: Tell students that **avoir de la chance** is an expression meaning "to be lucky."

Learning from Photos

(page R40 right) The windsurfer is on the island of Guadeloupe in the French Antilles. Ask the following questions about the photo. **Qu'est-ce que cet homme fait? Tu aimes faire de la planche à voile? Tu fais de la planche à voile où? Qu'est-ce qu'il faut avoir pour faire de la planche à voile?**

Conversation

Au bord de la mer

Julie: Qu'est-ce que tu as fait pendant les vacances?
Sophie: J'ai passé un mois au bord de la mer.
Julie: Super! Tu as de la chance.
Sophie: Oui. J'ai passé tout mon temps à la plage. J'ai beaucoup nagé et j'ai appris à faire de la planche à voile.
Julie: Et je vois que tu as bien bronzé!

Vous avez compris?

Répondez.
1. Sophie a passé ses vacances d'été où?
2. Elle a passé combien de temps au bord de la mer?
3. Elle a beaucoup nagé?
4. Qu'est-ce qu'elle a appris à faire?
5. Elle a pris des bains de soleil?
6. Elle a bien bronzé?

ANSWERS TO Vous avez compris?

1. Elle a passé ses vacances au bord de la mer.
2. Elle a passé un mois au bord de la mer.
3. Oui, elle a beaucoup nagé.
4. Elle a appris à faire de la planche à voile.
5. Oui, elle a pris des bains de soleil.
6. Oui, elle a bien bronzé.

Structure

Le passé composé des verbes réguliers avec avoir

1. In French, you use the **passé composé** to talk about an action completed in the past. The **passé composé** of most French verbs is formed by using the present tense of the verb **avoir** and the past participle of the verb. Review the formation of the past participle of regular verbs.

-er → é	-ir → i	-re → u
parler parlé	finir fini	perdre perdu
jouer joué	choisir choisi	vendre vendu

2. Now review the forms of the **passé composé** of regular French verbs.

JOUER	CHOISIR	PERDRE
j'ai joué	j'ai choisi	j'ai perdu
tu as joué	tu as choisi	tu as perdu
il/elle/on a joué	il/elle/on a choisi	il/elle/on a perdu
nous avons joué	nous avons choisi	nous avons perdu
vous avez joué	vous avez choisi	vous avez perdu
ils/elles ont joué	ils/elles ont choisi	ils/elles ont perdu

3. In the **passé composé**, the negative words, **ne... pas**, go around the verb **avoir**.

> Je **n'**ai **pas** parlé aux joueurs.
> Je **n'**ai **pas** choisi cette équipe.
> Ils **n'**ont **pas** perdu le match.

LES SPORTS

Révision E

Structure

Bellringer Review

Use BRR Transparency R.16 or write the following on the board.
Write all the things you can possibly do while at the beach.

Presentation

Le passé composé des verbes réguliers avec avoir

Step 1 Have students repeat the past participles in Item 1 after you.

Step 2 Write the forms of the verb **avoir** on the board.

Step 3 Put the past participles on the board with **avoir** and have students repeat aloud the forms of the **passé composé**.

Révision E

3 Historiette Lyon contre Bordeaux
Inventez une histoire.

1. Lyon a joué contre Bordeaux?
2. Vous avez regardé le match?
3. Lamart a donné un coup de pied dans le ballon?
4. Raglan a passé le ballon à Lamart?
5. Raglan a renvoyé le ballon?
6. Les Lyonnais ont marqué un but?
7. Le gardien n'a pas arrêté le ballon?
8. Les Bordelais ont égalisé le score?
9. L'arbitre a sifflé?
10. Il a déclaré un penalty contre Lyon?
11. Lyon a perdu le match?
12. Vous avez applaudi les gagnants?

Le stade Vélodrome à Marseille

4 Historiette Au grand magasin
Complétez en utilisant le passé composé.

1. Hier j'____ avec ma sœur. (parler)
2. Nous ____ d'acheter un cadeau pour mon père. (décider)
3. Nous ____ la maison à midi pour aller à La Samaritaine. (quitter)
4. J'____ le prix d'une chemise au vendeur. (demander)
5. Le vendeur ____ à ma question. (répondre)
6. J'____ une chemise blanche pour mon père. (choisir)
7. J'____ la chemise. (acheter)
8. Ma sœur et moi, nous n'____ pas ____ la même chose pour lui. (acheter)
9. Elle ____ des tennis pour lui. (choisir)
10. Nous ____ à la caisse. (payer)
11. Mon père ____ son anniversaire. (célébrer)

Le grand magasin La Samaritaine à Paris

Les participes passés irréguliers

1. The past participles of regular verbs end in the sounds /é/, /i/, or /ü/. Note that many irregular past participles also end in the sounds /i/ or /ü/ even though they are not all spelled the same way.

Infinitif → participe passé /i/		Infinitif → participe passé /ü/	
dire	dit	avoir	eu
écrire	écrit	croire	cru
		voir	vu
mettre	mis	boire	bu
permettre	permis	devoir	dû
		pouvoir	pu
prendre	pris	lire	lu
apprendre	appris	recevoir	reçu
comprendre	compris	vouloir	voulu

Elle a appris à jouer au tennis.
Elle a pris des leçons.
Il a voulu prendre des leçons de tennis aussi.

2. The verbs **être** and **faire** have irregular past participles.

| être → été | faire → fait |

Il a fait beaucoup de progrès.
Le moniteur a été très content de ses progrès.

5 Historiette À la plage Répondez que oui.

1. Mathilde et ses copines ont passé la journée à la plage?
2. Mathilde a pris un bain de soleil?
3. Elle a mis de la crème solaire?
4. Elles ont fait du ski nautique?
5. Elles ont appris à faire de la planche à voile?
6. Elles ont pris des leçons?
7. Elles ont eu une bonne monitrice?
8. Elles ont pu faire du surf?

Révision E

6 Historiette En route!
Complétez en utilisant le passé composé.

Mon ami Stéphane __1__ (dire) que Pralognan est une belle station de sports d'hiver. Il __2__ (lire) le guide Michelin et il __3__ (voir) Pralognan sur une carte de France. Pralognan est loin de Paris, mais il __4__ (vouloir) y aller tout de même. Les parents de Nicolas lui __5__ (permettre) de prendre leur voiture. Il __6__ (prendre) leur voiture. Il __7__ (faire) le voyage avec son copain Fabrice. Ils __8__ (mettre) leurs skis sur la voiture. Ils __9__ (prendre) l'autoroute. Ils n'__10__ pas __11__ (avoir) de problème.

Pralognan-la-Vanoise, une station de sports d'hiver

7 Vacances d'été
Donnez des réponses personnelles.

1. Tu as nagé?
2. Tu as nagé où?
3. Tu as pris des leçons de planche à voile?
4. Tu as eu un bon moniteur/une bonne monitrice?
5. Tu as beaucoup appris?
6. Tu as joué au tennis?
7. Tu as pris des leçons?
8. Tu as compris tout ce que le moniteur/la monitrice a dit?
9. Tu as vu la Coupe Davis à la télévision?
10. Tu as lu des articles sur le tennis?

Cédric Pioline, un joueur de tennis français professionnel

8 **L'été dernier** Get together with a classmate. Tell one another what you did last summer. Tell if you are going to do the same things next summer (**l'été prochain**).

9 **Ma saison préférée** Work with a classmate. Discuss your favorite season. Explain why you like it so much.

Des cyclistes en Provence

10 **Jeu Les sports** Divide into small groups. Take turns describing a sport without mentioning its name. The others have to guess what sport is being described.

 For more information about sports in the Francophone world, go to the Glencoe French Web site: french.glencoe.com

Révision F

Preview

This review covers vocabulary related to daily routines. This topic was first presented in **Bon voyage! Level 1**. The present and **passé composé** of reflexive verbs and the **passé composé** of verbs with **être** are reviewed.

National Standards

Communication

In Review F, students will communicate in spoken and written French on the following topics:
- Daily routines
- Home activities

Students will also narrate present and past events. They will obtain and provide information and engage in conversations about daily routines.

Révision F

La routine quotidienne

Révision F

R47

Révision F

Resource Manager

Workbook, pages R33–R38
Tests, pages R11–R12, R20, R30
ExamView® Pro

Vocabulaire

Bellringer Review

Use BRR Transparency R.17 or write the following on the board.
Choose the correct completion.
du savon / du dentifrice / du shampooing / une brosse à dents / un peigne / un gant de toilette
1. Je me lave la figure avec _____ et _____.
2. Je me lave les cheveux avec _____.
3. Je me brosse les dents avec _____ et _____.
4. Je me peigne avec _____.

Presentation

Step 1 Have students repeat the vocabulary words and sentences after you.

Step 2 Intersperse questions to get students using the vocabulary. Examples are: **Laure s'est réveillée tôt ou tard ce matin? Elle s'est levée quand?**

Révision F

Vocabulaire

Laure s'est réveillée tôt ce matin. Elle s'est levée tout de suite.

une glace
du savon
une brosse
un peigne

Elle s'est lavé la figure et les mains.

Ensuite, elle est sortie.

mettre la table

débarrasser la table

faire la vaisselle

Après le dîner, Jean a fait ses devoirs.

Il a allumé (mis) la télévision.

À onze heures, il s'est couché.

1 Historiette Le matin
Inventez une histoire.

1. Ce matin, Cédric s'est réveillé tôt?
2. Il s'est levé tout de suite?
3. Il est allé dans la salle de bains?
4. Il s'est lavé les mains et la figure?
5. Il s'est lavé les dents?
6. Il s'est peigné?
7. Il s'est regardé dans une glace quand il s'est peigné?
8. Il est sorti?
9. Il est allé à l'école?
10. Il est arrivé à l'école à l'heure?

Les élèves arrivent à l'école à Paris.

Julie aide sa mère à faire la vaisselle.

2 Historiette Vrai ou faux? Répondez.

1. On met la table après le dîner.
2. Le lave-vaisselle est presque toujours dans la cuisine.
3. On débarrasse la table avant le dîner.
4. Pour regarder une émission il faut éteindre la télévision.
5. On peut zapper pour éviter les publicités à la télévision.

LA ROUTINE QUOTIDIENNE

Révision F

Conversation

La matinée de Jean-Marc

Laurent: Tu te lèves à quelle heure le matin?
Jean-Marc: À quelle heure je me lève ou je me réveille?
Laurent: À quelle heure tu te lèves?
Jean-Marc: Je me lève à six heures et demie.
Laurent: Et tu quittes la maison à quelle heure?
Jean-Marc: À sept heures.
Laurent: Tu te laves, tu te laves les dents, tu te rases et tu prends ton petit déjeuner en une demi-heure!
Jean-Marc: Oui.
Laurent: Tu ne peux pas faire tout ça en une demi-heure!

Des lycéens devant le lycée Talma de Brunoy, près de Paris

Vous avez compris?

Répondez.

1. Jean-Marc se lève à quelle heure le matin?
2. Il quitte la maison à quelle heure?
3. Qu'est-ce qu'il fait avant de quitter la maison?
4. Il fait tout ça en combien de temps?

Structure

 ## Les verbes réfléchis au présent

1. A verb is reflexive when the subject both performs and receives the action of the verb. Since the subject also receives the action, an additional pronoun is needed. This is called the reflexive pronoun. Review the following.

SE LAVER	S'HABILLER
je me lave	je m'habille
tu te laves	tu t'habilles
il/elle/on se lave	il/elle/on s'habille
nous nous lavons	nous nous_z habillons
vous vous lavez	vous vous_z habillez
ils/elles se lavent	ils/elles s'habillent

Note that **me, te,** and **se** become **m', t',** and **s'** before a vowel or a silent **h.**

2. In the negative, **ne** comes before the reflexive pronoun. **Pas** follows the verb.

   Je me réveille, mais je ne me lève pas tout de suite.
   Il se lève, mais il ne s'habille pas tout de suite.

3. When a reflexive verb follows another verb, the reflexive pronoun agrees with the subject.

   Demain, nous allons nous lever tôt.
   Tu peux te réveiller tout seul?

LA ROUTINE QUOTIDIENNE

Révision F

3 Historiette Mon horaire Donnez des réponses personnelles.
1. Comment t'appelles-tu?
2. Tu te réveilles à quelle heure le matin?
3. Tu te lèves tout de suite?
4. Tu t'habilles avant ou après le petit déjeuner?
5. Quand est-ce que tu te laves les dents?
6. Tu te brosses les cheveux ou tu te peignes?
7. Tu te couches à quelle heure le soir?
8. Et ce soir, tu vas te coucher à quelle heure?
9. Demain matin tu vas te lever tôt ou tard?

4 Historiette La matinée de Chloé Complétez.

Bonjour! Je __1__ (s'appeler) Chloé et mon frère __2__ (s'appeler) Jérôme. Lui et moi, nous __3__ (se lever) à sept heures du matin. Quand je __4__ (se lever), je vais tout de suite dans la salle de bains. Là, je __5__ (se laver), je __6__ (se brosser) les dents et je __7__ (se peigner). Le matin, je __8__ (se dépêcher), je n'ai pas de temps à perdre. Je ne reste pas longtemps dans la salle de bains. Je sors, et tout de suite après, mon frère entre dans la salle de bains. Il __9__ (se laver), __10__ (se brosser) les dents et __11__ (se raser).

À quelle heure est-ce que tu __12__ (se lever) le matin? Tu as le même problème que nous? Tu __13__ (se dépêcher) pour ne pas être en retard à l'école?

Le passé composé avec être

1. Certain verbs form their **passé composé** with **être** instead of **avoir**. Many verbs that are conjugated with **être** express motion to or from a place.

ARRIVER	Il est arrivé.	PARTIR	Il est parti.
ENTRER	Il est entré.	SORTIR	Il est sorti.
MONTER	Il est monté.	DESCENDRE	Il est descendu.
ALLER	Il est allé.	RENTRER	Il est rentré.

2. The past participle of verbs conjugated with **être** must agree with the subject in number (singular or plural) and gender (masculine or feminine). Study the following forms.

Masculin	Féminin
je suis parti	je suis partie
tu es parti	tu es partie
il est parti	elle est partie
on est partis	on est parties
nous sommes partis	nous sommes parties
vous êtes parti(s)	vous êtes partie(s)
ils sont partis	elles sont parties

3. Although the following verbs do not express motion to or from a place, they are also conjugated with **être**.

RESTER	Il est resté huit jours.	*He stayed a week.*
TOMBER	Il est tombé.	*He fell.*
NAÎTRE	Elle est née en France.	*She was born in France.*
MOURIR	Elle est morte en 2001.	*She died in 2001.*

Bonnie est née à Paris.

Révision F

FUN FACTS
Grenoble has grown faster than any other French city since World War II. It has many new skyscrapers in a valley that is surrounded by mountains. Important industries in Grenoble are electronics, engineering, and nuclear research.

5 and 6 These activities can be done with books closed, open, or once each way. **Expansion:** Call on an individual to retell all the information in his or her own words.

Writing Development
You can have students write any or all of these activities in paragraph form.

Révision F

5 Historiette Un voyage à Grenoble
Répondez que oui.
1. Charlotte est allée à Grenoble?
2. Elle est arrivée à la gare de Lyon à 10 h?
3. Elle est allée sur le quai?
4. Elle est montée dans le train?
5. Le train est parti à l'heure?
6. Le train est arrivé à Grenoble à l'heure?
7. Charlotte est descendue du train à Grenoble?
8. Elle est sortie de la gare?
9. Elle est allée chez ses amis?

6 Historiette À l'école
Donnez des réponses personnelles.
1. Tu es allé(e) à l'école ce matin?
2. Tu es arrivé(e) à quelle heure?
3. Tu es entré(e) immédiatement?
4. Tu es sorti(e) de l'école à quelle heure hier?
5. Tu es allé(e) manger quelque chose avec tes copains après les cours?
6. Tu es rentré(e) chez toi à quelle heure?

La ville de Grenoble au pied des Alpes

7 Historiette Où est-ce qu'elle est allée?
Complétez en utilisant le passé composé.
1. Marine ____ de la maison. (sortir)
2. Je ____ avec elle. (sortir)
3. Nous ____ au gymnase. (aller)
4. Nous ____ au deuxième étage. (monter)
5. Tu ____ au gymnase aussi, Hugo? (aller)
6. Tu y ____ avec un copain? (aller)
7. Vous ____ au gymnase à quelle heure? (arriver)
8. Marine a fait de l'aérobic et ensuite elle ____ à la piscine. (descendre)
9. Marine et moi, nous ____ du gymnase vers six heures. (sortir)
10. Elle ____ à la maison à six heures et demie et moi, je ____ à sept heures moins le quart. (rentrer)

R54 RÉVISION F

ANSWERS TO Révision

5
1. Oui, Charlotte est allée à Grenoble.
2. Oui, elle est arrivée à la gare de Lyon à 10 h.
3. Oui, elle est allée sur le quai.
4. Oui, elle est montée dans le train.
5. Oui, le train est parti à l'heure.
6. Oui, le train est arrivé à Grenoble à l'heure.
7. Oui, Charlotte est descendue du train à Grenoble.
8. Oui, elle est sortie de la gare.
9. Oui, elle est allée chez ses amis.

6 *Answers will vary but may include:*
1. Oui, je suis allé(e) à l'école ce matin.
2. Je suis arrivé(e) à sept heures.
3. Oui, je suis entré(e) immédiatement.
4. Je suis sorti(e) de l'école à trois heures hier.
5. Oui, je suis allé(e) manger quelque chose avec mes copains après les cours.
6. Je suis rentré(e) chez moi à cinq heures et demie.

7
1. est sortie
2. suis sorti(e)
3. sommes allé(e)s
4. sommes monté(e)s
5. es allé
6. es allé
7. êtes arrivés
8. est descendue
9. sommes sorti(e)s
10. est rentrée, suis rentré(e)

Les verbes réfléchis au passé composé

1. You form the **passé composé** of reflexive verbs with the verb **être**. Note the agreement of the past participle.

SE LAVER

Masculin	Féminin
je me suis lavé	je me suis lavée
tu t'es lavé	tu t'es lavée
il s'est lavé	elle s'est lavée
on s'est lavés	on s'est lavées
nous nous sommes lavés	nous nous sommes lavées
vous vous êtes lavé(s)	vous vous êtes lavée(s)
ils se sont lavés	elles se sont lavées

2. Note that when a part of the body follows a reflexive verb, there is no agreement.

Agreement	No agreement
Marie s'est lavée.	Marie s'est lavé les mains.
Nous nous sommes brossés.	Nous nous sommes brossé les cheveux.

3. In a negative sentence, you put the negative words around the reflexive pronoun and the verb **être**.

> Je **ne** me suis **pas** levée tard.
> Mes amis **ne** se sont **jamais** amusés chez Paul.

LA ROUTINE QUOTIDIENNE

Révision F

Presentation

 Les verbes réfléchis au passé composé

Step 1 Lead students through Items 1–3.

Step 2 Ask students the following:
La fille s'est couchée tôt ou tard hier soir?
Elle s'est réveillée tôt ou tard?
Elle veut se lever?
Elle est fatiguée ou pas?
Elle veut dormir plus?

Révision F

8 Historiette Tôt!
Donnez des réponses personnelles.
1. Tu t'es réveillé(e) tôt ce matin?
2. Tu t'es levé(e) tout de suite?
3. Tu as pris une douche ou tu t'es lavé seulement la figure et les mains?
4. Tu t'es habillé(e) avant ou après le petit déjeuner?
5. Tu t'es peigné(e) ou tu t'es brossé les cheveux?
6. Tu t'es lavé les dents après le petit déjeuner?
7. Tes copains et toi, vous vous êtes bien amusés à l'école?
8. Vous vous êtes dépêchés de rentrer chez vous pour regarder la télévision?

9 Mes cousins Mettez au pluriel.
1. Il s'est levé.
2. Il s'est lavé.
3. Il s'est rasé.
4. Il s'est habillé.
5. Elle s'est levée tard.
6. Elle s'est maquillée.
7. Elle s'est vite habillée.
8. Elle s'est dépêchée.

10 Aujourd'hui Work with a classmate. Tell each other what you did today. Did you do anything different from your ordinary routine? If so, tell what.

Du sport au lycée Janson de Sailly à Paris

11 **Madame Nette** Madame Nette is a very organized woman whose daily routine is always the same. With your classmates, take turns describing Madame Nette's day from morning to night. The first student suggests her first activity of the day. The next student repeats that activity and adds another.

—Madame Nette se réveille à six heures.

—Madame Nette se réveille à six heures. Elle se lève tout de suite.

12 **Hier soir** You look really tired this morning. You got to bed quite late last night. Tell a classmate why. Tell what you did. Your classmate will then tell you if he or she had the same type of night.

13 **La révolte du samedi et du dimanche** When the weekend comes, everybody wants a change of pace. In small groups, discuss some of the things you do on weekends that are different from the things you do during the week. Then compare results with those of another group.

—Le samedi et le dimanche, je ne me lève pas à sept heures. Je me lève à neuf heures.

—Je ne prends pas le petit déjeuner à huit heures mais à onze heures.

For more information about daily life in the Francophone world, go to the Glencoe French Web site: french.glencoe.com

LA ROUTINE QUOTIDIENNE

R57

Planning for Chapter 1

SCOPE AND SEQUENCE, PAGES 1–31

Topics
* Cultural activities
* Movies, plays, museums

Culture
* Cultural activities in France
* African music—traditional and modern

Functions
* How to discuss movies, plays, and museums
* How to express what happens to you or someone else
* How to refer to people and things already mentioned

Structure
* The verbs **savoir** and **connaître**
* The pronouns **me, te, nous, vous**
* The pronouns **le, la, les**

National Standards
* Communication Standard 1.1 pages 4, 5, 8, 9, 11, 12, 13, 15, 16, 17, 19, 26
* Communication Standard 1.2 pages 4, 5, 8, 9, 11, 12, 13, 15, 16, 17, 18, 21, 23, 25
* Communication Standard 1.3 pages 4, 5, 8, 11, 13, 17, 26, 27
* Cultures Standard 2.1 pages 2, 20–21, 22–23
* Cultures Standard 2.2 pages 2, 3, 7, 9, 18, 19, 20–21, 22–23
* Connections Standard 3.1 pages 24–25
* Comparisons Standard 4.2 page 26
* Communities Standard 5.1 page 27

PACING AND PRIORITIES

> The chapter content is color coded below to assist you in planning.
> ■ required   ■ recommended   ■ optional

Vocabulaire (required)   *Days 1–4*
- ■ Mots 1
   - Au cinéma
   - Au théâtre
- ■ Mots 2
   - Au musée

Structure (required)   *Days 5–7*
- ■ Les verbes **savoir** et **connaître**
- ■ Les pronoms **me, te, nous, vous**
- ■ Les pronoms **le, la, les**

Conversation (required)
- ■ On va au cinéma?

Prononciation (recommended)
- ■ Le son /ü/

Lectures culturelles
- ■ Les loisirs culturels en France (recommended)
- ■ La musique africaine (optional)

Connexions (optional)
- ■ La musique

■ **C'est à vous** (recommended)

■ **Assessment** (recommended)

■ **On parle super bien!** (optional)

RESOURCE GUIDE

SECTION	PAGES	SECTION RESOURCES
Vocabulaire *Mots 1*		
Au cinéma	2–3	Vocabulary Transparencies 1.2–1.3
Au théâtre	3–5	Audio CD 2
		Audio Activities TE, pages 1–2
		Workbook, pages 1–2
		Quiz 1, page 1
		ExamView® Pro
Vocabulaire *Mots 2*		
Au musée	6–9	Vocabulary Transparencies 1.4–1.5
		Audio CD 2
		Audio Activities TE, page 3
		Workbook, pages 3–4
		Quiz 2, page 2
		ExamView® Pro
Structure		
Les verbes **savoir** et **connaître**	10–11	Audio CD 2
Les pronoms **me, te, nous, vous**	12–13	Audio Activities TE, pages 4–6
Les pronoms **le, la, les**	14–17	Workbook, pages 5–7
		Quizzes 3–5, pages 3–5
		ExamView® Pro
Conversation		
On va au cinéma?	18	Audio CD 2
		Audio Activities TE, page 7
		Interactive CD-ROM
Prononciation		
Le son /ü/	19	Audio CD 2
		Audio Activities TE, page 8
Lectures culturelles		
Les loisirs culturels en France	20–21	Audio CD 2
La musique africaine	22–23	Audio Activities TE, pages 8–9
		Tests, pages 4, 7
Connexions		
La musique	24–25	Tests, pages 8–9
C'est à vous		
	26–27	**Bon voyage!** Video, Episode 1
		Video Activities, Chapter 1
		French Online Activities
		french.glencoe.com
Assessment		
	28–29	Communication Transparency C 1
		Quizzes 1–5, pages 1–5
		Performance Assessment, Task 1
		Tests, pages 1–14
		ExamView® Pro
		Situation Cards, Chapter 1
		Marathon mental Videoquiz

Using Your Resources for Chapter 1

Transparencies

Bellringer 1.1–1.6

Vocabulary 1.1–1.5

Communication C 1

Workbook

Vocabulary,
pages 1–4

Structure,
pages 5–7

Enrichment,
pages 8–10

Audio Activities

Vocabulary,
pages 1–3

Structure,
pages 4–6

Conversation,
page 7

Pronunciation,
page 8

Cultural Reading,
pages 8–9

Additional Practice,
pages 10–11

Assessment

Vocabulary and Structure Quizzes, pages 1–5

Chapter Tests, pages 1–14

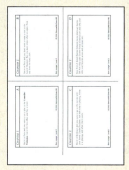
Situation Cards, Chapter 1

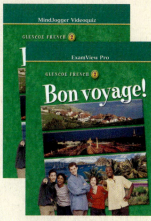
MindJogger Videoquiz, ExamView® Pro, Chapter 1

Timesaving Teacher Tools

TeacherWorks™

TeacherWorks™ is your all-in-one teacher resource center. Personalize lesson plans, access resources from the Teacher Wraparound Edition, connect to the Internet, or make a to-do list. These are only a few of the many features that can assist you in the planning and organizing of your lessons.

Includes:
- A calendar feature
- Access to all program blackline masters
- Standards correlations and more

ExamView® Pro

Test Bank software for Macintosh and Windows makes creating, editing, customizing, and printing tests quick and easy.

Technology Resources

In the Chapter 1 Internet activity, you will have a chance to learn more about the Francophone world. Visit **french.glencoe.com**.

On the Interactive Conversation CD-ROM, students can listen to and take part in a recorded version of the conversation in Chapter 1.

See the National Geographic Teacher's Corner on pages 138–139, 244–245, 372–373, 472–473 for reference to additional technology resources.

Bon voyage! Video and Video Activities, Chapter 1

Help your students prepare for the chapter test by playing the **Marathon mental** Videoquiz game show. Teams will compete against each other to review chapter vocabulary and structure and sharpen listening comprehension skills.

CHAPITRE 1

Preview

In this chapter, students will learn to discuss cultural events and express their cultural likes and dislikes. In order to do this, they will learn vocabulary associated with films, museums, and the theater. They will also learn to use the verbs **savoir** and **connaître** and the direct object pronouns.

National Standards

Communication
In Chapter 1, students will communicate in spoken and written French on the following topics:
• Going to the movies
• Visiting a museum
• Attending a theater performance
Students will also learn to tell whom and what they know. They will obtain and provide information and engage in conversations about their personal experiences with cultural events. They will also learn to use direct object pronouns.

Communities
After having learned about cultural preferences of the French, have students compare them with those of their own community.

LEVELING
The activities, conversations, and readings within each chapter are marked according to level of difficulty. **E** indicates easy. **A** indicates average. **C** indicates challenging. Some activities cover a range of difficulty. In some activities, for example, advanced students will be able to produce more extensive responses while students who learn at a different rate may give less detailed responses. The leveling indicators will help you individualize instruction to best meet your students' needs.

CHAPITRE 1

Les loisirs culturels

Objectifs
In this chapter you will learn to:
✔ discuss movies, plays, and museums
✔ tell what you know and whom you know
✔ tell what happens to you or someone else
✔ refer to people and things already mentioned
✔ talk about some cultural activities in Paris

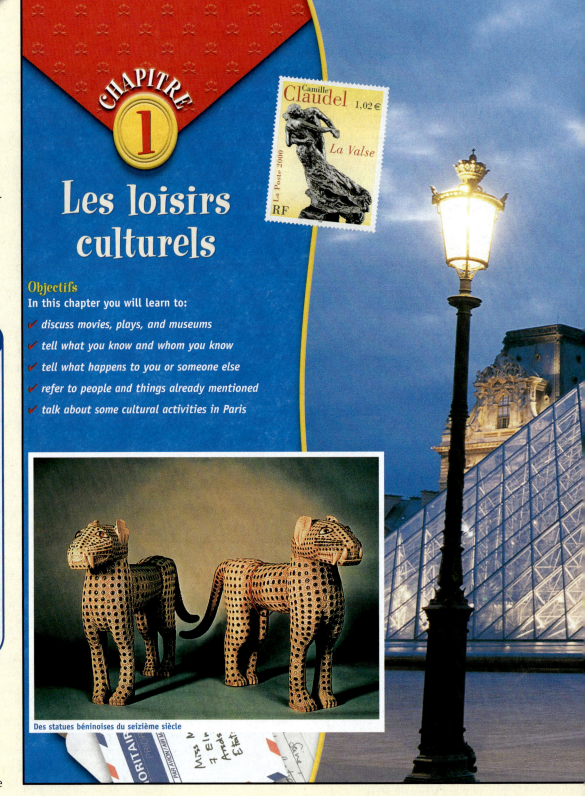

Des statues béninoises du seizième siècle

CHAPITRE 1

Spotlight on Culture

Photograph The Louvre is the world's largest museum, and at night, as seen here, it is beautifully illuminated by 70,000 lightbulbs. The Louvre as it stands today is the product of centuries of construction. It was originally built by Philippe-Auguste in the thirteenth century as a fortress. Throughout the centuries the palace has served many purposes, from the royal residence to empty apartments that were taken over by artists. Louis XVI and Marie-Antoinette fled from the palace, then called the **Palais des Tuileries**, in 1791, two years after the start of the Revolution. At the end of the eighteenth century, Napoleon made the Louvre into a museum, but three more French kings, Louis XVIII, Charles X, and Louis Philippe, continued to make the Louvre their home.

The Louvre's incredible collections include paintings, drawings, sculpture, furniture, coins, and jewelry.

Sculpture For much of its history, Bénin was known as Abomey, and later the kingdom of Dahomey. The cultural history of Bénin is very rich, and the art produced during the Dahomey era attracts international attention. Art served both a functional and spiritual purpose. The bronzes seen here are of leopards, and they date from the sixteenth century.

Vocabulaire *Mots 1*

1 Preparation

Resource Manager
Vocabulary Transparencies 1.2–1.3
Audio Activities TE, pages 1–2
Audio CD 2
Workbook, pages 1–2
Quiz 1, page 1
ExamView® Pro

Bellringer Review
Use BRR Transparency 1.1 or write the following on the board.
Make a list of activities you like to do in your free time.

2 Presentation

Step 1 Show Vocabulary Transparencies 1.2–1.3. Point to individual items and have the class repeat the words after you or Audio CD 2.

Step 2 Call on individual students to point to the corresponding illustration on the transparency as you say the word or expression.

Teaching Tip
Ask questions about students' personal preferences when practicing the vocabulary. For example:
Jacques, tu préfères les films policiers ou les documentaires? Qui aime les dessins animés?

Step 3 After presenting the vocabulary orally, have students open their books. Call on individuals to read. Ask questions such as: **On joue ce film étranger où? Le film est en V.O. ou on le voit avec des sous-titres?**

Step 4 Call on students to act out the short conversation.

Vocabulaire *Mots 1*

Au cinéma

Pierre est devant le guichet.
La prochaine séance est à treize heures.

Qui joue dans ce film?
On joue un film étranger au Rex.
Le film est en V.O. (version originale).
On le voit avec des sous-titres.
Dans un autre cinéma, le film est doublé.
On peut le voir en français.

Reaching All Students

Total Physical Response
(Student 1), levez-vous, s'il vous plaît.
Faites la queue devant le guichet.
Prenez votre billet.
Entrez dans le cinéma.
Choisissez une place.
Prenez votre place. Asseyez-vous.
Regardez le film.
Indiquez que le film est amusant.
Le film est fini. Levez-vous.
Sortez du cinéma.

Vocabulaire
Mots 1

un film de science-fiction

un film d'horreur

un film policier

un documentaire

un dessin animé

un film en vidéo
louer une vidéo (un DVD)

un film d'amour

un film d'aventures

Au théâtre

chanter
un chanteur
une chanteuse

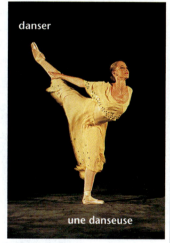
danser
une danseuse

On va monter *Roméo et Juliette*.
C'est une pièce de théâtre en trois actes.
Chaque acte a deux scènes.
Entre deux actes, il y a un entracte.
Roméo et Juliette est aussi un ballet.

Voici d'autres genres de pièces:
une tragédie
une comédie
un drame
une comédie musicale

trois 3

Vocabulaire

3 Practice

Quel est le mot?

Historiette Each time **Historiette** appears, it means that the answers to the activity form a short story. Encourage students to look at the title of the **Historiette**, since it can help them do the activity.

1, **3**, **5** With books closed, ask the questions to these activities and call on individuals to respond.

Note: Answers to these activities can be written at home.

2 and **4** Call on students to retell the information in their own words. Have students open books. Call on individuals to read aloud, completing the sentences with the appropriate words.

Attention!

Note that the activities are color-coded. All the activities in the text are communicative. However, the ones with blue titles are guided communication. The red titles indicate that the answers to the activity are more open-ended and can vary more. You may wish to correct students' mistakes more than in the guided activities than in the activities with a red title, which lend themselves to a freer response.

Vocabulaire

Quel est le mot?

1 Fana de cinéma ou pas? Donnez des réponses personnelles.

1. Tu vas souvent au cinéma?
2. Qu'est-ce que tu aimes comme films?
3. Quel est ton acteur préféré? Et ton actrice préférée? Il/Elle est très connu(e)?
4. Il y a un cinéma près de chez toi?
5. La première séance est à quelle heure?
6. Où est-ce que tu achètes les billets?
7. Tu fais souvent la queue devant le guichet?
8. Dans la salle de cinéma, tu aimes mieux une place près de l'écran ou loin de l'écran?
9. Si tu vas voir un film étranger, tu aimes mieux voir le film doublé ou en version originale avec des sous-titres?

Le cinéma Champollion, Paris

2 Historiette Au cinéma Complétez.

Ce soir, on __1__ un très bon film au Wepler. C'est un film étranger. Il n'est pas doublé. Il y a des __2__. Le film est en __3__ originale. La prochaine __4__ est à quelle heure? Les __5__ coûtent combien?

3 Tu aimes mieux quels genres de film? Donnez des réponses personnelles.

1. Tu aimes mieux (préfères) les documentaires ou les westerns?
2. Tu aimes mieux les films policiers ou les films d'horreur?
3. Tu aimes mieux les films comiques ou les films d'amour?
4. Tu aimes mieux les films d'aventures ou les films de science-fiction?
5. Tu vas voir quelquefois des dessins animés?
6. Tu loues quelquefois des films en vidéo ou DVD? Quels genres de film?

Les garçons louent un DVD.

4 quatre   CHAPITRE 1

ANSWERS TO Quel est le mot?

1 *Answers will vary but may include:*
1. Oui, je vais souvent au cinéma.
2. J'aime les films policiers.
3. Mon acteur préféré est _____. Mon actrice préférée est _____. Oui, ils sont très connus.
4. Oui, il y a un cinéma près de chez moi.
5. La première séance est à 19 h.
6. J'achète les billets au guichet.
7. Oui, je fais souvent la queue devant le guichet.
8. Dans la salle de cinéma j'aime mieux une place près de l'écran.
9. Si je vais voir un film étranger, j'aime mieux voir le film en version originale avec des sous-titres.

2
1. joue
2. sous-titres
3. version
4. séance
5. places

3 *Answers will vary but may include:*
1. J'aime mieux les westerns.
2. J'aime mieux les films policiers.
3. J'aime mieux les films comiques.
4. J'aime mieux les films de science-fiction.
5. Oui, je vais voir quelquefois des dessins animés.
6. Oui, je loue quelquefois des films en vidéo. Des films policiers.

Des pièces et des films Complétez.
1. Au lycée les élèves _____ une pièce tous les ans.
2. On voit un film au cinéma. On voit une pièce au _____.
3. Une _____ a des actes et les actes sont divisés en _____.
4. Entre deux actes, il y a un _____.
5. Un _____ joue le rôle de Roméo.
6. Une _____ joue le rôle de Juliette.
7. Dans une comédie musicale, les _____ chantent et les _____ dansent.

 Historiette Au théâtre Donnez des réponses personnelles.
1. Tu aimes le théâtre?
2. Tu vas souvent au théâtre?
3. Il y a un théâtre là où tu habites?
4. Ton école a un club d'art dramatique?
5. Tu es membre de ce club?
6. Le club monte combien de pièces par an?
7. Cette année, le club va monter quelle pièce?
8. C'est quel genre de pièce?
9. Il y a combien d'actes?
10. Il y a combien d'entractes?

 Mon film préféré Find out what a classmate's favorite movies are and why. Then find out which movies he or she dislikes and why. Take turns.

 For more practice using words from **Mots 1**, *do Activity 1 on page H2 at the end of this book.*

LES LOISIRS CULTURELS

cinq 5

Vocabulaire

Writing Development
Have students write the answers to Activities 2–5 in paragraph form.

Cognate Recognition
Have students scan the **Mots 1** words again and then identify and pronounce each cognate.

Reteaching
Show Vocabulary Transparencies 1.2–1.3 and let students say as much as they can about them in their own words.

Learning from Realia
(page 5 middle) You may wish to tell students that Molière was a famous seventeenth-century dramatist whose comedies are still very much appreciated today.

This *Infogap* activity will allow students to practice in pairs. The activity should be very manageable for them, since all vocabulary and structures are familiar to them.

LEVELING
E: Activities 1, 3, 5
A: Activities 2, 4, 5, 6

ANSWERS TO **Quel est le mot?**

4
1. montent
2. théâtre
3. pièce, scènes
4. entracte
5. acteur
6. actrice
7. chanteurs, danseurs

5 *Answers will vary but may include:*
1. Oui, j'aime le théâtre.
2. Oui, je vais souvent au théâtre.
3. Oui, il y a un théâtre là où j'habite.
4. Oui, mon école a un club d'art dramatique.
5. Oui, je suis membre de ce club.
6. Le club monte trois pièces par an.
7. Cette année le club va monter _____.
8. C'est _____.
9. Il y a _____ actes.
10. Il y a _____ entractes.

5

Vocabulaire Mots 2

1 Preparation

Resource Manager

Vocabulary Transparencies 1.4–1.5
Audio Activities TE, page 3
Audio CD 2
Workbook, pages 3–4
Quiz 2, page 2
ExamView® Pro

Bellringer Review

Use BRR Transparency 1.2 or write the following on the board.
Name your four favorite movies and tell what type of films they are.

2 Presentation

Step 1 Show Vocabulary Transparencies 1.4–1.5. Have students close their books and repeat the new words after you two or three times.

Step 2 Call a student to the front of the room. As you say a new word or phrase, have the student point to the appropriate item on the transparency.

Step 3 After presenting the vocabulary with the transparencies, have students open their books and read the words and sentences.

Vocabulaire Mots 2

Au musée

Une exposition de peinture et sculpture

6 six

CHAPITRE 1

Reaching All Students

Total Physical Response Before you begin, demonstrate **se promener**.
(Student 1), levez-vous et venez ici, s'il vous plaît.
Vous êtes devant le musée d'Art Moderne.
Entrez dans le musée.
Promenez-vous dans la grande salle.
Vous voyez un tableau que vous trouvez beau.
Arrêtez-vous.
Regardez le tableau.
Indiquez que vous aimez le tableau, que vous le trouvez beau.
Et voilà un autre tableau. Indiquez que vous n'aimez pas ce tableau. Vous ne le trouvez pas beau.

Je sais que le peintre s'appelle Duval.
Je ne le connais pas personnellement.
Je connais son œuvre (ses tableaux).
Ses tableaux, je les trouve extraordinaires!

Moi, je connais bien le musée du Centre Pompidou. Je le visite souvent. Je sais que le musée est fermé le mardi.

Le musée n'est pas ouvert le mardi.
Il est ouvert tous les jours sauf le mardi.

LES LOISIRS CULTURELS

Vocabulaire
Mots 2

Vocabulary Expansion

You may wish to give students the following additional vocabulary in order to talk about art.
- une gravure
- une lithographie
- de la poterie
- une aquarelle
- un portrait
- une peinture à l'huile

Cognate Recognition

Ask students to identify as many cognates as they can in **Mots 2**. Pay particular attention to their pronunciation of these cognates.

FOLDABLES Study Organizer — Dinah Zike's Study Guides

Your students may wish to use Foldable 12 to organize, display, and arrange data as they learn to describe cultural events. You may wish to encourage them to add information from each chapter as they continue to watch movies in French.

A *project board with tabs* foldable is also ideal for having students illustrate and describe scenes from other events that they will be learning about.

Chapter Projects

Une exposition Have groups research different French painters and/or sculptors. Each group can put on an art show, using prints by the artists.

Au musée Visit a local museum so that students can see different styles of art and, hopefully, some work by French artists.

Un film You may wish to rent a video of a French film in **version originale** and show it to the class. Your students might enjoy the following movies: *Au revoir les enfants, Les quatre cents coups, L'enfant sauvage, Le ballon rouge, Jean de Florette, La gloire de mon père, Cyrano de Bergerac*.

Vocabulaire

3 Practice

Quel est le mot?

8 You may wish to have students write their answers to this activity in paragraph form.

Reaching All Students

Additional Practice Have students quickly write down as many words associated with the movies, theater, or museums as they can. Then have them work in pairs, giving their partner one word at a time from their list. Their partner puts the word into a sentence.

Art Connection

Starting in 1890, Monet had built at his home in Giverny a beautiful garden and a pond, **un jardin d'eau**, which reflected his interest in Japanese art. He did many paintings of his **jardin d'eau**. Many of his paintings of **les nymphéas** *(water lilies)* can be seen today in the Orangerie in Paris.

Vocabulaire

Quel est le mot?

7 **Un peu de culture** Répondez d'après les dessins.

1. C'est un musée ou un théâtre?

2. Le musée est ouvert ou fermé?

3. Elle est peintre ou sculpteur?

4. C'est un tableau ou une statue?

8 **Historiette** Au musée
Inventez des réponses.
1. Michel sait comment s'appelle le peintre?
2. Il connaît le peintre personnellement?
3. Il connaît l'œuvre du peintre?
4. Annick sait dans quel musée il y a une exposition de Monet?
5. Elle trouve ses tableaux extraordinaires?
6. Elle connaît le musée de l'Orangerie?
7. Elle le visite souvent?
8. Elle sait que le musée est fermé le mardi?
9. Le musée de l'Orangerie est ouvert tous les jours sauf le mardi?

Claude Monet *Le bassin aux nymphéas*

ANSWERS TO Quel est le mot?

7
1. C'est un musée.
2. Le musée est ouvert.
3. Elle est sculpteur.
4. C'est un tableau.

8 *Answers will vary but may include:*
1. Non, Michel ne sait pas comment s'appelle le peintre.
2. Non, il ne connaît pas le peintre personnellement.
3. Oui, il connaît l'œuvre du peintre.
4. Oui, elle sait dans quel musée il y a une exposition de Monet.
5. Oui, elle trouve ses tableaux extraordinaires.
6. Oui, elle connaît le musée de l'Orangerie.
7. Oui, elle le visite souvent.
8. Oui, elle sait que le musée est fermé le mardi.
9. Oui, le musée de l'Orangerie est ouvert tous les jours sauf le mardi.

9 **L'art français** Work with a classmate. Discuss together what you have learned so far about French art and French artists. Find out who appreciates art more and who knows more about art.

Paul Cézanne *Pommes et oranges*

Art Connection

Early in his career, Paul Cézanne (1839–1906) also took part in the first exhibition of the Impressionists. Later studies led him to believe that Impressionist paintings lacked form, solidity, and structure. Cézanne wanted to paint nature, but he was not interested in reproducing exactly the shapes and colors found in nature. He began to experiment with still-life painting, often painting the same subject over and over until he was completely satisfied with it.

LEVELING

E: Activities 7, 8
A: Activities 8, 9, 10
C: Activity 10

Tours et crypte archéologique de Notre-Dame −12 ans : gratuit

Rue de Cloître, Paris 4ᵉ. **M°**: Cité, ou **RER C**: St. Michel. Tours: **tél**: 01 44 32 16 72, groupes: 01 44 32 16 72. **Horaires**: 9h30-19h30 du 1.04 au 30.09; 10h-17h du 1.10 au 31.03. Fermeture des caisses 45mn plus tôt. Crypte: **tél**: 01 43 29 83 51. **Horaires**: 9h30-18h du 1.04 au 30.09; 10h-16h30 du 1.10 au 31.03.
Du haut des tours: une vue exceptionnelle sur la cathédrale et la ville. . . Dans la crypte archéologique: l'histoire de Paris de l'époque gallo-romaine au XIXᵉ s.

Musée de l'Ordre de la Libération −12 ans : gratuit

Hôtel national des Invalides, 51 bis, boulevard de Latour-Maubourg, Paris 7ᵉ. **Tél**: 01 47 05 35 15. **M°**: Invalides. **Horaires**: 10h-17h.
Musée de la France Libre, de la Résistance et de la Déportation.

Musée d'Orsay − 18 ans : gratuit

1, rue de Bellechasse, Paris 7ᵉ. **Tél**: 01 40 49 48 14 . **M°**: Solférino, ou **RER C**: Musée d'Orsay. **Horaires**: 10h-18h, nocturne le jeudi jusqu'à 21h45. Le dimanche, et du 20.06 au 20.09: 9h-18h. Fermé le lundi.
Peintures impressionnistes et ensemble de la création artistique de 1848 à 1914.

---

10 **Renseignements** You're in Paris and you'd like to visit one of the museums listed in the brochure on the left. Call the museum and find out from the museum employee (your partner) where it's located, what time it opens and closes, what day it's closed, and how much a ticket costs. Your partner can use the information in the brochure to answer your questions.

 For more practice using words from **Mots 2**, *do Activity 2 on page H3 at the end of this book.*

LES LOISIRS CULTURELS

neuf 9

Answers to *Quel est le mot?*

9 Answers will vary depending upon the painter and/or works of art the students select.

10 Answers will vary.

Structure

1 Preparation

Resource Manager

Audio Activities TE, pages 4–6
Audio CD 2
Workbook, pages 5–7
Quizzes 3–5, pages 3–5
ExamView® Pro

Bellringer Review

Use BRR Transparency 1.3 or write the following on the board.
List everything you associate with the following.
le cinéma   le théâtre   un musée

2 Presentation

Les verbes savoir et connaître

Step 1 Lead students through Items 1–4 and the examples.

Step 2 Make two lists on the board, one of information that follows **connaître** (names of people, cities and other places, artistic and literary works), and the other with facts that follow **savoir** (dates, times, telephone numbers, addresses, infinitives, clauses).

Step 3 Give students the following words or expressions and have them say whether they would use **savoir** or **connaître**: André, sa famille, son adresse, son numéro de téléphone, le nom de son école, ses professeurs, sa ville.

Structure

Les verbes savoir et connaître
Telling whom and what you know

1. Study the following present-tense forms of the verbs **savoir** and **connaître**, both of which mean "to know."

SAVOIR		CONNAÎTRE	
je	sais	je	connais
tu	sais	tu	connais
il/elle/on	sait	il/elle/on	connaît
nous	savons	nous	connaissons
vous	savez	vous	connaissez
ils/elles	savent	ils/elles	connaissent

Note the **passé composé** of these verbs: **j'ai su, j'ai connu**.

2. You use **savoir** to indicate that you know a fact or that you know something by heart.

   Tu sais à quelle heure la séance commence?
   Tu sais le numéro de téléphone de Philippe?

3. You use **savoir** + infinitive to indicate that you know how to do something.

   Tu sais danser le tango?
   Il ne sait pas nager.

4. **Connaître** means "to know" in the sense of "to be acquainted with." You can use **connaître** only with nouns—people, places, and things. Compare the meanings of **connaître** and **savoir** in the sentences below.

   Je sais comment elle s'appelle. Nathalie.   Je connais bien Nathalie.
   Je sais où elle habite. À Grenoble.   Je connais bien Grenoble.
   Je sais le nom de l'auteur. Victor Hugo.   Je connais son œuvre.

Grenoble, France

10 ✦ dix

Learning from Photos

(page 10) Grenoble is the capital of Dauphiné in the Alps. It is a fast growing city with many new skyscrapers. It is home to several universities and major companies that specialize in electronics, engineering, and nuclear research. Surrounded by mountains, Grenoble is a modern, cosmopolitan city.

LEVELING

E: Activity 11
A: Activities 11, 12, 13, 14
C: Activity 14

Comment dit-on?

 Qu'est-ce que tu sais? Donnez des réponses personnelles.
1. Tu sais où habite ton ami(e)? Il/Elle habite dans quelle ville?
2. Tu connais bien cette ville?
3. Tu sais où on peut bien manger pour pas cher?
4. Tu sais le nom de l'auteur de *Hamlet*?
5. Tu connais les pièces de Shakespeare?
6. Tu connais *Hamlet*?

 On sait tout! Complétez.
1. Moi, je _____ où se trouve le théâtre.
2. Paul, tu _____ quel est le numéro de téléphone?
3. Nous ne _____ pas l'adresse exacte.
4. Nos amis _____ à quelle heure la pièce commence.
5. Vous _____ quelle pièce on joue en ce moment à la Comédie-Française?
6. Il faut demander à Julie. Elle _____ tout.

 Qu'est-ce que tu connais? Complétez.
1. Je _____ bien la France.
2. Les élèves de Mme Benoît _____ bien la peinture française.
3. Mais ils ne _____ pas très bien la littérature française.
4. Tu _____ la culture française?
5. Et Paul, il _____ la peinture française contemporaine?
6. Vous _____ les sculptures de Rodin?
7. Nous _____ des impressionnistes comme Monet, Manet et Renoir.
8. Tu _____ l'œuvre du peintre Edgar Degas?
9. Oui, je _____ son œuvre. J'adore ses danseuses.

 Tu le/la connais bien! Work with a classmate. Think of someone in the class whom you know quite well. Tell your partner some things you know about this person. Don't say who it is. Your partner will guess. Take turns.

Edgar Degas *Deux danseuses en scène*

 For more practice using **savoir** and **connaître**, do Activity 3 on page H4 at the end of this book.

LES LOISIRS CULTURELS

onze 11

Structure

3 Practice

Comment dit-on?

11 This activity can be done with books closed, open, or once each way.

12 and **13** After doing these activities with books open, have students close their books. You give sentence fragments, and the students say a complete sentence.
Example: **le numéro de téléphone**
Je sais le numéro de téléphone.

Reaching All Students

Additional Practice Have students write five things they know how to do using **savoir** + infinitive. Groups of students interview each other, then compile a report, and present it to the class. Students might then practice questioning techniques. For example: **Qui sait nager? Qui ne sait pas plonger? Qu'est-ce que Carole sait faire?**

This *Infogap* activity will allow students to practice in pairs. The activity should be very manageable for them, since all vocabulary and structures are familiar to them.

Art Connection

(page 11) Edgar Degas was born in Paris in 1834, and he died there in 1917. He studied law before dedicating himself to art. In his works, Degas was concerned with the line, form, and movement of the human body. This explains why so many of his famous paintings are of ballerinas.

ANSWERS TO Comment dit-on?

11 Answers will vary but may include:
1. Oui, je sais où habite mon amie. Elle habite à Chicago.
2. Oui, je connais bien cette ville.
3. Oui, je sais où on peut bien manger pour pas cher.
4. Oui, je sais le nom de l'auteur de *Hamlet*.
5. Oui, je connais les pièces de Shakespeare.
6. Oui, je connais *Hamlet*.

12
1. sais
2. sais
3. savons
4. savent
5. savez
6. sait

13
1. connais
2. connaissent
3. connaissent
4. connais
5. connaît
6. connaissez
7. connaissons
8. connais
9. connais

11

Structure

1 Preparation

Bellringer Review

Use BRR Transparency 1.4 or write the following on the board. List five things you know how to do.

2 Presentation

Les pronoms me, te, nous, vous

Note: The object pronouns **me, te, nous, vous** are introduced before the third person pronouns for two reasons. First, they are less complicated than the third person pronouns since they are both direct and indirect objects. Second, they are the only object pronouns that are truly necessary for communication. For example, if asked a question with **te** or **vous**, one must answer with **me** or **nous**. When speaking in the third person, however, one could respond with a noun instead of a pronoun: **Tu as invité Jean? Non, je n'ai pas invité Jean.**

Step 1 Lead students through Items 1–2 on page 12.

3 Practice

Comment dit-on?

15 and **16** Ask the questions with books closed and call on students to respond. Activities can be done again with books open for additional reinforcement.

Structure

Les pronoms me, te, nous, vous
Telling who does what for whom

1. The pronouns **me, te, nous,** and **vous** are object pronouns.

   Marie **t'**invite au théâtre?   Oui, elle **m'**invite au théâtre.
   Elle **te** parle au téléphone?   Oui, elle **me** parle au téléphone.
   Le prof **vous** regarde?   Oui, il **nous** regarde.
   Il **vous** explique la leçon?   Oui, il **nous** explique la leçon.

2. The object pronoun **me, te, nous,** or **vous** always comes right before the verb it is linked to.

   > Il **me** parle.
   > Il ne **me** parle pas.
   > Il veut **me** parler.
   > Il ne veut pas **me** parler.

Comment dit-on?

15 **Historiette** Une invitation
Répondez que oui.
1. Jean te téléphone?
2. Il te parle longtemps?
3. Il t'invite au cinéma?
4. Il te demande quel film tu veux voir?
5. Il te paie la place?
6. Après le film il t'invite au café?

16 **Historiette** En classe Répondez que oui.
1. En classe, la prof vous parle, à toi et aux autres élèves?
2. Elle vous apprend à lire et écrire en français?
3. Elle vous explique la grammaire?
4. Elle vous présente le vocabulaire?
5. Elle vous donne beaucoup de devoirs?
6. Elle vous donne trop de devoirs?
7. Elle vous parle toujours en français?

Une conversation au café

12 ✦ douze   CHAPITRE 1

ANSWERS TO Comment dit-on?

15
1. Oui, Jean me téléphone.
2. Oui, il me parle longtemps.
3. Oui, il m'invite au cinéma.
4. Oui, il me demande quel film je veux voir.
5. Oui, il me paie la place.
6. Oui, il m'invite au café.

16
1. Oui, la prof nous parle.
2. Oui, elle nous apprend à lire et écrire en français.
3. Oui, elle nous explique la grammaire.
4. Oui, elle nous présente le vocabulaire.
5. Oui, elle nous donne beaucoup de devoirs.
6. Oui, elle nous donne trop de devoirs.
7. Oui, elle nous parle toujours en français.

17 Au rayon des chemisiers Complétez avec **me** ou **vous**.

Je suis au rayon des chemisiers des Galeries Lafayette. La vendeuse __1__ parle. Elle __2__ demande:

La vendeuse: Vous désirez?
Moi: Je voudrais ce chemisier, s'il __3__ plaît. Je fais du 40.
La vendeuse: Je __4__ donne quelle couleur?
Moi: Qu'est-ce que vous __5__ proposez?
La vendeuse: Je ne sais pas. En bleu marine, il __6__ plaît?
Moi: Oui, il __7__ plaît.
La vendeuse: Mais je __8__ suggère d'essayer un 38.
Moi: D'accord. Je peux __9__ payer par carte de crédit?
La vendeuse: Mais bien sûr, mademoiselle!

 18 Pourquoi ça? Répondez d'après le modèle.

— Il me regarde!
— Il te regarde? Pourquoi?

1. Il me pose des questions!
2. Il me parle!
3. Il me téléphone!
4. Il me dit son numéro de téléphone!
5. Il me donne son adresse!

 19 Historiette C'est ton anniversaire.
Inventez une histoire.

1. Tes copains vont te téléphoner le jour de ton anniversaire?
2. Ils vont te voir?
3. Ils vont t'inviter au cinéma ou au concert?
4. Ils vont te dire «Joyeux anniversaire!» ?
5. Ils vont te faire un gâteau?
6. Ils vont te donner des cadeaux?

LES LOISIRS CULTURELS treize 13

Structure

1 Preparation

Bellringer Review

Use BRR Transparency 1.5 or write the following on the board. Answer.
1. Tu aimes aller au cinéma?
2. Tu vois beaucoup de films?
3. Tu as un acteur favori ou une actrice favorite?
4. C'est qui?
5. Il/Elle a joué dans quel film?
6. Tu as vu ce film?

2 Presentation

Les pronoms le, la, les

Step 1 Write a few example sentences from Item 1 on the board. Put a box around the noun object. Circle the object pronoun. Draw a line from the box to the circle. This helps students grasp the concept.

Step 2 Lead students through Items 1–2 on page 14.

Note: Students will learn the indirect object pronouns **lui** and **leur** in Chapter 2.

Structure

Les pronoms le, la, les
Referring to people and things already mentioned

1. You have already learned to use **le, la, l'**, and **les** as definite articles. These words are also used as direct object pronouns. A direct object receives the action of the verb. A direct object pronoun can replace either a person or a thing.

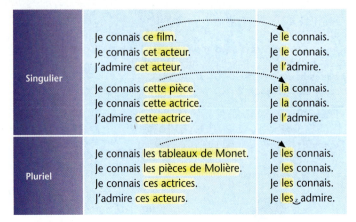

Singulier	Je connais ce film.	Je le connais.
	Je connais cet acteur.	Je le connais.
	J'admire cet acteur.	Je l'admire.
	Je connais cette pièce.	Je la connais.
	Je connais cette actrice.	Je la connais.
	J'admire cette actrice.	Je l'admire.
Pluriel	Je connais les tableaux de Monet.	Je les connais.
	Je connais les pièces de Molière.	Je les connais.
	Je connais ces actrices.	Je les connais.
	J'admire ces acteurs.	Je les admire.

2. Just as with the pronouns **me, te, nous, vous**, the pronouns **le, la, l'**, and **les** come right before the verb they are linked to.

Attention!
Note the elision and liaison with the direct object pronouns.
Vous **l'**admirez.   Vous **les** admirez.

Je **le** vois.
Je ne **le** vois pas.
Je veux **le** voir.
Je ne veux pas **le** voir.

Opéra Garnier, Paris

Learning from Photos
(page 14) You will read about l'Opéra Garnier in the cultural reading on pages 20–21.

Comment dit-on?

20 **Contacts** Répondez d'après le modèle.

Tu vois toujours Mélanie?

Oui, je la vois de temps en temps.

1. Tu vois toujours Sylvie?
2. Tu vois toujours tes copains tunisiens?
3. Tu vois toujours Marc?
4. Tu vois toujours tes cousines de Lyon?
5. Tu vois toujours tes professeurs de l'année dernière?

21 **En version originale** Complétez.

Paul: On va voir le film doublé ou en V.O.?
Annick: On va __1__ voir en V.O.
Paul: Tu connais l'actrice principale?
Annick: Tu rigoles! Bien sûr que je ne __2__ connais pas, mais je sais qui c'est!
Paul: Tu comprends l'espagnol?
Annick: Oui, je __3__ comprends un peu.
Paul: Tu __4__ comprends assez bien pour comprendre le film?
Annick: Non, mais il y a des sous-titres. Alors je __5__ lis quand je ne comprends pas les dialogues.

LES LOISIRS CULTURELS

quinze ❖ 15

Structure

3 Practice

Comment dit-on?

20 **Expansion:** After doing this activity, have students list some of their friends and classmates. They will then follow the example of the activity, substituting the names on their lists.

Learning from Realia

(page 15) Ask students the following questions about the ticket stubs.

- Quel est le nom du cinéma?
- Quel est le titre du film?
- À quelle heure est la séance?
- C'est un tarif réduit (moins cher)?

LEVELING

E: Activity 20
A: Activities 20, 21

ANSWERS TO Comment dit-on?

20
1. Oui, je la vois de temps en temps.
2. Oui, je les vois de temps en temps.
3. Oui, je le vois de temps en temps.
4. Oui, je les vois de temps en temps.
5. Oui, je les vois de temps en temps.

21
1. le
2. la
3. le
4. le
5. les

Structure

♻️ **Recycling**

Activity 22 also reviews the adjective **beau**.

Art Connection

🎨 Pierre Auguste Renoir (1841–1919) began his career as an artist copying the masters of the eighteenth century in the Louvre. In 1863 he went to study in the Gleyre Studio where he met Monet, Sisley, and Bazille. He went to paint with them in the Forest of Fontainebleau. He became very friendly with Monet, and they started to paint some of the same themes.

Renoir exhibited in the first exhibit of the Impressionists in 1874, and shortly thereafter he produced some of his best works, including *Bal du moulin de la Galette*, which he painted in 1876.

The **Moulin de la Galette**, made famous by Renoir's painting, still stands surrounded by shrubs on a hill in Montmartre. In Renoir's day, it was a popular open-air cabaret. It is now privately owned.

➡️ This *Infogap* activity will allow students to practice in pairs. The activity should be very manageable for them, since all vocabulary and structures are familiar to them.

Learning from Photos

(page 16) Ask students the following questions about the painting.
Qu'est-ce que les gens font? Ils s'amusent?

Structure

22 **Tout est très beau!**
Répondez d'après le modèle.

—Tu vois la statue?
—Oui, je la trouve très belle.
1. Tu vois le théâtre?
2. Tu vois les tableaux?
3. Tu vois l'acteur?
4. Tu vois l'actrice?
5. Tu vois les sculptures?

Jean-Antoine Houdon *Molière*

23 **Tout n'est pas très beau.** Refaites l'Activité 22 d'après le modèle.

—Tu vois la statue?
—Oui, mais je ne la trouve pas très belle.

Pierre Auguste Renoir *Bal du moulin de la Galette*

➡️ For more practice using pronouns, do Activity 4 on page H5 at the end of this book.

16 ⚜ *seize* CHAPITRE 1

ANSWERS TO *Comment dit-on?*

22
1. Oui, je le trouve très beau.
2. Oui, je les trouve très beaux.
3. Oui, je le trouve très beau.
4. Oui, je la trouve très belle.
5. Oui, je les trouve très belles.

23
1. Oui, mais je ne le trouve pas très beau.
2. Oui, mais je ne les trouve pas très beaux.
3. Oui, mais je ne le trouve pas très beau.
4. Oui, mais je ne la trouve pas très belle.
5. Oui, mais je ne les trouve pas très belles.

24 Demain Répondez d'après le modèle.

—Tu as vu ce film?
—Non, mais je vais le voir demain.

1. Tu as vu cette pièce?
2. Tu as vu cette exposition?
3. Tu as vu ces sculptures de Rodin?
4. Tu as vu ces tableaux?
5. Tu as vu l'exposition des tableaux de Gauguin?

25 Devinettes Devinez ce que c'est.

1. On le présente quand on va dans un pays étranger.
2. On le prend pour voyager très loin.
3. On les lave avant de manger.
4. On les lave avec une brosse à dents.
5. On la remplit avant de débarquer.
6. On l'écoute attentivement en classe.

26 Jeu Encore des devinettes Work in groups and make up riddles similar to those in Activity 25. Ask other groups your riddles. The group that guesses the most riddles wins.

27 L'artiste Have some fun. Pretend you are an artist. Draw something. Have a classmate give a critique of your artwork. Take turns.

Auguste Rodin *Le penseur*

Art Connection

Auguste Rodin (1840–1917) dominated the world of sculpture at the end of the nineteenth century and the beginning of the twentieth century. His technique in sculpture was similar to that of the Impressionists in painting. As he modeled in wax or clay, he added pieces bit by bit to construct his forms, just as the painters added dots and dashes of paint to create their pictures.

This statue, *Le penseur,* is one of his most famous. This sculpture, along with others, is located in the garden of **le musée Rodin** in the **7e arrondissement** of Paris. The museum is housed in a beautiful eighteenth-century mansion that was once Rodin's studio.

Allez-y!
At this point in the chapter, students have learned all the vocabulary and structure necessary to complete the chapter. The conversation and cultural readings that follow recycle all the material learned up to this point.

LEVELING
E: Activities 22, 23, 25
A: Activities 22, 23, 24, 25, 26, 27

Vous êtes sur le bon chemin. Allez-y!

dix-sept 17

ANSWERS TO Comment dit-on?

24
1. Non, mais je vais la voir demain.
2. Non, mais je vais la voir demain.
3. Non, mais je vais les voir demain.
4. Non, mais je vais les voir demain.
5. Non, mais je vais la voir demain.

25
1. son passeport
2. l'avion
3. les mains
4. les dents
5. la carte de débarquement
6. le prof, la prof

26 Answers will vary but may include:
On le donne à un ami pour son anniversaire. (le cadeau)
On les peigne le matin. (les cheveux)
On l'achète pour voir un film. (le billet)

27 Answers will vary but may include:
Je trouve ton dessin très beau. Je le trouve très intéressant.

17

Conversation

1 Preparation

Resource Manager
Audio Activities TE, page 7
Audio CD 2
CD-ROM

Bellringer Review
Use BRR Transparency 1.6 or write the following on the board. Write the following words under the correct category: **le cinéma** *or* **le théâtre**.
   une pièce, l'écran, les sous-titres, la scène, l'entracte, une séance, une tragédie

2 Presentation

Step 1 Tell students they are going to hear a conversation between Bruno and Léa, who are discussing going to a movie.

Step 2 Have them watch the conversation on the CD-ROM or listen as you read the conversation or play Audio CD 2.

Step 3 Have students work in pairs to practice the conversation. Then have several pairs present it to the class.

Step 4 You may have a more able student retell the conversation in narrative form in his or her own words.

Conversation

On va au cinéma?

Bruno: Qu'est-ce que tu veux faire?
Léa: Je ne sais pas, moi. Aller au cinéma.
Bruno: Qu'est-ce que tu veux voir?
Léa: Ça m'est égal. Comme tu veux. Qu'est-ce qu'il y a de bien?
Bruno: Attends. Je vais te dire… (*Il prend l'Officiel des Spectacles, il l'ouvre et il le lit…*) Il y a un film avec Ricki Dean.
Léa: Ah non, pas Ricki Dean. Je le déteste, ce type. Il est parfaitement ridicule et il ne le sait même pas!
Bruno: Il y a un film espagnol au Ciné-Élysées. Ça t'intéresse?
Léa: Oui, un film espagnol, ça me dit. On va pouvoir travailler notre espagnol.
Bruno: Alors, il faut se dépêcher. La prochaine séance est à seize heures.

Vous avez compris?

Répondez.

1. Qu'est-ce que Léa veut faire?
2. Qui a *l'Officiel des Spectacles*?
3. Qui le lit?
4. Léa aime Ricki Dean? Pour quelle raison?
5. Bruno et Léa vont voir quel film?
6. Pourquoi est-ce que Léa veut voir un film espagnol?
7. Ils vont aller à quelle séance?

ANSWERS TO *Vous avez compris?*

1. Elle veut aller au cinéma.
2. Bruno a *l'Officiel des Spectacles*.
3. Bruno le lit.
4. Non, elle n'aime pas Ricki Dean parce qu'il est ridicule.
5. Ils vont voir un film espagnol.
6. Ils vont pouvoir travailler leur espagnol.
7. Ils vont aller à la séance de seize heures.

Glencoe Technology

CD-ROM
On the CD-ROM, students can watch a dramatization of this conversation. They can then play the role of either one of the characters and record themselves in the conversation.

Parlons un peu plus

 On va au cinéma? Look at the movie guide. Decide which movie you'd like to see and invite a classmate to see it with you. Tell your partner when and where the movie is playing, whether it is dubbed or in the original language with subtitles. Discuss whether or not you both want to see the movie or figure out an alternative.

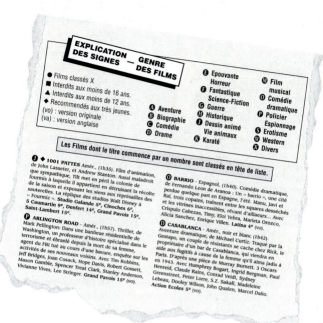

Prononciation

Le son /ü/

1. To say the sound /ü/, first say the sound /i/, then round your lips. Repeat the following words.

une statue	une sculpture	une peinture
une voiture	un musée	

2. The sound /ü/ also occurs in combination with other vowels. Repeat the following words.

   aujourd'hui   depuis   je suis   huit

3. Now repeat the following sentences.

   Tu as vu ces statues?
   C'est une sculpture très connue?
   Le musée est rue Sully depuis huit ans.

une statue

LES LOISIRS CULTURELS

Lectures culturelles

Resource Manager
Audio Activities TE, pages 8–9
Audio CD 2

National Standards

Cultures
The reading about cultural life in France on pages 20–21 and the related activities on page 21 allow students to find out more about museums, ballet, opera, and theater in France.

Presentation

Pre-reading
Step 1 Have students look at the photos on pages 20–21.

Step 2 Read and discuss the Reading Strategy, page 20. Have students identify the main idea of each section of the reading.

Step 3 Have students skim the reading quickly and silently.

Reading
Step 1 Lead students through the Lecture on pages 20–21 by having individuals read two to three sentences at a time. After each one reads, ask questions.

Step 2 Ask five or six questions that review the main points. Answers will give an organized summary of the **Lecture**.

LEVELING
E: Reading
A: Reading

Lectures culturelles

Les loisirs culturels en France

Les musées

Les musées en France sont toujours très fréquentés par les Français et par les touristes qui visitent la France. Tu connais les impressionnistes? Tu apprécies leurs tableaux? Alors il faut aller au musée d'Orsay. Le musée d'Orsay est une ancienne gare qui a été transformée en musée. C'est le musée du dix-neuvième siècle[1]. On trouve des tableaux, des sculptures, des meubles[2], tout du dix-neuvième siècle. Il y a une exposition permanente de tableaux des impressionnistes.

Si tu es fana d'art moderne, tu vas beaucoup aimer le centre Pompidou. Là, il y a toujours des expositions d'art moderne. Il y a aussi une vue extraordinaire sur Paris.

Mais la perle des musées français, c'est le Louvre. Au Louvre, tu peux admirer des tableaux et des sculptures de grands artistes de tous les siècles.

Le premier dimanche de chaque mois, l'entrée des musées nationaux est gratuite. Les autres dimanches, elle est demi-tarif[3]. C'est pourquoi les musées sont toujours combles le dimanche.

[1] siècle *century*
[2] meubles *furniture*
[3] demi-tarif *half-price*

Reading Strategy

Identifying the main idea

When reading, it is important to identify the main idea the author is expressing. Each paragraph usually discusses a different idea. The main idea is often found in the first or second sentence in each paragraph. First, skim the passage. Once you know the main idea of the passage, go back and read it again more carefully.

Centre Pompidou

Musée d'Orsay

Learning from Photos

(page 20 left) The **Centre Pompidou** is named after Georges Pompidou, the French president who launched the project to establish this museum of modern art. Most Parisians simply refer to it as **Beaubourg** because it is located on the plateau **Beaubourg**. The center was opened in 1977, and it soon attracted millions of visitors, five times more than had been estimated. The brightly painted exterior service pipes and the plastic tubing enclosing the escalator were in need of constant repair. In 1996 the government shut down the center for a complete renovation and expansion. It reopened in January 2000.

(page 20 right) The **musée d'Orsay** was once a railroad station. Today it houses the world's most complete collection of Impressionist paintings.

Le ballet et l'opéra

Si tu aimes la danse classique, il faut aller voir un ballet à l'opéra Garnier.

Si tu aimes l'opéra, il faut aller à l'opéra Bastille. On a inauguré le nouvel opéra sur la place de la Bastille en 1989 pour commémorer le bicentenaire de la Révolution française de 1789. Tu préfères l'architecture de quel opéra? De l'ancien opéra Garnier ou du nouvel opéra Bastille? L'architecture, c'est un art aussi, tu sais.

Le théâtre

Tu connais les grands auteurs dramatiques du dix-septième siècle: Racine, Corneille, Molière? Si tu as envie[4] d'aller voir une de leurs pièces, tu peux aller à la Comédie-Française, le plus vieux théâtre national du monde.

[4] as envie *feel like*

Opéra Garnier

Opéra Bastille

Comédie-Française

Vous avez compris?

A Les musées Répondez.
1. Qui fréquente les musées français?
2. Tu connais quelques peintres impressionnistes?
3. Tu apprécies leurs tableaux?
4. Tu connais leur œuvre?
5. Il y a une exposition permanente des impressionnistes dans quel musée?
6. Quel est le musée d'art moderne?
7. Quel est un autre musée très célèbre à Paris?
8. Qu'est-ce qu'il y a dans ce musée?
9. Les musées sont presque toujours combles le dimanche. Pourquoi?

B D'autres loisirs Répondez.
1. Tu es à Paris et tu veux voir un ballet. Tu vas où?
2. Tu veux voir un opéra. Tu vas où?
3. Tu veux voir une tragédie de Racine ou une comédie de Molière. Tu vas où?

Answers to Vous avez compris?

A
1. Les Français et les touristes qui visitent la France fréquentent les musées français.
2. Oui, je connais quelques peintres impressionnistes.
3. Oui, je les apprécie.
4. Oui, je la connais.
5. Il y a une exposition permanente des impressionnistes au musée d'Orsay.
6. Le musée d'art moderne est le centre Pompidou.
7. Le Louvre est un autre musée très célèbre à Paris.
8. Au Louvre il y a des tableaux et des sculptures de grands artistes de tous les siècles.
9. Les musées sont combles le dimanche parce que l'entrée est gratuite ou demi-tarif.

B
1. Je vais à l'opéra Garnier.
2. Je vais à l'opéra Bastille.
3. Je vais à la Comédie-Française.

Lectures culturelles

Post-reading

Have students do the **Vous avez compris?** activities on page 21 orally after reading the selection in class. Then assign these activities to be written at home. Go over them again the following day.

Vous avez compris?

A and **B** Allow students to refer to the story to look up the answers or you may use this activity as a testing device for factual recall.

Learning from Photos

(page 21 top) The **Opéra Garnier** is the original opera house of Paris. Built at the behest of Napoleon III, construction was begun in 1862 but not completed until 1875. It is named after its architect, Charles Garnier. It is a beautiful building with a mélange of many architectural styles. Most operas are now performed at the new **Opéra Bastille**, but there are still occasional performances at the Garnier, which is more often used for ballets.

(page 21 middle) The **Opéra Bastille** on the **place de la Bastille** was designed by the Argentine-born architect Carlos Ott. It opened in 1989 and it seats more than 3,000 people. Many Parisians are not fond of its glass façade that looks like a modern office building.

(page 21 bottom) The **Comédie-Française** theater building dates from 1790. The **Comédie-Française** Acting Company was created by Louis XIV and dates back to 1680. The **Comédie-Française** is the setting for performances of classical French dramas. The comedies of Molière and the tragedies of Racine and Corneille are performed regularly.

Lecture supplémentaire

La musique africaine

Quand on parle de musique africaine, on parle de deux sortes de musique—la musique traditionnelle et la musique moderne pop. Il y a une grande différence entre les deux.

La musique traditionnelle

La musique traditionnelle est la musique de la brousse[1], des villages ruraux. Cette musique traditionnelle accompagne toutes les activités de la vie quotidienne ainsi que[2] les événements mémorables de la vie sociale. Il y a de la musique pour les femmes, par exemple, de la musique pour les jeunes, pour les chasseurs[3], etc. À toutes ces festivités, les griots, des poètes musiciens, racontent des histoires et jouent de la musique. Tous les instruments de musique sont souvent faits à la main par les griots eux-mêmes[4].

Un griot

La musique moderne

La musique pop africaine est devenue[5] très populaire au-dehors des pays africains, surtout en Europe. La première fois que vous l'entendez, vous pensez que c'est un mélange de rythmes latins et afro-américains des États-Unis comme le rock et le jazz. C'est vrai. Pourquoi? Parce que la musique africaine est à l'origine de la musique latino-américaine et de la musique afro-américaine d'aujourd'hui.

[1] brousse *brush*
[2] ainsi que *as well as*
[3] chasseurs *hunters*
[4] eux-mêmes *themselves*
[5] est devenue *has become*

Un musicien joue du kora, Gambie

Youssou N'Dour

Le chanteur sénégalais Youssou N'Dour a un très grand succès. Il est né dans le quartier pauvre de la Médina à Dakar. Il est fils et petit-fils de griots, les poètes musiciens en Afrique. C'est lui le plus grand interprète de la musique «fusion pop». C'est une fusion d'un rythme africain, le m'balax, avec des rythmes de reggae, de rock et de jazz.

Vous avez compris?

La musique africaine Vrai ou faux?
1. La musique traditionnelle d'Afrique, c'est la musique des grandes villes cosmopolites.
2. La musique traditionnelle varie selon l'événement.
3. Les griots sont des poètes et des musiciens.
4. Les griots jouent toujours de la guitare électrique.
5. La musique moderne africaine est très populaire en Europe.
6. Le rock et le jazz ont influencé la musique africaine.
7. Youssou N'Dour est un chanteur sénégalais très connu.
8. La musique latino-américaine est une fusion de musique africaine avec du reggae, du rock et du jazz.

LES LOISIRS CULTURELS

National Standards

Connections
This reading about music on pages 24–25 establishes a connection with another discipline, allowing students to reinforce and further their knowledge of music through the study of French.

Attention!

The readings in the **Connexions** section are optional. They focus on some of the major disciplines taught in schools and universities. The vocabulary is useful for discussing such topics as history, literature, art, economics, business, science, etc. You may choose any of the following ways to do the readings in the **Connexions** section.

Independent reading Have students read the selections and do the post-reading activities as homework, which you collect. This option is least intrusive on class time and requires a minimum of teacher involvement.

Homework with in-class follow-up Assign the readings and post-reading activities as homework. Review and discuss the material in class the next day.

Intensive in-class activity This option includes a pre-reading vocabulary presentation, in-class reading and discussion, assignment of the activities for homework, and a discussion of the assignment in class the next day.

CONNEXIONS

Les Beaux-Arts

La musique

Like painting and literature, music is a form of art. Think of all the times you hear music each day. Music has been an integral part of the daily lives of people since the beginning of recorded history.

Before reading some general information about music, let's take a look at some of the many cognates that exist in the language of music.

un ballet

un orchestre symphonique

un opéra

une fanfare

un chœur

The names of many musical instruments are also cognates.

un piano	un saxophone	une trompette
une guitare	une flûte	une clarinette
un accordéon	un violon	une harpe

La musique

Les instruments musicaux
On peut classifier les instruments musicaux en quatre groupes principaux—les instruments à cordes, les instruments à vent, les instruments à percussion et les instruments à clavier.

Un orchestre ou une fanfare
Quelle est la différence entre un orchestre et une fanfare? Une fanfare n'a pas d'instruments à cordes. Il n'y a pas de violons, par exemple. Et dans une fanfare, il n'y a pas de flûtes ni de hautbois[1]. Les fanfares qui jouent de la musique pendant les événements sportifs et qui participent aux défilés[2] sont plus populaires aux États-Unis qu'en France.

[1] hautbois *oboes*   [2] défilés *parades*

Music Connection

Georges Bizet, the French composer, wrote the music to the opera *Carmen*. It is based on the short story *Carmen*, by Prosper Mérimée, published in 1845. It is the tragic love story of the bohemian Carmen and the brigadier don José in Seville, Spain. A scene from the opera is shown above.

Learning from Photos

(*page 25 middle*) This photo shows Céline Dion in concert. She is a popular French-Canadian singer who now resides in the U.S.

L'opéra *Carmen*

L'orchestre symphonique

Un orchestre symphonique est un grand orchestre composé d'instruments de tous les groupes musicaux. Une symphonie est une composition musicale pour orchestre. Une symphonie est en général une composition ambitieuse qui dure de vingt à quarante-cinq minutes.

L'opéra

Un opéra est une composition dramatique sans dialogue parlé. Dans un opéra, les acteurs chantent; ils ne parlent jamais. Ils chantent des airs d'une beauté extraordinaire. L'orchestre les accompagne. L'histoire est en général très tragique. Un opéra comique est un opéra avec des dialogues parlés. Un opéra comique n'est pas nécessairement très amusant. Un opéra bouffe est un opéra dont l'histoire est une comédie. *Carmen* de Georges Bizet et *Dialogue des Carmélites* de Francis Poulenc sont deux opéras français très célèbres.

La musique populaire

Il y a toutes sortes de musique populaire. Il y a des groupes de jazz, de rock et de rap, par exemple. De nos jours, le rap et la musique techno sont très populaires. Les chansons populaires ont souvent des thèmes romantiques. Il y a toujours une relation intime entre la musique populaire et la danse.

La chanteuse Céline Dion

Vous avez compris?

A Des instruments Nommez.
1. un instrument à cordes
2. quelques instruments à vent

B Vous le savez? Répondez.
1. Quelle est la différence entre un orchestre et une fanfare?
2. Qu'est-ce qu'un opéra?
3. Quels sont quelques types de musique populaire?

C'est à vous

Use what you have learned

♻ Recycling

These activities allow students to use the vocabulary and structure from this chapter in completely open-ended, real-life situations.

Learning from Photos

(page 26 top) The **Maison du Roi** is opposite the town hall (also seen in the photo) in Brussels. In spite of its name, no king ever lived there. The building is a sixteenth-century palace that houses the city museum. It has an excellent collection of ceramics and silverware. Brussels is famous for both ceramics and silverware.

LEVELING

These activities encompass all three levels. All students will be able to do them at a sophistication level commensurate with their ability in French. Some students will be able to speak for several minutes, and others may be able to give just a few sentences. This is to be expected when students are functioning completely on their own, generating their own language to the best of their ability.

C'est à vous

Use what you have learned

1 Pour t'amuser
✔ *Discuss movies, plays, and museums*

Work with a classmate. Pretend you're on vacation in Brussels in Belgium. You meet a Belgian teenager (your partner) who's interested in what you do for fun in your free time. Tell him or her about your leisure activities. Then your partner will tell you about what he or she does.

2 Une journée au musée
✔ *Ask and answer questions about a museum visit*

Work in groups of three or four. Pretend that one or two of you spent the day at a museum last Saturday. Other friends have some questions. Describe your museum visit and be sure to answer all their questions.

Maison du Roi, Bruxelles, Belgique

Musée du Louvre

3 Une affiche
✔ *Make a poster for a play*

Prepare a poster in French for your school play. Give all the necessary information to advertise **le spectacle**.

ANSWERS TO *C'est à vous*

1 Answers will vary depending upon student preferences.

2 Answers will vary depending upon the museum students choose.

CHAPITRE 1

4 Des renseignements, s'il vous plaît.
✓ *Write for information about cultural events*

You're going to spend a month in the French city of your choice. Write a letter or an e-mail to the tourist office (**le syndicat d'initiative**) asking for information about cultural events during your stay. Be sure to mention your age, what kind of cultural activities you like, and the dates of your stay.

Une colonne Morris, Paris

Writing Strategy

Persuasive writing Persuasive writing is writing that encourages a reader to do something or to accept an idea. Newspaper and magazine advertisements, as well as certain articles, are examples of persuasive writing. As you write, present a logical argument to encourage others to follow your line of thinking. Your writing should contain sufficient evidence to persuade readers to "buy into" what you are presenting. Explain how your evidence supports your argument; end by restating your argument.

5 Un reportage

Your local newspaper has asked you to write an article to attract French-speaking readers to a cultural event taking place in your community. You can write about a real or fictitious event. You have seen the event and you really liked it. Tell why as you try to convince or persuade your readers to go see it.

vingt-sept 27

Assessment

Resource Manager

Communication Transparencies C 1
Quizzes, pages 1–5
Tests, pages 1–14
ExamView® Pro
Situation Cards
Performance Assessment, Task 1
Marathon mental Videoquiz

✓ Assessment

This is a pre-test for students to take before you administer the chapter test. Answer sheets for students to do these pages are provided in your transparency binder. Note that each section is cross-referenced so students can easily find the material they have to review in case they made errors. You may wish to collect these assessments and correct them yourself or you may prefer to have the students correct themselves in class. You can go over the answers orally or project them on the overhead, using your Assessment Answers transparencies.

Assessment

Vocabulaire

1 Choisissez.

To review Mots 1, turn to pages 2–3.

1. On joue des films où?
   a. dans une séance
   b. dans une salle de cinéma
   c. dans un théâtre
2. Qui joue dans un film?
   a. des acteurs et des actrices
   b. des sous-titres
   c. des joueurs
3. Une pièce de théâtre est divisée en quoi?
   a. en version originale
   b. en entractes
   c. en actes et en scènes
4. Le film est doublé?
   a. Oui, il y a deux films.
   b. Non, il est en V.O.
   c. Oui, il y a des sous-titres.
5. Qu'est-ce que *l'Officiel des Spectacles*?
   a. un magazine
   b. une place
   c. un film

2 Identifiez.

To review Mots 2, turn to pages 6–7.

6.
7.
8.
9.
10.

28 vingt-huit   CHAPITRE 1

ANSWERS TO Assessment

1
1. b
2. a
3. c
4. b
5. a

2
6. un musée
7. une statue (une sculpture)
8. une peintre
9. un sculpteur
10. un tableau (une peinture)

Structure

3 Récrivez.

11. Je sais le numéro.
    Vous _____.
12. Vous connaissez mon ami?
    Il _____?

4 Complétez avec «savoir» ou «connaître».

13. Je ____ son numéro de téléphone.
14. Vous ____ où il habite, non?
15. Je ____ très bien l'œuvre de cet artiste.
16. Tu ____ Paris?
17. Ils ____ danser le tango.

To review the verbs savoir and connaître, turn to page 10.

5 Répondez avec un pronom.

18. Il te parle au téléphone? Oui, ____.
19. Tu invites Jean? Oui, ____.
20. Tu vas inviter sa petite amie aussi? Oui, ____.
21. Le prof vous donne beaucoup de devoirs? Oui, ____.
22. Tu vois la petite fille? Oui, ____.
23. Tu connais les pièces de Molière? Oui, ____.

To review the object pronouns, turn to pages 12–14.

Culture

6 Identifiez.

24. un musée à Paris
25. un auteur français dramatique du dix-septième siècle

To review this cultural information, turn to pages 20–21.

Musée du Louvre, Paris

Answers to Assessment

3
11. Vous savez le numéro.
12. Il connaît mon ami?

4
13. sais
14. savez
15. connais
16. connais
17. savent

5
18. Oui, il me parle au téléphone.
19. Oui, je l'invite.
20. Oui, je vais l'inviter aussi.
21. Oui, le prof nous donne beaucoup de devoirs.
22. Oui, je la vois.
23. Oui, je les connais.

6
24. le musée d'Orsay (le musée du Louvre, le Centre Pompidou)
25. Molière (Racine, Corneille)

CHAPITRE 1 Assessment

Glencoe Technology

MINDJOGGER VHS/DVD
You may wish to help your students prepare for the chapter test by playing the MindJogger game show. Teams will compete against each other to review chapter vocabulary and structure and sharpen listening comprehension skills.

On parle super bien!

This unique page gives students the opportunity to speak freely and say whatever they can, using the vocabulary and structures they have learned in the chapter. The illustration serves to remind students of precisely what they know how to say in French. There are no activities that students do not have the ability to describe or talk about in French. The art not only depicts the vocabulary and content of this chapter, but also reinforces what they learned in previous chapters.

You may wish to use this page in many ways. Some possibilities are to have students do the following:

1. Look at the illustration and identify items by giving the correct French words.
2. Make up sentences about what they see in the illustration.
3. Make up questions about the illustration. They can call on another class member to respond if you do this as a class activity, or you may prefer to allow students to work in small groups. This activity is extremely beneficial because it enables students to actively use interrogative words.
4. Answer questions you ask them about the illustration.
5. Work in pairs and make up a conversation based on the illustration.
6. Look at the illustration and give a complete oral review of what they see.
7. Look at the illustration and write a paragraph (or essay) about it.

You can also use this page as an assessment or testing tool, taking into account individual differences by having students go from simple to quite complicated tasks. The assessment can be either oral or written. You may wish to use the rubrics provided on pages T20–T21 as you give students the following directions.

On parle super bien!

Tell all you can about this illustration.

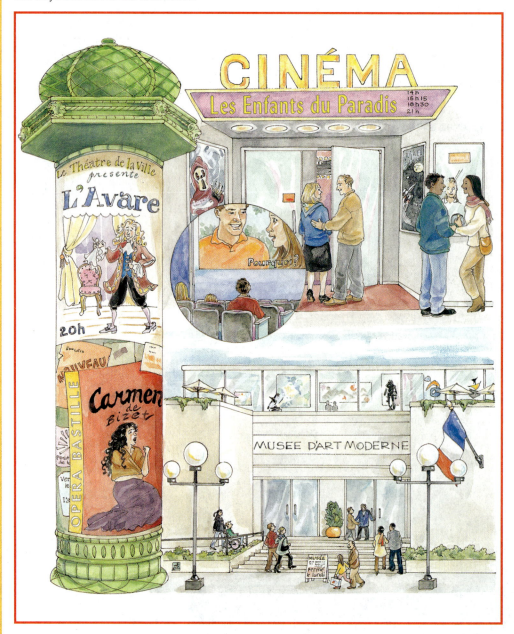

1. Identify the topic or situation of the illustration.
2. Give the French words for as many items as you can.
3. Think of as many sentences as you can to describe the illustration.
4. Go over your sentences and put them in the best sequencing to give a coherent story based on the illustration.

Vocabulaire

Discussing a movie

un cinéma	un film comique	un documentaire	jouer un film
une salle de cinéma	policier	un dessin animé	louer une vidéo
un guichet	d'horreur	étranger	
une place	de science-fiction	en V.O.	
une séance	d'aventures	doublé	
un écran	d'amour	avec des sous-titres	

Describing a play

un théâtre	un danseur	une comédie
une pièce	une danseuse	un drame
un acteur	une scène	monter une pièce
une actrice	un acte	chanter
un chanteur	un entracte	danser
une chanteuse	une tragédie	

Describing a museum visit

un musée	une œuvre
une exposition	une peinture
un tableau	un(e) peintre
une sculpture	un sculpteur (m. et f.)
une statue	

Other useful words and expressions

connaître	célèbre
savoir	connu
ouvert	sauf
fermé	ça (m')est égal

How well do you know your vocabulary?
- Choose the name of a cultural event or artistic profession.
- Have a classmate tell you his or her favorite in the category you chose.

VIDÉOTOUR
Épisode 1
In this video episode, you will join Chloé and Vincent as they experience some cultural wonders. See page 500 for more information.

LES LOISIRS CULTURELS

trente et un ❖ 31

Vocabulaire

Vocabulary Review

The words and phrases in the **Vocabulaire** have been taught for productive use in this chapter. They are summarized here as a resource for both student and teacher. This list also serves as a convenient resource for the **C'est à vous** activities on pages 26–27, as well as for talking about the illustration on page 30. There are approximately twenty-two cognates in this vocabulary list. Have students find them.

Attention!

You will notice that the vocabulary list here is not translated. This has been done intentionally, since we feel that by the time students have finished the material in the chapter they should be familiar with the meanings of all the words. If there are several words they still do not know, we recommend that they refer to the **Mots 1** and **2** sections in the chapter or go to the dictionaries at the back of this book to find the meanings. However, if you prefer that your students have the English translations, please refer to Vocabulary Transparency 1.1, where you will find all these words listed with their translations.

VIDÉO VHS/DVD
The Video Program allows students to see how the chapter vocabulary and structures are used by native speakers. For maximum reinforcement, show the video episode as a final activity for Chapter 1.

Planning for Chapter 2

SCOPE AND SEQUENCE, PAGES 32–63

Topics
✦ Health and medicine
✦ Prescriptions

Culture
✦ Doctors make house calls in France
✦ Discussing the relationship between culture and health
✦ Medical services in France

Functions
✦ How to describe an illness
✦ How to give commands
✦ How to refer to people, places, and things already mentioned

Structure
✦ The pronouns **lui, leur**
✦ The verbs **souffrir** and **ouvrir**
✦ The imperative
✦ The pronoun **en**

National Standards
✦ Communication Standard 1.1 pages 36, 37, 40, 41, 43, 44, 46, 47, 48, 49, 51, 58
✦ Communication Standard 1.2 pages 36, 37, 40, 41, 43, 44, 47, 49, 50, 53, 54, 57
✦ Communication Standard 1.3 pages 36, 40, 41, 43, 44, 58, 59
✦ Cultures Standard 2.1 pages 52–53, 54, 55
✦ Connections Standard 3.1 pages 56–57
✦ Connections Standard 3.2 page 54
✦ Comparisons Standard 4.2 page 54
✦ Communities Standard 5.1 page 59

PACING AND PRIORITIES

The chapter content is color coded below to assist you in planning.

■ required   ■ recommended   ■ optional

Vocabulaire *(required)*   Days 1–4
- Mots 1
  On est malade.
- Mots 2
  Chez le médecin
  À la pharmacie

Structure *(required)*   Days 5–7
- Les pronoms **lui, leur**
- Les verbes **souffrir** et **ouvrir**
- L'impératif
- Le pronom **en**

Conversation *(required)*
- Chez le médecin

Prononciation *(recommended)*
- Les sons /u/ et /ü/

Lectures culturelles
- Une consultation *(recommended)*
- Culture et santé *(optional)*
- Les services médicaux en France *(optional)*

Connexions *(optional)*
- La diététique

C'est à vous *(recommended)*

Assessment *(recommended)*

On parle super bien! *(optional)*

RESOURCE GUIDE

SECTION	PAGES	SECTION RESOURCES
Vocabulaire *Mots 1*		
On est malade.	34–37	Vocabulary Transparencies 2.2–2.3 Audio CD 2 Audio Activities TE, pages 12–14 Workbook, pages 11–12 Quiz 1, page 7 ExamView® Pro
Vocabulaire *Mots 2*		
Chez le médecin À la pharmacie	38–39 39–41	Vocabulary Transparencies 2.4–2.5 Audio CD 2 Audio Activities TE, pages 15–16 Workbook, page 12 Quiz 2, page 8 ExamView® Pro
Structure		
Les pronoms **lui**, **leur** Les verbes **souffrir** et **ouvrir** L'impératif Le pronom **en**	42–43 44 45–47 48–49	Audio CD 2 Audio Activities TE, pages 17–19 Workbook, pages 13–17 Quizzes 3–6, pages 9–12 ExamView® Pro
Conversation		
Chez le médecin	50	Audio CD 2 Audio Activities TE, pages 19–20 Interactive CD-ROM
Prononciation		
Les sons /u/ et /ü/	51	Audio CD 2 Audio Activities TE, page 20
Lectures culturelles		
Une consultation Culture et santé Les services médicaux en France	52–53 54 55	Audio CD 2 Audio Activities TE, page 21 Tests, pages 18, 21
Connexions		
La diététique	56–57	Tests, page 23
C'est à vous		
	58–59	**Bon voyage!** Video, Episode 2 Video Activities, Chapter 2 French Online Activities french.glencoe.com
Assessment		
	60–61	Communication Transparency C 2 Quizzes 1–6, pages 7–12 Performance Assessment, Task 2 Tests, pages 15–28 ExamView® Pro Situation Cards, Chapter 2 **Marathon mental** Videoquiz

Using Your Resources for Chapter 2

Transparencies

Bellringer 2.1–2.8

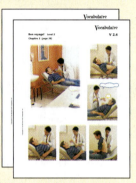
Vocabulary 2.1–2.5

Communication C 2

Workbook

Vocabulary,
pages 11–12

Structure,
pages 13–17

Enrichment,
pages 18–20

Audio Activities

Vocabulary,
pages 12–16

Structure,
pages 17–19

Conversation,
pages 19–20

Pronunciation,
page 20

Cultural Reading,
page 21

Additional Practice,
page 22

Assessment

Vocabulary and Structure Quizzes, pages 7–12

Chapter Tests, pages 15–28

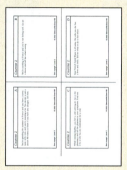
Situation Cards, Chapter 2

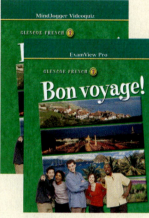
MindJogger Videoquiz, ExamView® Pro, Chapter 2

Timesaving Teacher Tools

TeacherWorks™

TeacherWorks™ is your all-in-one teacher resource center. Personalize lesson plans, access resources from the Teacher Wraparound Edition, connect to the Internet, or make a to-do list. These are only a few of the many features that can assist you in the planning and organizing of your lessons.

Includes:
- A calendar feature
- Access to all program blackline masters
- Standards correlations and more

ExamView® Pro

Test Bank software for Macintosh and Windows makes creating, editing, customizing, and printing tests quick and easy.

Technology Resources

In the Chapter 2 Internet activity, you will have a chance to learn more about the Francophone world. Visit <u>french.glencoe.com</u>.

On the Interactive Conversation CD-ROM, students can listen to and take part in a recorded version of the conversation in Chapter 2.

See the National Geographic Teacher's Corner on pages 138–139, 244–245, 372–373, 472–473 for reference to additional technology resources.

Bon voyage! Video and Video Activities, Chapter 2

Help your students prepare for the chapter test by playing the **Marathon mental** Videoquiz game show. Teams will compete against each other to review chapter vocabulary and structure and sharpen listening comprehension skills.

32D

Preview

In this chapter, students will learn to talk about routine illnesses and to describe their symptoms to a doctor. In order to do this, they will learn vocabulary associated with medical exams, prescriptions, and minor ailments such as colds, the flu, and headaches. Students will learn the indirect object pronouns **lui** and **leur,** the present and **passé composé** of verbs like **ouvrir** and **souffrir,** and the imperative forms of verbs.

Communication
In Chapter 2, students will communicate in spoken and written French on the following topics:
- Describing symptoms of minor ailments
- Getting a prescription at a pharmacy

Students will obtain and provide information and engage in conversations about their personal health. They will also learn to tell others what to do. Students will also learn to use indirect object pronouns.

La santé et la médecine

Objectifs
In this chapter you will learn to:
- explain a minor illness to a doctor
- have a prescription filled at a pharmacy
- tell for whom something is done
- talk about some more activities
- give commands
- refer to people, places, and things already mentioned
- discuss medical services in France

Édouard Vuillard *Le docteur Viau dans son cabinet*

CHAPITRE 2

 Spotlight on Culture

Photograph This old-style pharmacy is on the lovely **rue des Francs-Bourgeois**, one of the main, though narrow, streets in the Marais section of Paris. The sign with the serpent is called **un caducée**. It is a symbol for pharmacists and physicians.

Painting Édouard Jean Vuillard (1868–1940) was a painter and engraver. He also became a decorator, and he worked for **le Théâtre-Libre**. He also did some large murals. He was a friend of many symbolist painters, but in his own paintings he preferred intimate scenes with a bourgeois background. He enjoyed doing street scenes and portraits. In this painting we see Doctor Viau in his dental surgical suite.

LEVELING

The activities, conversations, and readings within each chapter are marked according to level of difficulty. **E** indicates easy. **A** indicates average. **C** indicates challenging. Some activities cover a range of difficulty. In some activities, for example, advanced students will be able to produce more extensive responses while students who learn at a different rate may give less detailed responses. The leveling indicators will help you individualize instruction to best meet your students' needs.

Vocabulaire — Mots 1

1 Preparation

Resource Manager
Vocabulary Transparencies 2.2–2.3
Audio Activities TE, pages 12–14
Audio CD 2
Workbook, pages 11–12
Quiz 1, page 7
ExamView® Pro

Bellringer Review

Use BRR Transparency 2.1 or write the following on the board. Draw a stick figure of a person and label all the body parts you can.

2 Presentation

Teaching Tip
You may wish to bring a handkerchief, tissues, and throat lozenges to class to use in the presentation of the **Mots 1** vocabulary.

Step 1 Point to yourself to model the following parts of the body: **la bouche, le nez, la gorge, l'oreille, les yeux, le ventre.**

Step 2 Use gestures to teach the following expressions: **avoir de la fièvre; avoir des frissons; il est très malade; il n'est pas en bonne santé; il a mal au ventre; il tousse; il éternue; il a mal à la tête; il a mal aux oreilles; elle a le nez qui coule; elle a les yeux qui piquent; elle a la gorge qui gratte.**

LEVELING
A: Vocabulary

Vocabulaire — Mots 1

On est malade.

la tête
une oreille
un œil
le nez
la bouche
la gorge
le ventre

avoir de la fièvre

Atchoum!   À tes souhaits!

un mouchoir

Paul a un rhume.
Il est enrhumé.
Il éternue.
Il a besoin d'un kleenex ou d'un mouchoir.

David tousse.

Reaching All Students

Total Physical Response Before you begin, demonstrate the meaning of **toucher**.
(Student 1), venez ici, s'il vous plaît.
  Montrez-moi votre bouche.
  Montrez-moi votre main.
  Montrez-moi votre nez.
  Montrez-moi votre pied.
  Montrez-moi votre ventre.
  Montrez-moi votre gorge.
  Montrez-moi vos yeux.
  Levez la main.
  Ouvrez la bouche.
  Fermez les yeux.
  Mettez la main sur la tête.
  Touchez vos pieds avec vos mains.
  Merci, (Student 1). Retournez à votre place et asseyez-vous, s'il vous plaît.

Vocabulaire
Mots 1

Christophe a très mal à la gorge.
Il a une angine.

La pauvre Miriam, qu'est-ce qu'elle a?
Elle a la grippe.
Elle a de la fièvre.
Elle a des frissons.

Elle a mal à la tête.

un médicament

Martin n'est pas en bonne santé.
Il est en mauvaise santé.
Il est très malade, le pauvre.
Il ne se sent pas bien. Il se sent très mal.

Note
Study the following cognates related to health and medicine:

allergique
bactérien(ne)
viral(e)
une allergie
un antibiotique

un sirop
de l'aspirine
une infection
de la pénicilline
la température

Elle a mal au ventre.

Elle a mal aux oreilles.

Elle a le nez qui coule.

Elle a les yeux qui piquent.

Elle a la gorge qui gratte.

LA SANTÉ ET LA MÉDECINE

trente-cinq ❖ 35

Step 3 Have students repeat the cognates carefully after you or Audio CD 2. These are the words they are most likely to anglicize.

Step 4 Ask several volunteers to come to the front of the room. Have each one mime a different ailment. The rest of the class describes the symptoms and suggests what he or she needs. Use as many props as possible. Guide the class with questions when necessary. For example: **La pauvre Isabelle! Elle a un rhume. Elle a besoin de quoi? Elle a besoin de beaucoup de kleenex.**

Step 5 Ask each volunteer to recapitulate his or her illness, symptoms, and needs. Cue key words or ask the class for help as necessary. For example: **J'ai un rhume. J'ai le nez qui coule. J'ai besoin d'aspirine,** etc.

Vocabulary Expansion

Tourists often experience stomach problems. If you wish, you may give students the following useful words and expressions.
Vous avez des nausées (mal au cœur)?
Vous avez la diarrhée?
Vous êtes constipé(e)?
Vous vomissez?

FRENCH Online

The **Glencoe World Languages Web site** (french.glencoe.com) offers options that enable you and your students to experience the French-speaking world via the Internet. For each chapter, there are activities, games, and quizzes. In addition, an *Enrichment* section offers students an opportunity to visit Web sites related to the theme of the chapter.

FUN FACTS

You may wish to introduce the colloquial expression **Mon œil!** to students. It means, "Come on, do you think I'm going to believe that?" When people say it, they usually put their finger up to their eye.

About the French Language

The word **angine** can sometimes cause confusion. When used alone it means a bad sore throat. Angina *(heart pain)* is **une angine de poitrine.** ❖

Vocabulaire

3 Practice

Quel est le mot?

Attention!

When students are doing the **Quel est le mot?** activities, accept any answer that makes sense. The purpose of these activities is to have students use the new vocabulary. They are not factual recall activities. Thus, it is not necessary for students to remember specific factual information from the vocabulary presentation when answering.

 2 and **3** Do these activities first with books closed. Ask the questions and call on individuals to answer. Students can write the activities for homework. Go over them the next day with books closed.
Expansion: Have students retell the information in Activities 2 and 3 in their own words.

Writing Development
Have students write the answers to Activities 2–3 in paragraph form.

Vocabulaire

Quel est le mot?

1 Qu'est-ce que c'est?
Identifiez.

2 **Historiette** Qu'est-ce qu'il a?
Inventez une histoire.
1. David est malade?
2. Il ne se sent pas bien?
3. Qu'est-ce qu'il a?
4. Il a de la fièvre et des frissons?
5. Il a la gorge qui gratte?
6. Il a les yeux qui piquent et le nez qui coule?
7. Il a mal à la tête?
8. Il a mal au ventre?
9. Il a mal aux oreilles?

3 **Historiette** La santé Donnez des réponses personnelles.
1. Tu es en bonne santé ou en mauvaise santé?
2. Quand tu es enrhumé(e), tu as le nez qui coule?
3. Tu as les yeux qui piquent?
4. Tu as la gorge qui gratte?
5. Tu tousses?
6. Tu éternues?
7. Qu'est-ce qu'on te dit quand tu éternues?
8. Tu as mal à la tête?
9. Tu ne te sens pas bien?
10. Tu as de la fièvre quand tu as un rhume?
11. Et quand tu as la grippe, tu as de la fièvre?
12. Quand tu as de la fièvre, tu as quelquefois des frissons?

36 *trente-six* CHAPITRE 2

Answers to Quel est le mot?

1
1. la tête
2. l'œil
3. le nez
4. la bouche
5. l'oreille
6. la gorge
7. le ventre

2 Answers will vary but may include:
1. Oui, David est malade.
2. Il ne se sent pas bien.
3. Il a un rhume.
4. Oui, il a de la fièvre et des frissons.
5. Oui, il a la gorge qui gratte.
6. Oui, il a les yeux qui piquent et le nez qui coule.
7. Oui, il a mal à la tête.
8. Oui, il a mal au ventre.
9. Oui, il a mal aux oreilles.

3 Answers will vary but may include:
1. Je suis en bonne santé.
2. Oui, quand je suis enrhumé(e), j'ai le nez qui coule.
3. Oui, j'ai les yeux qui piquent.
4. Oui, j'ai la gorge qui gratte.
5. Non, je ne tousse pas.
6. Oui, j'éternue.
7. On me dit «À tes souhaits!»

Vocabulaire

 On a mal. Complétez.
1. On prend de l'aspirine quand on a mal à la ____.
2. Si on a très mal à la gorge, on a une ____.
3. La ____ est un antibiotique.
4. L'aspirine et les antibiotiques sont des ____.
5. On ne peut pas prendre de pénicilline quand on est ____ à la pénicilline.
6. Si on a une température de 40° Celsius, on a de la ____.
7. Quand on est toujours malade, on est en ____.
8. On donne des antibiotiques comme la pénicilline pour combattre des infections bactériennes, pas des infections ____.
9. Quand on a le nez qui coule, on a besoin d'un ____ ou d'un ____.
10. Quand on a un rhume, on ____ et on ____.
11. Quand on est enrhumé ou quand on écoute la musique trop fort, on a mal aux ____.

 Qu'est-ce que tu as? Work with a classmate. Ask him or her what the matter is. Your classmate will tell you. Then suggest something he or she can do to feel better. Take turns.

 Devinette Have some fun! Work with a classmate and look at the following illustrations and French sayings. Together come up with some English equivalents.

Je ne suis pas dans mon assiette aujourd'hui.

Tu vas vite être sur pied.

Il a une fièvre de cheval.

Ça fait mal. Aïe aïe aïe!

J'ai un chat dans la gorge.

 For more practice using words from *Mots 1*, do Activity 5 on page H6 at the end of this book.

LA SANTÉ ET LA MÉDECINE

Vocabulaire

6 Expansion: Practice the expressions in this activity by miming or supplying the literal statement and having students supply the informal expression. For example: **Je ne peux pas parler. (Vous avez un chat dans la gorge.) Je ne me sens pas bien. (Vous n'êtes pas dans votre assiette.)** Clutch your arm and say «Aïe!» (Ça fait mal.)

Reteaching
Show Vocabulary Transparencies 2.2–2.3 and let students say as much as they can about them in their own words.

Vocabulary Expansion
Tell students the word "sofa" is the same in French: **un sofa**, but one also frequently hears **un canapé** or **un divan**.

 This *Infogap* activity will allow students to practice in pairs. The activity should be very manageable for them, since all vocabulary and structures are familiar to them.

LEVELING
E: Activities 1, 2, 3, 4, 5, 6
A: Activities 3, 4, 6

ANSWERS TO Quel est le mot?

(continued)
8. Oui, j'ai mal à la tête.
9. Non, je ne me sens pas bien.
10. Non, je n'ai pas de fièvre quand j'ai un rhume.
11. Oui, quand j'ai la grippe j'ai de la fièvre.
12. Oui, quand j'ai de la fièvre j'ai quelquefois des frissons.

4
1. tête
2. angine
3. pénicilline
4. médicaments
5. allergique
6. fièvre
7. mauvaise santé
8. virales
9. kleenex, mouchoir
10. tousse, éternue
11. oreilles

5 Answers will vary but may include:
—Qu'est-ce que tu as?
—Je ne sais pas. J'ai le nez qui coule et la gorge qui gratte.
—Je crois que tu es enrhumé!
Tu as besoin de beaucoup de kleenex!

6 Answers will vary but may include:
1. I don't feel so hot today.
2. You'll be back on your feet in no time.
3. He has a high fever.
4. That hurts! Ow, ow, ow!
5. I have a frog in my throat. (I have a scratchy throat.)

Vocabulaire
Mots 2

1 Preparation

Resource Manager

Vocabulary Transparencies 2.4–2.5
Audio Activities TE, pages 15–16
Audio CD 2
Workbook, page 12
Quiz 2, page 8
ExamView® Pro

Bellringer Review

Use BRR Transparency 2.2 or write the following on the board.
Write down what part(s) of the body you associate with the following.
1. des lunettes
2. un bonnet de ski
3. un kleenex
4. des chaussures

2 Presentation

Step 1 Have students keep their books closed. Dramatize the following expressions from **Mots 2: ouvrir la bouche; examiner la gorge; souffrir; tousser; respirer à fond.** Ask students to imitate each of your dramatizations and repeat each corresponding word.

Step 2 As you present the new words in sentences, ask questions such as: **Qui examine le malade? Qui ouvre la bouche? Qu'est-ce que le médecin examine?**

Vocabulaire
Mots 2

Chez le médecin

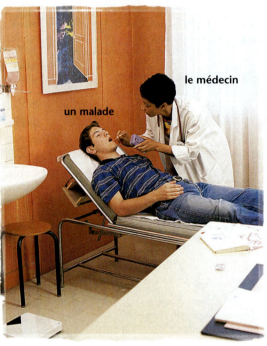

le médecin
un malade

Le médecin examine le malade.
Le malade ouvre la bouche.
Le médecin examine la gorge du malade.

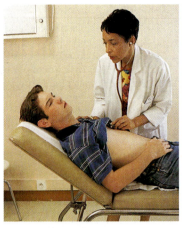

Elle ausculte le malade.
Il souffre, le pauvre.

Où avez-vous mal?
Là!

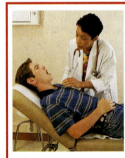 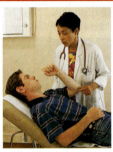 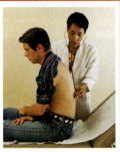

Le médecin parle.   Ouvrez la bouche!   Toussez!   Respirez à fond!

Reaching All Students

Total Physical Response
(Student 1), **levez-vous et venez ici, s'il vous plaît.**
Vous allez chez le médecin. Moi, je suis le médecin. Je vais vous examiner.
Je vais vous ausculter. Respirez à fond. Encore une fois.
(Student 1), **asseyez-vous, s'il vous plaît.**

Ouvrez la bouche.
Dites «Ah».
Ouvrez les yeux.
Et maintenant, fermez les yeux.
Merci, (Student 1). **C'est très bien. Vous êtes un(e) bon(ne) patient(e).**
Retournez à votre place, s'il vous plaît.
(continued)

Vocabulaire
Mots 2

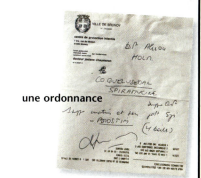

une ordonnance

Le médecin fait un diagnostic.
Sébastien a une sinusite aiguë.
Le médecin lui prescrit des antibiotiques.
Elle lui fait une ordonnance.

À la pharmacie 🎧

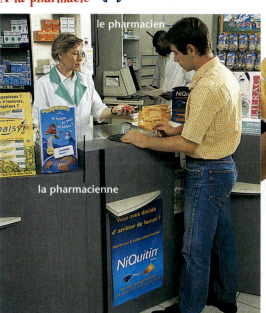

le pharmacien

la pharmacienne

un comprimé

avaler un comprimé

Sébastien prend les médicaments.
Il va mieux.

Qu'est-ce que la pharmacienne donne à Sébastien?
Elle lui donne des médicaments.

LA SANTÉ ET LA MÉDECINE

trente-neuf ❖ 39

Recycling
Bring back previously learned vocabulary by asking **Tu as mal où?** and pointing to your hand, foot, eyes, ear, nose, stomach, head, or throat. Have students respond using the correct word.

Step 3 Have students open their books. Have them read along and repeat the new material after you or Audio CD 2.

Reaching All Students

Kinesthetic Learners
Have students get up and dramatize many of the expressions in this vocabulary section.

Vocabulary Expansion
You may wish to give students the following expressions related to physical exams.
prendre la tension
prendre le pouls
faire une piqûre
faire une prise de sang
faire un électrocardiogramme

Chapter Projects
La santé Obtain a video on first aid, health, or nutrition in French or English from the health department in your school or county. Use it as a springboard for discussing health and illnesses with the new vocabulary from this chapter.

Reaching All Students

Total Physical Response
(Student 2), venez ici, s'il vous plaît.
Vous allez mimer ce que je dis.
Respirez à fond.
Toussez.
Éternuez.
Vous avez mal à la tête.
Vous avez de la fièvre.
Vous avez des frissons.
Vous avez les yeux qui piquent.
Vous avez le nez qui coule.
Prenez un kleenex.
Prenez un comprimé.
Merci, (Student 2). Très bien. Retournez à votre place, s'il vous plaît.

Vocabulaire

3 Practice

Quel est le mot?

8 You may wish to have students write their answers to this activity in paragraph form.

Learning from Photos

(page 40 bottom) This green type of cross with neon lights is the symbol in France for a pharmacy. When a pharmacy in France is closed for a holiday, late hour, etc., there is always a notice on the door informing you of the nearest open pharmacy—**la pharmacie de garde**.

Paired Activity
Have students work in pairs. Have them take turns telling each other that they think they have the flu or a bad cold. They should explain why they think they are sick by explaining their symptoms. The partner should respond by giving advice.

40

Vocabulaire

Quel est le mot?

7 Il est malade. Choisissez.

1. Où est le malade?
   a. au travail   b. à la crémerie   c. chez le médecin
2. Qui souffre?
   a. le médecin   b. le malade   c. le pharmacien
3. Qu'est-ce que le médecin examine?
   a. la fièvre   b. la grippe   c. la gorge
4. Qu'est-ce que le malade ouvre?
   a. le ventre   b. la bouche   c. l'oreille
5. Quand le médecin l'ausculte, comment respire le malade?
   a. à fond   b. rien   c. bien
6. Qui est-ce que le médecin ausculte?
   a. le malade   b. le pharmacien   c. la pharmacienne
7. Que fait le médecin?
   a. des comprimés   b. des médicaments   c. des diagnostics
8. Qu'est-ce qu'il a, le malade?
   a. une cassette   b. une sinusite aiguë   c. un grand nez
9. Qu'est-ce que le médecin lui fait?
   a. un pharmacien   b. une ordonnance   c. des antibiotiques
10. Qu'est-ce qu'elle prescrit?
    a. des yeux   b. des ordonnances   c. des comprimés

Une pharmacie

8 Historiette Chez le médecin
Donnez des réponses personnelles.

1. Tu vas chez le médecin quand tu es malade?
2. Le médecin te demande où tu as mal?
3. Qu'est-ce que tu réponds au médecin?
4. Quand tu as une angine, tu as mal où?
5. Qu'est-ce que le médecin te dit quand il t'ausculte?
6. Le médecin fait un diagnostic?
7. Il te prescrit des antibiotiques?
8. Tu vas à la pharmacie pour acheter des médicaments?
9. Tu prends quelquefois de l'aspirine? Quand?
10. Pour avaler des comprimés, qu'est-ce que tu bois?
11. Après quelques jours, tu vas mieux?

40 ✦ quarante   CHAPITRE 2

ANSWERS TO Quel est le mot?

7
1. c
2. b
3. c
4. b
5. a
6. a
7. c
8. b
9. b
10. c

8 Answers will vary but may include:
1. Oui, je vais chez le médecin quand je suis malade.
2. Oui, le médecin me demande où j'ai mal.
3. Je lui réponds: «J'ai mal à la gorge».
4. Quand j'ai une angine, j'ai mal à la gorge.
5. Quand le médecin m'ausculte il me dit: «Respirez à fond».
6. Oui, le médecin fait un diagnostic.
7. Oui, il me prescrit des antibiotiques.
8. Oui, je vais à la pharmacie pour acheter des médicaments.
9. Oui, je prends quelquefois de l'aspirine quand j'ai de la fièvre.
10. Pour avaler des comprimés, je bois de l'eau.
11. Oui, après quelques jours je vais mieux.

9   **Je ne suis pas dans mon assiette.** Work with a classmate. Yesterday you did something that made you feel ill today. Using the first list below, tell a classmate what you did. He or she has to guess what's wrong with you, choosing from the second list.

trop regarder la télé →
—Hier, j'ai trop regardé la télé.
—Tu as mal aux yeux.

lire pendant six heures
manger trop de chocolat
passer beaucoup d'examens
faire une longue promenade
étudier jusqu'à trois heures du matin
écouter de la musique trop fort
jouer dans la neige en t-shirt

être enrhumé(e)
avoir mal aux yeux
avoir mal aux pieds
être fatigué(e)
avoir mal aux oreilles
avoir mal à la tête
avoir mal au ventre

10 **Qu'est-ce que tu as?** You were absent from school today. Your classmate, a French exchange student, is concerned about you and calls to find out how you are feeling. Let him or her know and tell all that you are doing to get better.

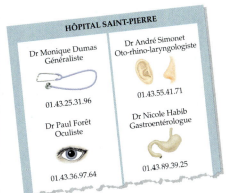

11   **Quel médecin?** While on a trip to France, you get sick. Describe your symptoms. A classmate will look at the list of doctors at the Hôpital Saint-Pierre and tell you which one to call and what the phone number is.

—J'ai mal à la gorge.
—On va appeler le docteur Simonet au 01.43.55.41.71.

12   **Au cabinet de consultation** Work with a classmate. You're sick. The doctor (your partner) will ask you questions about your symptoms. Answer the doctor's questions as completely as you can. Then reverse roles.

 For more practice using words from Mots 2, do Activity 6 on page H7 at the end of this book.

LA SANTÉ ET LA MÉDECINE

Structure

1 Preparation

Resource Manager

Audio Activities TE, pages 17–19
Audio CD 2
Workbook, pages 13–17
Quizzes 3–6, pages 9–12
ExamView® Pro

Bellringer Review

Use BRR Transparency 2.3 or write the following on the board.
You don't want to go to school today. Try to convince your mom or dad that you are sick. Be as descriptive as possible.

2 Presentation

Les pronoms lui, leur

Step 1 Write the sentences in Item 1 on the board. Use arrows as in the examples to help students understand the concept of direct versus indirect objects. As students look at these sentences, say: **Remarquez. Il ne lance pas Luc. Il lance le ballon. Il lance le ballon à qui? Il lance le ballon à Luc. «Le ballon», c'est l'objet direct. «Luc», c'est l'objet indirect.**

Step 2 Lead students through Items 1–2 and the accompanying examples.

Structure

Les pronoms lui, leur
Telling what you do for others

1. You have already learned the direct object pronouns **le, la,** and **les.** Now, you will learn the indirect object pronouns **lui** and **leur.** Observe the difference between a direct and an indirect object in the following sentences.

Paul lance le ballon à Luc.

Paul lance → le ballon.

Paul lance → le ballon ↗ à Luc.

In the preceding sentence, **le ballon** is the direct object because it is the direct receiver of the action of the verb. What does Paul throw? The ball. The indirect object indicates to whom the ball is thrown. **Luc** is the indirect object of the verb. To whom does Paul throw the ball? To Luc. Note that the indirect object is preceded by the preposition **à**—**à Luc.**

2. The indirect object pronouns in French are **lui** and **leur.** Note that the masculine and feminine forms are the same. Study the following chart.

Singulier	Le médecin parle à Pierre. Le médecin parle à Marie.	Il lui parle.
Pluriel	Le médecin parle à ses patients. Le médecin parle à ses patientes.	Il leur parle.

Just like the direct object pronouns, the indirect object pronouns **lui** and **leur** come right before the verb they are linked to.

Je lui parle.
Je ne lui parle pas.
Je veux lui parler.
Je ne veux pas lui parler.

Rappelez-vous que...
The object pronouns **me, te, nous, vous** are both direct and indirect.
Je te vois.
Je te parle.

42 quarante-deux   CHAPITRE 2

Note: Be sure students learn that **lui** and **leur** are both masculine and feminine. **Leur** as an indirect object never has an **s**.

LEVELING
A: Activities 13, 14, 15, 16
C: Activity 16

Comment dit-on?

  Historiette Une consultation
Répondez en utilisant **lui**.
1. Le médecin parle à Paul?
2. Il demande à Paul s'il a de la fièvre?
3. Paul explique ses symptômes au médecin?
4. Le médecin dit à Paul qu'il a de la fièvre?
5. Il donne une ordonnance à Paul?
6. Paul téléphone à la pharmacienne?

 Un match de foot Complétez avec **lui** ou **leur**.
1. Il lance le ballon à Marianne? Oui, il ___ lance le ballon.
2. Les joueurs parlent à l'arbitre? Oui, ils ___ parlent.
3. Et l'arbitre parle aux joueurs? Oui, il ___ parle.
4. L'arbitre explique les règles aux joueuses? Oui, il ___ explique les règles.
5. L'employée au guichet parle à un spectateur? Oui, elle ___ parle.

 Personnellement Répondez en utilisant **lui** ou **leur**.
1. Tu parles souvent à tes professeurs?
2. Tu dis toujours bonjour à ton professeur de français?
3. Tu vas téléphoner à ton copain/ta copine ce week-end?
4. Tu aimes parler à tes copains au téléphone?
5. Tu parles souvent à tes copains?
6. Tu vas écrire à tes grands-parents?

 Des cadeaux pour tout le monde? Work with a classmate. Describe your favorite friends or relatives. Then tell what you buy or give to each one as a gift.

 For more practice using **lui** and **leur**, do Activity 7 on page H8 at the end of this book.

LA SANTÉ ET LA MÉDECINE

quarante-trois 43

Structure

1 Preparation

Bellringer Review

Use BRR Transparency 2.4 or write the following on the board.
Your friend seems to get things mixed up when he or she speaks French. Correct your friend's statements.
1. La pharmacienne m'ausculte.
2. J'ai le nez qui pique et les yeux qui coulent.
3. J'ai mal à la tête. Elle est très rouge.
4. Je ne suis pas dans mon verre.

2 Presentation

Les verbes souffrir et ouvrir

Step 1 Lead students through Items 1–2. Have them repeat the forms after you.

Step 2 Explain to students that as with any regular **-er** verb the **je, tu, il, ils** forms of these verbs are all pronounced the same.

Expansion: You may wish to explain to students that **couvrir, découvrir,** and **offrir** follow the same pattern as **ouvrir** and **souffrir**.

3 Practice

Comment dit-on?

17 You may wish to have students retell the activity in their own words.

Structure

Les verbes souffrir et ouvrir
Describing more activities

1. The verbs **souffrir** and **ouvrir** are conjugated the same way as regular **-er** verbs in the present.

SOUFFRIR		OUVRIR	
je	souffre	j'	ouvre
tu	souffres	tu	ouvres
il/elle/on	souffre	il/elle/on	ouvre
nous	souffrons	nous	ouvrons
vous	souffrez	vous	ouvrez
ils/elles	souffrent	ils/elles	ouvrent

2. Note the past participles.

   souffrir → **souffert**   Ils ont beaucoup **souffert**.
   ouvrir → **ouvert**   Il a **ouvert** la bouche.

Comment dit-on?

17 **Historiette** Elle est malade.
Inventez des réponses.
1. Caroline souffre d'une angine?
2. Quand tu souffres d'une angine, tu as mal où?
3. Caroline va chez le médecin?
4. Quand le médecin lui examine la gorge, Caroline ouvre la bouche?
5. Le médecin lui donne une ordonnance?
6. Caroline va à la pharmacie?
7. Elle donne l'ordonnance au pharmacien?
8. Le pharmacien lui donne un paquet de comprimés?
9. Caroline ouvre le paquet?
10. Elle avale un comprimé?
11. Elle ne souffre plus?

À la pharmacie

44 ❀ quarante-quatre   CHAPITRE 2

ANSWERS TO Comment dit-on?

17 Answers will vary but may include:
1. Oui, Caroline souffre d'une angine.
2. Quand je souffre d'une angine j'ai mal à la gorge.
3. Oui, Caroline va chez le médecin.
4. Oui, quand le médecin lui examine la gorge, Caroline ouvre la bouche.
5. Oui, le médecin lui donne une ordonnance.
6. Oui, Caroline va à la pharmacie.
7. Oui, elle lui donne l'ordonnance.
8. Oui, le pharmacien lui donne un paquet de comprimés.
9. Oui, Caroline l'ouvre.
10. Oui, elle l'avale.
11. Non, elle ne souffre plus.

L'impératif
Telling people what to do

1. You use the imperative to give commands and make suggestions. The forms are usually the same as the **tu, vous,** and **nous** forms. Note that the **nous** form means "Let's . . ."

PARLER	FINIR	ATTENDRE
Parle à ton prof!	Finis tes devoirs!	Attends ton ami.
Parlez à votre prof!	Finissez vos devoirs!	Attendez votre ami.
Parlons à notre prof!	Finissons nos devoirs!	Attendons notre ami.

2. Note that with **-er** verbs, you drop the final **s** of the **tu** form. The same is true for **aller** and verbs like **ouvrir**.

   Regarde!
   Va voir le médecin!
   Ouvre la bouche!

3. In negative commands, you put the **ne… pas** or any other negative expression around the verb.

   Ne respirez plus!
   Ne dis rien.

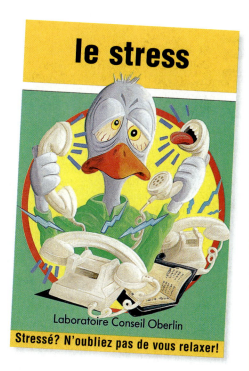

LA SANTÉ ET LA MÉDECINE

quarante-cinq 45

Structure

1 Preparation

Bellringer Review

Use BRR Transparency 2.5 or write the following on the board. Complete the sentences with the correct form of **ouvrir, souffrir,** or **offrir**.
1. Tu _____ un cadeau à ta mère?
2. Elle _____ le livre à la page 12.
3. Ils sont très malades. Ils _____ beaucoup.
4. J'ai _____ le réfrigérateur.

2 Presentation

L'impératif

Note: Students should have little trouble learning the imperative since they are already familiar with the verb forms. The only thing that will be new to them is the dropping of the **s** in the spelling of the **tu** form of **-er** verbs.

Step 1 Have students open their books to page 45. Lead them through Items 1–3.

Step 2 Illustrate the difference between singular and plural imperatives by giving commands to one student and to groups or pairs of students. For example: **Yvonne, prends ton livre de français. Va au tableau. Ouvre le livre à la page 15. Guillaume et Martine, sortez.**

Step 3 Practice the negative forms by calling out commands and having students change them to the negative. Then reverse the procedure.

LEVELING
E: Activity 17

Learning from Realia
(page 45) Explain that this type of card is provided by drug companies and distributed free at pharmacies. Have students pick out all the cognates and make up sentences using **stressé, se relaxer**.

45

Structure

3 Practice

Comment dit-on?

18 and **19** You may wish to have students work in pairs and then in groups. The recipient(s) of the command should show comprehension by miming the activity suggested in the command.

Reaching All Students

Additional Practice
Students work in groups of three. One student tells another what to do. That student dramatizes the command. The third student describes the scene. Rotate roles.
  Student 1: *(Student 2),* **ouvre la bouche.**
  (Student 2 dramatizes)
  Student 3: *(Student 2)* **ouvre la bouche, mais moi, je n'ouvre pas la bouche.**

Learning from Realia
(page 46) Ask students what the important message is on the cover of this brochure.

Structure

Comment dit-on?

18 **La loi, c'est moi!** Donnez un ordre à un copain ou à une copine d'après le modèle.

—regarder
—Regarde!
1. téléphoner à Jean
2. passer l'examen
3. parler français
4. travailler plus
5. préparer le dîner
6. ouvrir la porte
7. mettre la table
8. choisir un film
9. faire le travail
10. écrire l'exercice

19 **Et vous aussi**
Donnez un ordre d'après le modèle.

—regarder
—Regardez.
1. téléphoner à Jean
2. passer l'examen
3. parler français
4. travailler plus
5. préparer le dîner
6. ouvrir la porte
7. mettre la table
8. choisir un film
9. faire le travail
10. écrire l'exercice

 For more practice using the commands, do Activity 8 on page H9 at the end of this book.

46 ❦ quarante-six   CHAPITRE 2

ANSWERS TO Comment dit-on?

1. Téléphone à Jean!
2. Passe l'examen!
3. Parle français!
4. Travaille plus!
5. Prépare le dîner!
6. Ouvre la porte!
7. Mets la table!
8. Choisis un film!
9. Fais le travail!
10. Écris l'exercice!

1. Téléphonez à Jean!
2. Passez l'examen!
3. Parlez français!
4. Travaillez plus!
5. Préparez le dîner!
6. Ouvrez la porte!
7. Mettez la table!
8. Choisissez un film!
9. Faites le travail!
10. Écrivez l'exercice!

20 Ne fais pas ça! Donnez un ordre à un copain ou à une copine d'après le modèle.

—regarder
—Ne regarde pas!

1. lire le journal
2. écrire une lettre
3. prendre le métro
4. attendre devant la porte
5. descendre
6. aller plus vite
7. faire attention
8. entrer
9. sortir

21 Ne faites pas ça! Refaites l'Activité 20 d'après le modèle.

—regarder
—Ne regardez pas!

22 Allons-y! Répondez d'après le modèle.

On invite Marie?
D'accord, invitons Marie!

1. On va à la plage?
2. On nage?
3. On fait du ski nautique?
4. On prend notre petit déjeuner?
5. On dîne au restaurant?
6. On sort?

  Jacques a dit... This game is called "Simon Says" in English. Play in groups of five people or more. Give orders to your classmates. If you say **Jacques a dit** first, they have to obey the order. If you don't say **Jacques a dit** first, they should not obey your order. If they do, they are eliminated.

LA SANTÉ ET LA MÉDECINE

quarante-sept ❖ 47

YEUX ROUGES, YEUX IRRITES
DÉCOUVREZ CE COLLYRE EN MONODOSES!
ANTALYRE
Collyre en monodoses

ANSWERS TO *Comment dit-on?*

20
1. Ne lis pas le journal!
2. N'écris pas de lettre!
3. Ne prends pas le métro!
4. N'attends pas devant la porte!
5. Ne descends pas!
6. Ne va pas plus vite!
7. Ne fais pas attention!
8. N'entre pas!
9. Ne sors pas!

21
1. Ne lisez pas le journal!
2. N'écrivez pas de lettre!
3. Ne prenez pas le métro!
4. N'attendez pas devant la porte!
5. Ne descendez pas!
6. N'allez pas plus vite!
7. Ne faites pas attention!
8. N'entrez pas!
9. Ne sortez pas!

22
1. D'accord, allons à la plage!
2. D'accord, nageons!
3. D'accord, faisons du ski nautique!
4. D'accord, prenons notre petit déjeuner!
5. D'accord, dînons au restaurant!
6. D'accord, sortons!

Structure

✓ Assessment

As an informal assessment, you may wish to have students quickly make up as many commands as they can. If they can make up logical (and reasonable) commands, you could comply. For example: Students say **Ouvrez la porte.** You open the door.

Learning from Realia

(page 47) Ask students what the product in this ad is used for.

ENCORE PLUS This *Infogap* activity will allow students to practice in pairs. The activity should be very manageable for them, since all vocabulary and structures are familiar to them.

LEVELING

E: Activities 18, 19, 20, 21, 22, 23
A: Activities 18, 20, 21, 22, 23

Structure

1 Preparation

Bellringer Review

Use BRR Transparency 2.6 or write the following on the board.
You are babysitting a five-year-old. Write six things you tell him or her to do or not do.

2 Presentation

Le pronom en

Step 1 Have students open their books to page 48. Lead them through the explanation.

Step 2 Read the sample sentences with **en** and have students repeat them in unison.

3 Practice

Comment dit-on?

24 This can be done as a paired activity.

Structure

Le pronom en
Referring to people, places, and things already mentioned

1. The pronoun **en** is used to replace a noun that is introduced by **de** or any form of **de—du, de la, de l', des**. **En** refers mostly to things.

Tu as de l'aspirine?	Oui, j' en ai.
Il parle de sa santé?	Oui, il en parle.
Vous sortez de l'hôpital?	Oui, j' en sors.
Tu prends des médicaments?	Oui, j' en prends.

2. You also use the pronoun **en** with numbers or expressions of quantity. Note that in this case **en** refers not only to things but also to people.

   Tu as des frères?   Oui, j'en ai deux.
   Il prend combien de comprimés?   Il en prend trois par jour.
   Il a combien de CD?   Il en a beaucoup.

3. Just like other pronouns, **en** comes directly before the verb whose meaning it is linked to.

   Il en parle.
   Il n'en parle pas.
   Il veut en parler.
   Il ne veut pas en parler.

Savez-vous que... ?

En comes after **y** in the expression **il y a**.
Il y en a deux.
Il y en a beaucoup.
Il n'y en a pas.

Comment dit-on?

24 **Historiette** La fête de Laurence Répondez d'après le modèle.

 —Laurence sert du coca?
—Oui, elle en sert.

1. Elle sert de l'eau minérale?
2. Elle sert des sandwichs?
3. Elle sert de la pizza?
4. Elle sert de la salade?
5. Elle sert du fromage?
6. Elle sert des chocolats?
7. Elle sert de la glace?
8. Elle sert de la mousse au chocolat?

Answers to Comment dit-on?

1. Oui, elle en sert.
2. Oui, elle en sert.
3. Oui, elle en sert.
4. Oui, elle en sert.
5. Oui, elle en sert.
6. Oui, elle en sert.
7. Oui, elle en sert.
8. Oui, elle en sert.

LEVELING
E: Activities 24, 25, 27
A: Activities 25, 26, 27

25 Dans le frigo Répondez d'après le modèle.

du coca →
—Il y a du coca dans ton frigo?
—Non, il n'y en a pas.

1. de l'eau minérale
2. de la glace
3. des légumes surgelés
4. du jambon
5. des tartes
6. de la viande

26 Historiette Tu es malade?
Répondez d'après le modèle.

Tu manges du chocolat? (trop)
Oui, j'en mange trop!

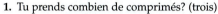

1. Tu prends combien de comprimés? (trois)
2. Tu bois de l'eau? (un litre)
3. Tu manges des fruits? (beaucoup)
4. Tu lis des magazines? (deux ou trois)
5. Tu regardes des vidéos? (trop)

27 Devinettes Devinez ce que c'est.

1. On en prend quand on est malade.
2. On en boit beaucoup quand on a de la fièvre.
3. On en utilise pour se laver les mains.
4. On en met sur une brosse à dents pour se laver les dents.
5. On en donne au vendeur quand on achète quelque chose.

Vous êtes sur le bon chemin. Allez-y!

quarante-neuf 49

ANSWERS TO Comment dit-on?

25
1. Non, il n'y en a pas.
2. Non, il n'y en a pas.
3. Non, il n'y en a pas.
4. Non, il n'y en a pas.
5. Non, il n'y en a pas.
6. Non, il n'y en a pas.

26
1. J'en prends trois!
2. Oui, j'en bois un litre!
3. Oui, j'en mange beaucoup!
4. Oui, j'en lis deux ou trois.
5. Oui, j'en regarde trop.

27
1. des comprimés
2. de l'eau
3. du savon
4. du dentifrice
5. de l'argent

Structure

25 You may wish to remind students to answer questions based on what is or is not in the refrigerator.
Expansion: Ask additional questions about what is or is not in the refrigerator:
Il y a des yaourts?
Oui, il y en a.
Il y a des pommes?
Non, il n'y en a pas.

 Dinah Zike's Study Guides

Your students may wish to use Foldable 9 to organize, display, and arrange data as they learn how to talk about how they feel in French. You may wish to encourage them to add information from each chapter as they continue to expand upon their ability to describe situations and emotions.

A *paper file folder organizer* foldable is also ideal for having students add information to different categories over a period of time.

Allez-y!
At this point in the chapter, students have learned all the vocabulary and structure necessary to complete the chapter. The conversation and cultural readings that follow recycle all the material learned up to this point.

49

Conversation

1 Preparation

Resource Manager
Audio Activities TE, pages 19–20
Audio CD 2
CD-ROM

Bellringer Review

Use BRR Transparency 2.7 or write the following on the board. Rewrite the following sentences with a pronoun.
1. Le médecin examine *le malade.*
2. Le malade ouvre *la bouche.*
3. Le malade lit *l'ordonnance.*
4. Il donne *l'ordonnance* au pharmacien.
5. Le pharmacien donne *les médicaments* au malade.

2 Presentation

Step 1 Tell students they are going to hear a conversation between Sylvie and her doctor.

Step 2 Have them listen as you read the conversation or play Audio CD 2.

Step 3 Have students work in pairs to practice the conversation. Then have several pairs present it to the class.

Glencoe Technology

CD-ROM
On the CD-ROM, students can watch a dramatization of this conversation. They can then play the role of either one of the characters and record themselves in the conversation.

Conversation

Chez le médecin

Sylvie: Bonjour, docteur.
Médecin: Bonjour, Sylvie. Alors, qu'est-ce qui ne va pas?
Sylvie: Je ne sais pas… Je ne me sens pas bien du tout.
Médecin: Tu as mal où?
Sylvie: Ben, j'ai mal un peu partout, mais surtout à la gorge.
Médecin: Tu as mal à la tête?
Sylvie: Oui, à la tête aussi. Et j'ai froid, j'ai des frissons…
Médecin: Tu dois avoir de la fièvre. Ouvre la bouche, s'il te plaît. Dis «Aaa…»
Sylvie: Aaa…
Médecin: Tu as la gorge très rouge. C'est certainement une angine.
Sylvie: Une angine!
Médecin: Oui, mais ce n'est pas grave. Je vais te donner des antibiotiques. Tu vas en prendre trois par jour pendant une semaine.

Vous avez compris?

Répondez.
1. Qui est malade?
2. Quels sont ses symptômes?
3. Elle a mal où?
4. Sylvie ouvre la bouche. Pourquoi?
5. Qu'est-ce que le médecin lui donne?
6. Sylvie doit prendre combien de comprimés par jour?
7. Pendant combien de temps?

ANSWERS TO Vous avez compris?

1. Sylvie est malade.
2. Elle a froid et elle a des frissons.
3. Elle a mal partout, mais surtout à la gorge et à la tête.
4. Elle ouvre la bouche parce que le médecin veut examiner sa gorge.
5. Le médecin lui donne des antibiotiques.
6. Elle doit en prendre trois par jour.
7. Pendant une semaine.

Learning from Photos

(page 50) You may wish to ask the following questions about the photo:
Qui examine la malade?
Elle lui parle?
La malade explique ses symptômes au médecin?
Qu'est-ce qu'elle lui dit? Elle a mal où?

Parlons un peu plus

A **Tu dois ou tu ne dois pas être médecin.** Work with a classmate. Interview each other and decide who would make a good doctor. Make a list of questions for your interview. One question you may want to ask is: **Tu as beaucoup de patience ou très peu de patience?**

B **Je suis très malade.** Imagine you're sick with a cold, the flu, or a sore throat. Tell the doctor (your partner) what your symptoms are. He or she makes a diagnosis and tells you what to do to get better. Use the model as a guide.

J'ai de la fièvre et des frissons.

Vous avez la grippe. Restez au lit et prenez de l'aspirine.

Prononciation

Les sons /u/ et /ü/

1. It is important to make a distinction between the sounds /u/ and /ü/, since many words differ only in these two sounds. Repeat the following pairs of words.

   vous / vu   dessous / dessus   roux / rue
   loue / lu   tout / tu

2. Now repeat the following sentences.

   Tu as beaucoup de température?
   J'éternue toutes les deux minutes.

souffrir

température

LA SANTÉ ET LA MÉDECINE

cinquante et un 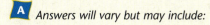 51

Lectures culturelles

Resource Manager
Audio Activities TE, page 21
Audio CD 2

Bellringer Review

Use BRR Transparency 2.8 or write the following on the board.
Choose the correct completion.

 ouvre   avale
 respire   souffre
 prend

1. Il _____ la bouche.
2. Il est très malade. Il _____ beaucoup.
3. Il _____ à fond.
4. Il _____ les comprimés avec de l'eau.
5. Il _____ ses médicaments.

National Standards

Cultures
The reading about a visit with the doctor on pages 52–53 and the related activities give students an understanding of health services in France.

Comparisons
The reading will allow students to make comparisons between the French and American medical systems.

About the French Language

Explain to students that **les honoraires** is the term used for the fees of professionals such as doctors and lawyers.

Lectures culturelles

Le Québec

Reading Strategy
Identifying important concepts
A quick way to identify the important concepts in a passage is to first read the questions that follow it. This will tell you what ideas the author is emphasizing and what type of information you should look for as you read.

Une consultation

La pauvre Mélanie. Elle est très malade! Elle tousse. Elle éternue. Elle a mal à la tête. Elle a de la température. Elle a des frissons. Elle n'est pas du tout dans son assiette. Elle veut appeler le médecin, mais c'est le week-end et son médecin ne donne pas de consultations le week-end. La seule solution, c'est d'appeler S.O.S. Médecins.

S.O.S. Médecins est un service qui envoie des médecins à domicile[1]. Un médecin arrive chez Mélanie et l'examine. Elle l'ausculte, elle lui prend sa température. Elle lui dit qu'elle a la grippe. Mais ce n'est pas grave. Elle va être vite sur pied. Le médecin lui fait une ordonnance. Elle prescrit des

[1] à domicile *to the home*

Le médecin ausculte la malade.

LEVELING
E: Reading

antibiotiques: trois comprimés par jour pendant une semaine. Mélanie va en prendre un à chaque repas.

Mélanie paie le médecin. Mais en France, la Sécurité Sociale rembourse les honoraires des médecins, c'est-à-dire l'argent qu'on donne aux médecins. Les honoraires et tous les frais[2] médicaux sont remboursés de 80 à 100% (pour cent) par la Sécurité Sociale.

[2] frais *expenses*

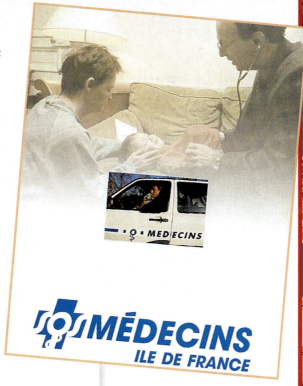

Vous avez compris?

A Autrement dit
Dites d'une autre façon.

1. Mélanie a *de la fièvre*.
2. Elle *ne se sent pas bien*.
3. Elle veut *téléphoner au* médecin.
4. Le médecin *ne voit pas de malades* le week-end.
5. S.O.S. Médecins envoie des médecins *chez les malades*.
6. Le médecin *écoute la respiration de* Mélanie.
7. La grippe n'est pas une maladie *alarmante*.
8. Mélanie va vite *se sentir mieux*.

B La pauvre Mélanie Répondez.
1. Mélanie est très malade?
2. Elle a de la fièvre?
3. Elle a mal au ventre?
4. Elle veut appeler le médecin?
5. Son médecin donne des consultations tous les jours?
6. Mélanie téléphone à qui?
7. Le médecin lui prescrit de l'aspirine?
8. Les frais médicaux ne sont pas remboursés en France?

C En France Qu'est-ce que vous avez appris sur les médecins et les services médicaux en France?

Lecture supplémentaire 1

National Standards

Cultures
This selection familiarizes students with cultural differences dealing with health matters.

Comparisons
This selection makes a comparison between typical health concerns of Americans and French people.

Attention!

This reading is optional. You may skip it completely, have the entire class read it, have only several students read it and report to the class, or assign it for extra credit.

Learning from Realia

(page 54 top) Point to the rabbit and say: **C'est un lapin. Qu'est-ce qu'il a, le lapin? Qu'est-ce qu'il a mangé? Il a mangé trop de carottes? Tu aimes les carottes? Tu manges beaucoup de carottes? On dit que les carottes sont bonnes pour les yeux?**

Lecture supplémentaire 1

Culture et santé

La culture influence la santé et la médecine? Certainement. Par exemple, en France tout le monde parle de son foie[1]. Les Français disent souvent, «J'ai mal au foie.» Aux États-Unis, on n'entend jamais dire ça. Pourquoi? Parce qu'aux États-Unis, une maladie du foie, c'est grave. Mais quand un Français dit qu'il a mal au foie, il veut dire tout simplement qu'il a un trouble digestif. Rien de grave. Il n'est peut-être pas dans son assiette aujourd'hui, mais il va vite être sur pied!

Aux États-Unis, par contre, on parle beaucoup d'allergies. De nombreux Américains souffrent d'une petite allergie. Les symptômes d'une allergie ressemblent aux symptômes d'un rhume. On éternue et on a souvent mal à la tête. Une allergie, c'est désagréable, mais d'habitude ce n'est pas grave. En France, on parle moins souvent d'allergies. Pourquoi? Qui sait? Vive la différence!

[1] foie *liver*

LES TROUBLES DIGESTIFS

Amis ou ennemis?

Vous avez compris?

Des différences Répondez.
1. On dit souvent qu'on a mal au foie dans quel pays?
2. Que veut dire un Français quand il dit qu'il a mal au foie?
3. Et pour un Américain, qu'est-ce que cela veut dire «J'ai mal au foie»?
4. Qui parle souvent d'allergies?
5. Quels sont les symptômes d'une allergie?

Answers to Vous avez compris?

1. en France
2. qu'il a un trouble digestif
3. que c'est une maladie grave
4. les Américains
5. On éternue, on a les yeux qui piquent et on a mal à la tête.

LEVELING

A: Reading 1, Reading 2

Lecture supplémentaire 2

Les services médicaux en France

En France, il y a de grands hôpitaux avec tout l'équipement haut de gamme[1] nécessaire à la pratique d'une médecine moderne. On compte plus de 3 500 établissements de soins polyvalents[2]. Il y a à peu près 900 établissements hospitaliers publics et plus de 2 500 cliniques privées. Beaucoup de ces cliniques ressemblent à des hôtels.

En France, on fait beaucoup de recherches médicales et pharmaceutiques. C'est à l'Institut Pasteur de Paris que le docteur Montagnier a isolé le virus du sida[3]. Aujourd'hui à l'Institut Pasteur on continue à faire des recherches contre cette terrible maladie.

[1] haut de gamme *state of the art*
[2] soins polyvalents *general care*
[3] sida *AIDS*

Un laboratoire de recherche à l'Institut Pasteur

L'Institut Pasteur, Paris

Vous avez compris?

Des mots apparentés Trouvez les mots apparentés dans la lecture.

LA SANTÉ ET LA MÉDECINE

Connexions

 National Standards

Connections
This reading about nutrition establishes a connection with another discipline, allowing students to reinforce and further their knowledge of natural sciences through the study of French.

Attention!

The readings in the **Connexions** section are optional. They focus on some of the major disciplines taught in schools and universities. The vocabulary is useful for discussing such topics as history, literature, art, economics, business, science, etc. You may choose any of the following ways to do the readings in the **Connexions** section.

Independent reading Have students read the selections and do the post-reading activities as homework, which you collect. This option is least intrusive on class time and requires a minimum of teacher involvement.

Homework with in-class follow-up Assign the readings and post-reading activities as homework. Review and discuss the material in class the next day.

Intensive in-class activity This option includes a pre-reading vocabulary presentation, in-class reading and discussion, assignment of the activities for homework, and a discussion of the assignment in class the next day.

Connexions

Les sciences naturelles

La diététique

Good nutrition is very important. What we eat can determine if we will enjoy good health or poor health. For this reason, it is most important to have a balanced diet and avoid the temptation to eat "junk food."

Read the following information about nutrition in French. Before reading this selection, however, look at the following groups of related words. Often if you know the meaning of one word you can guess the meaning of several words related to it.

individuel, individu
actif, activité
consommation, consommer, consommateur
adolescent, adolescence
âge, âgé

Un bon régime[1]

Il est très important d'avoir une alimentation équilibrée[2] pour être en bonne santé. Un régime équilibré comporte une variété de légumes et de fruits, des céréales, de la viande et du poisson.

Tout le monde a besoin de calories, mais le nombre idéal dépend de l'individu—de son métabolisme, de sa taille, de son âge et de son activité physique. Les adolescents, par exemple, ont besoin de plus de calories que les personnes âgées. Ils ont besoin de plus de calories parce qu'ils sont plus actifs et ils sont en période de croissance[3].

Les protéines

Les protéines sont particulièrement importantes pour les enfants et les adolescents parce qu'ils sont en pleine croissance. Les protéines aident à fabriquer des cellules. La viande et les œufs contiennent des protéines.

[1] régime *diet* [2] équilibrée *balanced* [3] croissance *growth*

Class Motivator

Des aliments Those students who are interested in nutrition may prepare a food chart with the following headings:

    Aliments hauts en calories
    Aliments bas en calories
    Graisses
    Hydrates de carbone
    Vitamine A
    Vitamine B
    Vitamine C
    Vitamine D
    Vitamine E

Under each heading they can put photos or drawings of the appropriate foods labeled in French that they have already learned to identify.

Les glucides (les hydrates de carbone)

Les glucides (les pommes de terre, les pâtes comme les spaghettis, le riz[4]) sont la source d'énergie la plus efficace pour le corps humain.

Les lipides (les graisses)

Les lipides sont aussi une bonne source d'énergie. Mais pour les personnes qui ont un taux de cholestérol élevé[5], les graisses ne sont pas bonnes. Il faut faire un régime sans graisse. Il faut les éliminer.

Les minéraux

Beaucoup de minéraux sont essentiels pour le corps humain. Le calcium est absolument nécessaire pour les os[6] et les dents.

L'eau

L'eau est absolument essentielle au corps humain qui est fait de 65% d'eau.

Les vitamines

Les vitamines sont indispensables au bon fonctionnement du corps humain. Ce tableau indique la source de quelques vitamines importantes.

[4] riz *rice*   [5] élevé *elevated, high*   [6] os *bones*

Vitamines	Sources
A	légumes, lait, quelques fruits
B	viande, œufs, céréales, légumes verts
C	fruits, tomates, salade verte
D	lait, œufs, poisson
E	huiles, légumes, œufs, céréales

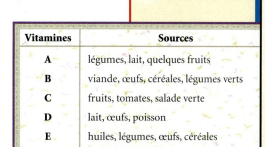

Vous avez compris?

A **La diététique** Répondez.

1. Qu'est-ce qu'on doit manger tous les jours?
2. Le nombre de calories pour chaque individu dépend de quoi?
3. Qui a particulièrement besoin de calories? Pourquoi?
4. Quelle est une source importante d'énergie?
5. Pourquoi faut-il contrôler la consommation de graisses?
6. Quel est un minéral important pour les os et les dents?
7. Qu'est-ce qui est indispensable au bon fonctionnement du corps humain?

B **Assez de vitamines?** Faites une liste de tout ce que vous avez mangé hier. Vous avez eu toutes les vitamines nécessaires?

LA SANTÉ ET LA MÉDECINE

C'est à vous

Use what you have learned

 Recycling

These activities allow students to use the vocabulary and structure from this chapter in completely open-ended, real-life situations.

Presentation

Encourage students to say as much as possible when they do these activities. Tell them not to be afraid to make mistakes, since the goal of these activities is real-life communication. If someone in the group makes an error, allow the others to politely correct him or her. Let students choose the activities they would like to do.

You may wish to separate students into pairs or groups. Encourage students to elaborate on the basic theme and to be creative. They may use props, pictures, or posters if they wish.

C'est à vous

Use what you have learned

1 Tout le monde est malade.
✔ *Describe cold symptoms and minor ailments*

Work with a classmate. Choose one of the people in the illustrations. Describe him or her. Your partner will guess which person you're talking about and say what's the matter with the person. Take turns.

1.    2.

3.    4.

2 Une ordonnance
✔ *Discuss a prescription with a pharmacist*

You are in a pharmacy in Bordeaux. Your classmate will be the pharmacist. Make up a conversation about your prescription. Explain why and how you have to take the medicine.

3 Jeu Je suis malade comme un chien!
✔ *Talk about how you are feeling*

Work with a partner. Make gestures to indicate how you're feeling today. Your partner will ask you why you feel that way. Tell him or her. Be as creative and humorous as possible.

58 *cinquante-huit*   CHAPITRE 2

ANSWERS TO C'est à vous

 1 *Answers will vary but may include:*

—Le pauvre! Il a très mal au ventre. Il a aussi de la fièvre. Sa mère va téléphoner au médecin.
—C'est le dessin numéro 1. Il a la grippe.

2 *Answers will vary but may include:*

—J'ai une angine. Le médecin m'a donné cette ordonnance.
—Ah, oui. C'est un très bon antibiotique.

—Il faut prendre combien de comprimés?
—Trois par jour. Et vous allez être vite sur pied.

 3 *Answers will vary but may include:*

Student points to his or her stomach.
—Tu as mal au ventre?
—Oui. Hier je suis allé(e) à une fête et j'ai beaucoup mangé. Je sais que j'ai mangé trop de gâteau au chocolat.

CHAPITRE 2

4 Excusez-moi...
✓ *Write a note describing a minor illness*

You're supposed to take a French test today but you're not feeling well. Write a note to your French teacher explaining why you can't take the test, and mention some symptoms you have.

Une ambulance du SAMU

Writing Strategy

Writing a personal essay In writing a personal essay, a writer has several options: to tell a story, describe something, or encourage readers to think a certain way or to do something. Whatever its purpose, a personal essay allows a writer to express a viewpoint based on his or her own experience. Your essay will be much livelier if you choose interesting details and vivid words to relay your message.

5 Des bénévoles

Your French club has a community service requirement. You have decided to work in the emergency room **(le service des urgences)** at your local hospital. You serve as a translator or interpreter for patients who speak only French. Write a flyer for your French club. Tell about your experience with one or more patients. Give your feelings about the work you do and try to encourage other club members to volunteer their services, too.

LA SANTÉ ET LA MÉDECINE

cinquante-neuf 59

Assessment

Resource Manager

Communication Transparencies C 2
Quizzes, pages 7–12
Tests, pages 15–28
ExamView® Pro
Situation Cards
Performance Assessment, Task 2
Marathon mental Videoquiz

✓ Assessment

This is a pre-test for students to take before you administer the chapter test. Answer sheets for students to do these pages are provided in your transparency binder. Note that each section is cross-referenced so students can easily find the material they have to review in case they made errors. You may wish to collect these assessments and correct them yourself or you may prefer to have the students correct themselves in class. You can go over the answers orally or project them on the overhead, using your Assessment Answers transparencies.

Assessment

Vocabulaire

1 Choisissez.

To review Mots 1, turn to pages 34–35.

1. ____ Elle a mal à la tête.
2. ____ Elle a mal au ventre.
3. ____ Elle tousse.
4. ____ Elle est enrhumée.

2 Identifiez.

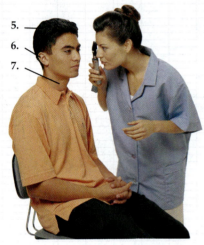

5.
6.
7.

3 Complétez.

To review Mots 2, turn to pages 38–39.

8. Le médecin ____ le malade.
9. Le malade ouvre la ____ quand le médecin lui examine la gorge.
10. Le médecin fait un ____. Il dit que Nathalie a une sinusite aiguë.
11. Le médecin lui fait une ____ pour des antibiotiques.
12. Elle va à la ____ pour acheter ses médicaments.

60 ⚜ *soixante* CHAPITRE 2

ANSWERS TO Assessment

1
1. c
2. a
3. d
4. b

2
5. la tête
6. l'oreille
7. la gorge

3
8. examine
9. bouche
10. diagnostic
11. ordonnance
12. pharmacie

CHAPITRE 2 Assessment

Structure

4 Complétez.

13. Le médecin parle au malade?
    Oui, il ____ parle.
14. Le médecin donne une ordonnance à ses patients?
    Oui, il ____ donne une ordonnance.
15. Paul donne son ordonnance à la pharmacienne?
    Oui, il ____ donne son ordonnance.

*To review **lui** and **leur**, turn to page 42.*

5 Complétez.

16. Ils ____ beaucoup, les pauvres. (souffrir)
17. J'____ le livre à la page 100. (ouvrir)
18. Vous ____ la bouche quand le médecin vous examine? (ouvrir)

*To review **souffrir** and **ouvrir**, turn to page 44.*

6 Complétez avec l'impératif.

19. (ouvrir) Paul, ____ ton livre.
    Luc et Louise, ____ vos livres aussi.
20. (attendre) Carole, ____ un moment.
    Sandrine et Maïa, ____ avec Carole.
21. (dire) Luc, ____ au médecin où tu as mal.
    Vous deux, ____ au médecin où vous avez mal.

To review commands, turn to page 45.

7 Répondez avec un pronom.

22. Tu as de l'aspirine?
    Oui, _____.
23. Tu as douze comprimés?
    Oui, _____.
24. Tu peux sortir de l'hôpital demain?
    Oui, _____.
25. Il a beaucoup d'argent?
    Oui, _____.

*To review the use of **en**, turn to page 48.*

LA SANTÉ ET LA MÉDECINE soixante et un 61

Glencoe Technology

MINDJOGGER VHS/DVD

You may wish to help your students prepare for the chapter test by playing the MindJogger game show. Teams will compete against each other to review chapter vocabulary and structure and sharpen listening comprehension skills.

ANSWERS TO Assessment

4
13. lui
14. leur
15. lui

5
16. souffrent
17. ouvre
18. ouvrez

6
19. ouvre, ouvrez
20. attends, attendez
21. dis, dites

7
22. Oui, j'en ai.
23. Oui, j'en ai douze.
24. Oui, je peux en sortir demain.
25. Oui, il en a beaucoup.

On parle super bien!

This unique page gives students the opportunity to speak freely and say whatever they can, using the vocabulary and structures they have learned in the chapter. The illustration serves to remind students of precisely what they know how to say in French. There are no activities that students do not have the ability to describe or talk about in French. The art not only depicts the vocabulary and content of this chapter, but also reinforces what they learned in previous chapters.

You may wish to use this page in many ways. Some possibilities are to have students do the following:

1. Look at the illustration and identify items by giving the correct French words.
2. Make up sentences about what they see in the illustration.
3. Make up questions about the illustration. They can call on another class member to respond if you do this as a class activity, or you may prefer to allow students to work in small groups. This activity is extremely beneficial because it enables students to actively use interrogative words.
4. Answer questions you ask them about the illustration.
5. Work in pairs and make up a conversation based on the illustration.
6. Look at the illustration and give a complete oral review of what they see.
7. Look at the illustration and write a paragraph (or essay) about it.

You can also use this page as an assessment or testing tool, taking into account individual differences by having students go from simple to quite complicated tasks. The assessment can be either oral or written. You may wish to use the rubrics provided on pages T20–T21 as you give students the following directions:

On parle super bien!

Tell all you can about this illustration.

1. Identify the topic or situation of the illustration.
2. Give the French words for as many items as you can.
3. Think of as many sentences as you can to describe the illustration.
4. Go over your sentences and put them in the best sequencing to give a coherent story based on the illustration.

Vocabulaire

Describing minor health problems

la santé	une sinusite aiguë	éternuer	avoir de la fièvre
en bonne santé	une allergie	avoir mal	le nez qui coule
en mauvaise santé	un mouchoir	à la tête	les yeux qui piquent
une infection	un kleenex	au ventre	la gorge qui gratte
un frisson	se sentir bien	aux oreilles	malade
la grippe	mal	à la gorge	viral(e)
un rhume	être enrhumé(e)		bactérien(ne)
une angine	tousser		allergique

Speaking with the doctor

le médecin	souffrir	respirer
le/la malade	ouvrir	prescrire
un diagnostic	examiner	
une ordonnance	ausculter	

Identifying more parts of the body

la tête	une oreille
un œil, des yeux	la gorge
le nez	le ventre
la bouche	

Speaking with a pharmacist

un(e) pharmacien(ne)	un sirop
une pharmacie	de la pénicilline
un médicament	de l'aspirine (f.)
un comprimé	avaler
un antibiotique	

Other useful words and expressions

À tes souhaits!	le/la pauvre
Qu'est-ce qu'il a?	à fond

How well do you know your vocabulary?
- Find as many cognates as you can in the list.
- Use five cognates to write several sentences.

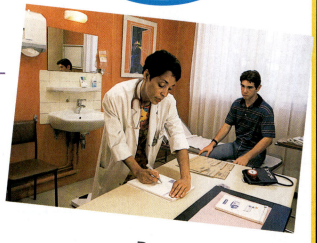

VIDÉOTOUR
Épisode 2
In this video episode, you will join Vincent as he experiences a strange nightmare. See page 501 for more information.

LA SANTÉ ET LA MÉDECINE

Planning for Chapter 3

SCOPE AND SEQUENCE, PAGES 64–95

Topics
- Technology
- Telecommunications

Culture
- The telephone—yesterday and today
- Telephone cards
- Communication advances

Functions
- How to describe habitual and continuous actions in the past
- How to narrate in the past

Structure
- **L'imparfait** of regular verbs
- Uses of **l'imparfait**

National Standards
- Communication Standard 1.1 pages 68, 69, 72, 73, 75, 76, 77, 81, 83, 90
- Communication Standard 1.2 pages 68, 69, 72, 73, 75, 76, 77, 79, 80, 82, 85, 86, 87, 89
- Communication Standard 1.3 pages 68, 69, 72, 73, 76, 77, 80, 81, 83, 90, 91
- Cultures Standard 2.1 pages 71, 83, 84–85, 87
- Cultures Standard 2.2 pages 79, 83, 86
- Connections Standard 3.1 pages 88–89
- Comparisons Standard 4.1 page 89
- Communities Standard 5.1 page 91

PACING AND PRIORITIES

The chapter content is color coded below to assist you in planning.

■ required   ■ recommended   ■ optional

Vocabulaire (required)   *Days 1–4*
- ■ Mots 1
  - L'ordinateur
  - Le télécopieur, le fax
- ■ Mots 2
  - Le téléphone

Structure (required)   *Days 5–7*
- ■ L'imparfait
- ■ Les emplois de l'imparfait

Conversation (required)
- ■ Des devoirs difficiles

Lectures culturelles
- ■ Le téléphone d'hier et d'aujourd'hui (recommended)
- ■ La télécarte (optional)
- ■ Les communications avant et maintenant (optional)

Connexions (optional)
- ■ L'ordinateur

■ **C'est à vous** (recommended)

■ **Assessment** (recommended)

■ **On parle super bien!** (optional)

RESOURCE GUIDE

SECTION	PAGES	SECTION RESOURCES
Vocabulaire *Mots 1*		
L'ordinateur	66–67	Vocabulary Transparencies 3.2–3.3
Le télécopieur, le fax	67–69	Audio CD 3
		Audio Activities TE, pages 23–25
		Workbook, pages 21–22
		Quiz 1, page 13
		ExamView® Pro
Vocabulaire *Mots 2*		
Le téléphone	70–73	Vocabulary Transparencies 3.4–3.5
		Audio CD 3
		Audio Activities TE, pages 25–27
		Workbook, pages 23–24
		Quiz 2, page 14
		ExamView® Pro
Structure		
L'imparfait	74–77	Audio CD 3
Les emplois de l'imparfait	78–81	Audio Activities TE, pages 28–29
		Workbook, pages 25–28
		Quizzes 3–4, pages 15–16
		ExamView® Pro
Conversation		
Des devoirs difficiles	82–83	Audio CD 3
		Audio Activities TE, pages 29–30
		Interactive CD-ROM
Lectures culturelles		
Le téléphone d'hier et d'aujourd'hui	84–85	Audio CD 3
La télécarte	86	Audio Activities TE, pages 30–31
Les communications avant et maintenant	87	Tests, pages 31, 35
Connexions		
L'ordinateur	88–89	Tests, page 36
C'est à vous		
	90–91	**Bon voyage!** Video, Episode 3
		Video Activities, Chapter 3
		French Online Activities
		french.glencoe.com
Assessment		
	92–93	Communication Transparency C 3
		Quizzes 1–4, pages 13–16
		Performance Assessment, Task 3
		Tests, pages 29–42
		ExamView® Pro
		Situation Cards, Chapter 3
		Marathon mental Videoquiz

Using Your Resources for Chapter 3

Transparencies

Bellringer 3.1–3.5   Vocabulary 3.1–3.5   Communication C 3

Workbook

Vocabulary, pages 21–24   Structure, pages 25–28   Enrichment, pages 29–32

Audio Activities

Vocabulary, pages 23–27   Structure, pages 28–29   Conversation, pages 29–30   Cultural Reading, pages 30–31   Additional Practice, pages 32–33

Assessment

Vocabulary and Structure Quizzes, pages 13–16

Chapter Tests, pages 29–42

Situation Cards, Chapter 3

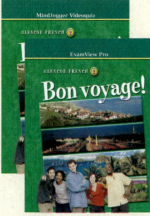
MindJogger Videoquiz, ExamView® Pro, Chapter 3

Timesaving Teacher Tools

TeacherWorks™

TeacherWorks™ is your all-in-one teacher resource center. Personalize lesson plans, access resources from the Teacher Wraparound Edition, connect to the Internet, or make a to-do list. These are only a few of the many features that can assist you in the planning and organizing of your lessons.

Includes:

- A calendar feature
- Access to all program blackline masters
- Standards correlations and more

ExamView® Pro

Test Bank software for Macintosh and Windows makes creating, editing, customizing, and printing tests quick and easy.

Technology Resources

 In the Chapter 3 Internet activity, you will have a chance to learn more about the Francophone world. Visit <u>french.glencoe.com</u>.

 On the Interactive Conversation CD-ROM, students can listen to and take part in a recorded version of the conversation in Chapter 3.

 See the National Geographic Teacher's Corner on pages 138–139, 244–245, 372–373, 472–473 for reference to additional technology resources.

 Bon voyage! Video and Video Activities, Chapter 3

 Help your students prepare for the chapter test by playing the **Marathon mental** Videoquiz game show. Teams will compete against each other to review chapter vocabulary and structure and sharpen listening comprehension skills.

CHAPITRE 3

Preview

In this chapter, students will learn to talk about computers, e-mail, and the Internet. They will learn how to send a fax and make a telephone call in France. Students will also learn the formation and uses of the imperfect tense.

National Standards

Communication

In Chapter 3, students will communicate in spoken and written French on the following topics:
- Computers, e-mail, and the Internet
- Using the telephone and fax machine
- Activities that they did frequently Students will obtain and provide information and engage in conversations dealing with computers and the telephone as they fulfill the chapter objectives listed on this page.

LEVELING

The activities, conversations, and readings within each chapter are marked according to level of difficulty. **E** indicates easy. **A** indicates average. **C** indicates challenging. Some activities cover a range of difficulty. In some activities, for example, advanced students will be able to produce more extensive responses while students who learn at a different rate may give less detailed responses. The leveling indicators will help you individualize instruction to best meet your students' needs.

CHAPITRE 3

Les télécommunications

Objectifs

In this chapter you will learn to:

✔ talk about computers, e-mail, the Internet, faxes, and telephones

✔ talk about habitual and continuous actions in the past

✔ narrate in the past

✔ discuss today's telecommunications

Maurice de Vlaminck *La route*

CHAPITRE 3

Spotlight on Culture

Photograph These phone booths are near the Forum des Halles in the 1st arrondissement of Paris.

Painting Maurice de Vlaminck (1876–1958) was a French painter, engraver, and writer. In his early years he was both a bicycle racer and an accomplished violinist. He started to paint for fun. In 1907, he met Henri Matisse. He was much impressed by the works of both Matisse and Van Gogh. He painted landscapes, urban sites, and scenes of streets.

Learning from Photos
(pages 64–65)
- **Recycling:** Have students say as much as they can about the clothing the people are wearing in the photo.
- After presenting **Mots 2** vocabulary, have students identify the following people in the photo on pages 64–65:
  1. Il fait un appel d'une cabine téléphonique.
  2. Il se sert de son portable.
  3. Ils font la queue devant une cabine téléphonique.

National Standards

Communities
Have students prepare a pamphlet in French for French-speaking visitors to the United States that explains how to make calls from a public telephone. Send it to your local Chamber of Commerce or the nearest foreign exchange student organization.

Vocabulaire Mots 1

1 Preparation

Resource Manager

Vocabulary Transparencies 3.2–3.3
Audio Activities TE, pages 23–25
Audio CD 3
Workbook, pages 21–22
Quiz 1, page 13
ExamView® Pro

Bellringer Review

Use BRR Transparency 3.1 or write the following on the board. Write five sentences about what you did last weekend. Be sure to use the passé composé.

2 Presentation

Step 1 Have students close their books. Introduce the **Mots 1** vocabulary using Vocabulary Transparencies 3.2–3.3. Have students repeat each word after you or the recording on Audio CD 3 two or three times as you point to the appropriate illustration on the transparencies.

Step 2 When presenting the sentences, intersperse questions to enable students to use the new words immediately. Build from simple to more complex questions.

Teaching Tip
When introducing material, proceed from the easiest to the most difficult type of question. Begin with *yes/no* or *either/or* questions. **(C'est un écran?)** Save information questions **(Qu'est-ce que c'est?)** until students have had a chance to produce or at least hear the new vocabulary several times.

Vocabulaire Mots 1

L'ordinateur

La jeune fille allume l'ordinateur.
Elle met une disquette dans le lecteur.

Elle utilise l'ordinateur pour faire ses devoirs.
Elle tape son texte (ses données).

Elle ne perd pas son texte.
Elle le sauvegarde.

Elle retire la disquette.

Chapter Projects

Bonjour! Your students may enjoy sending electronic postcards and greeting cards from french.glencoe.com.

Vocabulaire Mots 1

Ensuite, elle va sur Internet.
Elle clique sur ses messages.
Elle répond à quelques messages.
Elle envoie quelques (e-)mails.

Enfin, elle éteint son ordinateur.

Le télécopieur, le fax 🎧

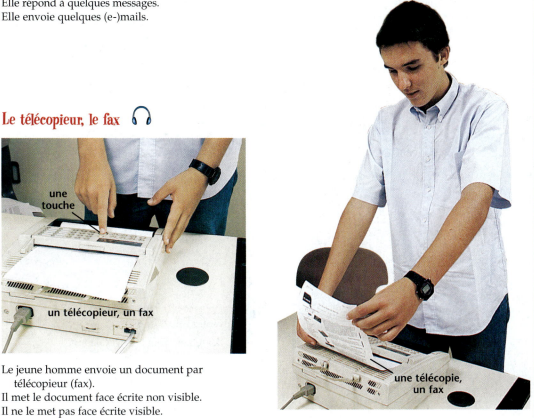

une touche

un télécopieur, un fax

Le jeune homme envoie un document par télécopieur (fax).
Il met le document face écrite non visible.
Il ne le met pas face écrite visible.
Il appuie sur la touche.

une télécopie, un fax

Il transmet (envoie) le document.

LES TÉLÉCOMMUNICATIONS

soixante-sept 67

Step 3 Have students open their books and read the new words and sentences aloud.

Teaching Tips
- If you have a computer in class, you can use it to teach much of this vocabulary.
- When presenting the fax vocabulary on page 67, use a sheet of paper to show **face écrite visible** vs. **face écrite non visible**.

About the French Language

Both **mail** and **e-mail** are used in French, but **mail** is actually more common. ⚜

Learning from Photos

(pages 66–67) All photos for the vocabulary section were taken in Brunoy, France.

Teacher note: We have varied the **tu** and **vous** forms with the TPR activities so students hear both forms. If you prefer to use **tu** with an individual student, change the commands in later activities to **tu**.

LEVELING
A: Vocabulary

Reaching All Students

Total Physical Response
(Student 1), lève-toi et viens ici, s'il te plaît.
On va imaginer que c'est un ordinateur.
Allume l'ordinateur.
Mets une disquette.

Tape ton texte.
Retire la disquette.
Éteins l'ordinateur.

(Student 2), lève-toi et viens ici, s'il te plaît.
Tu vas envoyer un fax.

Mets le document dans le télécopieur.
Tu l'as mis face écrite visible.
Retire le document.
Remets le document face écrite non visible.
Appuie sur la touche pour envoyer le document.

67

Vocabulaire

3 Practice

Quel est le mot?

Attention!

When students are doing the **Quel est le mot?** activities, accept any answer that makes sense. The purpose of these activities is to have students use the new vocabulary. They are not factual recall activities.

1 Go over this activity orally in class with books closed. Then have students write the answers for homework and go over the activity once again the following day.

2 Students can do this activity on their own and then read their answers.

3 This activity can also be done as a paired activity. One student asks the question and another responds.

Vocabulaire

Quel est le mot?

1 **L'ordinateur** Donnez des réponses personnelles.

1. Tu as un ordinateur chez toi ou tu utilises un ordinateur à l'école?
2. Tu utilises un ordinateur pour faire tes devoirs?
3. Tu as un dictionnaire ou une encyclopédie sur CD-ROM?
4. Quand tu tapes ton texte, tu regardes l'écran ou le clavier?
5. Quand tu commences à travailler, tu allumes ou tu éteins l'ordinateur?
6. Tu mets ta disquette où?
7. Tu vas quelquefois sur Internet?
8. Tu envoies des e-mails à tes amis?
9. Tu retires la disquette quand tu as fini tes devoirs?
10. Tu as une imprimante? Tu imprimes tes devoirs?

2 **Les instructions à suivre** Mettez les phrases suivantes en ordre.

1. On met une disquette dans le lecteur.
2. On tape les données.
3. On allume l'ordinateur.
4. On retire la disquette.
5. On éteint l'ordinateur.
6. On sauvegarde les données.
7. On clique sur l'icône du logiciel avec la souris.

3 **Historiette** **Au bureau**
Inventez une histoire.

1. La femme veut envoyer un fax?
2. Elle utilise un ordinateur ou un télécopieur?
3. Le télécopieur est allumé?
4. La femme met le document face écrite visible ou non visible?
5. Elle appuie sur quoi?
6. Qu'est-ce qu'elle fait de son document?

68 ✦ soixante-huit   CHAPITRE 3

ANSWERS TO Quel est le mot?

1 *Answers will vary but may include:*

1. Oui, j'ai un ordinateur chez moi et j'utilise un ordinateur à l'école.
2. Oui, j'utilise un ordinateur pour faire mes devoirs.
3. Oui, j'ai une encyclopédie sur CD-ROM.
4. Quand je tape mon texte, je regarde l'écran.
5. Quand je commence à travailler, j'allume l'ordinateur.
6. Je mets ma disquette dans le lecteur.
7. Oui, je vais quelquefois sur Internet.
8. Oui, j'envoie des (e-)mails à mes amis.
9. Oui, je retire la disquette quand j'ai fini mes devoirs.
10. Oui, j'ai une imprimante. J'imprime mes devoirs.

2 *Answers may vary slightly in order:*

1. On allume l'ordinateur.
2. On met une disquette dans le lecteur.
3. On clique sur l'icône du logiciel avec la souris.
4. On tape les données.
5. On sauvegarde les données.
6. On retire la disquette.
7. On éteint l'ordinateur.

3 *Answers will vary but may include:*

1. Oui, la femme veut envoyer un fax.
2. Elle utilise un télécopieur.
3. Oui, le télécopieur est allumé.
4. La femme met le document face écrite non visible.
5. Elle appuie sur la touche.
6. Elle transmet le document.

4 Comment utiliser un ordinateur Un(e) élève du Québec passe un an dans votre école. Il/Elle veut savoir comment utiliser votre ordinateur. Vous lui expliquez ce qu'il faut faire.

5 Comment envoyer un fax Vous travaillez quelques heures par semaine dans un bureau. Un copain y travaille aussi. Pour travailler votre français, vous discutez en français de tout ce qu'il faut faire pour envoyer un fax (une télécopie).

Un cours d'informatique

6 Logiciels Avec un copain, parlez de tout ce que vous faites sur votre ordinateur. Vous faites vos devoirs? Vous jouez à des jeux? Vous envoyez des e-mails à vos amis? Quels sont les logiciels que vous utilisez? Ensuite, regardez l'écran à gauche. Décrivez ce que vous voyez sur l'écran.

 *For more practice using words from **Mots 1**, do Activity 9 on page H10 at the end of this book.*

LES TÉLÉCOMMUNICATIONS   soixante-neuf ❖ 69

Vocabulaire

4 You may wish to briefly review **tu** form commands, which were presented in **Bon voyage! Level 1,** Chapter 14, and **Bon voyage! Level 2,** Chapter 2. Write the **tu** forms of the computer-related verbs on the board: **tu allumes, tu mets, tu tapes, tu retires, tu éteins, tu sauvegardes, tu cliques.** Remind students to drop the **s** from **-er** verbs.

Writing Development
Have students write the answers to Activity 3 in paragraph form.

Cognate Recognition
Have students scan the **Mots 1** words again and then identify and pronounce each cognate.

Reteaching
Show Vocabulary Transparencies 3.2–3.3 and let students say as much as they can about them in their own words.

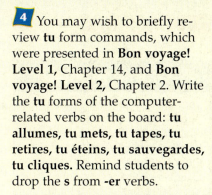 This *Infogap* activity will allow students to practice in pairs. The activity should be very manageable for them, since all vocabulary and structures are familiar to them.

LEVELING
E: Activities 1, 3
A: Activities 2, 4, 5, 6

ANSWERS TO *Quel est le mot?*

 Answers will vary but may include:
Allume l'ordinateur. Puis, mets une disquette dans le lecteur. Clique sur l'icône du logiciel «Word» avec la souris. Tape ton texte et sauvegarde ton texte. Retire la disquette et éteins l'ordinateur.

 Answers will vary but may include:
—Pour envoyer une télécopie il faut allumer le télécopieur.
—Oui, et puis il faut mettre le document face écrite non visible dans le télécopieur.
—Puis il faut appuyer sur la touche.
—Et voilà, le fax transmet le document.

 Answers will vary but may include:
—Moi, j'aime beaucoup utiliser mon ordinateur. Je fais tous mes devoirs sur mon ordinateur.
—Moi, je préfère jouer à des jeux. J'ai beaucoup de jeux sur CD-ROM.
—J'envoie aussi des mails à mes amis qui habitent loin d'ici.
—Oui, j'adore répondre à mes mails.
—J'utilise beaucoup de logiciels différents.
—À gauche sur l'écran je vois un mail. Un copain de Benjamin lui écrit une lettre. Je vois des icônes.

69

Vocabulaire Mots 2

1 Preparation

Resource Manager

Vocabulary Transparencies 3.4–3.5
Audio Activities TE, pages 25–27
Audio CD 3
Workbook, pages 23–24
Quiz 2, page 14
ExamView® Pro

Bellringer Review

Use BRR Transparency 3.2 or write the following on the board.
Answer the following.
1. Tu aimes téléphoner à tes amis?
2. Tu parles beaucoup au téléphone?
3. Tu as un ordinateur dans ta chambre à coucher?
4. Tu préfères parler au téléphone ou envoyer des mails?

2 Presentation

Step 1 Show Vocabulary Transparencies 3.4–3.5. Have students close their books and repeat the words after you or Audio CD 3 as you point to the appropriate illustration on the transparency.

Step 2 If possible, use props such as a telephone, a telephone book, coins, a telephone card, etc., to help teach the new vocabulary.

Step 3 Ask *yes/no* or *either/or* questions to elicit the new vocabulary. For example: **Je décroche ou je raccroche? C'est un annuaire ou une télécarte?**

Point out to students that they must dial 33 when making a call to France. This is the country code for France.

70

Vocabulaire Mots 2

Le téléphone

un annuaire

une cabine téléphonique

faire un appel (téléphonique), donner un coup de fil

une télécarte

mettre la télécarte dans la fente

un portable

une pièce de monnaie

un téléphone (à touches)

décrocher   attendre la tonalité

un répondeur automatique

un numéro de téléphone

composer (faire)   raccrocher
le numéro

l'indicatif régional
(33) 01 44 20 60 98
l'indicatif du pays (France)
le bon numéro
01 44 20 60 98
01 44 60 60 18
le mauvais numéro, une erreur

70 ❖ *soixante-dix*

Reaching All Students

Total Physical Response You may wish to bring in a play telephone and a phone book to use as props.
(Student 1), **venez ici, s'il vous plaît.**
Prenez l'annuaire.
Ouvrez l'annuaire.
Regardez dedans.
Cherchez un numéro.
Allez au téléphone.
Ouvrez la porte de la cabine téléphonique. Entrez.
Mettez votre télécarte dans la fente.
Décrochez. Attendez la tonalité.
Faites le numéro que vous voulez.
Parlez. Raccrochez.
Merci, (Student 1). **Retournez à votre place et asseyez-vous.**

Quand Nathalie était petite, elle aimait bien
   parler au téléphone.
Elle se servait souvent du téléphone.
Elle voulait toujours téléphoner à son grand-père.
Mais elle ne savait pas faire le numéro.
Alors son père l'aidait à faire le numéro.

LES TÉLÉCOMMUNICATIONS

Vocabulaire

3 Practice

Quel est le mot?

7 Have students work in pairs. Then call on pairs to present a portion of the activity to the class.

Learning from Photos
(page 72 top and page 73) Have students imagine the telephone conversations the people in the photos are having.

Assessment
As an informal assessment, you may wish to have individuals give simple instructions in their own words for making a telephone call, using the computer, and sending a fax.

Vocabulaire

Quel est le mot?

7 **Des coups de fil**
Donnez des réponses personnelles.

1. Tu téléphones souvent?
2. Tu te sers d'un portable?
3. De temps en temps, tu téléphones d'une cabine téléphonique?
4. Tu donnes des coups de fil à qui?
5. Quel est ton numéro de téléphone?
6. Quel est ton indicatif régional?
7. Tu fais un mauvais numéro de temps en temps?
8. Tu vérifies un numéro de téléphone dans quoi?
9. Si tu téléphones à quelqu'un qui habite dans un autre pays, qu'est-ce que tu dois savoir?
10. Tu as un répondeur automatique?
11. Quand il n'y a pas de réponse, tu laisses un message sur le répondeur automatique?

8 **Comment faire un appel téléphonique**
Mettez les phrases suivantes en ordre.

1. À la fin de la conversation, on raccroche le téléphone.
2. On compose le numéro.
3. On commence à parler.
4. Si c'est un téléphone public, on met la télécarte dans la fente.
5. On attend la tonalité.
6. La personne à qui on téléphone répond.
7. On décroche le téléphone.

Answers to Quel est le mot?

7 Answers will vary but may include:
1. Oui, je téléphone souvent.
2. Oui, je me sers d'un portable.
3. Oui, de temps en temps je téléphone d'une cabine téléphonique.
4. Je donne des coups de fil à mon copain Jacques.
5. Mon numéro de téléphone est le _____.
6. Mon indicatif régional est le _____.
7. Oui, je fais un mauvais numéro de temps en temps.
8. Je vérifie un numéro de téléphone dans l'annuaire.
9. Si je téléphone à quelqu'un qui habite dans un autre pays, je dois savoir l'indicatif du pays.
10. Oui, j'ai un répondeur automatique.
11. Oui, quand il n'y a pas de réponse, je laisse un message sur le répondeur automatique.

8
1. On décroche le téléphone.
2. Si c'est un téléphone public, on met la télécarte dans la fente.
3. On attend la tonalité.
4. On compose le numéro.
5. La personne à qui on téléphone répond.
6. On commence à parler.
7. À la fin de la conversation, on raccroche le téléphone.

Vocabulaire

9 Conversations téléphoniques Choisissez la réponse la plus logique.

1. Allô?
   a. Allô, oui!
   b. C'est de la part de qui?
   c. Il est là?
2. Je voudrais parler à Monsieur Delacroix, s'il vous plaît.
   a. Zut! Ça sonne occupé.
   b. Je suis désolé, il n'est pas là.
   c. Raccrochez, s'il vous plaît.
3. Monsieur Caron est là, s'il vous plaît?
   a. Oui, de la part de qui, s'il vous plaît?
   b. Oui, raccrochez, s'il vous plaît.
   c. Oui, composez le numéro.
4. C'est de la part de qui, s'il vous plaît?
   a. Il est parti.
   b. Ça sonne occupé.
   c. De Bernard Gaye.
5. Madame Burth, s'il vous plaît.
   a. Un instant, ne quittez pas.
   b. C'est occupé.
   c. De son mari.
6. Allô, Marc?
   a. Je regrette, mais c'est une erreur.
   b. Je voudrais parler à Marc.
   c. Ça sonne occupé.
7. Vous avez fait un mauvais numéro, monsieur.
   a. Je peux laisser un message?
   b. Oh, excusez-moi, madame.
   c. C'est de la part de qui?

10 Comment faire? Vous êtes dans la rue, dans une ville américaine. Vous voyez un(e) touriste français(e)—votre camarade de classe—qui essaie de faire un appel téléphonique dans une cabine.

- Le/La touriste vous demande comment faire pour téléphoner.
- Vous lui dites ce qu'il faut faire: s'il faut mettre une carte téléphonique ou des pièces de monnaie.
- Vous lui demandez de répéter les instructions pour être sûr(e) qu'il/elle a bien compris.

11 On sort ensemble? Vous êtes en France et vous avez rencontré un garçon ou une fille avec qui vous voulez sortir. Vous lui téléphonez pour voir s'il/si elle est libre. Avec un(e) autre élève, préparez votre conversation téléphonique.

LES TÉLÉCOMMUNICATIONS   soixante-treize ❖ 73

Structure

1 Preparation

Resource Manager
Audio Activities TE, pages 28–29
Audio CD 3
Workbook, pages 25–28
Quizzes 3–4, pages 15–16
ExamView® Pro

2 Presentation

 L'imparfait

Step 1 Read Items 1–2 to the students.

Step 2 In Item 2, write the infinitives on the board. Beneath them, write the **nous** form. Then cross out the **-ons** ending, leaving just the stem.

Step 3 Now pronounce the **je, tu, il/elle, ils/elles** forms of the verb.

Step 4 Write these four forms on the board in paradigm order, leaving space for the **nous** and **vous** forms. Indicate that the pronunciation remains the same even though the spelling changes.

Step 5 Now add the **nous** and **vous** forms.

Step 6 Alongside the paradigms, write the endings. Have students repeat all the forms after you.

Step 7 When going over Item 3, have students quickly repeat the **nous** forms in the present.

Structure

 L'imparfait
Narrating in the past

1. In French, several tenses are used to express past actions. You have already learned the **passé composé**. The **passé composé** is used to express actions that started and ended at a specific time in the past. You are now going to learn the imperfect tense.

2. First, let's look at how the imperfect tense is formed. To get the stem for the imperfect, you drop the **-ons** ending from the **nous** form of the present tense. You add the imperfect endings to this stem. Study the following.

	PARLER	FINIR	ATTENDRE
Present	nous parlons	nous finissons	nous attendons
Stem	parl-	finiss-	attend-
	je parlais	je finissais	j' attendais
	tu parlais	tu finissais	tu attendais
	il/elle/on parlait	il/elle/on finissait	il/elle/on attendait
	nous parlions	nous finissions	nous attendions
	vous parliez	vous finissiez	vous attendiez
	ils/elles parlaient	ils/elles finissaient	ils/elles attendaient

Note that the **je, tu, il,** and **ils** forms of the imperfect are pronounced the same way. They are, however, spelled differently.

3. The imperfect of all verbs, except for the verb **être**, is formed the same way.

AVOIR	nous avons	→	j'avais
COMMENCER	nous commençons	→	je commençais
FAIRE	nous faisons	→	je faisais
MANGER	nous mangeons	→	je mangeais
CROIRE	nous croyons	→	je croyais

4. Note the forms of **être**.

j'étais	nous étions
tu étais	vous étiez
il était	ils étaient

Les jeunes filles parlent avec leurs mains.

LEVELING
E: Activities 12, 13

5. In French, you use the imperfect to describe or reminisce about habitual or continuous actions. You also use the imperfect to describe emotional and physical conditions or states in the past. The time at which these actions or states began or ended is not important.

>Quand j'**étais** au collège, j'**avais** un très bon professeur de français. Elle s'**appelait** Madame Castex. Elle **était** un peu stricte, mais nous l'**aimions** beaucoup. Elle nous **racontait** toujours des histoires intéressantes et nous l'**écoutions** pendant des heures avec beaucoup d'attention.

Comment dit-on?

12 **Tu parles français?** Répétez la conversation.

Nina, tu parlais français quand tu étais petite, non?

Pas vraiment. On parlait anglais à la maison. Mes grands-parents parlaient français, mais ils habitaient à Québec.

Alors, tu parlais français quand tu allais les voir.

Bien sûr, parce que, eux, ils ne savaient pas un mot d'anglais.

13 **Le français ou l'anglais?** Répondez d'après la conversation.
1. On parlait anglais ou français chez Nina?
2. Qui parlait français dans sa famille?
3. Où habitaient ses grands-parents?
4. Quand est-ce que Nina parlait français?
5. Pourquoi est-ce qu'elle ne pouvait pas parler anglais avec ses grands-parents?

LES TÉLÉCOMMUNICATIONS

soixante-quinze 75

Structure

Step 8 When going over Item 4, explain to students that it is very important for them to learn these forms of the verb **être**, since they will use this verb frequently.

Step 9 Have students read aloud the paragraph in Item 5. Then give the person a name and ask questions such as: **Quand Henri était au collège, il avait un bon ou mauvais professeur de français? Elle s'appelait comment?**

Then ask: Why is this entire paragraph in the imperfect? Have students choose from the following:
a. It tells what Henri did one day when he was in school.
b. It reminisces about and describes Henri's days in school.

Have students repeat the model sentences in Item 5 after you.

Teaching Tip
It is strongly recommended that you not give the students the English equivalents for the imperfect tense. We want students to grasp the concept that the imperfect is used to express an ongoing, continuing action. Its beginning and end points are unimportant. When students hear that "used to" is an English equivalent of the imperfect, it confuses them and interferes with the concept because "used to" implies "but no longer," suggesting an end at a given point in time.

3 Practice

Comment dit-on?

12 Have students repeat the conversation after you. Then call on a pair of students to read it.

13 Note that this activity deals only with the third person forms.

ANSWERS TO Comment dit-on?

12 *Students will repeat the conversation.*

13
1. On parlait anglais chez Nina.
2. Les grands-parents de Nina parlaient français.
3. Ses grands-parents habitaient à Québec.
4. Nina parlait français quand elle allait voir ses grands-parents.
5. Elle ne pouvait pas parler anglais avec ses grands-parents parce qu'ils ne savaient pas un mot d'anglais.

About the French Language

The province of Quebec in French always uses the article with it: **le Québec**. The city of **Québec**, however, does not require an article. Compare: **Je vais au Québec** and **Je vais à Québec**. The first sentence refers to the province, the second to the city. Ask students which they think Nina is talking about in Activity 12.

Structure

3 Practice (continued)

14 This activity can be done with books closed, open, or once each way. It contrasts the **tu/je** forms and reincorporates the third person forms.

15 After completing this activity, call on one student to do the entire activity and retell the story in his or her own words.
Note: Activity 15 reintroduces the pronouns **le** and **lui**.

Writing Development
Have students write out Activities 14–15 in paragraph form.

Learning from Photos
(page 76) Saint-Malo is a very picturesque Breton town. It stands on a peninsula and is surrounded by ramparts that date from the thirteenth century. The old city of Saint-Malo was severely bombed during the Allied siege in August of 1944, but it has been carefully restored.

Structure

14 Historiette Quand j'étais petit(e)
Donnez des réponses personnelles.
1. Quand tu étais petit(e), tu téléphonais souvent à tes grands-parents?
2. Tu leur écrivais de temps en temps?
3. Tu les voyais souvent?
4. Tu leur achetais de petits cadeaux?
5. Qui choisissait les cadeaux pour ta grand-mère?
6. Qui choisissait les cadeaux pour ton grand-père? C'était toi, ton frère ou ta sœur?
7. Tes grands-parents t'invitaient souvent chez eux?

15 Historiette Gilles adorait sa grand-mère. Complétez.

Quand Gilles __1__ (être) petit, il __2__ (habiter) à Paris. Sa grand-mère __3__ (habiter) à Saint-Malo en Bretagne. Gilles __4__ (adorer) sa grand-mère et sa grand-mère l' __5__ (adorer) aussi. Il __6__ (aimer) téléphoner à sa grand-mère. Il lui __7__ (téléphoner) presque toujours de la maison. Mais quand il __8__ (vouloir) lui dire un secret, il l' __9__ (appeler) d'une cabine téléphonique. Sa grand-mère __10__ (être) toujours contente quand Gilles lui __11__ (donner) un coup de fil. Quand le téléphone __12__ (sonner), elle __13__ (entendre) la sonnerie et elle __14__ (répondre) tout de suite.

Saint-Malo en Bretagne

Answers to Comment dit-on?

14 Answers will vary but may include:
1. Quand j'étais petit(e), je téléphonais souvent à mes grands-parents.
2. Je leur écrivais de temps en temps.
3. Je les voyais souvent.
4. Je leur achetais de petits cadeaux.
5. Je choisissais les cadeaux pour ma grand-mère.
6. Mon frère choisissait les cadeaux pour mon grand-père.
7. Oui, mes grands-parents m'invitaient souvent chez eux.

15
1. était
2. habitait
3. habitait
4. adorait
5. adorait
6. aimait
7. téléphonait
8. voulait
9. appelait
10. était
11. donnait
12. sonnait
13. entendait
14. répondait

16 **On va parler au prof.** Posez des questions à votre professeur d'après le modèle.

aller à quelle école →
Quand vous étiez jeune, vous alliez à quelle école?

1. parler quelle langue
2. aimer vos cours
3. faire du français
4. recevoir de bonnes notes
5. lire beaucoup
6. écrire beaucoup
7. avoir beaucoup d'amis
8. sortir beaucoup
9. aller souvent au cinéma
10. s'amuser

17 **Les loisirs** Donnez des réponses personnelles.

1. Quand tu étais petit(e), où est-ce que tu allais en vacances? À la mer, à la montagne, chez tes grands-parents, ou est-ce que tu restais chez toi?
2. En hiver, qu'est-ce que tu faisais comme sport(s)? Du ski? Du hockey? Du patin à glace?
3. En été, tu faisais de la natation? Du ski nautique? De la planche à voile?
4. Tu aimais mieux les sports d'hiver ou les sports d'été?
5. Tu prenais quelquefois le train ou l'avion? Pour aller où?
6. Ta famille et toi, qu'est-ce que vous faisiez ensemble?
7. Vous vous amusiez bien?

Tu jouais dans la neige quand tu étais petit(e)?

Structure

1 Preparation

Bellringer Review

Use BRR Transparency 3.3 or write the following on the board.
Rewrite in the **passé composé**.
1. Je descends mes bagages.
2. Tous les voyageurs descendent du train.
3. Elle sort avec ses amis.
4. Il monte au deuxième étage.
5. Il ne prend pas l'ascenseur.

2 Presentation

Les emplois de l'imparfait

Step 1 Emphasize the fact that the imperfect is used for description in the past. Read the sentences for Item 2 as if they were part of an ongoing story in the past.

Learning from Photos

(page 78) The young man in this photo is from Cameroon.

The **Glencoe World Languages Web site (french.glencoe.com)** offers options that enable you and your students to experience the French-speaking world via the Internet. For each chapter, there are activities, games, and quizzes. In addition, an *Enrichment* section offers students an opportunity to visit Web sites related to the theme of the chapter.

Structure

Les emplois de l'imparfait
Describing things in the past

1. As you have already learned, the imperfect is used to describe continuous, repeated, or habitual actions in the past.

   Quand Germain **était** enfant, il **se couchait** toujours de bonne heure et il **se levait** très tôt pour aller à l'école.

2. You also use the imperfect to describe persons, things, places, situations, and physical and emotional conditions or states in the past.

location	Il **habitait** à Paris.
age	Il **avait** dix ans.
appearance	Il **était** très grand pour son âge.
physical condition	Il **était** en bonne santé.
attitude, emotions, and desires	Il **voulait** toujours faire du sport.
time	C'**était** le mois de décembre.
weather	Il **faisait** froid.

3. Verbs that describe mental or emotional states are often used in the imperfect. The following are some of the most common.

   aimer (mieux) = **préférer**
   vouloir
   pouvoir
   savoir
   croire

Germain fait toujours du sport!

78 soixante-dix-huit

LEVELING
A: Activity 18
C: Activity 18

Comment dit-on?

18 **Historiette** Un petit garçon bien triste
Complétez à l'imparfait.

Quel âge __1__ (avoir) le petit garçon? Il __2__ (être) très jeune. Il n'avait pas quatre ans. Il __3__ (habiter) tout près de Paris. Sa famille __4__ (avoir) une maison en banlieue. Mais le petit garçon __5__ (être) souvent triste. Il __6__ (vouloir) apprendre à lire, mais il ne __7__ (pouvoir) pas. Pourquoi? Il n' __8__ (être) pas intelligent? Au contraire, il __9__ (être) très intelligent. Mais il ne __10__ (pouvoir) pas lire parce qu'il ne __11__ (pouvoir) pas voir: il __12__ (être) aveugle. Et il __13__ (avoir) très envie d'apprendre à lire comme les autres enfants de son âge.

Plus tard, quand il __14__ (avoir) vingt ans, il __15__ (avoir) une idée fixe: il __16__ (être) professeur à l'institut des aveugles et il __17__ (vouloir) inventer un système d'écriture (un alphabet) pour ses élèves. Il __18__ (travailler) nuit et jour pour développer et perfectionner son alphabet.

Tous ses collègues __19__ (croire) qu'il __20__ (essayer) de faire quelque chose d'impossible. Mais le jeune homme ne les __21__ (écouter) pas. Il __22__ (continuer) son travail. Mais qui __23__ (être) donc ce jeune homme? Vous voulez le savoir? Eh bien, il __24__ (s'appeler) Louis Braille. C'est lui qui a créé le système d'écriture pour les aveugles. Ce système porte son nom: le système Braille. Vous ne __25__ (savoir) pas que l'inventeur du système Braille __26__ (être) un jeune Français?

Monument à Louis Braille à Coupvray

Un livre pour apprendre le braille

LES TÉLÉCOMMUNICATIONS

soixante-dix-neuf 79

Structure

3 Practice

Comment dit-on?

18 Have students close their books. Read the story to them, filling in the correct verb forms yourself as you go along. When you get to **Mais qui était donc ce jeune homme?**, ask if anyone knows who the story is about.

Then call on students to read and fill in the verb forms. Have each individual do two or three sentences until the activity is completed.

Call on a student to retell the life of Braille in his or her own words.

Note: The word **aveugle** in Activity 18 is new. Students should be able to guess the meaning because of what precedes the word in the text: **Mais il ne pouvait pas lire parce qu'il ne pouvait pas voir: il était aveugle.**

Reaching All Students

Additional Practice Have students retell orally as much as they can about Louis Braille.

History Connection

You may wish to have students get some more information about Louis Braille.

ANSWERS TO Comment dit-on?

18

1. avait
2. était
3. habitait
4. avait
5. était
6. voulait
7. pouvait
8. était
9. était
10. pouvait
11. pouvait
12. était
13. avait
14. avait
15. avait
16. était
17. voulait
18. travaillait
19. croyaient
20. essayait
21. écoutait
22. continuait
23. était
24. s'appelait
25. saviez
26. était

Structure

3 Practice (continued)

Comment dit-on?

20 Expansion: After students have made their own list of activities, have them use their list to interview several other classmates. Have them report back what they have found out about their respective childhood abilities. Example: **Moi, je ne savais pas nager, mais maintenant, je sais nager. Monique savait nager quand elle était jeune, mais Julie et Roger ne savaient pas nager.**

Attention!

This spelling change from **y** to **i** is very common, but it is not obligatory.

Reaching All Students

For the Younger Students Have students bring in vacation photos to elicit descriptions of the weather, places, times, or things using the imperfect.

LEVELING
E: Activities 19, 20, 21, 22
A: Activities 21, 22

Structure

19 **Historiette** Le beau jeune homme
Racontez une histoire d'après le dessin.
1. Il était quelle heure?
2. Il faisait quel temps?
3. Où était le jeune homme?
4. Il était comment?
5. Il pensait à qui?
6. Elle s'appelait comment?
7. Elle avait quel âge?
8. C'était sa petite amie?

20 Ce que je ne savais pas faire
Dites des choses que vous ne saviez pas faire quand vous étiez petit(e), mais que vous savez faire maintenant.

Attention!

Note the spelling of the verbs **appuyer**, **envoyer**, and **payer**.

j'appuie	j'envoie	je paie
tu appuies	tu envoies	tu paies
il appuie	il envoie	il paie
nous appuyons	nous envoyons	nous payons
vous appuyez	vous envoyez	vous payez
ils appuient	ils envoient	ils paient

Complétez.
1. J'____ sur la touche. J'____ mon fax et je ____. (appuyer, envoyer, payer)
2. Si vous ____ un fax, vous ____ sur cette touche. (envoyer, appuyer)

80 quatre-vingts   CHAPITRE 3

ANSWERS TO Comment dit-on?

19 Answers will vary but may include:
1. Il était midi.
2. Il pleuvait.
3. Le jeune homme était dans sa chambre à coucher.
4. Il était brun et grand.
5. Il pensait à sa copine.
6. Elle s'appelait Monique.
7. Elle avait seize ans.
8. Oui, c'était sa petite amie.

20 Answers will vary but may include:
Quand j'étais petit(e), je ne savais pas taper. Je ne savais pas utiliser l'ordinateur. Maintenant, je sais taper. J'utilise un ordinateur tous les jours.

ANSWERS TO  Attention!

1. appuie, envoie, paie
2. envoyez, appuyez

Structure

21 **Je ne voulais pas.** Travaillez avec un copain ou une copine. Dites tout ce que vous aimiez manger (et ce que vous ne vouliez pas manger) quand vous étiez petit(e). Décidez si vous aviez des goûts en commun.

22 **Qu'est-ce que tu aimais faire?** Demandez à un copain ou à une copine ce qu'il/elle aimait faire quand il/elle était enfant.

Tu allais souvent au parc quand tu étais petit(e)?

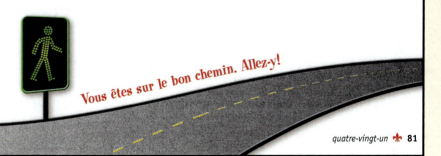

Vous êtes sur le bon chemin. Allez-y!

Structure

22 **Expansion:** Have students ask you the same questions to practice the **vous** form.

Learning from Photos
(page 81) These young children are in the Luxembourg gardens in Paris.

FOLDABLES **Dinah Zike's Study Guides**

Your students may wish to use Foldable 6 to organize, display, and arrange data as they develop communication skills in French. You may wish to encourage them to add information from each chapter as they continue to expand their ability to describe, explain, and discuss all the different topics they are studying.

A *miniature matchbook* foldable is ideal in helping students give more complex descriptions about topics they have studied in French.

 Allez-y!
At this point in the chapter, students have learned all the vocabulary and structure necessary to complete the chapter. The conversation and cultural readings that follow recycle all the material learned up to this point.

Answers to Comment dit-on?

21 *Answers will vary.*
Students will use the imperfect tense and foods they have learned to identify in French.

22 *Answers will vary but may include:*
—Qu'est-ce que tu aimais faire quand tu étais petit(e)?
—Moi, j'aimais jouer dans le jardin. J'aimais jouer avec mes amis. J'aimais aussi aller au parc.

Conversation

1 Preparation

Resource Manager
Audio Activities TE, pages 29–30
Audio CD 3
CD-ROM

Bellringer Review

Use BRR Transparency 3.4 or write the following on the board:
Change the verbs in the following sentences to the **imparfait**.
1. J'ai quinze ans.
2. Je vais au lycée tous les jours.
3. Je fais du ski en hiver.
4. Mon ami Marc fait du ski avec moi.

2 Presentation

Step 1 Have students close their books. Have them listen as you read the conversation aloud or play Audio CD 3.

Step 2 Have students read along as you model the conversation a second time.

Step 3 Allow time for pairs of students to practice the conversation. Then call on one or two pairs to read it to the class in as realistic a manner as possible.

Step 4 After several pairs of students have presented the conversation, ask the comprehension questions. Then you may have a more able student retell the conversation in narrative form in his or her own words.

Conversation

Des devoirs difficiles

Hugo: Tu comprends quelque chose, toi?
Joël: Rien du tout.
Hugo: À qui on téléphone?
Joël: À Marie. Elle est bonne en maths.
Hugo: C'est quoi, son numéro?
Joël: C'est le 03 44 51 60 84.
Hugo: Dis donc, tu le sais par cœur. Tu lui téléphones souvent?
Joël: Euh… de temps en temps.

Vous avez compris?

Répondez.

1. Que font les deux garçons?
2. Ils sont forts en maths?
3. Ils vont téléphoner à qui?
4. Pourquoi est-ce qu'ils vont lui téléphoner?
5. Quel est son numéro de téléphone?
6. Qui savait le numéro de Marie par cœur?
7. D'après vous, pourquoi est-ce qu'il téléphone à Marie assez souvent?

Answers to Vous avez compris?

1. Ils font leurs devoirs de maths.
2. Non, ils ne sont pas forts en maths.
3. Ils vont téléphoner à Marie.
4. Ils vont lui téléphoner parce qu'elle est forte en maths.
5. Son numéro de téléphone est le 03 44 51 60 84.
6. Joël savait son numéro par cœur.
7. Il téléphone à Marie assez souvent parce qu'il l'aime. (C'est sa petite amie/sa copine, etc.)

Glencoe Technology

CD-ROM
On the CD-ROM, students can watch a dramatization of this conversation. They can then play the role of either one of the characters and record themselves in the conversation.

Parlons un peu plus

A **Le répondeur** Vous voulez inviter un(e) ami(e) chez vous, mais quand vous lui téléphonez, c'est son répondeur automatique (votre camarade) qui vous répond. Laissez un message. Votre camarade va écrire votre message, puis il/elle va vous relire votre message.

- Laissez votre nom.
- Donnez la date et l'heure.
- Dites pourquoi vous téléphonez.
- Donnez votre numéro de téléphone.

B **La jeunesse de mes grands-parents** Dites tout ce que vous savez de la vie de vos grands-parents quand ils étaient jeunes—comment ils étaient, où ils habitaient, ce qu'ils faisaient, etc. Ensuite, votre camarade va vous parler de ses grands-parents.

C **Les renseignements** Vous n'avez pas d'annuaire et vous voulez savoir le numéro de téléphone de plusieurs personnes. Vous téléphonez au 12, le service des renseignements. Votre camarade vous répond.

—Les renseignements, bonjour.
—Bonjour (madame/monsieur). Je voudrais le numéro de téléphone de Monsieur Dab, 13 rue Quentin.
—Vous pouvez épeler le nom, s'il vous plaît?
—D comme Denise, A comme Adèle, B comme Béatrice.
—C'est le 01 24 35 57 86.

Pour vous aider, voici la liste officielle des noms à utiliser:

A comme Adèle	N comme Noémie
B comme Béatrice	O comme Odette
C comme Caroline	P comme Pierre
D comme Denise	Q comme Quentin
E comme Eugène	R comme Robert
F comme François	S comme Simone
G comme Georges	T comme Thomas
H comme Hector	U comme Ursule
I comme Isidore	V comme Victor
J comme Jacques	W comme William
K comme Karl	X comme Xavier
L comme Léon	Y comme Yves
M comme Marie	Z comme Zoé

LES TÉLÉCOMMUNICATIONS

quatre-vingt-trois ❖ 83

Lectures culturelles

Resource Manager
Audio Activities TE, pages 30–31
Audio CD 3

Bellringer Review
Use BRR Transparency 3.5 or write the following on the board.
List five things you always did when you were five years old.

National Standards
Cultures
The reading about the telephone on pages 84–85 and the related activity on page 85 familiarize students with the French telephone system, both now and in the past.

Presentation

Pre-reading
Step 1 Give students a brief oral summary (in French) of the reading.

Step 2 Read and discuss the Reading Strategy on page 84.

Step 3 Have students skim the reading quickly and silently.

Reading
Step 1 Call on an individual to read two or three sentences.

Step 2 Ask questions about the sentences just read and call on volunteers to answer them.

Step 3 Continue in this way until the entire selection has been read and discussed.

TEKS Correlations
01.B.02. demonstrate understanding of simple clearly written language such as simple stories, high-frequency commands, and brief instructions when dealing with familiar topics
SE Reading, Activities A–B, pp. 84–85

Lectures culturelles

Reading Strategy

Asking questions
There are several types of questions you can ask about a reading selection. One type is an inference question. An inference question can be answered by logical reasoning from information given in the text. You can also ask questions involving an opinion or thought. Asking any number of these different types of questions will usually aid comprehension.

Le téléphone d'hier et d'aujourd'hui

Bonjour. Je m'appelle Jean Charpentier. Je trouve incroyable comme la vie a changé depuis mon enfance. Quand j'étais petit, je me souviens[1] bien que j'aimais utiliser le téléphone. Ça m'amusait beaucoup. Maman me permettait de téléphoner à ma grand-mère. Je composais le numéro moi-même, mais maman m'aidait un peu. Sinon, je composais de temps en temps le mauvais numéro. Notre téléphone était un téléphone à cadran et souvent, mon petit doigt[2] ratait un numéro.

De temps en temps, je téléphonais à ma grand-mère d'une cabine téléphonique publique. Il n'y avait pas encore de télécarte. On devait avoir beaucoup de pièces parce que ma grand-mère habitait loin.

[1] je me souviens *I remember*
[2] doigt *finger*

Quand Jean était petit, il téléphonait toujours à sa grand-mère.

Un téléphone à cadran

Un téléphone public à pièces

Reaching All Students

Additional Practice
After reading and discussing the **Lecture** and completing the activities, have students summarize in their own words the steps Jean took to place a phone call.

Paired Activity
Have students work in pairs. One student plays the role of a small child. The other plays the grandparent. Have them make up a telephone conversation.

LEVELING
E: Reading

Papa me prenait dans ses bras et me soulevait[3] parce que je n'arrivais pas à mettre les pièces dans la fente. Papa décrochait et me donnait le téléphone. C'était lui qui faisait le numéro.

La vie a bien changé! Moi, je ne suis pas vieux. Je suis étudiant à l'université. Quand je parle des coups de téléphone que je donnais à ma grand-mère, il n'y a pas si longtemps de ça[4]. Aujourd'hui, avoir beaucoup de pièces de monnaie pour faire un appel? Absolument pas! Maintenant, on achète une télécarte pour faire des appels d'une cabine téléphonique. À la maison, notre téléphone n'a pas de cadran. C'est un téléphone à touches. Et on peut mettre en mémoire les numéros qu'on appelle souvent.

Je suis aux Tuileries. J'ai mon portable. Je crois que je vais téléphoner à ma grand-mère. Je l'adorais et je l'adore toujours. «Allô, Mamie? C'est Jean… »

[3] soulevait *lifted*
[4] il n'y a pas si longtemps de ça *it wasn't so long ago*

Un portable

Vous avez compris?

A Quand il était petit… Répondez.
1. Qui parle?
2. Qu'est-ce qu'il aimait utiliser quand il était petit?
3. À qui est-ce qu'il téléphonait souvent?
4. Sa mère l'aidait à composer le numéro? Pourquoi?
5. Qu'est-ce qu'on devait avoir pour téléphoner d'une cabine téléphonique?
6. Le père de Jean le soulevait. Pourquoi?
7. Qu'est-ce que Jean mettait dans la fente?
8. Qu'est-ce que le père de Jean lui donnait quand il décrochait?
9. Comment est-ce que Jean appelle sa grand-mère?

B Qu'en pensez-vous? Répondez.
1. Comment est-ce qu'on sait que Jean aimait sa grand-mère et qu'il l'aime toujours?
2. Comment est-ce que les parents de Jean l'aidaient à être souvent en contact avec sa grand-mère?
3. À votre avis, quels sont les rapports de Jean et de sa grand-mère?

Lecture supplémentaire 1

La télécarte

De nos jours, on n'a pas besoin de monnaie pour faire un appel d'une cabine téléphonique. On achète une télécarte. On demande la quantité d'unités qu'on désire. Avant de composer le numéro, on introduit la télécarte dans la fente. On peut utiliser une télécarte pour faire des appels urbains, interurbains et internationaux.

On peut acheter une télécarte dans un bureau de tabac ou dans un kiosque à journaux.

Un bureau de tabac

Un téléphone public à Tahiti

Vous avez compris?

A **Une comparaison** Expliquez comment on utilisait un téléphone public avant et comment on utilise un téléphone public maintenant.

B **Quel est le mot?** Trouvez l'équivalent en français.
1. local call
2. toll call
3. international call

Lecture supplémentaire 2

Les communications avant et maintenant

Depuis toujours, les hommes essaient de communiquer. Les Romains envoyaient des messagers à pied ou à cheval[1]. Les Indiens utilisaient des signaux de fumée[2]. Les Africains, eux, jouaient du tam-tam. Au dix-neuvième siècle[3], on utilisait le morse—inventé par l'Américain Samuel Morse. Puis c'est le télégraphe et enfin… le téléphone. Au début[4], la qualité des communications n'était pas très bonne, mais avec l'invention du microphone, elle s'est beaucoup améliorée[5].

Aujourd'hui, on utilise encore très souvent le téléphone. Mais de plus en plus, c'est l'ordinateur qu'on utilise pour communiquer. Non seulement on peut envoyer des messages à ses amis sur Internet, mais on peut aussi chercher des renseignements, réserver des places de cinéma ou de théâtre, ou acheter toutes sortes de produits. L'Internet offre des possibilités immenses de communication.

Comment donner une adresse e-mail en français? Voici comment on doit dire l'adresse suivante: veronique.perse@wanadoo.fr = Véronique (point) Perse (arrobase) wanadoo (point) fr. Et vous, vous avez une adresse e-mail?

[1] à cheval *on horseback*
[2] fumée *smoke*
[3] siècle *century*
[4] Au début *In the beginning*
[5] s'est… améliorée *got better*

Vous avez compris?

A Devinez. D'après le contexte, quelle est la signification des mots suivants?
1. des messages de fumée
2. au dix-neuvième siècle
3. le morse

B Votre adresse e-mail Donnez votre adresse e-mail (ou celle de votre école) à votre ami(e) français(e)—votre camarade.

Connexions

National Standards

Connections
This reading about changes in computer technology and the prevalence of English in the field of computer science establishes a connection with another discipline, allowing students to reinforce and further their knowledge of technology through the study of French.

Comparisons
This reading points out how much of the computer vocabulary in French has been derived from English and gives students a better understanding of the interrelatedness of the two languages.

Attention!

The readings in the **Connexions** section are optional. They focus on some of the major disciplines taught in schools and universities. The vocabulary is useful for discussing such topics as history, literature, art, economics, business, science, etc. You may choose any of the following ways to do the readings in the **Connexions** section.

Independent reading Have students read the selections and do the post-reading activities as homework, which you collect. This option is least intrusive on class time and requires a minimum of teacher involvement.

Homework with in-class follow-up Assign the readings and post-reading activities as homework. Review and discuss the material in class the next day.

Intensive in-class activity This option includes a pre-reading vocabulary presentation, in-class reading and discussion, assignment of the activities for homework, and a discussion of the assignment in class the next day.

Connexions

La technologie

L'ordinateur

It's hard to imagine life before the computer. The computer has revolutionized many fields, including travel, medicine, architecture, the military, banking, and commerce. Even agriculture and the arts make extensive use of the new technology. The changes have been tremendous. Because the United States has led the way in computer science, much of the vocabulary used worldwide is in English or derived from English. Let's read about some of these changes in technology and the prevalence of English in this domain.

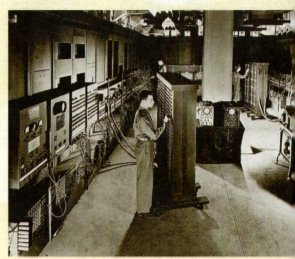

L'ordinateur ENIAC, 1946

Les progrès des télécommunications

Les ordinateurs d'il y a trente ans étaient énormes. Un ancien ordinateur comme le premier ENIAC exécutait moins d'instructions qu'une calculatrice actuelle[1] et occupait toute une salle! Aujourd'hui, il y a des ordinateurs portables qui pèsent moins de deux kilos. Ce qui a facilité le progrès en informatique, c'est la miniaturisation. Une seule micropuce[2] peut emmagasiner[3] des centaines de millions d'informations. Les premiers télécopieurs aussi étaient très grands et les télécopies qu'on recevait étaient souvent illisibles[4].

Marianne Silberfeld travaille pour un ministère du gouvernement français. Le bâtiment[5] est du dix-neuvième siècle, mais les appareils[6]

[1] actuelle *of today* [3] emmagasiner *store* [5] bâtiment *building*
[2] micropuce *microchip* [4] illisibles *illegible* [6] appareils *machines*

Learning from Photos

(page 88) ENIAC stood for *Electronic Numerical Integrator and Computer*. ENIAC, with its thousands of tubes, was the first electronic digital computer.

LEVELING

A: Reading
C: Reading

que Marianne utilise sont modernes. Elle a un ordinateur et un fax. À l'université, Marianne a fait des études d'anglais. Une bonne idée, parce qu'il y a beaucoup de mots anglais en informatique. Par exemple, il faut «cliquer» sur une «icône» pour accéder au «software». Un «virus» peut infecter les programmes. Voici d'autres exemples de la prédominance de l'anglais dans le monde de l'informatique: une disquette, la mémoire, un format, le hardware, un processeur, un bogue, un mail. Vous savez comment on dit tout ça en anglais?

Un ordinateur aujourd'hui

Un portable

Vous avez compris?

A En français Donnez le mot en français.

1. e-mail
2. fax
3. software
4. virus
5. hardware
6. format
7. memory
8. to access
9. to click
10. icon

B Définitions Dites d'une autre façon.

1. un petit ordinateur qu'on peut transporter facilement
2. qu'on ne peut pas lire
3. des machines
4. accumuler, mettre en réserve
5. un télécopieur ou une télécopie

LES TÉLÉCOMMUNICATIONS

C'est à vous

 Recycling

These activities allow students to use the vocabulary and structure from this chapter in completely open-ended, real-life situations.

Presentation

Encourage students to say as much as possible when they do these activities. Tell them not to be afraid of making mistakes since the goal of these activities is real-life communication. If someone in the group makes an error, allow the others to politely correct him or her. Let students choose the activities they would like to do.

You may wish to divide students into pairs or groups. Encourage students to elaborate on the basic theme and to be creative. They may use props, pictures, or posters if they wish.

Writing Development
Have students keep a notebook containing their best written work from each chapter. These selected writings can be based on assignments from the Student Textbook and the Workbook. The three activities on page 91 are examples of writing assignments that may be included in each student's portfolio. In the Workbook, students will develop an organized autobiography (**Mon autobiographie**). These workbook pages may also become a part of their portfolio.

C'est à vous

Use what you have learned

 1 Qu'est-ce qu'on fait?

✔ *Talk about computers, e-mail, the Internet, faxes, and telephones*

Choisissez une photo et décrivez-la à votre camarade.

1.   2.   3.

 2 Les étés de mon enfance

✔ *Talk about past habitual actions*

Demandez à un(e) camarade ce qu'il/elle faisait d'habitude en été quand il/elle était petit(e). Demandez-lui où il/elle allait, avec qui, ce qu'il/elle faisait, etc. Changez ensuite de rôle.

 3 Vos amis et vous

✔ *Talk about today's telecommunications and how you keep in touch with your friends*

Expliquez à un(e) camarade comment vous restez en contact avec vos amis. Dites-lui si vous avez un portable, un répondeur ou une adresse e-mail. Dites-lui aussi si vous téléphonez à vos amis tous les jours ou si vous leur envoyez des e-mails. Ensuite demandez-lui comment il/elle reste en contact avec ses amis.

 4 Le jeu du téléphone

✔ *Describe routine actions*

Divide into teams by row. Using the imperfect, the last person in each row whispers to the person in front of him or her one sentence about what he or she used to do in the past. Each person whispers the sentence to the next person until the message reaches the front of the row. The first person in each row says the sentence to the class. The team whose final sentence most closely resembles the original wins!

quatre-vingt-dix   CHAPITRE 3

Answers to C'est à vous

1 *Answers will vary but may include:*
(photo three) L'homme vérifie un numéro de téléphone dans l'annuaire. Il a un téléphone dans la main. Il veut téléphoner à un restaurant.

2 *Answers will vary but may include:*
—Tu allais où quand tu étais petit(e)?
—J'allais à la plage avec ma famille.
—Qu'est-ce que vous faisiez à la plage?
—Nous prenions des bains de soleil, nous nagions, et nous nous amusions.

3 *Answers will vary but may include:*
Je téléphone souvent à mes amis parce que j'ai un portable. Quand je ne suis pas chez moi, mes amis me laissent un message sur mon répondeur. J'envoie aussi des (e-)mails à mes amis. J'aime recevoir des (e-)mails!

4 *Students will play the game.*

CHAPITRE 3

5 Souvenirs d'enfance
✓ **Write about people and events in the past**

Quand vous étiez petit(e), est-ce que vous alliez quelquefois chez vos cousins ou chez un(e) ami(e)? En un paragraphe, décrivez chez qui vous alliez, comment étaient les gens et leur maison et ce que vous faisiez d'habitude chez eux.

6 Une petite histoire
✓ **Narrate in the past**

Écrivez une histoire en utilisant les catégories ci-dessous comme guide.
- Date
- Temps
- Personnages et lieu
- Description physique ou émotionnelle des personnages
- Attitudes
- Désirs
- Actions habituelles

C'était le 3 janvier. Il faisait...

7 Un job intéressant

You had a job this past summer with a service organization dealing with French-speaking countries. You got the job because you speak French. Write to Christophe, your French pen pal, and explain some of the things you did in the office and what equipment you used. Since you know that Christophe has never worked in an office and is not familiar with office machines, be as clear and as logical as you can in your explanation.

Writing Strategy

Expository writing Expository writing explains and informs. It helps readers to understand a topic. Before you write, two important questions to ask about your topic are "how to" and "why." Use familiar terms in your definitions and descriptions. Be careful not to omit important facts and steps and to present the steps in order. These measures will help you present a clear and concise explanation that readers will find interesting and informative.

LES TÉLÉCOMMUNICATIONS

quatre-vingt-onze 91

Assessment

Vocabulaire

1 Identifiez.

To review Mots 1, turn to pages 66–67.

1.

2.

3.

4.

5.

To review Mots 2, turn to pages 70–71.

2 Choisissez.

6. _____ le numéro   a. donner
7. _____ le téléphone   b. téléphoner
8. _____ un coup de fil   c. mettre
9. _____ à quelqu'un   d. décrocher
10. _____ la télécarte dans la fente   e. composer

Answers to Assessment

1
1. un écran
2. un clavier
3. une souris
4. une imprimante
5. une disquette

2
6. e
7. d
8. a
9. b
10. c

Structure

3 Récrivez à l'imparfait.

11–12. Quand il est petit, il habite à Nice.
13. On va toujours à la plage.
14. Je prends un bain de soleil.
15. Mes copains font du surf.
16. Nous aimons bien aller à la plage.

To review verb forms in the imperfect tense, turn to pages 74–75.

4 Complétez au passé.

Quand Françoise __17__ (avoir) trois ans, elle __18__ (aller) à l'école maternelle. Elle __19__ (vouloir) tout apprendre et elle __20__ (aimer) jouer avec les autres petits enfants. Elle __21__ (habiter) dans une belle maison, tout près de l'école. Quand il __22__ (faire) beau, elle __23__ (aller) à l'école à pied.

To review the use of the imperfect tense, turn to page 78.

Culture

5 Vrai ou faux?

24. Les télécommunications ont beaucoup changé en France.
25. Aujourd'hui, il faut avoir beaucoup de pièces de monnaie pour faire un appel d'un téléphone public.

To review this cultural information, turn to pages 84–85.

Glencoe Technology

MINDJOGGER VHS/DVD
You may wish to help your students prepare for the chapter test by playing the MindJogger game show. Teams will compete against each other to review chapter vocabulary and structure and sharpen listening comprehension skills.

LES TÉLÉCOMMUNICATIONS

ANSWERS TO Assessment

3
11–12. Quand il était petit, il habitait à Nice.
13. On allait toujours à la plage.
14. Je prenais un bain de soleil.
15. Mes copains faisaient du surf.
16. Nous aimions bien aller à la plage.

4
17. avait
18. allait
19. voulait
20. aimait
21. habitait
22. faisait
23. allait

5
24. vrai
25. faux

On parle super bien!

This unique page gives students the opportunity to speak freely and say whatever they can, using the vocabulary and structures they have learned in the chapter. The illustration serves to remind students of precisely what they know how to say in French. There are no activities that students do not have the ability to describe or talk about in French. The art not only depicts the vocabulary and content of this chapter, but also reinforces what they learned in previous chapters.

You may wish to use this page in many ways. Some possibilities are to have students do the following:

1. Look at the illustration and identify items by giving the correct French words.
2. Make up sentences about what they see in the illustration.
3. Make up questions about the illustration. They can call on another class member to respond if you do this as a class activity, or you may prefer to allow students to work in small groups. This activity is extremely beneficial because it enables students to actively use interrogative words.
4. Answer questions you ask them about the illustration.
5. Work in pairs and make up a conversation based on the illustration.
6. Look at the illustration and give a complete oral review of what they see.
7. Look at the illustration and write a paragraph (or essay) about it.

You can also use this page as an assessment or testing tool, taking into account individual differences by having students go from simple to quite complicated tasks. The assessment can be either oral or written. You may wish to use the rubrics provided on pages T20–T21 as you give students the following directions.

On parle super bien!

Tell all you can about this illustration.

1. Identify the topic or situation of the illustration.
2. Give the French words for as many items as you can.
3. Think of as many sentences as you can to describe the illustration.
4. Go over your sentences and put them in the best sequencing to give a coherent story based on the illustration.

Vocabulaire

Describing a computer

un ordinateur	une disquette	une imprimante
un clavier	un lecteur	un CD-ROM
un écran	une souris	un logiciel

Using a computer

allumer	envoyer	sauvegarder
mettre une disquette	un e-mail	retirer
taper	un mail	éteindre
cliquer	un texte	
	des données (f. pl.)	

Sending a fax

appuyer (sur)	un document
envoyer, transmettre	face écrite visible
un télécopieur, un fax	face écrite non visible
une télécopie, un fax	une touche

Describing a telephone

un téléphone	un répondeur	un portable
à touches	automatique	une cabine
public, publique	une fente	téléphonique

Giving a telephone number

un annuaire	un indicatif régional	une erreur
le numéro	le bon numéro	
l'indicatif du pays (m.)	le mauvais numéro	

Making a telephone call

téléphoner à	décrocher	rappeler
faire un appel	composer le numéro	une télécarte
téléphonique	faire le numéro	une pièce de monnaie
donner un coup	sonner	la tonalité
de fil	raccrocher	occupé

Other useful words and expressions

Allô?	Ce n'est pas grave.	se servir de
C'est de la part de qui?	désolé(e)	aider
Ne quittez pas.		

How well do you know your vocabulary?
- Choose words to describe your favorite method of communication.
- Write a brief explanation of either sending an e-mail or making a telephone call to a friend or family member.

VIDÉOTOUR
Épisode 3
In this video episode, we see technology at work on a small and large scale. Let's join Christine and Mme Séguin at the school office. See page 502 for more information.

LES TÉLÉCOMMUNICATIONS

Vocabulary Review

The words and phrases in the **Vocabulaire** have been taught for productive use in this chapter. They are summarized here as a resource for both student and teacher. This list also serves as a convenient resource for the **C'est à vous** activities on pages 90–91, as well as for talking about the illustration on page 94. There are approximately twenty cognates in this vocabulary list. Have students find them.

Attention!

You will notice that the vocabulary list here is not translated. This has been done intentionally, since we feel that by the time students have finished the material in the chapter they should be familiar with the meanings of all the words. If there are several words they still do not know, we recommend that they refer to the **Mots 1** and **2** sections in the chapter or go to the dictionaries at the back of this book to find the meanings. However, if you prefer that your students have the English translations, please refer to Vocabulary Transparency 3.1, where you will find all these words with their translations.

VIDÉO VHS/DVD

The Video Program allows students to see how the chapter vocabulary and structures are used by native speakers. For maximum reinforcement, show the video episode as a final activity for Chapter 3.

Planning for Chapter 4

SCOPE AND SEQUENCE, PAGES 96–129

Topics
* Train travel
* Air travel

Functions
* How to describe past events
* How to identify cities, countries, and continents

National Standards
* Communication Standard 1.1 pages 100, 101, 104, 105, 106, 107, 108, 110, 111, 112, 114, 115, 117, 124
* Communication Standard 1.2 pages 100, 101, 104, 105, 106, 107, 108, 110, 111, 112, 114, 115, 117, 123, 125, 126, 127, 123
* Communication Standard 1.3 pages 100, 101, 104, 105, 107, 108, 110, 111, 115, 117, 124, 125
* Cultures Standard 2.1 pages 118–119, 120, 121
* Cultures Standard 2.2 pages 98, 99, 103, 118–119, 122–123
* Connections Standard 3.1 pages 122–123
* Comparisons Standard 4.2 pages 99, 118–119, 120, 121
* Communities Standard 5.1 page 125

Culture
* Train travel—yesterday and today
* Thomas takes a trip to Switzerland
* A trip to Benin
* **Reflets de la France**

Structure
* Comparing **l'imparfait** and the **passé composé**
* Narrating in the past
* The verb **venir**
* Using prepositions with cities, countries, and continents

PACING AND PRIORITIES

The chapter content is color coded below to assist you in planning.

■ required   ■ recommended   ■ optional

Vocabulaire *(required)*   Days 1–4
- ■ Mots 1
    Les trains d'hier et d'aujourd'hui
- ■ Mots 2
    À l'aéroport
    À bord de l'avion
    À l'arrivée

Structure *(required)*   Days 5–7
- ■ L'imparfait et le passé composé
- ■ Raconter une histoire au passé
- ■ Le verbe **venir**
- ■ Les prépositions avec les noms géographiques

Conversation *(required)*
- ■ À l'aéroport

Lectures culturelles
- ■ Les trains d'hier et d'aujourd'hui *(recommended)*
- ■ Un voyage en Suisse *(optional)*
- ■ Un voyage au Bénin *(optional)*

Connexions *(optional)*
- ■ L'archéologie

■ **C'est à vous** *(recommended)*

■ **Assessment** *(recommended)*

■ **On parle super bien!** *(optional)*

RESOURCE GUIDE

SECTION	PAGES	SECTION RESOURCES
Vocabulaire *Mots 1*		
Les trains d'hier et d'aujourd'hui	98–101	Vocabulary Transparencies 4.2–4.3 Audio CD 3 Audio Activities TE, pages 34–35 Workbook, pages 33–34 Quiz 1, page 17 ExamView® Pro
Vocabulaire *Mots 2*		
À l'aéroport À bord de l'avion À l'arrivée	102 102 103–105	Vocabulary Transparencies 4.4–4.5 Audio CD 3 Audio Activities TE, pages 36–38 Workbook, pages 35–36 Quiz 2, page 18 ExamView® Pro
Structure		
L'imparfait et le passé composé Raconter une histoire au passé Le verbe **venir** Les prépositions avec les noms géographiques	106–108 109–111 112 113–115	Audio CD 3 Audio Activities TE, pages 38–42 Workbook, pages 37–41 Quizzes 3–4, pages 19–20 ExamView® Pro
Conversation		
À l'aéroport	116–117	Audio CD 3 Audio Activities TE, pages 43–44 Interactive CD-ROM
Lectures culturelles		
Les trains d'hier et d'aujourd'hui Un voyage en Suisse Un voyage au Bénin	118–119 120 121	Audio CD 3 Audio Activities TE, pages 44–45 Tests, pages 45, 50
Connexions		
L'archéologie	122–123	Tests, page 51
C'est à vous		
	124–125	**Bon voyage!** Video, Episode 4 Video Activities, Chapter 4 French Online Activities french.glencoe.com
Assessment		
	126–127	Communication Transparency C 4 Quizzes 1–4, pages 17–20 Performance Assessment, Task 4 Tests, pages 43–56 ExamView® Pro Situation Cards, Chapter 4 **Marathon mental** Videoquiz

Using Your Resources for Chapter 4

Transparencies

Bellringer 4.1–4.8　　Vocabulary 4.1–4.5　　Communication C 4

Workbook

Vocabulary, pages 33–36　　Structure, pages 37–41　　Enrichment, pages 42–44

Audio Activities

Vocabulary, pages 34–38　　Structure, pages 38–42　　Conversation, pages 43–44　　Cultural Reading, pages 44–45　　Additional Practice, pages 46–47

Assessment

Vocabulary and Structure Quizzes, pages 17–20

Chapter Tests, pages 43–56

Situation Cards, Chapter 4

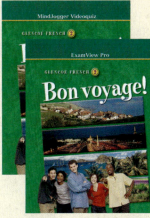
MindJogger Videoquiz, ExamView® Pro, Chapter 4

Timesaving Teacher Tools

TeacherWorks™

TeacherWorks™ is your all-in-one teacher resource center. Personalize lesson plans, access resources from the Teacher Wraparound Edition, connect to the Internet, or make a to-do list. These are only a few of the many features that can assist you in the planning and organizing of your lessons.

Includes:
- A calendar feature
- Access to all program blackline masters
- Standards correlations and more

ExamView® Pro

Test Bank software for Macintosh and Windows makes creating, editing, customizing, and printing tests quick and easy.

Technology Resources

In the Chapter 4 Internet activity, you will have a chance to learn more about the Francophone world. Visit **french.glencoe.com**.

On the Interactive Conversation CD-ROM, students can listen to and take part in a recorded version of the conversation in Chapter 4.

See the National Geographic Teacher's Corner on pages 138–139, 244–245, 372–373, 472–473 for reference to additional technology resources.

Bon voyage! Video and Video Activities, Chapter 4

Help your students prepare for the chapter test by playing the **Marathon mental** Videoquiz game show. Teams will compete against each other to review chapter vocabulary and structure and sharpen listening comprehension skills.

Preview
In this chapter, students will communicate about train and plane travel. They will distinguish between local and long-distance trains, modern and old-fashioned trains, services on trains and planes, and boarding and disembarking from planes. They will learn the difference between the imperfect and the **passé composé**. They will learn the verb **venir** and the prepositions used with geographic names.

 National Standards

Communication
In Chapter 4, students will communicate in spoken and written French on the following topics:
- Traveling on board a train
- Services on board an airplane
- Arriving at an airport
- Geography

Students will obtain and provide information and engage in conversations dealing with train and plane travel as they fulfill the chapter objectives listed on this page.

LEVELING
The activities, conversations, and readings within each chapter are marked according to level of difficulty. **E** indicates easy. **A** indicates average. **C** indicates challenging. Some activities cover a range of difficulty. For example, advanced students may produce more extensive responses while others may give less detailed responses. The leveling indicators will help you individualize instruction.

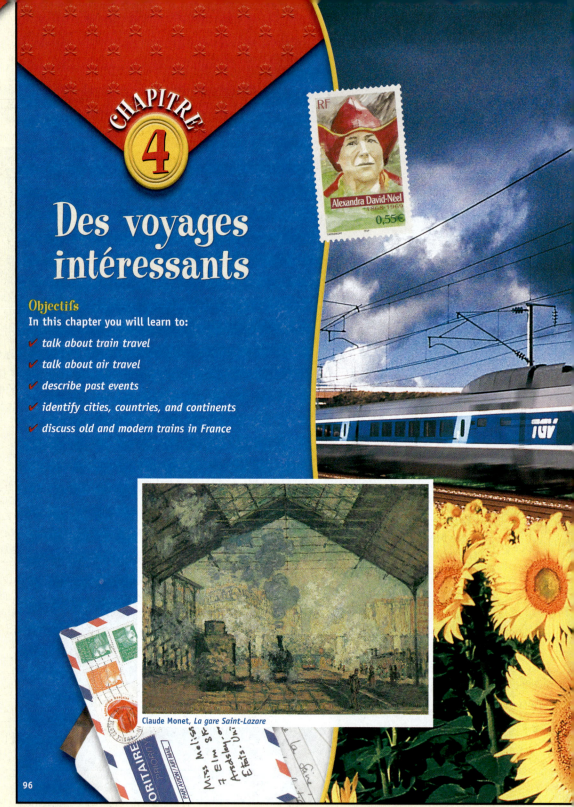

Des voyages intéressants

Objectifs
In this chapter you will learn to:
✓ talk about train travel
✓ talk about air travel
✓ describe past events
✓ identify cities, countries, and continents
✓ discuss old and modern trains in France

Claude Monet, *La gare Saint-Lazare*

CHAPITRE 4

 Spotlight on Culture

Photograph The photo shows the **TGV (le train à grande vitesse)**. The **TGV**, a train designed and manufactured in France, is one of the fastest trains in the world.

Painting Claude Monet (1840–1926) is one of the most famous French Impressionists. He loved to paint outdoors. In 1877, Monet decided to undertake the task of painting the interior of the gare Saint-Lazare, a building that symbolized both the industrialization and the glass and metal architectural style of the era. In the painting seen here, Monet is interested in both the building and the locomotive. He shows the puffs of smoke that escape from the engine forming clouds that dance in the light.

National Standards

Communities
Have students create a huge poster of a cutaway train or plane filled with passengers (self-portraits). All parts of the train or plane should be labeled in French. Hang the poster in the main hallway of the school for National Foreign Language Week (the first full week in March).

Vocabulaire Mots 1

1 Preparation

Resource Manager

Vocabulary Transparencies 4.2–4.3
Audio Activities TE, pages 34–35
Audio CD 3
Workbook, pages 33–34
Quiz 1, page 17
ExamView® Pro

Bellringer Review

Use BRR Transparency 4.1 or write the following on the board.
List all telecommunication equipment you have in your home or in your school.

2 Presentation

Recycling Some of the vocabulary dealing with rail travel was taught in **Bon voyage! Level 1,** Chapter 9. In this chapter it is recycled, expanded upon, and used in the imperfect and **passé composé**.

Step 1 Have students close their books. Introduce the **Mots 1** vocabulary using Vocabulary Transparencies 4.2–4.3. Have students repeat each word after you or the recording on Audio CD 3 two or three times as you point to the appropriate illustration on the transparencies.

Step 2 Now ask **Qu'est-ce que c'est?** as you point to the item on the transparency and have students come up with the new words themselves.

Step 3 Have students open their books and read the new words and sentences aloud.

Vocabulaire Mots 1

Les trains d'hier et d'aujourd'hui

le tableau des lignes de banlieue

Les lignes de banlieue sont les trains qui desservent les villages et les petites villes autour d'une grande ville.

Les grandes lignes sont les trains qui desservent les grandes villes en France et dans les autres pays.

le tableau des grandes lignes

Ah zut! J'ai raté le train! Le train est déjà parti.

un siège réglable

le couloir

La voiture d'un train moderne a un couloir central.
Il y a deux sièges de chaque côté.
Le contrôleur est entré dans la voiture.
Il a contrôlé les billets.

98 ✦ quatre-vingt-dix-huit

CHAPITRE 4

Reaching All Students

Additional Practice Using props, pictures, and various areas of the classroom, guide students with TPR techniques in acting out as many of the vocabulary phrases as possible. For example: **Indiquez un passager assis. Indiquez un passager debout. Indiquez une place libre. Vous êtes le contrôleur: Entrez dans la voiture. Vérifiez les billets,** etc.

LEVELING
A: Vocabulary

Vocabulaire
Mots 1

Les vieux trains avaient des compartiments.
De temps en temps, il n'y avait pas de places disponibles.
Tous les compartiments étaient complets.
Il y avait des voyageurs debout dans le couloir.

Le TGV est un train à grande vitesse.
Il roule très vite.
Le paysage est splendide.

DES VOYAGES INTÉRESSANTS

quatre-vingt-dix-neuf 99

Step 4 Have students close their books again. Ask someone in the classroom to stand up. Point to the person and say **debout**. Now point to a student who is seated and say **assis(e)**.

Step 5 Ask for individual repetitions of the words and phrases. Intersperse the repetitions with *yes/no, either/or,* or interrogative-word questions. For example: **Tous les compartiments étaient complets? Il y avait des places libres? Tous les passagers étaient assis ou debout? Les passagers étaient debout où?**

Step 6 After you have introduced the **Mots 1** vocabulary using the Vocabulary Transparencies, have students open their books and read the words and sentences on these pages.

✓ Assessment

As an informal assessment, you may wish to show the Vocabulary Transparencies for **Mots 1** again and let students identify items at random. Now have students make up questions about what they see on the transparencies. You may answer the questions or have them call on other students to answer.

Chapter Projects

Comparaisons Bring brochures from a local travel agency about American and French rail service to class. Ask students to compare and contrast the rail service in the two countries.

Le train If passenger train travel is nonexistent in your area, have students find out in which areas passenger service is available.

Un voyage Have groups plan a rail trip through France using a guide such as the one from Eurail (available at many travel agencies). Give them a time limit and have them include at least one overnight stay. They should plan arrival and departure times and the length of each stop on the itinerary. Groups can describe their trip to the class.

99

Vocabulaire

3 Practice

Quel est le mot?

Attention!

When students are doing the **Quel est le mot?** activities, accept any answer that makes sense. The purpose of these activities is to have students use the new vocabulary. They are not factual recall activities. Thus, it is not necessary for students to remember specific factual information from the vocabulary presentation when answering. If you wish, have students use the photos on this page as a stimulus, when possible.

1 and **2** It is suggested that you go over these activities orally in class with books closed. Then have students write the answers for homework and go over the activities once again the following day.

2 The information on the departure board in the photo on page 100 gives students the answer to number 2 of this activity.

Learning from Photos

(page 100 top) The train in which the conductor is checking the tickets is on the Paris to Dijon route. Have students imagine a dialogue between the people in the photo.

(page 100 bottom) This departure board is at the gare Montparnasse. In addition to serving destinations to the west of Paris, the gare Montparnasse has become the major terminus for trains to Southwest France with the introduction of the **TGV–Atlantique** service.

Vocabulaire

Quel est le mot?

1 Historiette Le voyage du père de Sylvain
Inventez une histoire.
1. Le père de Sylvain a fait un voyage en train quand il était jeune?
2. Il est allé de Paris à Dijon?
3. Le train avait des compartiments?
4. Tous les voyageurs étaient assis?
5. Il y avait des places disponibles?
6. Le père de Sylvain a trouvé une place?
7. Le contrôleur est entré dans le compartiment?
8. Il a contrôlé les billets?
9. Le train est arrivé à Dijon à l'heure?

Un contrôleur dans le train de Paris à Dijon

2 Historiette À la gare Répondez.
1. Charlotte va voyager en train. Elle est à la gare ou à l'aéroport?
2. Elle va de Paris à Chartres. Elle va consulter le tableau des grandes lignes ou le tableau des lignes de banlieue?
3. Elle va partir. Elle regarde le tableau des arrivées ou le tableau des départs?
4. Charlotte est montée dans le train sur le quai ou dans la salle d'attente?
5. Elle est arrivée à la gare à l'heure. Elle a raté son train ou pas?

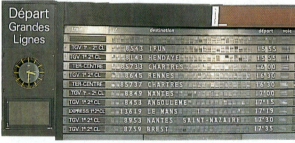

Tableau des départs à la gare Montparnasse à Paris

100 cent   CHAPITRE 4

ANSWERS TO Quel est le mot?

1 *Answers will vary but may include:*
1. Oui, le père de Sylvain a fait un voyage en train quand il était jeune.
2. Oui, il est allé de Paris à Dijon.
3. Oui, le train avait des compartiments.
4. Non, tous les voyageurs n'étaient pas assis.
5. Oui, il y avait des places disponibles.
6. Oui, le père de Sylvain a trouvé une place.
7. Oui, le contrôleur est entré dans le compartiment.
8. Oui, il a contrôlé les billets.
9. Oui, le train est arrivé à Dijon à l'heure.

2
1. Elle est à la gare.
2. Elle va consulter le tableau des grandes lignes.
3. Elle regarde le tableau des départs.
4. Elle est montée dans le train sur le quai.
5. Elle n'a pas raté son train.

Vocabulaire

3 Les trains Vrai ou faux?
1. Les vieux trains avaient un couloir avec deux sièges de chaque côté.
2. Il y a beaucoup de places disponibles quand le train est complet.
3. Il y a des voyageurs debout quand il n'y a plus de places disponibles.
4. Les voyageurs aiment avoir un siège réglable s'ils veulent dormir un peu.
5. Les lignes de banlieue desservent toutes les grandes villes.
6. Les voyageurs prennent la correspondance quand ils doivent changer de train.
7. Le TGV est un petit train qui dessert les villages de banlieue.
8. Quand on voyage en train, on peut regarder le paysage.
9. Le TGV roule très vite.

4 À la gare Travaillez avec un copain ou une copine. Vous êtes à la gare. Vous allez prendre le train de Nice à Grenoble. Décrivez ce que vous faites à la gare. Vous pouvez utiliser les expressions suivantes.

5 Mon train! Travaillez avec un(e) camarade. Regardez le dessin et décrivez tout ce que vous y voyez.

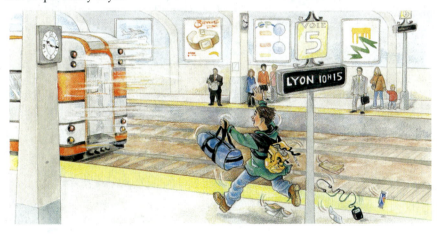

 For more practice using words from **Mots 1**, do Activity 10 on page H11 at the end of this book.

DES VOYAGES INTÉRESSANTS

cent un 101

Answers to Quel est le mot?

3
1. faux
2. faux
3. vrai
4. vrai
5. faux
6. vrai
7. faux
8. vrai
9. vrai

4 *Answers will vary but may include:*
À la gare j'achète un billet aller-retour au guichet. J'achète un magazine au kiosque. J'attends un peu dans la salle d'attente. Je composte mon billet et puis je cherche le quai numéro 3. Je monte dans le train et je trouve ma place.

5 *Answers will vary but may include:*
Il est dix heures et quart. Le train pour Lyon part de la voie numéro cinq. Le train part à l'heure. Le jeune homme est en retard. Il rate son train. Il perd des choses sur le quai.

Vocabulaire Mots 2

1 Preparation

Resource Manager

Vocabulary Transparencies 4.4–4.5
Audio Activities TE, pages 36–38
Audio CD 3
Workbook, pages 35–36
Quiz 2, page 18
ExamView® Pro

Bellringer Review

Use BRR Transparency 4.2 or write the following on the board.
Complete with the **passé composé**.
1. Hier je _____ à Versailles. (aller)
2. J'_____ le train. (prendre)
3. Le train _____ à l'heure. (arriver)
4. Mes amis et moi, nous _____ le château. (visiter)
5. Nous _____ une promenade dans les jardins. (faire)

2 Presentation

Note: The vocabulary in this section emphasizes words needed on board the plane and at the airport upon arrival. The vocabulary needed for the departure airport was presented in **Bon voyage! Level 1,** Chapter 8.

Step 1 Show Vocabulary Transparencies 4.4–4.5. Have students close their books and repeat the words after you or Audio CD 3 as you point to the appropriate illustration on the transparency.

Step 2 Call on students to point out the correct item on the transparency as you say the new word or expression.

Vocabulaire Mots 2

À l'aéroport

embarquer

le décollage

À bord de l'avion

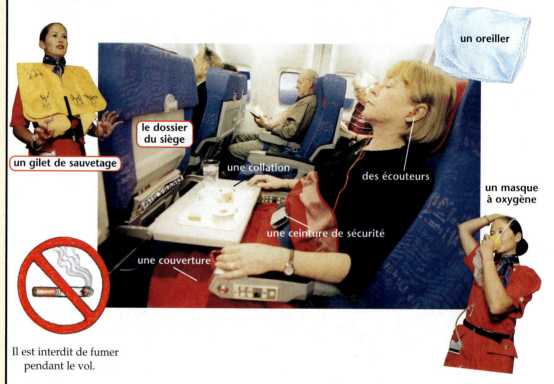

un oreiller
le dossier du siège
des écouteurs
un masque à oxygène
une ceinture de sécurité
une collation
une couverture
un gilet de sauvetage

Il est interdit de fumer pendant le vol.

Reaching All Students

Total Physical Response

(Student 1), venez ici, s'il vous plaît.
On va imaginer que votre vol vient d'arriver à Paris.
Détachez votre ceinture de sécurité.
Levez-vous. Débarquez de l'avion.
Dites «au revoir» à l'hôtesse de l'air.
Vous êtes au contrôle des passeports.
Montrez votre passeport.
Vous allez récupérer vos bagages.
Cherchez un chariot.
Mettez vos bagages sur le chariot.
Poussez le chariot.
Vous passez par la douane sans aucun problème.
Vous êtes maintenant devant l'aérogare.
Attendez votre ami(e) qui vient vous chercher à l'aéroport.

Vocabulaire Mots 2

À l'arrivée

l'atterrissage

L'avion atterrit.

débarquer

Après l'atterrissage, les passagers débarquent.

la douane

récupérer ses bagages

un chariot (à bagages)

Rémi récupère ses bagages. Les autres passagers passent à la douane.

C'était un vol sans escale. Il n'a pas fait escale dans une seule ville entre Dakar et Paris.

Rémi et les autres passagers passent au contrôle des passeports.
Ils vont en France.
Ils viennent du Sénégal.

Un ami est venu le chercher à l'aéroport.

Rémi a pris le vol Dakar–Paris.
L'avion est parti avec deux heures de retard.
Mais le vol n'a pas été annulé.

DES VOYAGES INTÉRESSANTS

cent trois 103

Vocabulaire

Quel est le mot?

6 Historiette Un voyage Inventez une histoire.

1. Aurélie a pris l'avion de Fort-de-France à Paris?
2. Elle a fait escale à New York?
3. L'avion est parti en retard?
4. Le vol a été annulé?
5. Pendant le vol, Aurélie a dormi un peu?
6. Elle a demandé un oreiller et une couverture à l'hôtesse de l'air?
7. Pendant le vol, on a servi un dîner ou une collation?
8. L'avion a atterri à l'heure?
9. Après le vol, Aurélie a récupéré ses bagages?
10. Elle a mis ses bagages sur un chariot?
11. Aurélie est passée au contrôle des passeports et à la douane?
12. Un ami est venu la chercher à l'aéroport?

Aurélie récupère ses bagages.

7 À bord de l'avion Choisissez.

1. En cas d'un changement de pression dans la cabine, _____ tombent automatiquement.
   a. les gilets de sauvetage   b. les couvertures   c. les masques à oxygène
2. En cas d'un atterrissage dans la mer ou dans l'océan, c'est-à-dire un amerrissage, il faut mettre _____.
   a. son gilet de sauvetage   b. le dossier de son siège   c. sa ceinture de sécurité
3. Pendant le décollage et l'atterrissage, il faut attacher _____.
   a. son masque à oxygène   b. son gilet de sauvetage   c. sa ceinture de sécurité
4. _____ de chaque passager doit être en position verticale pendant le décollage et l'atterrissage.
   a. Le masque à oxygène   b. Le dossier du siège   c. Le coffre à bagages
5. Une collation, c'est _____.
   a. un petit repas   b. le départ de l'avion   c. un grand dîner
6. Pendant le vol, il est interdit de _____.
   a. fumer   b. parler au personnel de bord   c. dormir

104 cent quatre CHAPITRE 4

Vocabulaire

8 Pendant le vol Répondez **Absolument!** ou **J'espère bien que non!**

1. Les passagers vont mettre leur gilet de sauvetage pendant le vol.
2. Les passagers vont attacher leur ceinture de sécurité pendant le décollage et l'atterrissage.
3. Le personnel de bord va servir une collation et des boissons.
4. Les hôtesses de l'air ou les stewards vont distribuer des écouteurs.
5. Les masques à oxygène vont tomber pendant le vol.
6. Les passagers vont débarquer ou embarquer pendant le vol.

À bord d'un avion

9 À l'aéroport Travaillez avec un copain ou une copine. Décrivez tout ce que vous voyez sur les dessins. Vous pouvez utiliser les mots suivants.

le comptoir de la compagnie aérienne
l'agent
le billet
les bagages à main

passer par le contrôle de sécurité
la porte d'embarquement
la carte d'embarquement
à bord de l'avion

1.   2.   3.   4.

10 C'est son premier vol. Travaillez avec un copain ou une copine. C'est la première fois qu'il/elle prend l'avion et il/elle a beaucoup de questions. Vous, vous avez beaucoup d'expérience. Répondez à toutes ses questions et dites-lui tout ce qui se passe pendant un vol.

DES VOYAGES INTÉRESSANTS

Structure

1 Preparation

Resource Manager

Audio Activities TE, pages 38–42
Audio CD 3
Workbook, pages 37–41
Quizzes 3–4, pages 19–20
ExamView® Pro

Bellringer Review

Use BRR Transparency 4.3 or write the following on the board.
Write the opposite.
l'atterrissage   debout
une ligne de   embarquer
  banlieue

2 Presentation

L'imparfait et le passé composé

Step 1 Lead students through Items 1–3 on page 106.

Step 2 For Item 2, draw a timeline on the board. Each time you give a verb in the **passé composé,** write an abrupt slash through the timeline to indicate termination or completion.

Step 3 As you go over the sentences in Item 3, put another timeline on the board. Each time you give a verb in the imperfect, draw a long shaded box on the timeline to indicate duration.

Learning from Photos

(page 106) Dordogne is the name of both a river and a **département** in southwest France. The valley passes through the Massif Central. In some areas of the valley there are magnificent châteaux.

Structure

L'imparfait et le passé composé
Talking about actions in the past

1. The decision to use the **passé composé** or the imperfect tense depends upon whether you are describing an action or event that took place at a definite time in the past or whether you are describing or reminiscing about a continuous, recurring action in the past.

2. You use the **passé composé** to relate actions or events that began and ended at a specific time in the past.

   **L'été dernier, nous sommes allés en Dordogne.
   Nous avons pris le train.
   Nous y sommes restés quinze jours.**

3. You use the imperfect to describe a continuous or repeated action in the past. When the action began or ended is not important.

   **Quand j'étais petit nous allions toujours en Dordogne.
   Nous prenions souvent le train.
   Nous y restions quinze jours.**

Comment dit-on?

 11 Avant et après Inventez des réponses.

1. Avant, le train arrivait à l'heure?
   Et hier, il est arrivé à l'heure?
2. Avant, le train partait toujours de la voie N° 14?
   Et ce matin, il est parti de la voie N° 14?
3. Avant, tu allais au cinéma tous les vendredis soirs?
   Et vendredi dernier, tu es allé(e) au cinéma?
4. Avant, ton prof allait en France tous les étés?
   Et l'été dernier, il est allé en France?
5. Avant, tu regardais la télé tous les soirs?
   Et hier soir, tu as regardé la télé?
6. Avant, tu recevais une lettre de ta grand-mère tous les mois?
   Et le mois dernier, tu as reçu une lettre de ta grand-mère?

Un château en Dordogne

ANSWERS TO Comment dit-on?

11 Answers will vary. Students can respond in either the affirmative or the negative.

1. Oui, avant, le train arrivait à l'heure, mais hier il n'est pas arrivé à l'heure.
2. Oui, avant, le train partait toujours de la voie N° 14, mais ce matin il n'est pas parti de la voie N° 14.
3. Oui, avant, j'allais au cinéma tous les vendredis soirs, mais vendredi dernier, je suis allé(e) au théâtre.
4. Oui, avant, mon prof allait en France tous les étés, mais l'été dernier il n'est pas allé en France.
5. Non, avant, je ne regardais pas la télé tous les soirs, mais hier soir j'ai regardé la télé.
6. Oui, avant, je recevais une lettre de ma grand-mère tous les mois, mais le mois dernier je n'ai pas reçu de lettre de ma grand-mère.

12 **Historiette** *Mes vacances* Donnez des réponses personnelles.
Quand tu étais petit(e), pendant les vacances…

1. tu allais toujours à la montagne?
2. tu prenais le train?
3. tu allais où?
4. tu écrivais des cartes postales?
5. tu faisais du ski?
6. tu avais un bon moniteur?
7. tu jouais dans la neige?
8. tu t'amusais bien?

Et l'année dernière…

1. tu es allé(e) à la montagne?
2. tu as pris le train?
3. tu es allé(e) où?
4. tu as écrit des cartes postales?
5. tu as fait du ski?
6. tu as eu un bon moniteur?
7. tu as joué dans la neige?
8. tu t'es bien amusé(e)?

Un train près de Chamonix dans les Alpes

13 **Historiette** *Hier* Lisez.

Hier, je me suis levé(e) de bonne heure. J'ai fait ma toilette, je me suis habillé(e), j'ai pris mon petit déjeuner et j'ai quitté la maison. Je suis allé(e) à la gare où j'ai attendu le train. Je suis descendu(e) sur le quai. Le train est arrivé et je suis monté(e) en voiture. Je suis arrivé(e) en ville une demi-heure plus tard. Je suis entré(e) dans mon bureau à neuf heures précises.

14 *Avant* Dans l'Activité 13, remplacez **Hier** par **Quand j'habitais en banlieue…**

L'entrée de la station de métro Luxembourg

DES VOYAGES INTÉRESSANTS

cent sept 107

Structure

15 As you do this activity with the students, have them identify the **imparfait** and **passé composé** "markers" (souvent / imparfait; l'été dernier / passé composé). You may wish to have students make two running columns of these words to help them distinguish between the usage of the two forms.

Note: If you are having the students write the answers to this activity, you will need to point out that in the **nous** and **vous** forms of the imparfait of verbs that end in **-ger**, you drop the **e** from the stem before adding the endings: **Nous nageons**; the stem is **nage-**: **je nageais**, but: **nous nagions, vous nagiez**.

16 Have pairs of students share their dialogues with the class.

About the French Language

The following types of time expressions are often used with the **passé composé**.

hier	à huit heures
hier soir	l'année dernière
ce matin	vendredi dernier
un jour	

These time expressions are often used with the **imparfait**.

de temps en temps
tous les jours
fréquemment
tous les mois
souvent
toutes les semaines ⚜

Learning from Photos

(page 108) Colmar is a lovely Alsatian town with many painted, carved houses as seen here in the photo.

Baron Haussmann, who designed the magnificent boulevards of Paris, was born in Colmar.

Structure

15 **Pas toujours** Suivez le modèle.

arriver →
Avant, tu arrivais toujours à l'heure.
Mais hier, tu es arrivé(e) en retard.

1. **prendre**
   On ____ souvent le train quand on allait en vacances.
   Mais l'été dernier, on ____ l'avion.
2. **aller**
   Tu ____ au cinéma tous les vendredis quand tu étais plus jeune.
   Mais vendredi dernier, tu ____ au théâtre.
3. **passer**
   De temps en temps, Madame Napier ____ ses vacances en Dordogne.
   Mais l'été dernier, Madame Napier ____ ses vacances en Alsace.
4. **voyager**
   Avant, nous ____ toujours en seconde classe.
   Mais cette année, nous ____ en première classe!
5. **arriver**
   Quand nous sortions ensemble, mes amis ____ toujours en retard.
   Mais le week-end dernier, ils ____ à l'heure.

Colmar en Alsace

16 **Avant et hier aussi?** Travaillez avec un copain ou une copine. Dites-lui ce que vous faisiez quand vous étiez petit(e). Dites-lui si vous avez fait la même chose récemment. Ensuite, changez de rôle.

108 ⚜ cent huit

CHAPITRE 4

ANSWERS TO Comment dit-on?

15

1. prenait, a pris
2. allais, es allé(e)
3. passait, a passé
4. voyagions, avons voyagé
5. arrivaient, sont arrivés

16 *Answers will vary but may include:*

Quand j'étais petit(e), j'aidais toujours ma mère à préparer le dîner. Hier aussi, j'ai aidé ma mère à préparer le dîner. Et toi? Qu'est-ce que tu faisais quand tu étais petit(e)?

Raconter une histoire au passé
Telling a story in the past

1. When telling a story about any past event, you will almost always use both the imperfect and the **passé composé**. Pretend you are describing a scene from a movie. To describe the setting and scenery, you use the imperfect. To tell what happened (the action), you use the **passé composé**.

Le décor (imparfait)

Il était midi dans le petit village de Barbizon.
Il faisait beau.
Il n'y avait personne dans les rues.

Au Café de la Poste, les clients déjeunaient tranquillement.

L'action (passé composé)

Soudain, une grosse voiture noire est arrivée.
Elle s'est arrêtée devant le Café de la Poste.

Un homme est descendu et est entré dans le café.

Tout le monde l'a regardé.

Et tout le monde a reconnu le grand acteur Gérard Auteuil.
Tout le monde a commencé à applaudir.

DES VOYAGES INTÉRESSANTS

cent neuf ✦ 109

Structure

1 Preparation

Bellringer Review

Use BRR Transparency 4.4 or write the following on the board.
Give five words associated with train travel and five words associated with plane travel.

2 Presentation

Raconter une histoire au passé

Step 1 Go through Item 1 with the students.

Step 2 After reading the narrative on page 109, ask the following questions about it. After a student answers, have him or her tell if it deals with **la scène** or **l'action**.

Il était quelle heure?
Il faisait quel temps à Barbizon?
Il y avait beaucoup de monde dans les rues?
Que faisaient les clients au Café de la Poste?
Qu'est-ce qui est arrivé?
Elle s'est arrêtée où?
Qui est descendu?
Il est entré où?
Qui l'a regardé?
Tout le monde l'a reconnu?

LEVELING
A: Activities 15, 16
C: Activities 15, 16

Structure

2. Study the difference between the imperfect and **passé composé** in the following sentences. The first set tells what you were doing (imperfect) when you heard the explosion. The second set tells what you did when you heard the explosion (**passé composé**).

   Il y a eu une explosion.
   Quand vous avez entendu l'explosion, qu'est-ce que vous faisiez?
   Je lisais. (Je regardais la télévision, Je faisais la vaisselle…)

   Il y a eu une explosion.
   Quand vous avez entendu l'explosion, qu'est-ce que vous avez fait?
   Je me suis levé(e). (Je suis allé[e] à la fenêtre, J'ai téléphoné à la police…)

Comment dit-on?

17 Historiette Quand j'étais petit(e) Donnez des réponses personnelles.
1. Quand tu étais petit(e), tu allais à quelle école primaire?
2. Quand la maîtresse parlait, tu écoutais?
3. Tu parlais quand elle parlait?
4. Tu levais la main quand elle posait des questions?
5. Maintenant, tu es élève dans une école secondaire. Tu n'as plus de maîtresse, tu as un professeur. Hier, ton professeur t'a posé une question difficile. Tu lui as donné la bonne réponse?
6. Tu as levé la main quand le professeur a posé cette question?
7. Tu as répondu aux autres questions du professeur?
8. Tu as dit au revoir au professeur quand tu as quitté la classe?

Une école primaire à Porto Novo au Bénin

18 Le téléphone a sonné et…
Répondez d'après le modèle.

Papa / travailler →
Papa n'a pas répondu. Il travaillait.
1. Papa / travailler dans le jardin
2. Maman / faire la cuisine
3. Amélie / lire le journal
4. Paul / écrire un paragraphe
5. Anne et Sylvie / s'habiller
6. Je / prendre une douche
7. Tu / dormir

19 Historiette Dans l'avion Répondez.
1. Tu écoutais de la musique quand le steward t'a servi une collation? Tu as pris la collation?
2. Ton voisin dormait quand l'hôtesse a fait des annonces? Il s'est réveillé quand il a entendu les annonces?
3. Tu parlais avec ta voisine quand l'hôtesse t'a donné des écouteurs? Tu as mis les écouteurs?
4. Beaucoup de passagers dormaient quand l'avion a commencé à atterrir? Ils se sont réveillés pendant l'atterrissage?
5. Tu as attaché ta ceinture de sécurité quand l'avion a commencé à atterrir?

20 Historiette Dans le petit village de Monéteau
Complétez en utilisant le passé composé ou l'imparfait.

Il __1__ (être) midi dans le petit village de Monéteau. Il __2__ (faire) très beau et le soleil __3__ (briller) dans le ciel bleu. Il n'y __4__ (avoir) pas beaucoup de monde dans les rues du village. Les rues __5__ (être) presque désertes.

Grégoire __6__ (être) dans son jardin. Il ne __7__ (travailler) pas. Il __8__ (se reposer). Il __9__ (lire) un magazine. Soudain, il __10__ (entendre) quelque chose. Il __11__ (lever) la tête et il __12__ (voir) son amie Séverine dans la rue. Il lui __13__ (dire) d'entrer. Ils __14__ (discuter) tout l'après-midi au soleil!

21 Ce que je faisais Vous parlez à un(e) camarade et vous lui racontez quelque chose qui est arrivé hier. Dites-lui ce que vous faisiez quand c'est arrivé.

22 Une histoire Avec un(e) camarade inventez une histoire. Utilisez la présentation de l'imparfait et du passé composé à la page 109 comme modèle.

DES VOYAGES INTÉRESSANTS

Structure

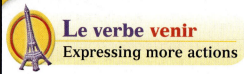

Le verbe venir
Expressing more actions

1. Study the forms of the present tense of **venir** (*to come*).

VENIR			
je	viens	nous	venons
tu	viens	vous	venez
il/elle/on	vient	ils/elles	viennent

Tu viens avec nous au cinéma?
Tous les ans, beaucoup de touristes viennent en France.

2. The verbs **revenir** (*to come back*) and **devenir** (*to become*) are conjugated the same way as **venir**. Their past participles are **venu**, **revenu**, and **devenu**. These verbs are conjugated with **être** in the **passé composé**.

Elle est devenue très riche et elle est revenue dans son village natal.

Comment dit-on?

23 **Oui, il vient.** Répondez.

1. Jacques vient ce soir?
2. Il vient avec qui?
3. Il n'est pas venu la semaine dernière avec Mélanie?
4. Ils ne sont pas venus ensemble?
5. Et toi, tu viens ce soir?
6. Ils viennent avec toi?

Les deux copains sont de Chalon-sur-Saône en Bourgogne.

Les prépositions avec les noms géographiques
Talking about cities, countries, and continents

1. With names of cities, you use the preposition **à** to express "in" or "to." You use **de** to express "from."

   Il est **à** Lyon aujourd'hui.   Il revient **de** Lyon demain.
   Elle arrive **à** Nice demain.   Elle part **de** Paris.

2. The names of all continents end in a silent **e** and they are feminine: **l'Europe, l'Asie, l'Afrique.** Almost all countries whose names end in a silent **e** are also feminine. All other countries are masculine.

Féminin	Masculin
la France	le Canada
la Belgique	le Sénégal
la Suisse	le Mali
l'Italie	le Luxembourg
l'Espagne	l'Iran

   Savez-vous que... ? Le Mexique is an exception. It ends in a silent **e**, but it is masculine.

3. You use **en** to express "in" or "to," and **de (d')** to express "from" with all continents and countries with the exception of masculine countries that begin with a consonant.

J'habite **en** Europe.	Je reviens **d'**Europe.
Je vais **en** Belgique.	Je viens **de** Belgique.
J'habite **en** Israël.	Je reviens **d'**Israël.
Je vais **en** Iran.	Je viens **d'**Iran.

4. You use **au** to express "to" or "in," and **du** to express "from" with all masculine countries that begin with a consonant.

J'habite **au** Canada.	Je reviens **du** Canada.
Je vais **au** Japon.	Je viens **du** Japon.

   Savez-vous que... ? You use the plural **aux** and **des** with **les États-Unis.** J'habite **aux** États-Unis. Je viens **des** États-Unis.

DES VOYAGES INTÉRESSANTS

cent treize ❖ 113

Note: You may want to give students the preposition for your state. To say "in" with a state in French, use **dans** before most states preceded by **le** or **l'**, for example: **dans le Connecticut, dans l'Oregon** (exceptions: **au Nouveau-Mexique, au Texas**). Use **en** without the article with states preceded by **la**, for example: **en Virginie.** With Hawaii, use **à Hawaii.**

l'Alabama	la Géorgie	le Minnesota	la Pennsylvanie
l'Alaska	Hawaii	le Mississippi	le Rhode Island
l'Arizona	l'Idaho	le Missouri	le Tennessee
l'Arkansas	l'Illinois	le Montana	le Texas
la Californie	l'Indiana	le Nebraska	l'Utah
la Caroline du Nord	l'Iowa	le Nevada	le Vermont
la Caroline du Sud	le Kansas	le New Hampshire	la Virginie
le Colorado	le Kentucky	le New Jersey	la Virginie Occidentale
le Connecticut	la Louisiane	l'état de New York	l'état de Washington
le Dakota du Nord	le Maine	le Nouveau-Mexique	le Wisconsin
le Dakota du Sud	le Maryland	l'Ohio	le Wyoming
le Delaware	le Massachusetts	l'Oklahoma	
la Floride	le Michigan	l'Oregon	

Structure

Comment dit-on?

24 **Les pays** Complétez avec **le, la** ou **l'**.
1. ___ France
2. ___ Espagne
3. ___ Maroc
4. ___ Chili
5. ___ Colombie
6. ___ Sénégal
7. ___ Côte d'Ivoire
8. ___ Iran
9. ___ Canada
10. ___ Grèce
11. ___ Chine
12. ___ Japon

Le marché Djemaa El Fna à Marrakech au Maroc

25 **Un peu de géographie** Répondez.
1. Paris est en France ou au Maroc?
2. Rome est en Italie ou en Israël?
3. Madrid est au Chili ou en Espagne?
4. Tokyo est en Chine ou au Japon?
5. Montréal est au Mexique ou au Canada?
6. Dakar est au Sénégal ou en Tunisie?
7. Chicago est aux États-Unis ou au Panama?

26 **Pas très fort(e) en géographie** Répondez.
1. Tu vas à Chartres? C'est dans quel pays?
2. Tu vas à Barcelone? C'est dans quel pays?
3. Tu vas à Ottawa? C'est dans quel pays?
4. Tu vas à Tel-Aviv? C'est dans quel pays?
5. Tu vas à Carthage? C'est dans quel pays?
6. Tu es à Abidjan? C'est dans quel pays?
7. Tu es à Milan? C'est dans quel pays?
8. Tu es à Acapulco? C'est dans quel pays?
9. Tu es à Shanghai? C'est dans quel pays?
10. Tu es à Fort Worth? C'est dans quel pays?

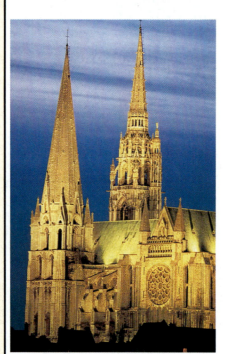

La cathédrale Notre-Dame de Chartres

FRENCH Online

For more information about Chartres and other cathedrals in the Francophone world, go to the Glencoe French Web site: french.glencoe.com

27 **C'est quel continent?** Complétez.
1. Le Japon est ____ Asie et la Chine est ____ Asie aussi.
2. L'Italie et l'Espagne sont ____ Europe. Le Portugal est aussi ____ Europe.
3. Le Brésil, le Chili et l'Argentine sont ____ Amérique du Sud.
4. Les États-Unis et le Canada sont ____ Amérique du Nord.
5. Le Sénégal et la Côte d'Ivoire sont ____ Afrique.

Un Bédouin dans le Sahara au Maroc

28 **D'où viennent ces touristes?** Répondez d'après le modèle.

l'Italie →
Ces touristes viennent d'Italie.

1. l'Espagne
2. Rome
3. Nice
4. la France
5. Tokyo
6. le Japon
7. le Maroc
8. le Mexique
9. New York
10. les États-Unis

29 **Des voyages** Travaillez avec un copain ou une copine. Dites-lui dans quels pays et dans quelles villes vous voulez aller un jour. Dites-lui aussi les pays et les villes où vous êtes déjà allé(e). Ensuite changez de rôle.

30 **Mes grands-parents** Parlez à un(e) camarade. Dites-lui de quel continent ou de quel(s) pays viennent vos grands-parents.

 l'Italie
 l'Espagne
 le Maroc
 la France
 le Canada
 le Japon
 le Mexique

Vous êtes sur le bon chemin. Allez-y!

cent quinze · 115

Conversation

1 Preparation

Resource Manager
Audio Activities TE, pages 43–44
Audio CD 3
CD-ROM

Bellringer Review
Use BRR Transparency 4.7 or write the following on the board.
Say that the following people are coming back from the following places.
1. M. Moreau / Maroc
2. Mme Duprée / France
3. Mlle Dupont / Italie
4. M. Demoulin / États-Unis
5. M. et Mme Charpentier / Canada

2 Presentation

Step 1 Have students close their books and listen as you read the conversation aloud, or play Audio CD 3. Have students listen carefully to the recorded version and pay particular attention to the intonation.

Step 2 Have students repeat each line after you or the recorded version as you model the conversation a second time.

Conversation

À l'aéroport

Vincent: Leïla! Leïla! Par ici!
Leïla: Vincent! Quelle surprise! Tu es venu me chercher à l'aéroport. C'est sympa. Mais mon pauvre, tu as attendu longtemps.
Vincent: Oui, il y avait un problème?
Leïla: Oui. Il faisait très mauvais à Fort-de-France et on est parti avec deux heures de retard.
Vincent: Tu as fait bon voyage?
Leïla: Oui, le personnel était sympa… Le film n'était pas trop mauvais…
Vincent: Tu as faim?
Leïla: Non, j'ai mangé comme douze! On a eu un dîner et une collation. Mais je suis fatiguée.
Vincent: Tu n'as pas dormi?
Leïla: Je ne peux pas dormir dans l'avion. J'ai essayé, mais je n'ai pas pu.
Vincent: Bon, je vais chercher la voiture. Reste ici avec les bagages, je reviens tout de suite.

Vous avez compris?

Répondez.
1. Qui est arrivé de Fort-de-France?
2. Son vol a eu du retard? Pourquoi?
3. Elle a fait bon voyage?
4. Elle a aimé le film?
5. Elle a mangé?
6. Elle a dormi?
7. Qui va chercher la voiture?

Answers to Vous avez compris?
1. Leïla est arrivée de Fort-de-France.
2. Oui, son vol a eu du retard parce qu'il faisait très mauvais à Fort-de-France.
3. Oui, elle a fait bon voyage.
4. Oui, elle a assez aimé le film.
5. Oui, elle a beaucoup mangé.
6. Non, elle n'a pas dormi.
7. Vincent va chercher la voiture.

Glencoe Technology

CD-ROM
On the CD-ROM, students can watch a dramatization of this conversation. They can then play the role of either one of the characters and record themselves in the conversation.

Parlons un peu plus

A **Un voyage en avion** Regardez l'horaire et choisissez une destination. Posez des questions au sujet de votre vol à l'agent de la compagnie aérienne (votre camarade). Il/Elle va vous répondre d'après l'horaire. Vous voulez savoir:
- l'heure de départ du vol
- la durée du vol
- l'heure d'arrivée du vol

B **Un travail intéressant?** Travaillez avec un(e) camarade. Parlez du travail que fait une hôtesse de l'air ou un steward. Décidez si c'est un travail qui vous intéresse ou pas. Si possible, expliquez pourquoi.

La cabine de première classe

DES VOYAGES INTÉRESSANTS

cent dix-sept ✦ 117

Conversation

Step 3 Allow time for pairs of students to practice the conversation. Then call on one or two pairs to read it to the class in as realistic a manner as possible.

Step 4 Ask for volunteers to present an improvised version of the conversation to the class.

3 Practice

Parlons un peu plus

These activities enable students to use the vocabulary and structures learned in the chapter in open-ended exchanges. You may wish to assign different activities to different groups or allow the students to choose the activities they wish to do.

A Before beginning this activity, discuss the lengths of the three flights. Have students look at the map on page 280 in **Bon voyage! Level 1** to determine the time zones.

Florence, Paris   same
Fort-de-France   5 hours earlier
Ft. Lauderdale   6 hours earlier

Geography Connection

🌐 Ask students if they can identify the area shown on the map that is projected on the screen in the photo on page 117.

LEVELING
E: Conversation

ANSWERS TO Parlons un peu plus

A Answers will vary but may include:
—Bonjour, monsieur/madame. Je voudrais aller à Fort Lauderdale. Vous pouvez me dire l'heure du départ du vol?
—Oui. Il y a trois vols par jour. Le premier vol part à dix heures quinze. Le vol dure treize heures et vingt-cinq minutes. Il arrive à dix-sept heures quarante.

B Answers will vary but may include:
—Les stewards ou les hôtesses de l'air doivent beaucoup travailler. Ils expliquent comment utiliser les gilets de sauvetage et les masques à oxygène. Ils distribuent les oreillers, les écouteurs et les couvertures. Ils servent un repas ou une collation, et après ils ramassent les plateaux. C'est un travail difficile. Ça ne m'intéresse pas.
—Oui, ils voyagent tout le temps! Ils vont en Asie, en Afrique, en Europe, partout! Ça c'est très intéressant!

Lectures culturelles

Resource Manager
Audio Activities TE, pages 44–45
Audio CD 3

Bellringer Review

Use BRR Transparency 4.8 or write the following on the board.
In the following sentences, some of the verbs are missing. Fill in the blanks with a verb that makes sense using either the imperfect or passé composé.
1. Quand j'étais petit(e) je voyais souvent ma tante qui _____ à Chicago.
2. Ma tante et moi, nous _____ souvent au cinéma ensemble.
3. Je _____ le journal quand le téléphone a sonné.
4. Quand je _____ à la maison après la fête, mes parents dormaient.

National Standards

Cultures
The reading about trains in France on pages 118–119 and the related activities on page 119 allow students to demonstrate an understanding of the importance of train travel in France.

Presentation

Pre-reading
Step 1 Ask students who among them has traveled by train. Ask them to tell the class a few details in French about their trip. Share you own train experiences in the same way.

Lectures culturelles

Reading Strategy
Questioning
As you read, question anything you do not understand and reread any confusing passages. Be aware that reading further may clear up any difficulties. Ask yourself what point the author is making in the passage and how this new concept relates to information that has already been given.

Les trains d'hier et d'aujourd'hui

L'été dernier, Ashley et d'autres copains qui faisaient du français avec Madame Carrigan sont allés en France. Ils y ont passé trois semaines fabuleuses. Ils se sont bien amusés.

Ils ont fait plusieurs voyages en train. Une fois, ils ont pris le TGV—le train à grande vitesse. Ils ont pris le TGV de Bordeaux à Paris. C'est un train extrêmement rapide: il roule à plus de 300 kilomètres à l'heure. Pour prendre le TGV, il faut payer un supplément et louer (réserver) sa place à l'avance. Ashley et ses amis ont pris des billets de seconde. Voyager en première classe coûte très cher.

Ce n'était pas la première fois que Madame Carrigan voyageait en France. Quand elle était étudiante, elle y allait souvent. Et elle voyageait toujours en train. Mais les vieux trains étaient bien différents du TGV. D'abord, il n'y avait pas de couloir central. Les vieux trains avaient des compartiments. Dans les compartiments de première, il y avait six places et dans les compartiments de seconde, il y en avait huit.

Le château de Beychevelle, près de Bordeaux

Geography Connection
Burgundy is famous for its vineyards and undulating countryside. Along the road from Dijon to Beaune, a distance of some 40 km, one encounters some of the most famous vineyards of the world.

Learning from Photos
(page 118) The area around the bustling, elegant city of Bordeaux, on the Garonne River, has many villages with vineyards that produce the famous Bordeaux wines, including Château de Beychevelle, seen in this photo.

La gare Saint-Lazare

Madame Carrigan voyageait toujours en seconde. Elle trouvait ça beaucoup plus sympa. Pourquoi? Parce que tout le monde montait en voiture muni de provisions[1]: un filet ou deux pleins de fromage, de jambon, de pâté et de fruits. Tous les voyageurs du même compartiment se parlaient et faisaient connaissance[2]. Si quelqu'un n'avait rien à manger, on partageait[3]. De temps en temps, on sortait dans le couloir pour se dégourdir les jambes[4] et bavarder avec les voyageurs des autres compartiments.

Ces vieux trains existent toujours? Oui, il y en a encore quelques-uns. Mais ils commencent à disparaître. Les TGV deviennent de plus en plus nombreux et ils desservent de plus en plus de villes. Tout le monde adore la vitesse.

[1] muni de provisions *loaded with food*
[2] faisaient connaissance *got to know one another*
[3] partageait *shared*
[4] se dégourdir les jambes *to stretch one's legs*

Un TGV en Bourgogne

Vous avez compris?

A Le voyage d'Ashley Répondez.
1. Quand est-ce qu'Ashley est allée en France?
2. Elle y est allée avec qui?
3. Ils y ont passé combien de temps?
4. Ils ont pris quel train pour aller de Bordeaux à Paris?
5. C'est un train qui roule très vite?
6. Il roule à combien de kilomètres à l'heure?
7. Que faisait Madame Carrigan quand elle était étudiante?
8. Comment étaient les vieux trains?
9. Madame Carrigan voyageait en quelle classe? Pourquoi?
10. Tous les voyageurs montaient en voiture munis de quoi?
11. Qu'est-ce qu'on partageait?
12. Comment est-ce que les passagers faisaient connaissance?

B Le TGV Décrivez le TGV. Dites tout ce que vous savez sur ce train.

DES VOYAGES INTÉRESSANTS

Lecture supplémentaire 1

Un voyage en Suisse

Thomas a fait un voyage en Suisse. Il a pris l'avion de Paris à Genève. Il a trouvé que c'était une expérience super. L'avion a survolé les Alpes et Thomas a eu des vues superbes des sommets des montagnes couvertes de neige.

Après une courte visite de Genève, il a pris le train pour Lausanne. Pendant le voyage, les vues du lac Léman étaient très belles.

De Lausanne, Thomas est passé par la région du Valais. Le paysage alpin de cette région est d'une extrême beauté. Avant, le Valais était un canton (une région) difficilement accessible. Mais maintenant, il y a un très bon réseau[1] de routes, de chemins de fer et de funiculaires.

À Visp, Thomas a pris un autre train pour aller à Zermatt. C'est un chemin de fer à voie étroite[2]. Le train monte les pentes[3] jusqu'à Zermatt, une station de sports d'hiver fabuleuse. Les voitures privées sont interdites dans ce petit village pittoresque.

Thomas a remarqué à Visp que les gens ne parlaient plus français. Ils parlaient allemand. En Suisse, il y a quatre langues officielles: le français, l'allemand, l'italien et le romanche.

[1] réseau *network*
[2] à voie étroite *narrow gauge*
[3] pentes *slopes*

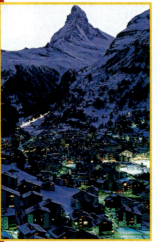
Zermatt en Suisse

Un train dans le massif de la Bernina en Suisse

Le Cervin en Suisse

Vous avez compris?

Des renseignements Trouvez les informations suivantes dans la lecture.
1. deux villes suisses francophones
2. quatre langues parlées en Suisse
3. une station de sports d'hiver très connue
4. un canton suisse
5. un lac en Suisse

Lecture supplémentaire 2

Un voyage au Bénin

Regardez une carte d'Afrique. Cherchez le Bénin. Ensuite, cherchez Cotonou, la ville principale du pays. Tout près de Cotonou, sur une jolie lagune, il y a un petit village de 12 000 habitants qui s'appelle Ganvié. Pour aller à Ganvié, on ne prend pas le train. On y va en pirogue—un genre de long canoë en bois. Tous les habitants du village habitent dans des huttes de bambou sur pilotis. Les habitants vivent[1] presque exclusivement de la pêche[2].

Que font les femmes du village? Elles vendent les poissons que les hommes attrapent. Elles vendent aussi des légumes, des fruits et des épices[3]. Le matin, il y a un marché, un marché où il y a des pirogues, pas des étals[4]. Les femmes vendent leurs produits dans des pirogues.

Ganvié est très pittoresque et beaucoup de touristes européens qui visitent le Bénin passent par ce village.

[1] vivent *live*
[2] la pêche *fishing*
[3] épices *spices*
[4] étals *stalls*

Une maison sur pilotis à Ganvié

Une pirogue à Ganvié

Vous avez compris?

Le Bénin Vrai ou faux?
1. Le Bénin est un pays africain.
2. Le Bénin est en Afrique occidentale, sur la côte de l'océan Atlantique.
3. Ganvié est la ville principale du Bénin.
4. Les maisons à Ganvié sont construites sur pilotis.
5. Les femmes de Ganvié vont à la pêche.
6. Une pirogue est un petit train en bois.

DES VOYAGES INTÉRESSANTS

CONNEXIONS

Les sciences sociales

L'archéologie

Archaeology is a fascinating field. Many interesting trips that tourists take include visits to famous ruins discovered by archaeologists. Archaeologists travel to every corner of the globe to excavate and study the ruins of ancient civilizations. The French-speaking world is no exception. There have been excellent finds of Roman ruins, particularly in France and in some of the French-speaking areas of North Africa.

L'archéologie

L'archéologie est la science qui étudie et analyse les vestiges[1] des civilisations anciennes découvertes par les archéologues. Les archéologues font des fouilles[2] pour déterrer[3] des ruines et des objets anciens faits par des êtres humains. En France et en Afrique du Nord, beaucoup de touristes visitent des sites où il y a des ruines magnifiques de l'Empire romain.

En France

Il y a un amphithéâtre à Arles et un autre à Nîmes. Ces amphithéâtres, appelés aussi des arènes, pouvaient recevoir entre vingt mille et vingt-cinq mille spectateurs. C'est là où avaient lieu des combats de gladiateurs. De nos jours on y donne des concerts, des manifestations sportives et des corridas[4].

C'est l'empereur Auguste qui a fait construire le théâtre à Arles. Les deux colonnes qui survivent sont très impressionnantes. Même aujourd'hui on continue à y présenter des spectacles et en été le théâtre accueille des

[1] vestiges *remains*
[2] fouilles *digs*
[3] déterrer *unearth*
[4] corridas *bullfights*

Le théâtre romain à Arles

National Standards

Connections
This reading about archaeology establishes a connection with another discipline, allowing students to reinforce and further their knowledge of the social sciences through the study of French.

Comparisons
This reading allows students to make comparisons between the ancient history of France and North Africa.

Attention!

The readings in the **Connexions** section are optional. They focus on some of the major disciplines taught in schools and universities. The vocabulary is useful for discussing such topics as history, literature, art, economics, business, science, etc. You may choose any of the following ways to do the readings in the **Connexions** section.

Independent reading Have students read the selections and do the post-reading activities as homework, which you collect. This option is least intrusive on class time and requires a minimum of teacher involvement.

Homework with in-class follow-up Assign the readings and post-reading activities as homework. Review and discuss the material in class the next day.

Intensive in-class activity This option includes a pre-reading vocabulary presentation, in-class reading and discussion, assignment of the activities for homework, and a discussion of the assignment in class the next day.

Learning from Photos

(page 122) The two beautiful columns seen here in the **théâtre romain** in Arles are affectionately called **les deux veuves** (the two widows).

LEVELING
A: Reading

festivals de musique, de photographie et de film.

La Maison Carrée à Nîmes est un temple construit par Agrippa, un général romain.

Le pont du Gard est un aqueduc romain construit en 19 avant J.-C. pour apporter de l'eau à Nîmes.

En Tunisie

En Tunisie on peut voir beaucoup de vestiges de la civilisation romaine. C'est à Carthage où les Romains ont battu[5] les Carthaginois après la troisième guerre punique en 146 avant J.-C.

À Dougga, il y a les ruines de toute une ville romaine. On peut voir des temples, des bains, des maisons privées et le forum—le marché romain.

[5] ont battu *beat*

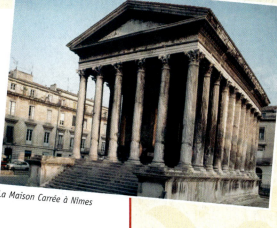
La Maison Carrée à Nîmes

Les ruines romaines à Carthage

Les ruines romaines à Dougga

Vous avez compris?

Un peu d'histoire Discutez.
There is some interesting historical information in this selection about the Roman influence on both France and North Africa. Discuss some of these interesting facts. You can have your discussion in English.

DES VOYAGES INTÉRESSANTS

C'est à vous

Use what you have learned

 Recycling

These activities allow students to use the vocabulary and structure from this chapter in completely open-ended, real-life situations.

Presentation

Encourage students to say as much as possible when they do these activities. Tell them not to be afraid to make mistakes, since the goal of these activities is real-life communication. Let students choose the activities they would like to do.

You may wish to separate students into pairs or groups. They may use props, pictures, or posters if they wish.

Learning from Photos

(page 124) Québec City is perched on a cliff above a narrow point in the St. Lawrence River. There is both the lower town and the upper town. The Château Frontenac is one of the city's most celebrated landmarks. Several buildings stood on this site before the present château was constructed beginning in 1893. It was built as a hotel and still functions as such. It owes its name to the Comte de Frontenac, governor of the French colony between 1672 and 1698.

Reaching All Students

Additional Practice
Display Communication Transparency C 4. Have students work in groups to make up questions about the illustration. Have groups take turns asking and answering the questions.

C'est à vous

Use what you have learned

1 Un voyage super
✔ *Talk about air or train travel*

Vous parlez à des amis d'un voyage que vous avez fait en avion ou en train. Expliquez à vos camarades où vous étiez, avec qui, ce que vous avez fait, etc.

2 Un pays francophone
✔ *Talk about a French-speaking country you'd like to visit*

Travaillez avec un(e) camarade. Choisissez un pays francophone que vous voulez visiter un jour. Trouvez des renseignements sur ce pays dans une encyclopédie, sur Internet, etc. Ensuite, dites pourquoi vous voulez visiter ce pays, comment vous l'imaginez…

3 Un peu de géographie
✔ *Identify French-speaking countries and cities*

Travaillez avec un(e) camarade. Posez des questions sur les villes et pays francophones que vous connaissez. Vous en connaissez beaucoup.

Le château Frontenac à Québec

ANSWERS TO C'est à vous

 Answers will vary but may include:
J'ai fait un voyage en train avec mon copain Jacques. Nous sommes allés à New York parce que nous voulions visiter le musée d'art moderne. Nous étions très contents et il faisait très beau. Nous lisions quand le contrôleur est venu nous demander nos billets. Jacques dormait quand le train est arrivé à New York. Je l'ai réveillé quand nous sommes arrivés. Nous nous sommes bien amusés.

 Answers will vary.
Students can pick any destination they wish.

 Answers will vary.
Students can recall information about the many areas of the French-speaking world they are now familiar with from their study of French.

CHAPITRE 4 C'est à vous

4 Préparons notre voyage
✔ *Write for information on a French-speaking country you'd like to visit*

Reprenez le pays que vous avez choisi dans l'Activité 2, page 124. Écrivez un e-mail à une agence de voyage pour demander tous les renseignements nécessaires: quelles villes visiter, en quelle saison, quels vêtements prendre, etc.

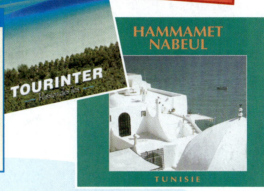

> **Writing Strategy**
>
> **Identifying sources for a research paper**
> To write a research paper, you must plan, set goals, and gather information. When you find a source, skim it to see whether it has any useful information. If it does, record the publication information on an index card so you can find the source easily when you begin your research. Be sure to use all resources available to you—both in print and nonprint. Your school library will be an excellent place to begin looking for sources for your research paper.

5 Mon état

You have to write a brief description of the interesting sites in your state for a French-speaking audience. Your school librarian will help you select the most appropriate print resources—encyclopedias, almanacs, geography books. The Internet is also an excellent resource. Your state's Web sites are a good place to start. Once you have assembled your resources, scan them for the information you need. Remember to include references at the end of your report. Prepare a draft of your report in French and ask your French teacher to review it for you. After you have seen your teacher's comments, prepare the final version of your report.

DES VOYAGES INTÉRESSANTS   cent vingt-cinq ❖ 125

> **Writing Strategy**
>
> **Identifying sources for a research paper** Have students read the Writing Strategy on page 125. Have students refer to the vocabulary list on page 129 if they need more ideas to write this selection.

> **Writing Development**
> Have students keep a notebook containing their best written work from each chapter. These selected writings can be based on assignments from the Student Textbook and the Workbook. The two activities on page 125 are examples of writing assignments that may be included in each student's portfolio. In the Workbook, students will develop an organized autobiography **(Mon autobiographie)**. These workbook pages may also become a part of their portfolio.

LEVELING
These activities encompass all three levels. All students will be able to do them at a sophistication level commensurate with their ability in French. Some students will be able to speak for several minutes, and others may be able to give just a few sentences. This is to be expected when students are functioning completely on their own, generating their own language to the best of their ability.

ANSWERS TO C'est à vous

4 *Answers will vary.*

5 *Answers will vary.*

Assessment

Vocabulaire

1 Complétez.

1. Les lignes ____ desservent les petites villes autour d'une grande ville.
2. Il a ____ son train. Le train est parti une minute avant son arrivée.
3. ____ vérifie ou contrôle les billets dans le train.
4. Toutes les places sont occupées. Il n'y a plus de places ____.
5. Dans une gare il y a ____ qui indique les arrivées et un autre qui indique les départs.

To review Mots 1, turn to pages 98–99.

2 Identifiez.

To review Mots 2, turn to pages 102–103.

6.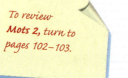
7.
8.
9.
10.

Structure

3 Choisissez la bonne réponse.

To review the imperfect and the passé composé, turn to pages 106, 109–110.

11–12. Quand ____ petit, les trains ____ des compartiments.
    a. j'étais, avaient
    b. j'ai été, ont eu

13–14. Hier nous ____ dans le train et il ____.
    a. montions, partait
    b. sommes montés, est parti

15. Hier vous ____ le train quand je vous ai vu à la gare?
    a. preniez
    b. avez pris

126 cent vingt-six   CHAPITRE 4

ANSWERS TO Assessment

1
1. de banlieue
2. raté
3. Le contrôleur
4. disponibles
5. un tableau

2
6. un oreiller
7. une couverture
8. une ceinture de sécurité
9. un gilet de sauvetage
10. un masque à oxygène

3
11–12. a. j'étais, avaient
13–14. b. sommes montés, est parti
15. a. preniez

CHAPITRE 4 Assessment

4 Complétez avec «venir».

16. Tes copains ____ à quelle heure?
17. Et vous, vous ____ avec eux?
18. Il est ____ hier.

To review the verb venir, turn to page 112.

5 Complétez.

19–20. Je suis allé(e) ____ France et ____ Israël.
21. Mais, mes amis sont allés ____ Maroc.
22. Leur vol arrive ____ Canada.
23. Elle vient ____ Espagne.

To review use of prepositions with country names, turn to page 113.

Culture

6 Choisissez.

24. Le TGV est ____.
    a. un avion supersonique
    b. un train français qui roule très vite
    c. un compartiment dans un train
25. Tout le monde montait en voiture muni de provisions, c'est-à-dire qu'ils montaient ____.
    a. avec tous leur bagages
    b. avec beaucoup de munitions
    c. avec des choses à manger

To review this cultural information, turn to pages 118–119.

Learning from Photos

(page 127) The train station seen here is quite new. It was built to accommodate the TGV. The first route of the TGV was Paris-Lyon.

Glencoe Technology

MINDJOGGER VHS/DVD
You may wish to help your students prepare for the chapter test by playing the MindJogger game show. Teams will compete against each other to review chapter vocabulary and structure and sharpen listening comprehension skills.

La gare TGV Lyon-Satolas

DES VOYAGES INTÉRESSANTS

ANSWERS TO Assessment

4	5	6
16. viennent	19. en	24. b
17. venez	20. en	25. c
18. venu	21. au	
	22. du	
	23. d'	

On parle super bien!

This unique page gives students the opportunity to speak freely and say whatever they can, using the vocabulary and structures they have learned in the chapter. The illustration serves to remind students of precisely what they know how to say in French. There are no activities that students do not have the ability to describe or talk about in French. The art not only depicts the vocabulary and content of this chapter, but also reinforces what they learned in previous chapters.

You may wish to use this page in many ways. Some possibilities are to have students do the following:

1. Look at the illustration and identify items by giving the correct French words.
2. Make up sentences about what they see in the illustration.
3. Make up questions about the illustration. They can call on another class member to respond if you do this as a class activity, or you may prefer to allow students to work in small groups. This activity is extremely beneficial because it enables students to actively use interrogative words.
4. Answer questions you ask them about the illustration.
5. Work in pairs and make up a conversation based on the illustration.
6. Look at the illustration and give a complete oral review of what they see.
7. Look at the illustration and write a paragraph (or essay) about it.

You can also use this page as an assessment or testing tool, taking into account individual differences by having students go from simple to quite complicated tasks. The assessment can be either oral or written. You may wish to use the rubrics provided on pages T20–T21 as you give students the following directions.

1. Identify the topic or situation of the illustration.
2. Give the French words for as many items as you can.
3. Think of as many sentences as you can to describe the illustration.
4. Go over your sentences and put them in the best sequencing to give a coherent story based on the illustration.

On parle super bien!

Tell all you can about this illustration.

128 cent vingt-huit

CHAPITRE 4

Vocabulaire

Getting around a train station

un tableau	un TGV (train à grande vitesse)
une ligne de banlieue	
une grande ligne	

On board the train

un compartiment	une place	assis(e)
le couloir	disponible	debout
un contrôleur	complet, complète	
un siège réglable		

Getting around an airport

embarquer	un décollage
débarquer	un atterrissage
récupérer les bagages	un chariot
le contrôle des passeports	la douane

On board the plane

un oreiller	un masque à oxygène
une couverture	un gilet de sauvetage
des écouteurs (m. pl.)	une ceinture de sécurité
une collation	
le dossier du siège	

Other useful words and expressions

desservir	venir	de chaque côté
rouler	Il est interdit de fumer	annulé(e)
rater	un paysage	sans escale
faire escale	splendide	

How well do you know your vocabulary?
- Choose words to describe a train trip.
- Write a brief description for someone who is traveling by train for the first time.

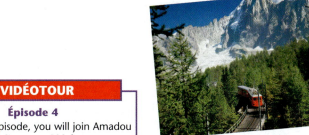

VIDÉOTOUR
Épisode 4
In this video episode, you will join Amadou on a train trip. See page 503 for more information.

DES VOYAGES INTÉRESSANTS

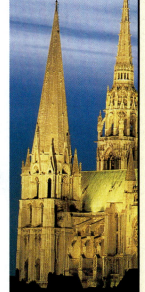

VIDÉO VHS/DVD
The Video Program allows students to see how the chapter vocabulary and structures are used by native speakers. For maximum reinforcement, show the video episode as a final activity for Chapter 4.

Révision

Conversation

Une sortie

Emma: Allô, Julie? Salut, c'est Emma.
Julie: Ah, bonjour, ça va?
Emma: Ça va. On va toujours au concert ce soir?
Julie: Oui, mais Cyril ne peut pas venir avec nous.
Emma: Pourquoi?
Julie: Il m'a envoyé un mail ce matin. Son train arrive à minuit.
Emma: Son train? Où est-ce qu'il est allé?
Julie: Voir sa grand-mère. Et pendant qu'il était chez elle, elle est tombée malade.
Emma: Rien de grave, j'espère.
Julie: Non, elle va mieux maintenant.

Vous avez compris?

Emma et Julie Choisissez la bonne réponse.

1. Emma _____ à Julie.
   a. envoie un mail
   b. donne un coup de fil
   c. envoie un fax
2. Emma va aller _____ ce soir.
   a. à un concert
   b. au théâtre
   c. chez sa grand-mère
3. Julie a reçu _____ de Cyril.
   a. un mail
   b. une carte postale
   c. un fax
4. Cyril ne peut pas aller au concert parce qu'il _____.
   a. va rester chez sa grand-mère qui est malade
   b. va s'occuper de sa grand-mère
   c. ne va pas arriver à l'heure
5. Le train va arriver _____.
   a. avec du retard
   b. trop tard
   c. à l'heure
6. Quand Cyril était chez sa grand-mère, elle _____.
   a. est tombée malade
   b. est allée à l'hôpital
   c. a eu un accident grave

130 cent trente   CHAPITRES 1–4

CHAPITRES 1–4

Structure

Les pronoms

1. **Le, la, (l'), les** are direct object pronouns. A direct object receives the action of the verb. Remember that **le, la, l', les** can replace people or things.

Marie regarde **l'horaire**.	Elle **le** regarde.
Elle regarde **l'ordonnance**.	Elle **la** regarde.
Elle regarde **les magazines**.	Elle **les** regarde.
Elle regarde **les cartes postales**.	Elle **les** regarde.
Marie regarde **Ludovic**.	Elle **le** regarde.
Ludovic regarde **Marie**.	Il **la** regarde.

2. **Lui, leur** are indirect objects. An indirect object is the indirect receiver of the action of the verb. Remember that **lui** and **leur** replace **à** + a person.

Je donne un cadeau **à Éric**.	Je **lui** donne un cadeau.
Je donne un cadeau **à Emma**.	Je **lui** donne un cadeau.
Je donne un cadeau **aux garçons**.	Je **leur** donne un cadeau.
Je donne un cadeau **aux filles**.	Je **leur** donne un cadeau.

3. The pronouns **me (m'), te (t'), nous,** and **vous** can be either direct or indirect objects.

Cyril **te** regarde?	Oui, il **me** regarde, mais il ne **me** parle pas.
Cyril **vous** regarde?	Oui, il **nous** regarde, mais il ne **nous** parle pas.

4. An object pronoun always comes right before the verb it is linked to.

   > Je **lui parle**.
   > Je ne **te parle** pas.
   > Je veux **les voir**.
   > Je ne veux pas **leur parler**.

Presentation

Les pronoms

Step 1 Write the examples on the board. Circle the nouns and draw a box around the object pronouns. Draw a line from the noun to the corresponding pronoun.

Step 2 Read each sentence on the left and have students answer you with the sentences on the right.

Révision

Art Connection

Pierre Auguste Renoir (1841–1919), one of the famous French Impressionist painters, loved to paint portraits and scenes. He delighted in showing the happiest sides of nature. He once said, "For me, a picture must be an amiable thing, joyous and pretty, yes, pretty! There are enough troublesome things in life without inventing them."

Renoir loved to paint. He did so up to the day he died, even though he was crippled with arthritis and sometimes had to have his brushes tied to his wrists.

Learning from Photos
(page 132) Have students say everything they can about the photo.

Révision

1 Super! Répondez d'après le modèle.

—Tu vois le tableau?

—Oui, je le vois. Il est très beau.

1. Tu vois la statue?
2. Tu entends le concert?
3. Tu lis le poème?
4. Tu vois l'actrice?
5. Tu regardes les tableaux?
6. Tu regardes le ballet?

Pierre Auguste Renoir *Portrait de Margot*

Un cinéma à Aix-en-Provence

2 Historiette En version originale
Répondez d'après le modèle.

—Tu veux voir ce film? (oui)
—Oui, je veux le voir.

1. Tu vas voir ce film? (oui)
2. Tu vas voir ce film en version originale? (oui)
3. Tu comprends le français? (oui, un peu)
4. Tu comprends le français assez bien pour comprendre le film? (non)
5. Tu lis les sous-titres? (oui)

3 Qu'est-ce que tu fais?
Répondez en utilisant **lui** ou **leur**.

1. Tu parles souvent à ton meilleur ami au téléphone?
2. Tu parles souvent à ta meilleure amie aussi?
3. Tu téléphones à tes cousins?
4. Tu donnes un cadeau à ta mère pour son anniversaire?
5. Tu achètes un chemisier à ta mère?

132 ✣ *cent trente-deux* CHAPITRES 1–4

ANSWERS TO Révision

1
1. Oui, je la vois. Elle est très belle.
2. Oui, je l'entends. Il est très beau.
3. Oui, je le lis. Il est très beau.
4. Oui, je la vois. Elle est très belle.
5. Oui, je les regarde. Ils sont très beaux.
6. Oui, je le regarde. Il est très beau.

2
1. Oui, je vais le voir.
2. Oui, je vais le voir en version originale.
3. Oui, je le comprends un peu.
4. Non, je ne le comprends pas assez bien pour le comprendre.
5. Oui, je les lis.

3
1. Oui, je lui parle souvent au téléphone.
2. Oui, je lui parle souvent aussi.
3. Oui, je leur téléphone.
4. Oui, je lui donne un cadeau pour son anniversaire.
5. Oui, je lui achète un chemisier.

4 **Vraiment?** Complétez en utilisant un pronom.

Charles: Mélanie, Guillaume __1__ cherche.
Mélanie: Guillaume __2__ cherche? Qu'est-ce qu'il veut?
Charles: Il veut __3__ dire quelque chose.
Mélanie: Qu'est-ce qu'il veut __4__ dire? Il sait bien que je ne veux plus __5__ voir.
Charles: Oui, mais il __6__ adore!
Mélanie: Et moi, je ne __7__ adore pas!
Charles: Et moi, je ne __8__ crois pas!

L'imparfait et le passé composé

1. The use of the imperfect or **passé composé** depends on whether the speaker sees the past action as an event or an action with a beginning and an end; or as an action in progress, a state, a situation with no real beginning or end. Compare the following sentences.

   Jean lisait quand il a entendu l'explosion.
   Jean est allé à la fenêtre quand il a entendu l'explosion.

   The first sentence states what happened (**passé composé**) and describes what was going on (imperfect) when the event occurred. The second sentence tells what the person did (**passé composé**) when the event occurred.

2. The following time expressions are often used with the indicated tenses.

Passé composé	Imparfait
hier	souvent
lundi (l'an) dernier	tous les jours (mois, ans)
pendant une heure (un mois)	de temps en temps
à trois heures	toujours

3. The difference between the imperfect and the **passé composé** is best shown in context. The more you are exposed to examples in context, the more you will get a feel for when to use one tense or the other.

Révision

5 **Que faisait-il?** Complétez d'après le modèle.

lire →
Quand il a entendu l'explosion, il ____.
Quand il a entendu l'explosion, il lisait.

1. faire une promenade à vélo
2. travailler
3. être au téléphone
4. regarder la télévision
5. écrire un mail
6. prendre un bain
7. mettre le couvert
8. dormir

6 **Qu'avez-vous fait?** Répondez d'après le modèle.

aller à la fenêtre →
Quand j'ai entendu l'explosion, je ____.
Quand j'ai entendu l'explosion, je suis allé(e) à la fenêtre.

1. se lever
2. téléphoner à la police
3. sortir dehors
4. regarder par la fenêtre
5. se réveiller

7 **Historiette** **Une rencontre à Paris** Complétez en utilisant le passé composé ou l'imparfait.

Steffi __1__ (rencontrer) Mark à Paris. Quand elle l' __2__ (rencontrer), il __3__ (porter) une chemise bleue. C'est Steffi qui __4__ (parler) la première. Elle __5__: (dire)

Steffi: Je crois que je vous __6__ déjà __7__ (voir) quelque part (*somewhere*).
Mark: Ah non, je ne crois pas, je ne __8__ jamais __9__ (venir) ici avant. Vous __10__ (voir) quelqu'un qui me ressemble, peut-être.
Steffi: Non, je crois bien que je vous __11__ (voir) quelque part. Mais ce n'est peut-être pas ici que je vous __12__ (voir) la première fois. Voyons, vous __13__ déjà __14__ (aller) à la tour Eiffel?
Mark: Oui, nous y __15__ (aller), ma sœur et moi, hier.
Steffi: Alors, vous voyez, j' __16__ (avoir) raison! Je vous __17__ déjà __18__! (voir) Moi aussi, j' __19__ (être) à la tour Eiffel hier avec mon frère. Nous __20__ (passer) toute la matinée à regarder Paris du haut du deuxième étage. Le temps __21__ (être) magnifique. Il ne __22__ (faire) pas trop froid… Mais vous le savez, vous y __23__ (être) aussi. Vous êtes américain?

Answers to Révision

5
1. Quand il a entendu l'explosion, il faisait une promenade à vélo.
2. Quand il a entendu l'explosion, il travaillait.
3. Quand il a entendu l'explosion, il était au téléphone.
4. Quand il a entendu l'explosion, il regardait la télévision.
5. Quand il a entendu l'explosion, il écrivait un mail.
6. Quand il a entendu l'explosion, il prenait un bain.
7. Quand il a entendu l'explosion, il mettait le couvert.
8. Quand il a entendu l'explosion, il dormait.

6
1. Quand j'ai entendu l'explosion, je me suis levé(e).
2. Quand j'ai entendu l'explosion, j'ai téléphoné à la police.
3. Quand j'ai entendu l'explosion, je suis sorti(e) dehors.
4. Quand j'ai entendu l'explosion, j'ai regardé par la fenêtre.
5. Quand j'ai entendu l'explosion, je me suis réveillé(e).

7
1. a rencontré
2. a rencontré
3. portait
4. a parlé
5. a dit
6. ai
7. vu
8. suis
9. venu
10. avez vu
11. ai vu
12. ai vu

Teacher's notes:

5 In this activity, you may wish to discuss with students why the first verb is in the **passé composé** and the second in the imperfect. One way to demonstrate the difference is to ask students which activity began first and continued for some time, and which was more sudden, with a clear start and finish.

6 In this activity, emphasize that both actions were short, separate, and independent, with clear starting and ending points. They are cause and effect actions.

7 Allow students time to prepare this activity before working together on it. Then have each student read two or three sentences as you write the verb forms on the board.
Expansion: Assign the roles to individuals and have them read the finished activity.
Note: Tell students **avoir raison** means **donner la bonne réponse, répondre correctement.**

Des touristes près de la place de la Concorde à Paris

Mark: Oui. Et vous, allemande?
Steffi: Non, suisse.
Mark: Ah, vraiment? Quelle coïncidence! Nous __24__ (passer) la semaine dernière en Suisse.
Steffi: Et vous __25__ (aimer) la Suisse?
Mark: Beaucoup. Nous __26__ (aller) à Genève, Lausanne, Neuchâtel et aussi à Zermatt. C'est splendide.
Steffi: Oui, mais il faut venir en hiver. C'est là où c'est bien. Vous faites du ski?
Mark: Oui, j'adore le ski. Quand j' __27__ (être) petit, nous __28__ (habiter) dans le Vermont et je __29__ (faire) du ski tout le temps.

8 **Chez le médecin** Travaillez avec un(e) camarade. Parlez de votre dernière visite chez le médecin. Dites comment vous vous sentiez, ce que vous avez dit au médecin et ce qu'il/elle a fait.

9 **Une critique** Vous parlez à des amis d'un film que vous avez vu. Expliquez à vos copains qui jouait dans le film et ce qui s'est passé.

LITERARY COMPANION *You may wish to read the excerpt about train travel from* Le livre de mon père, *written by Émile Henriot. You will find this literary selection on page 476.*

Preview

The section **Reflets de la France** was prepared by the National Geographic Society. Its purpose is to give students greater insight, through these visual images, into the culture and people of France. Have students look at the photographs on pages 136–139 for enjoyment. If they would like to talk about them, let them say anything they can, using the vocabulary they have learned to this point.

 National Standards

Cultures
The **Reflets de la France** photos and the accompanying captions allow students to gain insights into the people and culture of France.

About the Photos

1. Champs de lavande en Provence When one thinks of Provence, beauty and color are what most frequently come to mind—the Mediterranean landscapes with their bright colors, red roofed **mas** *(country homes)* surrounded by cypress trees, and beautifully scented lavender fields, which inspired the famous paintings of Cézanne and Van Gogh.

2. Le célèbre toit de l'hôtel-Dieu à Beaune en Bourgogne Beaune is the capital of the Côte de Beaune region, home of many famous vineyards. The **hôtel-Dieu** was built in 1450 and served as a hospital until 1971. During this time, nurses in the hospital continued to wear the medieval dresses they wore in the fifteenth century. There is a museum in the **hôtel-Dieu** that displays medical instruments used a century ago.

3. Les remparts d'Antibes sur la Côte d'Azur Antibes is a picturesque old town half-way between Nice and Cannes on the Côte

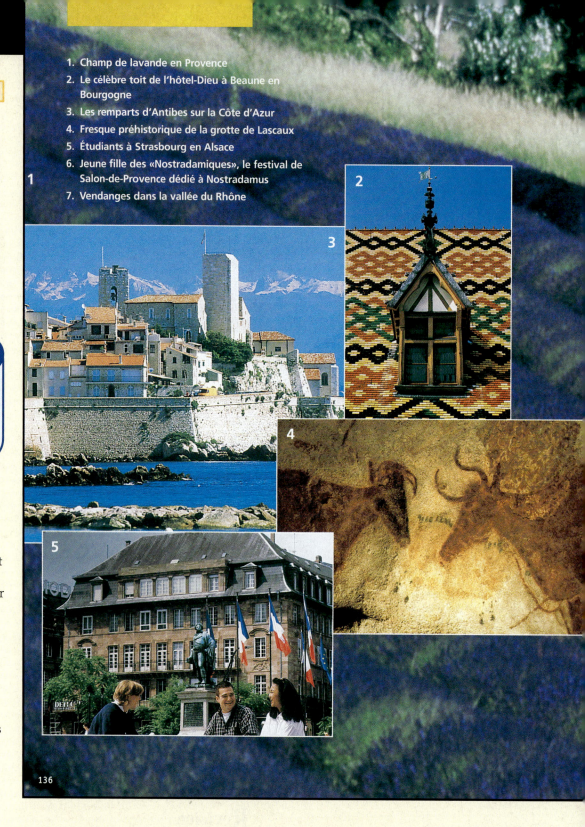

1. Champ de lavande en Provence
2. Le célèbre toit de l'hôtel-Dieu à Beaune en Bourgogne
3. Les remparts d'Antibes sur la Côte d'Azur
4. Fresque préhistorique de la grotte de Lascaux
5. Étudiants à Strasbourg en Alsace
6. Jeune fille des «Nostradamiques», le festival de Salon-de-Provence dédié à Nostradamus
7. Vendanges dans la vallée du Rhône

REFLETS
de la France

d'Azur. In its early days, Antibes was a strategic military place as evidenced by these ramparts.

4. Fresque préhistorique de la grotte de Lascaux Lascaux, in the Périgord region, is known for its prehistoric art. In the area there are many caves and caverns in which archaeologists have uncovered bones, utensils, and paintings of Cro-Magnon people. The caves of Lascaux were discovered in 1940. They contain the finest prehistoric paintings in Europe. It is believed that some are 30,000 years old. In 1963 it was discovered that in spite of precautions, some of the paintings had begun to deteriorate. The caves were closed, and an exact replica of the caves was constructed.

5. Étudiants à Strasbourg en Alsace Strasbourg is the capital of Alsace. Strasbourg is a charming city with many medieval streets with timbered houses, reminiscent of the architecture of many areas of Germany. It was in Strasbourg that Rouget de Lisle composed the words and music for *La Marseillaise,* the French national anthem.

6. Jeune fille des «Nostradamiques», le festival de Salon-de-Provence dédié à Nostradamus Salon-de-Provence is a market town near Aix-en-Provence. This small town was the home of the famous astrologer Nostradamus. The house where he lived is now a museum devoted to him. He is buried in the fourteenth century church of St. Laurent in Salon-de-Provence.

7. Vendanges dans la vallée du Rhône The Rhône valley has a recorded history that dates back to the time of the Romans. It is an area known for its excellent restaurants and fine wines. The northern part of the Rhône valley produces the light tasting Beaujolais wine.

137

8. Menton sur la Côte d'Azur
9. Un «nez» testant un parfum à Paris
10. Fortifications de la haute-ville et le port de Bonifacio, en Corse
11. Les jardins décoratifs du château d'Angers, dans la vallée de la Loire
12. Source naturelle à Contrexéville, une station thermale des Vosges
13. La plage de Deauville, en Normandie
14. Le pont du Gard à Nîmes

8. Menton sur la Côte d'Azur Menton is just a very short distance from the Italian border at the tip of the Côte d'Azur. Part of Menton is still a sleepy fishing village. Another part has wide avenues, upscale hotels, and a lovely beach. Many well-to-do retired people live in Menton.

9. Un «nez» testant un parfum à Paris France is famous for its perfume industry. The perfumes are made from flowers that grow in Provence.

10. Fortifications de la haute-ville et le port de Bonifacio, en Corse The island of Corsica is known for its natural beauty. It is now a **département** of France, and has a population of some 250,000. Bonifacio is an ancient fortress town situated on high chalk cliffs. It still has an active garrison. Napoleon was born in Ajaccio, the major town of the island.

11. Les jardins décoratifs du château d'Angers, dans la vallée de la Loire The Loire Valley is famous for its beautiful **châteaux** with their magnificent geometrical French gardens. The Château d'Angers has the appearance of a fortress, but it also has an elegant hibiscus-filled garden. The Château was originally built by one of the Comtes d'Anjou, but it was rebuilt by Louis IX, in the thirteenth century. It is an excellent example of feudal architecture.

12. Source naturelle à Contrexéville, une station thermale des Vosges Contrexéville is a thermal bath resort in the Vosges mountains, in Lorraine.

 **Teacher's Corner**

Index to the NATIONAL GEOGRAPHIC MAGAZINE

The following related articles may be of interest:

- "France's Paradox Island: Corsica," by Peter Ross Range, April 2003.
- "France's Magical Ice Age Art: Chauvet Cave," by Jean Clottes, August 2001.
- "Art Treasures from the Ice Age: Lascaux Cave," by Jean-Philippe Rigaud, October 1998.
- "Essence of Provence," by Bill Bryson, September 1995.
- "Europe Faces an Immigrant Tide," by Peter Range, May 1993.
- "Darcey: A Village That Refuses to Die," by William S. Ellis, July 1989.
- "Tour de France—An Annual Madness," by Gilbert Duclos-Lassalle, July 1989.
- "Paris: *La Belle Époque*," by Eugen Weber, July 1989.

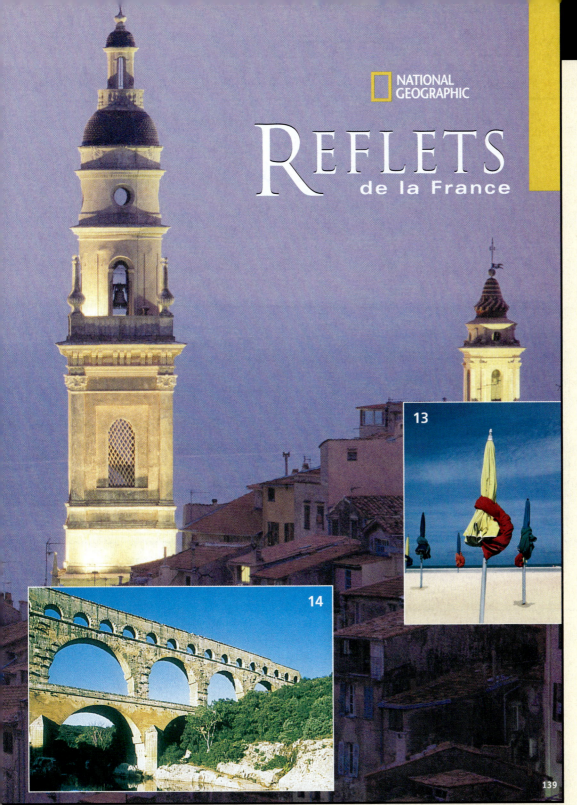

REFLETS
de la France

13. La plage de Deauville, en Normandie Deauville is famous for its sandy beach dotted with brightly colored tents and sun umbrellas. Along the beach there are **planches,** wooden walkways for parading up and down to see and be seen. Deauville has a rather aristocratic ambiance.

14. Le pont du Gard à Nîmes Le pont du Gard was built by the Romans some two thousand years ago as an aqueduct. It is 49 meters high, and for almost five centuries it carried water from Uzès to the city of Nîmes.

Products available from Glencoe/McGraw-Hill
To order the following products, call Glencoe/McGraw-Hill at 1-800-334-7344.
CD-ROM
- Picture Atlas of the World

Transparency Set
- NGS MapPack: Geography of Europe

Products available from National Geographic Society
To order the following products, call National Geographic Society at 1-800-368-2728.
Books
- National Geographic World Atlas for Young Explorers
- National Geographic Satellite Atlas of the World

Software
- ZingoLingo: French Diskette

Video
- France
- Europe

Planning for Chapter 5

SCOPE AND SEQUENCE, PAGES 140–171

Topics
* Bank and postal services

Functions
* How to use expressions related to bank and postal services
* How to refer to people and things already mentioned
* How to express what you and others do for one another
* How to make negative statements

National Standards
* Communication Standard 1.1 pages 144, 145, 148, 149, 151, 152, 154, 156, 157, 159, 166
* Communication Standard 1.2 pages 144, 145, 148, 149, 151, 152, 154, 156, 157, 158, 161, 162, 163, 165, 166
* Communication Standard 1.3 pages 154, 166, 167
* Cultures Standard 2.1 pages 142, 143, 158, 160–161, 162, 163
* Connections Standard 3.1 pages 164–165
* Comparisons Standard 4.2 pages 163, 167
* Communities Standard 5.1 page 167

Culture
* Mélanie and her weekly allowance
* Foreign currencies
* Discussing differences between postal services in the United States and France

Structure
* The relative pronouns **qui** and **que**
* Agreement of the past participle
* Reciprocal actions
* Negative expressions: **personne ne** and **rien ne**

PACING AND PRIORITIES

The chapter content is color coded below to assist you in planning.

■ required   ■ recommended   ■ optional

Vocabulaire (required)   Days 1–4
- ■ Mots 1
  - À la banque
  - Au bureau de change
  - Sandrine et Luc
- ■ Mots 2
  - À la poste

Structure (required)   Days 5–7
- ■ Les pronoms relatifs **qui** et **que**
- ■ L'accord du participe passé
- ■ Les actions réciproques
- ■ Personne ne… et rien ne…

Conversation (required)
- ■ Au bureau de change

Lectures culturelles
- ■ La semaine des jeunes Français (recommended)
- ■ Les devises étrangères (optional)
- ■ La Poste (optional)

Connexions (optional)
- ■ Les finances

■ C'est à vous (recommended)

■ Assessment (recommended)

■ On parle super bien! (optional)

RESOURCE GUIDE

SECTION	PAGES	SECTION RESOURCES
Vocabulaire *Mots 1*		
À la banque Au bureau de change Sandrine et Luc	142 143 143–145	Vocabulary Transparencies 5.2–5.3 Audio CD 4 Audio Activities TE, pages 48–50 Workbook, page 51 Quiz 1, page 21 ExamView® Pro
Vocabulaire *Mots 2*		
À la poste	146–149	Vocabulary Transparencies 5.4–5.5 Audio CD 4 Audio Activities TE, pages 50–52 Workbook, pages 52–54 Quiz 2, page 22 ExamView® Pro
Structure		
Les pronoms relatifs **qui** et **que** L'accord du participe passé Les actions réciproques **Personne ne…** et **rien ne…**	150–152 153–154 155–156 157	Audio CD 4 Audio Activities TE, pages 52–53 Workbook, pages 55–58 Quizzes 3–6, pages 23–26 ExamView® Pro
Conversation		
Au bureau de change	158–159	Audio CD 4 Audio Activities TE, page 54 Interactive CD-ROM
Lectures culturelles		
La semaine des jeunes Français Les devises étrangères La Poste	160–161 162 163	Audio CD 4 Audio Activities TE, page 55 Tests, pages 70, 73
Connexions		
Les finances	164–165	Tests, page 74
C'est à vous		
	166–167	**Bon voyage!** Video, Episode 5 Video Activities, Chapter 5 French Online Activities french.glencoe.com
Assessment		
	168–169	Communication Transparency C 5 Quizzes 1–6, pages 21–26 Performance Assessment, Task 5 Tests, pages 67–80 ExamView® Pro Situation Cards, Chapter 5 **Marathon mental** Videoquiz

Using Your Resources for Chapter 5

Transparencies

Bellringer 5.1–5.8

Vocabulary 5.1–5.5

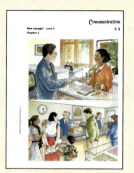
Communication C 5

Workbook

Vocabulary, pages 51–54

Structure, pages 55–58

Enrichment, pages 59–62

Audio Activities

Vocabulary, pages 48–52

Structure, pages 52–53

Conversation, page 54

Cultural Reading, page 55

Additional Practice, pages 56–57

Assessment

Vocabulary and Structure Quizzes, pages 21–26

Chapter Tests, pages 67–80

Situation Cards, Chapter 5

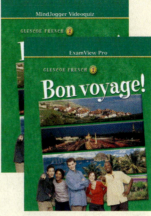
MindJogger Videoquiz, ExamView® Pro, Chapter 5

Timesaving Teacher Tools

TeacherWorks™

TeacherWorks™ is your all-in-one teacher resource center. Personalize lesson plans, access resources from the Teacher Wraparound Edition, connect to the Internet, or make a to-do list. These are only a few of the many features that can assist you in the planning and organizing of your lessons.

Includes:
- A calendar feature
- Access to all program blackline masters
- Standards correlations and more

ExamView® Pro

Test Bank software for Macintosh and Windows makes creating, editing, customizing, and printing tests quick and easy.

Technology Resources

In the Chapter 5 Internet activity, you will have a chance to learn more about the Francophone world. Visit <u>french.glencoe.com</u>.

On the Interactive Conversation CD-ROM, students can listen to and take part in a recorded version of the conversation in Chapter 5.

See the National Geographic Teacher's Corner on pages 138–139, 244–245, 372–373, 472–473 for reference to additional technology resources.

Bon voyage! Video and Video Activities, Chapter 5

Help your students prepare for the chapter test by playing the **Marathon mental** Videoquiz game show. Teams will compete against each other to review chapter vocabulary and structure and sharpen listening comprehension skills.

140D

Preview

In this chapter, students will learn to communicate with postal and bank clerks, write letters, address an envelope in French, exchange money, and carry out simple banking transactions. Structure points presented are the pronouns **qui** and **que**, the agreement of the past participle, reciprocal actions, and negative statements.

 National Standards

Communication

In Chapter 5, students will communicate in spoken and written French on the following topics:
• Personal banking
• Using the postal service
Students will obtain and provide information and engage in conversations dealing with money, banking, correspondence, and the post office as they fulfill the chapter objectives listed on this page.

Communities

If you live in an area where foreign language materials are available, have students look for French greeting cards. Prepare a bulletin board using these cards.

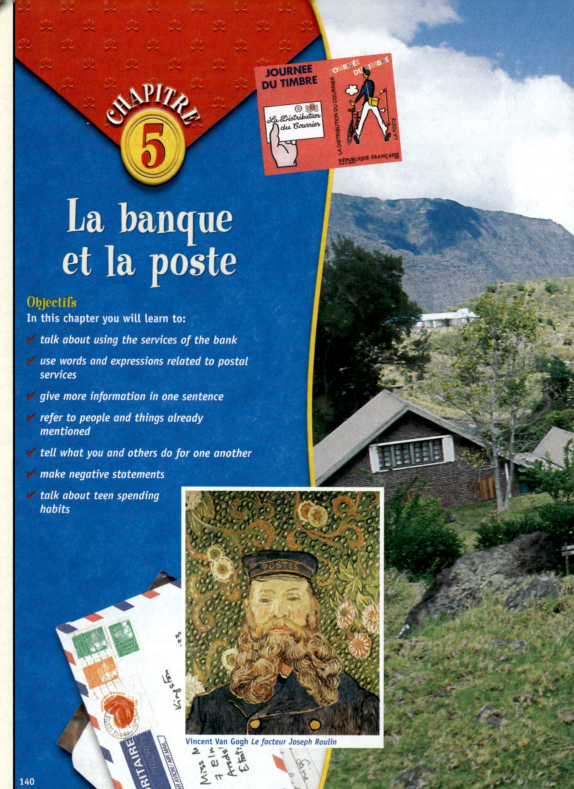

La banque et la poste

Objectifs
In this chapter you will learn to:

✓ talk about using the services of the bank
✓ use words and expressions related to postal services
✓ give more information in one sentence
✓ refer to people and things already mentioned
✓ tell what you and others do for one another
✓ make negative statements
✓ talk about teen spending habits

Vincent Van Gogh *Le facteur Joseph Roulin*

CHAPITRE 5

Spotlight on Culture

Photograph In this photo, we see a letter carrier delivering mail in the mountainous town of Cirque de Mafate on the island of la Réunion in the Indian Ocean. The town has two letter carriers, who make their rounds delivering mail completely on foot.

Painting As a young man, Van Gogh worked as a lay missionary in a poor mining village in Belgium. He became quite an introvert and turned to his true love of art. His early paintings, done in drab hues, showed peasants going about their daily routines.

In 1866 Van Gogh went to live in Paris to be with his brother, Theo, an art dealer. Theo immediately recognized his brother's artistic talents and provided him with an allowance so he could continue painting. Van Gogh's paintings became less somber and he began to use brighter colors. In 1888 he went to Arles, where he developed his own painting style marked by bright colors, bold brushstrokes, and twisting lines.

Van Gogh was an unstable individual who suffered from epilepsy and depression. He sold only one painting in his lifetime, but his work inspired many future artists.

LEVELING

The activities, conversations, and readings within each chapter are marked according to level of difficulty. **E** indicates easy. **A** indicates average. **C** indicates challenging. Some activities cover a range of difficulty. In some activities, for example, advanced students will be able to produce more extensive responses while students who learn at a different rate may give less detailed responses. The leveling indicators will help you individualize instruction to best meet your students' needs.

Vocabulaire Mots 1

1 Preparation

Resource Manager

Vocabulary Transparencies 5.2–5.3
Audio Activities TE, pages 48–50
Audio CD 4
Workbook, page 51
Quiz 1, page 21
ExamView® Pro

Bellringer Review

Use BRR Transparency 5.1 or write the following on the board.
Match the city to its country. Then write a complete sentence to indicate in which country each city is located.
1. Oslo — États-Unis
2. Nantes — Mexique
3. Acapulco — Norvège
4. Portland — Angleterre
5. Londres — France

2 Presentation

Step 1 Have students close their books. Introduce the **Mots 1** vocabulary using Vocabulary Transparencies 5.2–5.3. Have students repeat each word after you or the recording on Audio CD 4 two or three times as you point to the appropriate illustration on the transparencies.

Step 2 Ask **Qu'est-ce que c'est?** as you point to the item on the transparency and have students come up with the new words themselves.

Step 3 Have students open their books and read the new words and sentences aloud. Ask questions such as: **Jean est allé où? Qu'est-ce qu'il a donné à la caissière?**

Vocabulaire Mots 1

À la banque

des euros

Pour écrire un chèque, il faut avoir un compte courant. Jean donne le chèque à la caissière et elle lui donne de l'argent liquide. Il touche le chèque.

Jean parle à la caissière.

Magali a ouvert un compte d'épargne. Elle a versé de l'argent sur son compte.

Sophie a retiré de l'argent au distributeur automatique.

142 cent quarante-deux   CHAPITRE 5

Reaching All Students

Total Physical Response
Have students dramatize the following:
(Student 1), **venez ici, s'il vous plaît.**
Vous avez de l'argent?
Montrez-moi un billet.
Montrez-moi une pièce.
Imaginez que vous avez un chèque. Signez votre chèque.
Et maintenant, imaginez que vous êtes fauché(e). Indiquez-moi que vous n'avez pas de fric.

LEVELING
E: Vocabulary
A: Vocabulary

Vocabulaire Mots 1

Au bureo de change

un porte-monnaie
une pièce

Charlene est allée au bureau de change.
Le cours du change: Aujourd'hui, le dollar est à un euro cinq.
Elle a changé des dollars.
La caissière lui a donné des euros.
Charlene a pris les billets et elle les a comptés.
Elle a pris les pièces et elle les a mises dans son porte-monnaie.

Sandrine et Luc

Sandrine fait toujours des économies.
Elle ne dépense pas tout son argent.
Elle aime mettre de l'argent de côté.
Elle a plein de fric (beaucoup d'argent).

Mais Luc? Il n'a jamais de fric (d'argent).
Il est toujours fauché.

Tu peux me prêter de l'argent?

emprunter prêter

Luc, tu me dois du fric. Tu ne m'as pas rendu l'argent que je t'ai prêté.

Tu es sûre?

LA BANQUE ET LA POSTE

cent quarante-trois 143

Vocabulaire

Quel est le mot?

Le bureau de poste à Yerres dans la banlieue parisienne

1 Historiette À la banque
Répondez que oui.

1. Cédric est allé à la banque?
2. Il a parlé au caissier?
3. Il a touché un chèque?
4. Il aime mettre de l'argent de côté?
5. Il a ouvert un compte d'épargne?
6. Il a versé de l'argent sur son compte?

2 Historiette Au bureau de change
Répondez d'après les indications.
1. Le touriste est allé à la banque ou au bureau de change? (au bureau de change)
2. Qu'est-ce qu'il voulait faire? (changer de l'argent)
3. Quel était le cours du change? (un euro dix)
4. Il a changé combien d'argent? (100 dollars américains)
5. Le caissier lui a donné combien d'euros? (110)
6. Il a reçu combien de billets? (onze billets de dix euros)
7. Il les a trouvés beaux? (oui)
8. Il les a comptés? (oui)
9. Le caissier lui a donné des pièces aussi? (oui)
10. Il les a mises où? (dans son porte-monnaie)

Des euros

3 Les monnaies Vrai ou faux?

1. La monnaie américaine, c'est le dollar.
2. La monnaie européenne, c'est l'euro.
3. Il y a des billets américains de trois dollars.
4. Il y a des pièces américaines de deux euros.
5. Si on veut toucher (encaisser) un chèque, il faut le signer au verso (l'endosser).
6. Il faut avoir de l'argent dans un compte courant pour pouvoir écrire des chèques.
7. Quelqu'un qui fait des économies dépense tout son argent.
8. Une personne qui aime mettre de l'argent de côté ouvre un compte d'épargne.
9. Une personne qui fait des économies retire souvent de l'argent à un distributeur automatique.

Vocabulaire

4 Antonymes Choisissez.

1. de l'argent liquide
2. faire des économies
3. verser
4. emprunter
5. avoir plein de fric

a. dépenser
b. être fauché(e)
c. un chèque ou une carte de crédit
d. retirer
e. prêter

5 Au bureau de change Travaillez avec un(e) camarade. L'un(e) de vous est un(e) touriste, l'autre est un(e) employé(e) dans un bureau de change. Le/La touriste veut changer de l'argent. Conversez ensemble.

Un bureau de change à Paris

6 Tu me dois de l'argent. Travaillez avec un copain ou une copine. Décidez qui a prêté de l'argent et qui a emprunté de l'argent. Discutez de ce problème ensemble.

 For more practice using words from *Mots 1*, do Activity 11 on page H12 at the end of this book.

LA BANQUE ET LA POSTE

cent quarante-cinq 145

Vocabulaire

5 You may wish to set up a **bureau de change** in your classroom and have pairs present their dialogues for the class. If possible, bring in real euros for students to use.

Writing Development
Have students write the answers to Activities 1–2 in paragraph form.

Reteaching
Show Vocabulary Transparencies 5.2–5.3 and let students say as much as they can about them in their own words.

Learning from Realia
(page 145) Here, students see some French checks and a credit card, **une carte bleue**, which is a debit card.

This *Infogap* activity will allow students to practice in pairs. The activity should be very manageable for them, since all vocabulary and structures are familiar to them.

LEVELING
E: Activities 1, 2, 3
A: Activities 2, 4, 5
C: Activity 6

Answers to Quel est le mot?

4
1. c
2. a
3. d
4. e
5. b

5 *Answers will vary but may include:*
—Bonjour. Je voudrais changer des dollars.
—Oui, monsieur/mademoiselle. Combien, s'il vous plaît?
—Cent dollars. Quel est le cours du change aujourd'hui?
—Le dollar est à un euro dix. Ça fait cent dix euros.
—Merci beaucoup.

6 *Answers will vary.*
Remind students to decide which one borrowed the money and which one lent the money before they make up their conversation reincorporating vocabulary learned in this **Mots** section.

145

Vocabulaire Mots 2

1 Preparation

Resource Manager
Vocabulary Transparencies 5.4–5.5
Audio Activities TE, pages 50–52
Audio CD 4
Workbook, pages 52–54
Quiz 2, page 22
ExamView® Pro

Bellringer Review
Use BRR Transparency 5.2 or write the following on the board. Write at least three different ways you can earn some extra money.

2 Presentation

Step 1 Show Vocabulary Transparencies 5.4–5.5. Have students close their books and repeat the words after you or Audio CD 4 as you point to the appropriate illustration on the transparency.

Step 2 Call on students to point out the correct item on the transparency as you say the new word or expression.

Step 3 As you present the new vocabulary, ask questions such as the following: **Qui a mis une lettre à la poste? Elle a mis la lettre où? Elle l'a envoyée quand?**, etc.

Vocabulaire Mots 2

À la poste

un bureau de poste = la poste

C'est un petit colis.
Il ne pèse pas beaucoup.

146 cent quarante-six

CHAPITRE 5

Reaching All Students

Total Physical Response
(Student 1) et (Student 2), venez ici, s'il vous plaît.
(Student 1), vous êtes un(e) employé(e) des postes.
(Student 2), vous avez quelque chose à envoyer. Allez à la poste. Dites «bonjour» à l'employé(e).
(Student 1), répondez-lui. Demandez-lui ce qu'il/elle veut.
(Student 2), dites-lui ce que vous voulez envoyer. Dites-lui où vous voulez l'envoyer.
(Student 1), dites-lui combien ça va coûter.
(Student 2), payez l'employé(e). Donnez-lui de l'argent.
(Student 1), donnez-lui des timbres.
(Student 2), regardez bien les timbres. Il y a un problème. L'employé(e) ne vous a pas donné assez de timbres. Expliquez le problème à l'employé(e).

Vocabulaire
Mots 2

C'est combien, une carte postale pour les États-Unis?

un guichet

Serge a acheté des timbres.
Il les a achetés à la poste.

mettre une lettre à la poste

Danièle a envoyé une lettre.
Elle l'a mise dans la boîte aux lettres.
Elle l'a envoyée ce matin.

une factrice

C'est la factrice qui distribue le courrier.
C'est aussi le facteur qui le distribue.

LA BANQUE ET LA POSTE

Monsieur Vaillant a regardé la lettre que la factrice lui a donnée.
Il l'a ouverte et il l'a lue.

Cross-Cultural Comparison
Point out that when you address an envelope to someone in France, the **code postal**, the French equivalent of the zip code, precedes the name of the city. **En France le code postal précède le nom de la ville.**

Reteaching
Ask students to describe the people in the photos in their own words.

Assessment
As an informal assessment, refer students to the photos on pages 146–147. Ask them to make up as many questions as they can. Questions may be directed toward the teacher or a classmate, who will respond.

FRENCH Online
The **Glencoe World Languages Web** site (**french.glencoe.com**) offers options that enable you and your students to experience the French-speaking world via the Internet. For each chapter, there are activities, games, and quizzes. In addition, an *Enrichment* section offers students an opportunity to visit Web sites related to the theme of the chapter.

Reaching All Students

Additional Practice The following are additional questions you may ask after presenting the **Mots 2** vocabulary: Qui a acheté des timbres? Il les a achetés où? Danièle a mis la lettre à la poste? Elle l'a mise dans la boîte aux lettres? Qui a mis la lettre dans la boîte aux lettres? Elle l'a mise où? Elle l'a envoyée quand? Elle l'a envoyée hier?

Vocabulaire

3 Practice

Quel est le mot?

8 Go over this activity with books closed. Then have students read the activity aloud for additional reinforcement.

Paired Activity
Have students role-play in pairs. The first partner plays the role of a person waiting excitedly for the letter carrier to arrive. The second partner wants to find out what the other is waiting for. Allow partners time to prepare the skit, then have them present it to the class.

Writing Development
Have students write the answers to the questions in Activity 8 in paragraph form.

Chapter Projects

À la poste Have students make a list of services offered by the U.S. Postal Service and ask them to explain them in French.

LEVELING
E: Activities 7, 8, 9, 10, 11
A: Activities 9, 10, 11

Vocabulaire

Quel est le mot?

7 **Qu'est-ce que c'est?** Identifiez.

1. C'est un facteur ou une factrice?

2. C'est un colis ou une boîte aux lettres?

3. C'est un code postal ou le numéro de la rue?

4. C'est une boîte aux lettres ou un distributeur automatique?

5. C'est une enveloppe ou une carte postale?

8 **Historiette** **Au bureau de poste**
Répondez que oui.
1. Matthieu a écrit une lettre?
2. Il l'a mise dans une enveloppe?
3. Il a écrit le nom et l'adresse sur l'enveloppe?
4. Il est allé au bureau de poste?
5. Il a acheté des timbres au guichet?
6. L'employée des postes lui a rendu la monnaie?
7. Matthieu a mis la lettre à la poste?
8. Il l'a mise dans la boîte aux lettres?
9. Le facteur a distribué le courrier?
10. La petite amie de Matthieu a reçu la lettre qu'il lui a écrite?

Le facteur distribue le courrier à Yerres.

148 cent quarante-huit CHAPITRE 5

ANSWERS TO Quel est le mot?

7
1. C'est un facteur.
2. C'est une boîte aux lettres.
3. C'est un code postal.
4. C'est un distributeur automatique.
5. C'est une carte postale.

8
1. Oui, Matthieu a écrit une lettre.
2. Oui, il l'a mise dans une enveloppe.
3. Oui, il a écrit le nom et l'adresse sur l'enveloppe.
4. Oui, il est allé au bureau de poste.
5. Oui, il a acheté des timbres au guichet.
6. Oui, l'employée des postes lui a rendu la monnaie.
7. Oui, Matthieu a mis la lettre à la poste.
8. Oui, il l'a mise dans la boîte aux lettres.
9. Oui, le facteur a distribué le courrier.
10. Oui, la petite amie de Matthieu a reçu la lettre qu'il lui a écrite.

Vocabulaire

9 **Invitations** Choisissez.
1. Julie a mis l'invitation dans ___.
   a. une enveloppe
   b. un timbre
   c. un colis
2. Elle a acheté des timbres ___.
   a. au distributeur automatique
   b. à la boîte aux lettres
   c. à la factrice
3. Elle a mis ___ sur l'enveloppe.
   a. un distributeur automatique
   b. un timbre
   c. un facteur
4. Julie a mis l'invitation ___.
   a. au guichet
   b. dans le distributeur automatique
   c. dans la boîte aux lettres
5. Elle a envoyé un colis aussi. Elle a mis le colis ___ pour le peser.
   a. dans le distributeur automatique
   b. sur la balance
   c. dans la boîte aux lettres

10 **L'adresse** Travaillez avec un(e) camarade. Regardez cette enveloppe. L'un(e) de vous pose des questions sur la personne qui va recevoir cette lettre. L'autre répond.

Monsieur Paul Rivière
121, rue Saint-Julien-le-Pauvre
75005 Paris

11 **À la poste** Avec un copain ou une copine, discutez de tout ce que vous voyez sur ce dessin.

LA BANQUE ET LA POSTE

cent quarante-neuf 149

Structure

1 Preparation

Resource Manager
Audio Activities TE, pages 52–53
Audio CD 4
Workbook, pages 55–58
Quizzes 3–6, pages 23–26
ExamView® Pro

Bellringer Review
Use BRR Transparency 5.3 or write the following on the board.
Write the steps involved in writing and mailing a letter. Be very specific.

2 Presentation

Les pronoms relatifs qui et que

Step 1 Write the sentences from Item 1 on the board. Tell students that the first example in each pair consists of two separate sentences, each with a separate subject. The second example in each pair combines these two sentences into one, using a relative pronoun.

Step 2 Circle the pronoun, draw a box around its antecedent, and connect the two with a line to demonstrate their relationship. After a few examples, ask a student whether the relative pronoun in each sentence functions as the subject or the object of the clause.

Step 3 Go over Item 2 the same way. Ask students which relative pronoun functions as the subject and which one functions as the object.

Structure

Les pronoms relatifs qui et que
Giving more information in one sentence

1. The relative pronoun **qui** can replace either a person or a thing. It joins two short sentences into one longer sentence. **Qui** is always the subject of the clause it introduces.

QUI
Je parle à un employé.   Il travaille à la poste.
Je parle à un employé qui travaille à la poste.
Ma sœur a lu la lettre.   Elle est sur la table.
Ma sœur a lu la lettre qui est sur la table.

2. The relative pronoun **que** can also refer to people or things. It is also used to join two short sentences into a longer one, but **que** is always the direct object of the clause it introduces.

QUE
Je parle à un employé.   Vous connaissez cet employé.
Je parle à un employé que vous connaissez.
Vous avez ouvert le colis.   Le facteur l'a apporté.
Vous avez ouvert le colis que le facteur a apporté.

Le bureau de poste à Neauphle-le-Vieux

Attention!
Elision occurs with **que** but never with **qui**.
Voilà la femme qu'il admire.
Voilà une femme qui adore sa famille.

Learning from Photos
(page 150) Ask students the following questions about the photo: **D'après vous, cette poste est dans une grande ville ou dans un petit village? Expliquez.**

Chapter Projects
Des économies Have students draw up a personal budget and keep a diary of their expenditures as you do this chapter. At the chapter's end, have them tell or write what they learned about themselves by doing this. You may ask them to convert their expenditures into euros.

Comment dit-on?

12 **Historiette** C'est la même fille qui lit et qui écrit.
Répondez que oui.
1. La fille qui parle maintenant est très intelligente?
2. Tu aimes le poème qu'elle lit?
3. Le poème qu'elle lit est intéressant?
4. C'est Sylvie qui a écrit ce poème?
5. Tu aimes le poème que Sylvie a écrit?

13 **Historiette** Martin Faites une seule phrase en utilisant **qui** ou **que**.

Martin est un ami. Il aime écrire. →
Martin est un ami qui aime écrire.

1. C'est Martin. Il m'écrit.
2. Il m'écrit des lettres. Ses lettres sont intéressantes.
3. Le facteur me donne les lettres. Martin m'envoie les lettres.
4. Martin m'envoie aussi des photos. Les photos sont très jolies.
5. J'aime regarder les photos. Martin m'envoie les photos.

14 **Qui ou que?** Complétez.
1. Robert a écrit la lettre _____ vous lisez.
2. La personne _____ distribue le courrier est le facteur ou la factrice.
3. L'enveloppe _____ est sur la table est trop petite.
4. Les cartes postales _____ vous voulez envoyer n'ont pas de timbre.

LA BANQUE ET LA POSTE

cent cinquante et un ❖ **151**

Structure

Learning from Photos
(page 151) Ask these questions about the photo on page 151: **C'est Sylvie? Elle est où? Qu'est-ce qu'elle lit? Qu'est-ce qu'il y a sur la table devant elle? D'après vous, elle lit une lettre sérieuse ou pas sérieuse?** Have students describe Sylvie in their own words.

3 Practice

Comment dit-on?

12 Have students do this activity once with books closed and then again with books open.

Writing Development
Have students write the answers to Activities 12 and 13 in paragraph form.

LEVELING
E: Activity 12
A: Activities 13, 14
C: Activity 14

ANSWERS TO Comment dit-on?

12 Answers will vary but may include:
1. Oui, la fille qui parle maintenant est très intelligente.
2. Oui, j'aime le poème qu'elle lit.
3. Oui, le poème qu'elle lit est intéressant.
4. Oui, c'est Sylvie qui a écrit ce poème.
5. Oui, j'aime le poème que Sylvie a écrit.

13
1. C'est Martin qui m'écrit.
2. Il m'écrit des lettres qui sont intéressantes.
3. Le facteur me donne les lettres que Martin m'envoie.
4. Martin m'envoie aussi des photos qui sont très jolies.
5. J'aime regarder les photos que Martin m'envoie.

14
1. que
2. qui
3. qui
4. que

Structure

15 Historiette Du courrier pour moi? Faites une phrase en utilisant **qui** ou **que**.

1. Je vois le facteur. Il distribue le courrier dans notre quartier.
2. Aujourd'hui j'ai reçu une carte postale. Elle est très jolie.
3. Un ami m'a envoyé une carte. Il est en vacances en Bretagne.
4. La Bretagne est une jolie province. Elle est au nord-ouest de la France.

Une vue de Saint-Malo en Bretagne

16 Historiette Ma journée
Complétez en utilisant **qui** ou **que**.

Tous les matins, c'est mon père __1__ se lève le premier, à six heures. Ma mère, __2__ aime rester au lit, se lève à six heures et demie. À sept heures, je prends mon petit déjeuner __3__ je prépare moi-même. Je donne à manger à notre chat Minouche. C'est un chat __4__ j'aime beaucoup et __5__ a toujours faim le matin. Pour aller à l'école, je prends le bus __6__ passe juste devant la maison. Quand j'arrive à l'école, je vais au cours de maths. Pour moi, c'est un cours __7__ est difficile.

17 Jeu **Définitions** Travaillez avec un(e) camarade. Inventez des définitions. Votre camarade doit deviner ce que c'est ou qui c'est.

C'est une personne qui distribue le courrier.

C'est le facteur/la factrice.

152 ◆ cent cinquante-deux   CHAPITRE 5

L'accord du participe passé
Referring to people and things already mentioned

1. In French, the past participle of verbs conjugated with **avoir** must agree in gender and in number with the direct object when the direct object comes before the verb.

No agreement	Agreement
J'ai écrit une lettre.	Je l'ai écrite ce matin.
	Voilà la lettre que j'ai écrite ce matin.
Tu as reçu mes lettres?	Tu les as reçues?
	Ce sont les lettres que tu as reçues?
Elle a acheté des timbres.	Elle les a achetés hier.
	Voilà les timbres qu'elle a achetés hier.

Attention!
Most of the time agreement is only written, not heard. The agreement is heard only with the feminine form of a past participle that ends in a consonant:

écrit fait
écrite faite

La lettre? Il l'a envoyée, mais il ne l'a pas écrite.

Un bureau de poste à Marrakech au Maroc

LA BANQUE ET LA POSTE

cent cinquante-trois 153

Structure

1 Preparation

Bellringer Review

Use BRR Transparency 5.4 or write the following on the board. Choose the correct completion.
1. Quand _____ petit(e), _____ faire de petits voyages.
   a. j'étais   a. j'aimais
   b. j'ai été   b. j'ai aimé
2. _____ de la chance parce que mes parents _____ souvent.
   a. J'avais   a. voyageaient
   b. J'ai eu   b. ont voyagé
3. Une fois, nous _____ en Bretagne.
   a. allions
   b. sommes allés

2 Presentation

L'accord du participe passé

Step 1 We suggest that you not spend a great deal of time on this structure point. As students write more and more French, it will be necessary to remind them frequently to make the past participle agree with the preceeding direct object.

Learning from Photos
(page 153) Marrakesh is a beautiful city in southern Morocco. Marrakesh has several wonderful palaces, mosques, souks, and gardens. The terrain has a beautiful pink color and in the distance one has spectacular views of the snow-capped Atlas Mountains. Marrakesh is a very popular tourist destination.

Reaching All Students

Additional Practice Give two cards or slips of paper to each student, one with the word **qui**, the other with **que**. On the board or overhead, show sample complex sentences with the relative pronoun missing. Students hold up the card showing the appropriate pronoun. After some practice, try cueing the model sentences orally instead of visually.

Structure

3 Practice

Comment dit-on?

Note: Since participle agreement is a written concern, have students write the activities first and then read their responses. As the student says the past participle, write it on the board. Underline the ending when applicable.

18 Have students indicate which past participles show agreement as they do this activity. Then have them tell what the preceeding direct object is for each case of agreement.

Learning from Realia
(page 154 top) Have students tell what this brochure cover is advertising.

LEVELING
E: Activity 18
A: Activity 19
C: Activity 19

154

Structure

Comment dit-on?

18 **Historiette** La lettre que j'ai écrite
Répondez.

1. Tu as écrit une lettre?
2. Tu l'as écrite hier?
3. Tu l'as lue?
4. Tu as lu la lettre que tu as écrite?
5. Tu as mis la lettre dans une enveloppe?
6. Tu l'as mise dans une grande enveloppe?
7. Tu as écrit l'adresse sur l'enveloppe?
8. Tu l'as écrite clairement?
9. Tu as envoyé la lettre?
10. Tu l'as envoyée par avion?

19 Historiette Les photos que j'ai prises Complétez.

J'ai pris _1_ des photos. J'ai envoyé _2_ les photos que j'ai pris _3_ à mon amie Catherine. Je les ai envoyé _4_ la semaine dernière. Je les ai mis _5_ dans une grande enveloppe. J'ai écrit _6_ l'adresse de Catherine sur l'enveloppe. Je sais que je l'ai écrit _7_ clairement. Mais, zut! Je ne sais pas si j'ai mis _8_ le code postal. Je crois que je l'ai mis _9_, mais je n'en suis pas sûr. Je vais téléphoner à Catherine pour savoir si elle a reçu _10_ mes photos.
(Au téléphone)

Marc: Catherine, tu as reçu _11_ l'enveloppe que je t'ai envoyé _12_?
Catherine: Oui, je l'ai reçu _13_. Et je trouve que les photos que tu as pris _14_ sont super. Je les ai déjà regardé _15_ dix fois!

154 cent cinquante-quatre

CHAPITRE 5

Answers to Comment dit-on?

18 Answers will vary but may include:
1. Oui, j'ai écrit une lettre.
2. Oui, je l'ai écrite hier.
3. Oui, je l'ai lue.
4. Oui, j'ai lu la lettre que j'ai écrite.
5. Oui, j'ai mis la lettre dans une enveloppe.
6. Oui, je l'ai mise dans une grande enveloppe.
7. Oui, j'ai écrit l'adresse sur l'enveloppe.
8. Oui, je l'ai écrite clairement.
9. Oui, j'ai envoyé la lettre.
10. Oui, je l'ai envoyée par avion.

19
1. –
2. –
3. es
4. es
5. es
6. –
7. e
8. –
9. –
10. –
11. –
12. e
13. e
14. es
15. es

Les actions réciproques
Telling what we do for one another

1. Reflexive pronouns can also express a reciprocal action or interaction between two or more people. They can be either a direct object or an indirect object.

   Rappelez-vous que... The reflexive pronouns are **me, te, se, nous, vous,** and **se.**

Direct object	
Jean voit souvent son ami. Son ami voit souvent Jean.	Jean et son ami se voient souvent.

Indirect object	
Tu parles souvent à Marie. Marie te parle souvent.	Vous vous parlez souvent.

2. In the **passé composé** reciprocal verbs are conjugated with **être**. The past participle agrees with the reciprocal pronoun when it is the direct object of the sentence. There is no agreement when the pronoun is an indirect object.

Direct → Agreement	
Jean a vu son ami. Et son ami a vu Jean.	Jean et son ami **se** sont **vus**.

Indirect → No agreement	
Jean a parlé à son ami. Et son ami a parlé à Jean.	Jean et son ami **se** sont **parlé**.

LA BANQUE ET LA POSTE — cent cinquante-cinq ◆ 155

Reaching All Students

Additional Practice Tell students they are going to be copy editors. It is the job of a copy editor to catch and correct all errors. Give students this short paragraph to read carefully and have them make all necessary corrections.

Julie a reçu une lettre. Elle l'a reçu d'une copine qui habite à Paris. Julie a regardé l'enveloppe et elle l'a ouvert tout de suite. Sa copine lui a envoyé des photos. Julie les a regardé. Elle ne sait pas si c'est sa copine qui les a pris.

Structure

1 Preparation

Bellringer Review

Use BRR Transparency 5.5 or write the following on the board. Write the answers to these questions.
1. **Tu habites où?**
2. **Quelle est ton adresse?**
3. **Il y a un bureau de poste dans ta ville (ton village)?**
4. **Où est la poste?**
5. **Le facteur distribue le courrier chez toi quand?**

2 Presentation

Les actions réciproques

Step 1 Call two boys to the front of the room. Have them look at each other. Point from one to the other and say: **Jean voit Luc. Et Luc voit Jean.** Then wave your hand back and forth between them as you say: **Luc et Jean se voient. Ils se voient.**

Step 2 Now bring an outgoing boy and girl up front. (Or use photos of two dating/married movie stars.) The boy looks at the girl and says: **Je t'aime.** The girl says: **Moi aussi je t'aime.** Then they hold hands and say: **Nous nous aimons.**

Step 3 It is recommended that you not wait to move on until all students learn to make the past participle agree perfectly. This is a point that will take a great deal of reinforcement throughout the students' study of French.

Structure

3 Practice

Comment dit-on?

21 Ask students to analyze each sentence and explain why the past participle agrees or doesn't agree.

22 Have students write down their answers to this activity first, then ask for students to give their answers orally.

♻ Recycling

Ask students to look at the letter on page 156 and say where Benoît is from. Have students write or say as much as they can about Nice. Remind them that Nice is on the Mediterranean. They can review all the vocabulary they learned in **Bon voyage! Level 1** about the beach and summer activities.

About the French Language

As you explain the grammar point on page 157, you may wish to tell students that the answer to **Qu'est-ce qui se passe?** is often just **Rien.**

LEVELING
E: Activities 21, 23
A: Activities 20, 22, 23
C: Activity 22

Structure

Comment dit-on?

20 **De bons amis** Faites une seule phrase d'après le modèle.

**Tu adores Isabelle. Isabelle t'adore. →
Vous vous adorez.**

1. Pierre parle à Marie. Marie parle à Pierre.
2. Pierre aime Marie. Marie aime Pierre.
3. Je t'aime. Tu m'aimes.
4. Je te vois. Tu me vois.
5. Camille regarde Guillaume. Guillaume regarde Camille.
6. J'écris à Daniel. Daniel m'écrit.
7. Claire ne dit rien à Lucie. Lucie ne dit rien à Claire.
8. Tu téléphones à Pierre. Pierre te téléphone.

21 **Les deux copains**
Répondez que oui ou non.

1. Les deux copains se sont vus souvent?
2. Ils se sont dit bonjour?
3. Ils se sont parlé?
4. Ils se sont téléphoné régulièrement?
5. Ils se sont écrit de temps en temps?

22 **Pendant longtemps**
Refaites les phrases au passé composé.

1. Nous nous écrivons souvent.
2. Elles se voient.
3. Elles se parlent.
4. Ils se regardent.
5. Vous vous parlez souvent au téléphone.
6. Elles se téléphonent.
7. Nous nous voyons de temps en temps.

Les quais de la Seine à Paris

Answers to Comment dit-on?

20
1. Ils se parlent.
2. Ils s'aiment.
3. Nous nous aimons.
4. Nous nous voyons.
5. Ils se regardent.
6. Nous nous écrivons.
7. Elles ne se disent rien.
8. Vous vous téléphonez.

21
1. Oui, ils se sont vus souvent.
2. Oui, ils se sont dit bonjour.
3. Oui, ils se sont parlé.
4. Oui, ils se sont téléphoné régulièrement.
5. Oui, ils se sont écrit de temps en temps.

22
1. Nous nous sommes écrit souvent.
2. Elles se sont vues.
3. Elles se sont parlé.
4. Ils se sont regardés.
5. Vous vous êtes parlé souvent au téléphone.
6. Elles se sont téléphoné.
7. Nous nous sommes vu(e)s de temps en temps.

Personne ne... et rien ne...
Making negative statements

1. You use the negative expressions **personne ne...** and **rien ne...** as the subject of a sentence. Note that you do not use **pas** after the verb.

   Personne ne répond au téléphone.
   Rien n'a changé ici.

2. **Rien ne...** is often used as a response to a question with **se passer** and **arriver,** which both mean "to happen."

   Qu'est-ce qui se passe?   Rien ne se passe.
   Qu'est-ce qui est arrivé?   Rien n'est arrivé.

Comment dit-on?

 23 **Non!** Répondez au négatif.

1. Quelqu'un est allé à la poste?
2. Quelqu'un a acheté des timbres?
3. Quelqu'un a envoyé le colis?
4. Quelqu'un a vu le facteur?
5. Quelque chose est arrivé ce matin?
6. Qu'est-ce qui s'est passé?
7. Qu'est-ce qui a changé?

Le bureau de poste près de l'Opéra à Paris

Vous êtes sur le bon chemin. Allez-y!

cent cinquante-sept 157

Critical Thinking Activity

Making inferences, drawing conclusions
Read the following to the class or write it on the board or on a transparency:
De nos jours, les gens des pays industrialisés écrivent de moins en moins de lettres. Pourquoi? Donnez plusieurs raisons.

ANSWERS TO Comment dit-on?

1. Non, personne n'est allé à la poste.
2. Non, personne n'a acheté de timbres.
3. Non, personne n'a envoyé le colis.
4. Non, personne n'a vu le facteur.
5. Non, rien n'est arrivé ce matin.
6. Rien ne s'est passé.
7. Rien n'a changé.

Structure

1 Preparation

Bellringer Review

Use BRR Transparency 5.6 or write the following on the board. Write four things you must put on an envelope before you send a letter.

2 Presentation

Personne ne... et rien ne...

Step 1 When presenting this structure point, you may wish to contrast the affirmative and the negative. You can use the following examples: **Quelqu'un a répondu au téléphone. (Personne n'a répondu au téléphone.) Quelqu'un est arrivé. (Personne n'est arrivé.) Quelque chose est arrivé. (Rien n'est arrivé.)**

3 Practice

Comment dit-on?

23 **Expansion:** Have students make new questions related to the bank based on this activity:
1. Quelqu'un est allé à la banque?, etc.

 Allez-y!
At this point in the chapter, students have learned all the vocabulary and structure necessary to complete the chapter. The conversation and cultural readings that follow recycle all the material learned up to this point.

157

Conversation

1 Preparation

Resource Manager
Audio Activities TE, page 54
Audio CD 4
CD-ROM

Bellringer Review
Use BRR Transparency 5.7 or write the following on the board.
List five things you recently bought. Then say where you bought each item. For example: **une chemise Je l'ai achetée chez Target.**

2 Presentation

Step 1 Tell students they will hear a conversation between Charlene and a currency exchange teller. Have students close their books. They will watch the conversation on the CD-ROM or listen as you read the conversation or play Audio CD 4.

Learning from Photos
(page 158) This **bureau de change** is located in the **1ᵉ arrondissement** of Paris. Have students say everything they can about the photo.

Conversation

Au bureau de change

Charlene: Je voudrais changer cent dollars en euros, s'il vous plaît.
Le caissier: Vous avez des chèques de voyage ou de l'argent liquide?
Charlene: Des chèques de voyage. Le dollar est à combien aujourd'hui?
Le caissier: À un euro dix.
Charlene: D'accord.
Le caissier: Votre passeport, s'il vous plaît. Et signez votre chèque. Votre adresse à Paris?
Charlene: Hôtel Molière, rue Molière dans le 1ᵉʳ arrondissement.
Le caissier: Un billet de cent euros, ça va?
Charlene: Vous n'avez pas cinq billets de vingt euros?

Vous avez compris?

Répondez.

1. Où est allée Charlene?
2. Elle veut changer combien de dollars?
3. Elle a des chèques de voyage ou de l'argent liquide?
4. Elle veut changer ses dollars en quelle monnaie?
5. Quel est le cours du change?
6. Qu'est-ce que le caissier veut voir?
7. Charlene est à quel hôtel? À quelle adresse?

158 ❖ cent cinquante-huit   CHAPITRE 5

ANSWERS TO Vous avez compris?

1. Charlene est allée au bureau de change.
2. Elle veut changer cent dollars.
3. Elle a des chèques de voyage.
4. Elle veut changer ses dollars en euros.
5. Le dollar est à un euro dix.
6. Le caissier veut voir son passeport.
7. Charlene est à l'hôtel Molière, rue Molière dans le 1ᵉ arrondissement.

Glencoe Technology

CD-ROM
On the CD-ROM, students can watch a dramatization of this conversation. They can then play the role of either one of the characters and record themselves in the conversation.

Parlons un peu plus

A **Des euros** Vous voyagez en France. Vous n'avez pas assez d'euros et vous savez que vous allez en avoir besoin. Allez au bureau de change pour changer de l'argent. Votre camarade est le caissier (la caissière). Ensuite changez de rôle.

B **À la poste** Vous êtes à Abidjan, en Côte d'Ivoire. Vous voulez envoyer des cartes postales à vos amis. Vous ne savez pas combien ça coûte pour envoyer des cartes postales dans votre pays. Vous voulez aussi de beaux timbres pour vos cartes postales. Préparez une conversation au bureau de poste. Votre camarade est l'employé(e). Ensuite changez de rôle.

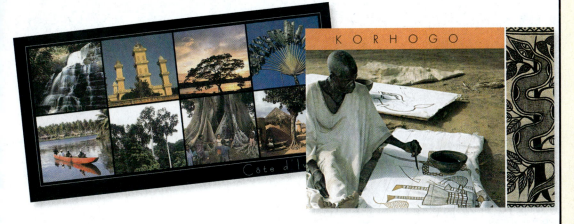

LA BANQUE ET LA POSTE

cent cinquante-neuf ✤ 159

Conversation

Step 2 Have pairs of students role-play Charlene and the teller, repeating their lines after you.

Step 3 Have two students read the conversation to the class.

Step 4 Write a different amount of money exchanged, rate of exchange, and local address for Charlene on the board. Then call on pairs to role-play with books open, making the substitutions. Have them research today's exchange rates.

3 Practice

Parlons un peu plus

These activities enable students to use the vocabulary and structures learned in the chapter in open-ended exchanges. You may wish to assign different activities to different groups or allow students to choose the activities.

B Expansion: You may wish to have students create their own postcard image, messages, and stamp, which they will then "mail" during their dialogue.

Learning from Realia

(page 159) Korhogo is about a nine-hour bus ride north from Abidjan. It is the capital of the Senoufo people, and it dates from the thirteenth century. The Senoufo people are famous for their woodcarvings and Korhogo cloth (**la toile de Korhogo**), made of raw cotton. It is rough, like burlap, and painted with mud-colored designs. The weavers use a natural vegetable dye made from leaves and mud.

LEVELING
E: Conversation

Answers to Parlons un peu plus

A Answers will vary but may include:
—Bonjour. Je voudrais changer cinquante dollars en euros, s'il vous plaît.
—Oui. Vous avez des chèques de voyage?
—Non, j'ai de l'argent liquide. Quel est le cours du change?
—Le dollar est à un euro dix.
—D'accord. Voilà mon passeport.
—Merci. Et voilà cinquante-cinq euros.
—Merci.

B Answers will vary but may include:
—C'est combien une carte postale pour les États-Unis?
—Soixante-quinze.
—Je voudrais dix timbres, s'il vous plaît. Vous avez de beaux timbres?
—Mais oui.
—Où est la boîte aux lettres, s'il vous plaît?
—À gauche de l'entrée.
—Merci.

Lectures culturelles

Resource Manager
Audio Activities TE, page 55
Audio CD 4

Bellringer Review

Use BRR Transparency 5.8 or write the following on the board. Match each expression in the first column with its opposite in the second column. Then choose one expression from each column and use it in a sentence about yourself.

quelque chose	jamais
toujours	personne
quelqu'un	rien
souvent	jamais

National Standards

Cultures
This reading familiarizes students with the spending and saving habits of a young French person.

Presentation

Pre-reading
Step 1 Take a survey to see which students receive a weekly allowance, which ones work part-time for spending money, what they use their money for, etc.

Reading
Step 1 Have students read the **Lecture** silently. Allow five minutes. Encourage them to read for the main ideas and important details only, not to use dictionaries, and not to stop each time they have difficulty. Tell them they will have a chance to reread.

Step 2 Call on an individual to read several sentences. Then ask other students about the sentences the student has just read.

Lectures culturelles

Reading Strategy
Evaluating
As you read, make judgments about the passage. You can do this by asking yourself questions such as: Is this fact or opinion? Does the passage have a logical conclusion based on what the writer said? In what way has this reading been of value to me? If you evaluate a work while reading it, you will increase your comprehension of the issues in the passage.

La semaine des jeunes Français

Qu'est-ce que la semaine? C'est la période de sept jours ou, comme disent les Français, huit jours. Mais la semaine, c'est aussi autre chose. C'est de l'argent. La semaine, c'est la somme d'argent qu'un jeune Français ou une jeune Française reçoit chaque semaine de ses parents. C'est son argent de poche[1].

Les jeunes Français reçoivent combien par semaine? Il est difficile de répondre à cette question d'une façon générale. Ça dépend d'abord de la générosité des parents et aussi de la situation économique de la famille.

Les parents de Mélanie lui donnent de l'argent toutes les semaines. Avec l'argent qu'elle a économisé, Mélanie a acheté un T-shirt et un CD. Mélanie achète souvent des CD parce qu'elle aime beaucoup la musique. Elle est allée aussi au café et a pris un pot[2] avec ses copains.

[1] argent de poche *pocket money* [2] un pot *refreshment, drink*

Dans une boutique de la rue de Rivoli à Paris

Dans un magasin de musique à Montgeron

Learning from Photos
(pages 160–161) Have students look at the photos and say as much as they can about them.

Critical Thinking Activity

Supporting statements with reasons
Put the following on the board or on a transparency.
- À ton avis, il est important ou pas de mettre de l'argent de côté, de faire des économies? Pourquoi?
- Il est important ou pas de devenir riche? Pourquoi?

Mélanie a un compte d'épargne à la poste. Ses parents lui ont ouvert son compte. Mélanie aime faire des économies et mettre de l'argent de côté. Quand elle reçoit de l'argent pour son anniversaire, par exemple, elle en dépense une partie, mais pas tout. Elle verse le reste sur son compte d'épargne. Personne ne peut dire que Mélanie jette[3] l'argent par les fenêtres!

[3] jette *throws*

des livrets de caisse d'épargne

Vous avez compris?

A La semaine Vrai ou faux?
1. La semaine, c'est une période de temps.
2. La semaine, c'est aussi de l'argent.
3. C'est le prof qui donne leur semaine aux jeunes.
4. Tous les jeunes Français reçoivent la même somme.
5. La générosité n'a rien à voir avec la somme que les parents donnent à leurs enfants.

B Mélanie Répondez.
1. Cette semaine, comment est-ce que Mélanie a dépensé son argent?
2. Mélanie aime faire des économies et mettre de l'argent de côté?
3. Qu'est-ce que les parents de Mélanie lui ont ouvert?
4. Qu'est-ce qu'elle fait quand elle reçoit de l'argent pour son anniversaire?
5. Qu'est-ce qu'on ne peut pas dire de Mélanie?

Lecture supplémentaire 1

Les devises étrangères

La monnaie change d'un pays à l'autre. Aux États-Unis, c'est le dollar américain (US$). Au Canada, c'est le dollar canadien (CAN$). En Tunisie et en Algérie, c'est le dinar. Au Maroc, c'est le dirham. En Europe, les pays de l'Union européenne ont une monnaie commune, l'euro(€).

Le Conseil de l'Europe à Strasbourg en Alsace

Vous avez compris?

Devises étrangères Identifiez les billets que vous voyez. Ils viennent d'où? Quel est le nom de la monnaie de ce pays?

Lecture supplémentaire 2

La Poste

En France comme aux États-Unis, la Poste est une administration publique qui assure le service de distribution du courrier. Du bureau de poste, on peut envoyer des lettres, des colis, des mandats[1]... En France, la Poste se charge aussi d'un grand nombre d'opérations bancaires. On dit que la Poste est peut-être la banque numéro un en France. Elle gère[2] vingt millions de comptes d'épargne, et le service des chèques postaux gère aujourd'hui dix millions de comptes courants. Beaucoup de Français paient leurs achats et leurs factures[3] avec des chèques postaux et pas avec des chèques bancaires parce que les chèques postaux ne coûtent presque rien.

Un petit bureau de poste en Bretagne

[1] mandats *money orders*
[2] gère *manages*
[3] factures *bills*

Vous avez compris?

Différences Décrivez la différence entre le service postal en France et aux États-Unis.

CONNEXIONS

L'économie

Les finances

At one point or another we must all get involved in matters of money and finances. A bank is a good provider of financial services. We may want to pay some bills by check or put some money aside and open a savings account. These are two of the many services offered by a bank. Today many of our banking needs can be taken care of without even entering the bank. We can do our transactions at an ATM, or automated teller machine.

Let's learn a few commonly used banking terms in French.

une carte de crédit

acheter à crédit

un relevé de compte

un carnet de chèques

Le Crédit Lyonnais, une grande banque française

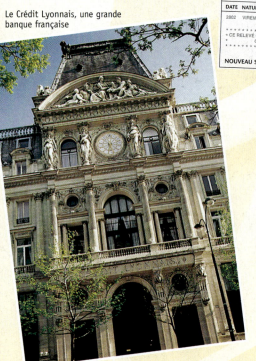

Le compte courant

Les services qu'une banque offre à ses clients sont importants. Il est facile et pratique de payer ses factures[1] par chèque.

Pour écrire des chèques, il faut avoir un compte courant dans une banque. Mais attention, il faut avoir assez d'argent sur son compte pour ne pas faire de chèque sans provisions[2].

La banque envoie à ses clients un relevé de compte mensuel, c'est-à-dire tous les mois. Il faut s'assurer que le solde de la banque correspond au solde que vous avez sur votre carnet de chèques.

[1] factures *bills*
[2] chèque sans provisions *bounced check*

Le compte d'épargne

Vous aimez faire des économies et mettre de l'argent de côté? Alors vous devez avoir un compte d'épargne. Pour être plus précis, en France on dit qu'on a un livret de caisse d'épargne. C'est très simple. Vous versez de l'argent sur votre compte, et la banque ou la Poste vous paie des intérêts. De cette façon, votre solde monte et vous devenez de plus en plus riche!

Les emprunts

De temps en temps, il faut emprunter de l'argent—pour acheter une voiture ou une maison, par exemple, et aux États-Unis pour payer ses études.

Une hypothèque est un emprunt pour acheter une maison. C'est un exemple d'emprunt à long terme. Pendant vingt ou vingt-cinq ans, on paie des traites, c'est-à-dire qu'on fait des paiements mensuels. Le taux[3] d'intérêt varie selon le type d'emprunt. Le taux d'intérêt pour un emprunt à long terme est plus bas que le taux d'intérêt pour un emprunt à court terme.

[3] taux *rate*

Vous avez compris?

L'argent Choisissez.

1. Renaud veut mettre de l'argent de côté pour l'avenir. Il doit ouvrir _____.
   a. un compte courant
   b. un compte d'épargne
   c. une banque
2. Si Renaud veut économiser de l'argent, il doit _____.
   a. emprunter de l'argent de son compte
   b. retirer de l'argent de son compte
   c. verser de l'argent sur son compte
3. Renaud ne paie pas toujours en liquide ou par carte de crédit. Il paie _____.
   a. avec des billets
   b. par chèque
   c. avec des pièces
4. Renaud n'a plus beaucoup de chèques. Il commande un autre _____.
   a. compte
   b. emprunt
   c. carnet
5. Si Renaud n'a pas assez d'argent sur son compte et qu'il écrit un chèque, c'est _____.
   a. un chèque sans provisions
   b. une hypothèque
   c. un versement
6. Une hypothèque est un emprunt pour _____.
   a. acheter une voiture
   b. acheter une maison
   c. payer ses études

LA BANQUE ET LA POSTE

CONNEXIONS

Presentation

L'économie
Les finances

Note: You may have students who are interested in finance, accounting, or banking read this selection. You may wish to have all students look at the vocabulary words presented here, since they are quite useful.

Step 1 Have students read the introduction in English on page 164.

Step 2 Have students scan the reading for cognates. Then have them do the reading again, this time for comprehension.

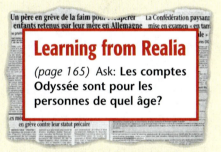

Learning from Realia

(page 165) Ask: **Les comptes Odyssée sont pour les personnes de quel âge?**

Career Connection

Banking is an industry where knowledge of French can be very helpful. Have students write to one of the large banks in the area, asking about careers in international banking. Be sure to have them ask what courses are necessary to be qualified for the positions.

ANSWERS TO Vous avez compris?

1. b
2. c
3. b
4. c
5. a
6. b

C'est à vous

 Recycling

These activities allow students to use the vocabulary and structure from this chapter in completely open-ended, real-life situations.

Presentation

Encourage students to say as much as possible when they do these activities. Tell them not to be afraid of making mistakes since the goal of these activities is real-life communication. If someone in the group makes an error, allow the others to politely correct him or her. Let students choose the activities they would like to do.

You may wish to divide students into pairs or groups. Encourage students to elaborate on the basic theme and to be creative. They may use props, pictures, or posters if they wish.

LEVELING

These activities encompass all three levels. All students will be able to do them at a sophistication level commensurate with their ability in French. Some students will be able to speak for several minutes, and others may be able to give just a few sentences. This is to be expected when students are functioning completely on their own, generating their own language to the best of their ability.

C'est à vous

Use what you have learned

1 À la poste
✔ *Use words and expressions related to postal services*

Vous êtes en vacances en France et vous voulez envoyer un colis. Vous allez à la poste où vous parlez à un(e) employé(e) des postes (votre camarade).

2 Un compte d'épargne
✔ *Talk about bank services*

Vous ne dépensez pas tout votre argent. Vous aimez mettre de l'argent de côté. Vous décidez d'ouvrir un compte d'épargne. Travaillez avec un copain ou une copine. Dites-lui pourquoi vous voulez avoir un compte d'épargne. Ensuite changez de rôle.

3 Ma semaine
✔ *Talk about teen spending habits*

Conversez avec un(e) camarade. Discutez d'où vient votre argent de poche. Vos parents vous donnent de l'argent? Vous le gagnez vous-même? Les deux? Dites aussi comment vous le dépensez.

4 Facile ou difficile?
✔ *Discuss saving money*

Écrivez un paragraphe intitulé «Pourquoi il faut faire des économies». Écrivez ensuite un deuxième paragraphe où vous expliquez s'il vous est facile ou difficile de mettre de l'argent de côté.

166 ✦ cent soixante-six

CHAPITRE 5

Answers to C'est à vous

 1 *Answers will vary.*
Students will make up a conversation using the specific vocabulary they learned in **Mots 2** of this chapter. They can use the following words and expressions.
  peser un colis
  mettre le colis sur la balance
  envoyer le colis
  combien de timbres
  ça coûte

 2 *Answers will vary.*
Students will use vocabulary presented in **Mots 1**.

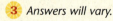 **3** *Answers will vary.*

 4 *Answers will vary.*

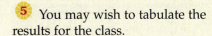

CHAPITRE 5 — C'est à vous

5 ÉCRIRE

Vous êtes comme la cigale ou la fourmi?
✔ *Analyze your spending habits*

Faites ce petit test pour voir si vous êtes comme la cigale ou la fourmi.

TEST:
1. Pour avoir l'argent de poche...
   a. Je ne fais rien. Mes parents me donnent de l'argent.
   b. Je travaille dans un magasin (un restaurant, etc.).
2. Quand je vois quelque chose que j'aime beaucoup...
   a. Je l'achète immédiatement.
   b. Je réfléchis avant de l'acheter.
3. Quand je reçois de l'argent comme cadeau...
   a. Je le dépense tout de suite.
   b. J'en mets de côté.
4. Quand je veux faire ou acheter quelque chose de spécial...
   a. J'emprunte de l'argent à mes amis ou à mes parents.
   b. Je mets de l'argent de côté à l'avance.
5. Quand j'emprunte de l'argent à mes copains...
   a. J'oublie souvent de les rembourser.
   b. Je les rembourse tout de suite.

SCORE:
Une majorité de a: Tu es une vraie cigale! Tu aimes beaucoup t'amuser dans ta vie. Tu dois peut-être essayer de penser un peu plus au futur.
Une majorité de b: Tu es une petite fourmi, responsable et toujours bien organisée. Tu es sûr(e) de t'amuser assez dans la vie?

la fourmi

la cigale

Writing Strategy

Writing informally Writing to friends is a good way to improve your communication skills and learn something about yourself at the same time. A personal message to a friend is different from a formal letter or e-mail to the bank, for example. It should include personal details about yourself, your thoughts, and your experiences. As you write, try to use words that are friendly and casual, just as you would when speaking face-to-face with a friend.

6 ÉCRIRE

Lettres ou e-mails?

International communication has changed greatly in recent years. Through e-mail, people from all over the world can communicate in a matter of seconds or minutes. As a result, letter writing is becoming less common, and sending e-mails is extremely popular.

Write an e-mail to a key pal in France telling him or her how you spend your money. Then ask your key pal questions about his or her spending habits.

Writing Development
Have students keep a notebook containing their best written work from each chapter. These selected writings can be based on assignments from the Student Textbook and the Workbook. The three activities on pages 166–167 are examples of writing assignments that may be included in each student's portfolio. In the Workbook, students will develop an organized autobiography (**Mon autobiographie**). These workbook pages may also become a part of their portfolio.

Writing Strategy

Writing informally
Have students read the Writing Strategy on page 167. Have students refer to the vocabulary list on page 171 if they need more ideas to write this selection.

Reaching All Students

For the Younger Students
Set up a "bank" and/or a "post office" in the classroom, with students playing the role of tellers at a new accounts window, a currency exchange window, and a letter/packages window. Distribute play money, photocopied checks, travelers' checks, and any other forms you can get from a local bank. Have students prepare postcards, letters, and packages to mail. Have other students act as customers engaging in various bank and post office transactions covered in this chapter.

5 You may wish to tabulate the results for the class.

Answers to C'est à vous

5 Answers will vary.

6 Answers will vary.

Assessment

Resource Manager

Communication Transparencies C 5
Quizzes, pages 21–26
Tests, pages 67–80
ExamView® Pro
Situation Cards
Performance Assessment, Task 5
Marathon mental Videoquiz

✓ Assessment

This is a pre-test for students to take before you administer the chapter test. Answer sheets for students to do these pages are provided in your transparency binder. Note that each section is cross-referenced so students can easily find the material they have to review in case they made errors. You may wish to collect these assessments and correct them yourself or you may prefer to have the students correct themselves in class. You can go over the answers orally or project them on the overhead, using your Assessment Answers transparencies.

Assessment

Vocabulaire

1 Identifiez.

1.    2.

To review Mots 1, turn to pages 142–143.

2 Choisissez.

a. Le caissier m'a donné 200 euros en liquide.
b. Je suis toujours fauché.
c. Le caissier m'a donné 10 billets de dix.
d. J'aime mettre de l'argent de côté.

3. _____ J'ai touché un chèque de 200 euros.
4. _____ J'ai changé un billet de 100 dollars.
5. _____ Je fais des économies.
6. _____ Je n'ai jamais de fric.

3 Identifiez.

7.    8.

To review Mots 2, turn to pages 146–147.

9.

168 ✦ cent soixante-huit   CHAPITRE 5

ANSWERS TO Assessment

1
1. des pièces
2. des billets

2
3. a
4. c
5. d
6. b

3
7. une boîte aux lettres
8. un colis
9. un timbre

CHAPITRE 5 Assessment

4 Vrai ou faux?
10. On met une lettre dans un distributeur automatique.
11. Avant d'envoyer une lettre il faut la mettre dans une enveloppe.
12. C'est le facteur qui vend les timbres à la poste.
13. Il faut écrire le nom et l'adresse sur l'enveloppe.

Structure

5 Complétez avec «qui» ou «que».
14. C'est le facteur ___ arrive.
15. Il parle de la lettre ___ son cousin écrit.
16. Où est le colis ___ je veux envoyer?
17. Je crois que c'est le colis ___ est sur la table.
18. Je ne sais pas si c'est le même garçon ___ vous connaissez.

To review qui and que, turn to page 150.

6 Récrivez au passé composé.
19. Voilà la lettre qu'il écrit.
20. Les timbres que vous achetez sont très beaux.

To review agreement in the passé composé, turn to page 153.

7 Récrivez au passé composé.
21. Les deux amis se voient.
22. Ils se parlent tout de suite.

To review reciprocal verbs, turn to page 155.

Culture

8 Vrai ou faux?
23. La semaine, c'est l'argent de poche qu'un(e) jeune Français(e) reçoit de ses parents.
24. Tous les jeunes en France reçoivent la même somme d'argent.
25. Les jeunes qui dépensent tout leur argent ont un compte d'épargne.

To review this cultural information, turn to pages 160–161.

Glencoe Technology

MINDJOGGER VHS/DVD
You may wish to help your students prepare for the chapter test by playing the MindJogger game show. Teams will compete against each other to review chapter vocabulary and structure and sharpen listening comprehension skills.

FOLDABLES Study Organizer — Dinah Zike's Study Guides

Your students may wish to use Foldable 7 to organize, display, and arrange data as they learn to write more extensively in French. You may wish to encourage them to add information from each chapter as they continue to write about and illustrate all the different topics they will be studying.

A *single picture frame* foldable will help different types of learners organize. When it comes to writing, it may help students begin to gather their thoughts to depict what it is they want to write about.

LA BANQUE ET LA POSTE — cent soixante-neuf 169

ANSWERS TO Assessment

4
10. faux
11. vrai
12. faux
13. vrai

5
14. qui
15. que
16. que
17. qui
18. que

6
19. Voilà la lettre qu'il a écrite.
20. Les timbres que vous avez achetés sont très beaux.

7
21. Les deux amis se sont vus.
22. Ils se sont parlé tout de suite.

8
23. vrai
24. faux
25. faux

On parle super bien!

This unique page gives students the opportunity to speak freely and say whatever they can, using the vocabulary and structures they have learned in the chapter. The illustration serves to remind students of precisely what they know how to say in French. There are no activities that students do not have the ability to describe or talk about in French. The art not only depicts the vocabulary and content of this chapter, but also reinforces what they learned in previous chapters.

You may wish to use this page in many ways. Some possibilities are to have students do the following:

1. Look at the illustration and identify items by giving the correct French words.
2. Make up sentences about what they see in the illustration.
3. Make up questions about the illustration. They can call on another class member to respond if you do this as a class activity, or you may prefer to allow students to work in small groups. This activity is extremely beneficial because it enables students to actively use interrogative words.
4. Answer questions you ask them about the illustration.
5. Work in pairs and make up a conversation based on the illustration.
6. Look at the illustration and give a complete oral review of what they see.
7. Look at the illustration and write a paragraph (or essay) about it.

You can also use this page as an assessment or testing tool, taking into account individual differences by having students go from simple to quite complicated tasks. The assessment can be either oral or written. You may wish to use the rubrics provided on pages T20–T21 as you give students the following directions.

170

On parle super bien!

Tell all you can about this illustration.

170 ❖ cent soixante-dix

CHAPITRE 5

1. Identify the topic or situation of the illustration.
2. Give the French words for as many items as you can.
3. Think of as many sentences as you can to describe the illustration.
4. Go over your sentences and put them in the best sequencing to give a coherent story based on the illustration.

Vocabulaire

Talking about the bank
une banque	de la monnaie	un chèque	faire la monnaie
de l'argent (m.) liquide	un distributeur	verser de l'argent sur	prêter
un billet	automatique	son compte	emprunter
une pièce	un compte d'épargne	retirer	devoir
un euro	un compte courant	toucher un chèque	rendre

Changing currency
un bureau de change	une monnaie
le cours du change	changer de l'argent
un caissier, une caissière	compter

Talking about saving and spending money
un porte-monnaie	avoir plein de fric
faire des économies	être fauché(e)
mettre de l'argent de côté	dépenser

How well do you know your vocabulary?
Choose words to describe a trip to the bank or the ATM machine. Will you deposit or withdraw money from your account?

Talking about the post office
la poste	une lettre	un timbre	mettre une lettre à la poste
un bureau de poste	une enveloppe	une boîte aux lettres	distribuer le courrier
un guichet	une adresse	un colis	
un(e) employé(e) des postes	le numéro	une balance	
un facteur, une factrice	la rue	peser	
une carte postale	la ville	envoyer	
	le code postal		

VIDÉOTOUR
Épisode 5
In this video episode, you will join Christine and Amadou as they do some errands. See page 504 for more information.

LA BANQUE ET LA POSTE

cent soixante et onze 171

Planning for Chapter 6

SCOPE AND SEQUENCE, PAGES 172–203

Topics
- Foods
- Food preparation

Culture
- A gastronomic voyage through France
- Dinner with a family from the Maghreb
- A recipe for lamb stew

Functions
- How to describe future events
- How to refer to people and things already mentioned
- How to tell what you have others do

Structure
- The future tense
- Two pronouns in the same sentence
- The verb **faire** + infinitive

National Standards
- Communication Standard 1.1 pages 176, 177, 180, 181, 183, 184, 186, 188, 189, 191, 198
- Communication Standard 1.2 pages 176, 177, 180, 181, 183, 184, 186, 188, 189, 190, 193, 194, 195, 197
- Communication Standard 1.3 pages 177, 180, 181, 183, 184, 188, 194, 198, 199
- Cultures Standard 2.1 pages 192–193, 194
- Cultures Standard 2.2 pages 189, 190, 192–193, 194, 195
- Connections Standard 3.1 pages 196–197
- Comparisons Standard 4.1 pages 181, 199
- Comparisons Standard 4.2 pages 181, 194, 199
- Communities Standard 5.1 page 199

PACING AND PRIORITIES

The chapter content is color coded below to assist you in planning.

■ required   ■ recommended   ■ optional

Vocabulaire *(required)*   *Days 1–4*
- ■ Mots 1
  - Dans la cuisine
  - Des aliments
- ■ Mots 2
  - Faisons la cuisine!
  - D'autres aliments

Structure *(required)*   *Days 5–7*
- ■ Le futur simple
- ■ Deux pronoms dans la même phrase
- ■ **Faire** + infinitif

Conversation *(required)*
- ■ La cuisine et moi, ça fait deux!

Lectures culturelles
- ■ Un voyage gastronomique *(recommended)*
- ■ Un dîner chez une famille maghrébine *(optional)*
- ■ Navarin d'agneau *(optional)*

Connexions *(optional)*
- ■ La littérature

■ **C'est à vous** *(recommended)*

■ **Assessment** *(recommended)*

■ **On parle super bien!** *(optional)*

RESOURCE GUIDE

SECTION	PAGES	SECTION RESOURCES
Vocabulaire *Mots 1*		
Dans la cuisine Des aliments	174 174–177	Vocabulary Transparencies 6.2–6.3 Audio CD 4 Audio Activities TE, pages 58–59 Workbook, page 63 Quiz 1, page 27 ExamView® Pro
Vocabulaire *Mots 2*		
Faisons la cuisine! D'autres aliments	178 179–181	Vocabulary Transparencies 6.4–6.5 Audio CD 4 Audio Activities TE, pages 60–61 Workbook, pages 64–65 Quiz 2, page 28 ExamView® Pro
Structure		
Le futur simple Deux pronoms dans la même phrase **Faire** + infinitif	182–184 185–186 187–189	Audio CD 4 Audio Activities TE, pages 62–64 Workbook, pages 66–69 Quizzes 3–5, pages 29–31 ExamView® Pro
Conversation		
La cuisine et moi, ça fait deux!	190–191	Audio CD 4 Audio Activities TE, pages 64–65 Interactive CD-ROM
Lectures culturelles		
Un voyage gastronomique Un dîner chez une famille maghrébine Navarin d'agneau	192–193 194 195	Audio CD 4 Audio Activities TE, pages 66–67 Tests, pages 83, 87
Connexions		
La littérature	196–197	Tests, page 88
C'est à vous		
	198–199	**Bon voyage!** Video, Episode 6 Video Activities, Chapter 6 French Online Activities french.glencoe.com
Assessment		
	200–201	Communication Transparency C 6 Quizzes 1–5, pages 27–31 Performance Assessment, Task 6 Tests, pages 81–94 ExamView® Pro Situation Cards, Chapter 6 **Marathon mental** Videoquiz

Using Your Resources for Chapter 6

Transparencies

Bellringer 6.1–6.7   Vocabulary 6.1–6.5   Communication C 6

Workbook

Vocabulary, pages 63–65   Structure, pages 66–69   Enrichment, pages 70–72

Audio Activities

Vocabulary, pages 58–61   Structure, pages 62–64   Conversation, pages 64–65   Cultural Reading, pages 66–67   Additional Practice, pages 67–68

Assessment

Vocabulary and Structure Quizzes, pages 27–31

Chapter Tests, pages 81–94

Situation Cards, Chapter 6

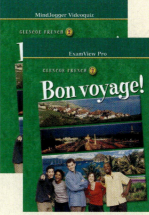
MindJogger Videoquiz, ExamView® Pro, Chapter 6

Timesaving Teacher Tools

TeacherWorks™

TeacherWorks™ is your all-in-one teacher resource center. Personalize lesson plans, access resources from the Teacher Wraparound Edition, connect to the Internet, or make a to-do list. These are only a few of the many features that can assist you in the planning and organizing of your lessons.

Includes:
- A calendar feature
- Access to all program blackline masters
- Standards correlations and more

ExamView® Pro

Test Bank software for Macintosh and Windows makes creating, editing, customizing, and printing tests quick and easy.

Technology Resources

 In the Chapter 6 Internet activity, you will have a chance to learn more about the Francophone world. Visit <u>french.glencoe.com</u>.

 On the Interactive Conversation CD-ROM, students can listen to and take part in a recorded version of the conversation in Chapter 6.

 See the National Geographic Teacher's Corner on pages 138–139, 244–245, 372–373, 472–473 for reference to additional technology resources.

 Bon voyage! Video and Video Activities, Chapter 6

 Help your students prepare for the chapter test by playing the **Marathon mental** Videoquiz game show. Teams will compete against each other to review chapter vocabulary and structure and sharpen listening comprehension skills.

Preview

In this chapter, students will learn to talk about food and its preparation. Students will also increase their communication skills by learning the future tense, the placement of two object pronouns in the same sentence, and the construction **faire** + infinitive.

 National Standards

Communication
In Chapter 6, students will communicate in spoken and written French on the following topics:
- Foods
- Food preparation

Students will obtain and provide information about these topics and engage in conversations that would typically take place in a kitchen as they fulfill the chapter objectives listed on this page.

LEVELING
The activities, conversations, and readings within each chapter are marked according to level of difficulty. **E** indicates easy. **A** indicates average. **C** indicates challenging. Some activities cover a range of difficulty. In some activities, for example, advanced students will be able to produce more extensive responses while students who learn at a different rate may give less detailed responses. The leveling indicators will help you individualize instruction to best meet your students' needs.

CHAPITRE 6
La gastronomie

Objectifs
In this chapter you will learn to:

✔ talk about foods and food preparation
✔ describe future events
✔ refer to people and things already mentioned
✔ tell what you have others do
✔ discuss the cuisine of various French provinces

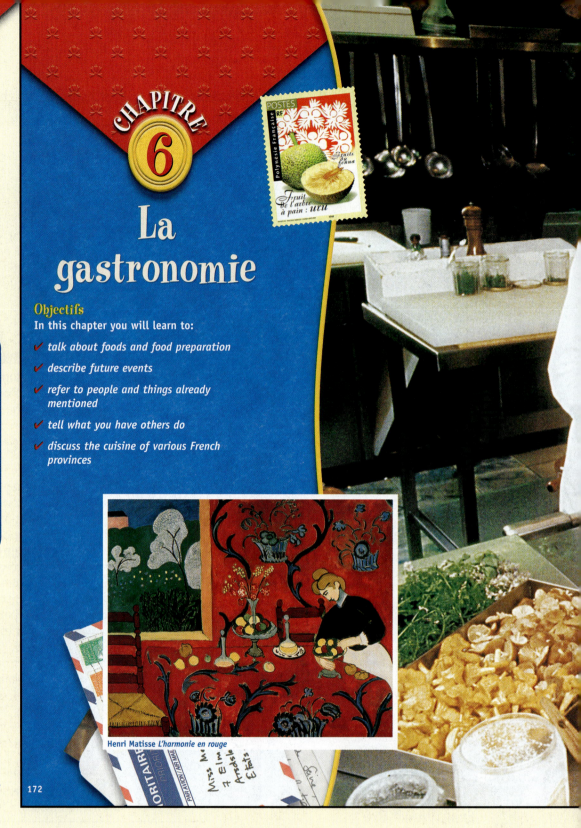

Henri Matisse *L'harmonie en rouge*

CHAPITRE 6

Spotlight on Culture

Photograph This photo shows the French chef Philippe Jousse at the culinary school in Paris. After completing the vocabulary sections, have students say everything they can about the photo.

Painting The turn of the century saw a new series of art movements in Europe. The first movement started in 1905, when a group of young painters under the tutelage of Henri Matisse (1869–1954) exhibited in Paris. The paintings were very simple in design and brightly colored. They were also very loose in brushwork. An enraged critic called the artists **fauves** or "wild beasts."

Henri Matisse was the leader of the Fauves. He was born to a middle-class couple from northern France. Matisse convinced his family to allow him to study art rather than law. Early on, Matisse developed a style that made use of broad areas of color, as seen here in ***L'harmonie en rouge,*** that were not meant to look like the shapes or colors found in nature.

Vocabulaire   Mots 1

1 Preparation

Resource Manager

Vocabulary Transparencies 6.2–6.3
Audio Activities TE, pages 58–59
Audio CD 4
Workbook, page 63
Quiz 1, page 27
ExamView® Pro

Bellringer Review

Use BRR Transparency 6.1 or write the following on the board. Divide this list of words into three categories:
fruits/légumes/viandes

une banane	une pomme
une carotte	du saucisson
une orange	des haricots verts
du poulet	
un oignon	une pomme de terre
une salade	
du bœuf	une tomate

Vocabulaire   Mots 1

Dans la cuisine

Des aliments

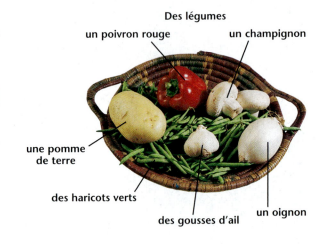

174 ✤ cent soixante-quatorze   CHAPITRE 6

Chapter Projects

 Un repas français Have students select a French recipe to prepare at home. You may assign or have them select a region of France from which a dish is representative. Groups could work together at home to make the recipe, bring it to class, and present information about the region and the ingredients.

Qu'est-ce qu'on mange? Have students work in small groups. Each group will determine their favorite fruits, vegetables, meats, and fish. Each group will complete its lists and determine their favorite foods. Are they healthy foods or not?

 Mon repas favori Have students prepare a menu for their favorite American meal. If a student is from another ethnic background, he or she may choose to prepare the menu for a meal from his or her ethnic group.

Au restaurant If there is a French restaurant in your area, you may wish to plan a field trip to allow students to experience eating at a French restaurant.

Vocabulaire
Mots 1

de l'huile d'olive
du persil
des pâtes
du laurier
du thym
des fines herbes

de la choucroute avec des saucisses

Quand Maman sera là.

Quand est-ce qu'on va dîner?

Quand elle rentrera, elle regardera d'abord le journal télévisé. Après, elle lira son courrier. On ne mangera pas encore avant neuf heures!

une recette

RÔTI DE PORC CUIT DANS LE LAIT
4 PERSONNES, PRÉPARATION 30 MINUTES, CUISSON 1 HEURE 15 MINUTES, FACILE

1 rôti de porc de 800 g, 1 litre de lait entier, 20 g de beurre, 2 cuil. à soupe d'huile d'olive, 1 branche de thym, 2 feuilles de sauge, 1 feuille de laurier, sel et poivre

- Dans une casserole, mettez le lait à bouillir.
- Dans une cocotte, faites chauffer le mélange de beurre et d'huile. Faites-y colorer sur feu vif le rôti.
- Ajoutez le laurier, la sauge, et le thym. Salez et poivrez. Versez le lait bouillant sur la viande. Couvrez et laissez cuire à tout petits bouillons.
- À mi-cuisson, retournez la viande. En réduisant, le lait va donner une belle sauce.
- Comme garniture, vous pouvez servir des légumes verts de saison ou alors des pâtes ou des pommes de terre.

ma recette favorite

LA GASTRONOMIE

cent soixante-quinze 175

Vocabulaire

3 Practice

Quel est le mot?

Attention!

When students are doing the **Quel est le mot?** activities, accept any answer that makes sense. The purpose of these activities is to have students use the new vocabulary. They are not factual recall activities. If you wish, have students use the photos on this page as a stimulus.

 This *Infogap* activity will allow students to practice in pairs. The activity should be very manageable for them, since all vocabulary and structures are familiar to them.

Recycling

Have students say as much as they can about the photo of the market stall on page 177. Have them create a dialogue with the **marchand.**

Reteaching

Show Vocabulary Transparencies 6.2–6.3 and let students say as much as they can about them in their own words.

Vocabulaire

Quel est le mot?

 1 Au magasin d'électroménager Travaillez avec un(e) camarade. Quels sont les appareils que vous pouvez trouver sur cette photo?

Le magasin Electrostar à Bonneuil-sur-Marne

 2 Historiette Dans la cuisine
Répondez d'après la photo.
1. Il y a quelqu'un dans la cuisine?
2. C'est une cuisine moderne?
3. C'est une cuisinière électrique ou à gaz?
4. Il y a aussi un four?
5. Le réfrigérateur a combien de portes?
6. Il y a un congélateur dans le réfrigérateur?

 For more practice using words from *Mots 1*, do Activity 12 on page H13 at the end of this book.

176 ❦ cent soixante-seize   CHAPITRE 6

ANSWERS TO Quel est le mot?

Il y a des réfrigérateurs (des frigos, des frigidaires), des congélateurs (des congés), des fours à micro-ondes, des fours et des cuisinières.

1. Non, il n'y a personne dans la cuisine.
2. Oui, c'est une cuisine moderne.
3. C'est une cuisinière électrique.
4. Oui, il y a aussi un four.
5. Le réfrigérateur a deux portes.
6. Oui, il y a un congélateur dans le réfrigérateur.

3 **Quelle catégorie?** Choisissez.

un légume   un fruit   une herbe aromatique

1. une pomme de terre
2. un citron
3. un champignon
4. un poivron vert ou rouge
5. du thym
6. du laurier
7. du raisin
8. des haricots verts
9. un pamplemousse
10. des oignons

4 **Ce que j'aime** Donnez des réponses personnelles.

1. Tu aimes la salade de fruits avec des bananes et des pamplemousses?
2. Tu aimes les pâtes avec de la sauce tomate?
3. Tu aimes l'ail dans la sauce tomate? Tu y mets combien de gousses d'ail?
4. Tu aimes la salade avec de l'huile et du vinaigre?
5. Tu aimes les pommes de terre avec du beurre et du persil?
6. Tu aimes la choucroute avec des saucisses?
7. Tu prépares un repas de temps en temps?
8. Tu as une recette favorite? Quelle est cette recette?
9. Tu as un plat favori? Quel est ce plat?

Le marché d'Arpajon

5 **Les aliments** Jouez avec un copain ou une copine. Vous avez appris les noms de beaucoup d'aliments. Vous avez trois minutes pour préparer une liste des noms de tous les aliments que vous avez appris. Celui qui a la plus longue liste gagne.

LA GASTRONOMIE

Vocabulaire Mots 2

1 Preparation

Resource Manager
Vocabulary Transparencies 6.4–6.5
Audio Activities TE, pages 60–61
Audio CD 4
Workbook, pages 64–65
Quiz 2, page 28
ExamView® Pro

Bellringer Review
Use BRR Transparency 6.2 or write the following on the board.
Write your two favorite meals. List the ingredients of each.

2 Presentation

Step 1 Show Vocabulary Transparencies 6.4–6.5. Have students close their books and repeat the words after you or Audio CD 4 as you point to the appropriate illustration on the transparency.

Step 2 Dramatize the meaning of these words: **éplucher, couper, hacher, râper, verser, remuer.**

Step 3 When students have produced the new vocabulary several times, have them open their books to pages 178–179 and call on volunteers to read the words, phrases, and sentences. Model pronunciation as necessary.

178

Vocabulaire Mots 2

Faisons la cuisine!

éplucher des pommes de terre
couper en morceaux
un morceau

hacher de la viande
râper du fromage

couper en rondelles
une rondelle

verser du lait
remuer une sauce
un couvercle
une poêle
une casserole

ajouter de l'eau

J'espère que ça sera bon!

M. Arnaud est bon cuisinier.
Il va faire cuire les carottes.
Il fait bouillir l'eau à feu vif.
Il met les carottes dans l'eau bouillante.

Il laisse bouillir les carottes à feu doux.

178 ❖ cent soixante-dix-huit

CHAPITRE 6

Vocabulaire
Mots 2

D'autres aliments

La viande

- le veau
- une côtelette de veau

- le bœuf
- un rôti de bœuf

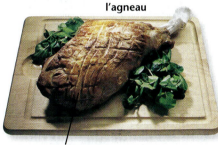
- l'agneau
- un gigot d'agneau

- le porc
- une côtelette de porc

Les poissons et les fruits de mer

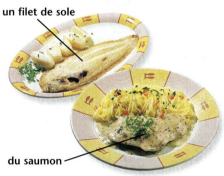
- un filet de sole
- du saumon

- une moule
- un homard
- une huître
- un crabe

French Online

The **Glencoe World Languages Web site** (french.glencoe.com) offers options that enable you and your students to experience the French-speaking world via the Internet. For each chapter, there are activities, games, and quizzes. In addition, an *Enrichment* section offers students an opportunity to visit Web sites related to the theme of the chapter.

Reaching All Students

Total Physical Response You may wish to bring some kitchen items to use for this activity.

(Student 1), venez ici, s'il vous plaît.
C'est une pomme de terre.
Lavez la pomme de terre.
Épluchez la pomme de terre.
Et maintenant, coupez la pomme de terre. Coupez-la en tranches.
Mettez les tranches dans une casserole.
Ajoutez de l'eau.
Allumez le feu.
Merci, (Student 1). C'est très bien. Vous pouvez retourner à votre place.
(Student 2), venez ici, s'il vous plaît.
C'est du fromage.
Coupez le fromage. Faites des gros morceaux.
Prenez une casserole.
Mettez un peu de lait dans le casserole.
Ajoutez le fromage.
Mettez la casserole sur le feu.
Remuez la sauce.
Remuez-la vite.
Versez un peu plus de lait.
Merci, (Student 2).

Vocabulaire

3 Practice

Quel est le mot?

6 You may wish to have students correct any false statements.

Writing Development
Have students write the answers to questions in Activity 7 in paragraph form.

Learning from Photos

(pages 180–181) Have students identify everything they can in the photos.

(page 180 top) Saint-Paul-de-Vence is a beautiful small town in the hills to the north of Nice. Have students note how beautifully produce is displayed in many French markets.

Vocabulaire

Quel est le mot?

6 **En cuisine**
Indiquez si ça se fait ou si ça ne se fait pas.

1. On coupe un concombre en rondelles.
2. On coupe l'eau en petits morceaux.
3. On met de l'eau dans une casserole pour faire bouillir quelque chose.
4. On fait les frites dans de l'eau.
5. On râpe le fromage avant de le mettre sur les pâtes.
6. On fait les hamburgers avec de la viande hachée.
7. On fait bouillir l'eau dans une poêle.
8. On verse du lait dans un couvercle.
9. On remue une sauce.
10. On épluche les pommes de terre et les carottes avant de les faire cuire.

Un marché de fruits et légumes à Saint-Paul-de-Vence

7 **Historiette** **Un bon cuisinier**
Inventez une histoire.

1. Luc aime faire la cuisine?
2. Il est bon cuisinier?
3. C'est lui qui va préparer le repas pour l'anniversaire de sa copine?
4. Qu'est-ce qu'il va préparer, de la viande ou du poisson?
5. Qu'est-ce qu'il préfère, la viande ou le poisson? Et sa copine?
6. Qu'est-ce qu'il va servir comme légumes?
7. Qu'est-ce qu'il va servir comme dessert?

Cuisine in France varies from region to region. To learn more about the differences of some of these regions, go to the Glencoe French Web site: french.glencoe.com

180 cent quatre-vingts   CHAPITRE 6

ANSWERS TO Quel est le mot?

6
1. Oui, on coupe un concombre en rondelles.
2. Non, on ne coupe pas l'eau en petits morceaux.
3. Oui, on met de l'eau dans une casserole pour faire bouillir quelque chose.
4. Non, on ne fait pas les frites dans de l'eau.
5. Oui, on râpe le fromage avant de le mettre sur les pâtes.
6. Oui, on fait les hamburgers avec de la viande hachée.
7. Non, on ne fait pas bouillir l'eau dans une poêle.
8. Non, on ne verse pas de lait dans un couvercle.
9. Oui, on remue une sauce.
10. Oui, on épluche les pommes de terre et les carottes avant de les faire cuire.

7 Answers will vary but may include:
1. Oui, Luc aime faire la cuisine.
2. Oui, il est bon cuisinier.
3. Oui, c'est lui qui va préparer le repas pour l'anniversaire de sa copine.
4. Il va préparer du poisson.
5. Il préfère la viande. Sa copine préfère le poisson.
6. Il va servir des haricots verts.
7. Il va servir un gâteau au chocolat.

Vocabulaire

8 J'aime ça.
Donnez des réponses personnelles.

1. Quels sont les poissons que tu aimes?
2. Quels sont les fruits de mer que tu aimes?
3. Quelles sont les viandes que tu aimes?
4. Quels sont tes fruits favoris?
5. Quels sont tes légumes favoris?

Le marché d'Arpajon

9 Nos repas favoris
Avec un copain ou une copine, parlez de vos repas favoris. Ensuite, décidez si vous mangez des aliments qui sont bons pour la santé.

10 Un repas américain Vous êtes à Carcassonne, en France, chez les Lebrun. Monsieur Lebrun (votre copain) ou Madame Lebrun (votre copine) vous demande de décrire un repas typiquement américain. Faites-le et expliquez-lui, si possible, comment on le prépare. Ensuite changez de rôle.

Carcassonne dans le sud-ouest de la France

LA GASTRONOMIE

Structure

1 Preparation

Resource Manager
Audio Activities TE, pages 62–64
Audio CD 4
Workbook, pages 66–69
Quizzes 3–5, pages 29–31
ExamView® Pro

Bellringer Review
Use BRR Transparency 6.3 or write the following on the board.
Name at least one food item that goes logically with each action below.
1. faire bouillir   4. hacher
2. râper   5. verser
3. éplucher

2 Presentation

 Le futur simple

Step 1 Review **aller** + infinitive as discussed in the **Rappelez-vous que…** section. Remind students that these actions will take place in the near future. Write some examples on the board.

Step 2 Go over Item 1. Stress that the **e** is dropped from **-re** verbs.

Step 3 Have students repeat the verb forms after you.

Step 4 Ask students what the future endings remind them of. Write the forms of **avoir** on the board and point out the similarity.

LEVELING
E: Activities 11, 12, 13

Structure

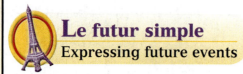
Le futur simple
Expressing future events

Rappelez-vous que…
You already learned that the future can be expressed in French by using **aller** + infinitive.
Vendredi, je vais sortir avec Émilie.

1. To form the future tense in French, you add the future endings to the entire infinitive of verbs that end in **-er** or **-ir**. You drop the **e** before adding the endings to **-re** verbs. Study the following.

	PARLER	FINIR	ATTENDRE
Infinitive	parler	finir	attendre
Stem	parler-	finir-	attendr-
	je parler**ai**	je finir**ai**	j' attendr**ai**
	tu parler**as**	tu finir**as**	tu attendr**as**
	il/elle/on parler**a**	il/elle/on finir**a**	il/elle/on attendr**a**
	nous parler**ons**	nous finir**ons**	nous attendr**ons**
	vous parler**ez**	vous finir**ez**	vous attendr**ez**
	ils/elles parler**ont**	ils/elles finir**ont**	ils/elles attendr**ont**

2. The verbs **être, faire, aller,** and **avoir** have an irregular stem in the future tense.
   ÊTRE   je serai, tu seras, il sera, nous serons, vous serez, ils seront
   FAIRE je ferai, tu feras, il fera, nous ferons, vous ferez, ils feront
   ALLER j'irai, tu iras, il ira, nous irons, vous irez, ils iront
   AVOIR j'aurai, tu auras, il aura, nous aurons, vous aurez, ils auront

3. The future tense is not commonly used in spoken French. You use **aller** + the infinitive more often to express the future. However, you must use the future tense after **quand** when the main verb in the sentence is in the future tense.
   Je te ferai un bon repas quand tu seras à Paris.
   Quand tout le monde sera là, je mettrai la viande au four.

About the French Language
You may wish to explain to students that the present tense of **aller** is frequently used to express the future.
J'y vais demain mais Robert y va la semaine prochaine.

Writing Development
Have students write Activities 11 and 12 in paragraph form.

Comment dit-on?

11 **Historiette** Un de ces jours... Répondez que oui.
1. Un de ces jours, Sandra voyagera en France?
2. Elle prendra l'avion pour y aller?
3. Elle passera quelques semaines à Paris?
4. Elle visitera les monuments?
5. Elle s'amusera?
6. Sa copine Liz l'accompagnera?
7. Elles sortiront souvent?
8. Elles dîneront dans de bons restaurants?

PARIS

12 **Historiette** Une bonne cuisinière
Inventez des réponses.
1. Sandra ira dans une école culinaire quand elle sera à Paris?
2. Elle apprendra à faire des plats français quand elle sera à Paris?
3. Elle préparera des repas exquis quand elle rentrera aux États-Unis?
4. Elle invitera ses amis à dîner?
5. Elle leur fera de la cuisine française quand elle les invitera?

Une fondue au fromage

Un marché à Aix-en-Provence

13   Une salade de fruits Répondez que oui.
1. Tu feras une bonne salade de fruits?
2. Tu mettras des oranges, des pommes et du raisin?
3. Tu laveras les fruits?
4. Tu éplucheras les pommes?
5. Tu couperas les bananes en rondelles?
6. Tu ajouteras du sucre?
7. Tu serviras de petits gâteaux avec ta salade de fruits?

LA GASTRONOMIE

cent quatre-vingt-trois 183

Structure

3 Practice (continued)

14 Expansion: Have students work in pairs. One asks the questions, the other answers each question.

16 Expansion: Have students invent original sentences telling what they will do at the beach. For example: **J'irai à la plage où je prendrai un bain de soleil.**

LEVELING
E: Activities 14, 15, 16, 17
A: Activities 15, 16, 17, 18

---

14 Pour ton anniversaire?
Posez des questions à Laurent d'après le modèle.

donner une fête →
Laurent, tu donneras une fête?

1. inviter des amis
2. préparer des hors-d'œuvre
3. jouer de la guitare
4. chanter
5. mettre des CD
6. danser

Le restaurant Julien à Paris

15 Historiette Au restaurant
Répondez d'après les indications.

1. Tu iras au restaurant à quelle heure demain soir? (à neuf heures)
2. C'est toi qui choisiras le restaurant? (oui)
3. Tu y dîneras seul? (non, avec Julie)
4. Vous prendrez une table avant l'arrivée de vos amis? (oui)
5. Vous demanderez la carte aussi? (non)
6. Vous attendrez vos amis? (absolument)

16 Un voyage à la Martinique Répondez que oui.

1. L'hiver prochain Émilie aura des vacances?
2. Elle fera un voyage?
3. Elle ira à la Martinique?
4. Elle fera le voyage en avion?
5. Elle sera fatiguée après le vol?
6. Tu feras ce voyage avec Émilie?
7. Vous irez ensemble à la Martinique?
8. Vous y ferez des excursions ensemble?
9. Vous irez à la plage?
10. Vous prendrez des bains de soleil?
11. Vous serez bronzé(e)s?

17 De bonnes résolutions
Vous avez décidé de prendre de bonnes résolutions pour le nouvel an. Par exemple: **Je serai gentil(le) avec ma sœur.** Faites une liste et comparez-la avec la liste d'un(e) camarade. Quelles sont les résolutions qui sont les mêmes?

18 J'espère…
Travaillez avec un(e) camarade. Dites ce que vous espérez pour l'avenir. Par exemple: **J'espère que je n'aurai plus de devoirs l'année prochaine.**

184 cent quatre-vingt-quatre CHAPITRE 6

ANSWERS TO Comment dit-on?

14
1. Laurent, tu inviteras des amis?
2. Laurent, tu prépareras des hors-d'œuvre?
3. Laurent, tu joueras de la guitare?
4. Laurent, tu chanteras?
5. Laurent, tu mettras des CD?
6. Laurent, tu danseras?

15
1. J'irai au restaurant à neuf heures.
2. Oui, c'est moi qui choisirai le restaurant.
3. Non, j'y dînerai avec Julie.
4. Oui, nous prendrons une table avant l'arrivée de nos amis.
5. Non, nous ne demanderons pas la carte.
6. Absolument, nous attendrons nos amis.

16
1. Oui, elle aura des vacances l'hiver prochain.
2. Oui, elle fera un voyage.
3. Oui, elle ira à la Martinique.
4. Oui, elle fera le voyage en avion.
5. Oui, elle sera fatiguée après le vol.
6. Oui, je ferai ce voyage avec Émilie.
7. Oui, nous irons ensemble à la Martinique.
8. Oui, nous y ferons des excursions ensemble.
9. Oui, nous irons à la plage.
10. Oui, nous prendrons des bains de soleil.
11. Oui, nous serons bronzé(e)s.

17 Answers will vary.

18 Answers will vary.

Structure

Deux pronoms dans la même phrase
Referring to people and things already mentioned

1. It is possible to use both a direct and an indirect object pronoun in the same sentence. Study the following sentences.

   Le serveur **me** donne **la carte**.   Il **me la** donne.
   Il **nous** sert **la soupe**.   Il **nous la** sert.

2. The pronouns **me, te, nous, vous** precede the pronouns **le, la, les**.

   Elle { me / te / nous / vous } { le / la / les } donne.

3. The double object pronouns, the same as a single pronoun, come directly before the verbs they are linked to. Study the following sentences.

Affirmatif	Négatif
Il me le donne.	Il ne me le donne pas.
Il va me le donner.	Il ne va pas me le donner.
Il me l' a donné.	Il ne me l' a pas donné.

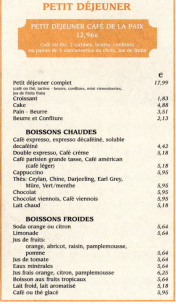

Rappelez-vous que...

In the **passé composé**, the past participle must agree with the preceding direct object.

Il t'a donné la recette?
Oui, il me l'a donnée.

LA GASTRONOMIE

cent quatre-vingt-cinq **185**

Structure

1 Preparation

Bellringer Review

Use BRR Transparency 6.4 or write the following on the board. List five things you will do next summer.

2 Presentation

Deux pronoms dans la même phrase

Step 1 Go over Items 1, 2, and 3 with the class and have students repeat the model sentences.

Note: The use of **lui** and **leur** in sentences with two pronouns will be taught in the next chapter.

Learning from Realia

(page 185) Have students find the present exchange rate for the euro, and then calculate the price in U.S. dollars of several items on this menu.

You may wish to explain to students that prices are a bit high because the Café de la Paix is considered quite ritzy. Also, prices in any café are higher when taken at a table. Prices are lower at the counter.

Structure

3 Practice

Comment dit-on?

19 Expansion: Change this activity to practice the **passé composé** and to review stores:
—Tu as le thym?
—Oui, je l'ai. Je l'ai acheté à l'épicerie hier.

> **Learning from Photos**
>
> *(page 186)* Have students identify the ingredients of the salad. Then have them say whether they would eat a salad like this one.
>
> This is a photo of a **salade niçoise**. Some of the ingredients are: **de la laitue, des tomates, des poivrons, des œufs durs, du thon, des haricots verts.**

LEVELING
E: Activities 19, 20
A: Activities 19, 20, 21
C: Activity 21

Structure

Comment dit-on?

19 Oui, je l'ai.
Suivez le modèle.
—Tu as le thym?
—Oui, je l'ai.
—Tu me le passes, s'il te plaît.
1. Tu as le fromage?
2. Tu as les champignons?
3. Tu as le persil?
4. Tu as la poêle?
5. Tu as l'huile?

20 Je vais vous aider.
Suivez le modèle.
—Il faut remuer la sauce.
—Je peux vous la remuer.
1. Il faut laver la salade.
2. Il faut râper le fromage.
3. Il faut éplucher les carottes.
4. Il faut préparer la sauce vinaigrette.
5. Il faut laver le persil.
6. Il faut laver les haricots verts.

21 Qui te l'a acheté? Suivez le modèle.
—J'ai de nouvelles lunettes.
—Qui te les a achetées?
1. J'ai une nouvelle voiture.
2. J'ai un nouveau téléviseur.
3. J'ai un nouveau magnétoscope.
4. J'ai de nouveaux skis.
5. J'ai un nouvel ordinateur.
6. J'ai une nouvelle calculatrice.
7. J'ai de nouvelles chaussures.

ANSWERS TO Comment dit-on?

19
1. —Oui, je l'ai.
   —Tu me le passes, s'il te plaît.
2. —Oui, je les ai.
   —Tu me les passes, s'il te plaît.
3. —Oui, je l'ai.
   —Tu me le passes, s'il te plaît.
4. —Oui, je l'ai.
   —Tu me la passes, s'il te plaît.
5. —Oui, je l'ai.
   —Tu me la passes, s'il te plaît.

20
1. —Je peux vous la laver.
2. —Je peux vous le râper.
3. —Je peux vous les éplucher.
4. —Je peux vous la préparer.
5. —Je peux vous le laver.
6. —Je peux vous les laver.

21
1. —Qui te l'a achetée?
2. —Qui te l'a acheté?
3. —Qui te l'a acheté?
4. —Qui te les a achetés?
5. —Qui te l'a acheté?
6. —Qui te l'a achetée?
7. —Qui te les a achetées?

Faire + infinitif
Telling what you have others do

1. You use **faire** + an infinitive to express what you have someone else do for you.

Je lave ma chemise moi-même. 　　Je ne lave pas ma chemise moi-même.
　　　　　　　　　　　　　　　　Je **fais laver** ma chemise.

Jean répare le lave-vaisselle.　　Jean ne répare pas le lave-vaisselle.
　　　　　　　　　　　　　　　　Il **fait réparer** le lave-vaisselle.

2. You use **faire** + an infinitive in many cooking expressions.

La viande cuit.　　　　　　　　Le cuisinier **fait cuire** la viande.

3. If there is an object pronoun in the sentence, the pronoun precedes the verb **faire**.

　　Je fais bouillir **l'eau**.　　Je **la** fais bouillir à feu vif.

LA GASTRONOMIE

Structure

1 Preparation

Bellringer Review

Use BRR Transparency 6.5 or write the following on the board. Answer.
1. Tu aimes faire les courses?
2. Qu'est-ce que tu achètes à la boulangerie?
3. Pour acheter de la viande, tu vas où?
4. Tu bavardes un peu avec les marchands?

2 Presentation

Faire + infinitif

Step 1 Lead students through the Items on page 187.

Step 2 Tell students that when someone performs an action himself or herself, only one verb is used. If a person has someone else do the action, **faire** is used with the verb.

Reaching All Students

Kinesthetic Learners
When explaining the **faire** construction, have students get involved. Example: Call one student to the front of the room and say (Student 1), **lavez votre chemise** and the student will do it. Call another. (Student 2), **vous n'allez pas laver votre chemise. Faites laver votre chemise. Donnez-la à** (Student 1). (Student 1), **vous allez laver la chemise pour** (Student 2).

Structure

3 Practice

Comment dit-on?

22 Tu le fais toi-même ou tu le fais faire?
Répondez d'après les indications.

1. Tu laves ton pantalon toi-même? (non)
2. Tu le fais laver? (oui)
3. Elle fait sa robe elle-même? (non)
4. Elle la fait faire? (oui)
5. Il répare le congélateur lui-même? (non)
6. Il le fait réparer? (oui)
7. Il répare le four à micro-ondes lui-même? (non)
8. Il le fait réparer? (oui)
9. Tu fais ton travail toi-même? (non)
10. Tu le fais faire? (oui)

Les lavages publics du Banco à Abidjan en Côte d'Ivoire

23 Historiette Dans la cuisine Inventez une histoire.

1. Le cuisinier fait cuire la viande au four?
2. Il la fait cuire à feu doux?
3. Il fait cuire des poivrons?
4. Il les fait cuire dans de l'huile d'olive?
5. Il fait bouillir la soupe?
6. Il la fait bouillir à feu vif?

Learning from Photos

(*page 188*) The **parc du Banco** is on the northwestern edge of Abidjan. It is a rainforest preserve and a pleasant place for a stroll. Near the park is this interesting outdoor launderette.

Everyday some 375 washermen called **fanicos** get together in this small stream. They rub the clothes vigorously on large stones held in place by old car tires. Afterward, they spread the clothes over rocks and grass in an area that covers at least a half kilometer. Once the clothing is dry, they iron it, never mixing up a piece. There are strict rules imposed by the washer's trade union. It is this union that allocates positions, and anyone who does not respect the rules is fired.

The work of the **fanicos** starts at dawn when they make their rounds in various parts of Abidjan to collect the laundry. The washing in the stream starts at about 6:30 A.M. The **fanicos** are almost all **burkinabé** (from Burkina Faso); none are Ivoirian.

22 Expansion: Have students answer the odd-numbered questions using object pronouns.

ANSWERS TO Comment dit-on?

22
1. Non, je ne lave pas mon pantalon moi-même.
2. Oui, je le fais laver.
3. Non, elle ne fait pas sa robe elle-même.
4. Oui, elle la fait faire.
5. Non, il ne répare pas le congélateur lui-même.
6. Oui, il le fait réparer.
7. Non, il ne répare pas le four à micro-ondes lui-même.
8. Oui, il le fait réparer.
9. Non, je ne fais pas mon travail moi-même.
10. Oui, je le fais faire.

23 Answers will vary but may include:
1. Oui, le cuisinier fait cuire la viande au four.
2. Oui, il la fait cuire à feu doux.
3. Oui, il fait cuire des poivrons.
4. Oui, il les fait cuire dans de l'huile d'olive.
5. Oui, il fait bouillir la soupe.
6. Oui, il la fait bouillir à feu vif.

24 **Un prof exigeant** Votre professeur de français vous fait faire beaucoup de choses. Avec un(e) camarade, parlez de tout ce qu'il/elle vous fait faire en classe. Vous pouvez utiliser les mots et expressions suivantes.

beaucoup parler	faire des devoirs
écrire des paragraphes	bien prononcer
passer des examens	répéter les phrases
répondre à trop de questions	lire des lectures
écrire au tableau noir	

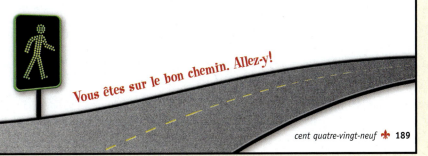

Vous êtes sur le bon chemin. Allez-y!

cent quatre-vingt-neuf ✦ 189

Structure

Learning from Realia

(page 189) This is a report card from a French lycée in the United States. You may wish to explain to students that in France, all of the grades would be given in numbers rather than letters, usually on a scale of 1 to 20.

Have students look at the report card and read the teacher's comments. What seems to be the problem the student is having?

✓ Assessment

As an informal assessment, you may wish to ask students if the subject is acting alone or having someone else perform the action: (Tell them that **repasser** means *to iron*.)
1. Je lave ma chemise.
2. Je fais laver ma chemise.
3. Je repasse ma chemise.
4. Je fais repasser ma chemise.
5. Je lave ma voiture.
6. Je fais laver ma voiture.

 Allez-y!
At this point in the chapter, students have learned all the vocabulary and structure necessary to complete the chapter. The conversation and cultural readings that follow recycle all the material learned up to this point.

ANSWERS TO *Comment dit-on?*

24 Answers will vary but may include:
Il/Elle nous fait faire beaucoup de devoirs.
Il/Elle nous fait répondre à trop de questions.
Il/Elle nous fait passer des examens difficiles.

LEVELING
E: Activities 22, 23
A: Activities 22, 23, 24
C: Activity 24

Conversation

1 Preparation

Resource Manager
Audio Activities TE, pages 64–65
Audio CD 4
CD-ROM

Bellringer Review
Use BRR Transparency 6.6 or write the following on the board. Imagine you won the lottery. Give five things you will do as a result.

2 Presentation

Step 1 Tell students they will hear a conversation between Serge and Peter. Have students close their books and listen as you read the conversation aloud or play Audio CD 4. Have students listen carefully to the recorded version and pay particular attention to the intonation.

Step 2 Have pairs of students role-play Serge and Peter, repeating their lines after you.

Step 3 Have two students read the conversation to the class.

Conversation

La cuisine et moi, ça fait deux!

Serge: Tu aimes faire la cuisine, toi, Peter, non?
Peter: Moi? Faire la cuisine! Tu rigoles! Jamais de la vie!
Serge: Moi, j'aime bien de temps en temps.
Peter: Qu'est-ce que tu sais faire comme plats?
Serge: Ben, le couscous, la bouillabaisse…
Peter: La bouillabaisse? Qu'est-ce que c'est?
Serge: C'est la spécialité de Marseille. C'est une soupe de poissons avec des tomates, des oignons, de l'ail et du pain.
Peter: Alors quand est-ce qu'on la mange, cette bouillabaisse?
Serge: Ben si tu veux, j'en ferai une la semaine prochaine.

Vous avez compris?

Répondez.
1. Est-ce que Peter aime faire la cuisine?
2. Quels plats est-ce que Serge sait faire?
3. Qu'est-ce que la bouillabaisse?
4. Qu'est-ce qu'on met dans la bouillabaisse?
5. Marseille est sur la mer Méditerranée ou sur l'océan Atlantique?
6. Quand est-ce que Serge fera une bouillabaisse?

Glencoe Technology

CD-ROM
On the CD-ROM, students can watch a dramatization of this conversation. They can then play the role of either one of the characters and record themselves in the conversation.

Answers to Vous avez compris?

1. Non, Peter n'aime pas faire la cuisine.
2. Serge sait faire le couscous et la bouillabaisse.
3. C'est la spécialité de Marseille.
4. On met du poisson, des tomates, des oignons, de l'ail et du pain.
5. Marseille est sur la mer Méditerranée.
6. Serge fera une bouillabaisse la semaine prochaine.

Parlons un peu plus

A **La cafétéria de l'école**
 Votre copain ou votre copine est chargé(e) de préparer les menus pour la cafétéria de votre école. Dites-lui les plats que vous aimez et les plats que vous n'aimez pas. Faites-lui aussi des suggestions. Ensuite, changez de rôle.

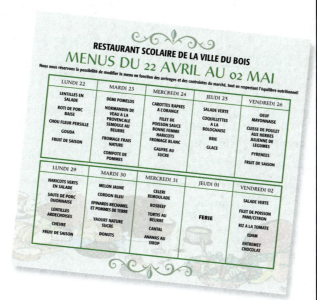

B **Au restaurant** Travaillez avec un(e) camarade. Regardez le dessin de la cuisine du restaurant. Ensemble, parlez de tout ce que vous voyez sur le dessin.

LA GASTRONOMIE

Lectures culturelles

Un voyage gastronomique

Charles Smith est un étudiant américain à l'université du Michigan. Il fait du français parce qu'il s'intéresse au commerce international. Charles a toujours eu envie d'aller en France pour travailler son français. L'été prochain, il réalisera son rêve[1] quand il passera deux mois en France. Il voyagera dans toute la France.

Charles est un vrai gourmand, c'est-à-dire qu'il aime bien manger. Il sait que la France est connue dans le monde entier pour sa bonne cuisine. Chaque région a ses spécialités.

Alsace

Charles va commencer son voyage à Strasbourg, en Alsace, près de la frontière allemande. Là, il prendra sans doute une choucroute avec du jambon, des lardons[2] et des saucisses. La cuisine alsacienne ressemble à la cuisine allemande.

Provence

Ensuite, Charles ira dans le sud, en Provence. Quelle différence! En Provence on mange des pâtes et même de la pissaladière, un genre de pizza. Dans les plats provençaux, on utilise ce qu'on appelle les herbes de Provence: du thym, du laurier, du basilic, du romarin[3]. On utilise aussi des tomates, des oignons et de l'ail. La cuisine est toujours faite à l'huile d'olive. On n'utilise pas de beurre.

[1] rêve *dream*
[2] lardons *bacon bits*
[3] romarin *rosemary*

Reading Strategy

Making connections
When you read a piece of nonfiction, think about what you have already read on the subject, as well as your personal knowledge and experiences. Ask yourself if the information supports or refutes what you already know. How does the passage enhance your understanding of the topic? Can you make connections between what you've learned and other areas of knowledge?

Map labels: Normandie, Bretagne, Alsace, Bourgogne, Provence

Bourgogne

Après huit jours en Provence, Charles visitera la Bourgogne. La Bourgogne est une région de vignobles[4]. Les vins de Bourgogne sont très appréciés et on les utilise beaucoup dans la cuisine bourguignonne. Bien sûr, Charles va manger un bœuf bourguignon—une des spécialités de la région. On prépare le bœuf bourguignon avec du bœuf, bien sûr, mais aussi avec du vin rouge, des oignons, du thym et du laurier. On le sert avec des pommes de terre cuites à l'eau ou à la vapeur[5]. Un vrai régal[6]!

Bretagne

Ensuite Charles ira en Bretagne, dans le nord-ouest. Il visitera de jolis villages de pêcheurs, comme Cancale, par exemple. Et qu'est-ce qu'il va manger en Bretagne? Il aura l'occasion de manger les meilleurs fruits de mer du monde—des huîtres, des moules et des coquilles Saint-Jacques[7].

Normandie

Avant de rentrer à Paris, Charles passera par la Normandie. Comme la Normandie est une région de pâturages, il y a beaucoup de vaches[8]. Pour cette raison, les Normands préparent leurs sauces avec de la crème et du beurre. Une escalope[9] à la normande est une escalope de veau avec une sauce à la crème et des champignons. C'est délicieux!

Quand notre gourmand sera en France, il apprendra sans doute que «la cuisine en France, c'est un art». Et quand il rentrera aux États-Unis, il aura certainement pris quelques kilos de plus.

[4] vignobles *vineyards*
[5] à la vapeur *steamed*
[6] régal *treat*
[7] coquilles Saint-Jacques *scallops*
[8] vaches *cows*
[9] escalope *cutlet*

Le port de Guilvinec en Bretagne

Vous avez compris?

A Le voyage de Charles Répondez.
1. Le français sera utile à Charles plus tard? Pourquoi?
2. Il ira en France quand?
3. Il visitera quelles régions?
4. Qu'est-ce qu'il apprendra quand il sera en France?

B Provinces et plats Donnez les informations suivantes.
1. le nom des provinces françaises que Charles visitera
2. un plat qu'il mangera dans chaque province

Lecture supplémentaire 1

Un dîner chez une famille maghrébine

Dans les pays du Maghreb, on se rassemble autour de la meïda pour manger. La meïda est une table ronde basse en bois[1] sculpté. Sur la table, on met un plateau en cuivre[2].

Le repas est pris en commun et tout est servi dans le même plat. Avant de commencer à manger on prononce la formule «Bis'millâh», pour s'assurer de la protection de Dieu[3].

On mange ce qui est devant soi. On ne mange jamais ce qui est au milieu de la table, c'est-à-dire, de la meïda. On laisse toujours des restes pour pouvoir donner de la nourriture aux pauvres. On ne doit pas trop parler pendant le repas. À la fin du repas, on remercie Dieu par un «El-Hamdoullâh».

Une table marocaine

À la fin, comme au début du repas, on verse l'eau d'un pot en cuivre sur les mains des invités pour qu'ils se lavent les mains.

Si vous êtes invité(e) dans une famille maghrébine, on vous servira peut-être un couscous. Le couscous est une semoule[4] qu'on accompagne de légumes, de poulet ou de mouton et parfois de raisins secs. On sert le couscous avec une sauce rouge très épicée[5], la harissa.

Un couscous dans un restaurant marocain

[1] bois *wood*
[2] cuivre *copper*
[3] Dieu *God*
[4] semoule *semolina (grain made from wheat)*
[5] épicée *spicy*

Vous avez compris?

A **Les coutumes** Dites en anglais ce qu'on doit faire quand on est à table chez une famille maghrébine.

B **Comparaisons** Comparez un dîner chez vous et un dîner chez une famille maghrébine.

Lecture supplémentaire 2

Navarin d'agneau

Vous dites que vous n'aimez pas beaucoup l'agneau? Mangez un bon navarin d'agneau et vous changerez certainement d'avis! Voici une recette pour préparer ce plat délicieux et assez facile à faire. Allons-y!

Navarin d'agneau

1,5 kg de mouton (agneau) coupé en morceaux
1 kg de navets[1]
2 oignons
3 carottes
60 g de beurre
1 cuillerée à café de farine[2]
2 verres de consommé de poulet
Thym, laurier, persil, sel et poivre

Préparation: 20 minutes   Cuisson: 1 h 30 - Cocotte (casserole)

Faites fondre[3] le beurre dans la cocotte. Ajoutez la viande. Faites-la bien revenir[4] des deux côtés. Ajoutez un peu de farine des deux côtés. Ajoutez le consommé, le sel et le poivre. Remuez bien. Faites cuire pendant 10 minutes. Ajoutez les carottes, les oignons, le thym, le laurier et le persil. Couvrez et faites cuire pendant 30 minutes à feu doux. Ajoutez les navets épluchés et faites cuire encore environ 45 minutes, toujours à feu doux.
Retirez du feu et servez!

[1] navets *turnips*
[2] cuillerée à café de farine *teaspoon of flour*
[3] fondre *melt*
[4] revenir *brown*

Vous avez compris?

À votre avis Répondez.
1. C'est facile ou difficile de préparer un navarin d'agneau?
2. Quels sont les ingrédients de cette recette que vous aimez?
3. Il y a des ingrédients que vous n'aimez pas? Quels ingrédients?

LA GASTRONOMIE

Connexions

National Standards

Connections
This reading about **Gargantua** by Rabelais establishes a connection with another discipline, allowing students to reinforce and further their knowledge of literature through the study of French.

Attention!

The readings in the **Connexions** section are optional. They focus on some of the major disciplines taught in schools and universities. The vocabulary is useful for discussing such topics as history, literature, art, economics, business, science, etc. You may choose any of the following ways to do the readings in the **Connexions** section.

Independent reading Have students read the selections and do the post-reading activities as homework, which you collect. This option is least intrusive on class time and requires a minimum of teacher involvement.

Homework with in-class follow-up Assign the readings and post-reading activities as homework. Review and discuss the material in class the next day.

Intensive in-class activity This option includes a pre-reading vocabulary presentation, in-class reading and discussion, assignment of the activities for homework, and a discussion of the assignment in class the following day.

Connexions

La littérature

Gargantua de Rabelais

François Rabelais, gravure d'un artiste inconnu

Have you ever heard the expression "gargantuan appetite" used to describe a person who eats a lot? The word "gargantuan" comes from the name of the main character in a book written by François Rabelais, a famous French author of the sixteenth century. An enlightened thinker of the Renaissance period, Rabelais challenged the constraints of medieval thought, particularly in the field of education. As we shall see, the character of Gargantua shows how education can transform an individual. Gargantua exhibits gross and animalistic behavior until he comes under the tutelage of a Renaissance humanist named Ponocrates.

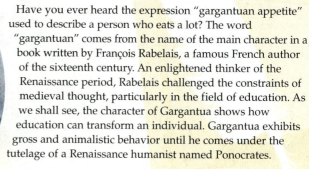

Gargantua

Gargantua est le fils de Grangousier et de Gargamelle. Tous deux sont des gros mangeurs et buveurs. Ils adorent manger et boire. Ce trait est transmis à leur fils. Dès l'instant[1] qu'il est né, il crie «À boire, à boire, à boire!» Son père l'entend et dit «Que grand tu as!»—et de là vient le nom de Gargantua. Le «petit» enfant a bu le lait de 17 913 vaches. Il s'est développé vite et il est devenu énorme—un véritable géant.

Quand il se réveillait, il sautait[2] dans son lit comme un mouton. Pour lui:

> peigner, laver et nettoyer[3] était perdre
> son temps en ce monde. Puis rotait[4], crachait[5], toussait,
> éternuait, et déjeunait: belles tripes frites[6], belles
> carbonnades [grillades], beaux jambons.

[1] Dès l'instant *From the moment*
[2] sautait *jumped up and down*
[3] nettoyer *clean*
[4] rotait *burped*
[5] crachait *spit*
[6] tripes frites *fried tripe*

cent quatre-vingt-seize

CHAPITRE 6

Gargantua aime manger, mais il n'aime pas du tout faire de l'exercice. Quand on lui dit de faire de l'exercice, il répond:

> Quoi! n'ai-je fait suffisant exercice?
> Je me suis vautré[7] six ou sept tours
> parmi le lit[8] avant de me lever.
> N'est-ce assez?

La vie et le comportement de Gargantua changent complètement quand son père décide de confier son éducation au sage[9] humaniste Ponocrates. Gargantua apprend alors à se laver, se peigner, s'habiller et se parfumer. Il assouplit[10] son corps par toutes sortes d'exercices physiques. On stimule son esprit par des jeux. Il rend visite aux artisans et converse avec les savants.

[7] Je me suis vautré *I rolled around*
[8] tours parmi le lit *times in bed*
[9] sage *wise*
[10] assouplit *loosens up*

La Devinière, le village natal de Rabelais

Vous avez compris?

Gargantua Répondez.

1. Quel est un trait des parents de Gargantua?
2. Ce trait a été transmis à leur fils?
3. Quand Gargantua est né, qu'est-ce qu'il a crié?
4. On lui a donné quel nom?
5. Qu'est-ce qu'il a bu?
6. Qu'est-ce qu'il est devenu?
7. Qu'est-ce qu'il faisait quand il se réveillait?
8. Qu'est-ce qu'il mangeait?
9. Il aimait faire de l'exercice?
10. Quand est-ce que tout cela a changé?

LA GASTRONOMIE

CONNEXIONS

Attention!

Connexions This selection is more difficult than the selections in other chapters. It is recommended that you have only your most able students read it. You may wish to have one or two students prepare a simple résumé of the selection and present it to the class.

Presentation

La littérature
Gargantua de Rabelais

Step 1 Have students read the introduction in English on page 196.

Step 2 Have students scan the reading for cognates. Then have them do the reading again, this time for comprehension.

LEVELING
A: Reading
C: Reading

ANSWERS TO Vous avez compris?

1. Les parents de Gargantua sont des gros mangeurs et buveurs.
2. Oui, ce trait a été transmis à leur fils.
3. Il a crié «à boire, à boire!»
4. On lui a donné le nom de Gargantua.
5. Il a bu le lait de 17 913 vaches.
6. Il est devenu énorme.
7. Quand il se réveillait il sautait dans son lit.
8. Il mangeait tripes frites, carbonnades et jambons.
9. Non, il n'aimait pas faire de l'exercice.
10. Tout cela a changé quand son père a décidé de confier son éducation à Ponocrates.

C'est à vous

Use what you have learned

1 Au marché
✓ **Talk about foods and food preparation**

Vous êtes au marché à Carpentras. Vous voulez acheter les ingrédients pour préparer votre plat favori. Votre camarade est le/la marchand(e). Dites-lui ce que vous voulez et en quelle quantité. Dites-lui aussi ce que vous allez préparer.

2 L'avenir (Le futur)
✓ **Describe future events**

On ne sait jamais ce que nous réserve l'avenir. Mais on a des aspirations et des souhaits *(wishes)*. Conversez avec un(e) camarade. Dites-lui ce que vous ferez quand vous aurez votre diplôme d'études secondaires. Ensuite changez de rôle. Vous avez les mêmes aspirations et les mêmes souhaits?

Le marché à Carpentras

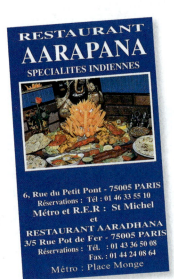

3 Cuisines étrangères
✓ **Describe a dish that you like**

Est-ce qu'il y a près de chez vous des restaurants qui servent des plats de différentes régions du monde? Si oui, préparez une liste de ces restaurants avec votre camarade. Indiquez le genre de cuisine qu'on y sert. Décrivez un plat que vous aimez.

198 cent quatre-vingt-dix-huit   CHAPITRE 6

CHAPITRE 6

ÉCRIRE

4 Un repas délicieux
✔ *Describe the cuisine of one of the French provinces*

Vous faites un voyage en Normandie. Vous passez quelques jours à Dieppe. Vous avez dîné dans un très bon restaurant qu'un ami français vous a recommandé. Vous lui écrivez un petit mot pour le remercier. Vous lui décrivez ce que vous avez mangé et vous lui dites combien vous avez aimé le restaurant et pourquoi.

Le port de plaisance de Dieppe en Normandie

FORMULE BUFFET
1 Entrée + 1 Plat 12,04 €
La soupe de poisson du pêcheur
Les 6 huîtres de Normandie
Servies sur glace pilée
Au choix   La salade cocktail
Crevettes roses - Saumon fumé

Le jambon à l'os à la Normande
Pommes frites - Champignons à la crème
L'entrecôte grillée
Pommes frites - Salade
Sauce beurre maître d'hôtel, ou aux deux poivres, ou roquefort, ou barbecue.

Writing Strategy

Writing about a process When you write an explanation of a process, keep in mind that your readers should be able to follow your explanation from start to finish. Present the steps of the process in a logical order and include as many details as possible. Remember to define any terms that may be unfamiliar to your readers.

ÉCRIRE

5 Un(e) Américain(e) à Colmar

You are living with a French family in Colmar, in Alsace. One day last week you prepared your favorite American dish for them. They loved it! They want you to write down the recipe for them before you return to the United States. Since they don't know much English, you'll have to write the recipe in French. Be sure to explain all the steps as clearly as possible so that they can prepare something delicious rather than a disaster!

LA GASTRONOMIE

cent quatre-vingt-dix-neuf ✦ 199

Assessment

Resource Manager

Communication Transparencies C 6
Quizzes, pages 27–31
Tests, pages 81–94
ExamView® Pro
Situation Cards
Performance Assessment, Task 6
Marathon mental Videoquiz

✓ Assessment

This is a pre-test for students to take before you administer the chapter test. Answer sheets for students to do these pages are provided in your transparency binder. Note that each section is cross-referenced so students can easily find the material they have to review in case they made errors. You may wish to collect these assessments and correct them yourself or you may prefer to have the students correct themselves in class. You can go over the answers orally or project them on the overhead, using your Assessment Answers transparencies.

Assessment

Vocabulaire

To review Mots 1, turn to pages 174–175.

1 Complétez.

1–2. ____ et ____ sont des légumes.
3–4. ____ et ____ sont des fruits.
5. ____ est une fine herbe.

2 Choisissez.

a.  b.

c.  d.

To review Mots 2, turn to pages 178–179.

6. ____ remuer   8. ____ éplucher
7. ____ couper   9. ____ râper

3 Identifiez.

10.
11.
12.

13.    14.

Answers to Assessment

1 *Answers will vary but may include:*
1. Un poivron rouge
2. un champignon
3. Un pamplemousse
4. un citron
5. Le thym

2
6. d
7. c
8. b
9. a

3
10. un couvercle
11. une casserole
12. un rôti
13. un homard
14. des huîtres

CHAPITRE 6 Assessment

Structure

4 **Complétez avec le futur.**

15. Je _____ au chef. (parler)
16. Il me _____ la recette. (lire)
17. Vous _____ à faire le plat? (apprendre)
18. On _____ un plat pas trop compliqué. (choisir)

To review the future tense, turn to page 182.

5 **Répondez avec des pronoms.**

19. Il te donnera la recette?
20. Elle va me préparer les champignons?

To review using pronouns, turn to page 185.

6 **Complétez.**

21. Moi, je ne répare pas l'évier. Je _____ l'évier.
22. Elle ne prépare pas le dîner. Elle _____ le dîner.

To review faire + an infinitive, turn to page 187.

Culture

7 **Choisissez la région.**

l'Alsace   la Provence   la Bourgogne   la Normandie

23. Sa cuisine utilise beaucoup de fines herbes et d'épices.
24. La choucroute y est un plat très apprécié.
25. Beaucoup de ses recettes sont à base de crème et de beurre.

To review this cultural information, turn to pages 192–193.

Le marais vernier en Normandie

LA GASTRONOMIE

Answers to Assessment

4
15. parlerai
16. lira
17. apprendrez
18. choisira

5
19. Oui, il me la donnera.
20. Oui, elle va me les préparer.

6
21. fais réparer
22. fait préparer

7
23. la Provence
24. l'Alsace
25. la Normandie

Glencoe Technology

MINDJOGGER VHS/DVD

You may wish to help your students prepare for the chapter test by playing the MindJogger game show. Teams will compete against each other to review chapter vocabulary and structure and sharpen listening comprehension skills.

FOLDABLES Study Organizer — Dinah Zike's Study Guides

Your students may wish to use Foldable 2 to organize, display, and arrange data as they learn about the foods in French. You may wish to encourage them to add information from each chapter as they continue to learn vocabulary that can be used to describe meals and foods.

A *forward-backward book* foldable is an ideal reference for students to organize what they know about foods. They can write the name of a food group (meat, vegetable, fruit) on the cover and on the opposite page list the foods they can name in French for that particular food group.

On parle super bien!

This unique page gives students the opportunity to speak freely and say whatever they can, using the vocabulary and structures they have learned in the chapter. The illustration serves to remind students of precisely what they know how to say in French. There are no activities that students do not have the ability to describe or talk about in French. The art not only depicts the vocabulary and content of this chapter, but also reinforces what they learned in previous chapters.

You may wish to use this page in many ways. Some possibilities are to have students do the following:

1. Look at the illustration and identify items by giving the correct French words.
2. Make up sentences about what they see in the illustration.
3. Make up questions about the illustration. They can call on another class member to respond if you do this as a class activity, or you may prefer to allow students to work in small groups. This activity is extremely beneficial because it enables students to actively use interrogative words.
4. Answer questions you ask them about the illustration.
5. Work in pairs and make up a conversation based on the illustration.
6. Look at the illustration and give a complete oral review of what they see.
7. Look at the illustration and write a paragraph (or essay) about it.

You can also use this page as an assessment or testing tool, taking into account individual differences by having students go from simple to quite complicated tasks. The assessment can be either oral or written. You may wish to use the rubrics provided on pages T20–T21 as you give students the following directions.

On parle super bien!

Tell all you can about this illustration.

1. Identify the topic or situation of the illustration.
2. Give the French words for as many items as you can.
3. Think of as many sentences as you can to describe the illustration.
4. Go over your sentences and put them in the best sequencing to give a coherent story based on the illustration.

Vocabulaire

Identifying some kitchen appliances and utensils

la cuisine	un frigidaire, un frigo	une casserole
une cuisinière	un four	un couvercle
un congé(lateur)	(à micro-ondes)	
un réfrigérateur	une poêle	

Talking about some cooking procedures

faire la cuisine	couper	une rondelle
faire cuire	râper	un morceau
faire bouillir	ajouter	une recette
éplucher	remuer	un plat
hacher	verser	

Identifying more foods

un aliment	des fines herbes	une côtelette
un légume	du persil	un rôti
un poivron rouge	du laurier	un gigot
un oignon	du thym	un poisson
une gousse d'ail	de l'huile (f.) d'olive	un filet de sole
un champignon	des pâtes (f. pl.)	du saumon
une pomme de terre	de la choucroute	des fruits (m. pl.)
un haricot vert	une sauce	de mer
un fruit	la viande	un homard
un citron	une saucisse	une moule
une orange	le bœuf	un crabe
un pamplemousse	le veau	une huître
du raisin	le porc	
une herbe	l'agneau (m.)	

Other useful words and expressions

à feu vif
à feu doux
bouillant(e)

How well do you know your vocabulary?
- Choose words from the list and describe a meal you would like to serve.
- Describe as many steps in the preparation of the meal as you can.

VIDÉOTOUR

Épisode 6
In this video episode, you will witness some of Manu's secret cooking skills. See page 505 for more information.

Vocabulaire

Vocabulary Review

The words and phrases in the **Vocabulaire** have been taught for productive use in this chapter. They are summarized here as a resource for both student and teacher. This list also serves as a convenient resource for the **C'est à vous** activities on pages 198–199, as well as for talking about the illustration on page 202. There are approximately sixteen cognates in this vocabulary list. Have students find them.

Attention!

You will notice that the vocabulary list here is not translated. This has been done intentionally, since we feel that by the time students have finished the material in the chapter they should be familiar with the meanings of all the words. If there are several words they still do not know, we recommend that they refer to the **Mots 1** and **2** sections in the chapter or go to the dictionaries at the back of this book to find the meanings. However, if you prefer that your students have the English translations, please refer to Vocabulary Transparency 6.1, where you will find these words listed with their translations.

LA GASTRONOMIE   deux cent trois 203

VIDÉO VHS/DVD

The Video Program allows students to see how the chapter vocabulary and structures are used by native speakers. For maximum reinforcement, show the video episode as a final activity for Chapter 6.

Planning for Chapter 7

SCOPE AND SEQUENCE, PAGES 204–235

Topics
- Cars and driving
- Giving directions

Functions
- How to talk about what would happen
- How to describe future events
- How to refer to something already mentioned

National Standards
- Communication Standard 1.1 pages 208, 209, 213, 215, 218, 219, 220, 221, 223, 230
- Communication Standard 1.2 pages 208, 209, 212, 213, 215, 217, 218, 219, 220, 221, 222, 225, 227, 229
- Communication Standard 1.3 pages 208, 209, 213, 215, 219, 223, 230, 231
- Cultures Standard 2.1 pages 206, 213, 217, 224–225, 226–227, 228–229
- Cultures Standard 2.2 pages 206, 224–225, 226–227
- Connections Standard 3.1 pages 226–227, 228–229
- Comparisons Standard 4.2 page 206
- Communities Standard 5.1 page 231

Culture
- Driving in France
- Tunisian adventure
- **Reflets du Maghreb**

Structure
- The conditional tense
- The future and conditional of irregular verbs
- Clauses with **si**
- Two pronouns in the same sentence

PACING AND PRIORITIES

The chapter content is color coded below to assist you in planning.

■ required   ■ recommended   ■ optional

Vocabulaire *(required)* — Days 1–4
- ■ Mots 1
  - La voiture
  - À la station-service
- ■ Mots 2
  - En ville
  - Sur la route

Structure *(required)* — Days 5–7
- ■ Le conditionnel
- ■ Le futur et le conditionnel des verbes irréguliers
- ■ Les propositions introduites par **si**
- ■ Deux pronoms dans la même phrase

Conversation *(required)*
- ■ À la station-service

Lectures culturelles
- ■ La conduite en France *(recommended)*
- ■ Partez à l'aventure en Tunisie! *(optional)*

Connexions *(optional)*
- ■ L'écologie

■ **C'est à vous** *(recommended)*

■ **Assessment** *(recommended)*

■ **On parle super bien!** *(optional)*

RESOURCE GUIDE

SECTION	PAGES	SECTION RESOURCES
Vocabulaire Mots 1		
La voiture À la station-service	206–207 207–209	Vocabulary Transparencies 7.2–7.3 Audio CD 5 Audio Activities TE, pages 69–71 Workbook, pages 73–74 Quiz 1, page 33 ExamView® Pro
Vocabulaire Mots 2		
En ville Sur la route	210 211–213	Vocabulary Transparencies 7.4–7.5 Audio CD 5 Audio Activities TE, pages 72–73 Workbook, pages 75–76 Quiz 2, page 34 ExamView® Pro
Structure		
Le conditionnel Le futur et le conditionnel des verbes irréguliers Les propositions introduites par **si** Deux pronoms dans la même phrase	214–215 216–218 218–219 220–221	Audio CD 5 Audio Activities TE, pages 74–75 Workbook, pages 77–79 Quizzes 3–6, pages 35–38 ExamView® Pro
Conversation		
À la station-service	222–223	Audio CD 5 Audio Activities TE, pages 76–77 Interactive CD-ROM
Lectures culturelles		
La conduite en France Partez à l'aventure en Tunisie!	224–225 226–227	Audio CD 5 Audio Activities TE, pages 77–78 Tests, pages 97, 101
Connexions		
L'écologie	228–229	Tests, page 94
C'est à vous		
	230–231	**Bon voyage!** Video, Episode 7 Video Activities, Chapter 7 French Online Activities french.glencoe.com
Assessment		
	232–233	Communication Transparency C 7 Quizzes 1–6, pages 33–38 Performance Assessment, Task 7 Tests, pages 95–108 ExamView® Pro Situation Cards, Chapter 7 **Marathon mental** Videoquiz

Using Your Resources for Chapter 7

Transparencies

Bellringer 7.1–7.9

Vocabulary 7.1–7.5

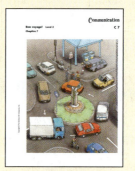
Communication C 7

Workbook

Vocabulary,
pages 73–76

Structure,
pages 77–79

Enrichment,
pages 80–82

Audio Activities

Vocabulary,
pages 69–73

Structure,
pages 74–75

Conversation,
pages 76–77

Cultural Reading,
pages 77–78

Additional Practice,
pages 79–80

Assessment

Vocabulary and Structure Quizzes, pages 33–38

Chapter Tests, pages 95–108

Situation Cards, Chapter 7

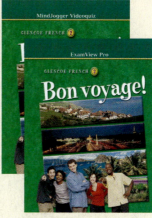
MindJogger Videoquiz, ExamView® Pro, Chapter 7

Timesaving Teacher Tools

TeacherWorks™

TeacherWorks™ is your all-in-one teacher resource center. Personalize lesson plans, access resources from the Teacher Wraparound Edition, connect to the Internet, or make a to-do list. These are only a few of the many features that can assist you in the planning and organizing of your lessons.

Includes:

- A calendar feature
- Access to all program blackline masters
- Standards correlations and more

ExamView® Pro

Test Bank software for Macintosh and Windows makes creating, editing, customizing, and printing tests quick and easy.

Technology Resources

 In the Chapter 7 Internet activity, you will have a chance to learn more about the Francophone world. Visit **french.glencoe.com**.

 On the Interactive Conversation CD-ROM, students can listen to and take part in a recorded version of the conversation in Chapter 7.

 See the National Geographic Teacher's Corner on pages 138–139, 244–245, 372–373, 472–473 for reference to additional technology resources.

 Bon voyage! Video and Video Activities, Chapter 7

 Help your students prepare for the chapter test by playing the **Marathon mental** Videoquiz game show. Teams will compete against each other to review chapter vocabulary and structure and sharpen listening comprehension skills.

204D

Preview

In this chapter, students will learn to talk about cars, roads, and driving. They will learn vocabulary associated with different types of cars, gas station services, and city and highway driving. Students will also increase their communication skills by learning the conditional, the future forms of irregular verbs, how to form sentences with direct object pronouns and **lui** or **leur,** and clauses with **si.**

 National Standards

Communication

In Chapter 7, students will communicate in spoken and written French on the following topics:
- Cars and driving
- Giving directions
- Road travel in France

Students will obtain and provide information about these topics and engage in conversations that would typically take place when driving as they fulfill the chapter objectives listed on this page.

 Spotlight on Culture

Photograph In this photo we see le château d'Ussé, which is on the banks of the Indre River, about 1 kilometer south of the Loire. The château was built in the fifteenth and sixteenth centuries on the site of an old medieval fortress.

In 1807 the château was bought by the Duc and Duchesse of Duras. The Duchesse was a friend of the novelist Chateaubriand, who wrote most of the novel **Les mémoires d'outre tombe** at this château.

CHAPITRE 7

La voiture et la route

Objectifs
In this chapter you will learn to:

✔ talk about cars and driving

✔ give directions on the road

✔ talk about what would happen under certain conditions

✔ describe future events

✔ refer to something already mentioned

✔ talk about driving and highways in France

Tamara de Lempicka *Autoportrait*

CHAPITRE 7

Spotlight on Culture

Painting The artist Tamara de Lempicka had a very interesting life and lived in many different places. She was born in Warsaw, Poland, in 1898. After moving to Russia, she married a lawyer, Tadeusz Lempicka, who was arrested by the Bolsheviks during the Russian revolution of 1917. After he was released, they emigrated to Paris.

De Lempicka exhibited her art for the first time in the **Salon d'automne** in 1922. After her divorce from Lempicka in 1928, she met and married the Baron Kuffner, a collector of her paintings. She continued to exhibit her works in Parisian galleries until 1939, when the couple moved to the U.S.

This 1925 self-portrait is an example of her art deco style. In 1960 she changed art styles and began to paint abstract works using a knife rather than a brush.

National Standards

Connections
Borrow a driver's education film from the Driver's Ed. class. Have students view it and discuss it in French. Then have them make a poster illustrating good driving tips and label it in French. Have them share the poster with the Driver's Ed. class.

Vocabulaire Mots 1

1 Preparation

Resource Manager
Vocabulary Transparencies 7.2–7.3
Audio Activities TE, pages 69–71
Audio CD 5
Workbook, pages 73–74
Quiz 1, page 33
ExamView® Pro

Bellringer Review
Use BRR Transparency 7.1 or write the following on the board.
What will happen in your next French class? Write five predictions using the future tense. For example:
Le professeur ne nous donnera pas de devoirs.

2 Presentation

Step 1 Have students close their books. Introduce the **Mots 1** vocabulary using Vocabulary Transparencies 7.2–7.3. Have students repeat each word after you or the recording on Audio CD 5 two or three times as you point to the appropriate illustration on the transparencies.

Step 2 Point to items at random and ask **Qu'est-ce que c'est?** Have students identify each item with the appropriate word or expression.

Step 3 After students have produced the new vocabulary several times, have them open their books to pages 206–207. Call on volunteers to read the new words, phrases, and sentences.

LEVELING
E: Vocabulary
A: Vocabulary

206

Vocabulaire Mots 1

La voiture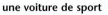

un camion

Le conducteur conduit le camion.

une voiture de sport

Renault et Peugeot sont deux marques françaises.

une moto
accélérer

un casque
un vélomoteur

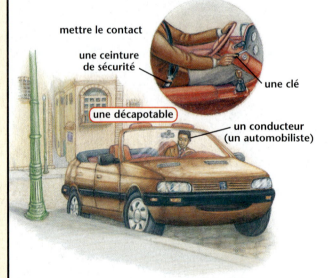
mettre le contact
une ceinture de sécurité
une clé
une décapotable
un conducteur (un automobiliste)
une auto-école

Le jeune homme prend des leçons de conduite.
Il apprend à se garer.

206 ❖ deux cent six   CHAPITRE 7

Reaching All Students

Total Physical Response Call a student to the front of the room and have him or her mimic the following, or you may wish to have the entire class do it.
  Prenez votre place dans la voiture.
  Attachez votre ceinture de sécurité.
  Prenez votre clé. Mettez le contact.
  Arrêtez-vous.

(Student 1), venez ici, s'il vous plaît.
Vous travaillez à mi-temps. Vous êtes pompiste dans une station-service.
Une voiture arrive.
Parlez au conducteur. Vérifiez les niveaux. Vérifiez la pression des pneus.
Mettez de l'air dans les pneus.
Ouvrez le coffre. Vérifiez la pression de la roue de secours.

Vocabulaire
Mots 1

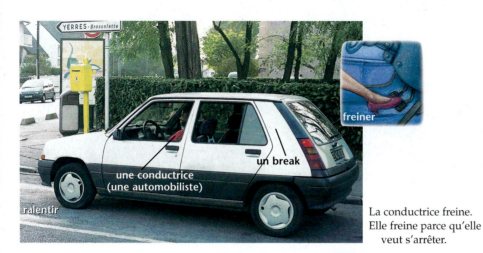

 freiner

un break
une conductrice (une automobiliste)
ralentir

La conductrice freine.
Elle freine parce qu'elle veut s'arrêter.

À la station-service

Le réservoir est vide.
Tu ne veux pas tomber en panne!
À ta place, je ferais le plein!

de l'essence
le pare-brise
le pompiste

Le pompiste a vérifié la pression des pneus.
Il met de l'air dans les pneus.

vérifier les niveaux d'huile et d'eau
une roue de secours
le coffre
 un pneu à plat
faire le plein

LA VOITURE ET LA ROUTE

deux cent sept 207

Teaching Tip
When a student cannot respond to a question, try asking **Qui sait?** Always have the original student repeat the correct model, and come back to him or her soon with the same item.

Step 4 Ask students personalized questions. For example: **Tu as ton permis de conduire? Tu prends des leçons de conduite? Où? Qui va à l'auto-école?**

Vocabulary Expansion

You may wish to give students some cognates:
le radiateur
la batterie
l'accélérateur
Other car parts:
le capot *(hood)*
la portière *(door)*
Other vehicle types:
un poids lourd *(tractor-trailer/big rig)*
une camionnette *(a van)*
un toit ouvrant *(a sun roof)*
une berline *(a sedan)*
  Students may be interested to know that the French have an equivalent for the slang word "cop." **C'est un flic. Voilà le flic qui arrive.**
  You may wish to give the students the word **une bagnole**, which is slang for "jalopy."

Cross-Cultural Comparison
Some cars in France, but not many, still take leaded gas, **essence plombée**. The following are the types of gases commonly used:
Super sans plomb 95
Super sans plomb 98
Gasoil (pour les moteurs diesel)

Reaching All Students

Additional Practice
Ask students the following questions:
1. On ne met pas d'essence dans le radiateur. Qu'est-ce qu'on met dans le radiateur? (de l'eau)
2. On ne met pas d'eau dans le moteur. Qu'est-ce qu'on met dans le moteur? (de l'huile)
3. Le conducteur ne veut pas rouler plus vite. Il veut rouler moins vite. Qu'est-ce qu'il fait? (Il freine, il ralentit.)
4. Le conducteur veut rouler plus vite. Qu'est-ce qu'il fait? (Il accélère.)

207

Vocabulaire

3 Practice

Quel est le mot?

Attention!
When students are doing the **Quel est le mot?** activities, accept any answer that makes sense. The purpose of these activities is to have students use the new vocabulary. They are not factual recall activities. If you wish, have students use the photos on this page as a stimulus.

Historiette Each time **Historiette** appears, it means that the answers to the activity form a short story. Encourage students to look at the title of the **Historiette**, since it can help them do the activity.

Learning from Realia
(page 208) Have students tell what the booklet is about.

Writing Development
Have students write the answers to Activities 2 and 3 in paragraph form.

Vocabulaire

Quel est le mot?

1 **Qu'est-ce que c'est?** Identifiez.

1. C'est un break ou une décapotable?

2. C'est une moto ou un vélomoteur?

3. C'est une voiture de sport ou un camion?

4. C'est un casque ou une ceinture de sécurité?

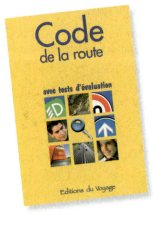

2 **Historiette** **Moi!** Donnez des réponses personnelles.
1. Tu as quel âge?
2. Tu as ton permis de conduire?
3. Dans ton état, il faut avoir quel âge pour passer son permis de conduire?
4. Tu as pris des leçons de conduite?
5. Tu es allé(e) à une auto-école?
6. Tu conduis bien?
7. Tu sais bien te garer?
8. Tu as une voiture?
9. Si tu n'as pas de voiture, ta famille a une voiture?
10. Elle est de quelle marque?
11. C'est quel type (modèle) de voiture?

208 ❖ deux cent huit

CHAPITRE 7

ANSWERS TO Quel est le mot?

1
1. C'est une décapotable.
2. C'est une moto.
3. C'est un camion.
4. C'est un casque.

2 *Answers will vary but may include:*
1. J'ai seize ans.
2. Oui, j'ai mon permis de conduire.
3. Dans mon état, il faut avoir seize ans pour passer son permis de conduire.
4. Oui, j'ai pris des leçons de conduite.
5. Non, je ne suis pas allé(e) à une auto-école.

6. Oui, je conduis bien.
7. Oui, je sais bien me garer.
8. Non, je n'ai pas de voiture.
9. Oui, ma famille a une voiture.
10. C'est _____.
11. C'est _____.

3 **Historiette À la station-service** Répondez.
1. Qui travaille dans une station-service?
2. Quand on fait le plein, on met de l'essence où?
3. Une voiture peut rouler si le réservoir est vide?
4. Qu'est-ce qu'on met dans les pneus?
5. On peut tomber en panne quand?

4 **La conduite** Vrai ou faux?
1. Il faut toujours rouler vite.
2. On freine pour accélérer.
3. On accélère pour s'arrêter.
4. On freine pour ralentir.
5. Il faut avoir une clé pour mettre le contact.
6. La roue de secours se trouve dans le réservoir.
7. On se sert de la roue de secours quand on a un pneu à plat.
8. On met de l'air dans les pneus quand la pression est basse.

5 **Ma voiture** Vous avez une voiture? Si vous n'avez pas de voiture, vous pensez en acheter une un jour? Décrivez la voiture de vos rêves *(dreams)* à un(e) camarade. Ensuite changez de rôle.

6 **Un petit job** Imaginez que vous travaillez de temps en temps dans une station-service. Dites à un(e) camarade tout ce que vous faites comme travail. Ensuite changez de rôle.

Une station-service sur l'autoroute A 10

 For more practice using words from Mots 1, do Activity 13 on page H14 at the end of this book.

LA VOITURE ET LA ROUTE

Vocabulaire Mots 2

1 Preparation

Resource Manager

Vocabulary Transparencies 7.4–7.5
Audio Activities TE, pages 72–73
Audio CD 5
Workbook, pages 75–76
Quiz 2, page 34
ExamView® Pro

Bellringer Review

Use BRR Transparency 7.2 or write the following on the board. Name as many car parts as you can.

2 Presentation

Step 1 Show Vocabulary Transparencies 7.4–7.5. Have students close their books and repeat the words after you or Audio CD 5 as you point to the appropriate illustration on the transparency.

Step 2 You may wish to use toy cars to demonstate **doubler, changer de voie, ralentir, accélérer, rouler vite.**

Step 3 Ask questions to elicit the vocabulary: **Cette voiture double? Elle accélère ou ralentit? Qu'est-ce que le motard porte sur la tête?**, etc.

Step 4 Use gestures and dramatizations to convey the meaning of **à droite, à gauche,** and **tourner.**

Chapter Projects

Le permis de conduire Have students prepare a chart or booklet comparing regulations for obtaining a driver's license in France with those of their state.

210

Vocabulaire Mots 2

En ville

un plan de la ville

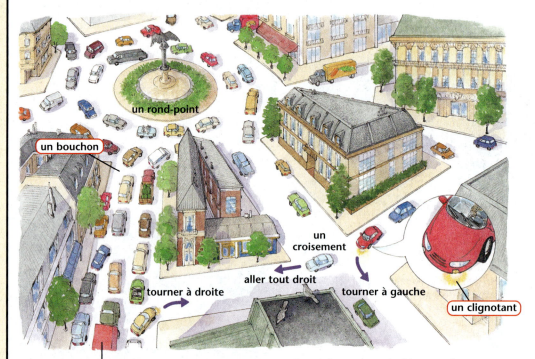

un rond-point
un bouchon
un croisement
aller tout droit
tourner à droite
tourner à gauche
un clignotant
une file de voitures

Il y a un bouchon.
Les voitures ne peuvent pas avancer.

Avant de tourner, n'oubliez pas de mettre votre clignotant.
Un conducteur va tout droit. Il ne tourne pas.

210 ❖ *deux cent dix* CHAPITRE 7

Reaching All Students

Total Physical Response Before you begin, set up a chair as a driver's seat. One student plays the part of a driver and the other a traffic police officer.

(Student 1), viens ici, s'il te plaît. Tu es un(e) automobiliste.
Monte dans la voiture. Mets le contact.
Roule, mais pas trop vite.
Maintenant, accélère.
Oh là là, tu as brûlé un feu rouge!
(Student 2), viens ici, s'il te plaît. Tu es un motard.
Dis à (Student 1) de s'arrêter.
Dis-lui qu'il/elle a brûlé un feu rouge.
Écris une contravention. Donne-lui la contravention. Dis au revoir.
(Student 1), que tu es furieux(se)! Dis quelque chose.
Merci, (Student 1) et (Student 2).

Vocabulaire Mots 2

Sur la route 🎧

Pour prendre l'autoroute, il faut payer un péage.

un péage

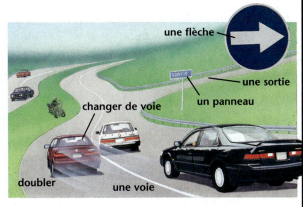

une flèche
une sortie
un panneau
changer de voie
doubler
une voie

Il y a deux voies dans chaque sens.
Le motard surveille la circulation.

Je sais que le motard me donnerait une contravention…

…si je brûlais un feu rouge.

une agglomération
une carte (routière)

…si je roulais trop vite.

…si je ne respectais pas la limitation de vitesse.

LA VOITURE ET LA ROUTE

Step 5 Ask the following questions that can be answered with one word. **Qui paie le péage, un motard ou un conducteur? Qui surveille la circulation, un motard ou un conducteur? Qui obéit à la limitation de vitesse, un motard ou un conducteur? Qui écrit des contraventions, un conducteur ou un motard?**

Step 6 Ask students personalized questions. For example: **Devant le lycée, quelle est la limitation de vitesse? Tu mets ta ceinture de sécurité quand tu es dans la voiture? Que fait ta mère à un feu rouge? Qui a des contraventions?**

Vocabulary Expansion

You may wish to give students the following additional vocabulary in order to talk about driving.
**un piéton/une piétonne
traverser la rue
une rue à sens unique
stationner
une contractuelle**

Cross-Cultural Comparison

If a police officer were to stop you in France for a traffic violation, he or she would say: **Permis de conduire et papiers du véhicule, s'il vous plaît.**

Reaching All Students

Additional Practice Have students match each verb on the left with the corresponding noun on the right.
1. circuler   a. la sortie
2. limiter   b. le ralentissement
3. conduire   c. la conduite
4. sortir   d. la limitation
5. ralentir   e. la circulation

Additional Practice Have students pretend they had a minor accident. They fill out an accident report including the following details:
Nom   Lieu
Âge   Vitesse
Date   Marque de voiture
Heure   Accidentés

Vocabulaire

3 Practice

Quel est le mot?

8 You may wish to have students correct false statements.

Learning from Photos

(page 212, Activity 7, number 4) You may wish to explain to students that these signs mean: **Il est interdit d'entrer. C'est exclusivement pour les autocars.**

FRENCH Online

The **Glencoe World Languages Web site (french.glencoe.com)** offers options that enable you and your students to experience the French-speaking world via the Internet. For each chapter, there are activities, games, and quizzes. In addition, an *Enrichment* section offers students an opportunity to visit Web sites related to the theme of the chapter.

Vocabulaire

Quel est le mot?

7 **Qu'est-ce que c'est?** Identifiez.

1. C'est un plan ou une carte?
2. C'est un bouchon ou une flèche?
3. C'est un rond-point ou un croisement?

4. C'est un panneau ou un péage?
5. C'est une route à deux voies ou à quatre voies?

8 **Sur la route** Vrai ou faux?

1. Il y a toujours un panneau pour indiquer la sortie de l'autoroute.
2. Il est interdit de changer de voie quand on veut doubler une autre voiture.
3. Quand il y a un bouchon, il y a beaucoup de circulation.
4. Il n'y a jamais de bouchon près des agglomérations.
5. Il faut ralentir pour doubler un camion.
6. Les motards surveillent la circulation sur l'autoroute.
7. Les flèches indiquent la direction qu'il faut prendre.
8. Les panneaux sont là pour la décoration de l'autoroute.
9. Il faut rouler vite et accélérer quand on arrive à un croisement dangereux.
10. Quand il y a un gros bouchon, il y a une longue file de voitures.
11. Si on brûle un feu rouge, on peut avoir une contravention.
12. Il faut mettre son clignotant pour signaler qu'on tourne à droite ou à gauche.

ANSWERS TO Quel est le mot?

7
1. C'est une carte.
2. C'est une flèche.
3. C'est un rond-point.
4. C'est un panneau.
5. C'est une route à deux voies.

8
1. vrai
2. faux
3. vrai
4. faux
5. faux
6. vrai
7. vrai
8. faux
9. faux
10. vrai
11. vrai
12. vrai

LEVELING

E: Activities 7, 9, 11
A: Activities 8, 9, 10, 11, 12

9 **Historiette** Une autoroute Répondez.
1. Il y a une autoroute près de chez vous?
2. C'est une autoroute à péage?
3. Les péages sont sur l'autoroute ou aux croisements?
4. Il y a beaucoup de circulation sur l'autoroute?
5. Qui surveille la circulation sur l'autoroute?
6. Quelle est la limitation de vitesse?
7. En général, est-ce que les conducteurs la respectent?
8. Sur l'autoroute, il y a combien de voies dans chaque sens?
9. Est-ce que les conducteurs qui roulent trop vite reçoivent une contravention?

10 **Avantages** En France, il faut payer un péage sur toutes les autoroutes. Sur les routes secondaires, il n'y a pas de péages. Avec un(e) camarade, expliquez pourquoi il vaut mieux (il est préférable de) prendre une autoroute et payer un péage. Quels sont les avantages?

11 **Une autoroute** Avec un(e) camarade, décrivez une autoroute près de chez vous. S'il y a un péage, c'est combien? Il y a combien de voies dans chaque sens? Cette autoroute va où?

12 **Les panneaux** Dites ce que ces panneaux signifient.

1.
2.
3.
4.
5.
6.

LA VOITURE ET LA ROUTE

Structure

1 Preparation

Resource Manager

Audio Activities TE, pages 74–75
Audio CD 5
Workbook, pages 77–79
Quizzes 3–6, pages 35–38
ExamView® Pro

Bellringer Review

Use BRR Transparency 7.3 or write the following on the board.
Rewrite the sentences in the future.
1. Je fais mes devoirs.
2. Je vais au cinéma.
3. J'ai le temps de te voir.
4. Je suis content(e).

2 Presentation

Le conditionnel

Step 1 Guide students through the Items on page 214. Have them repeat the verb forms after you.

Note: Students are already familiar with the verb stem from the future and with the endings from the imperfect. The conditional is used the same way in French as in English.

About the French Language

Pronunciation: Theoretically, the **ai** ending of the first person singular form of the future is pronounced /é/ and the **ais** ending of the first person conditional form is pronounced /è/. Most French speakers, however, do not make a distinction between **je parlerai** and **je parlerais**.

Structure

Le conditionnel
Expressing what would or could happen

1. You use the conditional in French, as you do in English, to express what would happen under certain circumstances. The conditional stem is the same as the future stem. The endings you add to this stem are the same as the endings for the imperfect tense. Study the following.

LE CONDITIONNEL

	PARLER	FINIR	ATTENDRE
Infinitive	parler	finir	attendre
Stem	parler-	finir-	attendr-
	je parler**ais**	je finir**ais**	j' attendr**ais**
	tu parler**ais**	tu finir**ais**	tu attendr**ais**
	il/elle/on parler**ait**	il/elle/on finir**ait**	il/elle/on attendr**ait**
	nous parler**ions**	nous finir**ions**	nous attendr**ions**
	vous parler**iez**	vous finir**iez**	vous attendr**iez**
	ils/elles parler**aient**	ils/elles finir**aient**	ils/elles attendr**aient**

Rappelez-vous que...

It is necessary to use **y** with **aller** when no place is mentioned. However, **y** is not used with the future or conditional.
J'y vais maintenant.
J'irais maintenant, mais je ne peux pas.

2. The verbs **être, faire, aller,** and **avoir** also have the same stem for the conditional as they have for the future.

ÊTRE je serais, tu serais, il serait,
nous serions, vous seriez, ils seraient

FAIRE je ferais, tu ferais, il ferait,
nous ferions, vous feriez, ils feraient

ALLER j'irais, tu irais, il irait,
nous irions, vous iriez, ils iraient

AVOIR j'aurais, tu aurais, il aurait,
nous aurions, vous auriez, ils auraient

3. As in English, you use the conditional in French to express what you or someone else would do.

Moi, je prendrais le train. Mais lui, il prendrait la voiture. Il conduirait.
Je le ferais mais je n'ai pas le temps.

214 ❧ deux cent quatorze

CHAPITRE 7

Learning from Photos

(page 215 bottom) Saint-Pierre, a lovely town on the coast of Martinique, was founded by a French explorer in 1635. At the turn of the nineteenth century, Saint-Pierre was a flourishing city with over 30,000 inhabitants. It was the most modern town in the Caribbean with electricity and phones. It was called the Paris of the West Indies. On May 8, 1902, the nearby volcano **la Montagne Pelée** erupted and split in half, emitting burning ash and poisonous gases. With temperatures over 3,600 degrees Fahrenheit, it vaporized everything. Some 30,000 people were killed in two minutes. The only survivor was a prisoner in the town jail. The thick walls of his underground cell saved him.

The prisoner, Cyparis, was later pardoned, and he went to work as a sideshow attraction in the Ringling Brothers and Barnum and Bailey Circus.

Comment dit-on?

13 **Historiette** **Un voyage en France**
Inventez une histoire.
1. Robert aimerait beaucoup visiter la France?
2. Il irait à quel moment de l'année?
3. Il y passerait combien de temps?
4. Il voyagerait dans tout le pays?
5. Il irait dans quelles régions?
6. Il louerait une voiture?
7. Il conduirait?
8. Il ferait ce voyage tout seul ou avec des copains?
9. Ses copains conduiraient aussi?
10. Ils consulteraient des cartes routières de temps en temps?

Une route dans les Alpes-Maritimes

14 **Historiette** **À ma place** Répondez d'après les indications.
1. Pour aller à Lyon, tu prendrais le train ou la voiture? (aller en voiture)
2. Tu louerais une voiture ou tu en emprunterais une? (louer)
3. Tu prendrais quelle route? (l'autoroute du sud)
4. Tu ferais le plein avant de partir ou sur l'autoroute? (avant de partir)
5. Qu'est-ce que tu ferais d'autre? (faire vérifier la pression des pneus)

Le village de Saint-Pierre à la Martinique

15 **Si c'était possible** Complétez au conditionnel.

Jacques __1__ (voyager). Il __2__ (aimer) beaucoup ça. Il __3__ (faire) beaucoup de voyages. Il __4__ (être) content d'être en France. Ses amis et lui __5__ (faire) beaucoup de voyages ensemble. Ils __6__ (visiter) beaucoup de villes intéressantes. Ils __7__ (apprendre) le français. Je __8__ (voyager) avec mes copains. Nous __9__ (aller) dans une île de la mer des Caraïbes. Je __10__ (prendre) des bains de soleil. Je __11__ (bronzer). Et toi, qu'est-ce que tu __12__ (faire)? Tu __13__ (aimer) mieux aller à la Martinique ou en France?

LA VOITURE ET LA ROUTE

deux cent quinze 215

Structure

3 Practice

Comment dit-on?

14 You can go over this activity once with books closed and then again with books open.

Writing Development
Have students write Activities 13 and 14 in paragraph form.

Learning from Photos
(page 215 top) The hairpin turns on this road are on the mountain road between Moulinet and Sospel.

LEVELING
E: Activity 13
A: Activities 14, 15
C: Activity 15

Answers to Comment dit-on?

13 Answers will vary but may include:
1. Oui, Robert aimerait beaucoup visiter la France.
2. Il irait en été.
3. Il y passerait deux mois.
4. Oui, il voyagerait dans tout le pays.
5. Il irait en Normandie et en Bretagne.
6. Oui, il louerait une voiture.
7. Oui, il conduirait.
8. Il ferait ce voyage avec des copains.
9. Oui, ses copains conduiraient aussi.
10. Oui, ils consulteraient des cartes routières de temps en temps.

14
1. Pour aller à Lyon, j'irais en voiture.
2. Je louerais une voiture.
3. Je prendrais l'autoroute du sud.
4. Je ferais le plein avant de partir.
5. Je ferais vérifier la pression des pneus.

15
1. voyagerait
2. aimerait
3. ferait
4. serait
5. feraient
6. visiteraient
7. apprendraient
8. voyagerais
9. irions
10. prendrais
11. bronzerais
12. ferais
13. aimerais

215

Structure

1 Preparation

Bellringer Review

Use BRR Transparency 7.4 or write the following on the board. What would you do if school were cancelled tomorrow? List five things.

2 Presentation

Le futur et le conditionnel des verbes irréguliers

Step 1 Guide students through the explanation and have them repeat the verb forms after you.

LEVELING

A: Attention!, 16

Structure

Attention!

Note the spelling and pronunciation of verbs like **acheter** and **se lever** in the future and conditional.

ACHETER	j'achèterai	nous achèterions
SE LEVER	je me lèverai	nous nous lèverions

Complétez.
1. Je ___ tôt demain matin. Et vous deux, vous ___ tôt aussi? (se lever)
2. Il ___ une grande voiture, mais il n'a pas assez d'argent. Et vous, qu'est-ce que vous ___ comme voiture? (acheter)

Le futur et le conditionnel des verbes irréguliers
Expressing more conditions and future events

1. The following verbs have an irregular stem for the future and the conditional. You will use many of these verbs frequently in the conditional. Their use in the future is less common.

Infinitive	Stem	Future	Conditional
savoir	saur-	je saurai, tu sauras	je saurais, tu saurais
voir	verr-	je verrai, tu verras	je verrais, tu verrais
envoyer	enverr-	j'enverrai, tu enverras	j'enverrais, tu enverrais
pouvoir	pourr-	je pourrai, tu pourras	je pourrais, tu pourrais
devoir	devr-	je devrai, tu devras	je devrais, tu devrais
recevoir	recevr-	je recevrai, tu recevras	je recevrais, tu recevrais
vouloir	voudr-	je voudrai, tu voudras	je voudrais, tu voudrais
venir	viendr-	je viendrai, tu viendras	je viendrais, tu viendrais
falloir	faudr-	il faudra	il faudrait

2. The conditional is often used in French to soften a request or an order or to make a suggestion. You already know the use of **Je voudrais…** Study the following sentences.

Vous pourriez fermer la porte, s'il vous plaît?	Could you close the door, please?
Je mangerais bien quelque chose.	I wouldn't mind eating something.
Tu devrais inviter Marie.	You should invite Marie.

ANSWERS TO Attention!

1. me lèverai, vous lèverez
2. achèterait, achèteriez

Comment dit-on?

16 **Historiette** **Vous irez à Nantes l'année prochaine.**
Mettez les verbes au futur.

Pour aller à Nantes, c'est très simple. Pour quitter Paris, vous __1__ (prendre) le boulevard Raspail jusqu'à la place Denfert-Rochereau. Vous __2__ (traverser) la place et vous __3__ (continuer) tout droit. Il y a quelques feux avant d'arriver au boulevard périphérique. Vous ne __4__ (prendre) pas le périphérique. Vous __5__ (continuer) tout droit et vous __6__ (voir) un panneau qui indique Chartres. C'est l'A 11. Vous __7__ (passer) par Chartres et vous __8__ (continuer) sur l'A 11 jusqu'au Mans. Là, vous __9__ (voir) un panneau qui indique la N 23. Vous __10__ (prendre) la N 23 jusqu'à Nantes. Je ne sais pas si vous __11__ (avoir) le temps, mais essayez de vous arrêter à Angers. Vous __12__ (aimer) beaucoup cette ville. Et attention! Il faut toujours respecter la limitation de vitesse. Sinon un motard vous __13__ (arrêter) et vous __14__ (recevoir) une contravention.

LA VOITURE ET LA ROUTE

Structure

3 Practice

Comment dit-on?

16 You may wish to have students prepare the activity individually and then go over it as a class activity.

ANSWERS TO Comment dit-on?

16

1. prendrez
2. traverserez
3. continuerez
4. prendrez
5. continuerez
6. verrez
7. passerez
8. continuerez
9. verrez
10. prendrez
11. aurez
12. aimerez
13. arrêtera
14. recevrez

Structure

3 Practice (continued)

17 Have students practice this activity with a partner, first with books open. Then have one student in each pair close his or her book and the other partner ask the questions in random order. Switch roles.

1 Preparation

Bellringer Review

Use BRR Transparency 7.5 or write the following on the board. List some things you can do but don't want to do.

2 Presentation

Les propositions introduites par si

Step 1 Write the sequence of tenses on the board and have students read the sample sentences aloud. Elicit and discuss other examples.

LEVELING

E: Activities 17, 18, 19, 20
A: Activities 17, 18, 20, 21, 22, 23

Structure

17 Suggestions Répondez selon le modèle et complétez les phrases.

—Tu devrais lui envoyer cette lettre.
—Je lui enverrais bien cette lettre, mais… (je n'ai pas son adresse).

1. Tu devrais écrire à Marie.
2. Tu devrais mettre ton pantalon noir.
3. Tu devrais sortir.
4. Tu devrais voir ce film.
5. Tu devrais venir avec nous.

18 Pas de sœur, pas de frère Complétez au conditionnel.

1. Je ____ faire tout ce que je veux. (pouvoir)
2. Je ____ plein de cadeaux. (recevoir)
3. Mes parents ____ me chercher à l'école en voiture. (venir)
4. Je ____ mes copains tous les jours après l'école. (voir)
5. Je ne ____ pas me coucher tôt tous les soirs. (devoir)

Les propositions introduites par si
Expressing conditions—possibilities or impossibilities

The **si** clauses, "if" clauses in English, have the following sequence of tenses.

Si + Présent → Futur

Si j'ai assez d'argent, je ferai un voyage.

Si + Imparfait → Conditionnel

Si j'avais assez d'argent, je ferais un voyage.

Si j'avais assez d'argent, j'irais dans cet hôtel.

deux cent dix-huit   CHAPITRE 7

ANSWERS TO Comment dit-on?

17 *Answers will vary but may include:*

1. J'écrirais bien à Marie, mais je n'ai pas le temps.
2. Je mettrais bien mon pantalon noir, mais je dois le laver.
3. Je sortirais bien, mais j'ai trop de devoirs à faire.
4. Je verrais bien ce film, mais je n'ai pas d'argent.
5. Je viendrais bien avec vous, mais je suis malade.

18
1. pourrais
2. recevrais
3. viendraient
4. verrais
5. devrais

Comment dit-on?

19 **Historiette** **Avec des si...**
Donnez des réponses personnelles.
1. Si tu reçois beaucoup d'argent, tu feras un grand voyage?
2. Si tu fais un voyage, tu iras en France?
3. Si tu vas en France, tu visiteras Paris?
4. Si tu visites Paris, tu monteras en haut de la tour Eiffel?
5. Si tu montes en haut de la tour Eiffel, tu prendras des photos?
6. Si tu fais des photos, tu me les montreras?

La tour Eiffel la nuit

20 **Historiette** **Moi, j'irais...**
Donnez des réponses personnelles.
1. Si tu avais beaucoup d'argent, tu ferais un grand voyage?
2. Si tu faisais un voyage, tu irais en France?
3. Si tu allais en France, tu visiterais Paris?
4. Si tu visitais Paris, tu monterais en haut de la tour Eiffel?
5. Si tu montais sur la tour Eiffel, tu prendrais des photos?
6. Si tu prenais des photos, tu me les montrerais?

21 **Historiette** **Sur la route** Répondez.
1. Si un motard te demandait de t'arrêter, tu t'arrêterais?
2. S'il te demandait ton permis de conduire, tu lui donnerais ton permis?
3. S'il te posait des questions, tu lui répondrais poliment?
4. Si tu devais payer une contravention, tu la paierais?

22 **Une enquête** Travaillez avec un(e) camarade. Il y a un billet de 100 dollars dans la rue. Demandez à cinq camarades ce qu'ils feraient s'ils trouvaient ce billet. Ensuite organisez vos réponses pour donner le résultat de votre enquête à la classe.

23 **Chaîne de mots** Faites des phrases en reprenant ce que la personne précédente a dit:
—Si j'avais mon permis de conduire, j'aurais une voiture.
—Si j'avais une voiture...

LA VOITURE ET LA ROUTE

deux cent dix-neuf ✦ 219

Structure

1 Preparation

Bellringer Review

Use BRR Transparency 7.6 or write the following on the board. Complete the following sentences.
1. Si je reçois de bonnes notes cette année...
2. Si je gagnais à la loterie...
3. Si je vais au cinéma ce week-end...
4. Si je visitais Paris...

2 Presentation

Deux pronoms dans la même phrase

Step 1 Lead students through the explanation on page 220.

Step 2 Point out that the order of direct and indirect objects in a sentence is the same for nouns as it is for pronouns: **Je donne le plan à Jean. Je le lui donne.** Nouns follow the verb, however, while pronouns precede it.

Step 3 You may wish to copy the model sentence pairs on the board. Circle direct object nouns and pronouns to show their relationship and positions in the sentences. Highlight indirect object nouns and pronouns with rectangles.

Note: Do not wait until all students have mastered this point before going on to new material. Students will need constant reinforcement of this concept throughout their study of French.

Structure

Deux pronoms dans la même phrase
Referring to something already mentioned

1. You have already seen that **me, te, nous,** and **vous** can be used with the direct object pronouns **le, la,** and **les.** You can also use **lui** and **leur** with **le, la,** and **les.**

   Je donne le plan à Jean. Je le lui donne.
   J'ai donné la clé à mes copains. Je la leur ai donnée.

2. The pronouns **le, la, les** always precede the pronouns **lui, leur.** Study the following.

	le	lui	
Elle	la		donne.
	les	leur	

3. These double object pronouns always come directly before the verb they are linked to. Study the following sentences.

Affirmatif	Négatif
Je le lui donne.	Je ne le lui donne pas.
Je le lui ai donné.	Je ne le lui ai pas donné.
Je vais le lui donner.	Je ne vais pas le lui donner.

Savez vous que... ?

In spoken French, the pronouns **le, la, les** are often dropped.
Tu lui as donné ton adresse?
Oui, je lui ai donné.

Comment dit-on?

24 **Tout pour mon copain**
Suivez le modèle.

le plan de la ville →
—Tu vas lui donner le plan de la ville?
—Oui, je vais le lui donner.

1. la carte routière
2. les clés
3. l'argent pour le péage
4. les directions

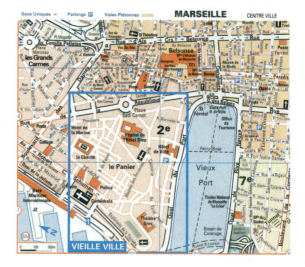

220 deux cent vingt

CHAPITRE 7

ANSWERS TO Comment dit-on?

24
1. —Tu vas lui donner la carte routière?
   —Oui, je vais la lui donner.
2. —Tu vas lui donner les clés?
   —Oui, je vais les lui donner.
3. —Tu vas lui donner l'argent pour le péage?
   —Oui, je vais le lui donner.
4. —Tu vas lui donner les directions?
   —Oui, je vais les lui donner.

Learning from Realia

(page 220) Have students identify the following on the map:
un rond-point un collège
un croisement un théâtre
une cathédrale l'hôtel de ville
un hôpital

25 **Que tu es généreux!** Répondez d'après le modèle en utilisant des pronoms.

Les billets de théâtre? Tu les as donnés à Michèle?

Oui, je les lui ai donnés.

1. Le portable? Tu l'as donné à Alain?
2. La télévision? Tu l'as donnée à Sylvie?
3. Les CD? Tu les as donnés à Marc?
4. La guitare? Tu l'as donnée à Philippe?
5. Les fraises? Tu les as données à tes amies?
6. Les livres? Tu les as donnés à tes cousins?
7. Les timbres? Tu les as donnés à tes cousines?
8. L'ordinateur? Tu l'as donné à tes frères?

26 **Non!** Répondez d'après le modèle en utilisant des pronoms.

—Tu as donné les clés à Jean-Paul?
—Non, je ne les lui ai pas données.

1. Tu as lu le livre au petit garçon?
2. Tu as vendu le magnétophone à Luc?
3. Tu as expliqué la pièce à Gilles?
4. Tu as écrit la lettre à tes parents?
5. Tu as montré les cartes à Vincent?
6. Tu as envoyé les livres à Jean?

To learn more about day trips by car from some major cities in the Francophone world, go to the Glencoe French Web site: french.glencoe.com

Vous êtes sur le bon chemin. Allez-y!

deux cent vingt et un 221

Conversation

1 Preparation

Resource Manager
Audio Activities TE, pages 76–77
Audio CD 5
CD-ROM

Bellringer Review

Use BRR Transparency 7.7 or write the following on the board.
Fill in the blanks with **qui** or **que**.
1. Je connais le garçon _____ travaille au supermarché.
2. Il a une voiture _____ j'aime beaucoup.
3. C'est la voiture _____ est garée devant sa maison.
4. Voilà le garçon _____ je connais.
5. C'est le garçon _____ a les cheveux blonds.

Reaching All Students

Additional Practice After completing the **Conversation** activity, ask a student to retell the situation of the conversation in his or her own words.

2 Presentation

Step 1 Have pairs of students practice reading the conversation with as much expression as possible.

Step 2 Have two students read the conversation to the class.

222

Conversation

À la station-service

Automobiliste: Bonjour, monsieur. Est-ce que vous pourriez me dire quelle sortie je dois prendre pour aller à Seignelay?
Pompiste: C'est Auxerre-Nord. Mais si j'étais vous, je sortirais à la sortie d'avant.
Automobiliste: Pourquoi?
Pompiste: Ben, parce qu'il y a un accident juste avant Auxerre-Nord. Il y a un bouchon de 10 kilomètres!
Automobiliste: Il n'y en aura peut-être plus quand on arrivera.
Pompiste: Ça m'étonnerait: il y a deux camions qui bloquent toute l'autoroute.
Automobiliste: On devrait peut-être s'arrêter pour déjeuner, alors.
Pompiste: À votre place, c'est ce que je ferais.
Automobiliste: Et la sortie avant Auxerre-Nord, c'est quoi?
Pompiste: Joigny, monsieur.
Automobiliste: Merci, monsieur. Au revoir.
Pompiste: Au revoir.

Vous avez compris?

Répondez.

1. Quelle est la sortie pour Seignelay?
2. Le pompiste recommande de sortir à la sortie d'avant. Pourquoi?
3. C'est un accident grave? Pourquoi?
4. À la place de l'automobiliste, qu'est-ce que le pompiste ferait?

222 ❦ deux cent vingt-deux

CHAPITRE 7

Glencoe Technology

CD-ROM
On the CD-ROM, students can watch a dramatization of this conversation. They can then play the role of either one of the characters and record themselves in the conversation.

ANSWERS TO Vous avez compris?

1. La sortie pour Seignelay est Auxerre-Nord.
2. Parce qu'il y a un accident juste avant la sortie Auxerre-Nord.
3. Oui, il y a deux camions qui bloquent toute l'autoroute.
4. À la place de l'automobiliste il s'arrêterait pour déjeuner.

Parlons un peu plus

A **En voyage** Travaillez avec un(e) camarade. Vous êtes sur la route. L'un(e) de vous conduit, l'autre regarde la carte ci-dessous et donne des instructions. Choisissez d'abord un itinéraire. Ensuite choisissez un deuxième itinéraire et changez de rôle.

B   **Au restaurant** Travaillez avec un(e) camarade. Vous êtes sur l'autoroute en France. Vous décidez de vous arrêter pour faire le plein et prendre quelque chose au restoroute. Ensemble, parlez de tout ce que vous allez faire.

Un restoroute près de Beaune

LA VOITURE ET LA ROUTE

Lectures culturelles

Resource Manager
Audio Activities TE, pages 77–78
Audio CD 5

Bellringer Review
Use BRR Transparency 7.8 or write the following on the board.
Make two lists: one of good driving habits, the other of bad ones.

Presentation

Pre-reading
Step 1 Ask how many students have their license.

Step 2 Discuss the highways and secondary roads in your area. Are there toll roads? Do you have traffic circles?

Reading
Step 1 Have students read the **Lecture** silently. Allow five minutes. Encourage them to read for the main ideas and important details only. Tell them they will have a chance to reread.

Step 2 Call on an individual to read several sentences. Then ask other students questions about the sentences the student has just read.

Geography Connection
Beaune is the capital of the region known as the **Côte de Beaune** where one finds the famous vineyards of Burgundy.

Lectures culturelles

La conduite en France

Les voitures
Presque toutes les familles françaises ont une voiture et même deux voitures. Par conséquent, il y a beaucoup de circulation sur les routes et les bouchons sont assez fréquents, surtout aux heures de pointe[1] et près des agglomérations.

Tu aimerais savoir quelles sont les marques de voitures préférées des Français? Il y a deux marques qui sont très populaires—Renault et Peugeot. On voit aussi beaucoup de voitures japonaises, mais très peu de voitures américaines.

Les routes
Il y a un très bon réseau[2] d'autoroutes en France. Les autoroutes ont deux ou trois voies dans chaque sens et elles sont toutes à péage. Mais les péages ne sont pas sur l'autoroute même; ils sont à la sortie. En France, il y a aussi des routes nationales qui sont des routes à grande circulation. Il y a aussi des routes départementales qui sont plus pittoresques parce qu'elles passent par beaucoup de petits villages. Mais il faut faire attention parce qu'il y a des croisements. Heureusement beaucoup de ces croisements ont été remplacés par des ronds-points qui sont beaucoup moins dangereux.

[1] heures de pointe *rush hours*
[2] réseau *network*

L'autoroute A 31 près de Beaune

National Standards

Cultures
This reading familiarizes students with driving in France.

Comparisons
Students learn that French teenagers must be 18 to get a license to drive a car, but that many drive mopeds at 16.

Learning from Photos
(page 225) Tell students that the beautiful tree-lined road in the photo is very typical of France. Plane trees **(les platanes)** often form an arch over the road. The trees grow in temperate regions of the northern hemisphere, particularly in Europe. A species that grows in North America is called the buttonwood or sycamore tree.

En France, comme partout³, il faut respecter la limitation de vitesse. Sur les routes, il y a beaucoup de motards. Si tu roules trop vite, ils te donneront une contravention.

Le permis de conduire

En France, pour passer son permis de conduire, il faut avoir dix-huit ans. Si tu habitais en France, tu pourrais avoir un permis de conduire? Beaucoup de jeunes Français ont un vélomoteur. Mais leur rêve⁴, c'est d'avoir une moto. On peut conduire une moto à partir de seize ans avec un permis spécial moto. Et le casque est obligatoire. Si tu habitais en France, tu aimerais avoir une moto?

³ partout *everywhere*
⁴ rêve *dream*

Une route pittoresque à Melun en France

Vous avez compris?

A Les voitures Vrai ou faux?
1. Très peu de familles françaises ont des voitures.
2. Il n'y a presque jamais de bouchons sur les autoroutes en France.
3. Il y a beaucoup de voitures américaines en France.
4. La plupart des autoroutes ont deux ou trois voies dans chaque sens.
5. Les autoroutes en France sont gratuites; il n'y a pas de péages.

B La conduite Répondez.
1. Les bouchons sont fréquents où et quand?
2. Les routes départementales sont plus pittoresques que les autoroutes. Pourquoi?
3. Qui surveille la circulation sur les autoroutes?
4. Qu'est-ce que les motards donnent aux automobilistes qui ne respectent pas la limitation de vitesse?
5. Il faut avoir quel âge pour passer son permis de conduire en France? Et là où tu habites?
6. Tu pourrais avoir une moto si tu habitais en France? Et là où tu habites?

Lectures culturelles

Cross-Cultural Comparison

In France, the minimum age requirement for driving various types of vehicles is the same throughout the entire country. In the United States, it varies from state to state.

- **Un cyclomoteur (une sorte de bicyclette avec un petit moteur): 14 ans**
- **Un vélomoteur: 16 ans**
- **Une moto: 16 ans**
- **Une voiture: 18 ans**

Student drivers must learn many things besides driving: the names of engine parts, how to change a flat tire, etc. All of this is part of the very difficult test to get a driver's license.

You may wish to give students the following information about the French police.

Le gendarme est toujours sur la route.

L'agent de police règle la circulation dans les villes. Il aide les gens à trouver leur chemin. Et il oblige tout le monde à respecter la loi.

Un C.R.S. (Compagnie républicaine de sécurité) porte un uniforme de combat. S'il y a une manifestation, le C.R.S. défend l'ordre public.

La police nationale dépend du ministère de l'Intérieur. La gendarmerie nationale est une force militaire et dépend du ministère de la Défense.

Most drivers fear the **motards**, motorcycle police officers. The **motards** mean business when they stop speeding motorists.

LEVELING

E: Reading

Answers to Vous avez compris?

A
1. faux
2. faux
3. faux
4. vrai
5. faux

B Answers will vary but may include:
1. Les bouchons sont fréquents aux heures de pointe et près des agglomérations.
2. Parce qu'elles passent par beaucoup de petits villages.
3. Les motards surveillent la circulation sur les autoroutes.
4. Ils leur donnent une contravention.
5. Il faut avoir 18 ans pour passer son permis de conduire en France. Où j'habite il faut avoir ____ ans pour passer son permis de conduire.
6. Oui, je pourrais avoir une moto si j'habitais en France. Où j'habite je (ne) pourrais (pas) avoir une moto.

Lecture supplémentaire

Partez à l'aventure en Tunisie!

Dans le désert saharien du sud de la Tunisie, il y a deux villages très intéressants—Nefta et Tozeur. Là où on ne voit que les dunes et le sable du désert, se trouvent ces deux villages, pleins de végétation et de verdure[1]. À l'entrée de Nefta, une large avenue bordée d'eucalyptus vous souhaite la bienvenue. Ici, le désert cède la place à des oasis où des sources[2] d'eau sortent du sable. Nefta compte 150 sources d'eau chaude et plus de 300 000 palmiers. C'est à Nefta qu'on cultive les deglas—les dattes réputées être les plus délicieuses du monde.

[1] verdure *greenery*
[2] sources *springs*

L'oasis de Nefta en Tunisie

Pas loin de Nefta, on trouve Tozeur—un village de 15 000 habitants et 250 000 palmiers. Les maisons de Tozeur sont d'une jolie couleur marron-rouge. On fait les briques de ces maisons avec le sable du désert. Les briques de la façade des maisons forment de très jolis dessins géométriques.

Si tu es courageux, et si tu veux faire un voyage extraordinaire, tu dois traverser le chott el-Djerid de Tozeur à Kebili—une distance de 90 kilomètres. Un chott, c'est un ancien lac salé[3], mais l'eau du lac s'est évaporée et il reste seulement une croûte de sel sèche et dure[4]. L'après-midi, l'air est chauffé[5] par le soleil et le sel brûlant[6]. Il déforme alors le paysage. On croit voir des îles, des palmiers et des villages où rien n'existe. Quelle sensation extraordinaire que de voir un mirage! Ces mirages ont égaré[7] beaucoup de caravanes de Bédouins[8] qui circulaient dans le désert. Alors, allez-y! Partez à l'aventure!

[3] salé *salt*
[4] sèche et dure *dry and hard*
[5] chauffé *heated*
[6] brûlant *burning*
[7] ont égaré *led astray*
[8] Bédouins *Bedouins (nomadic Arab tribes)*

Une rue à Tozeur

Des Bédouins dans le Sahara en Tunisie

Vous avez compris?

A Descriptions Décrivez.
1. Nefta
2. Tozeur
3. le chott el-Djerid

B Qu'est-ce que c'est?
Expliquez les mots suivants.
1. une oasis
2. un désert
3. une deglas
4. un chott

LA VOITURE ET LA ROUTE

deux cent vingt-sept 227

National Standards

Connections
This reading about air pollution establishes a connection with another discipline, allowing students to reinforce and further their knowledge of ecology through the study of French.

Attention!

The readings in the **Connexions** section are optional. They focus on some of the major disciplines taught in schools and universities. The vocabulary is useful for discussing such topics as history, literature, art, economics, business, science, etc. You may choose any of the following ways to do the readings in the **Connexions** section.

Independent reading Have students read the selections and do the post-reading activities as homework, which you collect. This option is least intrusive on class time and requires a minimum of teacher involvement.

Homework with in-class follow-up Assign the readings and post-reading activities as homework. Review and discuss the material in class the next day.

Intensive in-class activity This option includes a pre-reading vocabulary presentation, in-class reading and discussion, assignment of the activities for homework, and a discussion of the assignment in class the following day.

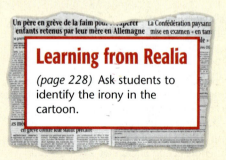

Learning from Realia
(page 228) Ask students to identify the irony in the cartoon.

CONNEXIONS

Les sciences

L'écologie

Ecology is a subject of great interest and concern to people around the world. People are increasingly aware of how pollution damages the environment. The automobile is a primary cause of air pollution. Recently, the French teen magazine *Phosphore* interviewed some students from different areas of France. They were asked whether cars should be banned. Let's see what they had to say.

Faut-il interdire les voitures?

Sylvain: 24 ans, étudiant en informatique à Paris, circule à vélo

Claire: 18 ans, étudiante à Marseille, circule à pied et en transports en commun

Nicolas: 21 ans, étudiant en économie à Nice, circule à pied et en voiture

Trouvez-vous qu'il y a trop de voitures dans votre ville? Est-ce que vous souffrez de la pollution automobile?

Sylvain: Oui, je trouve que les voitures sont dangereuses à Paris. Je vois souvent des automobilistes énervés qui ne respectent pas les limitations de vitesse, les feux… De plus, je ressens[1] la pollution dans ma chair[2], elle m'irrite comme la fumée[3], je sens que l'air n'est

pas pur. Je ne ressens pas ça en province et à la campagne.

Nicolas: Moi, je prends la voiture assez souvent pour aller dans le centre ou pour sortir. Mais pour trouver des places de parking, c'est toujours la galère[4]! Je n'ai jamais vraiment souffert de la pollution, même si je suis asthmatique. Sauf une fois, quand j'étais à Paris sur les Champs-Élysées. Je n'arrivais plus à respirer. Paris, c'est

[1] ressens *feel*
[2] chair *flesh*
[3] fumée *smoke*

[4] c'est la galère *it's a real hassle*

LEVELING
E: Reading
A: Reading

vraiment pollué. À Nice, la situation est en progrès. La municipalité a mis en place des bus au gaz naturel. C'est vraiment agréable.

Claire: Non, à Marseille, le mistral[5] chasse vite la pollution. Mais la situation est catastrophique dans des villes comme Mexico, par exemple.

Si vous aviez le choix entre la voiture et un mode de transport moins polluant, est-ce que vous adopteriez ce dernier par civisme[6]?

Sylvain: Il est normal que, si j'ai une opinion, je l'applique à moi-même. Mais je ne le fais pas par civisme. Un mode de transport moins polluant serait aussi plus agréable.

Claire: Je ne sais pas. Je vais au lycée en bus ou à pied. Mais la voiture, c'est important pour sortir et aller travailler. Ça dépend où on habite.

Nicolas: Il faut améliorer[7] les transports en commun[8]. Dans ce cas, je serais prêt[9].

[5] mistral *mistral, strong cold wind*
[6] civisme *civic duty*
[7] améliorer *to improve*
[8] transports en commun *mass transit*
[9] prêt *ready*

Vous avez compris?

A Un résumé Préparez un résumé des réponses des jeunes Français à la première question de l'interview.

B Recherches Faites des recherches sur les nouveaux moyens de propulsion des voitures (voitures électriques et voitures au gaz GPL).

LA VOITURE ET LA ROUTE

deux cent vingt-neuf ✦ 229

Connexions

Presentation

Les sciences
L'écologie

Note: You may wish to have all students scan this selection quickly. The topic is of great interest today and the reading selection is quite easy.

Step 1 Have students read the introduction in English on page 228.

Step 2 Have students scan the reading for cognates. Then have them do the reading again, this time for comprehension.

About the French Language

You may wish to point out to students that the inverted question format is almost always used in interview questions: **Faut-il interdire les voitures?** ✦

ANSWERS TO Vous avez compris?

A *Answers will vary but may include:*
Sylvain trouve qu'il y a trop de voitures à Paris. Il y a beaucoup de pollution.

Nicolas ne dit pas qu'il y a trop de voitures à Nice. Mais il n'y a pas assez de places de parking. Il n'a pas souffert de la pollution.

Claire dit qu'il n'y a pas de pollution à Marseille à cause du mistral.

B *Students will research the topic.*

C'est à vous

Use what you have learned

Bellringer Review

Use BRR Transparency 7.9 or write the following on the board.
Write the opposite of each term.
accélérer
stationner
tourner à gauche
brûler un feu rouge
prudemment
plein

 Recycling

These activities allow students to use the vocabulary and structure from this chapter in completely open-ended, real-life situations.

Presentation

Encourage students to say as much as possible when they do these activities. Tell them not to be afraid to make mistakes, since the goal of these activities is real-life communication. Let students choose the activities they would like to do.

You may wish to separate students into pairs or groups. Encourage them to use props, pictures, or posters.

1 Tell students that **mener** means *to lead*.

C'est à vous

Use what you have learned

PARLER 1

Près de chez vous
✓ *Talk about cars and driving*

Avec un(e) camarade, choisissez une ville près de chez vous. Décrivez les routes qui mènent à cette ville. Discutez s'il y a beaucoup de circulation. Quand? Pourquoi?

Des panneaux à la Martinique

PARLER 2

Jeu   Attention aux contraventions!
✓ *Talk about driving in France*

Regardez le dessin ci-dessous. Vous êtes un motard et vous donnez une contravention à un(e) des automobilistes (votre camarade) qui ne respecte pas les panneaux.

Votre permis de conduire, s'il vous plaît.

230 *deux cent trente*   CHAPITRE 7

ANSWERS TO C'est à vous

1 Answers will vary depending on the town or city students choose to describe. They will, however, be able to use the vocabulary presented in this chapter.

2 Answers will vary but may include the following problems:

Vous avez brûlé un feu rouge.
Il est interdit de tourner à droite.
Vous n'avez pas respecté la limitation de vitesse.
Il est interdit de doubler.

CHAPITRE 7

C'est à vous

PARLER
3

Quand j'aurai mon permis de conduire...
✔ Describe future events

Quand est-ce que vous aurez votre permis de conduire? Quelle sorte de conducteur/conductrice est-ce que vous serez? Qu'est-ce que vous ferez (ou ne ferez pas) quand vous aurez votre permis? Quand vous achèterez une voiture, quelle marque est-ce que vous choisirez? Pourquoi?

ÉCRIRE
4

Des invités
✔ Give directions

Un(e) de vos ami(e)s français(es) va bientôt venir vous voir avec sa famille. Vous lui écrivez pour lui expliquer comment venir chez vous de l'aéroport.

Writing Strategy

Developing a fictional narrative Like any other narrative, a fictional narrative tells a story. A short story is one kind of fictional narrative which centers on a single event. The writer creates a plot, characters, and a setting and describes them from a certain point of view. For some writers, the hardest part is coming up with the idea, but once they do, they must be sure that their stories contain all these elements.

ÉCRIRE
5

Très en retard!

You were driving to school with Antoine, the French high school exchange student living with you. You had some misadventures on the road and missed your first period class, which happens to be your Driver's Education class. To make matters worse, you had a test that day. Write an imaginative story explaining to your teacher why you and Antoine were late. It might be fun to use the road signs to help you make up the story. Be as humorous and creative as you can. Remember, you have to be convincing enough so your teacher will let you make up the exam rather than take a zero!

LA VOITURE ET LA ROUTE

deux cent trente et un 231

C'est à vous

Writing Development
Have students keep a notebook containing their best written work from each chapter. These selected writings can be based on assignments from the Student Textbook and the Workbook. The two activities on page 231 are examples of writing assignments that may be included in each student's portfolio.

Writing Strategy

Developing a fictional narrative Have students read the Writing Strategy on page 231. They may refer to the vocabulary list on page 235 if they need more ideas to write this selection.

Reaching All Students

Additional Practice Display Communication Transparency C 7. Have students work in groups to make up as many questions as they can about the illustration. Have groups take turns asking and answering the questions.

LEVELING
These activities encompass all three levels. All students will be able to do them at a sophistication level commensurate with their ability in French. Some students will be able to speak for several minutes, and others may be able to give just a few sentences. This is to be expected when students are functioning completely on their own generating their own language to the best of their ability.

ANSWERS TO C'est à vous

3 Answers will vary but may include:
Quand j'aurai mon permis de conduire, je conduirai prudemment. Je ne roulerai jamais trop vite. Je respecterai toujours la limitation de vitesse. J'achèterai _____. J'aime cette marque de voiture.

4 Answers will vary depending upon where the student lives. Students may use the following words:
l'autoroute, le péage, la sortie, prendre, continuer, tourner, à gauche, à droite, tout droit.

5 Answers will vary.

Assessment

Resource Manager

Communication Transparencies C 7
Quizzes, pages 33–38
Tests, pages 95–108
ExamView® Pro
Situation Cards
Performance Assessment, Task 7
Marathon mental Videoquiz

✓ Assessment

This is a pre-test for students to take before you administer the chapter test. Answer sheets for students to do these pages are provided in your transparency binder. Note that each section is cross-referenced so students can easily find the material they have to review in case they made errors. You may wish to collect these assessments and correct them yourself or you may prefer to have the students correct themselves in class. You can go over the answers orally or project them on the overhead, using your Assessment Answers transparencies.

Assessment

Vocabulaire

1 Identifiez.

1.
2.
3.
4.

To review Mots 1, turn to pages 206–207.

2 Choisissez.

5. Elle va à une auto-école.
6. Le réservoir est presque vide.
7. Elle veut ralentir.
8. Elle a eu un pneu à plat.

a. Mais elle a une roue de secours dans le coffre.
b. Elle prend des leçons de conduite.
c. Elle a besoin d'essence.
d. Elle doit freiner.

To review Mots 2, turn to pages 210–211.

3 Complétez.

9. Quand on conduit une voiture, il faut mettre _____ avant de tourner.
10. Sur l'autoroute il y a trois _____ dans chaque sens.
11. Il y a un _____ qui indique la sortie de l'autoroute.
12. On ne doit pas rouler trop vite. Il faut respecter _____.
13. Non, non. Ne tournez pas. Allez _____.

232 deux cent trente-deux

CHAPITRE 7

ANSWERS TO Assessment

1
1. une voiture de sport
2. un vélomoteur
3. une clé
4. une moto

2
5. b
6. c
7. d
8. a

3
9. son clignotant
10. voies
11. panneau
12. la limitation de vitesse
13. tout droit

CHAPITRE 7 Assessment

Structure

4 Complétez au conditionnel.

14. Il nous ____. (attendre)
15. Je te ____ un plan de la ville. (donner)
16. Vous ____ en voiture? (aller)
17. Elles ____ leur travail à l'heure. (finir)

To review verbs in the conditional, turn to page 214.

5 Récrivez au conditionnel.

18. Je veux y aller.
19. Ils reçoivent des contraventions.
20. Vous pouvez être là à six heures?

To review irregular verbs, turn to pages 216–217.

6 Complétez.

21. Je ferais le voyage si j'____ assez d'argent. (avoir)
22. Le motard te ____ une contravention si tu brûles un feu rouge. (donner)

To review clauses with si, turn to page 218.

7 Répondez avec des pronoms.

23. Il donnera sa voiture à son fils?
24. Elle montrera son permis de conduire à ses amis?

To review the position of pronouns, turn to page 220.

Culture

8 Complétez.

25. En France, il faut avoir ____ ans pour passer son permis de conduire mais on peut conduire une moto à partir de ____ ans.

To review this cultural information, turn to pages 224–225.

LA VOITURE ET LA ROUTE

deux cent trente-trois ❖ 233

Learning from Photos
(page 233) Have students say everything they can about the photo.

Glencoe Technology

MINDJOGGER VHS/DVD
You may wish to help your students prepare for the chapter test by playing the MindJogger game show. Teams will compete against each other to review chapter vocabulary and structure and sharpen listening comprehension skills.

FOLDABLES Study Organizer — Dinah Zike's Study Guides

Your students may wish to use Foldable 10 to organize, display, and arrange data as they learn to describe many situations in French. You may wish to encourage them to draw a picture from each chapter as they continue to gather facts and make observations about all the different topics they are studying.

An *envelope fold* is also ideal for collecting and reviewing information students have learned about particular subjects.

ANSWERS TO Assessment

4
14. attendrait
15. donnerais
16. iriez
17. finiraient

5
18. Je voudrais y aller.
19. Ils recevraient des contraventions.
20. Vous pourriez être là à six heures?

6
21. avais
22. donnera

7
23. Oui, il la lui donnera.
24. Oui, elle le leur montrera.

8
25. 18, 16

On parle super bien!

This unique page gives students the opportunity to speak freely and say whatever they can, using the vocabulary and structures they have learned in the chapter. The illustration serves to remind students of precisely what they know how to say in French. There are no activities that students do not have the ability to describe or talk about in French. The art not only depicts the vocabulary and content of this chapter, but also reinforces what they learned in previous chapters.

You may wish to use this page in many ways. Some possibilities are to have students do the following:

1. Look at the illustration and identify items by giving the correct French words.
2. Make up sentences about what they see in the illustration.
3. Make up questions about the illustration. They can call on another class member to respond if you do this as a class activity, or you may prefer to allow students to work in small groups. This activity is extremely beneficial because it enables students to actively use interrogative words.
4. Answer questions you ask them about the illustration.
5. Work in pairs and make up a conversation based on the illustration.
6. Look at the illustration and give a complete oral review of what they see.
7. Look at the illustration and write a paragraph (or essay) about it.

You can also use this page as an assessment or testing tool, taking into account individual differences by having students go from simple to quite complicated tasks. The assessment can be either oral or written. You may wish to use the rubrics provided on pages T20–T21 as you give students the following directions.

234

On parle super bien!

Tell all you can about this illustration.

234 🌼 *deux cent trente-quatre*   CHAPITRE 7

1. Identify the topic or situation of the illustration.
2. Give the French words for as many items as you can.
3. Think of as many sentences as you can to describe the illustration.
4. Go over your sentences and put them in the best sequencing to give a coherent story based on the illustration.

Vocabulaire

Talking about cars and other vehicles

une voiture	un camion	une marque française	un conducteur, une
une voiture de sport	une moto	une auto-école	conductrice
un break	un vélomoteur	une leçon de conduite	un(e) automobiliste
une décapotable	un casque	un permis de conduire	

Identifying parts of a car

une clé	le réservoir	un pneu (à plat)
une ceinture de sécurité	le coffre	une roue de secours
	le pare-brise	un clignotant

Talking about services at a gas station

une station-service	faire le plein
de l'essence (f.)	vérifier la pression
un(e) pompiste	les niveaux (m. pl.)
l'air (m.)	

Talking about driving

conduire	rouler	tourner
mettre le contact	se garer	à gauche
accélérer	doubler	à droite
freiner	changer de voie	aller tout droit
ralentir	tomber en panne	
s'arrêter	brûler un feu rouge	

Talking about driving on the highway

une carte (routière)	un péage	un bouchon	un rond-point
un plan (de la ville)	une sortie	une file de voitures	la limitation de vitesse
une autoroute	une flèche	une agglomération	un motard
une voie	un panneau	un croisement	une contravention

Other useful words and expressions

à (ta) place	vide
prudemment	respecter
dangereusement	oublier

How well do you know your vocabulary?
Make a list of words describing skills you would learn in a driver's education class. Write a few sentences about your first driving lesson.

 VIDÉOTOUR
Épisode 7
In this video episode, you will see Christine react to Mme Séguin's driving expertise. See page 506 for more information.

LA VOITURE ET LA ROUTE

deux cent trente-cinq 235

Vocabulaire

Vocabulary Review

The words and phrases in the **Vocabulaire** have been taught for productive use in this chapter. They are summarized here as a resource for both student and teacher. This list also serves as a convenient resource for the **C'est à vous** activities on pages 230–231, as well as for talking about the illustration on page 234. There are five cognates in this vocabulary list. Have students find them.

Attention!

You will notice that the vocabulary list here is not translated. This has been done intentionally, since we feel that by the time students have finished the material in the chapter they should be familiar with the meanings of all the words. If there are several words they still do not know, we recommend that they refer to the **Mots 1** and **2** sections in the chapter or go to the dictionaries at the back of this book to find the meanings. However, if you prefer that your students have the English translations, please refer to Vocabulary Transparency 7.1, where you will find all these words listed with their translations.

 VIDÉO VHS/DVD
The Video Program allows students to see how the chapter vocabulary and structures are used by native speakers. For maximum reinforcement, show the video episode as a final activity for Chapter 7.

235

Révision

Preview

This section reviews the salient points from Chapters 5–7. In the **Conversation,** students will review car and bank vocabulary, as well as the future and conditional. In the **Structure** sections, they will review the future, the conditional, and object pronouns.

Resource Manager

Workbook, Check-Up, pages 83–88
Tests, pages 109–117

Presentation

Conversation

Step 1 Have students open their books to page 236. Call on two students to read this short conversation aloud.

Step 2 Go over the activity in the **Vous avez compris?** section.

History Connection

The **banque de France** was created in 1800 and nationalized in 1945. It is the central bank of the country and the bank of the State Treasury.

Révision

Conversation

Une voiture

Aurore: On va prendre quelque chose au Sélect?
Jérôme: Désolé, mais j'ai rendez-vous à la banque.
Aurore: Pour quoi faire?
Jérôme: Pour demander un prêt.
Aurore: Tu as besoin d'argent?
Jérôme: Oui, pour acheter une voiture.
Aurore: Ah oui? Qu'est-ce que tu vas acheter?
Jérôme: La vieille Twingo de mon cousin.
Aurore: Tu ne vas pas te ruiner!
Jérôme: Ben si, justement. Je n'ai pas le fric que tu as, moi! Si je l'avais, je n'achèterais pas une vieille Twingo! Ça, tu peux en être sûre!

Vous avez compris?

Une nouvelle voiture Répondez.
1. Pourquoi est-ce que Jérôme ne peut pas aller au café avec Aurore?
2. Qu'est-ce qu'il va y faire?
3. Pour quoi faire?
4. Il va acheter quelle voiture?
5. D'après Aurore, c'est une voiture chère?
6. Si Jérôme avait de l'argent, il achèterait une vieille Twingo?

Answers to Vous avez compris?

1. Il a rendez-vous à la banque.
2. Il va demander un prêt.
3. Il va acheter une voiture.
4. Il va acheter la vieille Twingo de son cousin.
5. Non, ce n'est pas une voiture chère.
6. Non, si Jérôme avait de l'argent, il n'achèterait pas une vieille Twingo.

Fun Facts

The **Twingo** is a popular, rather inexpensive car. As one can see in this photo, it has the shape of a small station wagon or van. It is manufactured by Renault, and it is available in many vivid colors.

Structure

 ## Le futur et le conditionnel

1. The infinitive of **-er** and **-ir** verbs serves as the stem for the formation of the future and the conditional. Note that with **-re** verbs you drop the final **-e** of the infinitive. As in English, you use the future to express what will happen and the conditional to express what would or could happen under certain circumstances.

LE FUTUR

	PARLER	FINIR	ATTENDRE
Infinitive	parler	finir	attendre
Stem	parler-	finir-	attendr-
	je parlerai	je finirai	j' attendrai
	tu parleras	tu finiras	tu attendras
	il/elle/on parlera	il/elle/on finira	il/elle/on attendra
	nous parlerons	nous finirons	nous attendrons
	vous parlerez	vous finirez	vous attendrez
	ils/elles parleront	ils/elles finiront	ils/elles attendront

LE CONDITIONNEL

	PARLER	FINIR	ATTENDRE
Infinitive	parler	finir	attendre
Stem	parler-	finir-	attendr-
	je parlerais	je finirais	j' attendrais
	tu parlerais	tu finirais	tu attendrais
	il/elle/on parlerait	il/elle/on finirait	il/elle/on attendrait
	nous parlerions	nous finirions	nous attendrions
	vous parleriez	vous finiriez	vous attendriez
	ils/elles parleraient	ils/elles finiraient	ils/elles attendraient

Presentation

 Le futur et le conditionnel

Step 1 Quickly go over the verb forms that appear here.

Step 2 Have individuals read the verb forms aloud.

Révision

2. The following verbs have an irregular future and conditional stem.

ÊTRE	je serai	je serais
FAIRE	je ferai	je ferais
ALLER	j'irai	j'irais
AVOIR	j'aurai	j'aurais
SAVOIR	je saurai	je saurais
VOIR	je verrai	je verrais
ENVOYER	j'enverrai	j'enverrais
POUVOIR	je pourrai	je pourrais
DEVOIR	je devrai	je devrais
RECEVOIR	je recevrai	je recevrais
VOULOIR	je voudrai	je voudrais
VENIR	je viendrai	je viendrais
FALLOIR	il faudra	il faudrait

Rappelez-vous que...

When the main verb in the sentence is in the future, any verb after **quand** must also be in the future.
Je lui parlerai quand je le verrai.

3. Review the sequence of tenses with **si** clauses.

Si + Présent → Futur	Si + Imparfait → Conditionnel
Si j'ai assez d'argent, je ferai un voyage.	Si j'avais assez d'argent, je ferais un voyage.

Une baie à Tahiti

1 Un jour!
Répondez d'après le modèle.

voyager beaucoup →
Un jour, je voyagerai beaucoup.
Et vous, vous voyagerez beaucoup aussi?

1. gagner beaucoup d'argent
2. aller à Tahiti
3. faire un voyage au Maroc
4. voir les sept merveilles du monde
5. savoir beaucoup de choses
6. pouvoir parler dix langues
7. recevoir le prix Nobel

Révision

2 **Mes amis et moi** Répondez en utilisant **Mes amis et moi, on…**

1. Vous aimeriez aller à Washington?
2. Vous iriez en hiver ou au printemps?
3. Vous prendriez l'avion ou le train pour y aller?
4. Vous visiteriez la Maison Blanche?
5. Vous visiteriez les autres monuments de la capitale? Quels monuments?

Washington

QUE VOIR ET QUE FAIRE?
Le Capitole, la Maison Blanche, le cimetière d'Arlington, Lincoln Memorial, Washington Monument et son obélisque, Le Mall et les musées Smithsonian (gratuits).

Petit déjeuner américain. Visite guidée de Washington. Vous passez devant la Maison Blanche, l'édifice de la Cour Suprême, l'obélisque du Washington Monument, le mémorial de Jefferson. Déjeuner dans un restaurant typique. Après-midi libre pour la visite des musées du Smithsonian. Dîner libre.

PRÉSENTATION
Capitale des États-Unis, Washington est le siège du gouvernement fédéral et d'organisations nationales et internationales.

UN PEU D'HISTOIRE
Dessinée par un ingénieur français: Pierre-Charles L'Enfant, la ville a été créée en 1791 dans l'unique but de devenir capitale politique.

3 **Si on avait 10 000 dollars!**
Dites ce que chaque personne ferait.

1. moi
2. mon père
3. mes grands-parents
4. ma sœur
5. toi
6. mes copains et moi
7. vous deux

RÉVISION

deux cent trente-neuf ❖ 239

Révision

Presentation

Deux pronoms dans la même phrase

Step 1 Read the questions in Item 2 and have students read the responses.

Reaching All Students

Additional Practice
Replace the words in italics with pronouns.
1. Marc va apporter *le cadeau à Marie.*
2. Serge te prête *les cravates.*
3. Catherine nous a donné *les livres.*
4. Ma mère m'a prêté *la voiture.*
5. Mon père m'a donné *les clés.*

Learning from Photos

(page 240) Bouillabaisse is a fish stew from the Marseille area. An authentic bouillabaisse has about six different types of fish, including rascasse (scorpion fish) and eel, as well as langoustines, crabs, and lobster. They are all cooked together with olive oil, tomato, garlic, fennel, saffron, and a touch of anise. It is served with garlic toast and **rouille**—a type of mayonnaise flavored with garlic and red chili pepper.

Révision

 Deux pronoms dans la même phrase

1. When two pronouns are used in the same sentence, the order is as follows.

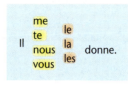

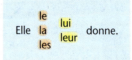

Il **me le** dit toujours.
Il ne **le lui** dit jamais.

2. Remember that the past participle must agree with a preceding direct object.

La recette? Je **la** lui ai donn**ée**.
Les 100 dollars? Elle me **les** a rendu**s**.

Une bouillabaisse

4 Une promesse Répondez d'après le modèle.

la bouillabaisse de Grand-Maman →
Moi, je te la prépare.
1. le bœuf bourguignon de Grand-Maman
2. la choucroute de Grand-Maman
3. les haricots verts de Grand-Maman
4. le couscous de Grand-Maman
5. la pizza de Grand-Maman

 LITERARY COMPANION You may wish to read the poems by Camara Laye and René Philombe. You will find the *Deux poèmes africains* on page 480.

ANSWERS TO Révision

4
1. Moi, je te le prépare.
2. Moi, je te la prépare.
3. Moi, je te les prépare.
4. Moi, je te le prépare.
5. Moi, je te la prépare.

 Literary Companion

When you finish this review section, if you wish, have students read the *Deux poèmes africains* on pages 480–485.

5 **Une carte** Répondez en utilisant des pronoms.

1. Tu voulais envoyer une carte et un cadeau d'anniversaire à ton ami(e). Tu as écrit la carte à ton ami(e)?
2. Tu lui as envoyé la carte?
3. Tu as donné la carte au facteur?
4. Tu as envoyé le cadeau?
5. Ton ami(e) a reçu la carte?
6. Il/Elle a reçu le cadeau?
7. Il/Elle a aimé la carte et le cadeau?
8. Ton ami(e) a montré la carte et le cadeau à ses autres amis?

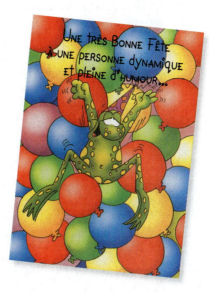

6 **L'avenir** Travaillez avec un(e) camarade. Parlez chacun de ce que sera votre avenir.

7 **Si je pouvais…** Avec un(e) camarade, dites tout ce que vous aimeriez faire si vous pouviez le faire.

8 **Quand j'aurai mon permis de conduire…** Quand est-ce que vous aurez votre permis de conduire? Quelle sorte de conducteur/conductrice est-ce que vous serez? Qu'est-ce que vous ferez (ou ne ferez pas) quand vous aurez votre permis? Quand vous achèterez une voiture, quelle marque est-ce que vous choisirez? Pourquoi?

FUN FACTS

The cars in the photo on page 241 are **deux chevaux.** They were extremely popular in the late 50s and 60s. They were quite small and economical. They are no longer manufactured, but they are today considered collector's items.

ANSWERS TO Révision

5 *Answers will vary but may include:*
1. Oui, je la lui ai écrite.
2. Oui, je la lui ai envoyée.
3. Oui, je la lui ai donnée.
4. Oui, je l'ai envoyé.
5. Oui, il l'a reçue.
6. Oui, il l'a reçu.
7. Oui, il les a aimés.
8. Oui, il les leur a montrés.

6 *Answers will vary.*
Students can use any vocabulary they have learned up to this point and put the verbs in the future.

7 *Answers will vary.*
Students will use the conditional with the imperfect after **si.**

8 *Answers will vary.*
Students can use the following types of expressions with the verbs in the future: **conduire prudemment, ne rouler pas trop vite, respecter la limitation de vitesse, acheter.**

Preview

This section, **Reflets du Maghreb**, was prepared by the National Geographic Society. Its purpose is to give students greater insight, through these visual images, into the culture and people of North Africa. Have students look at the photographs on pages 242–245 for enjoyment. If they would like to talk about them, let them say anything they can, using the vocabulary they have learned up to this point.

 National Standards

Culture
The **Reflets du Maghreb** photos and the accompanying captions allow students to gain insights into the people and culture of North Africa.

About the Photos

1. Palmiers dattiers de l'oasis de Nefta, en Tunisie Nefta is surrounded by undulating desert. When one approaches Nefta, it appears to be a stretch of green beside the chott (see below). Nefta is an artificial oasis, made possible by the boring of 2,100-foot wells during the 1960s. The oasis has some 300,000 palm trees, including 70,000 deglas, that are reputed to be among the world's best date palms. The original oasis of Roman days had 152 warm springs, dominated by a hilltop called the Corbeille. A **chott** is a salt flat. The Tunisian chotts are a distinctive geological feature on the northern fringe of the Sahara, and they stretch for about 200 miles from the Gulf of Gabes into Algeria. Some of them are lower than sea level.

1. Palmiers dattiers de l'oasis de Nefta, en Tunisie
2. Jeune fille tunisienne en costume traditionnel
3. La place Djemaa El Fna à Marrakech, au Maroc
4. Vendeur de pâtisseries aux dattes et au miel à Kairouan, en Tunisie
5. La mosquée de Bourguiba à Monastir, en Tunisie
6. Le quartier El Manar à Tunis, en Tunisie
7. Électroniciennes à Alger, en Algérie

2. Jeune fille tunisienne en costume traditionnel The young woman seen here is in a somewhat traditional Bedouin dress. Today it is not common to see Tunisian women go about their daily routine in such traditional dress, with the exception of some Berber women. The terms Bedouin (Beduin, in English) and Berber are often confused. Tunisia's aborigines were the Berbers. It is believed that around 10,000 B.C., dark-haired, brown-skinned Berbers settled in and around Tunisia. They subsequently interbred with the Blacks from the Sahara and blue-eyed, blond immigrants from the north. The offspring called themselves **Imazighen,** meaning "noble ones," but the Romans called them **Barbari** ("uncouth ones"). Bedui is the plural of the Arabic bedui, meaning "belonging to the desert." "Beduin" has come to be synonymous with "nomad," since many Berber groups were, and still are, nomadic herders. These two terms are loosely used as one, even in Tunisia itself.

REFLETS
du Maghreb

5. La mosquée de Bourguiba à Monastir, en Tunisie Monastir is a lovely coastal city with a university campus, film studios, and a stadium seating 20,000. A wide coastal boulevard skirts the beaches. There are several mosques in Monastir, including the **Mosquée de Bourguiba.** Adjoining this mosque is the Bourguiba family mausoleum, the final resting-place of Habib Bourguiba, who was born in Monastir. Bourguiba is considered the "Father of the Nation." He fought for and negotiated Tunisia's independence, which was recognized by France on March 20, 1956. On July 25, 1957, he declared himself president of the Republic. Bourguiba adapted Moslem traditions to modern life. He was overthrown in a bloodless coup in 1987, because of his advanced age and reports of senility.

6. Le quartier El Manar à Tunis, en Tunisie The El Manar area is a chic residential section of metropolitan Tunis.

7. Électroniciennes à Alger, en Algérie Algeria has had a turbulent history in comparison to other countries of the Maghreb. Algeria was not a French protectorate, but rather a part of metropolitan France. Prior to independence, some 3 million French settlers lived in Algeria, along with 7 million Moslems of great diversity. After a bloody civil war that lasted 7 years and cost 1 million lives, President DeGaulle considered the drain on France too great, and in March, 1962, Algerian independence was recognized. After independence, only 40,000 French remained, and many Algerians migrated to France. The political situation in Algeria is still unstable with much fighting between divergent groups of moderates, Islamic fundamentalists, and Berbers.

3. La place Djemaa El Fna à Marrakech, au Maroc The famous Djemaa El Fna square in Marrakech (often Marrakesh in English) is one of the liveliest and most colorful spots in Morocco. There are many little wooden-shuttered shops and stalls that belong to traveling merchants, in addition to dozens of little charcoal stoves that are kept burning all day to make couscous, brochettes, and boiling water for mint tea. In the afternoon the **Djemaa El Fna** becomes a gigantic sideshow of entertainers and storytellers.

4. Vendeur de pâtisseries aux dattes et au miel à Kairouan, en Tunisie Dates are well-known in Tunisia. Tunisians are also famous for their pastries, some of which are sweet. The city of Kairouan is a holy Islamic city with the Great Mosque and the shrines of several Moslem saints.

8. Un village dans la vallée du Dadès, au Maroc The Dadès Valley in the deep south of Morocco is a narrow band of cultivated land dotted with Ksour, or fortified villages, such as the one seen in this photo. The Dadès Valley also has many gorges.

9. Vendeur de pain sur l'île de Djerba, en Tunisie The island of Djerba today is a popular tourist destination. The island is covered with palm trees, orange and lemon orchards, and beautiful gardens.

10. Plage de Monastir, en Tunisie For information on Monastir, see number 5 on page 243.

11. Détail de la façade du Palais Royal à Fès, au Maroc Fez (**Fès,** in French) was founded as the first political capital of Morocco in 809. Although the capital has been moved several times, Fez continues to be a very important intellectual, cultural, and religious center. The beautiful Royal Palace, the Dar el Makhzen, is on a large square in the center of town. The medina of Fez was declared a World Patrimony by UNESCO in 1980.

12. Femme berbère filant la laine à Tinerhir, au Maroc At the beginning of the historical era, the Berbers were inhabitants of North Africa. There is not much known about their origin. Their language today is mostly a spoken language, but the Saharan Touaregs still write it. The town of Tinerhir is near the Todra gorges explained in number 8.

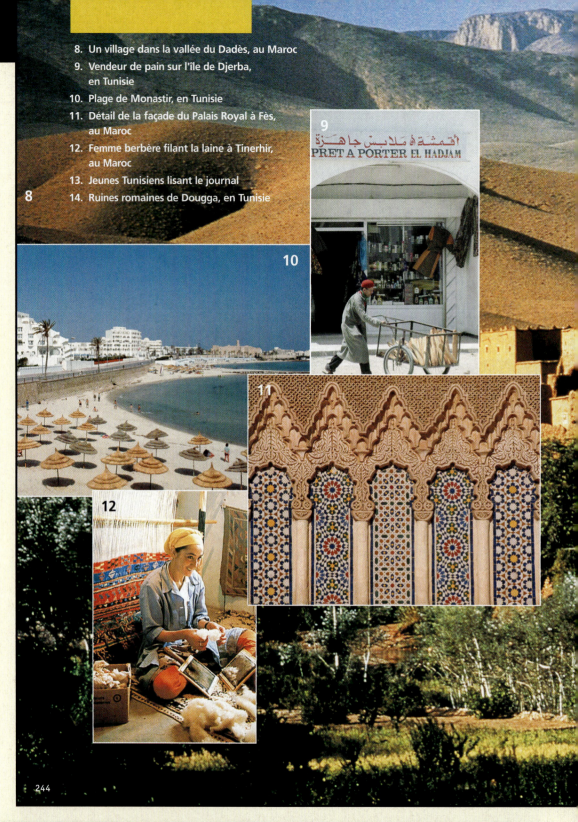

8. Un village dans la vallée du Dadès, au Maroc
9. Vendeur de pain sur l'île de Djerba, en Tunisie
10. Plage de Monastir, en Tunisie
11. Détail de la façade du Palais Royal à Fès, au Maroc
12. Femme berbère filant la laine à Tinerhir, au Maroc
13. Jeunes Tunisiens lisant le journal
14. Ruines romaines de Dougga, en Tunisie

 Teacher's Corner

Index to the NATIONAL GEOGRAPHIC MAGAZINE

The following related articles may be of interest:
- "In Focus: Central Africa's Cycle of Violence," by Mike Edwards, June 1997.
- "Hunting the Mighty Python," by Karen Lange, May 1997.
- "Morocco: North Africa's Timeless Mosaic," by Erla Zwingle, October 1996.
- "Below the Cliff of Tombs: Mali's Dogon," by David Roberts, October 1990.
- "Africa's Sahel: The Stricken Land," by William S. Ellis, August 1987.
- "Oasis of Art in the Sahara," by Henri Lhote, August 1987.
- "Senegambia: A Now and Future Nation," by Aubine Kirtley and Michael Kirtley, August 1985.
- "Finding West Africa's Oldest City," by Roderick McIntosh and Susan McIntosh, September 1982.
- "The Ivory Coast—African Success Story," by Aubine Kirtley and Michael Kirtley, July 1982.
- "Tunisia: Sea, Sand, Success," by Mike W. Edwards, February 1980.

REFLETS
du Maghreb

13. Jeunes Tunisiens lisant le journal As is the case with many young Tunisians, both male and female, these men are dressed in Western dress.

14. Ruines romaines de Dougga, en Tunisie Dougga, ancient name Thugga, was already an important town in the Punic era. Like all Roman towns in North Africa developed during the second and third centuries, it was densely populated. The remains date from that period. The principal remains are the theater, the Forum, and the temple of Caelestis. There are other temples, tombs, baths, and cisterns.

Products available from GLENCOE/MCGRAW-HILL
To order the following products, call Glencoe/McGraw-Hill at 1-800-334-7344.
CD-ROM
- Picture Atlas of the World

Transparency Set
- NGS MapPack: Geography of Africa

Products available from NATIONAL GEOGRAPHIC SOCIETY
To order the following products, call National Geographic Society at 1-800-368-2728.
Books
- National Geographic World Atlas for Young Explorers
- National Geographic Satellite Atlas of the World

Software
- ZingoLingo: French Diskette

Video
- Africa

Planning for Chapter 8

SCOPE AND SEQUENCE, PAGES 246–277

Topics
- Medical care
- Emergency room procedures

Functions
- How to describe accidents and medical problems
- How to ask different types of questions
- How to tell people what to do
- How to compare people and things

National Standards
- Communication Standard 1.1 pages 251, 254, 255, 257, 259, 260, 261, 263, 265, 272
- Communication Standard 1.2 pages 250, 251, 254, 255, 257, 259, 260, 261, 263, 264, 267, 269, 271
- Communication Standard 1.3 pages 251, 261, 263, 272, 273
- Cultures Standard 2.1 pages 266–267, 268–269, 271
- Connections Standard 3.1 pages 270–271
- Comparisons Standard 4.2 pages 266–267
- Communities Standard 5.1 page 273

Culture
- Hugo goes to the emergency room
- Doctors Without Borders

Structure
- Interrogative and relative pronouns
- Pronouns and commands
- Superlative adjectives
- Expressing **meilleur** and **mieux**

PACING AND PRIORITIES

> The chapter content is color coded below to assist you in planning.
> ■ required   ■ recommended   ■ optional

Vocabulaire *(required)*   *Days 1–4*
- ■ Mots 1
  - Un accident
  - Au service des urgences
  - Le corps
- ■ Mots 2
  - À l'hôpital
  - Une salle d'opération

Structure *(required)*   *Days 5–7*
- ■ Les pronoms interrogatifs et relatifs
- ■ Les pronoms et l'impératif
- ■ Le superlatif des adjectifs
- ■ Meilleur/mieux

Conversation *(required)*
- ■ Au service des urgences

Lectures culturelles
- ■ À l'Hôtel-Dieu, à toute vitesse! *(recommended)*
- ■ Médecins Sans Frontières *(optional)*

Connexions *(optional)*
- ■ Louis Pasteur et l'Institut Pasteur

■ **C'est à vous** *(recommended)*

■ **Assessment** *(recommended)*

■ **On parle super bien!** *(optional)*

RESOURCE GUIDE

SECTION	PAGES	SECTION RESOURCES
Vocabulaire *Mots 1*		
Un accident Au service des urgences Le corps	248 248 249–251	Vocabulary Transparencies 8.2–8.3 Audio CD 5 Audio Activities TE, pages 81–83 Workbook, pages 89–91 Quiz 1, page 39 ExamView® Pro
Vocabulaire *Mots 2*		
À l'hôpital Une salle d'opération	252 253–255	Vocabulary Transparencies 8.4–8.5 Audio CD 5 Audio Activities TE, pages 84–86 Workbook, page 91 Quiz 2, page 40 ExamView® Pro
Structure		
Les pronoms interrogatifs et relatifs Les pronoms et l'impératif Le superlatif des adjectifs Meilleur/mieux	256–257 258–260 261 262–263	Audio CD 5 Audio Activities TE, pages 86–89 Workbook, pages 92–96 Quizzes 3–5, pages 41–43 ExamView® Pro
Conversation		
Au service des urgences	264–265	Audio CD 5 Audio Activities TE, pages 89–90 Interactive CD-ROM
Lectures culturelles		
À l'Hôtel-Dieu, à toute vitesse! Médecins Sans Frontières	266–267 268–269	Audio CD 5 Audio Activities TE, pages 91–92 Tests, pages 121, 127
Connexions		
Louis Pasteur et l'Institut Pasteur	270–271	Tests, page 128
C'est à vous		
	272–273	**Bon voyage!** Video, Episode 8 Video Activities, Chapter 8 French Online Activities french.glencoe.com
Assessment		
	274–275	Communication Transparency C 8 Quizzes 1–5, pages 39–43 Performance Assessment, Task 8 Tests, pages 117–134 ExamView® Pro Situation Cards, Chapter 8 **Marathon mental** Videoquiz

Using Your Resources for Chapter 8

Transparencies

Bellringer 8.1–8.9   Vocabulary 8.1–8.5   Communication C 8

Workbook

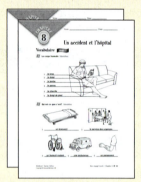  

Vocabulary, pages 89–91   Structure, pages 92–96   Enrichment, pages 97–100

Audio Activities

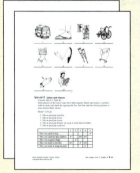    

Vocabulary, pages 81–86   Structure, pages 86–89   Conversation, pages 89–90   Cultural Reading, pages 91–92   Additional Practice, pages 92–93

246C

Assessment

Vocabulary and Structure Quizzes, pages 39–43

Chapter Tests, pages 117–134

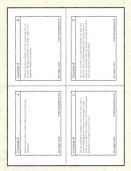
Situation Cards, Chapter 8

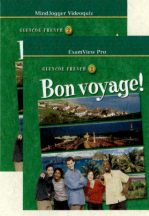
MindJogger Videoquiz, ExamView® Pro, Chapter 8

Timesaving Teacher Tools

TeacherWorks™

TeacherWorks™ is your all-in-one teacher resource center. Personalize lesson plans, access resources from the Teacher Wraparound Edition, connect to the Internet, or make a to-do list. These are only a few of the many features that can assist you in the planning and organizing of your lessons.

Includes:

- A calendar feature
- Access to all program blackline masters
- Standards correlations and more

ExamView® Pro

Test Bank software for Macintosh and Windows makes creating, editing, customizing, and printing tests quick and easy.

Technology Resources

In the Chapter 8 Internet activity, you will have a chance to learn more about the Francophone world. Visit <u>french.glencoe.com</u>.

On the Interactive Conversation CD-ROM, students can listen to and take part in a recorded version of the conversation in Chapter 8.

See the National Geographic Teacher's Corner on pages 138–139, 244–245, 372–373, 472–473 for reference to additional technology resources.

Bon voyage! Video and Video Activities, Chapter 8

Help your students prepare for the chapter test by playing the **Marathon mental** Videoquiz game show. Teams will compete against each other to review chapter vocabulary and structure and sharpen listening comprehension skills.

CHAPITRE 8

Preview

In this chapter, students will learn to report and describe certain accidents and talk about minor injuries. They will learn vocabulary associated with emergency hospital treatment. Students will learn to form questions using **qu'est-ce que** and **qu'est-ce qui.** They will also learn to use **ce qui** and **ce que,** express opinions using superlative statements about people and things, use the expressions **meilleur** and **mieux,** and use the imperative form of the verb with an object pronoun.

National Standards

Communication
In Chapter 8, students will communicate in spoken and written French on the following topics:
• Accidents and injuries
• Emergency room treatment
Students will obtain and provide information about these topics and engage in conversations that would typically take place at the scene of an accident or in a hospital emergency room as they fulfill the chapter objectives listed on this page.

LEVELING

The activities, conversations, and readings within each chapter are marked according to level of difficulty. **E** indicates easy. **A** indicates average. **C** indicates challenging. Some activities cover a range of difficulty. In some activities, for example, advanced students will be able to produce more extensive responses while students who learn at a different rate may give less detailed responses. The leveling indicators will help you individualize instruction to best meet your students' needs.

CHAPITRE 8

Un accident et l'hôpital

Objectifs
In this chapter you will learn to:
✓ talk about accidents and medical problems
✓ talk about emergency room procedures
✓ ask different types of questions
✓ tell people what to do
✓ compare people and things
✓ talk about a medical emergency in France

Jean Geoffroy *Le jour de la visite à l'hôpital*

246

CHAPITRE 8

Spotlight on Culture

Photograph L'hôpital la Salpêtrière, today called l'hôpital de la Pitié-Salpêtrière, is situated on a site that once housed a powder factory, from which it gets its name (saltpeter). The hospital was conceived by Louis XIV in 1656, as a general hospital for the poor of Paris.

Today it serves as a large general hospital with several areas of specialization. It was to this hospital that Lady Diana was brought after the horrible automobile accident in which she was killed.

The buildings are built around interior courtyards with classic French gardens and a central chapel, the dome of which can be seen in this photograph.

Painting *Le jour de la visite à l'hôpital* was painted in 1889 by the French painter Jean Geoffroy (1853–1924). The painting presently hangs in the **Hôtel de Ville** in Vichy. Geoffroy was very well known as an illustrator.

National Standards

Communities
Have students write a short article in French about health care where they live. They can write about their local hospital and first aid squad.

Vocabulaire
Mots 1

1 Preparation

Resource Manager

Vocabulary Transparencies 8.2–8.3
Audio Activities TE, pages 81–83
Audio CD 5
Workbook, pages 89–91
Quiz 1, page 39
ExamView® Pro

Bellringer Review

Use BRR Transparency 8.1 or write the following on the board.
Write as many words as you can remember related to health or health care.

2 Presentation

Step 1 Have students close their books. In addition to using Vocabulary Transparencies 8.2–8.3, you may wish to use gestures or dramatizations to introduce many of these terms. Those which lend themselves to easy dramatization are: **glisser, tomber, se couper le doigt, se fouler la cheville, se tordre le genou, se casser la jambe,** and **marcher avec des béquilles.**

Step 2 Refer to yourself or a student model to demonstrate **le bras, le genou, la jambe, le doigt, la cheville,** and **le doigt de pied.**

Vocabulaire
Mots 1

Un accident

glisser
tomber

appeler police secours
se fouler la cheville
la cheville

La pauvre Anne s'est foulé la cheville.

Au service des urgences

le service des urgences
une ambulance
un brancard

Les secouristes sont arrivés.
Ils ont emmené Anne à l'hôpital en ambulance.

Qu'est-ce qui t'est arrivé?
Je me suis fait mal. J'ai eu un accident.
T'en fais pas, c'est pas grave.

248 deux cent quarante-huit

CHAPITRE 8

Reaching All Students

Total Physical Response

(Student 1), venez ici, s'il vous plaît.
Montrez-moi votre bras.
Montrez-moi votre doigt.
Montrez-moi votre pied.
Montrez-moi votre genou.
Montrez-moi votre cheville.
Montrez-moi votre jambe.
Montrez-moi votre ventre.
Montrez-moi vos lèvres.
Montrez-moi vos yeux.
Merci, (Student 1).

(Student 2), venez ici, s'il vous plaît.
Vous allez appeler police secours.
Prenez votre portable.
Décrochez.
Composez le numéro.
Parlez. Dites ce qui est arrivé.
Merci, (Student 2).

Et maintenant (Student 3), venez ici, s'il vous plaît.
Mimez ce qui vous est arrivé.
Vous avez glissé.
Vous êtes tombé(e).
Vous vous êtes foulé la cheville.
Vous marchez avec des béquilles.
Merci, (Student 3).

Vocabulaire

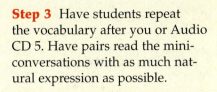

Le corps 🎧

- le bras
- le genou
- le pied
- le doigt de pied
- la jambe

se tordre le genou

- un fauteuil roulant
- une béquille

Émilie s'est cassé la jambe.
Elle marche avec des béquilles.

des points de suture

Vous avez mal où? Montrez-moi.
J'ai mal au doigt.
le doigt

Maryse s'est blessée.
Qu'est-ce qui lui est arrivé?
Elle s'est coupé le doigt.

Ça va mieux.
un pansement

L'infirmière la soigne.
Elle lui fait un pansement.
C'est une petite blessure.

UN ACCIDENT ET L'HÔPITAL

deux cent quarante-neuf 249

Vocabulaire

3 Practice

Quel est le mot?

Attention!
When students are doing the **Quel est le mot?** activities, accept any answer that makes sense. The purpose of these activities is to have students use the new vocabulary. They are not factual recall activities. Thus, it is not necessary for students to remember specific factual information from the vocabulary presentation when answering.

Historiette Each time **Historiette** appears, it means that the answers to the activity form a short story. Encourage students to look at the title of the **Historiette**, since it can help them do the activity.

2 and **3** Have students retell the stories in their own words.

Vocabulaire

Quel est le mot?

1 **Qu'est-ce que c'est?** Identifiez.

1. C'est une ambulance ou une voiture?

2. C'est une jambe ou une cheville?

3. C'est une salle d'opération ou le service des urgences?

4. C'est un brancard ou un fauteuil roulant?

5. C'est un bras ou un genou?

6. C'est un pansement ou un point de suture?

7. C'est un fauteuil roulant ou des béquilles?

8. C'est une blessure ou un pansement?

9. C'est un doigt ou un doigt de pied?

10. C'est un médecin ou une infirmière?

2 **Historiette** **Un petit accident** Répondez d'après les indications.

1. François est tombé? (oui)
2. Il a glissé sur quoi? (de l'eau)
3. Il s'est fait mal? (oui)
4. Il s'est blessé? (oui)
5. Il a pu se relever tout seul? (oui)
6. On a appelé police secours? (non)
7. Il est allé où? (à l'hôpital)
8. Qui l'a emmené à l'hôpital? (son copain)
9. Il est allé où, à l'hôpital? (au service des urgences)
10. On lui a fait combien de points de suture? (dix)

250 ♦ deux cent cinquante

CHAPITRE 8

ANSWERS TO Quel est le mot?

1
1. C'est une ambulance.
2. C'est une jambe.
3. C'est le service des urgences.
4. C'est un fauteuil roulant.
5. C'est un bras.
6. C'est un point de suture.
7. C'est (Ce sont) des béquilles.
8. C'est un pansement.
9. C'est un doigt.
10. C'est une infirmière.

2
1. Oui, François est tombé.
2. Il a glissé sur de l'eau.
3. Oui, il s'est fait mal.
4. Oui, il s'est blessé.
5. Oui, il a pu se relever tout seul.
6. Non, on n'a pas appelé police secours.
7. Il est allé à l'hôpital.
8. Son copain l'a emmené à l'hôpital.
9. À l'hôpital il est allé au service des urgences.
10. On lui a fait dix points de suture.

3 Historiette Tu as déjà eu un accident?
Donnez des réponses personnelles.

1. Tu es déjà tombé(e)?
2. Où est-ce que tu es tombé(e)?
3. Qu'est-ce qui t'est arrivé? Tu as glissé?
4. Tu t'es fait mal? Où?
5. Tu t'es cassé la jambe? Le bras? Le doigt?
6. Tu t'es foulé la cheville ou tordu le genou?
7. Tu t'es coupé le doigt ou le pied?
8. On t'a transporté(e) sur un brancard?
9. On t'a emmené(e) à l'hôpital en ambulance?
10. Tu es allé(e) au service des urgences?
11. Qui t'a soigné(e)?
12. Tu as dû marcher avec des béquilles?

Des secouristes à Paris

4 Un accident Vous voyagez en France avec un(e) ami(e). Vous faites un petit voyage à bicyclette. Votre ami(e) est tombé(e) et vous croyez qu'il/elle s'est cassé le bras. Un(e) secouriste—votre camarade—arrive sur la scène de l'accident. Décrivez ce qui est arrivé et répondez à toutes ses questions.

5 Jeu Un monstre Travaillez avec un(e) camarade. Décrivez un géant ou un monstre. Ensuite, décrivez votre monstre à la classe. Vous pouvez utiliser les mots suivants:

UN ACCIDENT ET L'HÔPITAL

Vocabulaire
Mots 2

1 Preparation

Resource Manager

Vocabulary Transparencies 8.4–8.5
Audio Activities TE, pages 84–86
Audio CD 5
Workbook, page 91
Quiz 2, page 40
ExamView® Pro

Bellringer Review

*Use BRR Transparency 8.2 or write the following on the board.
Imagine you have a cold. Describe your symptoms.*

Note: This Bellringer Review recalls vocabulary from Chapter 2.

2 Presentation

Step 1 Show Vocabulary Transparencies 8.4–8.5. Have students close their books and repeat the words after you or Audio CD 5 as you point to the appropriate illustration on the transparency.

Step 2 Practice some of the expressions by putting them into short sentences. For example: **Faire une piqûre: Le médecin lui a fait une piqûre. Faire une radio: Le médecin lui a fait une radio. Prendre la tension: Le médecin lui a pris la tension,** etc.

Step 3 You may wish to ask the following questions during your presentation: **Bruno est arrivé où? Qui a rempli le formulaire? On lui a fait une radio de l'os? Qu'est-ce qui lui est arrivé? Qu'est-ce que l'anesthésiste lui a fait? Et le chirurgien-orthopédiste?**

Vocabulaire
Mots 2

À l'hôpital

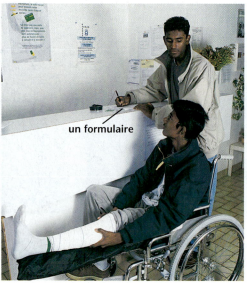

un formulaire

Bruno est arrivé au service des urgences.
Son frère a rempli un formulaire.

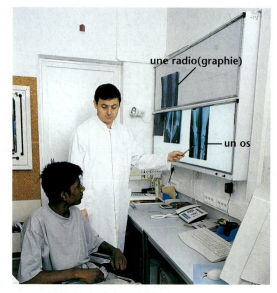

une radio(graphie)

un os

On lui a fait une radio de l'os.
Bruno s'est cassé la jambe.
Il a une fracture compliquée.

prendre le pouls

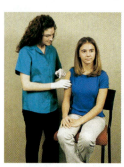

faire une piqûre

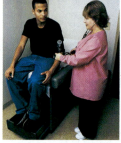

prendre la tension

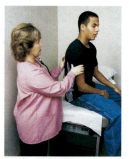

ausculter

252 ❧ *deux cent cinquante-deux*   CHAPITRE 8

Learning from Photos

(page 252) The photos of the young man in the hospital were taken at the **Hôtel-Dieu** in the **4ᵉ arrondissement** of Paris.

Une salle d'opération

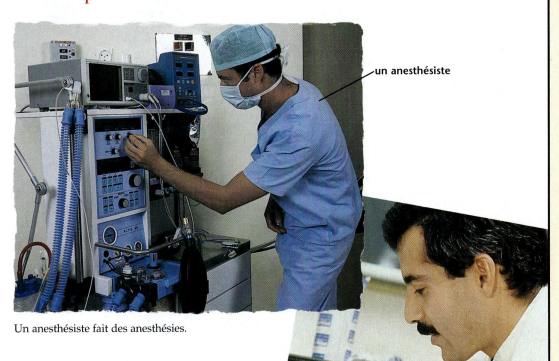

un anesthésiste

Un anesthésiste fait des anesthésies.

Le chirurgien-orthopédiste a remis
   l'os en place.
Il lui a mis la jambe dans le plâtre.
Il l'a plâtrée.

un chirurgien

UN ACCIDENT ET L'HÔPITAL

Vocabulaire
Mots 2

Pronunciation Note: Point out the difference in pronunciation between the singular and plural forms of **os**: **un os,** the final **s** is pronounced; **des os,** the final **s** is silent.

Reaching All Students

Kinesthetic Learners
Dramatize the following:
   remplir un formulaire
   prendre le pouls
   faire une piqûre
   prendre la tension
   ausculter

Additional Practice
Ask the following questions about the photos:
   Où est le malade? Où est la table d'opération? Le chirurgien regarde le malade? Qui va lui faire une anesthésie? Qu'est-ce qu'on peut voir sur la radio? Qui fait une piqûre à la fille? Qui lui prend le pouls? Qui prend la tension au garçon?

FRENCH Online

The **Glencoe World Languages Web site** (french.glencoe.com) offers options that enable you and your students to experience the French-speaking world via the Internet. For each chapter, there are activities, games, and quizzes. In addition, an *Enrichment* section offers students an opportunity to visit Web sites related to the theme of the chapter.

Chapter Projects

 Ça fait mal! Have students select a health problem or injury they learn about in this chapter and write a paragraph about it in French.

Vocabulaire

Quel est le mot?

6 Une visite médicale Jean-François est allé chez le médecin parce qu'il veut jouer dans l'équipe de football cette année. Qu'est-ce que le médecin lui a fait? Répondez.

1. Le médecin a ausculté Jean-François?
2. Le médecin lui a dit de respirer à fond?
3. Le médecin lui a pris le pouls?
4. Le médecin lui a pris sa tension?
5. Le médecin lui a fait une piqûre?
6. Le médecin lui a fait une radio?

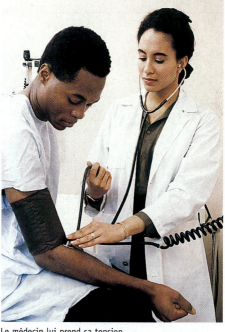

Le médecin lui prend sa tension.

7 Historiette À l'hôpital Choisissez.

1. On a emmené Jacques à l'hôpital en ___.
   a. camion   b. bicyclette   c. ambulance
2. Il est allé tout de suite ___.
   a. à la salle d'opération   b. chez le médecin   c. au service des urgences
3. Quand Jacques est arrivé à l'hôpital, son père a rempli ___ pour lui.
   a. un formulaire   b. une piqûre   c. un os
4. Jacques croit qu'il s'est cassé ___.
   a. les yeux   b. la bouche   c. la jambe
5. On lui a fait ___ de l'os.
   a. une radio   b. une fracture   c. une piqûre
6. Le chirurgien lui dit qu'il a ___.
   a. une fracture compliquée   b. une piqûre   c. un os
7. ___ lui a fait une anesthésie.
   a. Le chirurgien-orthopédiste   b. L'infirmier   c. L'anesthésiste
8. ___ a remis l'os en place.
   a. Le chirurgien-orthopédiste   b. L'infirmier   c. Le radiologue
9. Le chirurgien-orthopédiste lui a mis la jambe dans ___.
   a. les béquilles   b. le plâtre   c. le brancard

254 ❖ deux cent cinquante-quatre   CHAPITRE 8

8 C'est quel mot? Pour chaque définition, donnez le mot exact.
1. une personne qui opère, qui fait des interventions chirurgicales, qui fait des opérations
2. des personnes qui aident les médecins et soignent les malades dans un hôpital
3. le squelette humain en a 206
4. le négatif d'une photo d'un os, d'un organe

 9 À l'hôpital Vous êtes réceptionniste dans un hôpital. Le/La patient(e)—votre camarade—est blessé(e). Il/Elle vient du Québec et ne parle pas bien anglais. Posez-lui les questions nécessaires pour remplir le formulaire d'admission. Vous lui demandez son nom, son adresse, son âge, etc. Vous voulez savoir aussi ce qui lui est arrivé, où il/elle a mal, etc.

 10 Chez le médecin Vous n'avez pas eu d'accident, mais vous ne vous sentez pas bien. Vous croyez que vous avez la grippe et vous décidez d'aller chez le médecin (votre camarade). Le médecin vous pose des questions et vous lui décrivez vos symptômes. Vous pouvez utiliser les mots et expressions suivantes.

éternuer	des frissons	une ordonnance
tousser	de la fièvre	des comprimés
avoir mal à la tête	la gorge qui gratte	

 For more practice using words from Mots 1 and Mots 2, do Activity 14 on page H15 at the end of this book.

UN ACCIDENT ET L'HÔPITAL

deux cent cinquante-cinq ✤ 255

Structure

1 Preparation

Resource Manager

Audio Activities TE, pages 86–89
Audio CD 5
Workbook, pages 92–96
Quizzes 3–5, pages 41–43
ExamView® Pro

Bellringer Review

Use BRR Transparency 8.3 or write the following on the board. Complete.

Ah, zut! Le _____ de ma voiture est presque vide. J'ai besoin d'_____. Il faut aller à la _____. Je vais faire le _____. Et puis je vais _____ la pression des _____.

2 Presentation

Les pronoms interrogatifs et relatifs

Step 1 Students may find this point difficult. Go over it thoroughly, but do not strive for mastery at this point. Differentiating between **ce qui** and **ce que** takes a great deal of ear training. For this reason these expressions will be reintroduced often.

Structure

Les pronoms interrogatifs et relatifs
Expressing "what"

1. To ask the question "what" in French, you use the interrogative expressions **qu'est-ce qui** or **qu'est-ce que**. **Qu'est-ce qui** is the subject of the verb and **qu'est-ce que** is the object.

Sujet	Objet
Qu'est-ce qui intéresse Luc?	Qu'est-ce que Luc veut faire?
Qu'est-ce qui est arrivé?	Qu'est-ce qu'il a?

Rappelez-vous que...
Que becomes **qu'** before a vowel. **Qui** does not change.

2. To introduce an indirect question with "what" in French, you use **ce qui** or **ce que**. Note that **ce qui**, just like **qu'est-ce qui**, is used as the subject and that **ce que**, just like **qu'est-ce que**, is used as the object.

Sujet	Objet
Elle demande ce qui intéresse Luc.	Elle demande ce que Luc veut faire.
Il veut savoir ce qui se passe.	Il veut savoir ce qu'il a.

3. Compare the following forms.

	Question directe	Question indirecte
Sujet	Qu'est-ce qui se passe?	Je ne sais pas ce qui se passe.
Objet	Qu'est-ce que Luc a dit?	Je ne sais pas ce que Luc a dit.

Note that **ce qui** is usually followed by a verb and **ce que** is usually followed by a subject and a verb.

Comment dit-on?

11 Je n'ai pas entendu. Répondez en utilisant **qu'est-ce que** ou **qu'est-ce qui**. Suivez le modèle.

L'infirmier a mis *un pansement* sur la blessure. →
Qu'est-ce que l'infirmier a mis sur la blessure?

1. *Ton livre de biologie* est sur la table.
2. Le malade a eu *un accident*.
3. Il s'est cassé *le bras*.
4. *La science-fiction* intéresse Paul.
5. La mère de Romain s'est coupé *le doigt*.
6. *La médecine* intéresse beaucoup ma sœur.

12 Dis donc! Tu sais ce qui est arrivé?
Répondez que oui.

1. Tu sais ce qui est arrivé?
2. Tu sais ce qui se passe maintenant?
3. Tu sais ce que le médecin a dit à Charlotte?
4. Tu sais ce qu'il a fait?
5. Tu sais ce que le médecin a prescrit?
6. Tu sais ce qu'il a écrit sur l'ordonnance?
7. Tu as compris ce que le pharmacien a dit?

13 Je ne suis pas content(e)!
Complétez avec **ce qui** ou **ce que**.

1. Je sais bien ____ se passe.
2. Je ne comprends pas ____ tu dis.
3. Je ne veux pas savoir ____ est arrivé.
4. Je veux te dire ____ il a fait.
5. Je crois ____ je vois, c'est tout.
6. Je ne crois jamais ____ elle dit.

UN ACCIDENT ET L'HÔPITAL

deux cent cinquante-sept 257

Structure

1 Preparation

Bellringer Review

Use BRR Transparency 8.4 or write the following on the board. Complete with the correct pronoun.
1. L'ordonnance. Le médecin me _____ a donnée.
2. Les médicaments. Le pharmacien me _____ a vendus.
3. Les comprimés. Je _____ ai pris.
4. Le pansement. Je ne _____ touche pas.

2 Presentation

Les pronoms et l'impératif

Step 1 Guide students through Items 1–3.

Step 2 Provide students with this summary of pronoun use.
1. The pronoun always precedes the verb except in the affirmative command. There it follows the verb.
2. **Me** and **te** become **moi** and **toi** when they follow the verb.

Step 3 You may wish to have students do the following easy exercises before beginning the activities in the text. Tell them to follow the model:
Ne le regardez pas. Regardez-le.
   Ne le touchez pas.
   Ne le dites pas.
   Ne le faites pas.
Now tell them to follow this model: **Regardez-le. Non, ne le regardez pas.**
   Touchez-le.
   Dites-le.
   Faites-le.
Finally, have them follow this model: **Ne me regarde pas. Regarde-moi.**
   Ne m'écoute pas.
   Ne me parle pas.
   Ne me donne pas ça.

Structure

Les pronoms et l'impératif
Telling people what to do

1. In the affirmative command, object pronouns follow the verb. They are attached to the verb by a hyphen.

   La **piqûre**? Faites-**la** tout de suite!
   Les **radios**? Regarde-**les** maintenant!
   À **Paul**? Prends-**lui** sa température!

   Note that in the negative command, the pronouns precede the verb in the usual way.

   La piqûre? Ne **la** fais pas tout de suite!

2. In the affirmative command, **me** becomes **moi** and **te** becomes **toi**. Study the following.

Négatif	Affirmatif
Ne **me** dites pas ça!	Dites-**moi** ça!
Ne **me** donne pas ça!	Donne-**moi** ça!
Ne **te** couche pas!	Couche-**toi**!
Ne **te** lève pas!	Lève-**toi**!

3. In the affirmative command, the pronouns **le**, **la**, **les** always precede the other object pronouns—**lui**, **leur**, **moi**, **toi**, **nous**, **vous**. Note that in the negative command the order is the usual one.

Négatif	Affirmatif
Ne **me le** donnez pas!	Donnez-**le**-**moi**!
Ne **les leur** achète pas!	Achète-**les**-**leur**!

Rappelez-vous que...
Object pronouns come directly before the verb or the auxiliary.
La piqûre? Je **la** fais tout de suite.
À Paul? Je **lui** ai parlé il y a deux minutes.
Sa température? Je **la lui** prends tous les jours.

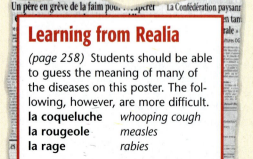

Learning from Realia

(page 258) Students should be able to guess the meaning of many of the diseases on this poster. The following, however, are more difficult.
la coqueluche   whooping cough
la rougeole   measles
la rage   rabies

Comment dit-on?

14 Bon! Fais-le si tu veux. Répondez d'après le modèle.

Je vais regarder la télé.

Bon! Regarde-la, si tu veux.

1. Je vais regarder ce film.
2. Je vais écouter ton CD.
3. Je vais lire mon magazine.
4. Je vais écrire ma lettre.
5. Je vais acheter les billets.
6. Je vais mettre le couvert.
7. Je vais faire la vaisselle.
8. Je vais aider Maman.

15 Ne le fais pas maintenant. Refaites l'Activité 14 d'après le modèle.

—Je vais regarder la télé.
—S'il te plaît, ne la regarde pas maintenant.

16 D'accord, vas-y! Répondez d'après le modèle.

Je voudrais écrire à Michel. D'accord, écris-lui.

1. Je voudrais téléphoner à mes grands-parents.
2. Je voudrais parler à Simone.
3. Je voudrais écrire à mon copain.
4. Je voudrais acheter quelque chose à mes parents.
5. Je voudrais dire bonjour au professeur de français.

Structure

3 Practice

Comment dit-on?

14 to **16** You may do these activities with books open or closed.

LEVELING
E: Activities 14, 15, 16
A: Activities 14, 15, 16

ANSWERS TO Comment dit-on?

14
1. Bon! Regarde-le, si tu veux.
2. Bon! Écoute-le, si tu veux.
3. Bon! Lis-le, si tu veux.
4. Bon! Écris-la, si tu veux.
5. Bon! Achète-les, si tu veux.
6. Bon! Mets-le, si tu veux.
7. Bon! Fais-la, si tu veux.
8. Bon! Aide-la, si tu veux.

15
1. S'il te plaît, ne le regarde pas maintenant.
2. S'il te plaît, ne l'écoute pas maintenant.
3. S'il te plaît, ne le lis pas maintenant.
4. S'il te plaît, ne l'écris pas maintenant.
5. S'il te plaît, ne les achète pas maintenant.
6. S'il te plaît, ne le mets pas maintenant.
7. S'il te plaît, ne la fais pas maintenant.
8. S'il te plaît, ne l'aide pas maintenant.

16
1. D'accord, téléphone-leur.
2. D'accord, parle-lui.
3. D'accord, écris-lui.
4. D'accord, achète-leur quelque chose.
5. D'accord, dis-lui bonjour.

Structure

3 Practice (continued)

17 Expansion: Have students redo the activity making negative commands.

18 Expansion: Have students redo the activity making positive commands.

19 Expansion: Have students redo the activity making negative commands.

Learning from Realia

(page 260 top) Have students find the commands in this little song.
   Prête-moi
   Ouvre-moi
Explain to students that **une plume** is **un stylo**. Have them look at the illustrations of the candle and the moon to figure out the meaning of the song.

(page 260 bottom) Have students identify all commands in the poster.

LEVELING
E: Activities 17, 18, 21, 22
A: Activities 17, 18, 19, 20, 21, 23

Structure

 17 Alors, fais-le! Répondez d'après le modèle.

—Je vais me maquiller.
—Alors, maquille-toi!

1. Je vais me lever.
2. Je vais me laver.
3. Je vais me brosser.
4. Je vais me raser.
5. Je vais me peigner.
6. Je vais m'habiller.
7. Je vais me coucher.

 18 Ce n'est pas nécessaire. Répondez d'après le modèle.

1. Je me lave?
2. Je me peigne?
3. Je me rase?
4. Je m'habille bien?

 19 Maintenant ou plus tard? Répondez d'après le modèle.

—Je vous passe le sel?
—Oui, passez-le moi, s'il vous plaît.

1. Je vous passe le beurre?
2. Je vous passe le lait?
3. Je vous passe le poivre?
4. Je vous passe le sucre?
5. Je vous passe la baguette?
6. Je vous passe la crème?
7. Je vous passe les olives?

 20 Attention à l'accident! Le pauvre Marc (votre camarade)! Il a toujours de petits accidents. Marc vous dira ce qui lui est arrivé et vous lui direz ce qu'il faut faire ou ne pas faire.

260 deux cent soixante   CHAPITRE 8

ANSWERS TO Comment dit-on?

17
1. Alors, lève-toi.
2. Alors, lave-toi.
3. Alors, brosse-toi.
4. Alors, rase-toi.
5. Alors, peigne-toi.
6. Alors, habille-toi.
7. Alors, couche-toi.

18
1. Non, ne te lave pas.
2. Non, ne te peigne pas.
3. Non, ne te rase pas.
4. Non, ne t'habille pas bien.

19
1. Oui, passez-le moi, s'il vous plaît.
2. Oui, passez-le moi, s'il vous plaît.
3. Oui, passez-le moi, s'il vous plaît.
4. Oui, passez-le moi, s'il vous plaît.
5. Oui, passez-la moi, s'il vous plaît.
6. Oui, passez-la moi, s'il vous plaît.
7. Oui, passez-les moi, s'il vous plaît.

20 Answers will vary. Students can use the vocabulary from this chapter.

Structure

Le superlatif des adjectifs
Comparing people and things

The superlative expresses "the most" or "the least." To form the superlative in French you use the definite article **le, la, les** with **plus** or **moins**. The superlative is followed by **de**. Study the following chart.

> Pierre est le plus sérieux de la classe.
> Marie est la moins sérieuse de la classe.
>
> Marc et Sophie sont les plus sérieux de la classe.
> Anne et Virginie sont les moins sérieuses de la classe.

Rappelez-vous que...
You use the comparative **plus** or **moins... que** to express "more," or "less . . . than."
Ce docteur est plus (moins) sympathique que l'autre.

21 Dans une boutique Conversez selon le modèle.

—La robe rose est très jolie.
—Oui, c'est la plus jolie de la boutique.

1. Le pantalon noir est très élégant.
2. Le pull rouge est très joli.
3. Les chaussures marron sont très chères.
4. Le manteau bleu marine est très beau.
5. La jupe bleue est très belle.
6. La robe noire est très habillée.

22 Historiette Ma famille Donnez des réponses personnelles.

1. Qui est le plus jeune ou la plus jeune de ta famille?
2. Qui est le plus âgé ou la plus âgée de ta famille?
3. Qui est le plus amusant ou la plus amusante de ta famille?
4. Qui est le plus beau ou la plus belle de ta famille?
5. Qui est le plus intelligent ou la plus intelligente de ta famille?
6. Qui est le plus timide ou la plus timide de ta famille?
7. Qui est le plus sérieux ou la plus sérieuse de ta famille?

23 Comparaisons Travaillez avec un(e) camarade. Comparez des personnes que vous connaissez ou que vous ne connaissez pas: une star de cinéma, un champion de basket-ball, par exemple.

UN ACCIDENT ET L'HÔPITAL   deux cent soixante et un ❖ 261

Structure

1 Preparation

Bellringer Review

Use BRR Transparency 8.5 or write the following on the board. List as many adjectives as you can that you can use to describe people.

2 Presentation

Le superlatif des adjectifs

Step 1 Lead students through the explanation on page 261.

Step 2 Have students share their word lists from the Bellringer Review activity.

Step 3 Draw three stick figures on the board and name them. Using their list of adjectives, have students make up sentences comparing one of the stick figures to the other two.

Step 4 Provide additional examples by comparing objects or students in the room. For example: **Regardez. Roland est le plus grand de la classe.**

Step 5 Tell students that the superlative is followed by **de** in French. Do not explain that it is **de** in French and "in" in English. When this comparison is not made, students tend not to use **dans**.

ANSWERS TO Comment dit-on?

21
1. Oui, c'est le plus élégant de la boutique.
2. Oui, c'est le plus joli de la boutique.
3. Oui, ce sont les plus chères de la boutique.
4. Oui, c'est le plus beau de la boutique.
5. Oui, c'est la plus belle de la boutique.
6. Oui, c'est la plus habillée de la boutique.

22 Answers will vary.
Students can use words such as **mon cousin, ma cousine, mon oncle, ma tante**, etc. Agreement will depend upon the relative selected.

23 Answers will vary.

Structure

1 Preparation

Bellringer Review

Use BRR Transparency 8.6 or write the following on the board. Rewrite the following commands using object pronouns.
1. Mets le contact.
2. Ne vérifie pas la pression.
3. Mets le clignotant.
4. Ne paie pas le péage.

2 Presentation

 Meilleur/mieux

Step 1 Lead students through Items 1 and 2 on page 262.

Learning from Photos
(page 262) Have students create a dialogue between the students shown in the photo.

Structure

Meilleur/mieux
Expressing "better"

1. The adjective **bon(ne)(s)** has irregular forms in the comparative and superlative—**meilleur(e)(s)** and **le (la, les) meilleur(e)(s)**.

   Charles est bon en maths.
   Mais Vincent est meilleur en maths que Charles.
   Caroline est la meilleure en maths de la classe.
   Caroline et son frère sont les meilleurs en maths de toute l'école!

2. The adverb **bien** also has an irregular comparative and superlative: **mieux, le mieux**.

   Luc chante bien. Mais moi, je chante mieux.
   Mais c'est Virginie qui chante le mieux.

   Note that **mieux,** just like **bien,** is an adverb and therefore is invariable.

Magali est meilleure en maths que Thomas.

262 ✦ deux cent soixante-deux

CHAPITRE 8

Comment dit-on?

24 **Toi ou quelqu'un d'autre?** Donnez des réponses personnelles.

1. Tu skies bien?
2. Qui skie mieux que toi?
3. Qui est un meilleur skieur ou une meilleure skieuse que toi?
4. De tous tes amis, qui skie le mieux?
5. Qui est le meilleur skieur ou la meilleure skieuse?
6. Tu nages bien?
7. Qui nage mieux que toi?
8. Qui est un meilleur nageur ou une meilleure nageuse que toi?
9. De tous tes amis, qui nage le mieux?
10. Qui est le meilleur nageur ou la meilleure nageuse?

To learn more about skiing and other winter sports in the Francophone world, go to the Glencoe French Web site: french.glencoe.com

Des skieurs dans les Alpes

Vous êtes sur le bon chemin. Allez-y!

deux cent soixante-trois 263

ANSWERS TO Comment dit-on?

24 *Answers will vary.*

Note: Agreement will vary depending upon the subject the student gives.

1. Oui, je skie bien.
2. _____ skie mieux que moi.
3. _____ est un meilleur skieur que moi.
4. _____ skie le mieux de tous mes amis.
5. _____ est la meilleure skieuse.
6. Oui, je nage bien.
7. _____ nage mieux que moi.
8. _____ est une meilleure nageuse que moi.
9. _____ nage le mieux de tous mes amis.
10. _____ est la meilleure nageuse.

Structure

3 Practice

Comment dit-on?

Reaching All Students

Additional Practice
You may wish to ask the following questions.
1. Qui est le meilleur danseur de la classe? Qui danse le mieux?
2. Qui est le meilleur joueur de foot de la classe? Qui joue le mieux au foot?
3. Qui est la meilleure danseuse de la classe? Qui danse le mieux?
4. Qui est la meilleure joueuse de foot? Qui joue le mieux au foot?

Learning from Photos
(page 263) Have students recall as much as they can about skiing. Call on students to give random sentences about this topic.

Allez-y!
At this point in the chapter, students have learned all the vocabulary and grammar necessary to complete the chapter. The conversation and cultural readings that follow recycle all the material learned up to this point.

LEVELING
E: Activity 24

263

Conversation

1 Preparation

Resource Manager
Audio Activities TE, pages 89–90
Audio CD 5
CD-ROM

Bellringer Review

Use BRR Transparency 8.7 or write the following on the board.
Identify the following people.
Il distribue le courrier.
Elle travaille à la banque.
Il fait le plein.
Il donne des contraventions.
Elle sert une collation à bord d'un avion.
Elle fait un pansement.

2 Presentation

Step 1 Tell students they will hear a conversation in an emergency room. Have students close their books and listen as you read the conversation aloud or play Audio CD 5. Have students listen carefully to the recorded version and pay particular attention to the intonation.

Step 2 Have pairs of students practice reading the conversation with as much expression as possible.

Step 3 Have two students read the conversation to the class.

Step 4 After going over the conversation, have students say as much as they can about the photograph.

Learning from Photos
(page 264) This photo was taken at the **Hôtel-Dieu** in the **4ᵉ arrondissment** of Paris.

Conversation

Au service des urgences

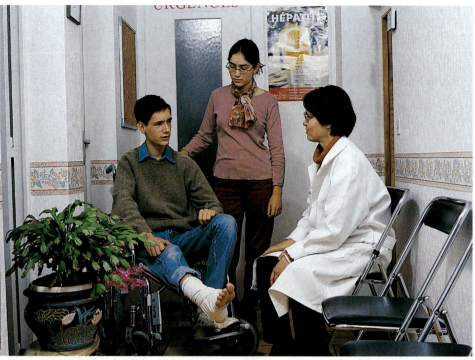

Juliette: Ben, mon pauvre vieux, qu'est-ce qui t'arrive?
Fabien: Oh, je suis tombé et je me suis fait mal à la cheville.
Juliette: Qu'est-ce que tu attends?
Fabien: Le résultat de mes radios.
Médecin: Fabien Morel, c'est vous?
Fabien: Oui, c'est moi.
Médecin: Alors, c'est bien une fracture.
Fabien: Je me suis cassé la cheville?
Médecin: Oui. Mais je vais vous arranger ça. Je vais vous plâtrer et vous pourrez rentrer tranquillement chez vous.
Fabien: Euh… ça va faire mal?
Médecin: Non, ne vous en faites pas! On va vous faire une petite anesthésie locale.
Fabien: Juliette, tu restes avec moi, hein?

Vous avez compris?

Répondez.

1. Fabien a mal où?
2. Comment est-ce qu'il s'est blessé?
3. Qu'est-ce qu'il attend?
4. Quel est le résultat des radios?
5. Qu'est-ce que le médecin va faire?
6. Pourquoi est-ce que ça ne va pas faire mal?
7. Est-ce que Fabien va passer la nuit à l'hôpital?

Reaching All Students

Additional Practice After completing the **Conversation** activity, ask a student to retell the situation of the conversation in his or her own words.

Answers to Vous avez compris?

1. Il a mal à la cheville.
2. Il est tombé.
3. Il attend le résultat de ses radios.
4. C'est une fracture.
5. Elle va plâtrer la cheville.
6. On va lui faire une petite anesthésie locale.
7. Non, il va pouvoir rentrer chez lui.

Parlons un peu plus

 A Ne vous en faites pas! Votre meilleur(e) ami(e) a eu un petit accident. Vous étiez ensemble quand ça s'est passé. C'est vous qui téléphonez aux parents de votre ami(e) pour leur dire ce qui est arrivé. Le père ou la mère de votre ami(e) (votre camarade) répond au téléphone et vous pose beaucoup de questions. Rassurez-le/la!

Il téléphone de l'Hôtel-Dieu à Paris.

Une visite médicale

  B Une visite médicale Vous avez obtenu une bourse *(scholarship)* pour aller en France. Mais avant de partir, il faut passer une visite médicale. Votre camarade est l'assistant(e) du médecin. Il/Elle vous pose des questions sur votre état de santé. Répondez à ses questions. Ensuite changez de rôle.

UN ACCIDENT ET L'HÔPITAL

deux cent soixante-cinq 265

Conversation

Glencoe Technology

 CD-ROM
On the CD-ROM, students can watch a dramatization of this conversation. They can then play the role of any one of the characters and record themselves in the conversation.

3 Practice

Parlons un peu plus

These activities enable students to use the vocabulary and structures learned in the chapter in open-ended exchanges. You may wish to assign different activities to different groups or allow the students to choose the activities they wish to do.

LEVELING
E: Conversation

  ANSWERS TO Parlons un peu plus

A and B
Answers to these open-ended activities will vary depending on the accident the student wishes to speak about and, in Activity B, the questions the students ask each other. Students can use the vocabulary presented in this chapter and also reincorporate vocabulary from Chapter 2.

Lectures culturelles

Resource Manager
Audio Activities TE, pages 91–92
Audio CD 5

Bellringer Review
Use BRR Transparency 8.8 or write the following on the board. Write that the following people are the most or best of the following categories.
1. Jeanne / intelligente / classe
2. Marc / bon / en maths / classe
3. Julie et Colette / sympathiques / toutes les filles

National Standards

Cultures
This reading about an emergency hospital visit in France familiarizes students with aspects of the health care system in France.

Comparisons
Students learn that, unlike in the United States, the majority of medical costs of French people are paid by the French social security system.

Presentation

Note: This **Lecture** provides many examples of the contrast between the **passé composé** and the imperfect.

Pre-reading

Step 1 Find out if any students have ever had a broken bone. Ask how the injury was treated.

Step 2 Have students look at a map of Paris or use the Map Transparency M 3. Say:
L'Hôtel-Dieu se trouve à Paris sur l'Île de la Cité tout près de Notre-Dame.

LEVELING
E: Reading

Lectures culturelles

Reading Strategy
Visualizing
Visualizing can help you to better understand a passage. As you read, use the details that the writer gives you to form mental pictures. Pause and really try to "see" the scene. If the passage includes characters, observe how they interact with each other. This attention to detail will help you clarify what you read.

À l'Hôtel-Dieu, à toute vitesse!

L'autre jour, j'étais avec mon ami Hugo quand il a eu un petit accident. Je dis un «petit» accident, mais en fait c'était assez grave. On était en ville et Hugo ne faisait pas très attention où il marchait. Il y avait des travaux[1] et il y avait un grand trou[2] dans le trottoir[3]. Hugo ne l'a pas vu et il est tombé dedans. Il s'est fait très mal et il ne pouvait pas se relever. Moi, j'étais sûr qu'il était blessé.

J'ai appelé police secours. J'ai composé le 17 et la police est arrivée en quelques minutes. Les secouristes ont allongé Hugo sur un brancard et l'ont emmené à l'Hôtel-Dieu, un grand hôpital en face de Notre-Dame. Je l'ai accompagné à l'hôpital dans l'ambulance. Quand nous sommes arrivés à l'hôpital, j'ai remarqué que Hugo souffrait beaucoup. Je l'ai aidé à remplir les formulaires nécessaires au service des urgences. Un médecin l'a examiné et nous a envoyés au service radio. La radio a indiqué une fracture compliquée. Nous sommes donc allés au service orthopédie où un

[1] travaux *construction work*
[2] trou *hole*
[3] trottoir *sidewalk*

La cour de l'Hôtel-Dieu à Paris

L'Hôtel-Dieu à Paris

Learning from Photos
Recycling
(page 266 right) Have students look at the sign **hôpitaux de Paris.** Have them give the singular and then review:

le journal	les journaux
le général	les généraux
le canal	les canaux

Cross-Cultural Comparison
Point out that many of the older hospitals in France look like beautiful châteaux. The newer medical centers look more like the hospitals in the United States.

chirurgien-orthopédiste et une anesthésiste nous attendaient. L'anesthésiste a fait une anesthésie locale à Hugo et le chirurgien a remis l'os en place. Hugo a pu quitter l'hôpital avec la cheville dans le plâtre et des béquilles. Le chirurgien lui a fait une ordonnance pour des comprimés contre la douleur[4].

Qui paie les frais[5] hospitaliers? C'est la Sécurité sociale, donc l'État[6]. En France, les frais médicaux sont remboursés à 80% par la Sécurité sociale.

[4] contre la douleur *for pain*
[5] frais *expenses*
[6] État *government*

Vous avez compris?

Un accident Répondez.
1. Qui a eu un accident?
2. Comment est arrivé cet accident?
3. Qu'est-ce que Hugo n'a pas vu?
4. L'ami de Hugo a appelé police secours. Pourquoi?
5. Comment est-ce que Hugo est allé à l'hôpital?
6. Qui l'a accompagné?
7. Où est-ce que les deux copains ont rempli des formulaires?
8. Qui s'est occupé de Hugo?
9. Qu'est-ce que la radio a indiqué?
10. Qui a mis la cheville de Hugo dans le plâtre?
11. Le chirurgien a fait une ordonnance pour quels médicaments?
12. Quel service rembourse les frais hospitaliers en France?

Lecture supplémentaire

Médecins Sans Frontières

C'est qui? C'est quoi?

L'organisation Médecins Sans Frontières (MSF) est née en 1971. Un groupe de médecins français invente l'aide médicale d'urgence. Ces médecins sont allés au Biafra en Afrique avec la Croix-Rouge[1]. En trente mois, ils ont vu mourir un million de Biafrais! Ils ont fait tout leur possible pour soigner les victimes des combats et de la famine. Mais la situation était désespérée. À leur retour en France, ils créent Médecins Sans Frontières.

Qui sont les Médecins Sans Frontières?

Au début, les Médecins Sans Frontières—les *French Doctors* comme on les appelle souvent maintenant—étaient peu nombreux. De nos jours, environ trois mille volontaires partent en mission avec Médecins Sans Frontières. Parmi eux, il y a des médecins, des chirurgiens, des infirmiers et infirmières. Mais les volontaires n'appartiennent[2] pas tous au corps médical. Il y a aussi des personnes responsables des questions de matériel et d'administration. Pour leur travail, les membres de Médecins Sans Frontières sont très peu payés.

[1] Croix-Rouge *Red Cross*
[2] appartiennent *belong*

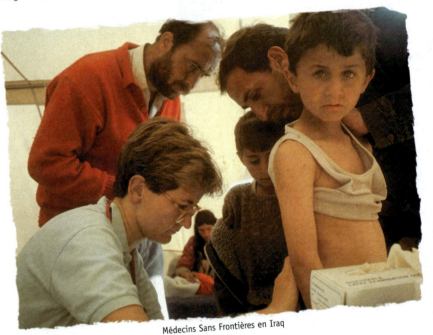
Médecins Sans Frontières en Iraq

Où intervient Médecins Sans Frontières?

Médecins Sans Frontières est présent actuellement[3] dans plus de soixante pays. Chaque année, de nouvelles missions ouvrent et d'autres ferment. Médecins Sans Frontières est la plus grande organisation médicale d'urgence. Elle se retrouve dans des zones de conflits, dans des camps de réfugiés et dans des régions qui ont été ravagées par une catastrophe naturelle comme un tremblement de terre[4], par exemple.

Le rôle de Médecins Sans Frontières est aussi d'alerter l'opinion publique. Tous les ans, l'organisation publie un rapport sur les populations en danger.

En 1999, Médecins Sans Frontières a reçu le prestigieux Prix Nobel de la Paix.

[3] actuellement *nowadays*
[4] tremblement de terre *earthquake*

Vous avez compris?

Une organisation non-gouvernementale (une O.N.G.)
Expliquez.
1. comment l'organisation Médecins Sans Frontières est née
2. qui sont les volontaires
3. où travaillent les volontaires
4. un deuxième rôle de Médecins Sans Frontières
5. le prix que l'organisation a reçu

CONNEXIONS

National Standards

Connections
This reading about Louis Pasteur and the Pasteur Institute establishes a connection with another discipline, allowing students to reinforce and further their knowledge of microbiology through the study of French.

Attention!

The readings in the **Connexions** section are optional. They focus on some of the major disciplines taught in schools and universities. The vocabulary is useful for discussing such topics as history, literature, art, economics, business, science, etc. You may choose any of the following ways to do the readings in the **Connexions** section.

Independent reading Have students read the selections and do the post-reading activities as homework, which you collect. This option is least intrusive on class time and requires a minimum of teacher involvement.

Homework with in-class follow-up Assign the readings and post-reading activities as homework. Review and discuss the material in class the next day.

Intensive in-class activity This option includes a pre-reading vocabulary presentation, in-class reading and discussion, assignment of the activities for homework, and a discussion of the assignment in class the next day.

CONNEXIONS

Les sciences

Louis Pasteur et l'Institut Pasteur

The Pasteur Institute in Paris is one of the world's renowned institutions for medical and pharmaceutical research. The Institute is named after a famous French scientist—Louis Pasteur. You may recognize his name from the word *pasteurized* (as in pasteurized milk). Pasteur is considered the founder of the science of microbiology—the study of germs. The young Frenchman, who thought he wanted to be an artist, was the first to develop a vaccine against rabies, which would save millions of lives.

L'Institut Pasteur à Paris

Louis Pasteur

Louis Pasteur (1822–1895)

Louis Pasteur est né en 1822 dans le Jura, près de la Suisse. Au collège, il n'était pas très bon élève. Ses cours ne l'intéressaient pas beaucoup, mais il aimait le dessin. On l'appelait «l'artiste». Après le lycée, Louis Pasteur pense devenir professeur et entre à l'École Normale, un institut qui forme les professeurs. À l'École Normale, il se passionne pour les sciences et passe son temps à faire de la recherche. Il se spécialise en chimie.

En 1854, il commence à étudier ce que nous appelons aujourd'hui des microbes. Pasteur, lui, appelait ces microbes des «germes». Une nouvelle science est née: la microbiologie!

En 1873, Pasteur présente à l'Académie de Médecine un rapport qui révolutionne la médecine. Avant ce rapport, on croyait que c'était le corps humain qui créait des maladies comme la typhoïde et le choléra. Mais au cours de ses recherches, Pasteur a découvert que toutes les maladies étaient causées par des micro-organismes. On leur a donné le nom de «microbes». Pour Pasteur, ces microbes sont partout. C'est pourquoi il dit aux chirurgiens de l'époque de se laver les mains avant d'opérer leurs patients et de laver soigneusement[1] tous leurs instruments, c'est-à-dire, de pratiquer l'asepsie. Malheureusement on ne l'écoute pas beaucoup. Pourquoi? Parce que Pasteur n'est pas médecin. Il est chimiste et biologiste.

[1] soigneusement *carefully*

Pasteur ne s'arrête pas là. Il continue ses recherches. Il veut lutter[2] contre les microbes. Ses recherches sur les maladies infectieuses des animaux le conduisent[3] à découvrir la vaccination. En 1885, il réalise le vaccin contre la rage[4]. Il vaccine alors pour la première fois un être humain, un petit garçon de neuf ans—Joseph Meister. Le petit Joseph a été mordu[5] par un chien enragé. Pasteur lui sauve la vie[6]. C'est la victoire, après quarante ans de recherches.

Vaccination contre la rage à l'Institut Pasteur

L'Institut Pasteur (1888)

L'enthousiasme est grand, non seulement en France, mais dans le monde entier. L'Académie des Sciences reçoit de l'argent de nombreux pays pour la construction d'un centre de recherches en microbiologie. L'Institut Pasteur est inauguré en 1888. Et qui est son concierge? C'est… Joseph Meister.

De nos jours, il y a des instituts Pasteur un peu partout dans le monde. À l'Institut Pasteur de Paris, il y a un centre de recherches et un centre d'enseignement[7]. En 1983, c'est à l'Institut Pasteur que le docteur Montagnier a isolé le virus du sida (syndrome immunodéficitaire acquis). Aujourd'hui, on continue à faire des recherches pour trouver une cure à cette terrible maladie.

[2] lutter *fight*
[3] conduisent *lead*
[4] rage *rabies*
[5] mordu *bitten*
[6] vie *life*
[7] enseignement *teaching*

La fabrication de vaccins à l'Institut Pasteur

Vous avez compris?

Des informations Trouvez les informations suivantes dans la lecture.

1. ce qui intéressait beaucoup Pasteur quand il était jeune
2. les deux sciences qu'il a étudiées
3. la science qu'il a fondée ou découverte
4. où il disait que les microbes se trouvaient
5. ce qu'est l'asepsie
6. le vaccin qu'il a réalisé
7. la découverte du professeur Montagnier

C'est à vous

Use what you have learned

Bellringer Review

Use BRR Transparency 8.9 or write the following on the board.
List as many things as you can that are found in a kitchen.

Recycling

These activities allow students to use the vocabulary and structure from this chapter in completely open-ended, real-life situations.

Presentation

Encourage students to say as much as possible when they do these activities. Tell them not to be afraid to make mistakes, since the goal of these activities is real-life communication. If someone in the group makes an error, allow the others to politely correct him or her. Let students choose the activities they would like to do.

You may wish to separate students into pairs or groups. Encourage students to elaborate on the basic theme and to be creative. They may use props, pictures, or posters if they wish.

Reaching All Students

Additional Practice
Display Communication Transparency C 8. Have students work in groups to make up as many questions as they can about the illustration. Have groups take turns asking and answering the questions.

C'est à vous

Use what you have learned

PARLER 1

Les services médicaux de la municipalité
✓ **Describe medical services**

Il y a un(e) jeune Québécois(e) (votre camarade) qui passe un semestre dans votre école. Il/Elle a quelques questions sur les services médicaux offerts par votre municipalité. Décrivez-lui l'hôpital de votre région. Si nécessaire, procurez-vous une brochure qui décrit les services offerts par cet hôpital pour répondre aux questions que vous pose votre camarade.

L'hôpital Royal Victoria à Montréal

PARLER 2

Je vais être interprète.
✓ **Ask questions about medical problems**

L'hôpital de votre région a un problème. De nombreux patients sont haïtiens et leur interprète de français est malade. Vous allez le remplacer pendant quelques jours. Votre camarade est votre premier patient ou votre première patiente. Posez-lui des questions. Aidez-le/la à remplir les formulaires nécessaires.

PARLER / ÉCRIRE 3

Un sketch *(skit)* comique
✓ **Talk about emergency room procedures and accidents**

Travaillez par groupes de quatre ou cinq personnes. Préparez une comédie très courte intitulée «Une journée au service des urgences». Présentez ensuite votre sketch à la classe.

deux cent soixante-douze   CHAPITRE 8

ANSWERS TO C'est à vous

1 *Answers will vary.*
Students can use the vocabulary from this chapter to discuss the local medical services.

2 *Conversations will vary but may include the following questions:*
Comment vous appelez-vous?
Votre âge?
Votre adresse?
Qu'est-ce que vous avez?
Quels sont vos symptômes?
Qui est votre médecin?
Vous avez des allergies?

3 *Answers will vary.*

CHAPITRE 8 — C'est à vous

4 Un formulaire
✔ *Fill out a medical form*

Remplissez ce formulaire d'un hôpital français. Remplissez-le sur une feuille de papier.

```
Imp.«AP»         ASSISTANCE   HÔPITAUX        B1-61
                 PUBLIQUE     DE PARIS

HOPITAL : ..................................................

N° d'ordre ..................    Année ..................
NOM et prénoms : ..........................................
Date de naissance ........................................
Profession : .............................................
Domicile : ...............................................
Salle : ..................................................
Diagnostic : .............................................
Opération : ..............................................
Entrée le ................................................
Sortie le ................................................
```

Dates	OBSERVATIONS

Writing Strategy

Writing a feature article

When writing a feature article, writers have two challenges: first, they must identify current topics that will bring the article to life, and second, they must give readers the background they need. An important aspect of feature writing is the use of an effective lead to describe the opening of the story. This will catch the readers' attention and draw them in.

5 Un article dans le journal

Your French pen pal has asked you to write a feature story on a person or place in your community to include in his or her school newspaper. Your parents recently had an accident and had to go to the emergency room. They were transported there by the First Aid Squad in your community. You were extremely pleased with the quality of service, beginning with the paramedics who arrived promptly and administered treatment at the scene. The care your parents received in the emergency room from the staff was equally good. Write an article about this experience.

Vocabulaire

1 Choisissez.

1. Il a eu un accident et on a appelé ____.
   a. un anesthésiste
   b. le service des urgences
   c. un fauteuil roulant

2. On a mis le blessé sur ____.
   a. son genou
   b. un pansement
   c. un brancard

3. Elle s'est cassé la jambe et elle marche avec ____.
   a. des béquilles
   b. des doigts
   c. des fauteuils

4. On lui a fait un pansement parce qu'il ____.
   a. est tombé
   b. s'est foulé la cheville
   c. s'est coupé

5. L'infirmière ____ le malade.
   a. emmène
   b. soigne
   c. blesse

To review Mots 1, turn to pages 248–249.

2 Identifiez.

To review Mots 2, turn to pages 252–253.

6.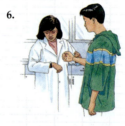

7.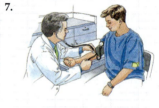

8.

9.

274 ✦ deux cent soixante-quatorze

CHAPITRE 8

ANSWERS TO Assessment

1
1. b
2. c
3. a
4. c
5. b

2
6. prendre le pouls
7. prendre la tension
8. faire une radio
9. plâtrer

Structure

3 Complétez avec l'équivalent de *what*.

10. _____ amuse les enfants?
11. _____ vous faites maintenant?
12. Elle me demande _____ se passe.
13. Je sais _____ vous voulez.

4 Récrivez avec des pronoms.

14. Ouvrez la bouche.
15. Donnez-moi cette ordonnance.
16. Parle au médecin.
17. Regardez les radios maintenant.

5 Récrivez au négatif.

18. Faites-la maintenant.
19. Dites-le-moi.
20. Lève-toi.

6 Répondez.

21. Quel est le garçon le plus sérieux de la classe?
22. Quelle est la fille la plus intelligente?

7 Complétez.

23. Charles est très bon en maths, mais sa sœur est _____.
24. Je crois que sa sœur est _____ de toute la classe.
25. Je comprends bien, mais vous comprenez _____ que moi.

Culture

8 Choisissez.

26. L'Hôtel-Dieu est _____.
    a. un hôtel   b. une cathédrale   c. un hôpital
27. On peut composer le 17 pour appeler _____.
    a. l'hôpital   b. police secours   c. le service radio
28. En France _____ paie les frais médicaux.
    a. l'hôpital   b. le malade   c. la Sécurité sociale

To review asking the question "what," turn to page 256.

To review pronouns in the imperative, turn to page 258.

To review the superlative, turn to page 261.

To review meilleur *and* mieux, *turn to page 262.*

To review this cultural information, turn to pages 266–267.

ANSWERS TO Assessment

3
10. Qu'est-ce qui
11. Qu'est-ce que
12. ce qui
13. ce que

4
14. Ouvrez-la.
15. Donnez-la-moi.
16. Parle-lui.
17. Regardez-les maintenant.

5
18. Ne la faites pas maintenant.
19. Ne me le dites pas.
20. Ne te lève pas.

6
21. Michel est le plus sérieux de la classe.
22. Monique est la plus intelligente de la classe.

7
23. meilleure
24. la meilleure
25. mieux

8
26. c
27. b
28. c

On parle super bien!

Tell all you can about this illustration.

1. Identify the topic or situation of the illustration.
2. Give the French words for as many items as you can.
3. Think of as many sentences as you can to describe the illustration.
4. Go over your sentences and put them in the best sequencing to give a coherent story based on the illustration.

Vocabulaire

Vocabulary Review

The words and phrases in the **Vocabulaire** have been taught for productive use in this chapter. They are summarized here as a resource for both student and teacher. This list also serves as a convenient resource for the **C'est à vous** activities on pages 272–273, as well as for talking about the illustration on page 276. There are approximately seven cognates in this vocabulary list. Have students find them.

Talking about an accident

glisser	se couper	se fouler la cheville	une fracture
tomber	se faire mal	se tordre le genou	(compliquée)
se blesser	se casser	un accident	une blessure

Talking about medical emergencies and a hospital

appeler police (f.) secours	un brancard	un hôpital
remplir un formulaire	un fauteuil roulant	le service des urgences
une ambulance	une béquille	la salle d'opération

Identifying some medical professions

un(e) secouriste	un chirurgien	un infirmier
un(e) anesthésiste	(-orthopédiste)	une infirmière

Talking about medical care

soigner	prendre la tension
ausculter	le pouls
faire une piqûre	une anesthésie
un pansement	remettre l'os en place
un point de suture	plâtrer
une radio(graphie)	mettre dans le plâtre

How well do you know your vocabulary?
- Identify words that describe emergency room procedures.
- Write a few sentences about the steps a doctor takes to treat a patient with a broken leg.

Identifying parts of the body

le bras	le genou	la cheville	le doigt de pied
le doigt	la jambe	le pied	un os

Other useful words and expressions

Qu'est-ce qui (t') est arrivé?	avoir mal (à la jambe, au genou, etc.)	emmener
Ne t'en fais pas.		montrer
Ce n'est pas grave.	aller mieux	

Attention!

You will notice that the vocabulary list here is not translated. This has been done intentionally, since we feel that by the time students have finished the material in the chapter they should be familiar with the meanings of all the words. If there are several words they still do not know, we recommend that they refer to the **Mots 1** and **2** sections in the chapter or go to the dictionaries at the back of this book to find the meanings. However, if you prefer that your students have the English translations, please refer to Vocabulary Transparency 8.1, where you will find all these words listed with their translations.

VIDÉOTOUR
Épisode 8
In this video episode, Vincent makes an unexpected trip to the hospital. See page 507 for more information.

UN ACCIDENT ET L'HÔPITAL

VIDÉO VHS/DVD

The Video Program allows students to see how the chapter vocabulary and structures are used by native speakers. For maximum reinforcement, show the video episode as a final activity for Chapter 8.

277

Planning for Chapter 9

SCOPE AND SEQUENCE, PAGES 278–307

Topics
* Hotels

Culture
* Valérie's trip to Nice
* Youth hostels in France
* Club Med resorts

Functions
* How to check into and out of your hotel
* How to express past actions
* How to refer to previously mentioned places
* How to describe how you do things

Structure
* The **passé composé** with **être** or **avoir**
* The pronoun **y**
* Pronoun + **en**
* Adverb formation

National Standards
* Communication Standard 1.1 pages 282, 283, 286, 287, 288, 290, 291, 292, 295, 302
* Communication Standard 1.2 pages 282, 283, 286, 287, 288, 289, 291, 292, 294, 297, 298, 299, 301
* Communication Standard 1.3 pages 282, 286, 291, 298, 303
* Cultures Standard 2.1 pages 294, 296–297, 298, 299, 300–301
* Cultures Standard 2.2 page 299
* Connections Standard 3.1 pages 300–301
* Comparisons Standard 4.1 pages 300–301
* Communities Standard 5.1 page 303

PACING AND PRIORITIES

The chapter content is color coded below to assist you in planning.

■ required   ■ recommended   ■ optional

Vocabulaire (required)   Days 1–4
- ■ Mots 1
   L'arrivée à l'hôtel
- ■ Mots 2
   Dans la chambre d'hôtel
   Dans la salle de bains

Structure (required)   Days 5–7
- ■ Le passé composé: **être** ou **avoir**
- ■ Le pronom **y**
- ■ Un pronom + **en**
- ■ La formation des adverbes

Conversation (required)
- ■ À la réception de l'hôtel

Lectures culturelles
- ■ L'Hôtel de la Gare (recommended)
- ■ Les auberges de jeunesse (optional)
- ■ Le Club Med (optional)

Connexions (optional)
- ■ Le langage

■ **C'est à vous** (recommended)

■ **Assessment** (recommended)

■ **On parle super bien!** (optional)

RESOURCE GUIDE

SECTION	PAGES	SECTION RESOURCES
Vocabulaire *Mots 1*		
L'arrivée à l'hôtel	280–283	Vocabulary Transparencies 9.2–9.3 Audio CD 6 Audio Activities TE, pages 94–96 Workbook, pages 101–102 Quiz 1, page 45 ExamView® Pro
Vocabulaire *Mots 2*		
Dans la chambre d'hôtel Dans la salle de bains	284 284–287	Vocabulary Transparencies 9.4–9.5 Audio CD 6 Audio Activities TE, pages 96–98 Workbook, page 103 Quiz 2, page 46 ExamView® Pro
Structure		
Le passé composé: **être** ou **avoir** Le pronom **y** Un pronom + **en** La formation des adverbes	288–289 289–291 291–292 292–293	Audio CD 6 Audio Activities TE, pages 98–100 Workbook, pages 104–106 Quizzes 3–6, pages 47–50 ExamView® Pro
Conversation		
À la réception de l'hôtel	294–295	Audio CD 6 Audio Activities TE, pages 100–101 Interactive CD-ROM
Lectures culturelles		
L'Hôtel de la Gare Les auberges de jeunesse Le Club Med	296–297 298 299	Audio CD 6 Audio Activities TE, pages 102–103 Tests, pages 138, 142
Connexions		
Le langage	300–301	Tests, page 143
C'est à vous		
	302–303	**Bon voyage!** Video, Episode 9 Video Activities, Chapter 9 French Online Activities french.glencoe.com
Assessment		
	304–305	Communication Transparency C 9 Quizzes 1–6, pages 45–50 Performance Assessment, Task 9 Tests, pages 135–150 ExamView® Pro Situation Cards, Chapter 9 **Marathon mental** Videoquiz

Using Your Resources for Chapter 9

Transparencies

Bellringer 9.1–9.8

Vocabulary 9.1–9.5

Communication C 9

Workbook

Vocabulary, pages 101–103

Structure, pages 104–106

Enrichment, pages 107–110

Audio Activities

Vocabulary, pages 94–98

Structure, pages 98–100

Conversation, pages 100–101

Cultural Reading, pages 102–103

Additional Practice, pages 103–105

Assessment

Vocabulary and Structure Quizzes, pages 45–50

Chapter Tests, pages 135–150

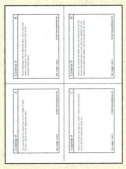
Situation Cards, Chapter 9

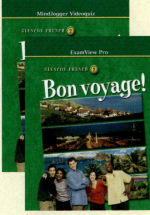
MindJogger Videoquiz, ExamView® Pro, Chapter 9

Timesaving Teacher Tools

TeacherWorks™

TeacherWorks™ is your all-in-one teacher resource center. Personalize lesson plans, access resources from the Teacher Wraparound Edition, connect to the Internet, or make a to-do list. These are only a few of the many features that can assist you in the planning and organizing of your lessons.

Includes:

- A calendar feature
- Access to all program blackline masters
- Standards correlations and more

ExamView® Pro

Test Bank software for Macintosh and Windows makes creating, editing, customizing, and printing tests quick and easy.

Technology Resources

In the Chapter 9 Internet activity, you will have a chance to learn more about the Francophone world. Visit <u>french.glencoe.com</u>.

On the Interactive Conversation CD-ROM, students can listen to and take part in a recorded version of the conversation in Chapter 9.

See the National Geographic Teacher's Corner on pages 138–139, 244–245, 372–373, 472–473 for reference to additional technology resources.

Bon voyage! Video and Video Activities, Chapter 9

Help your students prepare for the chapter test by playing the **Marathon mental** Videoquiz game show. Teams will compete against each other to review chapter vocabulary and structure and sharpen listening comprehension skills.

Preview

In this chapter, students will learn vocabulary associated with making a hotel reservation, checking in and out, identifying features of a hotel room, and requesting various hotel services. They will learn more about the **passé composé** of verbs conjugated with **être,** and the pronouns **y** and **en.** Students will also learn the formation of adverbs.

 National Standards

Communication

In Chapter 9, students will communicate in spoken and written French on the following topics:
- Making a reservation and checking into and out of a hotel
- Requesting various hotel services
- Discussing basic hotel features and facilities

Students will obtain and provide information about these topics and engage in conversations that would typically take place in a hotel as they fulfill the chapter objectives listed on this page.

CHAPITRE 9

L'hôtel

Objectifs
In this chapter you will learn to:

✓ check into and out of a hotel
✓ ask for things you may need while at a hotel
✓ talk about past actions
✓ refer to previously mentioned places
✓ talk about people and things already mentioned
✓ describe how you do things
✓ talk about hotels in France

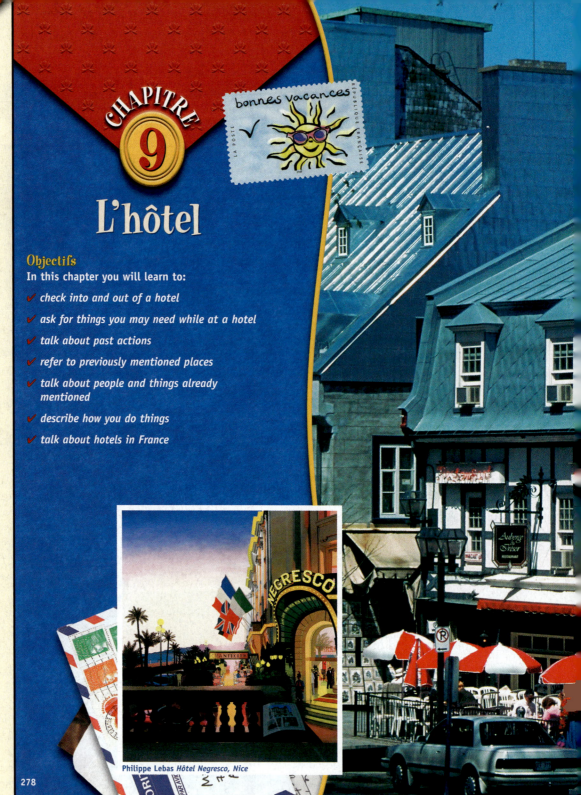

Philippe Lebas *Hôtel Negresco, Nice*

CHAPITRE 9

Spotlight on Culture

Photograph This photo is of the **Auberge du Trésor**, a restaurant and hotel in the old city of Québec.

Painting The Hôtel Negresco is the most famous hotel in Nice. Situated on the promenade des Anglais, it is a byword for old-world elegance. The hotel also has one of the best restaurants in France. This painting was done by the twentieth-century French artist Philippe Lebas.

LEVELING

The activities, conversations, and readings within each chapter are marked according to level of difficulty. **E** indicates easy. **A** indicates average. **C** indicates challenging. Some activities cover a range of difficulty. In some activities, for example, advanced students will be able to produce more extensive responses while students who learn at a different rate may give less detailed responses. The leveling indicators will help you individualize instruction to best meet your students' needs.

Vocabulaire
Mots 1

1 Preparation

Resource Manager

Vocabulary Transparencies 9.2–9.3
Audio Activities TE, pages 94–96
Audio CD 6
Workbook, pages 101–102
Quiz 1, page 45
ExamView® Pro

Bellringer Review

Use BRR Transparency 9.1 or write the following on the board.
What sort of treatment would you receive in the hospital for the following problems?
1. Tu t'es coupé le doigt.
2. Tu es tombé et tu t'es cassé la jambe.
3. On va remettre l'os en place et ça va faire très mal.

2 Presentation

Step 1 Have students close their books. Use Vocabulary Transparencies 9.2–9.3 to present **Mots 1**. Lead students through the new vocabulary by asking: **Qu'est-ce que c'est?** or **C'est qui?**

LEVELING
E: Vocabulary
A: Vocabulary

Vocabulaire
Mots 1

L'arrivée à l'hôtel

À la réception, Camille remplit soigneusement la fiche de police.

Camille a réservé une chambre.
Elle a versé des arrhes.
Elle a donné de l'argent à l'avance.

Camille est montée au troisième étage.
Elle a monté ses bagages.

Reaching All Students

Total Physical Response Before you begin, set up places in a hotel, such as **le hall, l'escalier, le couloir, la réception.** As props you might use a briefcase as a suitcase, a room key, and a fake passport.
  (Student 1) et (Student 2), **venez ici, s'il vous plaît.**
  (Student 1), **tu es un(e) client(e) qui arrive à l'hôtel.**
(Student 2), **tu es le/la réceptionniste.**
(Student 1), **va à la réception. Demande une chambre.**
(Student 2), **donne-lui la fiche de police. Demande son passeport.**
(Student 1), **mets ton passeport sur le comptoir.**
(Student 2), **ouvre son passeport et regarde-le.**
(Student 1), **signe la fiche de police. Donne la fiche au/à la réceptionniste.**
(Student 1), **prends ton passeport. Mets-le dans ta poche.**
(Student 2), **donne la clé au client/à la cliente.**
(Student 1), **prends tes bagages. Monte l'escalier.**
Merci, (Student 1) et (Student 2).

Vocabulaire
Mots 1

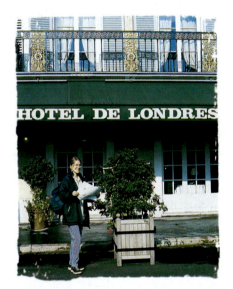

une chambre avec salle de bains

un lit

une chambre à un lit

Elle a défait son sac.

Ensuite elle est sortie de sa chambre.
Elle a fermé sa porte à clé.

Elle est descendue.
Elle a sorti un plan de la ville de son sac à dos.

Elle est allée visiter la ville.
Il y avait beaucoup de monde.

L'HÔTEL

deux cent quatre-vingt-un ❖ 281

Teaching Tip
You can also use *either/or* questions to introduce the new vocabulary by contrasting a new item with one known to students. For example: **C'est un ascenseur ou un escalier? (C'est un escalier.)**

Step 2 Have students open their books and repeat chorally as you model the entire **Mots 1** vocabulary or play Audio CD 6.

Step 3 While showing the Vocabulary Transparencies, call on students to read the vocabulary words and sentences.

Step 4 Ask **vrai ou faux** questions such as the following: **Le hall est dans le jardin de l'hôtel? La réception est dans le hall? La réceptionniste remplit une fiche de police? On peut monter plus vite dans l'ascenseur?**

✓ Assessment

After completing the vocabulary presentation, as an informal assessment you may wish to call on students to look at the photos and say as much as they can about them. Then check comprehension by mixing true and false statements about the photos. Students respond with «**C'est vrai.**» or «**C'est faux.**»

Learning from Photos

(page 280 top left) The photos that appear in this vocabulary section were taken at the small **Hôtel de Londres** in Fontainebleau. The proprietor seen here is Madame Ginette Columbier.

Have students look at the photo and say all they can about it.

Reaching All Students

Kinesthetic Learners Call on individuals to dramatize or pantomime the following:
  remplir une fiche   fermer la porte à clé
  monter l'escalier   descendre l'escalier
  monter les bagages   sortir quelque chose
  ouvrir un sac   d'un sac
  défaire le sac

About the French Language

In the bottom left photo on page 281, point out that the word **Hôtel** on the awning does not have the **circonflex** over the **o**. Accents are usually dropped when words are written in all capital letters. ⚜

281

Vocabulaire

3 Practice

Quel est le mot?

1 After completing the activity, have students take turns describing one of the illustrations.

2 Focus on the listening skill by having students work in pairs. One partner reads the questions in random order while the other answers with his or her book closed.

Art Connection

The small village of Barbizon is close to Fontainebleau on the outskirts of Paris. In the mid-nineteenth century, Barbizon was a favorite haunt of painters such as Corot, Théodore Rousseau, and Jean-Francois Millet. Rousseau and Millet both had studios in Barbizon. There is now a museum in the barn that once served as Rousseau's studio.

Vocabulaire

Quel est le mot?

 1 Qu'est-ce que c'est? Identifiez.

1. C'est le hall ou la réception?
2. C'est une clé ou une fiche de police?
3. C'est une porte ou une chambre?
4. C'est une chambre à un lit ou à deux lits?
5. La jeune fille fait ou défait ses bagages?

À la réception de l'hôtel Bas-Bréau à Barbizon

2 Historiette L'arrivée
Inventez une histoire.
1. Stéphane est arrivé à l'hôtel?
2. Il est entré dans le hall?
3. Il a trouvé la réception?
4. Il a demandé une chambre pour une personne?
5. Il a demandé le prix de la chambre? Le petit déjeuner est compris?
6. La réceptionniste lui a donné sa clé?
7. Elle lui a souhaité un bon séjour?
8. Stéphane est monté dans sa chambre?
9. Il a monté ses bagages?
10. Il a défait ses bagages?
11. Il a sorti un plan de la ville de sa valise?
12. Quand il est sorti, il a fermé la porte à clé?

282 ✦ *deux cent quatre-vingt-deux*   CHAPITRE 9

ANSWERS TO Quel est le mot?

1
1. C'est la réception.
2. C'est une clé.
3. C'est une porte.
4. C'est une chambre à un lit.
5. La jeune fille défait ses bagages.

2 *Answers will vary but may include:*
1. Oui, il est arrivé à l'hôtel.
2. Oui, il est entré dans le hall.
3. Oui, il a trouvé la réception.
4. Oui, il a demandé une chambre pour une personne.
5. Oui, il a demandé le prix de la chambre. Oui, le petit déjeuner est compris.
6. Oui, la réceptionniste lui a donné sa clé.
7. Oui, elle lui a souhaité un bon séjour.
8. Oui, il est monté dans sa chambre.
9. Oui, il a monté ses bagages.
10. Oui, il a défait ses bagages.
11. Oui, il a sorti un plan de la ville de sa valise.
12. Oui, quand il est sorti, il a fermé la porte à clé.

3 Le touriste Choisissez.

1. À l'hôtel, le touriste remplit ___.
   a. une fiche   b. une chambre   c. une clé
2. Pour monter dans sa chambre, il prend ___.
   a. la clé   b. l'ascenseur   c. la porte
3. Il ouvre la porte de sa chambre avec ___.
   a. sa fiche   b. son lit   c. sa clé
4. Il prend une douche dans ___.
   a. la salle de bains   b. le hall   c. l'escalier
5. Il dort dans ___.
   a. son lit   b. sa salle de bains   c. sa rue
6. Le matin, il se lève et prend ___.
   a. sa fiche   b. son lit   c. son petit déjeuner
7. Pour réserver une chambre, il faut verser ___.
   a. une carte de crédit   b. des arrhes   c. des taxes

HÔTEL Manoir Saint-Sauveur

SERVICE AUX CHAMBRES

PETIT DÉJEUNER
de 7 H 00 à 10 H 30

LE CONTINENTAL — 6,25 $
Choix d'un petit jus rafraîchi
Un croissant, un muffin et une chocolatine
Thé, café régulier ou décaféiné
Beurre et confitures

LE SAINT-SAUVEUR — 9,50 $
Choix d'un petit jus rafraîchi
Deux oeufs, bacon ou saucisses ou jambon
Rôties de pain de ménage
Pommes de terres rissolées
Thé, café régulier ou décaféiné

4 Une réservation

Votre classe de français pense faire un voyage en France. Chaque élève a quelque chose à faire pour aider à organiser le séjour. Votre camarade et vous, vous êtes chargé(e)s de réserver les chambres. Vous téléphonez à l'hôtel. Vous, vous êtes l'élève et votre camarade est le/la réceptionniste de l'hôtel. Mentionnez les dates d'arrivée et de départ, le nombre de chambres, le nombre d'élèves par chambre, les repas, le prix, et demandez s'il faut verser des arrhes, etc.

5 Dans le hall

Travaillez avec un(e) camarade. Décrivez tout ce que vous voyez sur le dessin.

L'HÔTEL

Vocabulaire Mots 2

1 Preparation

Resource Manager
Vocabulary Transparencies 9.4–9.5
Audio Activities TE, pages 96–98
Audio CD 6
Workbook, page 103
Quiz 2, page 46
ExamView® Pro

Bellringer Review
Use BRR Transparency 9.2 or write the following on the board.
Write something you could buy in each of the following places.
une pharmacie, une papeterie, une boutique, une boulangerie, une agence de voyages

2 Presentation

Step 1 Show Vocabulary Transparencies 9.4–9.5. Have students close their books and repeat the words after you or Audio CD 6 as you point to the appropriate illustration on the transparency.

Step 2 Point to the appropriate illustration and ask questions such as: **Qu'est-ce que la cliente demande? Qu'est-ce qu'elle vérifie? Elle paie avec quoi?**

Dans la chambre d'hôtel

- un cintre
- un placard
- un oreiller
- une couverture
- un drap
- l'air climatisé = la climatisation

Dans la salle de bains

se sécher

- un rouleau de papier hygiénique
- une serviette propre
- un gant de toilette
- du savon
- une serviette sale

Camille a demandé poliment une serviette propre. La femme de chambre lui en a donné une.

284 ❖ *deux cent quatre-vingt-quatre* CHAPITRE 9

Reaching All Students

Total Physical Response
(Student 1), venez ici, s'il vous plaît.
Vous allez quitter l'hôtel.
Allez à la caisse. Demandez votre note.
Regardez et vérifiez les frais.
Il y a quelque chose sur la note que vous ne comprenez pas. Indiquez le problème au/à la réceptionniste.
Le/La réceptionniste vous l'explique.

Vous comprenez. Sortez votre carte de crédit.
Donnez votre carte de crédit au/à la réceptionniste.
Merci, (Student 1). Retournez à votre place.
(Student 2), venez ici, s'il vous plaît.
Vous êtes dans un hôtel.
Vous êtes dans votre chambre.
Ouvrez la porte du placard.
Prenez un cintre. Accrochez votre veste.

Mettez-la dans le placard.
Fermez la porte du placard.
Allez dans la salle de bains.
Prenez le gant de toilette.
Prenez le savon. Lavez-vous la figure.
Regardez-vous dans la glace.
Prenez une serviette.
Séchez-vous la figure avec la serviette.
Merci, (Student 2). Retournez à votre place, s'il vous plaît.

Camille a libéré sa chambre.

les frais de téléphone

Camille a demandé la note.
La caissière la lui a donnée.
Camille a vérifié les frais de téléphone.
Elle a payé avec une carte de crédit.
Elle n'a pas payé en espèces (en liquide).

L'HÔTEL

deux cent quatre-vingt-cinq 285

Vocabulaire
Mots 2

Step 3 Using props as cues (a pillow, a wash mitt, soap, a towel, money, etc.), ask students what one needs in order to do various things. For example: **On va prendre une douche. On va prendre un bain. On va se laver la figure. On va se sécher. On va dormir. On va mettre nos vêtements dans le placard.**

Step 4 When presenting the sentences on page 285, ask questions in order to give students the opportunity to use the words. For example: **Camille est allée à l'hôtel. Qui est allé à l'hôtel? Elle est allée où? Elle est restée une semaine à l'hôtel? Elle est restée combien de temps à l'hôtel? Elle a libéré sa chambre? Elle est descendue où? C'est une note d'hôtel? Qu'est-ce que c'est? Qui a demandé la note? Elle a demandé la note à la réception? Elle a demandé la note où?**

Teaching Tip
When asking the questions above, direct the easier questions to the less able students and the more difficult questions to the more able students.

Vocabulary Expansion

You may wish to give students the following useful expressions.
**Je voudrais plus de cintres, s'il vous plaît.
J'ai besoin d'une autre couverture.
Un autre oreiller, s'il vous plaît.
Il n'y a pas de savon.
Il n'y a pas de papier hygiénique.**

Chapter Projects

 On va voyager! Have students use a Michelin Guide to plan hotel stays in different French cities.

 Un bon hôtel Have groups create their own hotel and describe it to the rest of the class, who rate it as to quality, price value, and cuisine.

Vocabulaire

Quel est le mot?

6 Qu'est-ce que c'est? Identifiez.

1. C'est un oreiller ou une couverture?

2. C'est un cintre ou un gant de toilette?

3. C'est du savon ou du shampooing?

4. C'est un gant de toilette ou du papier hygiénique?

5. C'est une note d'hôtel ou une serviette?

6. C'est une carte de crédit ou de l'argent liquide?

Mme Legrand paie sa note d'hôtel.

7 Historiette Elle a libéré la chambre. Inventez une histoire.

1. Mme Legrand a libéré la chambre?
2. Elle est descendue à la réception?
3. Elle a demandé ses frais de téléphone?
4. Elle a parlé au caissier?
5. Elle a vérifié sa note?
6. Elle a payé avec une carte de crédit ou en espèces?

8 C'est quel mot? Pour chaque définition, donnez le mot exact.

1. On se lave avec.
2. On se sèche avec.
3. On met ses vêtements dessus.
4. On se couche dedans.
5. On en met une sur son lit quand il fait froid.
6. Ça se présente en rouleau.
7. Le contraire de «propre».
8. On met ses vêtements dedans.
9. On la met quand il fait trop chaud dans la chambre.
10. On lui demande des serviettes propres.

 9 La chambre est libre! Votre camarade est réceptionniste dans un hôtel. Vous êtes le/la client(e). Vous avez libéré votre chambre. Vous demandez votre note et vous posez des questions. Le/La réceptionniste vous répond et vous demande comment vous voulez payer votre note.

 10 Un bon hôtel Avec un(e) camarade discutez de ce qui est important quand vous allez à l'hôtel. Vous pouvez utiliser les mots suivants.

la catégorie de l'hôtel	une piscine
la chambre	un gymnase
le prix	un restaurant
le petit déjeuner	le lit
l'air climatisé	le service

Une chambre dans un hôtel de luxe

Juan-les-Pins sur la Côte d'Azur

 11 Quel désastre! Vous avez passé une semaine dans un hôtel à Juan-les-Pins sur la Côte d'Azur. L'hôtel était une véritable horreur. Votre camarade vous pose des questions sur votre séjour dans cet hôtel. Vous pouvez exagérer un peu. Ensuite changez de rôle. Décidez qui a eu l'expérience la plus atroce.

 For more practice using words from *Mots 1* and *Mots 2*, do Activity 15 on page H16 at the end of this book.

Structure

1 Preparation

Resource Manager
Audio Activities TE, pages 98–100
Audio CD 6
Workbook, pages 104–106
Quizzes 3–6, pages 47–50
ExamView® Pro

Bellringer Review
Use BRR Transparency 9.3 or write the following on the board. Write six things you would expect to find in a hotel room.

2 Presentation

Le passé composé: être ou avoir

Step 1 Read the example sentences to the class. After each sentence have students tell if the sentence has a direct object. If it does, have students tell what the direct object is.

Step 2 Lead students through the explanation on page 288.

Step 3 Go on to the activities.

3 Practice

Comment dit-on?

12 Expansion: Have students do the activity again, changing the subject in both questions and answers first to **Agathe et Chantal** and then to **Ma mère et moi**.

Structure

Le passé composé: être ou avoir
Talking about past actions

Verbs like **descendre, monter, passer, rentrer,** and **sortir** are conjugated with **être** when they are not followed by a direct object. They are conjugated with **avoir,** however, when followed by a direct object. Note the difference in meaning in the following sentences.

Marie est descendue.   Elle a descendu ses bagages.   Ils sont sortis hier.   Ils ont sorti leurs billets.

Comment dit-on?

12 **Historiette** Agathe est arrivée.
 Répondez que oui.
1. Agathe est arrivée à l'hôtel?
2. Elle est allée à la réception?
3. Elle a sorti son passeport et sa carte de crédit?
4. Elle est montée dans sa chambre?
5. Elle a monté ses bagages?
6. Elle est descendue pour sortir?
7. Elle est sortie?
8. Elle est allée au musée?
9. Elle est rentrée à l'hôtel à six heures du soir?
10. Elle a sorti sa clé pour ouvrir la porte de sa chambre?

288 ✦ *deux cent quatre-vingt-huit*   CHAPITRE 9

ANSWERS TO Comment dit-on?

 12

1. Oui, elle est arrivée à l'hôtel.
2. Oui, elle est allée à la réception.
3. Oui, elle a sorti son passeport et sa carte de crédit.
4. Oui, elle est montée dans sa chambre.
5. Oui, elle a monté ses bagages.
6. Oui, elle est descendue pour sortir.
7. Oui, elle est sortie.
8. Oui, elle est allée au musée.
9. Oui, elle est rentrée à l'hôtel à six heures du soir.
10. Oui, elle a sorti sa clé pour ouvrir la porte de sa chambre.

13 **Historiette** En route!
Complétez au passé composé.

Les deux copines __1__ (sortir) de la maison à neuf heures. Elles __2__ (sortir) tous leurs bagages. Elles __3__ (attendre) un taxi. Quand le taxi __4__ (arriver), elles __5__ (mettre) leurs bagages dans le coffre. Puis les deux filles __6__ (monter) dans le taxi. Quand elles __7__ (arriver) à la gare, elles __8__ (descendre) du taxi. Elles __9__ (sortir) leurs billets et __10__ (monter) dans le train.

La gare de Lyon à Paris

 Le pronom y
Referring to places already mentioned

1. You use **y** to replace any location. Study the following examples.

Tu vas **à Paris**?	Oui, j'**y** vais.
Julien est **devant l'hôtel**?	Oui, il **y** est.
Il veut rester **dans sa chambre**?	Oui, il veut **y** rester.

Rappelez-vous que...

The verb **aller** cannot stand alone. You use **y** with **aller** to refer to places already mentioned.
—Tu vas au restaurant?
—Oui, j'y vais. On y va ensemble?

2. The pronoun **y**, like any other object pronoun, comes right before the verb it is linked to.

Affirmatif	Négatif
Il **y** va.	Il n'**y** va pas.
Il veut **y** aller.	Il ne veut pas **y** aller.
Il **y** est allé.	Il n'**y** est pas allé.

Savez-vous que... ?

In order to make the liaison, the final **s** is not dropped in the affirmative command of **-er** verbs and **aller** when **y** is used.
Restes-y! mais
N'y reste pas!

L'HÔTEL

deux cent quatre-vingt-neuf 289

Structure

3 Practice

Comment dit-on?

 You may wish to use the recorded version of this activity.

> **Learning from Photos**
>
> *(page 290)* The young women are in front of a healthclub in Évry, a suburb of Paris.

> ✓ **Assessment**
>
> As an informal assessment, you may wish to check for understanding by asking questions that would elicit a natural negative response. Ask each question three times: once in the present, once in the **passé composé**, and once in the **futur proche** (**aller** + infinitive). For example: **Tu vas à l'école en taxi?** (Non, je n'y vais pas en taxi.) **Tu y es allé(e) en taxi la semaine dernière?** (Non, je n'y suis pas allé(e) en taxi la semaine dernière.) **Tu vas y aller en taxi demain?** (Non, je ne vais pas y aller en taxi demain.)

LEVELING

E: Activities 14, 15, 16
A: Activity 17

Structure

Comment dit-on?

14 Au gymnase Répétez la conversation.

Tu vas au gymnase?

Oui, j'y vais tous les samedis.

Ton copain y va aussi?

Oui, il y va aussi. Il y va souvent, mais il n'y est pas allé hier.

ANSWERS TO Comment dit-on?

 Students will repeat the conversation.

Reaching All Students

Additional Practice Have students tell about a trip they took. They should mention the place by name in the first sentence and use **y** in succeeding ones. For example: **L'année dernière je suis allé(e) à New York. J'y suis allé(e) avec ma famille. Nous y sommes allé(e)s en avion. Nous y sommes resté(e)s deux semaines**, etc.

15 **Historiette À l'hôtel** Répondez en utilisant **y**.

1. David est arrivé à l'hôtel?
2. Il a mis ses bagages devant l'hôtel?
3. Il est entré dans le hall?
4. Il est allé à la réception?
5. Il a fait la queue à la réception?
6. Il est monté dans sa chambre?

16 À l'école Donnez des réponses personnelles en utilisant **y**.

1. Tu vas à l'école tous les jours?
2. Tu es à la maison en ce moment?
3. Tu attends tes amis dans la cour de l'école?
4. Tu vas à l'école à pied?
5. Tu aimes aller chez tes copains après les cours?

Un pronom + en
Referring to people and things already mentioned

1. When you use **en** with another pronoun, **en** always comes last.

   Tu **lui** as parlé **de l'hôtel**?   Oui, je **lui en** ai parlé.
   Elle **t'**a donné combien **de clés**?   Elle **m'en** a donné deux.

2. You will frequently use **en** with the expression **il y a**.

   Il y a **des chambres**?   Oui, **il y en a**, mais il n'y **en** a pas beaucoup.
   Il y a combien **de lits** dans la chambre?   **Il y en a** deux.

Comment dit-on?

17 **Historiette Je lui en ai parlé.** Complétez la conversation.

—Vous avez parlé à votre père de vos problèmes financiers?
—Oui, je __1__ ai parlé.
—Et il vous a prêté de l'argent?
—Oui, il __2__ a prêté.
—Il __3__ a prêté beaucoup?
—Bof! Il __4__ a prêté un peu!
—Et vous __5__ avez parlé combien de fois?
—Oh! Je __6__ ai bien parlé dix fois!

L'HÔTEL

Answers to Comment dit-on?

15
1. Oui, David y est arrivé.
2. Oui, il y a mis ses bagages.
3. Oui, il y est entré.
4. Oui, il y est allé.
5. Oui, il y a fait la queue.
6. Oui, il y est monté.

16 Answers will vary but may include:
1. Non, je n'y vais pas tous les jours.
2. Non, je n'y suis pas.
3. Oui, j'y attends mes amis.
4. Oui, j'y vais à pied.
5. Oui, j'aime y aller après les cours.

17
1. lui en
2. m'en
3. vous en
4. m'en
5. lui en
6. lui en

Structure

3 Practice (continued)

18 Expansion: Have pairs of students make up similar questions about their school. For example: **Il y a combien d'élèves dans cette école?**, etc.

> **Learning from Photos**
> (page 292) The old types of elevators like the one in the photo still exist in many French hotels and apartment buildings. This one is at the famous Negresco Hotel in Nice.

1 Preparation

Bellringer Review

Use BRR Transparency 9.6 or write the following on the board.
Write these sentences in the **passé composé**.
1. Alice monte ses valises.
2. Juliette monte au deuxième étage.
3. Claire sort avec Jim.
4. Claire sort les billets de sa poche.

2 Presentation

 La formation des adverbes

Step 1 Define the function of the adverb: to modify the meaning of the verb.

Step 2 Guide students through Items 1–3 on page 292. Have students read each word aloud with attention to pronunciation. Point out the spelling changes in Items 2 and 3.

292

Structure

 18 Il y en a combien?
 Répondez en utilisant un pronom.
1. Il y a combien de chambres dans cet hôtel? (cent)
2. Il y a combien de lits dans chaque chambre? (deux)
3. Il y a combien de placards dans chaque chambre? (un)
4. Il y a combien de cintres dans un placard? (quatre)
5. Il y a combien d'oreillers sur chaque lit? (deux)
6. Il y a combien d'ascenseurs dans l'hôtel? (pas assez)

Un ascenseur

 La formation des adverbes
Describing how you do things

1. You form most adverbs in French by adding **-ment** to the feminine form of the adjective.

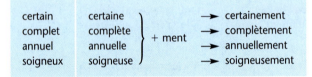

2. However, if the masculine form of the adjective ends in a vowel, you add **-ment** to the masculine form.

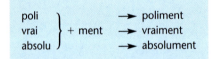

3. Note the spelling and the pronunciation of the adverbial form of the adjectives that end in **-ent** or **-ant**. The ending is always pronounced [amɑ̃] whether it's written **-emment** or **-amment**.

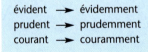

292 deux cent quatre-vingt-douze

CHAPITRE 9

ANSWERS TO Comment dit-on?

18
1. Il y en a cent.
2. Il y en a deux.
3. Il y en a un.
4. Il y en a quatre.
5. Il y en a deux.
6. Il n'y en a pas assez.

Comment dit-on?

19 **Un adolescent exemplaire**
Répondez d'après les indications.

1. Il conduit toujours comment? (prudemment)
2. Il parle toujours comment? (poliment)
3. Il écoute toujours comment? (patiemment)
4. Il fait toujours ses devoirs comment? (sérieusement)

Il étudie sérieusement?

  Le jeu des adverbes
 Un(e) de vos camarades sort. Vous choisissez un adverbe—par exemple, **sérieusement**. Votre camarade revient et vous mimez l'adverbe choisi. Votre camarade doit deviner quel est l'adverbe. Vous pouvez utiliser les adverbes correspondant aux adjectifs suivants.

- timide
- patient
- énergique
- facile
- furieux
- comique
- difficile

Vous êtes sur le bon chemin. Allez-y!

deux cent quatre-vingt-treize 293

Structure

The **Glencoe World Languages Web site** (french.glencoe.com) offers options that enable you and your students to experience the French-speaking world via the Internet. For each chapter, there are activities, games, and quizzes. In addition, an *Enrichment* section offers students an opportunity to visit Web sites related to the theme of the chapter.

Allez-y!

At this point in the chapter, students have learned all the vocabulary and structures necessary to complete the chapter. The conversation and cultural readings that follow recycle all the material learned up to this point.

LEVELING
E: Activities 18, 19, 20
A: Activity 20

ANSWERS TO Comment dit-on?

19
1. Il conduit toujours prudemment.
2. Il parle toujours poliment.
3. Il écoute toujours patiemment.
4. Il fait toujours ses devoirs sérieusement.

Conversation

À la réception de l'hôtel

Elizabeth: Bonjour, monsieur. J'ai réservé une chambre pour deux personnes.
Réceptionniste: C'est à quel nom, s'il vous plaît?
Elizabeth: Au nom de Collins.
Réceptionniste: Vous avez votre confirmation?
Elizabeth: Oui, la voilà. *(Elle lui montre sa confirmation.)*
Réceptionniste: Merci. J'ai une très jolie chambre au troisième qui donne sur la cour.
Elizabeth: C'est une chambre à deux lits?
Réceptionniste: Oui, avec salle de bains.
Elizabeth: Et c'est combien?
Réceptionniste: Cent cinquante euros. Le petit déjeuner est compris. Voilà votre clé. Je vous en donne une autre pour votre amie?
Elizabeth: Ah, bonne idée. Merci.
Réceptionniste: Voilà… Et je vous souhaite un bon séjour, mesdemoiselles…

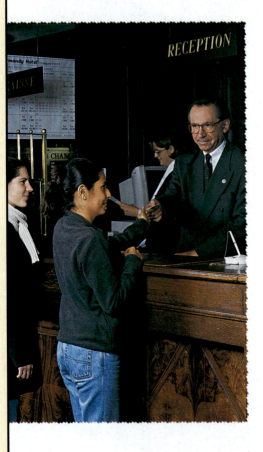

Vous avez compris?

Répondez.

1. Elizabeth veut une chambre pour combien de personnes?
2. Elle parle à qui?
3. Elle a réservé une chambre à quel nom?
4. Qu'est-ce qu'elle montre au réceptionniste?
5. La chambre est à quel étage?
6. Elle donne sur la rue?
7. C'est une chambre à combien de lits?
8. La chambre a une salle de bains?
9. La chambre coûte combien?
10. Le petit déjeuner est compris ou pas?
11. Elizabeth va avoir combien de clés?

Parlons un peu plus

 Un hôtel à Québec Cet été vous allez passer vos vacances à Québec avec votre famille. Vous montrez à votre camarade des brochures sur les hôtels de Québec. Expliquez à votre camarade quel hôtel vous avez choisi et pour quelles raisons. Ensuite, votre camarade vous dira s'il/si elle est d'accord avec vous ou pas, et pour quelles raisons.

 À la réception Avec votre camarade, préparez la conversation qu'on a quand on arrive à la réception d'un hôtel.

L'HÔTEL

Conversation

3 Practice

Parlons un peu plus

These activities enable students to use the vocabulary and structures learned in the chapter in open-ended exchanges. You may wish to assign different activities to different groups or allow students to choose the activities they wish to do.

A Have students look carefully at the three hotel brochures before they begin this activity. If necessary, help them identify the activities listed in each brochure.

FUN FACTS

Usually, breakfast is included in the price of a room in a French hotel. It is a continental breakfast with a choice of hot tea, coffee, or hot chocolate, a croissant, and bread. Breakfast is served in a small room on the ground floor or in the dining room. Breakfast can also be served in one's room.

LEVELING
E: Conversation

Reaching All Students

Additional Practice After completing the **Conversation** on page 294, ask a student to retell the situation of the conversation in his or her own words.

ANSWERS TO Parlons un peu plus

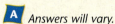 Answers will vary.

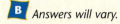 Answers will vary.

Students may refer to the **Conversation** on page 294 as a guide. All of the necessary vocabulary has been presented in this chapter.

Lectures culturelles

Resource Manager
Audio Activities TE, pages 102–103
Audio CD 6

Bellringer Review
Use BRR Transparency 9.8 or write the following on the board.
Rewrite the following sentences replacing the words in italics with pronouns.
1. Notre prof de français nous donne *des devoirs* tous les jours.
2. La fille met *du lait* dans le frigo.
3. J'ai beaucoup *d'argent*.

National Standards
Cultures
This reading about a visit to Nice familiarizes students with the French tourist bureau and this popular city on the Riviera.

Presentation

Pre-reading
Step 1 Ask students what resources they would use to plan a trip to France. If you have access to a Michelin Guide, share its rating system with the students.

Step 2 Have students look at the map of France on page xxxi (French 1A, 1B: page xxiv) or use Map Transparency M 2. Have them locate Nice.

Reading
Step 1 You may wish to divide the **Lecture** into two or three segments.

Step 2 Call on an individual to read several sentences. Then ask other students about the sentences the student has just read.

Lectures culturelles

Reading Strategy
Previewing
Often you can learn about the topic of a passage simply by looking at the titles and pictures before you begin to read. Previewing a reading selection will give you an overview of its purpose, organization, and content.

La gare de Nice

L'Hôtel de la Gare

Au syndicat d'initiative
Valérie est allée avec quelques copines à Nice. Quand elles sont arrivées, elles sont descendues du train et sont allées tout de suite au syndicat d'initiative. Le syndicat d'initiative est un bureau de tourisme qui se trouve souvent dans les gares ou près des gares. Les touristes vont au syndicat d'initiative pour trouver une chambre d'hôtel s'ils n'ont pas réservé de chambre à l'avance.

Valérie a expliqué à l'employée du syndicat d'initiative que ses copines et elle sont étudiantes. Elles ne veulent pas aller dans un hôtel de luxe qui coûte cher. Pas de problème. L'employée a téléphoné à l'Hôtel de la Gare où elle a réservé une chambre pour les filles. L'Hôtel de la Gare est un hôtel confortable mais pas trop cher. Et il est où, l'Hôtel de la Gare? En face de la gare, bien sûr! Dans beaucoup de villes en France, il y a un Hôtel de la Gare.

La promenade des Anglais
Valérie et ses copines sont sorties de la gare, elles ont traversé la rue et sont arrivées à l'hôtel en deux minutes. Elles ont rempli les fiches de police et ont monté leurs bagages dans leur chambre. Elles sont descendues tout de suite après et sont allées visiter la ville de Nice. Elles ont fait une promenade le long de la célèbre promenade des Anglais qui borde la jolie baie des Anges. Elles ont remarqué que sur la plage il n'y avait pas de sable, mais des galets[1].

[1] galets *pebbles, stones*

La promenade des Anglais à Nice

LEVELING
E: Reading

Le Vieux-Nice

Avant de rentrer à l'hôtel, les jeunes filles ont visité la vieille ville. Elles ont flâné[2] dans les petites ruelles[3] et elles sont allées au marché aux fleurs. Valérie avait faim, alors elles ont trouvé un petit café. Elles ont toutes commandé une salade niçoise— c'est une salade avec de la laitue, des tomates, des haricots verts, du thon[4], des œufs, des olives noires et des anchois[5].

Le marché aux fleurs à Nice

Henri Matisse *Cour du Moulin*

Cimiez

Demain, elles iront visiter Cimiez, un quartier où il y a deux musées intéressants. Le musée Matisse a une grande collection de tableaux et de sculptures de Henri Matisse.

L'autre musée est dédié à l'œuvre de Marc Chagall, un peintre français d'origine russe qui a passé une partie de sa vie sur la Côte d'Azur.

[2] ont flâné *wandered through*
[3] ruelles *narrow streets*
[4] thon *tuna*
[5] anchois *anchovies*

Vous avez compris?

A **Un séjour à Nice** Répondez.
1. Où sont allées Valérie et ses copines?
2. Elles sont allées à Nice comment?
3. Quand elles sont arrivées à la gare, où sont-elles allées?
4. Pourquoi sont-elles allées au syndicat d'initiative?
5. L'employée du syndicat d'initiative a téléphoné à quel hôtel?
6. Comment les filles sont-elles allées à l'hôtel? À pied, en autobus, en taxi?
7. Qu'est-ce qu'elles ont fait quand elles sont arrivées à l'hôtel?
8. Où sont-elles allées à Nice?
9. Il y a du sable sur la plage? Qu'est-ce qu'il y a?
10. Où iront-elles demain?

B **La ville de Nice** Vrai ou faux?
1. Nice est une ville de la Côte d'Azur, sur la mer Méditerranée dans le sud de la France.
2. La promenade des Anglais est dans la vieille ville.
3. Dans une salade niçoise, on met de la viande.
4. Marc Chagall est un peintre d'origine russe.
5. Henri Matisse est un peintre russe.

La cathédrale orthodoxe russe à Nice

Lectures culturelles

Vous avez compris?

A Allow students to refer to the story to look up the answers or you may use this activity as a testing device for factual recall.

B Have students correct any false statements.

Geography Connection

Nice is considered both the queen and the capital of the French Riviera. It is situated along the **baie des Anges,** and palatial hotels line the famous beachfront street, the **promenade des Anglais.**

Nice was once a mecca for the rich only, but today it also attracts many conferences and conventions. Traffic has been banned from much of the town center. Nice also has a lovely old town with picturesque narrow winding streets.

ANSWERS TO Vous avez compris?

A
1. Elles sont allées à Nice.
2. Elles y sont allées en train.
3. Elles sont allées au syndicat d'initiative.
4. Elles y sont allées pour trouver une chambre d'hôtel.
5. Elle a téléphoné à l'Hôtel de la Gare.
6. Elles y sont allées à pied.
7. Elles ont rempli les fiches de police.
8. Elles sont allées à la promenade des Anglais, et à la vieille ville.
9. Non, il n'y a pas de sable sur la plage. Il y a des galets.
10. Elles iront visiter Cimiez, un quartier où il y a deux musées intéressants.

B
1. vrai
2. faux
3. faux
4. vrai
5. faux

Lecture supplémentaire 1

Les auberges de jeunesse

Les jeunes qui voyagent en France vont souvent dans des auberges de jeunesse. Les auberges de jeunesse ont des dortoirs[1] et ne coûtent pas cher. Les randonneurs[2] ou les cyclistes peuvent louer une chambre ou simplement un lit. Mais, ce qui est bien dans les auberges de jeunesse, c'est qu'on rencontre[3] beaucoup de jeunes de pays différents.

Pour pouvoir aller dans une auberge de jeunesse, il faut avoir une carte d'adhésion internationale. Cette carte donne accès à des auberges de jeunesse non seulement en France, mais dans 66 pays du monde.

Cette même carte permet également d'obtenir des réductions dans les musées, les piscines, les transports, etc.

[1] dortoirs *dorms*
[2] randonneurs *hikers*
[3] rencontre *meet*

L'auberge de jeunesse Mont Alban à Nice

Vous avez compris?

A Les jeunes voyageurs Vrai ou faux?
1. Les auberges de jeunesse ont beaucoup de chambres particulières pour une personne.
2. Les prix dans les auberges de jeunesse sont relativement bas.
3. Les randonneurs voyagent en voiture.
4. Dans les auberges de jeunesse, il y a des jeunes de différentes nationalités.
5. Il faut avoir un passeport français pour aller dans une auberge de jeunesse.

B Une explication Expliquez les avantages d'avoir une carte d'adhésion internationale.

Lecture supplémentaire 2

Le Club Med

Le Club Méditerranée est une chaîne d'hôtels française qui a des établissements dans de nombreux pays du monde. Les clients du Club Med sont des jeunes, des personnes plus âgées et des familles avec enfants. Le Club Med offre toute une gamme d'activités sportives comme le volley-ball et le tennis. De nombreux clubs se trouvent au bord de la mer et offrent donc toutes sortes de sports nautiques—le ski nautique, la voile[1] et la planche à voile. Le Club Med de la Guadeloupe, qui s'appelle «la Caravelle», a même un laboratoire de langues où on peut faire du français.

Quand vous allez au Club Med, vous n'avez pas besoin d'argent. Pas d'argent? Non. Parce qu'on paie un prix forfaitaire. Cela veut dire que tout est compris—la chambre, les repas, les activités sportives, etc. On ne paie que[2] les boissons. Si on veut aller au Club Med, il faut y passer au moins une semaine. On ne peut pas y passer une ou deux nuits[3] comme dans un hôtel normal. Les Clubs Med sont en fait des villages de vacances où on va pour s'amuser et quelquefois pour se reposer[4].

[1] la voile *sailing*
[2] ne… que *only*
[3] nuits *nights*
[4] se reposer *to rest*

Une plage au Club Med à la Guadeloupe

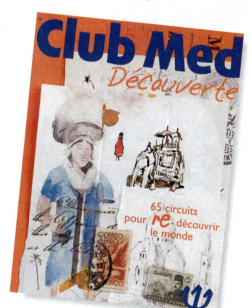

Vous avez compris?

Le Club Méditerranée Répondez.
1. Le Club Méditerranée est une chaîne d'hôtels française ou américaine?
2. Où se trouvent les Clubs Med?
3. On n'a pas besoin d'argent au Club Med. Pourquoi?
4. Il faut rester un minimum de combien de jours au Club Med?
5. Que sont les Clubs Med?

National Standards

Connections
This reading about the complexities of the French language establishes a connection with another discipline, allowing students to reinforce and further their knowledge of humanities through the study of French.

Attention!

The readings in the **Connexions** section are optional. They focus on some of the major disciplines taught in schools and universities. The vocabulary is useful for discussing such topics as history, literature, art, economics, business, science, etc. You may choose any of the following ways to do the readings in the **Connexions** section.

Independent reading Have students read the selections and do the post-reading activities as homework, which you collect. This option is least intrusive on class time and requires a minimum of teacher involvement.

Homework with in-class follow-up Assign the readings and post-reading activities as homework. Review and discuss the material in class the next day.

Intensive in-class activity This option includes a pre-reading vocabulary presentation, in-class reading and discussion, assignment of the activities for homework, and a discussion of the assignment in class the following day.

CONNEXIONS

Les lettres

Le langage

In a language, one word can often have more than one meaning. The word "bank" is an example of such a word in English. Give the meaning of the word "bank" in the following sentences.

I have an account in this bank.
Let's walk along the bank of the river.
There's a large bank of earth over there.
The plane is going into a rather severe bank.
You can't bank on that.

L'hôtel is a word in French that can have several meanings. Read the information on the next page and study the photos to learn about the different types of «hôtels».

Un petit hôtel à Yvoire

L'Hôtel-Dieu à Paris

Learning from Photos

(pages 300–301) Have students identify each type of **hôtel** in the photos.

LEVELING
E: Reading

Les différents sens d'un mot

Le mot «hôtel» a plusieurs sens[1]. Si on le cherche dans le dictionnaire, on voit que son premier sens est «maison meublée[2] où on loge les voyageurs». Mais un hôtel, cela peut être aussi un hôtel particulier, c'est-à-dire une grande maison luxueuse située dans une ville.

Un hôtel, c'est également n'importe quel[3] édifice destiné à des établissements publics. Un hôtel de ville, c'est la mairie[4] d'une grande ville.

Dans certaines villes, il y a un Hôtel-Dieu. L'Hôtel-Dieu, c'est l'hôpital principal de la ville. C'est toujours un vieil hôpital.

[1] sens *meaning*
[2] meublée *furnished*
[3] n'importe quel *any*
[4] mairie *town hall*

L'Hôtel de Ville de Paris

Un hôtel particulier à Paris

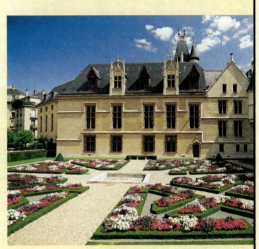
La cour de l'hôtel de Sens dans le Marais

Vous avez compris?

A Recherches Trouvez un mot anglais qui a plusieurs sens. Faites des phrases qui illustrent ces différents sens.

B Un mot français À l'aide d'un dictionnaire, trouvez les différents sens du mot français «note».

CONNEXIONS

Les lettres
Le langage

Step 1 Have students read the introduction in English on page 300.

Step 2 Ask students to think of other examples like the word "bank."

FUN FACTS

Many of the old elegant **hôtels particuliers** are now museums or embassies. Others have been subdivided into apartment (condo) units. There are still, however, **hôtels** that are occupied by a single family.

About the French Language

The word **hôtel** is also used in the expression **maître d'hôtel** which really has nothing to do with a hotel. It is the term for a headwaiter, or as we often say in English, *maître d'*.

ANSWERS TO Vous avez compris?

A *Answers will vary.*

B *Answers will vary but may include:*
1. un son musical
2. une courte communication écrite
3. une observation
4. une évaluation scolaire
5. une addition

C'est à vous

Use what you have learned

 Recycling

These activities allow students to use the vocabulary and structure from this chapter in completely open-ended, real-life situations.

Presentation

Encourage students to say as much as possible when they do these activities. Tell them not to be afraid to make mistakes, since the goal of these activities is real-life communication.

You may wish to separate students into pairs or groups. Encourage students to elaborate on the basic theme and to be creative. They may use props, pictures, or posters if they wish.

Learning from Photos

(page 302) Aix-en-Provence is a beautiful city with many classical buildings and historic monuments. Since Roman days it has been a spa town. It also has a major university, and it is the home of the world-famous drama festival that takes place every July.

The word **Aix** comes from the Latin **Aquae**, meaning *waters*.

C'est à vous

Use what you have learned

 PARLER **1**

Vous avez une chambre?
✔ *Reserve a hotel room*

Vous êtes à Aix-en-Provence. Vous n'avez pas réservé de chambre d'hôtel. Vous téléphonez à un hôtel et vous demandez s'il y a une chambre disponible. Vous demandez le prix, ce qui est compris dans le prix, comment aller à l'hôtel, etc. Le/La réceptionniste (votre camarade) répond poliment à vos questions.

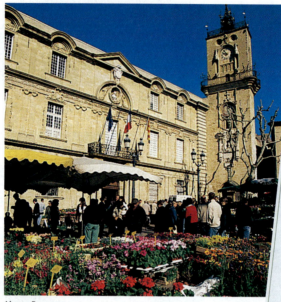
Aix-en-Provence

 PARLER **2**

La note, s'il vous plaît!
✔ *Check out of a hotel*

Vous quittez votre hôtel. Vous demandez la note. Le caissier ou la caissière (votre camarade) vous la présente. Vous trouvez qu'il y a des erreurs. Vous n'avez pas pris votre petit déjeuner à l'hôtel, vous n'avez pas acheté de brochure, etc.

302 trois cent deux

CHAPITRE 9

ANSWERS TO C'est à vous

 1 *Answers will vary but may include:*

—Bonjour, madame. Vous auriez une chambre pour deux personnes pour ce soir, s'il vous plaît?
—Une chambre à un ou deux lits?
—Une chambre à deux lits.
—Oui, j'ai une chambre avec salle de bains.
—D'accord. Le petit déjeuner est compris?
—Oui, absolument.
—C'est combien, la chambre?
—100 euros.
—Ça va. On va arriver tout de suite.

2 *Answers will vary.*

CHAPITRE 9

3 Un fax pour l'hôtel Château d'Esclimont
✓ *Obtain information about a hotel in France*

Les parents de votre ami(e) vont faire un voyage en France. Ils veulent descendre à l'hôtel Château d'Esclimont près de Chartres. Ils savent que vous faites du français et vous demandent de les aider à envoyer un fax. Avant d'écrire le fax, faites une liste de tous les renseignements que les parents de votre ami(e) veulent avoir. Rédigez ensuite le fax.

Le Château d'Esclimont

Writing Strategy

Writing an advertisement The purpose of an advertisement is to persuade people to buy a product or service. An effective ad will attract attention and create interest in the product. You can use a striking design to draw readers in. You can use facts and opinions to explain the product's features and to convince readers that they should buy your product instead of the competition's.

4 Une petite annonce

A hotel in your community wants to encourage French-speaking guests to stay there. They have asked you to prepare an advertisement describing the hotel and listing its best features. Use the advertisement shown as a guide, but be as original as you can. Be sure your ad reflects services offered by the hotel as well as activities and events in your community.

Assessment

Vocabulaire

1 Choisissez.

1. _____ une fiche de police   a. verser
2. _____ des arrhes   b. monter
3. _____ une chambre   c. remplir
4. _____ au troisième   d. réserver

To review Mots 1, turn to pages 280–281.

2 Identifiez.

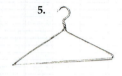 5.

 6.

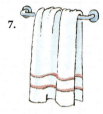 7.

 8.

 9.

To review Mots 2, turn to pages 284–285.

Structure

3 Choisissez.

10. Charles _____ sorti pour visiter la ville.
    a. est   b. a
11. Il _____ rentré à neuf heures du soir.
    a. est   b. a
12. Qui _____ descendu les bagages?
    a. est   b. a
13. Il _____ sorti sa clé de son sac-à-dos.
    a. est   b. a
14. Le petit garçon _____ monté l'escalier.
    a. est   b. a

To review these verbs in the passé composé, turn to page 288.

304 trois cent quatre   CHAPITRE 9

ANSWERS TO Assessment

1
1. c
2. a
3. d
4. b

2
5. un cintre
6. du savon
7. une serviette
8. un rouleau de papier hygiénique
9. un gant de toilette

3
10. a
11. a
12. b
13. b
14. b

CHAPITRE 9 Assessment

4 Répondez avec un pronom.
15. Tu veux aller à Paris?
16. Tu es allé(e) au Canada?
17. Tu veux rester dans ta chambre?

*To review the pronoun **y**, turn to page 289.*

5 Complétez.
18. Le réceptionniste t'a donné combien de clés?
    Il ____ a donné deux.
19. Il lui a parlé de sa visite?
    Oui, il ____ a parlé.
20. Il y a combien de chambres dans cet hôtel?
    Il ____ a vingt.

*To review the pronoun **en**, turn to page 291.*

Culture

6 Vrai ou faux?
21. Le syndicat d'initiative est une gare.
22. La promenade des Anglais est à Nice.
23. À Nice, il y a une belle plage de sable.
24. Dans une salade niçoise, il y a de la viande.
25. Marc Chagall est un peintre français d'origine russe.

To review this cultural information, turn to pages 296–297.

La baie des Anges à Nice

Assessment

This is a pre-test for students to take before you administer the chapter test. Answer sheets for students to do these pages are provided in your transparency binder. Note that each section is cross-referenced so students can easily find the material they have to review in case they made errors. You may wish to collect these assessments and correct them yourself or you may prefer to have students correct themselves in class. You can go over the answers orally or project them on the overhead, using your Assessment Answers transparencies.

Glencoe Technology

MINDJOGGER VHS/DVD
You may wish to help your students prepare for the chapter test by playing the MindJogger game show. Teams will compete against each other to review chapter vocabulary and structure and sharpen listening comprehension skills.

ANSWERS TO Assessment

4
15. Oui, je veux y aller.
16. Oui, j'y suis allé(e).
17. Oui, je veux y rester.

5
18. m'en
19. lui en
20. y en

6
21. faux
22. vrai
23. faux
24. faux
25. vrai

On parle super bien!

This unique page gives students the opportunity to speak freely and say whatever they can, using the vocabulary and structures they have learned in the chapter. The illustration serves to remind students of precisely what they know how to say in French. There are no activities that students do not have the ability to describe or talk about in French. The art not only depicts the vocabulary and content of this chapter, but also reinforces what they learned in previous chapters.

You may wish to use this page in many ways. Some possibilities are to have students do the following:

1. Look at the illustration and identify items by giving the correct French words.
2. Make up sentences about what they see in the illustration.
3. Make up questions about the illustration. They can call on another class member to respond if you do this as a class activity, or you may prefer to allow students to work in small groups. This activity is extremely beneficial because it enables students to actively use interrogative words.
4. Answer questions you ask them about the illustration.
5. Work in pairs and make up a conversation based on the illustration.
6. Look at the illustration and give a complete oral review of what they see.
7. Look at the illustration and write a paragraph (or essay) about it.

You can also use this page as an assessment or testing tool, taking into account individual differences by having students go from simple to quite complicated tasks. The assessment can be either oral or written. You may wish to use the rubrics provided on pages T20–T21 as you give students the following directions.

On parle super bien!

Tell all you can about this illustration.

1. Identify the topic or situation of the illustration.
2. Give the French words for as many items as you can.
3. Think of as many sentences as you can to describe the illustration.
4. Go over your sentences and put them in the best sequencing to give a coherent story based on the illustration.

Vocabulaire

Making a hotel reservation
réserver une chambre
verser des arrhes

une chambre
 à un lit
 à deux lits
 avec salle de bains

compris

Checking into a hotel
un hôtel
le hall
la réception
le/la réceptionniste

une fiche de police
une clé
un bagage
une valise

monter
descendre
défaire

Checking out of a hotel
libérer
la note
les frais (de téléphone)

une carte de crédit
en espèces
 (en liquide)

le caissier, la caissière

Talking about a hotel room
une porte
un placard
un cintre
un drap

une couverture
un oreiller
l'air climatisé
la climatisation

Talking about a bathroom
un gant de toilette
du savon
une serviette
un rouleau de papier
 hygiénique

propre
sale

Other useful words and expressions
une femme de
 chambre
un séjour
absolument
soigneusement

poliment
se sécher
fermer la porte à clé
souhaiter
du monde

How well do you know your vocabulary?

Identify words you would use when reserving a hotel room. Describe the type of room you would like to have and how you will pay for it.

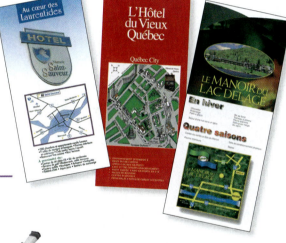

VIDÉOTOUR

Épisode 9

In this video episode, you will join Manu, who is helping out at his parents' hotel. See page 508 for more information.

L'HÔTEL · trois cent sept · 307

Planning for Chapter 10

SCOPE AND SEQUENCE, PAGES 308–337

Topics
* Public transportation

Culture
* Public transportation in Paris
* Discussing public transportation in Haiti and Africa

Functions
* How to request information formally and informally
* How to tell what you and others have just done
* How to find out how long someone has been doing something

Structure
* Forming questions
* **Venir de** + infinitive
* Expressing time

National Standards
* Communication Standard 1.1 pages 312, 313, 316, 317, 319, 320, 321, 322, 323, 325, 332
* Communication Standard 1.2 pages 312, 313, 316, 317, 319, 320, 321, 322, 323, 324, 327, 329, 331
* Communication Standard 1.3 pages 317, 322, 323, 331, 333
* Cultures Standard 2.1 pages 310, 311, 314, 315, 324, 325, 326–327, 328–329
* Cultures Standard 2.2 pages 310, 314, 315, 316, 325, 326–327, 328–329
* Connections Standard 3.1 pages 330–331
* Comparisons Standard 4.1 page 324
* Comparisons Standard 4.2 pages 317, 326–329
* Communities Standard 5.1 page 333

PACING AND PRIORITIES

The chapter content is color coded below to assist you in planning.

■ required   ■ recommended   ■ optional

Vocabulaire *(required)* *Days 1–4*
- ■ Mots 1
  Le métro
- ■ Mots 2
  L'autobus

Structure *(required)* *Days 5–7*
- ■ Les questions
- ■ **Venir de** + infinitif
- ■ Les expressions de temps

Conversation *(required)*
- ■ Le métro

Lectures culturelles
- ■ Les transports en commun à Paris *(recommended)*
- ■ Les transports en commun en Haïti et en Afrique *(optional)*

Connexions *(optional)*
- ■ La littérature

■ **C'est à vous** *(recommended)*

■ **Assessment** *(recommended)*

■ **On parle super bien!** *(optional)*

RESOURCE GUIDE

SECTION	PAGES	SECTION RESOURCES
Vocabulaire *Mots 1*		
Le métro	310–313	Vocabulary Transparencies 10.2–10.3 Audio CD 6 Audio Activities TE, pages 106–108 Workbook, pages 111–112 Quiz 1, page 51 ExamView® Pro
Vocabulaire *Mots 2*		
L'autobus	314–317	Vocabulary Transparencies 10.4–10.5 Audio CD 6 Audio Activities TE, pages 108–110 Workbook, pages 112–113 Quiz 2, page 52 ExamView® Pro
Structure		
Les questions **Venir de** + infinitif Les expressions de temps	318–321 321–322 323	Audio CD 6 Audio Activities TE, pages 110–111 Workbook, pages 114–117 Quizzes 3–5, pages 53–55 ExamView® Pro
Conversation		
Le métro	324–325	Audio CD 6 Audio Activities TE, pages 112–113 Interactive CD-ROM
Lectures culturelles		
Les transports en commun à Paris Les transports en commun en Haïti et en Afrique	326–327 328–329	Audio CD 6 Audio Activities TE, pages 113–114 Tests, page 154, 158
Connexions		
La littérature	330–331	Tests, page 159
C'est à vous		
	332–333	**Bon voyage!** Video, Episode 10 Video Activities, Chapter 10 French Online Activities french.glencoe.com
Assessment		
	334–335	Communication Transparency C 10 Quizzes 1–5, pages 51–55 Performance Assessment, Task 10 Tests, pages 151–166 ExamView® Pro Situation Cards, Chapter 10 **Marathon mental** Videoquiz

Using Your Resources for Chapter 10

Transparencies

Bellringer 10.1–10.7

Vocabulary 10.1–10.5

Communication C 10

Workbook

Vocabulary, pages 111–113

Structure, pages 114–117

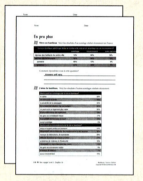
Enrichment, pages 118–120

Audio Activities

Vocabulary, pages 106–110

Structure, pages 110–111

Conversation, pages 112–113

Cultural Reading, pages 113–114

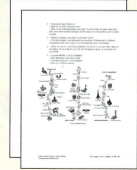
Additional Practice, pages 114–117

308C

Assessment

Vocabulary and Structure Quizzes, pages 51–55

Chapter Tests, pages 151–166

Situation Cards, Chapter 10

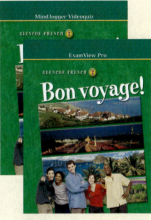

MindJogger Videoquiz, ExamView® Pro, Chapter 10

Timesaving Teacher Tools

TeacherWorks™

TeacherWorks™ is your all-in-one teacher resource center. Personalize lesson plans, access resources from the Teacher Wraparound Edition, connect to the Internet, or make a to-do list. These are only a few of the many features that can assist you in the planning and organizing of your lessons.

Includes:
- A calendar feature
- Access to all program blackline masters
- Standards correlations and more

ExamView® Pro

Test Bank software for Macintosh and Windows makes creating, editing, customizing, and printing tests quick and easy.

Technology Resources

In the Chapter 10 Internet activity, you will have a chance to learn more about the Francophone world. Visit **french.glencoe.com**.

On the Interactive Conversation CD-ROM, students can listen to and take part in a recorded version of the conversation in Chapter 10.

See the National Geographic Teacher's Corner on pages 138–139, 244–245, 372–373, 472–473 for reference to additional technology resources.

Bon voyage! Video and Video Activities, Chapter 10

Help your students prepare for the chapter test by playing the **Marathon mental** Videoquiz game show. Teams will compete against each other to review chapter vocabulary and structure and sharpen listening comprehension skills.

Preview

In this chapter, students will learn vocabulary associated with the public transportation system in a French-speaking country. They will increase their ability to ask and understand directions. They will learn more about the various ways of asking questions, learn to express the idea "to have just done something," and the time expression **depuis**.

National Standards

Communication
In Chapter 10, students will communicate in spoken and written French on the following topics:
- Using public transportation, including the subway and the bus
- Asking for directions

Students will obtain and provide information about these topics and engage in conversations that would typically take place using public transportation as they fulfill the chapter objectives listed on this page.

LEVELING

The activities, conversations, and readings within each chapter are marked according to level of difficulty. **E** indicates easy. **A** indicates average. **C** indicates challenging. Some activities cover a range of difficulty. In some activities, for example, advanced students will be able to produce more extensive responses while students who learn at a different rate may give less detailed responses. The leveling indicators will help you individualize instruction to best meet your students' needs.

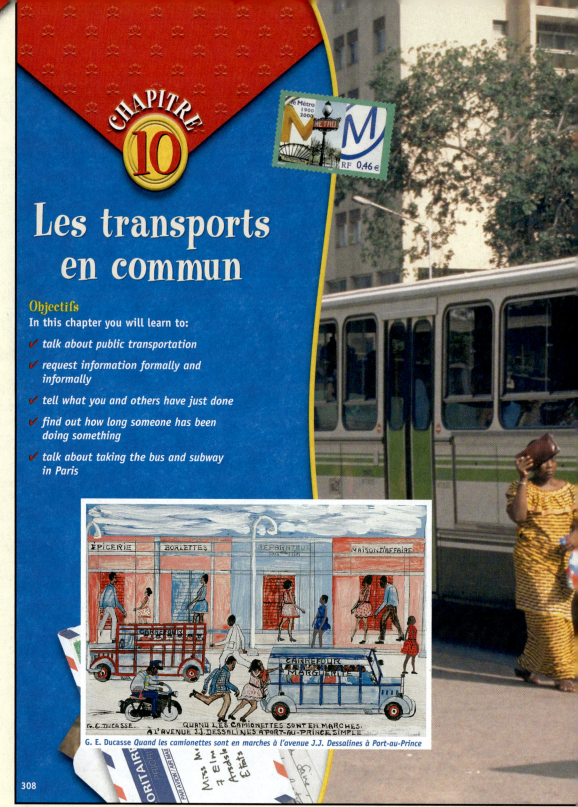

CHAPITRE 10
Les transports en commun

Objectifs
In this chapter you will learn to:

✔ talk about public transportation

✔ request information formally and informally

✔ tell what you and others have just done

✔ find out how long someone has been doing something

✔ talk about taking the bus and subway in Paris

G. E. Ducasse *Quand les camionettes sont en marches à l'avenue J.J. Dessalines à Port-au-Prince*

Spotlight on Culture

Photograph In this photo we see a public bus in Abidjan, the capital of Côte d'Ivoire. The public municipal buses are all yellow and green. The woman on the street is wearing a typical West African dress called a **boubou**.

Painting This painting was done by the twentieth-century Haitian folk artist G.E. Ducasse. This painting shows some buses or **camionnettes** known as **tap taps** in Haiti. They are on avenue Dessalines, a main street in the capital, Port-au-Prince. The street is named after Jean-Jacques Dessalines (1758–1806), a former slave who revolted against colonial domination. He fought the French and proclaimed Haitian independence on January 1, 1804. He was then crowned emperor of Haiti with the name Jacques I.

National Standards

Communities

If you live in an area with a public transportation system, have students prepare a brochure for French-speaking visitors on how to use it. Then send it to the local Chamber of Commerce or the nearest foreign student exchange organization.

Vocabulaire Mots 1

1 Preparation

Resource Manager

Vocabulary Transparencies
 10.2–10.3
Audio Activities TE, pages 106–108
Audio CD 6
Workbook, pages 111–112
Quiz 1, page 51
ExamView Pro®

Bellringer Review

Use BRR Transparency 10.1 or write the following on the board.
List all the words and expressions you can remember that have to do with train travel.

2 Presentation

Step 1 Have students close their books. Use Vocabulary Transparencies 10.2–10.3 to present **Mots 1**. Have students repeat the words, phrases, and sentences after you or Audio CD 6.

Step 2 Ask *either/or* and *yes/no* questions to elicit the vocabulary. Then point in random order to illustrations on the Vocabulary Transparencies and ask **Qu'est-ce que c'est?**

Step 3 Have students open their books and read pages 310–311. Model the correct pronunciation as necessary.

Step 4 Have students repeat the miniconversation with as much expression as possible. Point out that **un carnet** is a book of ten tickets.

Vocabulaire Mots 1

Le métro

Il faut valider son ticket.
Il faut le glisser dans le tourniquet.

310 ❖ *trois cent dix* CHAPITRE 10

Reaching All Students

Total Physical Response Call on individuals to mimic the following.
 Regardez le plan du métro.
 Prenez un ticket au distributeur automatique.
 Glissez le ticket dans le tourniquet.
 Attendez le métro sur le quai.
 Montez en voiture.
 Cherchez une place.
 Prenez votre place.
 Levez-vous.
 Descendez du métro.

310

Vocabulaire
Mots 1

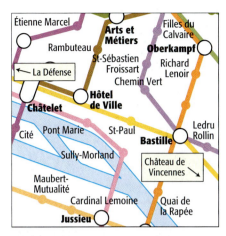

Pour aller à Bastille, il faut prendre la ligne N° 1, direction Vincennes.
Plusieurs lignes se croisent à Bastille.
Quand on prend la correspondance, on change de ligne.
On peut prendre la correspondance à Bastille.

un escalier mécanique

Les voyageurs descendent l'escalier mécanique.
Ils viennent d'acheter leurs tickets.

le quai

le métro

Les voyageurs attendent le métro.
Ils n'attendent pas longtemps.
Il y a un métro toutes les quatre minutes.

Excusez-moi, madame. Vous descendez à la prochaine?

Il y a beaucoup de gens dans le métro.
Aux heures de pointe, les métros sont bondés.

LES TRANSPORTS EN COMMUN

trois cent onze 311

Vocabulaire

Quel est le mot?

1 Qu'est-ce que c'est? Identifiez.

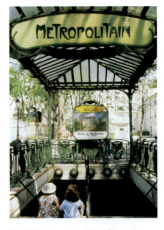

1. C'est un guichet ou un distributeur automatique?
2. C'est une station de métro ou le coin d'une rue?
3. C'est un ticket ou un carnet?

4. C'est un métro ou un autobus?
5. C'est un tourniquet ou un escalier mécanique?

2 Historiette Le métro Répondez que oui.

1. Il y a un escalier mécanique pour descendre sur le quai?
2. Il y a un guichet où on peut acheter des tickets de métro?
3. Il y a des distributeurs automatiques?
4. Il faut valider son ticket avant d'aller sur le quai?
5. Il faut passer par un tourniquet avant d'arriver sur le quai?
6. Les voyageurs attendent le métro sur le quai?
7. Le métro vient de partir?
8. Il y a un métro toutes les quatre minutes?
9. De temps en temps, il faut changer de ligne?
10. On peut prendre la correspondance dans une station où deux lignes se croisent?

3 **Historiette** **Dans la station de métro** Complétez.
1. Quand je ne sais pas où se trouve une ____ de métro, je demande à quelqu'un.
2. Je vais prendre le métro. Je descends sur le ____.
3. Je peux acheter un ticket au ____ ou au ____.
4. Je peux acheter un seul ticket ou un ____ de dix tickets.
5. Je prends l'____ pour descendre sur le quai de la station.
6. Si je ne sais pas quelle direction prendre, je regarde le ____.
7. On peut prendre la ____ dans une station où deux lignes se croisent.
8. Les métros sont souvent ____ aux heures de pointe.

4 **Pardon...** Vous êtes à Montréal. Votre camarade est canadien(ne). Vous voulez prendre le métro et vous demandez les renseignements suivants à votre camarade: **où prendre le métro; où acheter des tickets; comment aller sur le quai.**

5 **Quelle station?** Vous êtes un(e) touriste à Paris. Choisissez un monument ou un musée que vous voulez visiter. Demandez à quelqu'un dans le métro (votre camarade) à quelle station vous devez descendre. Ensuite changez de rôle.

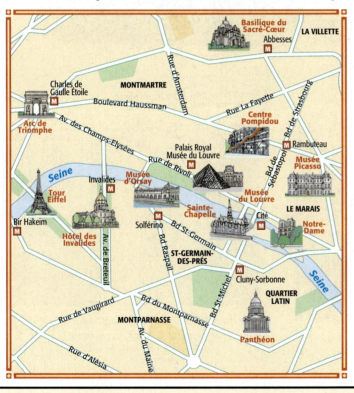

trois cent treize ❖ 313

Vocabulaire Mots 2

1 Preparation

Resource Manager

Vocabulary Transparencies 10.4–10.5
Audio Activities TE, pages 108–110
Audio CD 6
Workbook, pages 112–113
Quiz 2, page 52
ExamView Pro®

Bellringer Review

Use BRR Transparency 10.2 or write the following on the board. Write words and expressions associated with an airport.

2 Presentation

Step 1 Show Vocabulary Transparencies 10.4–10.5. Have students close their books and repeat the words after you or Audio CD 6 as you point to the appropriate illustration on the transparency.

Step 2 Ask students questions such as: **On attend l'autobus où? On attend le 48 à cet arrêt d'autobus? On met son ticket dans la machine ou le conducteur prend le ticket? On met le ticket dans l'appareil pour le valider? Pour demander un arrêt, on appuie sur le bouton ou s'appuie contre la porte? Il est interdit de s'appuyer contre la porte?**

Step 3 To elicit the new vocabulary on these pages, ask questions such as: **On descend de l'autobus par où? On monte par le milieu ou l'avant? Le jeune homme a poussé un homme? Qu'est-ce qu'il dit pour s'excuser?**

314

Vocabulaire Mots 2

L'autobus

un arrêt d'autobus
un autobus
un numéro

un conducteur   valider son ticket
une machine = un appareil

Ne poussez pas, jeune homme!
Excusez-moi, monsieur.
un bouton
une porte

Pour demander un arrêt, on appuie sur le bouton.
Il n'est pas prudent de s'appuyer contre la porte.

314 trois cent quatorze

CHAPITRE 10

Chapter Projects

On prend le métro! Have students study the Paris **métro** map on page 310. They should choose a starting point and destination and write directions to get from one to the other.

Je suis touriste. Have groups prepare questions they feel would be most useful when making their way about an unfamiliar French city.

Des comparaisons Have groups research and compare various aspects of French and American cities and suburbs. Possible topics might include: public transportation, populations of city centers vs. suburbs, etc.

Vocabulaire Mots 2

Le terminus est le dernier arrêt.
Le trajet est le voyage que fait un autobus d'un terminus à un autre.

Mélanie avait rendez-vous avec Julien à trois heures.
Il est trois heures et demie.
Julien n'est toujours pas là.
Mélanie l'attend depuis une demi-heure.

On descend de l'autobus par l'arrière ou le milieu.
La descente est interdite par l'avant.
On monte par l'avant.

LES TRANSPORTS EN COMMUN

trois cent quinze 315

Learning from Photos

(page 315) Point out to students the map on the bus. The map shows the bus route. The route is also indicated on the side of the bus.

Vocabulary Expansion

You may wish to teach the expression **faire exprès**. Have students look at the lower right illustration on page 314. Ask: **Le jeune homme a poussé l'homme? Il voulait le pousser? Il savait qu'il l'avait poussé? Oui. Alors il l'a fait exprès. Il savait ce qu'il faisait.**

Assessment

As an informal assessment, show Vocabulary Transparencies 10.4–10.5. Call on students to point to and identify various items at random.

The **Glencoe World Languages Web site** (french.glencoe.com) offers options that enable you and your students to experience the French-speaking world via the Internet. For each chapter, there are activities, games, and quizzes. In addition, an *Enrichment* section offers students an opportunity to visit Web sites related to the theme of the chapter.

Reaching All Students

Total Physical Response Call on students to mimic the following.
Montez dans l'autobus.
Validez votre ticket dans l'appareil.
Appuyez sur le bouton pour indiquer que vous voulez descendre.
Descendez de l'autobus.
Attendez votre ami(e).
Regardez votre montre.
Indiquez que vous devenez impatient(e).

Vocabulaire

3 Practice

Quel est le mot?

Learning from Realia

(page 316) Have students look at the bus schedule and route map as you ask: **Quels sont les terminus de cette ligne? L'autobus fait combien d'arrêts entre Luxembourg et Clisson?**

Reaching All Students

Additional Practice Have students listen to these definitions and supply a word or expression that means the same.

  le dernier arrêt
  le contraire de «monter»
  le voyage que fait un autobus
     d'un terminus à l'autre
  pardonnez-moi
  la partie antérieure d'un
     véhicule
  la partie postérieure d'un
     véhicule
  celui qui conduit l'autobus
  pas permis
  se servir de quelque chose
     comme support

Vocabulaire

Quel est le mot?

6 Un autobus parisien
Répondez d'après la photo.
1. De quelle couleur est l'autobus?
2. Quel est le numéro de l'autobus?
3. Quel est le terminus?

Un arrêt du 52 à Paris

7 Historiette À l'arrêt d'autobus
Répondez d'après le panneau.
1. Quel est l'arrêt entre les alpes et clisson?
2. Le premier bus commence à circuler à quelle heure du lundi au samedi?
3. Le dernier bus est à quelle heure?
4. Quel est l'un des terminus de cette ligne?

For more practice using words from **Mots 2**, *do Activity 16 on page H17 at the end of this book.*

316 ✦ trois cent seize

CHAPITRE 10

ANSWERS TO Quel est le mot?

6
1. L'autobus est bleu et blanc.
2. C'est le 52.
3. C'est le parc de Saint-Cloud.

7
1. Nationale est l'arrêt entre les alpes et clisson.
2. Le premier bus commence à circuler à 6 h 46 du lundi au samedi.
3. Le dernier bus est à 0 h 43.
4. Un terminus est Porte de Vitry.

8 **Historiette** **Les autobus parisiens** Répondez.
1. Les lignes des autobus parisiens sont numérotées?
2. Dans l'autobus, il y a un tableau qui indique tous les arrêts de la ligne?
3. Les autobus parisiens ont combien de portes?
4. Il faut le dire au conducteur quand on veut descendre?
5. Il y a un appareil à l'avant de l'autobus pour valider son ticket?
6. Pour demander un arrêt, il faut appuyer sur un bouton?
7. Il est interdit de descendre de l'autobus par l'arrière?
8. La descente est interdite par le milieu?
9. Beaucoup de voyageurs s'appuient contre la porte pendant le trajet?
10. Le terminus est le dernier arrêt qu'un autobus fait?
11. Il faut pousser tout le monde pour descendre de l'autobus?

Il faut valider son ticket.

9 **Les transports en commun** Travaillez avec un(e) camarade. Dites quels sont les transports en commun dans votre ville. Décidez si vous avez un bon réseau de transports en commun. Sinon, décidez comment on peut l'améliorer *(improve)*.

Le funiculaire à Montmartre

La station de métro Bougainville à Marseille

Un autobus en Nouvelle-Calédonie

10 **Un car scolaire** Travaillez avec un(e) camarade. Décrivez un car scolaire typique. Ensuite comparez ce car scolaire à un autobus parisien.

Structure

1 Preparation

Resource Manager

Audio Activities TE, pages 110–111
Audio CD 6
Workbook, pages 114–117
Quizzes 3–5, pages 53–55
ExamView Pro®

Bellringer Review

Use BRR Transparency 10.3 or write the following on the board. Complete the sentences with the conditional of the verbs in parentheses.
1. À sa place, je _____ au professeur. (parler)
2. Nous _____, mais nous devons aller à la gare. (attendre)
3. À ma place, qu'est-ce que tu _____? (faire)
4. Vous _____ à la fête si vous étiez invité(e)? (aller)

2 Presentation

Les questions

Step 1 Students have had a good deal of practice hearing and producing questions in the ways described in Item 1 and the second part of Item 5. You may wish to have students read this material silently. Then have them read the model questions aloud. The more students hear and form questions, the more comfortable they will be.

Structure

Les questions
Requesting information

1. You have been using questions since you began your study of French. The most common way to form a question in spoken French is simply to use a rising intonation at the end of a statement. If you use a question word such as **quand, comment,** etc., you put it at the end of the sentence.

   Sylvain part? Il part quand? Il part avec qui?

2. Another way to form a question in French is to place **est-ce que** before a statement. If a question word is used, it comes before **est-ce que.**

   Est-ce que Sylvain part?
   Quand est-ce qu'il part?
   Avec qui est-ce qu'il part?

3. A third way to ask a question is to use inversion, that is, to reverse the order of the subject and verb. Inversion is used mostly in formal French.

   Parlez-vous français?
   Où vas-tu?
   Pourquoi partent-ils maintenant?

4. When the verb is in the **passé composé,** you invert the subject and the auxiliary verb, **avoir** or **être: Combien as-tu payé?**

   The same rule applies to verbs followed by an infinitive: **Combien peux-tu payer?**

5. With a noun subject, you can use both the noun and the inverted subject. However, this type of inversion is used only in formal, written French.

   Marie parle-t-elle français?
   Les garçons vont-ils au match de foot?
   Combien ce chemisier coûte-t-il?

   You can simply invert the subject and the verb for questions beginning with question words (**où, combien, que, comment, à quelle heure,** etc.).

   Où habite Marie?
   Combien coûte ce chemisier?
   Que fait Paul?

Attention!

When the pronouns **il(s), elle(s),** and **on** are inverted, there is a /t/ sound between the subject and the verb. This /t/ sound is represented by the **t** or **d** already present at the end of the verb.
Comment vont-elles au bureau?
Où prend-il le métro?

However, if the verb ends in a vowel, you add a -t- between the subject and the verb.
À quelle station monte-t-elle?
Où va-t-on?

318 ❖ *trois cent dix-huit*   CHAPITRE 10

LEVELING
E: Activities 11, 12, 13
A: Activities 11, 12, 13

Comment dit-on?

11 J'ai des questions à vous poser. Posez des questions de trois façons différentes.

1. Vous êtes français.
2. Vous parlez français.
3. Vous habitez à Paris.
4. Vous avez un appartement en ville.
5. Vous travaillez à Paris.
6. Vous êtes peintre.
7. Vous allez au travail en bus.

12 Historiette Tous les jours Refaites les questions d'après le modèle.

À quelle heure Jean se lève-t-il?
À quelle heure est-ce que Jean se lève?

1. À quelle heure son frère se réveille-t-il?
2. Quand sa sœur se lave-t-elle les dents?
3. Comment s'habillent-ils?
4. À quelle heure partent-ils pour l'école?
5. Quand rentrent-ils à la maison?
6. À quelle heure se couchent-ils?
7. Et vous, à quelle heure vous couchez-vous?

13 Historiette Des questions Faites des questions d'après le modèle.

Marie habite *à Paris.*
Où habite Marie?

1. Marie habite *rue du Cloître-Notre-Dame.*
2. Marie est *très sympathique.*
3. Marie fait *de l'anglais.*
4. Son professeur d'anglais s'appelle *Madame Richards.*
5. Madame Richards vient *d'Angleterre.*
6. Le cours d'anglais de Marie est *à onze heures.*

La rue du Cloître-Notre-Dame à Paris

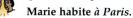

trois cent dix-neuf ✦ 319

Structure

14 **Un diplôme de quelle école?** Récrivez les questions suivantes en utilisant l'inversion.

1. Vous allez à quelle école?
2. Votre frère veut aller à quelle école?
3. Vous suivez combien de cours ce semestre?
4. Votre frère va suivre combien de cours?
5. Vous allez à l'école comment?
6. Votre frère va à l'école comment?
7. Vous faites du français avec quel professeur?
8. Votre frère pense faire du français avec qui?

Des universitaires à Abidjan en Côte d'Ivoire

15 **Historiette Un voyage** Faites une question en utilisant l'inversion.

1. Robert a fait un voyage à Avignon l'année dernière. (que)
2. Il est allé à l'aéroport avec ses copains. (où)
3. L'avion a fait deux escales. (combien)
4. Le vol était complet. (comment)
5. L'avion est arrivé à cinq heures du soir. (à quelle heure)
6. Robert était fatigué. (comment)
7. Il est allé récupérer ses bagages. (que)

Le pont Saint-Bénézet à Avignon

16 Des questions Travaillez avec un(e) camarade. Regardez le dessin ci-dessous. Faites des questions sur tout ce que vous voyez. Utilisez les mots suivants: **où, d'où, qu'est-ce que, qui, quand, comment, quoi, qu'est-ce qui.**

   17 Posons des questions! Travaillez par groupes de quatre ou cinq personnes. Vous avez cinq minutes pour préparer une liste de questions. Le groupe qui a le plus grand nombre de questions gagne.

 ## Venir de + infinitif
Telling what just happened

You use **venir** in the present tense with **de** + infinitive to indicate that an action has just taken place.

Les voyageurs viennent de descendre du métro.	*The passengers just got off the subway.*
Le métro vient de partir.	*The subway just left.*

LES TRANSPORTS EN COMMUN — trois cent vingt et un

Structure

3 Practice
Comment dit-on?

16 Expansion: After students prepare their questions, have them work in groups to ask and answer each others' questions.

1 Preparation

Bellringer Review

Use BRR Transparency 10.4 or write the following on the board. List everything you would see or do on a Parisian bus.

2 Presentation

 Venir de + infinitif

Step 1 Guide students through the explanation and have them read the model sentences aloud.

Step 2 You may wish to have students repeat one sentence, such as **Je viens d'arriver,** in all forms. For example: **Je viens d'arriver. Tu viens d'arriver. Il/Elle/On vient d'arriver,** etc.

ANSWERS TO Comment dit-on?

16 *Answers will vary.*
Students can use any word order they wish. In conversational French, the rising intonation with the question word at the end is the most common.

Answers may include:
Où les garçons vont-ils? Quelle heure est-il? Quel est le numéro de l'autobus? Qu'est-ce qu'on sert au café?, etc.

Structure

3 Practice

Comment dit-on?

18 and **19** These activities can be done with books either open or closed.

♻ Recycling

Have students form as many questions as they can about the girl in the photo on page 322.

Learning from Photos

(page 323) The village of Tinerhir is not far from the gorges of the Dadès Valley (see page 244). As one can see in the photo, Tinerhir has several palm groves. Once one leaves Tinerhir traveling north, the opposite direction of the gorges, there is not much change in the scenery of the stone desert.

LEVELING

E: Activities 18, 20, 22
A: Activities 19, 20, 21, 22

Structure

Comment dit-on?

18 **La journée d'Alexis** Répondez.
1. Il est sept heures et demie du matin. Alexis vient de se lever ou de se coucher?
2. Il est midi. Il vient de déjeuner ou de dîner?
3. Il est quatre heures et demie de l'après-midi. Il vient d'entrer en classe ou de rentrer du collège?
4. Il est sept heures du soir. Il vient de dîner ou de prendre son petit déjeuner?
5. Il est dix heures du soir. Il vient de regarder la télévision ou de dîner?
6. Il est onze heures du soir. Il vient de se lever ou de se coucher?

19 **Qu'est-ce qu'on vient de faire?** Répondez en utilisant **venir de**.
1. Moi, je ___.
2. Mon père ___.
3. Mes copains ___.
4. Nous ___.
5. Vous ___.
6. Et toi, tu ___.

20 **Récemment** Travaillez avec un(e) camarade. Dites tout ce que vous venez de faire. Décidez si vous venez tous les deux de faire les mêmes choses.

21 **Où suis-je allé(e)?** Dites à un(e) camarade plusieurs choses que vous venez de faire. Il/Elle vous dira où vous êtes allé(e). Ensuite changez de rôle.
—Je viens d'acheter des timbres.
—Tu es allé(e) à la poste.

Le bureau de poste à Évry près de Paris

ANSWERS TO Comment dit-on?

18
1. Il vient de se lever.
2. Il vient de déjeuner.
3. Il vient de rentrer du collège.
4. Il vient de dîner.
5. Il vient de regarder la télévision.
6. Il vient de se coucher.

19 *Answers will vary but may include:*
1. viens d'entrer en classe.
2. vient d'aller au travail.
3. viennent de parler avec le prof d'anglais.
4. venons de déjeuner.
5. venez d'arriver à l'école.
6. viens de me donner ton livre.

20 *Answers will vary depending upon what students just did.*

21 *Answers will vary but may include:*
—Je viens de faire les courses.
—Tu es allé(e) au marché.

Les expressions de temps
Expressing time

You use the expression **depuis** with the present tense to describe an action that began at some time in the past and continues into the present.

Vous attendez le bus depuis combien de temps?   Je l'attends depuis cinq minutes.

Depuis quand est-ce qu'elle habite ici?   Elle habite ici depuis 1999.

Comment dit-on?

 22 Depuis quand? Donnez des réponses personnelles.

1. Tu habites dans la même ville ou dans le même village depuis quand?
2. Tu habites dans la même maison ou dans le même appartement depuis quand?
3. Depuis combien de temps vas-tu à la même école?
4. Depuis combien de temps est-ce que tu fais du français?
5. Depuis combien de temps est-ce que tu as le même professeur?

Le village de Tinerhir au Maroc

Vous êtes sur le bon chemin. Allez-y!

trois cent vingt-trois ✦ 323

Vocabulary Expansion

The following are expressions that mean the same thing as **depuis**.
Il y a cinq ans que je travaille ici.
Voilà cinq ans que je travaille ici.
Ça fait cinq ans que je travaille ici.

ANSWERS TO Comment dit-on?

22 *Answers will vary but may include:*
1. J'habite dans la même ville depuis _____.
2. J'habite dans la même maison depuis _____.
3. Je vais à la même école depuis _____.
4. Je fais du français depuis _____.
5. J'ai le même professeur depuis _____.

Structure

1 Preparation

Bellringer Review

Use BRR Transparency 10.5 or write the following on the board. Write five questions you would like to ask your favorite movie or sports star if you could.

2 Presentation

Les expressions de temps

Step 1 It is recommended that you not translate these time expressions. Students tend to become confused when they think in terms of the present perfect progressive construction ("have been . . . ing"). Stress that actions that began in the past but are still going on in the present are considered present-tense actions by French speakers.

3 Practice

Comment dit-on?

22 Expansion: Have students ask each other the questions and tabulate the results.

Allez-y!
At this point in the chapter, students have learned all the vocabulary and structure necessary to complete the chapter. The conversation and cultural readings that follow recycle all the material learned up to this point.

323

Conversation

1 Preparation

Resource Manager
Audio Activities TE, pages 112–113
Audio CD 6
CD-ROM

Bellringer Review

Use BRR Transparency 10.6 or write the following on the board. Rewrite each sentence in the *passé composé*.
1. Je vais prendre le bus.
2. Je vais attendre le bus à l'arrêt Saint-Michel.
3. Le bus va arriver.
4. Je vais monter.
5. Je vais valider mon ticket.
6. Avant de descendre, je vais appuyer sur le bouton.
7. Je vais descendre du bus à Luxembourg.

2 Presentation

Step 1 Have students close their books and listen as you read the conversation aloud or play Audio CD 6. Have students listen carefully to the recorded version and pay particular attention to the intonation.

Step 2 Have students open their books and read along with you or Audio CD 6.

Step 3 Ask why Franck is confused. Have students tell where he shows his confusion.

Step 4 Call on a pair of volunteers to read the conversation to the class. Tell the student who plays Franck to sound confused when appropriate.

Conversation

Le métro

Franck: Pardon, mademoiselle. Je ne suis pas d'ici et je ne sais pas quelle ligne je dois prendre.
La femme: Vous voulez aller où?
Franck: À La Motte-Picquet-Grenelle.
La femme: Voilà! Vous êtes ici à Ternes. Vous allez prendre cette ligne direction Porte Dauphine jusqu'à Charles-de-Gaulle-Étoile.
Franck: Charles-de-Gaulle-Étoile?
La femme: Oui, c'est la prochaine station. À Charles-de-Gaulle-Étoile, vous prenez la correspondance.
Franck: Correspondance?
La femme: Oui, vous changez à Charles-de-Gaulle-Étoile. Vous prenez la direction Nation et vous descendez à La Motte-Picquet.
Franck: Merci, mademoiselle. Vous êtes très aimable.
La femme: Je vous en prie.

Vous avez compris?

Complétez d'après la conversation.

1. Franck n'est pas ____.
2. Il ne sait pas ____.
3. Il veut aller ____.
4. Franck est maintenant ____.
5. Il va prendre la correspondance à ____.
6. «Prendre la correspondance» veut dire ____.
7. À Charles-de-Gaulle-Étoile, il va prendre la direction ____.
8. Il va ____ à La Motte-Picquet-Grenelle.

ANSWERS TO Vous avez compris?

1. d'ici
2. quelle ligne il doit prendre
3. à La Motte-Picquet-Grenelle
4. à Ternes
5. Charles-de-Gaulle-Étoile
6. changer de ligne
7. Nation
8. descendre

Glencoe Technology

CD-ROM

On the CD-ROM, students can watch a dramatization of this conversation. They can then play the role of either one of the characters and record themselves in the conversation.

Parlons un peu plus

A **Jeu** Travaillez par petits groupes de trois ou quatre personnes. Écrivez autant de questions que possible sur le métro et les autobus à Paris. Posez vos questions à un autre groupe. Le groupe qui répond correctement au plus grand nombre de questions gagne.

B **Quelle station?** Travaillez avec un(e) camarade. Regardez le plan du métro parisien. Décidez où vous êtes et où vous voulez aller. Discutez comment vous allez faire pour y arriver.

Les Champs-Élysées

La Bibliothèque Nationale de France

La tour Eiffel

Le Louvre

LES TRANSPORTS EN COMMUN

Conversation

3 Practice

Parlons un peu plus

These activities enable students to use the vocabulary and structures learned in the chapter in open-ended exchanges. You may wish to assign different activities to different groups or allow students to choose the activities they wish to do.

B You may wish to give students some preselected trips as well, highlighting some of the metro stops closest to the tourist destinations.

Reaching All Students

Additional Practice
After completing the **Conversation** activity, ask a student to retell the situation of the conversation in his or her own words.

LEVELING
E: Conversation

Answers to Parlons un peu plus

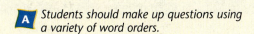

A Students should make up questions using a variety of word orders.

B Answers will vary depending upon where students decide they are and where they want to go.

Lectures culturelles

Les transports en commun à Paris

Le métro

Le métro parisien date de 1900. Il y a quatorze lignes qui traversent toute la ville. Toutes les lignes portent un numéro, mais on les appelle le plus souvent par les noms des stations des deux extrémités, c'est-à-dire le nom de leurs terminus.

Un métro est composé d'une suite de wagons appelée une rame de métro. Avant il y avait deux classes, la première classe qui coûtait plus cher et la deuxième classe. Maintenant, il n'y a plus qu'une[1] seule classe. On achète des tickets aux guichets ou dans les distributeurs automatiques à l'entrée de la station. On peut acheter un seul ticket ou un carnet de dix tickets. Ces tickets sont valables également dans les autobus. On peut aussi acheter une carte orange valable pour une semaine ou un mois. Avec la carte orange, on peut faire autant[2] d'allers–retours qu'on veut en bus ou en métro.

Pour prendre le métro, il faut glisser son ticket dans la fente d'un tourniquet avant de pouvoir aller sur le quai. Dans l'autobus, il faut le valider dans la machine qui se trouve à l'avant de l'autobus.

[1] plus qu'une *only one*   [2] autant *as many*

La station de métro Cité à Paris

Le métro à la station Bercy à Paris

Reading Strategy

Reviewing

As you read, ask yourself what the main ideas of the passage are. A good strategy for reviewing is to jot down the topics and the major points the author makes as you go through the selection. If you use this approach, when you have finished reading you will have a self-made review of the passage.

Aux heures de pointe (d'affluence), les métros et les autobus sont bondés. Il y a énormément de monde, mais heureusement, les métros et les autobus passent fréquemment.

Le bus

Les arrêts d'autobus sont facultatifs. Ils ne sont pas obligatoires. Il faut indiquer au chauffeur (au conducteur) qu'on veut descendre. Pour cela, il faut appuyer sur un bouton pour demander l'arrêt. Un signal «arrêt demandé» s'allume à l'avant de l'autobus. Il faut descendre de l'autobus par l'arrière ou par le milieu. À l'avant, la descente est interdite.

Dans le métro, les trains s'arrêtent à toutes les stations. Les stations de correspondance sont les stations où plusieurs lignes se croisent. C'est dans ces stations qu'on change de ligne: on prend la correspondance.

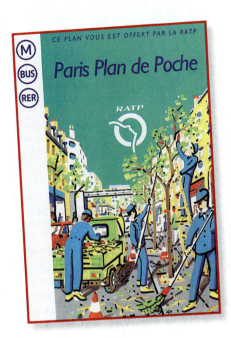

Vous avez compris?

A Le métro Répondez.
1. Depuis quand le métro parisien existe-t-il?
2. Il y a combien de lignes?
3. Quels noms les lignes portent-elles?
4. Combien de classes y a-t-il maintenant?
5. Où achète-t-on les tickets?
6. Que peut-on acheter aussi si on voyage beaucoup?
7. Que faut-il faire avant de pouvoir aller sur le quai?
8. Quand le métro est-il bondé?

B L'autobus Vrai ou faux?
1. On peut utiliser les mêmes tickets ou la même carte orange dans le métro ou l'autobus.
2. Dans le bus, on valide son billet dans une machine qui se trouve à l'avant.
3. Les autobus s'arrêtent à tous les arrêts, même si on ne demande pas un arrêt.
4. On descend de l'autobus par l'arrière et le milieu.
5. On peut descendre de l'autobus par l'avant.

LES TRANSPORTS EN COMMUN

trois cent vingt-sept 327

Lecture supplémentaire

Les transports en commun en Haïti et en Afrique

Le tap tap

Si vous vous trouvez dans une rue de Port-au-Prince, la capitale d'Haïti, vous verrez de petits camions aux couleurs vives[1]. Ce sont des taps taps. Le tap tap est le moyen de transport le plus important en Haïti. Chaque tap tap a un nom. C'est souvent un nom d'origine religieuse. Le chauffeur est presque toujours propriétaire du tap tap. Il en est très fier[2] et il l'entretient[3] très bien.

Le taxi brousse

Dans tous les pays d'Afrique occidentale, un moyen de transport important et indispensable, c'est le taxi brousse. Un taxi brousse peut être une Peugeot 504 assemblée au Nigeria. Dans ce cas, il a plusieurs noms: un 504, un Peugeot, un sept places ou un break. Un mini-bus est moins cher qu'un Peugeot. Et le moins cher de tous, c'est une bâche. Une bâche est un pick-up ou une camionnette couverte, avec des bancs en bois[4] des deux côtés. Les bâches sont toujours bondées—pas uniquement de personnes, mais aussi d'animaux et de provisions.

[1] vives *bright*
[2] fier *proud*
[3] entretient *maintains*
[4] bancs en bois *wooden benches*

Un tap tap à Port-au-Prince en Haïti

Un taxi brousse à Dakar au Sénégal

Une des gares routières à Abidjan en Côte d'Ivoire

Pour trouver un taxi brousse, il faut aller à une gare routière. La plupart de villes en ont plusieurs. Pour chaque route importante qui sort de la ville, il y a une gare routière qui la dessert.

Le bateau-bus

À Abidjan, il y a un excellent réseau[5] de bateaux-bus sur la lagune. Les bateaux-bus desservent presque tous les quartiers de la ville. Pour prendre le bateau-bus, on va à une des gares lagunaires qui se trouvent tout le long de la lagune. Il y a plusieurs départs par heure, de six heures du matin à huit heures et demie du soir.

[5] réseau *network*

Vous avez compris?

A Le tap tap Décrivez un tap tap.

B Le taxi brousse Répondez.
1. Il y a combien de types de taxis brousse?
2. Quel est le taxi le plus cher? Le Peugeot ou le mini-bus?
3. D'où partent les taxis brousse?
4. Il y a plus d'une gare routière dans chaque ville?

C Le bateau-bus Vrai ou faux?
1. À Abidjan, il y a un excellent réseau de bateaux-bus.
2. Les bateaux-bus desservent presque tous les quartiers de la ville d'Abidjan.
3. Les bateaux-bus partent d'une gare lagunaire une fois par heure.
4. Les bateaux-bus circulent 24 heures sur 24.

LES TRANSPORTS EN COMMUN

National Standards

Connections
This reading about literary genres and their characteristics establishes a connection with another discipline, allowing students to reinforce and further their knowledge of literature and the arts through the study of French.

Attention!

The readings in the **Connexions** section are optional. They focus on some of the major disciplines taught in schools and universities. The vocabulary is useful for discussing such topics as history, literature, art, economics, business, science, etc. You may choose any of the following ways to do the readings in the **Connexions** section.

Independent reading Have students read the selections and do the post-reading activities as homework, which you collect. This option is least intrusive on class time and requires a minimum of teacher involvement.

Homework with in-class follow-up Assign the readings and post-reading activities as homework. Review and discuss the material in class the next day.

Intensive in-class activity This option includes a pre-reading vocabulary presentation, in-class reading and discussion, assignment of the activities for homework, and a discussion of the assignment in class the following day.

CONNEXIONS

Les lettres
La littérature

If you ride the subway in Paris someday, you may make some interesting observations. For example, you'll notice that many people read as they ride to their destination. Rather than waste time, many riders choose to read the newspaper or a good novel.

Some of the names of the metro stations also have a literary connection. As you ride the metro around Paris, you'll see the names of French writers such as Voltaire, Victor Hugo, and Alexandre Dumas.

The literary genres that we read and learn about in our English classes are the same genres French students study and read—namely the novel, the short story, and poetry.

Les genres littéraires
Le roman

Le roman est une œuvre littéraire d'une certaine longueur en prose qui raconte[1] des événements imaginaires ou fictifs. L'intérêt du roman repose dans la narration d'aventures, l'étude de mœurs[2] et de caractère, et l'analyse des sentiments et des passions. Il y a des romans d'aventures, d'amour, d'histoire, de science-fiction, etc.

[1] raconte *tells* [2] mœurs *customs*

Les romans policiers sont aussi très populaires, surtout quand on veut lire quelque chose pour se distraire³, comme dans le métro, par exemple.

La nouvelle

La nouvelle, comme le roman, raconte des événements imaginaires ou fictifs. Mais la nouvelle est beaucoup plus courte qu'un roman. La nouvelle, comme le roman, a un ou plusieurs protagonistes. Le protagoniste est le personnage principal ou le personnage le plus important de l'œuvre. L'argument, c'est la narration de ce qui se passe dans le roman ou la nouvelle. C'est l'action.

La poésie

Un poème est un ouvrage en vers ou en prose qui évoque des sensations ou qui raconte une histoire. Pour cela, le poète emploie des images, des rimes, des sons⁴, etc. pour créer une réaction émotionnelle chez la personne qui lit le poème.

³ pour se distraire *for fun*   ⁴ sons *sounds*

Vous avez compris?

A Vos connaissances Est-ce que vous savez le nom d'autres écrivains français? Qu'est-ce qu'ils ont écrit? Vous avez lu des œuvres d'auteurs français au cours d'anglais? Quelles œuvres?

B Une nouvelle Vous allez écrire une nouvelle. Pour l'écrire suivez les instructions suivantes.

Protagoniste: Le/La protagoniste est la personne la plus importante de la nouvelle. Inventez votre protagoniste. Décrivez-le/la: dites comment il/elle s'appelle, quels sont ses traits physiques, comment est sa personnalité, ce qu'il/elle fait dans la vie.

Lieu: Indiquez d'où vient votre protagoniste. Indiquez aussi où l'action de votre histoire se passe. Décrivez le lieu, par exemple, la maison, le village ou la ville de votre protagoniste. Donnez le plus de détails possible.

Argument: Faites un résumé de l'action qui a lieu dans votre nouvelle. Écrivez ce que votre protagoniste fait ou ce qui lui arrive. Décrivez tout ce qui se passe.

Dénouement: Expliquez ce qui se passe à la fin de votre nouvelle—comment finit l'action.

C'est à vous

Use what you have learned

 Recycling

These activities allow students to use the vocabulary and structure from this chapter in completely open-ended, real-life situations.

Presentation

Encourage students to say as much as possible when they do these activities. Tell them not to be afraid to make mistakes, since the goal of these activities is real-life communication. Let students choose the activities they would like to do.

You may wish to separate students into pairs or groups. Encourage students to be creative. They may use props, pictures, or posters if they wish.

> **Learning from Realia**
>
> *(page 332 top)* Note the use of the word **poussette** in this piece of realia. **Une poussette** is a stroller. Note the touch of humor in including **une poussette** as a mode of transportation.
>
> Have students identify the types of transportation listed.

LEVELING

These activities encompass all three levels. All students will be able to do them at a sophistication level commensurate with their ability in French. Some students will be able to speak for several minutes, and others may be able to give just a few sentences. This is to be expected when students are functioning completely on their own, generating their own language to the best of their ability.

C'est à vous

Use what you have learned

 1 Sondage: Comment allez-vous...
✓ *Talk about public transportation with your classmates*

Travaillez par groupes de trois ou quatre personnes. Choisissez un chef et un(e) secrétaire. Le chef demande aux autres personnes du groupe comment leurs parents vont au travail et comment les membres du groupe vont à l'école. Le/La secrétaire présente les résultats à la classe.

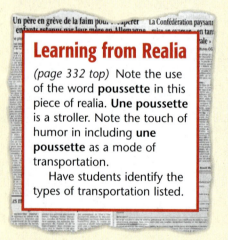

 2 Les transports en commun
✓ *Compare the public transportation system in your town to that of Paris*

Travaillez avec un(e) camarade. Comparez les transports en commun de votre ville—ou de la ville la plus proche—et ceux de Paris. Décidez quelle ville a les meilleurs transports en commun et justifiez votre réponse.

 3 Le bus ou le métro
✓ *Talk about taking the bus and subway in Paris*

Discutez avec un(e) camarade. Si vous habitiez Paris, aimeriez-vous mieux prendre le bus ou le métro? Expliquez pourquoi. Êtes-vous d'accord ou pas?

L'arrêt Charles-de-Gaulle-Étoile du 92

ANSWERS TO C'est à vous

1 *Answers will vary but may include:*
—Mes parents vont au travail en voiture.
—Ma mère va au travail en autobus, et mon père va au travail en métro.
—Et mon père va au travail à bicyclette.

2 *Answers will vary but may include:*

Dans notre ville il y a des autobus, mais pas beaucoup. Nous n'avons pas de métro. À Paris, il y a un très bon réseau de métro et d'autobus. On peut aller partout à Paris sans voiture.

3 *Answers will vary depending upon student preferences.*

CHAPITRE 10 C'est à vous

4 Prenez le bus ou le métro!
✔ *Encourage people to take public transportation*

Le club d'écologie de votre école fait une campagne pour encourager les gens à prendre le bus ou le métro. Avec un(e) camarade, dessinez une affiche. N'oubliez pas de donner plusieurs raisons pour lesquelles on devrait prendre le bus ou le métro.

Writing Strategy

Writing a survey In order to analyze a problem and present a solution, you first need to gather information about the problem. One way to gather information is to write a survey. First identify the problem and then ask yourself what its causes are and how the problem affects people, the environment, and the economy. Once you have answered these types of questions and know what kind of information you are looking for, you will be able to write a more concise survey.

5 Pour lutter contre la pollution

Today many people are concerned about the polluted air we breathe in many of the world's larger cities. The cause of much of the pollution is often the fumes emitted by cars. Write a survey to find out if your classmates and their families are doing their part to help fight pollution and then, based on their answers, try to come up with some solutions. Here are some questions you may wish to ask:

- When you go out, who drives?
- Do you go alone or with other people?
- How do you get to school?
- How do your parents get to work?

Now have your classmates fill out the questionnaire and share the results with the class.

LES TRANSPORTS EN COMMUN   trois cent trente-trois ❖ 333

Writing Development
Have students keep a notebook containing their best written work from each chapter. These selected writings can be based on assignments from the Student Textbook and the Workbook. The two activities on page 333 are examples of writing assignments that may be included in each student's portfolio.

Writing Strategy

Writing a survey
Have students read the Writing Strategy on page 333. Have students refer to the vocabulary list on page 337 if they need more ideas to write this selection.

Reaching All Students

Additional Practice
Display Communication Transparency C 10. Have students work in groups to make up as many questions as they can about the illustration. Have groups take turns asking and answering the questions.

About the French Language
You may wish to have students look at the brochure cover on this page. Tell them that the infinitive in French, here **contribuer**, is often used to express a command addressed to a general audience. ❖

ANSWERS TO C'est à vous

 Answers will vary.

 Answers will vary.

Assessment

Resource Manager

Communication Transparencies C 10
Quizzes, pages 51–55
Tests, pages 151–166
ExamView® Pro
Situation Cards
Performance Assessment, Task 10
Marathon mental Videoquiz

FOLDABLES Study Organizer — Dinah Zike's Study Guides

Your students may wish to use Foldable 5 to organize, display, and arrange data as they practice interrogatives. You may wish to encourage them to add information from each chapter as they continue to ask and answer questions in French.

Encourage students to keep this *tab book* foldable in a safe place so they can refer to it and add content as they acquire more knowledge.

Assessment

Vocabulaire

To review Mots 1, turn to pages 310–311.

1 Complétez.

1–2. On peut acheter des tickets de métro au _____ ou au _____.
3. Il faut _____ son ticket dans le tourniquet.
4. Les voyageurs changent de ligne. Ils prennent la _____.
5. Aux _____, de 16 h à 19 h, les métros sont toujours bondés.
6. Les voyageurs n'attendent pas _____ parce qu'il y a un métro toutes les quatre minutes.

To review Mots 2, turn to pages 314–315.

2 Choisissez.

7. Tous les autobus ont _____.
   a. un numéro   b. une correspondance   c. un seul arrêt
8. C'est _____ qui conduit l'autobus.
   a. le contrôleur   b. l'escalier mécanique   c. le conducteur
9. Il faut appuyer sur _____ pour demander un arrêt.
   a. le bouton   b. la porte   c. l'appareil
10. Dans les autobus parisiens, il y a _____ à l'avant, au milieu et à l'arrière.
    a. des machines   b. des portes   c. des appareils
11. Le dernier arrêt du bus, c'est _____.
    a. le trajet   b. la descente   c. le terminus

Structure

To review types of questions, turn to page 318.

3 Posez la question d'une autre façon.

12. Vous parlez français?
13. Quand part-il?
14. Elles prennent le métro où?
15. Tu as payé combien?

334 ❧ *trois cent trente-quatre*

CHAPITRE 10

ANSWERS TO Assessment

1
1–2. guichet, distributeur automatique
3. glisser
4. correspondance
5. heures de pointe
6. longtemps

2
7. a
8. c
9. a
10. b
11. c

3
12. Parlez-vous français? (Est-ce que vous parlez français?)
13. Quand est-ce qu'il part? (Il part quand?)
14. Où prennent-elles le métro? (Où est-ce qu'elles prennent le métro?)
15. Combien as-tu payé? (Combien est-ce que tu as payé?)

CHAPITRE 10 Assessment

4 Répondez d'après le modèle.

—Il est arrivé?
—Oui, il vient d'arriver.

16. Elles sont sorties?
17. Tu as déjeuné?
18. Le train est parti?

To review venir de + infinitive, turn to page 321.

5 Complétez.

19–20. Robert ____ le train ____ combien de temps?
21–22. Il ____ le train ____ quinze minutes.

To review expressing time, turn to page 323.

Culture

6 Vrai ou faux?

23. Maintenant il n'y a qu'une seule classe dans les métros parisiens.
24. Les arrêts d'autobus sont tous obligatoires.
25. On peut descendre de l'autobus par l'avant, par le milieu ou par l'arrière.

To review this cultural information, turn to pages 326–327.

LES TRANSPORTS EN COMMUN

On parle super bien!

This unique page gives students the opportunity to speak freely and say whatever they can, using the vocabulary and structures they have learned in the chapter. The illustration serves to remind students of precisely what they know how to say in French. There are no activities that students do not have the ability to describe or talk about in French. The art not only depicts the vocabulary and content of this chapter, but also reinforces what they learned in previous chapters.

You may wish to use this page in many ways. Some possibilities are to have students do the following:

1. Look at the illustration and identify items by giving the correct French words.
2. Make up sentences about what they see in the illustration.
3. Make up questions about the illustration. They can call on another class member to respond if you do this as a class activity, or you may prefer to allow students to work in small groups. This activity is extremely beneficial because it enables students to actively use interrogative words.
4. Answer questions you ask them about the illustration.
5. Work in pairs and make up a conversation based on the illustration.
6. Look at the illustration and give a complete oral review of what they see.
7. Look at the illustration and write a paragraph (or essay) about it.

You can also use this page as an assessment or testing tool, taking into account individual differences by having students go from simple to quite complicated tasks. The assessment can be either oral or written. You may wish to use the rubrics provided on pages T20–T21 as you give students the following directions.

On parle super bien!

Tell all you can about this illustration.

1. Identify the topic or situation of the illustration.
2. Give the French words for as many items as you can.
3. Think of as many sentences as you can to describe the illustration.
4. Go over your sentences and put them in the best sequencing to give a coherent story based on the illustration.

Vocabulaire

Taking the subway

le métro	un carnet	un plan du métro
une station (de métro)	un tourniquet	la correspondance
un guichet	un escalier mécanique	la direction
un distributeur automatique	le quai	les heures de pointe
	une ligne	valider
un ticket	une direction	changer de ligne

Taking the bus

un autobus	une machine	l'avant (m.)	un terminus
un arrêt d'autobus	un appareil	le milieu	un trajet
un numéro	une porte	l'arrière (m.)	appuyer sur
un conducteur, une conductrice	un bouton	la descente	

Other useful words and expressions

venir de	depuis
se croiser	longtemps
pousser	bondé(e)
s'appuyer contre	Vous descendez à la prochaine?
avoir (donner) rendez-vous	
là-bas	
au coin (de)	

How well do you know your vocabulary?
- List words you would use to describe taking the bus in Paris.
- Write a few sentences about getting on and off the bus.

VIDÉOTOUR

Épisode 10

In this video episode, you will join Chloé and Vincent as they try to find each other in the metro station. See page 509 for more information.

LES TRANSPORTS EN COMMUN

Planning for Chapter 11

SCOPE AND SEQUENCE, PAGES 338–365

Topics
* City life
* Country life

Culture
* The Fauvet family's farm in the south of France
* Life in Abidjan
* Life in Montréal
* **Reflets des Caraïbes**

Functions
* How to talk about city and country life
* How to ask questions to distinguish between two or more people or things
* How to describe activities

Structure
* **Lequel** and **celui-là**
* The verbs **suivre, conduire, vivre**
* Infinitives after prepositions

National Standards
* Communication Standard 1.1 pages 342, 343, 346, 347, 349, 350, 351, 353, 360
* Communication Standard 1.2 pages 342, 343, 346, 347, 349, 350, 351, 352, 355, 357, 359
* Communication Standard 1.3 pages 343, 353, 360, 361
* Cultures Standard 2.1 pages 354–355, 356, 357, 358–359
* Connections Standard 3.2 pages 358–359
* Comparisons Standard 4.2 page 361

PACING AND PRIORITIES

The chapter content is color coded below to assist you in planning.

■ required   ■ recommended   ■ optional

Vocabulaire (required) — Days 1–4
- ■ Mots 1
  - La ville
  - Au centre-ville / En ville
- ■ Mots 2
  - À la campagne
  - Des animaux

Structure (required) — Days 5–7
- ■ **Lequel** et **celui-là**
- ■ Les verbes **suivre, conduire, vivre**
- ■ L'infinitif après les prépositions

Conversation (required)
- ■ La ville ou la campagne?

Lectures culturelles
- ■ Une famille d'agriculteurs (recommended)
- ■ Abidjan (optional)
- ■ Montréal (optional)

Connexions (optional)
- ■ La démographie

■ **C'est à vous** (recommended)

■ **Assessment** (recommended)

■ **On parle super bien!** (optional)

RESOURCE GUIDE

SECTION	PAGES	SECTION RESOURCES
Vocabulaire *Mots 1*		
La ville Au centre-ville / En ville	340 340–343	Vocabulary Transparencies 11.2–11.3 Audio CD 7 Audio Activities TE, pages 118–120 Workbook, pages 121–122 Quiz 1, page 57 ExamView® Pro
Vocabulaire *Mots 2*		
À la campagne Des animaux	344 345–347	Vocabulary Transparencies 11.4–11.5 Audio CD 7 Audio Activities TE, pages 121–122 Workbook, pages 123–124 Quiz 2, page 58 ExamView® Pro
Structure		
Lequel et **celui-là** Les verbes **suivre, conduire, vivre** L'infinitif après les prépositions	348–349 350 351	Audio CD 7 Audio Activities TE, pages 123–124 Workbook, pages 125–127 Quizzes 3–5, pages 59–61 ExamView® Pro
Conversation		
La ville ou la campagne?	352–353	Audio CD 7 Audio Activities TE, pages 124–125 Interactive CD-ROM
Lectures culturelles		
Une famille d'agriculteurs Abidjan Montréal	354–355 356 357	Audio CD 7 Audio Activities TE, pages 125–126 Tests, page 170, 174
Connexions		
La démographie	358–359	Tests, page 175
C'est à vous		
	360–361	**Bon voyage!** Video, Episode 11 Video Activities, Chapter 11 French Online Activities french.glencoe.com
Assessment		
	362–363	Communication Transparency C 11 Quizzes 1–5, pages 57–61 Performance Assessment, Task 11 Tests, pages 167–182 ExamView® Pro Situation Cards, Chapter 11 **Marathon mental** Videoquiz

Using Your Resources for Chapter 11

Transparencies

 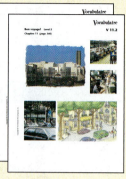 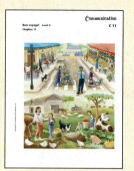

Bellringer 11.1–11.7 | Vocabulary 11.1–11.5 | Communication C 11

Workbook

Vocabulary, pages 121–124 | Structure, pages 125–127 | Enrichment, pages 128–130

Audio Activities

Vocabulary, pages 118–122 | Structure, pages 123–124 | Conversation, pages 124–125 | Cultural Reading, pages 125–126 | Additional Practice, pages 126–127

Assessment

Vocabulary and Structure Quizzes, pages 57–61

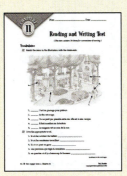
Chapter Tests, pages 167–182

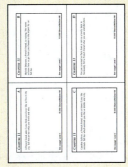
Situation Cards, Chapter 11

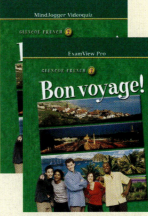
MindJogger Videoquiz, ExamView® Pro, Chapter 11

Timesaving Teacher Tools

TeacherWorks™

TeacherWorks™ is your all-in-one teacher resource center. Personalize lesson plans, access resources from the Teacher Wraparound Edition, connect to the Internet, or make a to-do list. These are only a few of the many features that can assist you in the planning and organizing of your lessons.

Includes:
- A calendar feature
- Access to all program blackline masters
- Standards correlations and more

ExamView® Pro

Test Bank software for Macintosh and Windows makes creating, editing, customizing, and printing tests quick and easy.

Technology Resources

 In the Chapter 11 Internet activity, you will have a chance to learn more about the Francophone world. Visit <u>french.glencoe.com</u>.

 On the Interactive Conversation CD-ROM, students can listen to and take part in a recorded version of the conversation in Chapter 11.

 See the National Geographic Teacher's Corner on pages 138–139, 244–245, 372–373, 472–473 for reference to additional technology resources.

 Bon voyage! Video and Video Activities, Chapter 11

 Help your students prepare for the chapter test by playing the **Marathon mental** Videoquiz game show. Teams will compete against each other to review chapter vocabulary and structure and sharpen listening comprehension skills.

Preview

In this chapter, students will learn to compare and contrast city and country life. Students will also learn the pronouns **celui** and **lequel**, the verbs **suivre**, **vivre**, and **conduire**, and the infinitive after a preposition.

Communication

In Chapter 11, students will communicate in spoken and written French on the following topics:
- City life
- Country life

Students will obtain and provide information about these topics and engage in conversations that would typically take place in urban or rural environments as they fulfill the chapter objectives listed on this page.

LEVELING

The activities, conversations, and readings within each chapter are marked according to level of difficulty. **E** indicates easy. **A** indicates average. **C** indicates challenging. Some activities cover a range of difficulty. In some activities, for example, advanced students will be able to produce more extensive responses while students who learn at a different rate may give less detailed responses. The leveling indicators will help you individualize instruction to best meet your students' needs.

À la ville et à la campagne

Objectifs
In this chapter you will learn to:

✓ talk about life in the city and give directions
✓ talk about life in the country
✓ ask questions to distinguish between two or more people or things
✓ describe some more activities
✓ talk about life on a farm in France

Ornement traditionnel du Mali

CHAPITRE 11

 Spotlight on Culture

Photograph This photo of a tractor on a tree-lined street in front of the village church was taken in the Côte d'Or area of Burgundy. This rural area is famous for its vineyards and superb Burgundy wines.

Headdress To appreciate African art, it is necessary to know the context in which an object is used. Almost all traditional African art has a practical purpose. It can involve religion, daily life, health, or successful crops. The piece seen here is a traditional harvest headdress from Mali. It is in the art museum in Bamako, the capital of Mali.

trois cent trente-neuf

Vocabulaire Mots 1

1 Preparation

Resource Manager

Vocabulary Transparencies
  11.2–11.3
Audio Activities TE, pages 118–120
Audio CD 7
Workbook, pages 121–122
Quiz 1, page 57
ExamView® Pro

Bellringer Review

Use BRR Transparency 11.1 or write the following on the board.
List all the words and expressions you can remember that have to do with taking the metro.

2 Presentation

Step 1 Have students close their books. Use Vocabulary Transparencies 11.2–11.3 to present **Mots 1**. Have students repeat the words, phrases, and sentences after you or Audio CD 7.

Step 2 Ask *either/or* and *yes/no* questions to elicit the vocabulary. Then point in random order to illustrations on the Vocabulary Transparencies and ask **Qu'est-ce que c'est?**

Step 3 Use gestures and dramatizations to convey the meaning of **à gauche, à droite, devant, derrière, tout droit, en face de, tourner,** and **faire demi-tour.**

Step 4 Have students repeat the miniconversation with as much expression as possible.

Vocabulaire Mots 1

La ville

une tour = un bâtiment très haut
un quartier d'affaires

La banlieue est l'ensemble des agglomérations qui entourent une grande ville.

une ouvrière
une usine

un bureau

Au centre-ville / En ville

L'agent de police règle la circulation.

un agent de police

une rue à sens unique
un coin
un feu
un piéton
un trottoir
un passage pour piétons
une rue

Avant de traverser la rue, il faut regarder à gauche et à droite.
Le feu va changer.
Les piétons traversent la rue dans un passage pour piétons.

Learning from Photos

(page 340 top left) The photo shows **la Défense**, the relatively new commercial business area beyond Neuilly.

LEVELING

E: Vocabulary

Vocabulaire
Mots 1

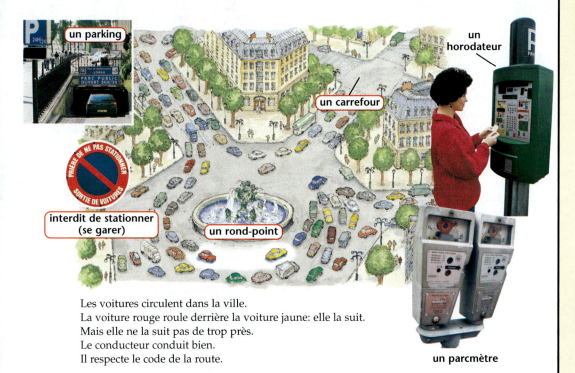

- un parking
- un horodateur
- un carrefour
- interdit de stationner (se garer)
- un rond-point
- un parcmètre

Les voitures circulent dans la ville.
La voiture rouge roule derrière la voiture jaune: elle la suit.
Mais elle ne la suit pas de trop près.
Le conducteur conduit bien.
Il respecte le code de la route.

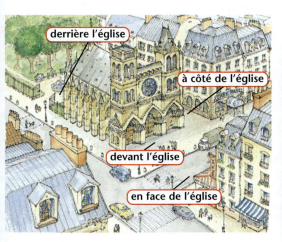

- derrière l'église
- à côté de l'église
- devant l'église
- en face de l'église

La rue Balzac, s'il vous plaît?

Ah, vous allez dans le mauvais sens, monsieur. Faites demi-tour. Allez tout droit jusqu'au prochain carrefour et là, tournez à gauche.

À LA VILLE ET À LA CAMPAGNE

trois cent quarante et un ❖ 341

Vocabulaire

3 Practice

Quel est le mot?

Attention!

When students are doing the **Quel est le mot?** activities, accept any answer that makes sense. The purpose of these activities is to have students use the new vocabulary. They are not factual recall activities. If you wish, have students use the photos on pages 342–343 as a stimulus.

 Recycling

Use Activity 1 as an object pronoun review. Redo the activity, and have students replace everything possible with object pronouns.
For example: **7. Oui, il leur en donne une.**

1 and **2** After completing these activities, have one student read each activity as a story.

Writing Development
Have students write the answers to Activities 1 and 2 in paragraph form.

LEVELING
E: Activities 1, 2, 3, 5, 6
A: Activities 4, 5, 6

Vocabulaire

Quel est le mot?

1 **Historiette** En ville, à pied
Répondez.
1. Avant de traverser, les piétons attendent sur le trottoir?
2. Ils attendent au coin, où il y a un feu?
3. Ils traversent la rue quand le feu est rouge?
4. Il faut regarder à gauche et à droite avant de traverser?
5. Les piétons traversent dans un passage pour piétons?
6. Est-ce qu'un agent de police règle la circulation?
7. Il donne une contravention aux automobilistes qui ne respectent pas le code de la route?

Le boulevard du Montparnasse à Paris

2 **Historiette** Le mauvais sens Répondez d'après les indications.
1. Il va dans le bon sens ou dans le mauvais sens? (le mauvais sens)
2. C'est une rue à sens unique? (oui)
3. Il doit aller tout droit ou faire demi-tour? (faire demi-tour)
4. Il doit aller jusqu'où? (au troisième carrefour)
5. Qu'est-ce qu'il y a là? (un feu)
6. Il doit continuer tout droit jusqu'où? (au rond-point)
7. S'il suit une autre voiture de trop près, il risque d'avoir un accident? (oui)
8. Il est interdit de stationner sur le rond-point? (oui)
9. Il peut se garer où? (au parking)

3 Où est le café? Répondez d'après le dessin.
1. Le café est à droite ou à gauche du théâtre?
2. Le cinéma est à côté du restaurant ou derrière le restaurant?
3. Le parc est à côté du restaurant ou en face du café?
4. La voiture est garée devant l'école ou derrière l'école?
5. Le cinéma est derrière le théâtre ou en face du théâtre?

ANSWERS TO Quel est le mot?

1 *Answers will vary but may include:*
1. Oui, avant de traverser, les piétons attendent sur le trottoir.
2. Oui, ils attendent au coin, où il y a un feu.
3. Non, ils ne traversent pas la rue quand le feu est rouge. Ils la traversent quand le feu est vert.
4. Oui, il faut regarder à gauche et à droite avant de traverser.
5. Oui, les piétons traversent dans un passage pour piétons.
6. Oui, un agent de police règle la circulation.
7. Oui, il donne une contravention aux automobilistes qui ne respectent pas le code de la route.

2
1. Il va dans le mauvais sens.
2. Oui, c'est une rue à sens unique.
3. Il doit faire demi-tour.
4. Il doit aller jusqu'au troisième carrefour.
5. Là, il y a un feu.
6. Il doit continuer tout droit jusqu'au rond-point.
7. Oui, s'il suit une autre voiture de trop près, il risque d'avoir un accident.
8. Oui, il est interdit de stationner sur le rond-point.
9. Il peut se garer au parking.

3
1. Le café est à droite du théâtre.
2. Le cinéma est à côté du restaurant.
3. Le parc est en face du café.
4. La voiture est garée derrière l'école.
5. Le cinéma est en face du théâtre.

Vocabulaire

La Grande Arche de la Défense

4 **Qu'est-ce que c'est?** Donnez le mot approprié.

1. un bâtiment très haut
2. un bâtiment destiné à la fabrication d'un produit (des voitures, des télévisions, etc.)
3. le quartier d'une ville où il y a beaucoup de bureaux, de magasins, de banques, etc.
4. la région autour d'une ville, les agglomérations
5. une personne qui marche
6. une personne qui travaille dans une usine
7. là où on met des pièces de monnaie pour se garer
8. là où les secrétaires travaillent

5 **Des instructions** Travaillez avec un(e) camarade. Expliquez-lui comment aller chez vous de l'école. Ensuite, changez de rôle.

6 **Au carrefour** Travaillez avec un(e) camarade. Expliquez tout ce qu'on doit faire quand on arrive à un carrefour en voiture. Vous pouvez utiliser les mots suivants.

ralentir	regarder le feu
freiner	regarder à gauche et à droite
s'arrêter	faire attention aux piétons

À LA VILLE ET À LA CAMPAGNE

trois cent quarante-trois 343

Vocabulaire Mots 2

1 Preparation

Resource Manager
Vocabulary Transparencies 11.4–11.5
Audio Activities TE, pages 121–122
Audio CD 7
Workbook, pages 123–124
Quiz 2, page 58
ExamView® Pro

Bellringer Review
Use BRR Transparency 11.2 or write the following on the board. Complete each sentence.
1. Si je pouvais, j'____ à Paris. (habiter)
2. Mais pas mon amie Émilie. Si elle ____ assez d'argent, elle aurait une maison dans un petit village de Provence. (avoir)
3. Nous ____ en Provence cet été si nous avons du temps libre. (aller)

2 Presentation

Step 1 Show Vocabulary Transparencies 11.4–11.5. Have students close their books and repeat the words after you or Audio CD 7 as you point to the appropriate illustration on the transparency.

Step 2 Call on students to point to items on the transparencies and identify them with the proper word or expression.

Step 3 You may wish to ask the following about the animals: **Testez vos connaissances: De tous les animaux que vous voyez sur cette page, lesquels donnent du lait?**

Note: For fun, the animal sounds are introduced in Activity 11, page 347.

Vocabulaire Mots 2

À la campagne

une grange
une ferme

Le fermier entrepose son matériel agricole dans un hangar.

un fermier, un agriculteur
la terre
un champ

L'agriculteur cultive (travaille) la terre.

le blé
les céréales
la récolte

un vignoble

un pré
un troupeau de moutons
de l'herbe

Le bébé d'un mouton, c'est un agneau.

Reaching All Students

Total Physical Response Have students listen to the following statements and raise their hands when the statement is true.
Le bébé d'une vache, c'est un agneau.
Un cheval est un animal.
Les vaches dorment dans une étable.
Les agriculteurs cultivent le trottoir.
On cultive des légumes dans un vignoble.
La récolte a lieu presque toujours au printemps.
Les agriculteurs travaillent la terre.
Les fermes sont à la campagne.

Vocabulaire
Mots 2

Des animaux 🎧

un cheval

Lequel des chevaux tu préfères?
Celui-là.

un lapin

une poule

Jules va faire du cheval.

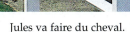
un cochon

une vache
un veau

À la ferme, les vaches dorment dans une étable.

À LA VILLE ET À LA CAMPAGNE

trois cent quarante-cinq 345

FUN FACTS

The **coq gaulois** has been the French national symbol since the French Revolution. The rooster's cry, **cocorico**, is an expression of victory, "Three cheers for France!"

Learning from Photos

(page 344 top left) This photo was taken on a farm in the **Limousin** region.

(page 344 bottom left) The grapes ripening on the vines are pinot noir grapes.

(page 344 bottom right) This photo was taken in the **Aquitaine** region in the foothills of the **Pyrénées**.

About the French Language

Un hangar is a farm building with open sides.
Une étable is the type of barn cattle would be kept in.
A horse barn with stables is **une écurie**.
A horseback rider is **un écuyer, une écuyère. Être bon(ne) écuyer(ère)** means to be a good rider.

Assessment

As an informal assessment, you may wish to show Vocabulary Transparencies 11.4–11.5. Call on students to point to and identify various items at random.

FUN FACTS

The average French person consumes 72 kilos of bread a year.

Vocabulaire

Quel est le mot?

7 Bâtiment, animal ou céréale? Choisissez.
1. une grange
2. une poule
3. une étable
4. du blé
5. un cochon
6. une vache
7. un hangar
8. un lapin

8 Historiette Une ferme Répondez.
1. On trouve des fermes à la campagne ou dans des villes?
2. Il y a souvent des champs autour d'une ferme?
3. Il y a des troupeaux de moutons et de vaches dans les prés?
4. Pour travailler la terre, l'agriculteur utilise des chevaux ou des tracteurs?
5. Les fermiers entreposent leur matériel agricole où?
6. Ils mettent les animaux où?
7. Ils mettent leur récolte où?
8. Les agriculteurs sont contents si la récolte est bonne?

Dans le pays d'Auge en Normandie

9 Parlons agriculture! Complétez.
1. Si on aime les chevaux, on aime faire du ____.
2. On peut dire un fermier ou un ____.
3. Le petit d'une vache, c'est un ____.
4. Le mouton, c'est le mâle. La brebis, c'est la femelle et le petit, c'est l'____.
5. Un agriculteur ____ la terre.
6. Les vaches mangent de l'____ quand elles sont dans les prés.
7. Dans un ____, on cultive du raisin.
8. On cultive des céréales comme le blé dans des ____.

For more practice using words from Mots 2, do Activity 17 on page H18 at the end of this book.

Ils montent à cheval.

346 trois cent quarante-six

CHAPITRE 11

Vocabulaire

10 **À la ferme** Vous parlez à un(e) ami(e) français(e) qui habitait dans une ferme quand il/elle était petit(e). Posez-lui des questions sur la ferme de sa famille. Ensuite, changez de rôle.

Une ferme en Dordogne

11 **Jeu** **C'est le cri de quel animal?** Travaillez avec un(e) camarade. Répétez chaque cri et attribuez-le à un animal.

À LA VILLE ET À LA CAMPAGNE trois cent quarante-sept ✦ **347**

Vocabulaire

Geography Connection

Dordogne is a **département** in the southwestern region of Aquitaine.

11 Students can have fun imitating the animal sounds. Have them compare how the French imitate the sounds in comparison to English speakers.

Chapter Projects

J'aimerais habiter... Have students choose a French-speaking city or town that they would like to live in, according to whether they prefer urban or rural life. Have them prepare a report on their city or town and ask them to explain why they selected it. Students should include photos and maps of the city or town in their report, if possible. The Internet is a good source for this information.

La cuisine régionale Have students make a large map of France. Ask students to bring in pictures of French food products from magazines and have them glue them in the appropriate region on the map.

ANSWERS TO Quel est le mot?

10 *Answers will vary but the type of questions students may ask are:*

La ferme était grande ou petite?
Tu avais quels animaux?
Ton père cultivait la terre?
Il avait quels matériels agricoles?
Tu aimais la vie à la ferme?
Tu aidais tes parents?

11 *Students will repeat the animal sounds.*

347

Structure

1 Preparation

Resource Manager
Audio Activities TE, pages 123–124
Audio CD 7
Workbook, pages 125–127
Quizzes 3–5, pages 59–61
ExamView® Pro

Bellringer Review
Use BRR Transparency 11.3 or write the following on the board.
List at least six things you see on a typical busy city street.

2 Presentation

Lequel et celui-là

Step 1 Go over the explanation in Item 1 with students as they follow along in their books.

Step 2 Write the forms of **lequel** on the board.

Step 3 Write the forms of the demonstrative pronouns on the board and go over the explanation with the students.

LEVELING
E: Activities 12, 13
A: Activity 14

Structure

Lequel et celui-là
Distinguishing between two or more people or things

1. To ask "which one" in French, you use a form of the interrogative pronoun **lequel**.

Masculin	J'aime beaucoup ce livre.	Ah oui? Lequel?
	J'aime beaucoup ces livres.	Ah oui? Lesquels?
Féminin	J'aime beaucoup cette photo.	Ah oui? Laquelle?
	J'aime beaucoup ces photos.	Ah oui? Lesquelles?

Rappelez-vous que…
Review the forms of the interrogative adjective "which" or "what."
Quel village?
Quelle ville?
Quels villages?
Quelles villes?

2. To answer a question with the interrogative **quel, quels, quelle,** or **quelles,** you can use the demonstrative pronouns **celui, ceux, celle, celles.** Study the following forms.

Masculin	Tu préfères quel livre?	Celui-là.
	Tu préfères quels livres?	Ceux-là.
Féminin	Tu préfères quelle photo?	Celle-là.
	Tu préfères quelles photos?	Celles-là.

Note that demonstrative pronouns can never stand alone. They are followed by:

- **-là** to single something or someone out.
  De toutes ces voitures, laquelle tu préfères? **Celle-là.**

- **de** to indicate possession.
  C'est ta voiture? Non, c'est **celle de** mon frère.

- the relative pronouns **qui** or **que (qu')** to identify which one.
  Lequel de ces garçons est ton frère? } **Celui qui** parle.
  Celui que tu vois, là-bas.

348 ❖ trois cent quarante-huit   CHAPITRE 11

About the French Language

Just as **ceci** is seldom used in spoken French in comparison to **cela** or **ça, celui-ci** is also seldom used. You may wish to explain to students that they could use **celui (celle)-ci** when specifically comparing two items: **Celui-ci est grand mais celui-là est petit.** ❖

Comment dit-on?

12 Aussi Répondez d'après le modèle.

—Sa ferme est immense. Et celle de son oncle?
—Elle est immense aussi.

1. Ta voiture est très jolie. Et celle de ton frère?
2. Ta maison est grande. Et celle de tes grands-parents?
3. Cet immeuble est très élégant. Et celui d'en face?
4. Ton appartement est au troisième étage. Et celui de ton cousin?
5. Ces rues sont très petites. Et celles de ton village?
6. Ces boulevards sont très longs. Et ceux de Paris?

13 Lequel tu préfères? Suivez le modèle.

ces deux magazines →
—De ces deux magazines, lequel tu préfères?
—Celui-là.

1. ces deux livres
2. ces deux journaux
3. ces deux cassettes
4. ces deux CD
5. ces deux vidéos
6. ces deux couleurs

14 Au village Complétez.

1. —Où est ta voiture?
   —Là-bas. C'est ____ ____ est garée devant l'église.
2. —Laquelle est la ferme de M. Gaston?
   —C'est ____ ____ on peut voir d'ici.
3. —C'est quel fils qui l'aide à la ferme?
   —C'est ____ ____ est encore à l'école du village.
4. —Il est très sympa!
   —C'est ____ ____ je préfère.
5. —Ce sont vos chevaux?
   —Non, ce sont ____ ____ M. Gaillard.
6. —Ce sont vos vaches?
   —Non, ce sont ____ ____ Mme Fort.

Une école dans un petit village de Provence

À LA VILLE ET À LA CAMPAGNE   trois cent quarante-neuf 349

Structure

1 Preparation

Bellringer Review

Use BRR Transparency 11.4 or write the following on the board. Complete each sentence.
1. Les piétons _____ la rue dans le _____ pour piétons.
2. Les automobilistes s'arrêtent quand ils _____ à un _____ rouge.
3. Il est _____ de stationner (se garer) sur le trottoir.
4. Vous allez dans le mauvais sens. Il faut faire _____.

2 Presentation

Les verbes suivre, conduire, vivre

Step 1 Guide students through Items 1 and 2 and write the paradigms on the board.

Step 2 Have students repeat the verb forms after you and call on volunteers to read the model sentences.

3 Practice

Comment dit-on?

15 and **16** It is recommended that you go over the activities in class before assigning them for homework. Activity 15 can be done with books either closed or open. Activity 16 is to be done with books open.

LEVELING
E: Activities 15, 17
A: Activities 15, 16, 18

Structure

Les verbes suivre, conduire, vivre
Expressing more actions

1. Study the forms of the verbs **suivre** (to follow), **conduire** (to drive), and **vivre** (to live).

SUIVRE	CONDUIRE	VIVRE
je suis	je conduis	je vis
tu suis	tu conduis	tu vis
il/elle/on suit	il/elle/on conduit	il/elle/on vit
nous suivons	nous conduisons	nous vivons
vous suivez	vous conduisez	vous vivez
ils/elles suivent	ils/elles conduisent	ils/elles vivent

2. The past participles are **suivi**, **conduit**, and **vécu**.
   Elle a **conduit** toute la journée.
   Elle a **suivi** une autre voiture devant elle.
   Il a **vécu** longtemps à la campagne.

Comment dit-on?

15 Qui vit où et de quoi? Répondez.
1. Est-ce que les agriculteurs vivent de la terre?
2. Ils vivent dans une ferme?
3. À ton avis, on vit bien aux États-Unis?
4. Tu vis dans une grande ville ou un petit village?
5. Est-ce que tu aimerais vivre dans une ferme?
6. Tu as déjà vécu dans un autre pays? Si oui, lequel?

16 Comment conduit-on? Complétez.
1. Je ne _____ jamais une autre voiture de trop près. (suivre)
2. Celui qui ne _____ pas une autre voiture de trop près _____ bien. (suivre, conduire)
3. Tout le monde dit qu'il _____ bien parce qu'il _____ une Porsche. (vivre, conduire)
4. Les agriculteurs _____ des tracteurs et _____ de la terre. (conduire, vivre)
5. Et vous, vous _____ prudemment? Vous ne _____ pas les autres voitures de trop près? (conduire, suivre)

350 ❖ trois cent cinquante   CHAPITRE 11

Un tracteur et le Mont-Saint-Michel

ANSWERS TO Comment dit-on?

15 Answers will vary but may include:
1. Oui, les agriculteurs vivent de la terre.
2. Oui, ils vivent dans une ferme.
3. Oui, à mon avis, on vit bien aux États-Unis.
4. Je vis dans une grande ville.
5. Non, je n'aimerais pas vivre dans une ferme.
6. Non, je n'ai jamais vécu dans un autre pays.

16
1. suis
2. suit, conduit
3. vit, conduit
4. conduisent, vivent
5. conduisez, suivez

About the French Language

The verb **habiter** means "to live" in the sense "to dwell." **Il habite à Paris. Vivre** can be used to express "to live" in its different meanings: **Il vit à Genève. Il vit bien. Il vit de l'agriculture.** ❖

L'infinitif après les prépositions
Describing two related activities

1. Review the ways in which you have already learned to use an infinitive.

   Julie va **faire** un petit voyage à la campagne.
   Elle veut **passer** une semaine dans une ferme.

2. You also use an infinitive after a preposition in French. Study the following.

   Elle est allée en ville **pour faire** des courses.
   Avant d'aller au magasin, elle est allée à la banque.
   On ne peut rien acheter **sans payer**.

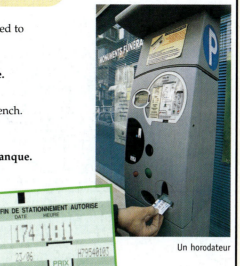

Un horodateur

Comment dit-on?

17 **Il conduit bien.** Répondez.
1. Le conducteur a ralenti avant d'arriver au carrefour?
2. Avant de continuer, il a regardé s'il y avait des piétons qui traversaient?
3. Dans un parking, on est obligé de payer?
4. Vous avez pu vous garer sans payer?

18 **Une étudiante sérieuse** Répondez d'après le modèle.

Elle fait d'abord ses devoirs. Ensuite elle regarde la télé. →
Elle fait ses devoirs avant de regarder la télé.
1. Elle fait d'abord ses devoirs. Ensuite elle téléphone à ses copains.
2. Elle fait d'abord ses devoirs. Ensuite elle écoute des CD.
3. Elle fait d'abord ses devoirs. Ensuite elle regarde un DVD.
4. Elle fait d'abord ses devoirs. Ensuite elle sort.
5. Elle fait d'abord ses devoirs. Ensuite elle lit un magazine.

Vous êtes sur le bon chemin. Allez-y!

trois cent cinquante et un ❖ 351

Structure

1 Practice

Bellringer Review
Use BRR Transparency 11.5 or write the following on the board.
Write a list of all the animals you know in French.

2 Presentation

L'infinitif après les prépositions

Step 1 Have students read the model sentences aloud.

Learning from Photos
(page 351) You use an **horodateur** to get a ticket so you can park legally. First, you put a coin or credit card in the **horodateur** and push a blue button for the amount of time you need. You then push a green button to get your ticket. You then place the ticket behind the windshield.

✓ Assessment
You may wish to have students make up some original sentences with **pour, avant de,** and **sans**.

Allez-y!
At this point in the chapter, students have learned all the vocabulary and grammar necessary to complete the chapter. The conversation and cultural readings that follow recycle all the material learned up to this point.

ANSWERS TO Comment dit-on?

17
1. Oui, le conducteur a ralenti avant d'arriver au carrefour.
2. Oui, avant de continuer, il a regardé s'il y avait des piétons qui traversaient.
3. Oui, dans un parking, on est obligé de payer.
4. Oui, j'ai pu me garer sans payer.

18
1. Elle fait ses devoirs avant de téléphoner à ses copains.
2. Elle fait ses devoirs avant d'écouter des CD.
3. Elle fait ses devoirs avant de regarder un DVD.
4. Elle fait ses devoirs avant de sortir.
5. Elle fait ses devoirs avant de lire un magazine.

351

Conversation

1 Preparation

Resource Manager
Audio Activities TE, pages 124–125
Audio CD 7
CD-ROM

Bellringer Review
Use BRR Transparency 11.6 or write the following on the board.
Where would you find the following things, **à la ville ou à la campagne?**
une tour, des piétons, un hangar, un bureau, une grange, un veau, un carrefour, un rond-point, un pré, un vignoble, une étable, une usine, un parking

2 Presentation

Step 1 Have students close their books and listen as you read the conversation aloud or play Audio CD 7.

Step 2 Have students open their books and read along with you or Audio CD 7.

Step 3 Call on volunteers to read the conversation to the class.
Note: Tell students **l'élevage** means *the raising of livestock.*

LEVELING
E: Conversation

Conversation

La ville ou la campagne?

Julie: Tu aimes vivre à la campagne?
Sophie: Beaucoup. J'adore les grands espaces et le bon air frais.
Julie: Tu ne trouves pas la vie un peu ennuyeuse?
Sophie: Pas du tout. Ici, il n'y a pas de bouchons. On n'a pas besoin de tourner en rond pendant trois heures pour trouver une place pour se garer.
Julie: C'est vrai. Mais moi, je ne pourrais jamais vivre sans les musées, les concerts, tout ça, quoi.
Sophie: Et moi, je ne pourrais jamais vivre sans pouvoir faire du cheval. Le cheval, c'est ma vie. Mon rêve, c'est de faire de l'élevage de chevaux. Peut-être un jour…

Vous avez compris?

Répondez.

1. Sophie aime vivre où?
2. Pourquoi?
3. Elle ne trouve pas la campagne ennuyeuse (monotone)?
4. Qu'est-ce que Sophie n'aime pas en ville?
5. Qu'est-ce que Julie aime faire en ville?
6. Qu'est-ce que Sophie aimerait faire plus tard?

ANSWERS TO Vous avez compris?

1. Sophie aime vivre à la campagne.
2. Elle adore les grands espaces et le bon air frais.
3. Elle ne trouve pas la campagne ennuyeuse.
4. Elle n'aime pas la circulation.
5. Julie aime aller au musée et au concert.
6. Sophie aimerait faire de l'élevage de chevaux.

Learning from Photos
(page 352) The young women in this photo are at the **Club hypique de Varennes-Jarcy.**
Have students answer the following questions about the photo:
1. Les jeunes filles viennent de faire quoi?
2. C'est quel type de bâtiment?
3. Lequel des chevaux préfères-tu?

Parlons un peu plus

A **J'aimerais vivre...** Travaillez avec un(e) camarade. Dites où vous aimeriez vivre, à la ville ou à la campagne. Donnez vos raisons.

B **Avantages et inconvénients** Travaillez par groupes de quatre ou cinq personnes. Discutez des avantages et des inconvénients de vivre à la ville et à la campagne.

Abidjan en Côte d'Ivoire

Un petit village dans le Roussillon

Montréal la nuit

À LA VILLE ET À LA CAMPAGNE

trois cent cinquante-trois 353

Conversation

3 Practice

Parlons un peu plus

These activities enable students to use the vocabulary and structures learned in the chapter in open-ended exchanges.

B After the groups have discussed the topic, have the class compile lists for each category.

Learning from Photos

(page 353 top) Abidjan, the major city of the Côte d'Ivoire, has been a modern city with an excellent harbor since the French constructed the Vridi Canal in 1951. The canal connects the Atlantic ocean with the lagoon. In this photo, we see one of the bridges over the lagoon. The skyscrapers in the background are part of Le Plateau, the modern commercial center of the city.

(page 353 right) Montreal's downtown area, or **centre-ville**, is very modern and cosmopolitan.

History Connection

Le Roussillon is a very historic region in the eastern area of the **Pyrénées.** It was occupied at various times by the Romans, Visigoths, and Arabs. For a period it was ceded to Aragon in Spain. It became a part of France with the signing of the Treaty of the Pyrenees in 1659. The major city of **le Roussillon** is Perpignan.

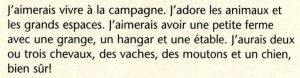
Montreal is the second-largest French-speaking city after Paris.

Glencoe Technology

CD-ROM
On the CD-ROM, students can watch a dramatization of this conversation. They can then play the role of either one of the characters and record themselves in the conversation.

Answers to Parlons un peu plus

A *Answers will vary but may include:*
J'aimerais vivre à la campagne. J'adore les animaux et les grands espaces. J'aimerais avoir une petite ferme avec une grange, un hangar et une étable. J'aurais deux ou trois chevaux, des vaches, des moutons et un chien, bien sûr!

B *Answers will vary depending upon students' opinions.*

Lectures culturelles

Resource Manager
Audio Activities TE, pages 125–126
Audio CD 7

Bellringer Review

Use BRR Transparency 11.7 or write the following on the board.
Complete with the verb **parler**.
1. Je _____ à ma sœur tous les jours.
2. Et j'_____ à ma sœur hier.
3. Et je suis sûr que je lui _____ demain aussi.
4. Quand nous étions petits, nous nous _____ tous les jours.

National Standards

Cultures
This reading about a French farming family familiarizes students with another segment of the French population.

Presentation

Pre-reading
Step 1 Ask students if they have ever visited or lived on a farm. Have them describe what they observed.

Step 2 Go over the Reading Strategy on page 354.

Reading
Step 1 You may wish to divide the **Lecture** into two or three segments.

Step 2 Call on an individual to read several sentences. Then ask other students about the sentences the student has just read.

Lectures culturelles

Reading Strategy
Responding
Examine your reaction to the facts and ideas as you read. Start to form an opinion of the ideas presented and decide how you can find out more about the topic. Once you have evaluated the reading, you should be able to agree or disagree with the writer's thesis and give your reasons.

Une famille d'agriculteurs

La famille Fauvet a une ferme à quelques kilomètres de Soual, dans le sud-ouest de la France. M. Fauvet est propriétaire[1] de sa ferme. Sa ferme n'est pas très grande.

Les Fauvet habitent dans une petite maison typique en pierre[2]. À côté de la maison, il y a une étable, une grange et un hangar où M. Fauvet entrepose le matériel. M. et Mme Fauvet se lèvent tôt et se couchent tôt; ils profitent des heures de jour pour cultiver la terre. Leur vie est réglée sur le lever et le coucher du soleil.

Les Fauvet ont deux enfants, Luc et Marie. Comme beaucoup d'enfants d'agriculteurs, Luc et Marie disent que la vie de fermier ne les intéresse pas. Après leurs études, ils veulent aller travailler à la ville.

[1] propriétaire *owner*
[2] pierre *stone*

Un village sur le Tarn dans le sud-ouest

Une famille d'agriculteurs

LEVELING
E: Reading

En 1960, 25 pour cent de la population active en France—c'est-à-dire la population qui travaille—était dans l'agriculture. Aujourd'hui, c'est moins de 6 pour cent. Mais il y a aussi des paysans[3] qui adorent la campagne. Ceux qui l'adorent ne changeraient leur vie pour rien au monde.

[3] paysans *peasants*

Des champs dans le sud-ouest de la France

On cultive des fraises dans le sud-ouest.

Vous avez compris?

A **Qui est-ce?** Identifiez.
1. celui qui se consacre à l'agriculture
2. celui qui a une propriété
3. celui qui a une ferme
4. celui qui vit à la campagne

B **Les Fauvet**
Répondez d'après la lecture.
1. Où est la ferme des Fauvet?
2. Où est Soual?
3. Que fait M. Fauvet?
4. Les Fauvet ont une maison en bois?
5. Qu'est-ce qu'il y a à côté de leur maison?
6. Où M. Fauvet entrepose-t-il son matériel?
7. Les Fauvet ont combien d'enfants?
8. Après leurs études, les enfants resteront à la ferme?

Lectures culturelles

Post-reading
Have students discuss the last paragraph of the reading. Does a similar situation exist in the United States?

Vous avez compris?

A and **B** Allow students to refer to the story to look up the answers or you may use these activities as a testing device for factual recall.

Geography Connection
Although the southwest of France has some industrial areas such as Toulouse, the region is mostly known for its agriculture. One of the favorite dishes of the area is a **cassoulet** made from goose, pork, sausage, and beans. It is a very hearty dish and best eaten at midday.

Critical Thinking Activity

Drawing conclusions, making inferences
Read the following to the class or write it on the board or on a transparency:
1. Le lever et le coucher du soleil sont très importants pour les fermiers. Pourquoi?
2. Qu'est-ce qui se passe si le fermier a une mauvaise récolte? Quelles en sont les conséquences?

ANSWERS TO Vous avez compris?

A
1. un agriculteur
2. un propriétaire
3. un fermier
4. un paysan

B
1. La ferme des Fauvet est à quelques kilomètres de Soual.
2. Soual est dans le sud-ouest de la France.
3. M. Fauvet est fermier.
4. Non, ils ont une maison en pierre.
5. À côté de leur maison il y a une étable, une grange et un hangar.
6. M. Fauvet entrepose son matériel dans le hangar.
7. Les Fauvet ont deux enfants.
8. Non, les enfants ne resteront pas à la ferme après leurs études.

Lecture supplémentaire 1

Abidjan

En 1951 Abidjan était une petite ville de moins de 100 000 habitants. Aujourd'hui, c'est une grande ville cosmopolite de plus de 2,9 millions d'habitants et la ville principale de la Côte d'Ivoire. On appelle Abidjan le Paris de l'Afrique occidentale. Cette ville tout proche de l'équateur a même une patinoire couverte.

Le Plateau

Abidjan est construite autour d'une jolie lagune. La zone commerciale du centre-ville s'appelle Le Plateau. Là, il y a des tours modernes. Près du Plateau se trouve Cocody, un quartier résidentiel très chic.

Un marché dans la rue à Abidjan

Treichville et Adjamé

Treichville et Adjamé sont deux quartiers très intéressants du point de vue du tourisme. Il y a deux grands ponts[1] qui relient ces deux quartiers au Plateau. On peut aussi prendre le bateau-bus. Treichville a le plus grand marché de la ville. Au marché, il vaut mieux[2] savoir quelques mots de dioula. Le dioula, c'est une langue spéciale qu'on parle uniquement sur les marchés africains. Adjamé a aussi un marché et une immense gare routière.

[1] ponts *bridges*
[2] il vaut mieux *you'd better*

Le Plateau à Abidjan

Vous avez compris?

Une ville cosmopolite Vrai ou faux?
1. Abidjan a toujours été une grande ville.
2. On n'est jamais loin de l'eau à Abidjan.
3. Il y a des tours modernes au centre-ville.
4. Adjamé est le nom du centre-ville.
5. Le plus grand marché d'Abidjan se trouve à Treichville.
6. Le dioula est la langue qu'on parle dans tous les quartiers d'Abidjan.

Lecture supplémentaire 2

Montréal

Montréal est la ville francophone la plus importante après Paris. La ville de Montréal est située sur une île du même nom—l'île de Montréal. Elle est née de la confluence de la rivière des Outaouais et du fleuve Saint-Laurent. Une quinzaine de ponts[1] relient l'île au continent. Montréal est un important centre industriel, commercial et financier.

Une ville souterraine à Montréal

Une patinoire à Montréal

Montréal en hiver

À Montréal, la température varie beaucoup d'une saison à l'autre. En hiver, il fait très froid et il neige beaucoup. Grâce à une «ville sous la ville», on peut flâner[2] dans un immense centre commercial sans souffrir des rigueurs du climat. La ville souterraine a des passages piétons qui permettent d'avoir accès aux principaux hôtels, aux bureaux, aux grands magasins, à des centaines de boutiques, à de nombreux cinémas et restaurants et à deux gares.

Le vieux Montréal

Le vieux Montréal est aujourd'hui un quartier très agréable. Les demeures[3] anciennes ont été rénovées et les vieux entrepôts[4] ont été convertis en appartements et en bureaux. Des calèches permettent aux touristes de visiter ces beaux quartiers du temps passé.

[1] ponts *bridges*
[2] flâner *wander around*
[3] demeures *abodes, dwellings*
[4] entrepôts *warehouses*

Une calèche devant l'hôtel de ville de Montréal

Vous avez compris?

Une ville importante Décrivez.
1. où est située la ville de Montréal
2. le temps qu'il y fait en hiver
3. la ville souterraine
4. le vieux Montréal

À LA VILLE ET À LA CAMPAGNE

National Standards

Connections
This reading about demographics in France establishes a connection with another discipline, allowing students to reinforce and further their knowledge of the social sciences through the study of French.

Comparisons
This reading contrasts certain demographic statistics of the United States with those of France, affording students a better understanding of the nature of both the size and age of the two populations.

Attention!

The readings in the **Connexions** section are optional. They focus on some of the major disciplines taught in schools and universities. The vocabulary is useful for discussing such topics as history, literature, art, economics, business, science, etc. You may choose any of the following ways to do the readings in the **Connexions** section.

Independent reading Have students read the selections and do the post-reading activities as homework, which you collect. This option is least intrusive on class time and requires a minimum of teacher involvement.

Homework with in-class follow-up Assign the readings and post-reading activities as homework. Review and discuss the material in class the next day.

Intensive in-class activity This option includes a pre-reading vocabulary presentation, in-class reading and discussion, assignment of the activities for homework, and a discussion of the assignment in class the next day.

CONNEXIONS

La sociologie

La démographie

Demography is the study of human populations, of their distribution, density, and vital statistics. Demographics explain where people choose to live and why. They also explain population shifts—why people move from place to place.

The demography of France is quite similar to that of most industrialized nations. The urban areas are becoming more populated because people are migrating from rural areas to the cities. Newly arrived immigrants from foreign countries also settle in the cities where employment is often more available.

La démographie

La démographie est l'étude des populations humaines. La démographie étudie où vivent les gens et les raisons pour lesquelles ils y vivent. La démographie explique quand et pourquoi les gens décident de déménager[1] et de s'installer ailleurs.

Déplacements de population

De nombreux agriculteurs se trouvent actuellement dans une situation économique précaire. Le matériel agricole qui est indispensable à une bonne exploitation de la terre coûte cher. Il faut souvent s'endetter pour acheter des machines, des tracteurs, etc., et le revenu que leur rapporte[2] leur petite propriété—surtout les années où la récolte n'est pas bonne—n'est pas suffisant pour couvrir les frais. Pour cette raison, de nombreux paysans[3] quittent les régions rurales pour aller chercher du travail dans les agglomérations urbaines. Au milieu du dix-neuvième siècle, les ruraux représentaient les 2/3 (les deux tiers) de la population totale de la France. Aujourd'hui, leur part est tombée à 6 pour cent.

[1] déménager *to move*
[2] rapporte *brings*
[3] paysans *peasants*

La cueillette des cerises

L'immigration

La France n'a jamais été un grand pays d'émigration. En revanche (au contraire), la France a fait appel à l'immigration pour se procurer la main-d'œuvre[4] nécessaire au développement de son économie. Pendant les années 80, la hausse du chômage[5] a provoqué l'arrêt de l'immigration. Récemment, l'immigration a repris[6], mais le nombre des immigrés de pays européens est en baisse[7]. La plupart des nouveaux arrivés sont du Maghreb, d'Afrique occidentale et d'Asie. Estimée à 4,3 millions de personnes, la population étrangère représente 7,4 pour cent de la population totale. De ces 4,3 millions, un million sont des jeunes de moins de 16 ans.

[4] main-d'œuvre *work force*
[5] hausse du chômage *rise in unemployment*
[6] a repris *started up again*
[7] en baisse *lower*

Des téléphones publics à Paris

Pays d'origine des étrangers résidant en France

Portugal	606 000
Algérie	572 000
Italie	523 000
Maroc	447 000
Espagne	413 000
Tunisie	182 000
Afrique occidentale	182 000
Turquie	159 000
Pays d'Asie	158 000
Yougoslavie	60 000
Pologne	40 000

Vous avez compris?

Discussion Discutez en anglais.

1. What is demography?
2. What migratory patterns exist within France?
3. Why did France call upon immigrants?

CONNEXIONS

Presentation

La sociologie
La démographie

Step 1 Have students read the introduction in English on page 358.

Step 2 Have students read the selection independently.

FUN FACTS

Most of the Asians residing in France are from Vietnam and Cambodia.

LEVELING

A: Reading

À LA VILLE ET À LA CAMPAGNE

C'est à vous

Use what you have learned

Presentation

Encourage students to say as much as possible when they do these activities. Tell them not to be afraid to make mistakes, since the goal of these activities is real-life communication. If someone in the group makes an error, allow the others to politely correct him or her. Let students choose the activities they would like to do.

You may wish to divide students into pairs or groups. Encourage students to elaborate on the basic theme and to be creative. They may use props, pictures, or posters if they wish.

LEVELING

These activities encompass all three levels. All students will be able to do them at a sophistication level commensurate with their ability in French. Some students will be able to speak for several minutes, and others may be able to give just a few sentences. This is to be expected when students are functioning completely on their own, generating their own language to the best of their ability.

C'est à vous

Use what you have learned

1 La ville
✔ Talk about life in the city

Avec un(e) camarade, parlez de tout ce que vous savez de Paris. Dites si vous aimeriez habiter à Paris et pourquoi.

Le Quartier latin à Paris

2 Une ville francophone
✔ Talk about life in an interesting Francophone city

Depuis que vous faites du français, vous avez «visité» plusieurs villes francophones. Choisissez une ville qui vous intéresse et décrivez-la à votre camarade. Ensuite, il/elle fera de même.

3 Jeu Comparaisons
✔ Talk about animals—an aspect of country life

Travaillez avec un(e) camarade. Essayez de deviner ce que les expressions suivantes veulent dire. (Vous en connaissez déjà quelques-unes.) Essayez ensuite de trouver leur équivalent en anglais.

avoir une faim de loup
avoir une fièvre de cheval
compter les moutons
être malade comme un chien
être mère poule
manger comme un cochon
jouer au chat et à la souris

Quand le chat n'est pas là, les souris dansent.
Il fait un temps de chien.

360 🪻 trois cent soixante

CHAPITRE 11

ANSWERS TO C'est à vous

1 *Answers will vary.*
Students can tell about the many monuments they have learned about, different areas of the city, museums, public transport, etc.

2 *Answers will vary depending upon the city students choose.*

3 *Answers will vary but may include:*
To be as hungry as a wolf
To be burning up with fever
To count sheep
To be as sick as a dog
To be a mother hen
To eat like a pig
To play cat and mouse
When the cat's away, the mice will play.
It's raining cats and dogs.

CHAPITRE 11   C'est à vous

Recycling
These activities allow students to use the vocabulary and structure from this chapter in completely open-ended, real-life situations.

4 Je ne pourrais jamais vivre...
✓ Give your opinion about city life vs. country life

Écrivez une rédaction intitulée «Je ne pourrais jamais vivre à la campagne (à la ville)». Donnez vos raisons.

Writing Strategy

Comparing and contrasting
Comparing and contrasting involves writing about similarities and differences between two or more related things. A Venn diagram will help you do this. First draw two intersecting circles; title the circles with the subjects to be compared. List unique features of each subject. Then list the similarities of the two subjects in the area where the circles intersect. This tool, or any other similar one you can think of, will help you organize your thoughts so you can clearly and effectively write your comparison.

5 Deux villes
Think of two cities you have visited. Write a paper comparing the two places. If you are not familiar with two different cities, compare the town where you live with a nearby city or other town. Be sure to organize your thoughts with a list or a graph, showing the similarities and differences.

Writing Development
Have students keep a notebook containing their best written work from each chapter. These selected writings can be based on assignments from the Student Textbook and the Workbook. The two activities on page 361 are examples of writing assignments that may be included in each student's portfolio. In the Workbook, students will develop an organized autobiography (**Mon autobiographie**). These workbook pages may also become a part of their portfolio.

Writing Strategy

Comparing and contrasting   Have students read the Writing Strategy on page 361. Have students refer to the vocabulary list on page 365 if they need more ideas to write this selection.

La ville de Luxembourg

Fort-de-France à la Martinique

À LA VILLE ET À LA CAMPAGNE   trois cent soixante et un ❖ 361

Learning from Photos
(page 361 left) Fort-de-France is the main city of Martinique—**un département français d'outre-mer (un D.O.M.)**. It is a colorful city on the Caribbean coast.

(page 361 right) Luxembourg is a small principality that serves as one of the financial capitals of Europe. Its residents speak three languages: Luxembourgish, German, and French. Luxembourg City is the capital.

Reaching All Students

Additional Practice
Display Communication Transparency C 11. Have students work in groups to make up as many questions as they can about the illustration. Have groups take turns asking and answering the questions.

Answers to C'est à vous

4   Answers will vary depending upon students' preferences.

5   Answers will vary depending upon the cities selected.

Assessment

Resource Manager

Communication Transparencies C 11
Quizzes, pages 57–61
Tests, pages 167–182
ExamView® Pro
Situation Cards
Performance Assessment, Task 11
Marathon mental Videoquiz

 Assessment

This is a pre-test for students to take before you administer the chapter test. Answer sheets for students to do these pages are provided in your transparency binder. Note that each section is cross-referenced so students can easily find the material they have to review in case they made errors. You may wish to collect these assessments and correct them yourself or you may prefer to have the students correct themselves in class. You can go over the answers orally or project them on the overhead, using your Assessment Answers transparencies.

Assessment

Vocabulaire

1 Identifiez.

To review Mots 1, turn to pages 340–341.

2 Complétez.

6. Vous allez dans le mauvais sens. Il faut faire _____.
7. Les piétons _____ la rue dans un passage pour piétons.
8. L'école n'est pas devant l'église. Elle est _____ l'église.

3 Répondez.

To review Mots 2, turn to pages 344–345.

9. Qui cultive la terre?
10. Donnez les noms de deux animaux.
11. Les fermiers mettent les animaux où?
12. Ils mettent leur récolte où?
13. Quel animal donne du lait?

362 trois cent soixante-deux   CHAPITRE 11

ANSWERS TO Assessment

1
1. une piétonne
2. le coin
3. le trottoir
4. un agent de police
5. un feu rouge

2
6. demi-tour
7. traversent
8. derrière

3 Answers will vary but may include:
9. un agriculteur (un fermier)
10. une vache, un mouton
11. dans une étable
12. dans une grange
13. une vache

CHAPITRE 11

Structure

4 Complétez la question et la réponse.

14–15. —Tu préfères ____ de ces deux livres?
—Moi, je préfère ____.

16–17. —De toutes ces voitures, ____ est ta favorite?
—Ma favorite, c'est ____ ____ mon frère.

18–19. —____ de ces deux hommes est le mari de la prof?
—____ ____ parle maintenant.

To review these pronouns, turn to page 348.

5 Complétez.

20–21. Je ____ bien et ils ____ bien aussi. (conduire)
22–23. Tu ____ bien et nous ____ bien aussi. (vivre)

To review these verbs, turn to page 350.

Culture

6 Répondez.

24. Qu'est-ce qu'il y a à côté de la maison d'un agriculteur typique?
25. Chaque année, il y a plus ou moins d'agriculteurs en France?

To review this cultural information, turn to pages 354–355.

Des champs près d'Albi

À LA VILLE ET À LA CAMPAGNE

trois cent soixante-trois 363

On parle super bien!

This unique page gives students the opportunity to speak freely and say whatever they can, using the vocabulary and structures they have learned in the chapter. The illustration serves to remind students of precisely what they know how to say in French. There are no activities that students do not have the ability to describe or talk about in French. The art not only depicts the vocabulary and content of this chapter, but also reinforces what they learned in previous chapters.

You may wish to use this page in many ways. Some possibilities are to have students do the following:

1. Look at the illustration and identify items by giving the correct French words.
2. Make up sentences about what they see in the illustration.
3. Make up questions about the illustration. They can call on another class member to respond if you do this as a class activity, or you may prefer to allow students to work in small groups. This activity is extremely beneficial because it enables students to actively use interrogative words.
4. Answer questions you ask them about the illustration.
5. Work in pairs and make up a conversation based on the illustration.
6. Look at the illustration and give a complete oral review of what they see.
7. Look at the illustration and write a paragraph (or essay) about it.

You can also use this page as an assessment or testing tool, taking into account individual differences by having students go from simple to quite complicated tasks. The assessment can be either oral or written. You may wish to use the rubrics provided on pages T20–T21 as you give students the following directions.

On parle super bien!

Tell all you can about this illustration.

364   *trois cent soixante-quatre*   CHAPITRE 11

1. Identify the topic or situation of the illustration.
2. Give the French words for as many items as you can.
3. Think of as many sentences as you can to describe the illustration.
4. Go over your sentences and put them in the best sequencing to give a coherent story based on the illustration.

Vocabulaire

Describing a city

la ville	un boulevard	un passage pour	une usine
le centre-ville	un coin	piétons	un ouvrier, une
un quartier d'affaires	un trottoir	un bâtiment	ouvrière
la banlieue	un piéton, une	une tour	traverser la rue
une rue	piétonne	un bureau	
une avenue			

Getting around by car

une rue	un parcmètre	conduire	se garer
à sens unique	un horodateur	régler	de près
un carrefour	un parking	circuler	
un rond-point	un agent de police	suivre	
la circulation	le code de la	respecter	
un feu	route	stationner	

Giving directions

faire demi-tour	devant	à côté de
le bon sens	derrière	en face de
le mauvais sens		

How well do you know your vocabulary?
Choose words to describe getting around a city by car. Write three or four sentences about what a good driver should and should not do.

Describing the country

la campagne	un champ	un hangar	entreposer
une ferme	un pré	du matériel agricole	cultiver
un fermier, une	de l'herbe (f.)	une récolte	
fermière	un vignoble	la terre	
un agriculteur, une	une grange	le blé	
agricultrice	une étable	les céréales (f. pl.)	

Identifying some farm animals

une vache	un agneau	un cochon
un mouton	une poule	un cheval
un veau	un lapin	un troupeau (de)

Other useful words and expressions

suivre
vivre
faire du cheval

 VIDÉOTOUR

Épisode 11
In this video episode, you will join Vincent and Manu on a treasure hunt. See page 510 for more information.

trois cent soixante-cinq ❖ 365

Révision

Preview

This section reviews the salient points from Chapters 8–11. In the **Conversation,** students will review hotel, public transportation, and direction giving vocabulary. In the **Structure** sections, they will review the **passé composé** with **avoir** and **être,** time expressions, **lequel,** and **celui.**

Resource Manager

Workbook, Check-Up, pages 131–136
Tests, pages 183–193

Presentation

Conversation

Step 1 Have students open their books to page 366. Call on two students to read this short conversation aloud.

Step 2 Go over the activity in the **Vous avez compris?** section.

Learning from Photos

(page 366) The agent in the photo is helping the young man locate a hotel on a map. The photo was taken at the **gare de l'Est** information center in Paris.

Révision

Conversation

Bureau du tourisme—gare de l'Est

Jimmy: Bonjour, monsieur. Je voudrais savoir comment je vais à l'hôtel Beauséjour.
Employé: Lequel? Des hôtels Beauséjour, il y en a beaucoup.
Jimmy: Euh, celui qui est avenue Parmentier.
Employé: Ah oui. J'espère que vous avez réservé. Je viens de téléphoner pour un autre touriste et tout est complet.
Jimmy: Oui, oui, j'ai une réservation depuis bien trois mois! Il y a un autobus qui y va?
Employé: Oui, mais c'est les heures de pointe maintenant, alors il vaut mieux prendre le métro.
Jimmy: D'accord.
Employé: Alors, voilà. Je vous donne un plan du métro. Regardez. Vous êtes ici à la gare de l'Est. Vous prenez la direction place d'Italie. Vous descendez à République. Ça fait deux stations. Vous me suivez bien?
Jimmy: Oui, oui, je vous suis.
Employé: À République, vous changez et vous prenez la direction Galliéni. Vous descendez à Parmentier. C'est une station, c'est tout. Vous sortez du métro et l'hôtel est juste à votre droite. C'est pas loin. Un quart d'heure, vingt minutes, maximum.
Jimmy: Merci. Au revoir, monsieur.

Vous avez compris?

Comment y aller? Répondez.

1. Où est Jimmy?
2. Où veut-il aller?
3. Il a réservé une chambre?
4. Il a une réservation depuis combien de temps?
5. Où est l'hôtel?
6. Comment peut-il y aller?
7. Jimmy va à quelle station pour prendre le métro?
8. Il va descendre à quelle station pour changer?
9. Il va sortir du métro à quelle station?

366 ❧ trois cent soixante-six   CHAPITRES 8–11

Answers to Vous avez compris?

1. Jimmy est au bureau de tourisme à la gare de l'Est.
2. Il veut aller à l'hôtel Beauséjour.
3. Oui, il a réservé une chambre.
4. Il a une réservation depuis trois mois.
5. L'hôtel est avenue Parmentier.
6. On peut y aller en autobus ou en métro.
7. Jimmy va à la station gare de l'Est.
8. Il va descendre à République.
9. Il va sortir du métro à Parmentier.

Structure

Avoir ou être

Verbs like **descendre, monter, sortir** are conjugated with **avoir** when they have a direct object. They are conjugated with **être** when they do not have a direct object.

Il a descendu ses bagages au rez-de-chaussée.
Il est descendu au rez-de-chaussée.

1 Historiette Elle va à l'hôtel.
Choisissez.

1. Elle _____ à la station George V.
   a. est descendue   b. a descendu
2. Elle _____ un magazine de son sac à dos.
   a. est sortie   b. a sorti
3. Elle _____ du métro à Bastille.
   a. est sortie   b. a sorti
4. Elle _____ ses bagages.
   a. est descendue   b. a descendu
5. Elle _____ dans la rue.
   a. est montée   b. a monté
6. Elle _____ l'escalier à toute vitesse.
   a. est montée   b. a monté
7. Elle _____ à l'hôtel.
   a. est rentrée   b. a rentré
8. Elle _____ son billet.
   a. est sortie   b. a sorti
9. Elle _____ dans sa chambre.
   a. est montée   b. a monté
10. Ensuite, elle _____ de l'hôtel pour visiter la ville.
    a. est sortie   b. a sorti

La station de métro Bastille

 LITERARY COMPANION *You may wish to read the excerpt from* **Vol de nuit,** *a novel by Antoine de Saint-Exupéry. You will find this literary selection on page 486.*

Révision

Expressions de temps

1. You use the present tense of **venir de** + infinitive to express what just happened.

   Le train vient d'arriver.
   Mes amis viennent de descendre du train.

2. You use the expression **depuis (que)** with the present tense to express an action that began in the past and continues into the present.

   Il habite à la campagne depuis quand?
   Il habite à la campagne depuis des années—
   depuis qu'il est tout petit.

 Toute la famille Répondez.
1. Ton père vient d'envoyer un fax?
2. Ta mère vient de rentrer du bureau?
3. Tes frères viennent de finir leurs devoirs?
4. Tu viens de rentrer de l'école?
5. Tout le monde vient de faire quelque chose de différent?

 Moi! Donnez des réponses personnelles.
1. Tu es dans la même école depuis quand?
2. Tu as le/la même prof de français depuis combien de temps?
3. Il/Elle enseigne le français depuis combien de temps?
4. Et toi, tu fais du français depuis combien de temps?

Des champs de lavande en Provence

Lequel et celui

Review the following forms of **lequel** (which one[s]) and **celui** (this/that one, these/those).

The forms of **lequel** are: lequel, laquelle, lesquels, lesquelles.

   De tous ces magazines, tu préfères lequel?
   De toutes ces photos, tu préfères lesquelles?

The forms of **celui** are: celui-là, celle-là, ceux-là, celles-là.

   De tous ces magazines, tu préfères lequel?
   Je préfère celui-là, celui qui est sur la table.
   De toutes ces photos, tu préfères lesquelles?
   Je préfère celles-là, celles de Mélanie.

368 trois cent soixante-huit   CHAPITRES 8–11

4 Préférences Complétez.

1. —J'ai deux magazines. Je vais t'en donner un. Tu veux lequel?
   —Je veux bien ____.
2. —De toutes les fermes que tu as visitées, tu préfères ____?
   —Je préfère ____ ____ la famille Fauvet.
3. —De toutes les chambres de cet hôtel, tu préfères ____?
   —Je préfère ____ ____ donnent sur la cour.
4. —De tous les hôpitaux de cette ville, ____ est le plus moderne?
   —____ ____ est le plus connu, c'est l'hôpital de la Croix, mais je ne sais pas si c'est le plus moderne.
5. —De toutes les photos que j'ai prises cet été, tu sais ____ ____ je préfère?
   —Non, ____?
   —____ ____ j'ai prises au Sénégal.
6. —De ces deux vues de Dakar, ____ tu préfères?
   —____.

La Grande Mosquée à Dakar au Sénégal

Le musée d'Art Africain à Dakar

5 Les transports en commun Travaillez en petits groupes. En cinq minutes, écrivez autant de questions que possible sur le métro et les autobus à Paris. Posez vos questions à un autre groupe. Le groupe qui répond correctement au plus grand nombre de questions gagne.

6 Un accident Décrivez un accident que vous avez eu ou qu'un autre membre de votre famille a eu. Dites ce qui est arrivé, comment, quand, etc. Dites tout ce que le médecin, l'infirmière/l'infirmier ou les secouristes ont fait ou dit.

7 À la ville ou à la campagne Faites deux listes: une des avantages et des inconvénients de la vie à la campagne, et une autre pour la vie à la ville. Expliquez où vous préféreriez habiter et pourquoi.

Preview

This section, **Reflets des Caraïbes,** was prepared by the National Geographic Society. Its purpose is to give students greater insight, through these visual images, into the culture and people of the French-speaking Caribbean. Have students look at the photographs on pages 370–373 for enjoyment. If they would like to talk about them, let them say anything they can, using the vocabulary they have learned to this point.

 National Standards

Culture
The **Reflets des Caraïbes** photos and the accompanying captions allow students to gain insights into the people and culture of the French-speaking areas of the Caribbean.

About the Photos

1. La plage de Sainte-Anne, à la Guadeloupe Guadeloupe is made up of two major islands, **Basse-Terre** and **Grande-Terre,** and a few smaller islands. The **plage de Sainte-Anne** is on **Grande-Terre.** The beach is protected by reefs and is excellent for snorkeling.

2. La cathédrale Saint-Louis à Fort-de-France, à la Martinique The Saint-Louis Cathedral in Fort-de-France is the sixth to be built on this same site. The others were destroyed by fire, earthquake, or hurricane. The present structure dates from 1878. It has impressive stained-glass windows, and several of Martinique's former governors are buried beneath the choir loft. The cathedral is on Rue Victor Schœlcher, which runs through the center of the shopping district.

1. La plage de Sainte-Anne, à la Guadeloupe
2. La cathédrale Saint-Louis à Fort-de-France, à la Martinique
3. Homme portant des anthuriums et autres fleurs exotiques à Fond-Saint-Denis, à la Martinique
4. La place de la Victoire à Pointe-à-Pitre, à la Guadeloupe
5. Jeune Haïtienne
6. Jeune violoniste de l'Orchestre Philharmonique Sainte Trinité, en Haïti
7. Artistes peintres exposant leurs tableaux à Port-au-Prince, en Haïti

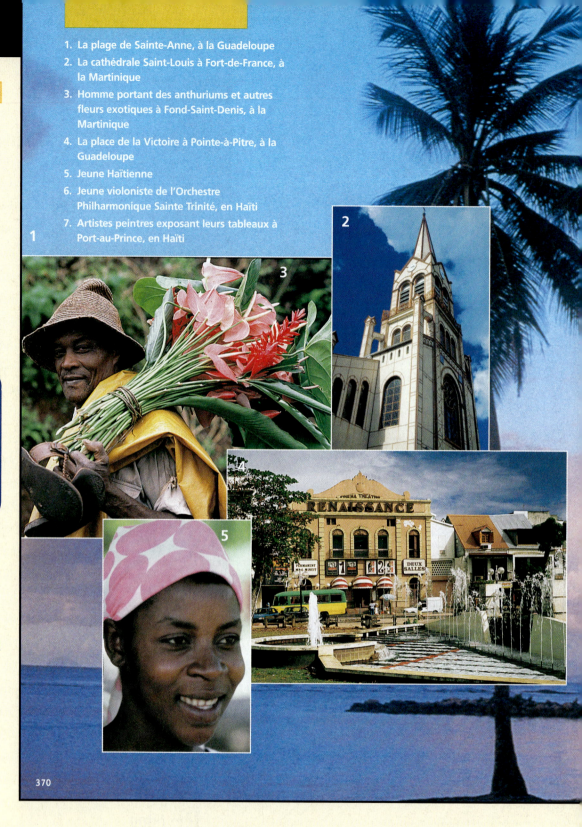

REFLETS
des Caraïbes

3. Homme portant des anthuriums et autres fleurs exotiques à Fond-Saint-Denis, à la Martinique Martinique is known for its exotic flora. In the capital, Fort-de-France, there is the **Parc Floral et Culturel** where one can learn about the many varieties of flowers that grow around the island.

4. La place de la Victoire à Pointe-à-Pitre, à la Guadeloupe Pointe-à-Pitre is a city of some 100,000 people on **Grande-Terre.** It is the island's commercial and industrial hub. The heart of the old city is the **place de la Victoire.** The square is surrounded by wood buildings, which have balconies and shutters. In the center of the square there is a palm-shaded park that is a popular gathering place.

5. Jeune Haïtienne Haiti occupies the western part of the island of Hispaniola, which it shares with the Dominican Republic. Its more than seven million people speak French and Creole. The people are extremely industrious, but Haiti has suffered from one political crisis after another. It is the poorest country in the Western Hemisphere.

6. Jeune violoniste de l'Orchestre Philharmonique Sainte Trinité, en Haïti In spite of the poverty in Haiti, its people find ways to express their talents, particularly in the fields of music and art. **Sainte Trinité** is the name of Port-au-Prince's cathedral. The major religions of Haiti are Roman Catholic and voodoo.

7. Artistes peintres exposant leurs tableaux à Port-au-Prince, en Haïti Many Haitians excel in art, and their paintings are popular in art galleries around the world. Many of the artists are self-taught, and their paintings depict scenes of everyday life or Biblical scenes. In Port-au-Prince, the **Centre d'art** is run by charitable groups, and it helps to promote Haitian art. Some of the artists are too poor to get canvas, and they paint on cardboard.

8. Ouvriers agricoles dans un champ de canne à sucre dans la région du Moule, à la Guadeloupe Although tourism is very popular in Guadeloupe, sugar is still Guadeloupe's principal source of income. Sugar harvest time is in February, and the fields are filled with workers cutting cane. The roads are clogged with trucks taking cane to factories and distilleries.

9. L'héliconia, une fleur exotique des Antilles There are many varieties of Heliconia. The one pictured is commonly known as "lobster claw." These beautiful flowers grow throughout the Caribbean.

10. Fresque décorant le mur d'une pharmacie de Fort-de-France, à la Martinique Here we see a painting done by a local resident on the wall of a pharmacy in Fort-de-France.

11. Courses de gommiers au large des côtes de la Martinique The boats seen in this race are **gommiers**. **Gommiers** are actually fishing boats that are made from the wood of a gum tree.

12. La bibliothèque Schœlcher à Fort-de-France, à la Martinique The **bibliothèque Schœlcher** is a rather elaborate building, incorporating several architectural styles. It is a public library, and it was named after Victor Schœlcher. Schœlcher was an Alsatian who led the fight for the abolition of slavery in the West Indies during the nineteenth century. The Fort-de-France suburb of Schœlcher is also named after him. It is a pleasant area, home to the University of the French West Indies and Guyana.

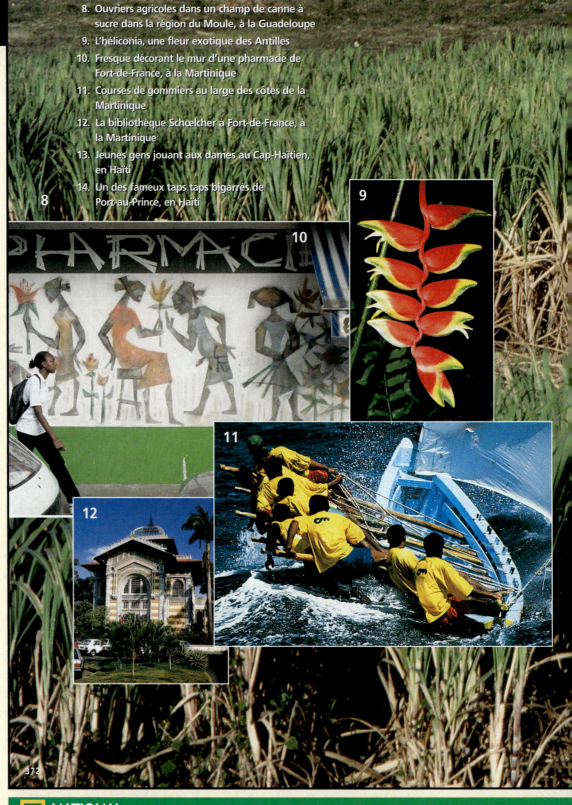

8. Ouvriers agricoles dans un champ de canne à sucre dans la région du Moule, à la Guadeloupe
9. L'héliconia, une fleur exotique des Antilles
10. Fresque décorant le mur d'une pharmacie de Fort-de-France, à la Martinique
11. Courses de gommiers au large des côtes de la Martinique
12. La bibliothèque Schœlcher à Fort-de-France, à la Martinique
13. Jeunes gens jouant aux dames au Cap-Haïtien, en Haïti
14. Un des fameux taps taps bigarrés de Port-au-Prince, en Haïti

 Teacher's Corner

Index to the NATIONAL GEOGRAPHIC MAGAZINE

The following related articles may be of interest:
- "Haiti—Against All Odds," by Charles E. Cobb, November 1987.
- "Searching for Columbus's Lost Colony: La Navidad," by Kathleen A. Deagan, November 1987.
- "The Caribbean: Sun, Sea, and Seething," by Noel Grove, February 1981.

REFLETS
des Caraïbes

13. Jeunes gens jouant aux dames au Cap-Haïtien, en Haïti
Cap-Haïtien is the second-largest city in Haiti, with a population of some 90,000. It was destroyed several times by fires and earthquakes. Above the city sits an old **Citadelle** reachable by donkey.

14. Un des fameux taps taps bigarrés de Port-au-Prince, en Haïti **Taps taps** are the major means of public transportation in Haiti. The brightly painted trucks of a wide variety of sizes are given creative names, many of which are religious in nature. Many of the **taps taps** are privately owned, and their owners are proud of them and maintain them very well.

Products available from
GLENCOE/MCGRAW-HILL
To order the following products, call Glencoe/McGraw-Hill at 1-800-334-7344.
CD-ROM
• Picture Atlas of the World
Transparency Set
• NGS MapPack: Geography of North America

Products available from
NATIONAL GEOGRAPHIC SOCIETY
To order the following products, call National Geographic Society at 1-800-368-2728.
Books
• National Geographic World Atlas for Young Explorers
• National Geographic Satellite Atlas of the World
Software
• ZingoLingo: French Diskette

Planning for Chapter 12

SCOPE AND SEQUENCE, PAGES 374–403

Topics
- Holidays and celebrations

Culture
- Celebrations and holidays in France
- **Carnaval** in France, the Caribbean, the United States, and Canada

Functions
- How to talk about things that may or may not happen
- How to express what you wish, hope, or would like others to do

Structure
- The subjunctive
- The subjunctive with expressions of wish or desire

National Standards
- Communication Standard 1.1 pages 378, 379, 382, 383, 386, 387, 388, 389, 391, 398
- Communication Standard 1.2 pages 378, 379, 382, 383, 386, 387, 388, 389, 390, 393, 395, 397
- Communication Standard 1.3 pages 378, 379, 383, 387, 389, 391, 398, 399
- Cultures Standard 2.1 pages 376, 377, 380, 381, 385, 386, 392–393, 394–395
- Connections Standard 3.1 pages 396–397
- Comparisons Standard 4.2 pages 379, 383, 391
- Communities Standard 5.1 page 399

PACING AND PRIORITIES

The chapter content is color coded below to assist you in planning.

■ required   ■ recommended   ■ optional

Vocabulaire (required)   *Days 1–4*
- ■ Mots 1
  - Le 14 juillet
  - Le carnaval
- ■ Mots 2
  - Noël
  - Hanouka
  - Le jour de l'An
  - Le mariage

Structure (required)   *Days 5–7*
- ■ Le subjonctif
- ■ Le subjonctif après les expressions de souhait ou de volonté

Conversation (required)
- ■ C'est bientôt le 14 juillet

Lectures culturelles
- ■ Des fêtes en France (recommended)
- ■ Carnaval (optional)

Connexions (optional)
- ■ Histoire et Littérature

■ **C'est à vous** (recommended)

■ **Assessment** (recommended)

■ **On parle super bien!** (optional)

RESOURCE GUIDE

SECTION	PAGES	SECTION RESOURCES
Vocabulaire *Mots 1*		
Le 14 juillet Le carnaval	376 377–379	Vocabulary Transparencies 12.2–12.3 Audio CD 7 Audio Activities TE, pages 128–130 Workbook, pages 137–138 Quiz 1, page 63 ExamView® Pro
Vocabulaire *Mots 2*		
Noël Hanouka Le jour de l'An Le mariage	380 381 381 381–383	Vocabulary Transparencies 12.4–12.5 Audio CD 7 Audio Activities TE, pages 131–133 Workbook, page 139 Quiz 2, page 64 ExamView® Pro
Structure		
Le subjonctif Le subjonctif après les expressions de souhait ou de volonté	384–387 388–389	Audio CD 7 Audio Activities TE, pages 133–135 Workbook, pages 140–142 Quizzes 3–4, pages 65–66 ExamView® Pro
Conversation		
C'est bientôt le 14 juillet	390–391	Audio CD 7 Audio Activities TE, pages 135–136 Interactive CD-ROM
Lectures culturelles		
Des fêtes en France Carnaval	392–393 394–395	Audio CD 7 Audio Activities TE, pages 136–138 Tests, pages 198, 202
Connexions		
Histoire et Littérature	396–397	Tests, page 203
C'est à vous		
	398–399	**Bon voyage!** Video, Episode 12 Video Activities, Chapter 12 French Online Activities french.glencoe.com
Assessment		
	400–401	Communication Transparency C 12 Quizzes 1–4, pages 63–66 Performance Assessment, Task 12 Tests, pages 195–210 ExamView® Pro Situation Cards, Chapter 12 **Marathon mental** Videoquiz

Using Your Resources for Chapter 12

Transparencies

Bellringer 12.1–12.8   Vocabulary 12.1–12.5   Communication C 12

Workbook

Vocabulary, pages 137–139   Structure, pages 140–142   Enrichment, pages 143–146

Audio Activities

Vocabulary, pages 128–133   Structure, pages 133–135   Conversation, pages 135–136   Cultural Reading, pages 136–138   Additional Practice, pages 139–141

Assessment

Vocabulary and Structure Quizzes, pages 63–66

Chapter Tests, pages 195–210

Situation Cards, Chapter 12

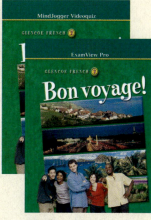

MindJogger Videoquiz, ExamView® Pro, Chapter 12

Timesaving Teacher Tools

TeacherWorks™

TeacherWorks™ is your all-in-one teacher resource center. Personalize lesson plans, access resources from the Teacher Wraparound Edition, connect to the Internet, or make a to-do list. These are only a few of the many features that can assist you in the planning and organizing of your lessons.

Includes:
- A calendar feature
- Access to all program blackline masters
- Standards correlations and more

ExamView® Pro

Test Bank software for Macintosh and Windows makes creating, editing, customizing, and printing tests quick and easy.

Technology Resources

In the Chapter 12 Internet activity, you will have a chance to learn more about the Francophone world. Visit **french.glencoe.com**.

On the Interactive Conversation CD-ROM, students can listen to and take part in a recorded version of the conversation in Chapter 12.

See the National Geographic Teacher's Corner on pages 138–139, 244–245, 372–373, 472–473 for reference to additional technology resources.

Bon voyage! Video and Video Activities, Chapter 12

Help your students prepare for the chapter test by playing the **Marathon mental** Videoquiz game show. Teams will compete against each other to review chapter vocabulary and structure and sharpen listening comprehension skills.

CHAPITRE 12

Preview

In this chapter, students will learn to describe and discuss several important holidays and family celebrations as well as to extend holiday greetings. Students will also be introduced to the subjunctive and its use to express wishes, preferences, and demands.

National Standards

Communication
In Chapter 12, students will communicate in spoken and written French on the following topics:
- Family social events
- Weddings
- Holiday customs

Students will obtain and provide information about these topics, express feelings, and engage in conversations that would typically take place at celebrations or on important holidays as they fulfill the chapter objectives listed on this page.

LEVELING

The activities, conversations, and readings within each chapter are marked according to level of difficulty. **E** indicates easy. **A** indicates average. **C** indicates challenging. Some activities cover a range of difficulty. In some activities, for example, advanced students will be able to produce more extensive responses while students who learn at a different rate may give less detailed responses. The leveling indicators will help you individualize instruction to best meet your students' needs.

CHAPITRE 12

Les fêtes

Objectifs
In this chapter you will learn to:
- ✓ talk about holidays and celebrations
- ✓ talk about things that may or may not happen
- ✓ express what you wish, hope, or would like others to do
- ✓ discuss some family celebrations

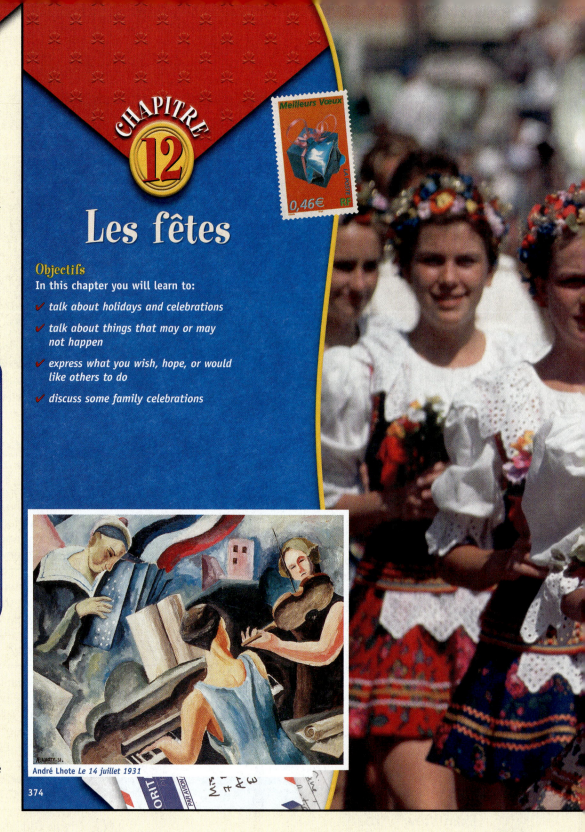

André Lhote *Le 14 juillet 1931*

CHAPITRE 12

Spotlight on Culture

Photograph The young women in the photo are marching in a parade during the Flower Festival in Digne, Provence.

Painting André Lhote (1885–1962) was both a painter and an art critic. Influenced by fauvists and cubists, he liked to use vivid colors to paint realistic human figures.

Students can send electronic greeting cards in French for various holidays from (french.glencoe.com).

trois cent soixante-quinze ❖ 375

Vocabulaire
Mots 1

1 Preparation

Resource Manager

Vocabulary Transparencies 12.2–12.3
Audio Activities TE, pages 128–130
Audio CD 7
Workbook, pages 137–138
Quiz 1, page 63
ExamView® Pro

Bellringer Review

Use BRR Transparency 12.1 or write the following on the board. Complete.
1. Aujourd'hui Marie a quinze ans. C'est son _____.
2. Marie donne une _____ et elle _____ ses amis.
3. Ses amis lui donnent des _____.
4. Il y a un _____ avec quinze bougies.

2 Presentation

Step 1 Have students close their books. Use Vocabulary Transparencies 12.2–12.3 to present **Mots 1**. Have students repeat the words, phrases, and sentences after you or Audio CD 7.

Learning from Photos

(page 376 top left) The photo is of a military band participating in the July 14th parade on the **Champs-Élysées**.

(page 376 top right) The marching band is playing at the Bastille Day celebrations in Beaune.

LEVELING

A: Vocabulary

Vocabulaire
Mots 1

Le 14 juillet

un drapeau
un défilé

C'est la fête nationale française.
La fête a lieu le 14 juillet.

une fanfare
une trompette
des cymbales
un tambour

La fanfare joue l'hymne national.
C'est «La Marseillaise».

un trombone   un soldat

des feux d'artifice

une tribune
le maire
le premier rang
les notables

Les soldats défilent.
Ils passent devant les tribunes.

376 ❖ trois cent soixante-seize   CHAPITRE 12

FUN FACTS

The **Garde républicaine de Paris**, pictured in the illustration on page 376, is an arm of the national police force under the Department of Defense. Their appearance, with gleaming sabers, shining helmets with plumes, varnished boots, and flashing breastplates, is impressive at state functions like the Bastille Day parade. They are also honored for their service as a riot squad and in battle.

Reaching All Students

Kinesthetic Learners
Pantomime Game Write these expressions on cards. Distribute them to students to mime. The others guess what instrument is being played.

jouer de la guitare   jouer du tambour
jouer du piano   jouer des cymbales
jouer de l'accordéon   jouer du violon
jouer du trombone

Vocabulaire Mots 1

Le carnaval

un char
lancer des confettis
des serpentins

Un défilé de chars traverse la ville.

Dans la rue, il y a des groupes masqués.

LES FÊTES trois cent soixante-dix-sept 377

Step 2 As you are presenting the vocabulary, you may wish to ask the following types of questions: La fête nationale française est le 4 ou le 14 juillet? Le 14 juillet, il y a un grand défilé? Les soldats défilent? Il y a beaucoup de monde dans les tribunes? Le maire et les notables regardent le défilé? Quels instruments y a-t-il dans une fanfare? Comment s'appelle l'hymne national français? Quand est-ce qu'il y a des feux d'artifice? Qu'est-ce qu'on lance pendant le carnaval?

Step 3 Have students open their books and read the new words and expressions.

About the French Language

Tell students that **jouer de** is used to express the meaning *to play a musical instrument*.
   On joue du piano.
   On joue du violon.
Review **jouer à** with a sport.
   On joue au foot. ⚜

Learning from Photos

(page 377) All of these photos were taken during the **carnaval** celebrations in Nice.

Assessment

As an informal assessment after completing the vocabulary presentation, call on students to look at the illustrations and say as much as they can about them.

Reaching All Students

Additional Practice You may wish to ask students the following additional questions about the **Mots 1** vocabulary: Il faut que tout le monde applaudisse après «La Marseillaise»? Qui joue l'hymne national, la fanfare ou l'orchestre? Il y a des tambours dans une fanfare? On tire des feux d'artifice le 14 ou le 4 juillet en France? Et aux États-Unis?

Vocabulary Expansion

You may wish to give students the names of these musical instruments:

un violon	une clarinette
un piano	un saxophone
une harpe	un cornet
un orgue	un tuba
une flûte	un triangle
un hautbois	une grosse caisse
un piccolo	

Vocabulaire

3 Practice

Quel est le mot?

Historiette Each time **Historiette** appears, it means that the answers to the activity form a short story. Encourage students to look at the title of the **Historiette**, since it can help them do the activity.

2 and **3** After completing these activities, have one student read each one as a story.

Learning from Photos

(page 378) The photos are as follows:
1. a float at the Mardi Gras Festival in New Orleans, Louisiana
2. fireworks in Paris for Bastille Day
3. French Foreign Legion marching band on Bastille Day in Paris

---

Writing Development
Have students write the answers to Activities 2 and 3 in paragraph form.

Vocabulaire

Quel est le mot?

 Qu'est-ce que c'est? Identifiez.

1. C'est un char ou des confettis?
2. C'est un drapeau ou un feu d'artifice?
3. C'est une tribune ou une fanfare?

4. C'est un tambour ou un drapeau?
5. C'est un soldat ou le maire?

 Historiette Le quatorze juillet Répondez.
1. La fête nationale française, c'est le 14 juillet?
2. Pour célébrer la fête nationale, il y a des défilés?
3. Est-ce que les soldats défilent?
4. Ils défilent au son d'une fanfare?
5. Les tribunes sont pleines de spectateurs?
6. Le défilé passe devant les tribunes?
7. Le maire est au premier rang?
8. Est-ce qu'il y a d'autres notables dans les tribunes?
9. La fanfare joue l'hymne national?
10. «La Marseillaise», c'est l'hymne national français?

 Historiette Une grande fête
Inventez une histoire.
1. Il y a beaucoup de monde dans la rue?
2. Un défilé de chars passe dans la rue?
3. Des gens masqués chantent et dansent dans la rue?
4. Il y a un orchestre qui joue dans la rue?
5. Il y a des feux d'artifice?

 For more practice using words from **Mots 1**, do Activity 18 on page H19 at the end of this book.

378 ❦ *trois cent soixante-dix-huit*

CHAPITRE 12

ANSWERS TO Quel est le mot?

1
1. C'est un char.
2. C'est un feu d'artifice.
3. C'est une fanfare.
4. C'est un drapeau.
5. C'est un soldat.

2
1. Oui, la fête nationale française, c'est le 14 juillet.
2. Oui, il y a des défilés.
3. Oui, les soldats défilent.
4. Oui, ils défilent au son d'une fanfare.
5. Oui, les tribunes sont pleines de spectateurs.
6. Oui, le défilé passe devant les tribunes.
7. Oui, le maire est au premier rang.
8. Oui, il y a d'autres notables dans les tribunes.
9. Oui, la fanfare joue l'hymne national.
10. Oui, «La Marseillaise» est l'hymne national français.

3
1. Oui, il y a beaucoup de monde dans la rue.
2. Oui, un défilé de chars passe dans la rue.
3. Oui, des gens masqués chantent et dansent dans la rue.
4. Oui, il y a un orchestre qui joue dans la rue.
5. Oui, il y a des feux d'artifice.

Deux fêtes nationales Vrai ou faux?

1. La fête nationale française a lieu le 14 juillet.
2. La fête nationale française est le même jour que la fête nationale américaine.
3. L'hymne national français s'appelle «La Marseillaise» et l'hymne national américain s'appelle «The Star-Spangled Banner».
4. Aux États-Unis le 4 juillet, il y a des feux d'artifice.
5. À Paris le 14 juillet, il y a un grand défilé militaire le matin et des feux d'artifice le soir.
6. Dans une fanfare, les musiciens jouent de la trompette, du trombone, du tambour, des cymbales.
7. Les soldats passent devant le maire et les notables.
8. Le 4 juillet, aux États-Unis, on joue «La Marseillaise».

Le 14 juillet aux Champs-Élysées

Le carnaval à Fort-de-France

 Une fête Travaillez avec un(e) camarade. Décrivez une fête qu'on célèbre là où vous habitez. Elle a lieu quand? Quelles sont les activités? Vous y participez ou pas?

 La fanfare de votre école Votre camarade est un(e) jeune Français(e) qui visite votre école. Décrivez-lui la fanfare de votre école. Dites-lui si elle est grande ou petite, quand elle joue et où. Dites-lui comment les musiciens sont habillés (ce qu'ils portent) et s'ils ont gagné des trophées. Ensuite changez de rôle.

Vocabulaire Mots 2

1 Preparation

Resource Manager
Vocabulary Transparencies 12.4–12.5
Audio Activities TE, pages 131–133
Audio CD 7
Workbook, page 139
Quiz 2, page 64
ExamView® Pro

Bellringer Review
Use BRR Transparency 12.2 or write the following on the board.
Look at the Paris metro map on page xxxiii. Find the Cité station, located on the Île de la Cité island in the Seine River. Write directions from that stop to the Opéra station.

2 Presentation

Step 1 Show Vocabulary Transparencies 12.4–12.5. Have students close their books and repeat the words after you or Audio CD 7 as you point to the appropriate illustration on the transparency.

Step 2 You may wish to ask the following questions during your presentation: **Qui apporte les cadeaux de Noël? Qui reçoit les cadeaux de Noël? Il faut qu'ils soient sages? Où sont les souliers? Les cadeaux de Noël sont dans les souliers et sous l'arbre de Noël? Quel est votre chant de Noël préféré? Quel est un autre nom pour la fête des Lumières? C'est une fête juive ou chrétienne? Qui allume les bougies de la menorah?**

Vocabulaire Mots 2

Noël

la messe de minuit

un chant de Noël

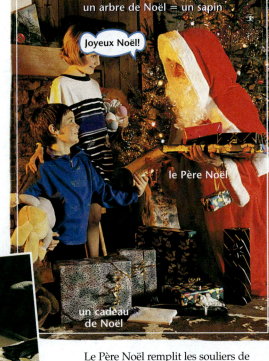

un arbre de Noël = un sapin

Joyeux Noël!

le Père Noël

une cheminée

un soulier

un cadeau de Noël

Le Père Noël remplit les souliers de cadeaux la veille de Noël.
Il faut que les enfants soient sages s'ils veulent recevoir des cadeaux de Noël.

Le réveillon est le repas qu'on fait la veille de Noël.
Ils réveillonnent.

Meilleurs Vœux!

une carte de vœux

380 ♦ trois cent quatre-vingts

CHAPITRE 12

Reaching All Students

Kinesthetic Learners
Pantomime Have students mime the following actions:
  Ouvrez votre cadeau de Noël.
  Chantez un chant de Noël.
  Allumez une bougie.
  Signez une carte de vœux.
  Souhaitez «Bonne Année» à quelqu'un.

Learning from Photos
(page 380 top left) The Midnight Mass is taking place at the church in Kayersberg in Alsace.

Hanouka

Hanouka est une fête juive.
C'est la fête des Lumières.
Pendant la fête, les enfants allument les bougies de la menorah.

une branche
une bougie
une menorah = un chandelier

Le jour de l'An

Bonne Année!
Bonne Santé!
s'embrasser

On réveillonne aussi la veille du jour de l'An.
Tout le monde se souhaite une bonne année et s'embrasse.

Le mariage

La cérémonie civile a lieu à la mairie.

une alliance

le garçon d'honneur
la demoiselle d'honneur
le marié
la mariée
les mariés

La cérémonie religieuse a lieu à l'église.
On se marie à la mairie et à l'église.

LES FÊTES   trois cent quatre-vingt-un 381

Vocabulaire

3 Practice

Quel est le mot?

7 and **9** These activities can be done with books closed or open.

Learning from Photos

(page 382 right) The photo of **Le Père Noël** arriving on his sleigh was taken in the small town of Pégomas.

Writing Development

Have students write the answers to Activities 7 and 9 in paragraph form.

LEVELING

E: Activities 7, 9, 10, 11
A: Activities 8, 11, 12

Vocabulaire

Quel est le mot?

7 **Historiette** Noël Répondez d'après les indications.

1. Noël, c'est quel jour? (le vingt-cinq décembre)
2. Qu'est-ce que les gens envoient à leurs amis? (des cartes de vœux)
3. La messe de minuit, c'est quel jour? (le vingt-quatre décembre)
4. Qui reçoit des cadeaux de Noël? (les enfants sages)
5. Où est-ce que les enfants laissent leurs souliers? (devant la cheminée)
6. Qui remplit les souliers de cadeaux? (le Père Noël)
7. Quel est l'arbre de Noël traditionnel? (le sapin)
8. Où vont les catholiques la veille de Noël? (à la messe de minuit)
9. Qu'est-ce qu'ils chantent pendant la messe de minuit? (des chants de Noël)
10. Qu'est-ce que les gens font après la messe de minuit? (Ils réveillonnent.)

Le repas du réveillon

Le Père Noël en Provence

8 **C'est quoi?** Identifiez.

1. une fête chrétienne qui célèbre la naissance de Jésus-Christ
2. une fête juive qui s'appelle aussi la fête des Lumières
3. celui qui arrive avec des cadeaux de Noël pour les enfants
4. ce que les enfants juifs allument pour célébrer la fête des Lumières
5. un grand repas qu'on fait la veille de Noël et la veille du jour de l'An
6. le premier janvier
7. ce que les mariés échangent pendant la cérémonie de mariage
8. une fête pendant laquelle on lance des confettis et des serpentins
9. une fête pendant laquelle on se souhaite une bonne année et on s'embrasse

382 ✤ trois cent quatre-vingt-deux CHAPITRE 12

ANSWERS TO Quel est le mot?

7
1. Noël est le vingt-cinq décembre.
2. Les gens envoient des cartes de vœux à leurs amis.
3. La messe de minuit est le vingt-quatre décembre.
4. Les enfants sages reçoivent des cadeaux de Noël.
5. Les enfants laissent leurs souliers devant la cheminée.
6. Le Père Noël remplit les souliers de cadeaux.
7. Le sapin est l'arbre de Noël traditionnel.
8. Les catholiques vont à la messe de minuit la veille de Noël.
9. Ils chantent des chants de Noël pendant la messe de minuit.
10. Après la messe de minuit, ils réveillonnent.

8
1. Noël
2. Hanouka
3. le Père Noël
4. les bougies
5. le réveillon
6. le jour de l'An
7. les alliances
8. le jour de l'An
9. le jour de l'An

9 Historiette Hanouka
Répondez d'après les indications.

1. La menorah ou le chandelier qu'on utilise pendant la fête des Lumières a combien de branches? (neuf)
2. Qui célèbre la fête des Lumières? (les juifs)
3. La fête des Lumières est quel mois? (au mois de décembre)
4. Elle dure combien de jours? (huit)
5. Qu'est-ce que les enfants allument? (les bougies de la menorah)

10 Le jour du mariage Vrai ou faux?

1. Le maire fait la cérémonie civile de mariage.
2. Il faut que le Père Noël soit présent au mariage.
3. La cérémonie religieuse a lieu à la mairie.
4. Les demoiselles d'honneur se marient avec les garçons d'honneur.
5. Le jour de la cérémonie les mariés vont d'abord à l'église et ensuite à la mairie.

Une menorah

11 Une grande fête de famille Travaillez avec un(e) camarade. Décrivez les traditions et les coutumes de votre famille pour célébrer une fête de fin d'année telle que Noël, Hanouka, Kwanzaa ou toute autre fête de ce genre. Décrivez tout ce que vous faites, ce que vous mangez, etc.

Le dîner *Thanksgiving* aux États-Unis

12 Thanksgiving *Thanksgiving* (le jour de grâce) au mois de novembre est une fête typiquement américaine. Votre camarade est un(e) jeune Français(e) qui visite votre école. Décrivez-lui ce que vous faites pour célébrer cette fête américaine. Ensuite, changez de rôle. Vous aurez peut-être besoin des mots suivants:

une dinde farcie
des canneberges
des patates douces

Structure

1 Preparation

Resource Manager

Audio Activities TE, pages 133–135
Audio CD 7
Workbook, pages 140–142
Quizzes 3–4, pages 65–66
ExamView® Pro

Bellringer Review

Use BRR Transparency 12.3 or write the following on the board.
Make up two sentences with **jouer de** and two sentences with **jouer à**.

2 Presentation

Le subjonctif

Note: The basic concept we wish to have students understand is that the subjunctive is used when we do not know if the action will take place. If we know that it is or will be a reality, we use the indicative. When students understand this concept, they will not have to memorize a long list of phrases that are followed by the subjunctive.

You may also wish to give students the following simple outline.

Indicative: indicates or points something out; factual, objective; stands alone, independent

Subjunctive: subjective, not objective, not factual; cannot stand alone, depends upon something else, dependent

Structure

Le subjonctif
Talking about facts or nonfacts

1. All verbs you have learned so far have been in the indicative mood. The indicative mood describes actions, events, or situations that are factual, that actually do, did, or will happen.

2. Now, you will learn the subjunctive mood. The subjunctive is used to express that which is not necessarily a fact. It describes actions, events, or situations that may or may not happen. Compare the following sentences.

   Le petit garçon est sage.   **Il faut** que le petit garçon **soit** sage.
   Il fait ses devoirs.   Ses parents **veulent** qu'il **fasse** ses devoirs.

   The sentences in the left column are in the indicative. They express factual information—the young boy is good, and he always does his homework. The sentences in the right column contain a dependent clause, and the verb in the dependent clause is in the subjunctive. It is in the subjunctive because the situation or action being described in the clause may or may not happen. Even though the young boy should be good and even though his parents want him to do his homework, we don't know if he is good and if he does indeed do his homework. For this reason, the verb must be in the subjunctive in French.

3. You form the present subjunctive of regular verbs by dropping the **-ent** ending from the **ils/elles** form of the present indicative and adding the subjunctive endings to this stem. Study the following.

	PARLER	FINIR	ATTENDRE
Present	ils parl**ent**	ils finiss**ent**	ils attend**ent**
Stem	parl-	finiss-	attend-
	que je parl**e**	que je finiss**e**	que j' attend**e**
	que tu parl**es**	que tu finiss**es**	que tu attend**es**
	qu'il/elle/on parl**e**	qu'il/elle/on finiss**e**	qu'il/elle/on attend**e**
	que nous parl**ions**	que nous finiss**ions**	que nous attend**ions**
	que vous parl**iez**	que vous finiss**iez**	que vous attend**iez**
	qu'ils/elles parl**ent**	qu'ils/elles finiss**ent**	qu'ils/elles attend**ent**

trois cent quatre-vingt-quatre

4. The subjunctive of most verbs is formed this way.

PARTIR	ils **partent**	que je parte, que nous partions
METTRE	ils **mettent**	que je mette, que nous mettions
LIRE	ils **lisent**	que je lise, que nous lisions
ÉCRIRE	ils **écrivent**	que j'écrive, que nous écrivions
SUIVRE	ils **suivent**	que je suive, que nous suivions
DIRE	ils **disent**	que je dise, que nous disions
CONDUIRE	ils **conduisent**	que je conduise, que nous conduisions
CONNAÎTRE	ils **connaissent**	que je connaisse, que nous connaissions

5. Few verbs are irregular in the subjunctive. Those that are, are very commonly used. Study the following irregular verbs in the present subjunctive.

ÊTRE	AVOIR	FAIRE	ALLER
que je sois	que j' aie	que je fasse	que j' aille
que tu sois	que tu aies	que tu fasses	que tu ailles
qu'il/elle/on soit	qu'il/elle/on ait	qu'il/elle/on fasse	qu'il/elle/on aille
que nous soyons	que nous ayons	que nous fassions	que nous allions
que vous soyez	que vous ayez	que vous fassiez	que vous alliez
qu'ils/elles soient	qu'ils/elles aient	qu'ils/elles fassent	qu'ils/elles aillent

To learn more about this and other French songs, go to the Glencoe French Web site: french.glencoe.com

LES FÊTES trois cent quatre-vingt-cinq 385

Structure

3 Practice

Comment dit-on?

 to These activities can be done with books closed or open. It is recommended that you go over each activity the first time with books closed. Then have students open their books and read the activities for additional reinforcement.

Note: The purpose of these activities is to give students initial practice with the verb forms of the subjunctive. For this reason, the introductory clause **il faut que** is constant.

> ### Learning from Photos
> *(page 386 bottom)* This civil wedding ceremony is taking place in the town of Lacanau near Bordeaux.
>
> *(pages 386–387)* Have students say as much as they can about the photos.

Structure

Comment dit-on?

13 **Pour avoir des cadeaux du Père Noël** Répondez que oui.
1. Il faut que les enfants soient sages toute l'année?
2. Il faut qu'ils aient de bonnes notes à l'école?
3. Il faut qu'ils décorent l'arbre de Noël?
4. Il faut qu'ils mettent leurs souliers devant la cheminée?
5. Il faut qu'ils aillent à la messe de minuit?
6. Il faut qu'ils réveillonnent avec leurs parents?
7. Il faut qu'ils chantent des chants de Noël?
8. Il faut qu'ils souhaitent «Joyeux Noël» à tout le monde?

14 **Le mariage en France** Répondez.
1. Il faut que les fiancés annoncent leur mariage?
2. Il faut qu'ils choisissent des alliances?
3. Il faut qu'ils aient une demoiselle ou un garçon d'honneur?
4. Il faut qu'ils disent «oui» devant le maire?
5. Il faut qu'ils aillent à l'église s'ils veulent une cérémonie religieuse?

À la mairie avant le mariage religieux

ANSWERS TO Comment dit-on?

13
1. Oui, il faut que les enfants soient sages toute l'année.
2. Oui, il faut qu'ils aient de bonnes notes à l'école.
3. Oui, il faut qu'ils décorent l'arbre de Noël.
4. Oui, il faut qu'ils mettent leurs souliers devant la cheminée.
5. Oui, il faut qu'ils aillent à la messe de minuit.
6. Oui, il faut qu'ils réveillonnent avec leurs parents.
7. Oui, il faut qu'ils chantent des chants de Noël.
8. Oui, il faut qu'ils souhaitent «Joyeux Noël» à tout le monde.

14 *Answers given are with* Oui, *but students may also answer with* Non.
1. Oui, il faut qu'ils annoncent leur mariage.
2. Oui, il faut qu'ils choisissent des alliances.
3. Oui, il faut qu'ils aient une demoiselle ou un garçon d'honneur.
4. Oui, il faut qu'ils disent «oui» devant le maire.
5. Oui, il faut qu'ils aillent à l'église s'ils veulent une cérémonie religieuse.

15 **Il faut que je fasse tellement de choses.** Donnez des réponses personnelles.

1. Il faut que tu te lèves de bonne heure?
2. Il faut que tu ailles à l'école?
3. Il faut que tu sois toujours à l'heure?
4. Il faut que tu dises «bonjour» au professeur?
5. Il faut que tu fasses tes devoirs?
6. Il faut que tu passes un examen?

16 **On doit le faire.** Suivez le modèle.

faire les devoirs →
Il faut qu'il fasse ses devoirs.
Il faut que vous fassiez vos devoirs aussi.

1. étudier pour demain
2. préparer la fête
3. choisir des cadeaux
4. aller au magasin
5. faire des achats
6. aller au marché
7. faire les courses
8. rentrer chez vous
9. préparer le dîner
10. mettre le couvert
11. servir le dîner

Ils ont acheté des cadeaux à Aix-en-Provence.

17 **Il faut qu'on fasse tellement de choses!** Travaillez avec un(e) camarade. Parlez de tout ce qu'il faut que vous fassiez. Dites aussi ce qu'il faut que vos parents fassent.

LES FÊTES

trois cent quatre-vingt-sept ✦ 387

Structure

Reaching All Students

Additional Practice Have students answer **oui** to the following.
1. Il faut qu'on écrive au Père Noël?
2. Il faut qu'on lise tes cartes de vœux?
3. Il faut qu'on aille au défilé?
4. Il faut qu'on se dise «Bonne Année»?
5. Il faut que nous mettions les cadeaux sous l'arbre de Noël?

LEVELING
E: Activities 13, 14, 15, 17
A: Activities 15, 16, 17

ANSWERS TO Comment dit-on?

15
1. Oui, il faut que je me lève de bonne heure.
2. Oui, il faut que j'aille à l'école.
3. Oui, il faut que je sois toujours à l'heure.
4. Oui, il faut que je dise «bonjour» au professeur.
5. Oui, il faut que je fasse mes devoirs.
6. Oui, il faut que je passe un examen.

16
1. Il faut qu'il étudie pour demain.
   Il faut que vous étudiiez pour demain aussi.
2. Il faut qu'il prépare la fête.
   Il faut que vous prépariez la fête aussi.
3. Il faut qu'il choisisse des cadeaux.
   Il faut que vous choisissiez des cadeaux aussi.
4. Il faut qu'il aille au magasin.
   Il faut que vous alliez au magasin aussi.
5. Il faut qu'il fasse des achats.
   Il faut que vous fassiez des achats aussi.
6. Il faut qu'il aille au marché.
   Il faut que vous alliez au marché aussi.
7. Il faut qu'il fasse les courses.
   Il faut que vous fassiez les courses aussi.
8. Il faut qu'il rentre chez lui.
   Il faut que vous rentriez chez vous aussi.
9. Il faut qu'il prépare le dîner.
   Il faut que vous prépariez le dîner aussi.
10. Il faut qu'il mette le couvert.
    Il faut que vous mettiez le couvert aussi.
11. Il faut qu'il serve le dîner.
    Il faut que vous serviez le dîner aussi.

Structure

1 Preparation

Bellringer Review

Use BRR Transparency 12.4 or write the following on the board.
Write five things the students in your French class must do. Start each sentence with **Il faut que**.

2 Presentation

Le subjonctif après les expressions de souhait ou de volonté

Step 1 Have students repeat the verbs aloud.

Step 2 Emphasize once again that the subjunctive is used because we don't know if the action of the verb will take place.

Step 3 Have students read the model sentences aloud.

Learning from Realia

(page 388) Have students identify the subjunctive forms of the verbs inside the greeting card.

Structure

Le subjonctif après les expressions de souhait ou de volonté
Expressing wishes and orders

The subjunctive is used with expressions such as **vouloir que, aimer mieux que (préférer que), souhaiter que.** You use the subjunctive because, even though you want, prefer, or wish that someone do something, it will not necessarily happen; the person may not do it.

   J'aimerais que tu **viennes**.
   Je souhaite que vous **soyez** heureux.

Comment dit-on?

18 **Historiette Ça me ferait plaisir!**
Complétez chaque phrase d'après le modèle.

   Tu viens avec nous, j'espère. →
   J'aimerais que tu viennes avec nous.
   1. Tu vas à la fête, j'espère.
   2. Tu es ponctuel, j'espère.
   3. Tu conduis, j'espère.
   4. Tu pars maintenant, j'espère.
   5. Tu ne dis rien à personne, j'espère.

19 **Historiette Oui, je préférerais.**
Répondez d'après le modèle.

   —Vous voulez que je le fasse?
   —Oui, je préférerais que vous le fassiez.
   1. Vous voulez que je lui dise ce qui se passe?
   2. Vous voulez que je lui écrive une lettre?
   3. Vous voulez que je mette la lettre dans une enveloppe?
   4. Vous voulez que j'aille à la poste?

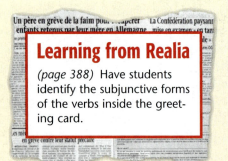

ANSWERS TO Comment dit-on?

18
1. J'aimerais que tu ailles à la fête.
2. J'aimerais que tu sois ponctuel.
3. J'aimerais que tu conduises.
4. J'aimerais que tu partes maintenant.
5. J'aimerais que tu ne dises rien à personne.

19
1. Oui, je préférerais que vous lui disiez ce qui se passe.
2. Oui, je préférerais que vous lui écriviez une lettre.
3. Oui, je préférerais que vous mettiez la lettre dans une enveloppe.
4. Oui, je préférerais que vous alliez à la poste.

Structure

20 Historiette Tout se passera bien. Répondez.
1. Tu préfères qu'il conduise?
2. Tu préfères que je lui écrive des instructions?
3. Tu aimerais qu'il soit là pour le 25?
4. Tu veux qu'il parte avec moi?

Noël à Paris

21 Mes parents le veulent. Dites à un(e) camarade tout ce que vos parents veulent que vous fassiez. Ensuite, demandez-lui ce que ses parents veulent qu'il/elle fasse. Comparez vos réponses. Est-ce que vous faites toujours ce que vos parents veulent que vous fassiez?

22 La prof le veut. Parlez avec un(e) camarade. Dites tout ce que votre professeur de français veut absolument que vous fassiez—ou que vous ne fassiez pas!

Vous êtes sur le bon chemin. Allez-y!

389

Conversation

1 Preparation

Resource Manager
Audio Activities TE, pages 135–136
Audio CD 7
CD-ROM

Bellringer Review

Use BRR Transparency 12.5 or write the following on the board. Write the following words under the appropriate heading.
le 14 juillet / Noël
un cadeau, un chant, une cheminée, un défilé, un drapeau, une fanfare, des feux d'artifice, la messe de minuit, un sapin, un soldat, des souliers, des tribunes

2 Presentation

Step 1 Have students close their books and listen as you read the conversation aloud or play Audio CD 7.

Step 2 Have students open their books and read along with you or Audio CD 7.

Step 3 Call on volunteers to read the conversation to the class.

LEVELING

E: Conversation

Conversation

C'est bientôt le 14 juillet

Carine: Tu vas au défilé du 14 juillet?
Sylvain: Bien sûr. Quelle question!
Carine: Pourquoi «Quelle question»? Tu n'es pas forcé d'y aller.
Sylvain: Bien sûr que si. Il faut que je joue.
Carine: Il faut que tu joues?
Sylvain: Ben, dans la fanfare.
Carine: Ah bon! Je ne savais pas. Tu joues de quel instrument?
Sylvain: De la trompette.
Carine: Ah, il faut que j'aille voir ça!
Sylvain: Si c'est pour rigoler, je préfère que tu restes chez toi!

Vous avez compris?

Répondez.

1. À qui parle Carine?
2. Qu'est-ce qu'elle veut savoir?
3. Pourquoi Sylvain va-t-il au défilé?
4. Est-ce que Carine savait qu'il jouait d'un instrument?
5. De quel instrument Sylvain joue-t-il?
6. Pourquoi ne veut-il pas que Carine vienne le voir?

390 ❖ trois cent quatre-vingt-dix

CHAPITRE 12

ANSWERS TO Vous avez compris?

1. Carine parle à Sylvain.
2. Elle veut savoir si Sylvain va au défilé du 14 juillet.
3. Il va au défilé parce qu'il joue dans la fanfare.
4. Non, elle ne savait pas qu'il jouait d'un instrument.
5. Sylvain joue de la trompette.
6. Il ne veut pas qu'elle vienne pour rigoler.

Glencoe Technology

CD-ROM
On the CD-ROM, students can watch a dramatization of this conversation. They can then play the role of either one of the characters and record themselves in the conversation.

Parlons un peu plus

A **Le 4 juillet** Parlez avec un(e) camarade. Décrivez comment on célèbre le 4 juillet là où vous habitez. Dites si vous y participez ou pas, et comment.

B **De bons copains** Parlez avec un(e) camarade. Dites ce que vous aimeriez que de bons copains fassent ou ne fassent pas. Dites quelle est votre réaction quand vos copains ne font pas ce que vous voulez. Comparez vos réactions.

Le 4 juillet à Austin dans le Texas

C **Une invitation** Vous êtes invité(e) à une réception de mariage! Vous y allez avec un(e) ami(e) (votre camarade) qui vous demande tous les renseignements. Regardez l'invitation et répondez.

LES FÊTES

trois cent quatre-vingt-onze ✦ 391

Conversation

3 Practice

Parlons un peu plus

B After the groups have discussed the topic, have the class compile lists on the board.

> **Learning from Photos**
> *(page 390)* This photo shows the Bastille Day Parade on the promenade des Anglais in Nice.

> **Learning from Realia**
> *(page 391)* In the wedding invitation, explain to students that **faire part** means *to announce*. The preposition *en* l'église (rather than *dans*) is used in a very formal way. The capitalization of the day and month on the announcement is for decorative purposes.
> You may wish to ask the following questions about the announcement:
> Comment s'appelait la mariée? Et le marié?
> Qui fait part de leur mariage?
> Ils se sont mariés quel jour? Où?

Cross-Cultural Comparison
Note that the invitation to the reception has the names of the mothers of the bride and of the groom. Both families share responsibility for the reception. Only the mothers' names appear on the invitation.
Note that this reception took place one month after the wedding. The reception is normally held the same day as the wedding.

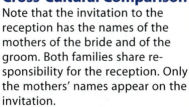

ANSWERS TO Parlons un peu plus

A *Answers will vary but may include:*
Dans mon village le 4 juillet, on a un défilé d'enfants. Les enfants décorent leurs bicyclettes et leurs poussettes et on défile et chante des chansons comme «Yankee Doodle Dandy». Après, il y a un grand pique-nique dans le parc et le soir, il y a des feux d'artifice. Nous y allons tous les ans!

B *Answers will vary but may include:*
J'aimerais que mes copains me téléphonent tous les jours. Je veux qu'ils m'écrivent des e-mails aussi. Quand ils ne me téléphonent pas, je ne suis pas content(e).

C *Answers will vary but may include:*
—Où est la réception?
—Elle est chez Maxim's.
—Quelle est la date de la réception?
—le mercredi 12 novembre.
—À quelle heure?
—À partir de 18 h 30.

Lectures culturelles

Resource Manager
Audio Activities TE, pages 136–138
Audio CD 7

Bellringer Review
Use BRR Transparency 12.6 or write the following on the board. Complete the sentences with the correct form and tense of the verb in parentheses.
1. Ce matin, j'_____ l'autobus pour aller au lycée. (prendre)
2. On _____ sur le bouton pour demander un arrêt. (appuyer)
3. Quand j'étais jeune, je _____ prendre le métro. (préférer)
4. Si j'avais une voiture, je la _____ prudemment. (conduire)
5. Demain je _____ à l'arrêt d'autobus. (être)

Presentation

Pre-reading
Step 1 Ask students if they have ever been to a wedding. Have them describe what they observed. Ask students who celebrate Christmas or Hanukkah to describe their celebrations.

Step 2 Go over the Reading Strategy on page 392.

Reading
Step 1 You may wish to divide the **Lecture** into three segments.

Step 2 Call on an individual to read several sentences. Then ask other students about the sentences the student has just read.

Post-reading
Have students compare the French celebrations to those in the U.S.

LEVELING
E: Reading
A: Reading

Lectures culturelles

Des fêtes en France

Le mariage
En France, quand on se marie, on a souvent deux cérémonies de mariage—une civile et une religieuse. Le mariage civil est le seul mariage obligatoire en France.

Il est célébré avant le mariage religieux. Seuls les mariés, leurs parents, les membres de leur famille et les témoins[1] assistent à la cérémonie qui est célébrée par le maire dans la salle des mariages de la mairie ou de l'hôtel de ville.

La cérémonie religieuse a lieu après le mariage civil. Elle est toujours célébrée dans un lieu religieux. À la campagne, il n'est pas rare que le cortège[2] aille à l'église à pied. À la ville, on va à l'église en voiture. Après la cérémonie religieuse, il y a une réception. La réception a lieu chez la mariée, dans une salle louée pour l'occasion ou dans un restaurant. Après un déjeuner ou un buffet superbe, la mariée coupe la pièce montée (le gâteau de mariage). On sert le champagne et on porte des toasts aux mariés.

Un mariage dans un petit village d'Aquitaine

Noël
Noël est la fête des enfants. Avant Noël, ils écrivent une lettre au Père Noël. Ils lui donnent une liste de tous les jouets qu'ils veulent recevoir pour Noël. La veille de Noël, ils mettent leurs souliers devant la cheminée. Ils veulent que le Père Noël les remplisse avec les cadeaux qu'ils ont demandés.

Le 24 décembre, beaucoup de gens vont à la messe de minuit. Après la messe, ils rentrent chez eux pour le réveillon. Ce repas traditionnel commence par des huîtres. Ensuite, il y a du boudin blanc[3]. Le plat traditionnel est une dinde farcie aux marrons[4]. Le dessert est une bûche de Noël.

Une bûche de Noël

[1] témoins *witnesses*
[2] cortège *bridal procession*
[3] boudin blanc *veal sausage*
[4] dinde farcie aux marrons *turkey stuffed with chestnuts*

National Standards

Cultures
This reading about major celebrations in France familiarizes students with important French customs.

Comparisons
The reading and the Reading Strategy on page 392 encourage students to make comparisons about weddings, Christmas, and Hanukkah in France and in the United States.

FUN FACTS
Have students look carefully at the **bûche de Noël.** It is a filled, rolled cake which is supposed to look like a log and is decorated with forest items like mushrooms (made of meringue, of course). The **bûche** comes from the same tradition as the Yule log. Ask the Home Economics or Family Living class to help your students prepare a **bûche de Noël.** Then invite them to share the cake with you.

Reading Strategy

Making comparisons
When you read cultural information about another country, you will notice that there are similarities and differences between our customs and those of the other country. Take note of these as you read. Doing so will make the ideas clearer and help you remember more of what you read.

On mange, on parle, on boit et on s'amuse beaucoup. Tout le monde est content d'être réuni et d'attendre l'arrivée du Père Noël.

Hanouka

Les juifs en France, comme les juifs du monde entier, célèbrent Hanouka. Cette fête commémore la reconsécration du temple de Jérusalem par les Maccabées après la révolte contre Antiochos, le roi[5] de Syrie, en 167 avant Jésus-Christ. Elle est appelée aussi la fête des Lumières.

Les enfants allument les bougies de la menorah—un chandelier à neuf branches. Ils allument une bougie chaque soir. La bougie au centre du chandelier est allumée le premier soir et elle sert à allumer les autres bougies. La fête dure huit jours. Hanouka est une fête joyeuse, surtout pour les enfants qui reçoivent un cadeau tous les jours. Mais il y a aussi des bonbons[6] et des cadeaux pour les adultes.

[5] roi *king*
[6] bonbons *candies*

Une famille juive du Marais

Vous avez compris?

A Le mariage Répondez.
1. En France, la plupart des couples ont combien de cérémonies de mariage?
2. En général, laquelle est célébrée la première?
3. La cérémonie religieuse a lieu où?
4. On y va comment à la campagne? Et à la ville?
5. Qu'est-ce qu'il y a après la cérémonie à l'église?
6. Qu'est-ce que la mariée coupe pendant la réception?

B Noël et Hanouka Vrai ou faux?
1. À Noël, les enfants mettent leurs souliers devant la porte d'entrée de la maison.
2. Le Père Noël arrive très tôt le matin du 25 décembre.
3. Les enfants veulent que le Père Noël remplisse leurs souliers de cadeaux.
4. La messe de minuit a lieu le soir du 25 décembre.
5. On mange souvent de la dinde à Noël.
6. Hanouka est une fête juive.
7. Ce sont les adultes qui allument les bougies de la menorah.
8. Les enfants allument une bougie tous les soirs.
9. Hanouka dure dix jours.
10. Les enfants reçoivent des cadeaux tous les jours.

Lecture supplémentaire

Carnaval

Le carnaval, c'est la période réservée aux divertissements[1] avant le début du Carême[2]. Pour les catholiques et les protestants, le Carême est une période d'environ quarante-six jours avant Pâques. Pendant ces quarante-six jours, on fait pénitence. Le Carême est presque toujours au mois de février.

En France, le carnaval de Nice est très célèbre. Les rues de cette belle ville de la Côte d'Azur sont décorées. Un long défilé de chars fleuris traverse la ville. Des groupes masqués font escorte à Sa Majesté Carnaval. Pendant plusieurs nuits, il y a des bals et des feux d'artifice. On lance des confettis et des serpentins. Tout le monde s'amuse bien avant le Carême.

[1] divertissements *amusements*
[2] Carême *Lent*

Le carnaval à Nice

Le carnaval à la Martinique

Le mardi gras à La Nouvelle-Orléans

À la Martinique, à la Guadeloupe et à La Nouvelle-Orléans en Louisiane, il y a aussi des carnavals célèbres. Les festivités sont à peu près les mêmes que celles de Nice. Le jour du mardi gras[3], il y a un grand défilé. Le carnaval de La Nouvelle-Orléans s'appelle aussi le Mardi-Gras.

Le carnaval d'hiver à Québec attire tous les ans des milliers de visiteurs. Il y a des festivités pendant dix-sept jours. Il y a un grand concours[4] de sculptures sur glace et des courses de canots sur le Saint-Laurent qui est en partie gelé[5]. À Québec, Sa Majesté Carnaval s'appelle Bonhomme Carnaval.

[3] mardi gras *Shrove Tuesday, "Fat Tuesday"*
[4] concours *contest*
[5] gelé *frozen*

Le Bonhomme Carnaval à Québec

Le carnaval à la Martinique

Vous avez compris?

Une fête amusante Vrai ou faux?
1. Le Carême est une période pendant laquelle on s'amuse.
2. Le carnaval précède le Carême.
3. Il y a un carnaval célèbre à Nice.
4. Les chars sont décorés de lumières.
5. Le matin, il y a des feux d'artifice.
6. Le carnaval de La Nouvelle-Orléans s'appelle aussi le Mardi-Gras.
7. Il fait chaud pendant le carnaval à Québec.
8. Au carnaval de Québec, il y a un concours de sculptures sur glace.

LES FÊTES

CONNEXIONS

Attention!
The readings in the **Connexions** section are optional. They focus on some of the major disciplines taught in schools and universities. The vocabulary is useful for discussing such topics as history, literature, art, economics, business, science, etc. You may choose any of the following ways to do the readings in the **Connexions** section.

Independent reading Have students read the selections and do the post-reading activities as homework, which you collect. This option is least intrusive on class time and requires a minimum of teacher involvement.

Homework with in-class follow-up Assign the readings and post-reading activities as homework. Review and discuss the material in class the next day.

Intensive in-class activity This option includes a pre-reading vocabulary presentation, in-class reading and discussion, assignment of the activities for homework, and a discussion of the assignment in class the next day.

Presentation
Les lettres
Histoire et Littérature

Step 1 Have students read the introduction in English on page 396.

Step 2 Have students read the selection independently.

CONNEXIONS

Les lettres
Histoire et Littérature

History has many stories of famous marriages—Napoleon and Josephine, Nicholas and Alexandra, Elizabeth Barrett and Robert Browning. Innumerable novels, short stories, and poems speak of love and marriage. Henry Wadsworth Longfellow's poem "Evangeline" tells the sad story of the young Evangeline's quest for the man who was to be her husband. Let's read about the real story of Evangeline, whose name was actually Emmeline.

La vraie histoire d'Évangéline

Au Canada

La triste histoire d'Évangéline que raconte le poète Henry Wadsworth Longfellow est basée sur une histoire vraie. C'est l'histoire des Français d'Acadie (de nos jours la Nouvelle-Écosse[1]) qui en 1755 ont perdu toutes leurs possessions et même leur famille.

Dans le village acadien de Grandpré habite une jeune fille, Emmeline Labiche, et son père. Sa mère est morte quand elle était enfant. Emmeline est très jolie et généreuse. À seize ans, elle se fiance avec son ami d'enfance, Louis Arceneaux.

L'Acadie est un territoire anglais depuis 1713. À cette époque au Canada, il y a beaucoup de rivalités entre les Français et les Anglais. Mais les Acadiens, les Français d'Acadie, ne participent pas à ces rivalités. Ils restent très indépendants dans leurs petites communautés françaises. Ils cultivent la terre, ils pêchent[2] et ne demandent rien à personne.

Henry Wadsworth Longfellow

Le Grand Dérangement

C'est alors qu'en 1755, un nouveau gouverneur anglais, Lawrence, décide de punir[3] les Acadiens pour leur attitude indépendante. Des soldats anglais chassent les Acadiens de leurs

La forteresse de Louisbourg en Nouvelle-Écosse

[1] Nouvelle-Écosse *Nova Scotia*
[2] pêchent *fish*
[3] punir *punish*

National Standards

Connections
This reading about the history of Acadia and the Cajuns establishes a connection with another discipline, allowing students to reinforce and further their knowledge of history through the study of French.

Chapter Projects

Les Acadiens You may wish to have students do some research on the **Grand Dérangement**. Students can also do research on the French influence in Louisiana.

maisons et les forcent à monter dans des bateaux et de partir vers le sud. Cette expulsion s'appelle le «Grand Dérangement». Les familles, les amis sont séparés! La pauvre Emmeline voit son fiancé, Louis, monter dans un bateau pour une destination inconnue. Elle et son père montent dans un autre bateau qui les emmène dans le Maryland. Là, pendant des années, elle essaie de retrouver Louis. Elle le cherche dans toutes les colonies anglaises, mais en vain.

En Louisiane

Les Acadiens ne veulent pas vivre dans les colonies anglaises. Ils décident de partir pour La Nouvelle-Orléans où on parle français. Ils partent en masse. Emmeline et son père sont avec eux. Le long voyage commence. Ils prennent d'abord la route vers l'ouest, jusqu'au Mississippi. Là ils construisent des canots et descendent le fleuve.

Emmeline ne reste pas à La Nouvelle-Orléans. Elle descend le bayou Tèche et arrive finalement à Saint-Martinville. Là, sous un grand chêne[4], Louis Arceneaux la regarde! Ils se reconnaissent avec émotion. Mais hélas, Louis lui dit qu'il croyait l'avoir perdue à jamais[5] et qu'il s'est marié avec une autre jeune fille.

Quelques mois plus tard, Emmeline meurt de chagrin[6].

[4] chêne *oak tree* [5] à jamais *forever* [6] meurt de chagrin *dies of grief*

L'embarquement des Acadiens

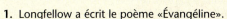
La statue d'Évangéline à Saint-Martinville en Louisiane

Vous avez compris?

Le Grand Dérangement   Répondez.

1. Qui a écrit le poème «Évangéline»?
2. Comment s'appelle l'Acadie de nos jours?
3. Quel est le véritable nom d'Évangéline?
4. Depuis 1713, l'Acadie est un territoire français ou anglais?
5. Pourquoi le gouverneur Lawrence décide-t-il de punir les Acadiens?
6. Que font les soldats anglais?
7. Qu'est-ce qui arrive à Louis et Emmeline?
8. Où Emmeline cherche-t-elle Louis?
9. Où les Acadiens décident-ils d'aller? Pourquoi?
10. Où Emmeline arrive-t-elle finalement?
11. Qui voit-elle?
12. Pourquoi meurt-elle de chagrin?

LES FÊTES

History Connection

La forteresse de Louisbourg, in Nova Scotia, was founded by the French in 1713. In subsequent decades it was strongly fortified. In 1745, during the war of the Austrian Succession, it was captured by New England colonials under Sir William Pepperell. It was returned to the French by the Treaty of **Aix-la-Chapelle** in 1748. In the Seven-Year War (1758), it was again taken by the English. The original fort has been reconstructed, and it is preserved as an historic attraction.

FUN FACTS

(page 397) This illustration comes from *A History of the United States* by William Cullen Bryant, published in 1888–1890. The etching is done with a technique called drypoint, a common technique used in books of the time.

Literature Connection

You may wish to have students read the poem *Évangéline*, by Longfellow. You may also want to have students research and bring in some samples of Cajun music and food.

LEVELING
A: Reading

Answers to Vous avez compris?

1. Longfellow a écrit le poème «Évangéline».
2. De nos jours, l'Acadie s'appelle la Nouvelle-Écosse.
3. Le véritable nom d'Évangéline est Emmeline Labiche.
4. Depuis 1713, l'Acadie est un territoire anglais.
5. Le gouverneur Lawrence décide de punir les Acadiens pour leur attitude indépendante.
6. Les soldats anglais chassent les Acadiens de leurs maisons.
7. Louis part dans un bateau pour une destination inconnue, et Emmeline et son père vont dans le Maryland.
8. Elle cherche Louis dans toutes les colonies anglaises.
9. Les Acadiens décident d'aller à la Nouvelle-Orléans parce qu'on y parle français.
10. Finalement, Emmeline arrive à Saint-Martinville.
11. Elle voit Louis Arceneaux.
12. Parce que Louis s'est marié avec une autre jeune fille.

C'est à vous

Use what you have learned

Preparation

Bellringer Review

Use BRR Transparency 12.7 or write the following on the board. Complete.
1. Il faut que je _____ mon travail. (finir)
2. Il faut que je _____ mes devoirs. (faire)
3. Il faut que je _____ sage. (être)
4. Je veux que le Père Noël me _____ visite. (rendre)
5. Je veux qu'il _____ beaucoup de cadeaux pour moi. (avoir)

Recycling

These activities allow students to use the vocabulary and structure from this chapter in completely open-ended, real-life situations.

Learning from Photos

(page 398 right) **La fête des Rois** is held on January 6 to commemorate the arrival of the wisemen bearing gifts for the infant Jesus. Dessert that day is the «Galette des rois», a large, round puff pastry filled with almond paste. Inside is a kidney bean or a charm. The person whose slice contains the hidden prize becomes "king" for a day. Ask students who found the prize in the photo.

C'est à vous

Use what you have learned

PARLER 1 — Ma fête préférée

✓ *Talk about your favorite holiday*

Travaillez avec un(e) camarade. Demandez-lui quelle est sa fête préférée et pourquoi. Ensuite changez de rôle.

La fête des Rois

Un mariage dans le Var

PARLER 2 — Mon mariage

✓ *Talk about a wedding*

Imaginez que vous allez vous marier avec un(e) Français(e). Votre camarade est un peu surpris(e) parce qu'il/elle ne le savait pas. Parlez-lui de votre fiancé(e), de la cérémonie et des festivités de votre mariage. Ensuite, changez de rôle.

PARLER 3 — De bonnes résolutions

✓ *Talk about New Year's resolutions*

Travaillez avec un(e) camarade. Imaginez que c'est le jour de l'An. Vous prenez chacun trois bonnes résolutions pour la nouvelle année. Dites ce que vous ferez ou ne ferez pas l'année prochaine.

ANSWERS TO C'est à vous

 1 Answers will vary but may include:
—Quelle est ta fête préférée?
—C'est Noël.
—Pourquoi?
—Parce que j'adore les sapins de Noël, les chants de Noël, et les cadeaux!

2 Answers will vary but students can use all the wedding vocabulary presented in this chapter.

3 Answers will vary depending upon what students plan to do. The verbs will be in the future tense.

CHAPITRE 12

4 Une invitation
✓ *Invite someone to a family celebration*

Préparez une invitation pour un anniversaire, un mariage ou toute autre fête. Donnez tous les renseignements nécessaires.

Un mariage au Maroc

Writing Strategy

Classifying a subject When writing, one way to organize your material effectively is to classify your subject. For example, if you are writing about clothing, you could choose from several categories: clothing for school, clothing for weekends, clothing for doing chores, and many more. By choosing a category and classifying your subject, you will be able to organize your information and construct a good paragraph or paper.

5 Les fêtes

You and your classmates celebrate many holidays throughout the year, though not always the same ones. Write a paper about holidays you celebrate and describe what these celebrations entail. Rather than writing about every holiday you celebrate, select a category for your holidays: **Mes fêtes préférées, Les fêtes religieuses, Les fêtes de fin d'année, Les fêtes de printemps, d'automne ou d'hiver,** or any other category you can think of. Include an introduction and a conclusion.

C'est à vous

4 Have students make and decorate a sample invitation.

Writing Development
Have students keep a notebook containing their best written work from each chapter. These selected writings can be based on assignments from the Student Textbook and the Workbook. The two activities on page 399 are examples of writing assignments that may be included in each student's portfolio. In the Workbook, students will develop an organized autobiography (**Mon autobiographie**). These workbook pages may also become a part of their portfolio.

Cross-Cultural Comparison
The marriage ceremonies in the Maghreb countries are complex, and they vary from region to region. Traditionally the young man's mother chooses the bride, but in towns and cities there are more opportunities for young people to meet and get to know one another. Negotiations leading to the marriage contract are still, however, the prerogative of the parents.

The marriage festivities are quite an event because, according to Koranic law, the bride leaves her family to enter a new one. Marriage is not just a union between individuals; it is a link between two families. The dowry is paid before a notary, and the money is used to purchase the bride's trousseau as well as furniture.

The festivities can last for days, and the men and women celebrate in different rooms.

LEVELING
These activities encompass all three levels. All students will be able to do them at a sophistication level commensurate with their ability in French. Some students will be able to speak for several minutes, and others may be able to give just a few sentences. This is to be expected when students are functioning completely on their own, generating their own language to the best of their ability.

Answers to C'est à vous

4 Have students make the invitation look like a real one.

5 Answers will vary depending upon the holiday or celebration students select.

Assessment

Resource Manager

Communication Transparencies C 12
Quizzes, pages 63–66
Tests, pages 195–210
ExamView® Pro
Situation Cards
Performance Assessment, Task 12
Marathon mental Videoquiz

Bellringer Review

Use BRR Transparency 12.8 or write the following on the board.
Write five sentences telling what your French teacher wants you to do in class today. Begin each sentence with **Le/La prof veut que nous…**

Assessment

This is a pre-test for students to take before you administer the chapter test. Answer sheets for students to do these pages are provided in your transparency binder. Note that each section is cross-referenced so students can easily find the material they have to review in case they made errors. You may wish to collect these assessments and correct them yourself or you may prefer to have the students correct themselves in class. You can go over the answers orally or project them on the overhead, using your Assessment Answers transparencies.

Assessment

Vocabulaire

1 Identifiez.

1.    2.

3.   4.

To review Mots 1, turn to pages 376–377.

2 Complétez.

5–6. Le Père Noël remplit les ____ de cadeaux la ____ de Noël.
7. On envoie une ____ à des amis pour Noël ou Hanouka.
8. Le repas qu'on fait la veille de Noël, c'est le ____.
9. Hanouka est une fête ____.
10. Les mariés choisissent un garçon d'honneur et une ____ d'honneur pour la cérémonie de leur mariage.

To review Mots 2, turn to pages 380–381.

Structure

3 Complétez.

11. Il faut qu'on ____ les souliers devant la cheminée. (mettre)
12. Il faut que tu ____ là. (être)
13. Il faut qu'ils y ____. (aller)
14. Il faut que je le ____. (finir)
15. Il faut que vous le ____. (dire)

To review the subjunctive, turn to pages 384–385.

400 ✦ quatre cents

CHAPITRE 12

ANSWERS TO Assessment

1
1. des drapeaux
2. des soldats
3. un trombone
4. un feu d'artifice

2
5. souliers
6. veille
7. carte de vœux
8. réveillon
9. juive
10. demoiselle

3
11. mette
12. sois
13. aillent
14. finisse
15. disiez

4 Suivez le modèle.

Ils sont là. J'aimerais… →
J'aimerais qu'ils soient là.

16. Il le lit. Je veux…
17. Je ne le fais pas. Mes parents préfèrent…
18. Vous avez un Joyeux Noël. Je souhaite…
19. Je conduis. Ils veulent…
20. Tu pars. Elle ne veut pas…

To review expressing wishes and orders, turn to page 388.

Culture

5 Complétez.

21. En France on a souvent deux cérémonies de mariage—une ____ et une ____.
22. Après la cérémonie de mariage, il y a une ____ qui est souvent un déjeuner ou un buffet.
23. Avant Noël, les enfants français écrivent une lettre au ____.
24. Le plat traditionnel pour le réveillon de Noël est ____.
25. Les enfants juifs allument les ____ de la menorah.

To review this cultural information, turn to pages 392–393.

Noël aux Champs-Élysées

On parle super bien!

This unique page gives students the opportunity to speak freely and say whatever they can, using the vocabulary and structures they have learned in the chapter. The illustration serves to remind students of precisely what they know how to say in French. There are no activities that students do not have the ability to describe or talk about in French. The art not only depicts the vocabulary and content of this chapter, but also reinforces what they learned in previous chapters.

You may wish to use this page in many ways. Some possibilities are to have students do the following:

1. Look at the illustration and identify items by giving the correct French words.
2. Make up sentences about what they see in the illustration.
3. Make up questions about the illustration. They can call on another class member to respond if you do this as a class activity, or you may prefer to allow students to work in small groups. This activity is extremely beneficial because it enables students to actively use interrogative words.
4. Answer questions you ask them about the illustration.
5. Work in pairs and make up a conversation based on the illustration.
6. Look at the illustration and give a complete oral review of what they see.
7. Look at the illustration and write a paragraph (or essay) about it.

You can also use this page as an assessment or testing tool, taking into account individual differences by having students go from simple to quite complicated tasks. The assessment can be either oral or written. You may wish to use the rubrics provided on pages T20–T21 as you give students the following directions.

On parle super bien!

Tell all you can about this illustration.

1. Identify the topic or situation of the illustration.
2. Give the French words for as many items as you can.
3. Think of as many sentences as you can to describe the illustration.
4. Go over your sentences and put them in the best sequencing to give a coherent story based on the illustration.

Vocabulaire

Describing a parade

un défilé	une trompette	le maire	un feu d'artifice
un soldat	un trombone	les notables (m. pl.)	un drapeau
une fanfare	un tambour	le premier rang	défiler
un hymne national	des cymbales (f. pl.)		
une fête nationale	une tribune		

Talking about carnival

le carnaval	un groupe masqué	des confettis (m. pl.)
un char	lancer	

Talking about Christmas

Noël	une cheminée	la messe de minuit
Joyeux Noël!	un soulier	réveillonner
une carte de vœux	la veille	
le Père Noël	le réveillon	
un arbre de Noël,	un cadeau de Noël	
un sapin	un chant de Noël	

Talking about Hanukkah

Hanouka	une branche
la fête des Lumières	une bougie
une menorah	juif, juive
un chandelier	allumer les bougies

Talking about New Year's

le jour de l'An	Bonne Santé!
un serpentin	s'embrasser
Bonne Année!	(se) souhaiter

Talking about a wedding

le mariage	une demoiselle	une cérémonie	religieux, religieuse
la mariée	d'honneur	la mairie	se marier
le marié	un garçon d'honneur	une église	
les mariés (m. pl.)	une alliance	civil(e)	

Other useful words and expressions

sage	avoir lieu

How well do you know your vocabulary?
- Choose words to describe a holiday you celebrated recently.
- Write a few sentences about what you and your friends or family did to celebrate.

VIDÉOTOUR

Épisode 12
In this video episode, Manu surprises Chloé on Christmas Eve. See page 511 for more information.

LES FÊTES

quatre cent trois 403

Planning for Chapter 13

SCOPE AND SEQUENCE, PAGES 404–433

Topics
- Social etiquette
- Introducing people

Functions
- How to describe feelings
- How to express opinions
- How to talk about things that may or may not happen
- How to express emotional reactions to what others do

National Standards
- Communication Standard 1.1 pages 408, 409, 412, 413, 415, 418, 419, 421, 428
- Communication Standard 1.2 pages 408, 409, 412, 413, 414, 415, 418, 419, 420, 423, 424, 425
- Communication Standard 1.3 pages 413, 414, 415, 418, 419, 427, 428, 429
- Cultures Standard 2.1 pages 407, 411, 421, 422–423, 424, 425, 426–427
- Connections Standard 3.1 pages 426–427
- Comparisons Standard 4.1 pages 424, 425
- Comparisons Standard 4.2 pages 422–423, 424, 425, 427, 429
- Communities Standard 5.1 page 429

Culture
- Discussing differences between etiquette and manners in the United States and France
- Use of **tu** and **vous** in France
- Customary greetings in West Africa

Structure
- The subjunctive with impersonal expressions
- Other verbs in the present subjunctive
- The subjunctive with expressions of emotion

PACING AND PRIORITIES

The chapter content is color coded below to assist you in planning.

■ required   ■ recommended   ■ optional

Vocabulaire (required)   Days 1–4
- ■ Mots 1
   - D'autres parties du corps
   - Bien ou mal élevé(e)?
   - Comment se tenir à table?
- ■ Mots 2
   - Les émotions
   - Les présentations

Structure (required)   Days 5–7
- ■ Le subjonctif après les expressions impersonnelles
- ■ D'autres verbes au présent du subjonctif
- ■ Le subjonctif après les expressions d'émotion

Conversation (required)
- ■ Il faut qu'on s'habille.

Lectures culturelles
- ■ Le savoir-vivre en France (recommended)
- ■ Le tutoiement (optional)
- ■ Les salutations en Afrique occidentale (optional)

Connexions (optional)
- ■ Étiquette

■ **C'est à vous** (recommended)

■ **Assessment** (recommended)

■ **On parle super bien!** (optional)

RESOURCE GUIDE

SECTION	PAGES	SECTION RESOURCES
Vocabulaire *Mots 1*		
D'autres parties du corps Bien ou mal élevé(e)? Comment se tenir à table?	406 406–407 407–409	Vocabulary Transparencies 13.2–13.3 Audio CD 8 Audio Activities TE, pages 142–144 Workbook, page 147 Quiz 1, page 67 ExamView® Pro
Vocabulaire *Mots 2*		
Les émotions Les présentations	410 411–413	Vocabulary Transparencies 13.4–13.5 Audio CD 8 Audio Activities TE, pages 145–147 Workbook, page 148 Quiz 2, page 68 ExamView® Pro
Structure		
Le subjonctif après les expressions impersonnelles D'autres verbes au présent du subjonctif Le subjonctif après les expressions d'émotion	414–415 416–417 418–419	Audio CD 8 Audio Activities TE, pages 147–149 Workbook, pages 149–151 Quizzes 3–5, pages 69–71 ExamView® Pro
Conversation		
Il faut qu'on s'habille.	420–421	Audio CD 8 Audio Activities TE, pages 149–150 Interactive CD-ROM
Lectures culturelles		
Le savoir-vivre en France Le tutoiement Les salutations en Afrique occidentale	422–423 424 425	Audio CD 8 Audio Activities TE, pages 150–151 Tests, pages 214, 218
Connexions		
Étiquette	426–427	Tests, page 219
C'est à vous		
	428–429	**Bon voyage!** Video, Episode 13 Video Activities, Chapter 13 French Online Activities french.glencoe.com
Assessment		
	430–431	Communication Transparency C 13 Quizzes 1–5, pages 67–71 Performance Assessment, Task 13 Tests, pages 211–226 ExamView® Pro Situation Cards, Chapter 13 **Marathon mental** Videoquiz

Using Your Resources for Chapter 13

Transparencies

Bellringer 13.1–13.7   Vocabulary 13.1–13.5   Communication C 13

Workbook

Vocabulary, pages 147–148   Structure, pages 149–151   Enrichment, pages 152–154

Audio Activities

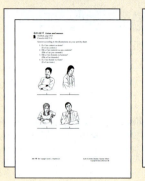    

Vocabulary, pages 142–147   Structure, pages 147–149   Conversation, pages 149–150   Cultural Reading, pages 150–151   Additional Practice, pages 152–153

Assessment

Vocabulary and Structure Quizzes, pages 67–71

Chapter Tests, pages 211–226

Situation Cards, Chapter 13

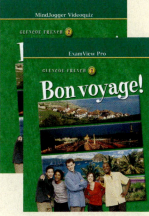
MindJogger Videoquiz, ExamView® Pro, Chapter 13

Timesaving Teacher Tools

TeacherWorks™

TeacherWorks™ is your all-in-one teacher resource center. Personalize lesson plans, access resources from the Teacher Wraparound Edition, connect to the Internet, or make a to-do list. These are only a few of the many features that can assist you in the planning and organizing of your lessons.

Includes:
- A calendar feature
- Access to all program blackline masters
- Standards correlations and more

ExamView® Pro

Test Bank software for Macintosh and Windows makes creating, editing, customizing, and printing tests quick and easy.

Technology Resources

In the Chapter 13 Internet activity, you will have a chance to learn more about the Francophone world. Visit **french.glencoe.com**.

On the Interactive Conversation CD-ROM, students can listen to and take part in a recorded version of the conversation in Chapter 13.

See the National Geographic Teacher's Corner on pages 138–139, 244–245, 372–373, 472–473 for reference to additional technology resources.

Bon voyage! Video and Video Activities, Chapter 13

Help your students prepare for the chapter test by playing the **Marathon mental** Videoquiz game show. Teams will compete against each other to review chapter vocabulary and structure and sharpen listening comprehension skills.

Preview

In this chapter, students will learn vocabulary associated with good manners and some French social customs. They will learn the subjunctive forms of some irregular verbs and the use of the subjunctive with expressions of necessity, possibility, and emotion.

 National Standards

Communication

In Chapter 13, students will communicate in spoken and written French on the following topics:
- Good manners
- Social customs
- Emotions

Students will obtain and provide information about these topics, express feelings, and engage in conversations that would typically take place in social settings as they fulfill the chapter objectives listed on this page.

LEVELING

The activities, conversations, and readings within each chapter are marked according to level of difficulty. **E** indicates easy. **A** indicates average. **C** indicates challenging. Some activities cover a range of difficulty. In some activities, for example, advanced students will be able to produce more extensive responses while students who learn at a different rate may give less detailed responses. The leveling indicators will help you individualize instruction to best meet your students' needs.

CHAPITRE 13

Le savoir-vivre

Objectifs
In this chapter you will learn to:

✔ talk about social etiquette

✔ introduce people to each other

✔ describe some feelings

✔ express opinions

✔ talk about more things that may or may not happen

✔ express emotional reactions to what others do

✔ compare etiquette in France and the United States

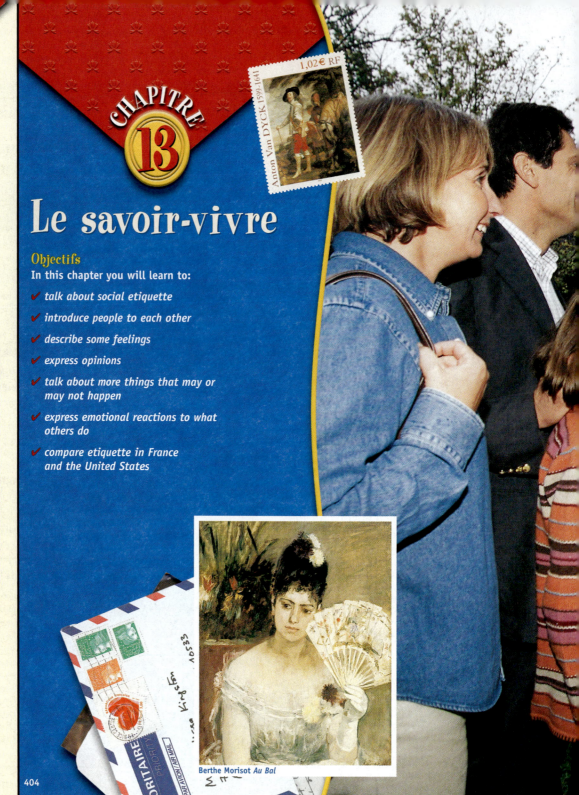

Berthe Morisot *Au Bal*

404

CHAPITRE 13

Spotlight on Culture

Photograph In this photo we see families visiting one another at the home of one of the couples in Brunoy, a residential suburb of Paris.

Painting Berthe Morisot (1841–1895), a granddaughter of Jean-Honoré Fragonard, was born into a family with a rich artistic tradition. From a very early age she was certain she would become a painter. At age fifteen she started to copy paintings in the Louvre. At this time, this was a common way to learn to paint. At the Louvre she met Édouard Manet. They became good friends, and several years later she married his brother Eugène.

Like Manet, Morisot concentrated on portraits and interior scenes. Her figures are attractive and properly reserved. Note how the woman in the painting *Au Bal* would not be so bold as to stare directly at you. She shyly lowers her gaze.

Morisot posed her models for short periods of time and then painted them from memory. She was thus able to avoid the somewhat stiff expressions displayed when poses were held over long periods of time.

quatre cent cinq ♦ **405**

Vocabulaire
Mots 1

1 Preparation

Resource Manager

Vocabulary Transparencies
 13.2–13.3
Audio Activities TE, pages 142–144
Audio CD 8
Workbook, page 147
Quiz 1, page 67
ExamView® Pro

Bellringer Review

Use BRR Transparency 13.1 or write the following on the board.
List all the parts of the body that you remember in French.

2 Presentation

Step 1 Have students close their books. Use Vocabulary Transparencies 13.2–13.3 to present **Mots 1.** Have students repeat the words, phrases, and sentences after you or Audio CD 8.

Step 2 Point to the parts of the body (**un doigt, la main, le poignet, l'avant-bras, le coude, le pouce, la joue, la bouche, la lèvre**).

Step 3 Dramatize the meaning of **bousculer, resquiller, se serrer la main, s'embrasser, manger la bouche fermée, manger la bouche ouverte, s'essuyer les lèvres.**

Step 4 Have students open their books and read the new words and expressions.

Vocabulaire
Mots 1

D'autres parties du corps

Bien ou mal élevé(e)?

mal élevée = malpolie

bien élevé = poli

bousculer

resquiller

Reaching All Students

Kinesthetic Learners
Pantomime Game
Have students do the following:
  Montrez-moi votre bouche.
  Montrez-moi votre pouce.
  Montrez-moi votre coude.
  Montrez-moi votre main.
  Montrez-moi vos lèvres.

Write the following words or phrases on index cards. Have a student pick a card and mime the action. The class will guess what the person is doing.

bousculer
resquiller
se serrer la main
s'embrasser

manger la bouche fermée
manger la bouche ouverte
s'essuyer les lèvres

Vocabulaire
Mots 1

Les amis ont rendez-vous dans un café.
Ils se retrouvent dans un café.
Les filles s'embrassent sur les deux joues.
Les garçons se serrent la main.

Les garçons et les filles partagent les frais quand ils sortent.

Note
tutoyer quelqu'un = dire «tu» à quelqu'un

Les jeunes se tutoient entre eux.

Le tutoiement est très courant, surtout entre adolescents.

Comment se tenir à table?

la bouche ouverte
Gloup, gloup
une serviette
la bouche fermée

Le garçon s'essuie la bouche avec sa serviette.

Les bonnes manières
- Il ne faut pas mettre ses coudes sur la table.
- Il faut mettre ses poignets sur la table.
- Il ne faut pas ouvrir la bouche quand on mange.
- Il vaut mieux manger la bouche fermée.
- Il ne faut pas parler la bouche pleine.
- Il ne faut pas faire de bruit quand on mange de la soupe.
- Il faut s'essuyer la bouche.

LE SAVOIR-VIVRE

Vocabulaire

3 Practice

Quel est le mot?

Historiette Each time **Historiette** appears, it means that the answers to the activity form a short story. Encourage students to look at the title of the **Historiette,** since it can help them do the activity.

 and You may wish to use the recorded version of these activities.

 If there is disagreement, let the students argue their viewpoints.

Reaching All Students

Verbal/Linguistic Learners
Have students who like to express themselves prepare a debate. Separate students into two teams, each team taking one of the following sides:
1. Les garçons et les filles doivent partager les frais quand ils sortent.
2. Les garçons et les filles ne doivent pas partager les frais. Ce sont les garçons (les filles) qui doivent payer.

Vocabulaire

Quel est le mot?

1 Le corps Identifiez.

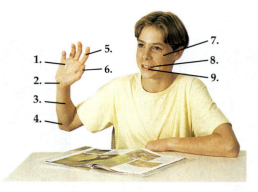

2 À vous de décider. Dites si la personne est bien ou mal élevée.
1. Alain se lève quand une personne âgée entre.
2. Caroline ne regarde jamais la personne à qui elle parle, à qui elle s'adresse.
3. Quand Sophie voit une personne âgée debout dans le métro, elle lui offre sa place.
4. Romain fait beaucoup de bruit quand il mange. Il mange d'une façon bruyante.
5. Cédric dit toujours merci quand on lui donne quelque chose ou quand on fait quelque chose pour lui.
6. Sylvie parle souvent la bouche pleine.
7. Michel ne met jamais ses coudes sur la table.
8. Sandrine ne met pas ses mains sous la table.

Les deux amis s'embrassent.

3 C'est poli ou malpoli? Décidez.
1. Quand on mange d'une façon bruyante, on montre qu'on apprécie ce qu'on mange.
2. On peut toujours faire beaucoup de bruit.
3. Quand on a rendez-vous avec des amis, on peut arriver avec une heure de retard.
4. Quand il y a beaucoup de monde, on bouscule les gens, on les pousse avec les coudes.
5. Quand on rencontre un ami, on lui serre la main.
6. On peut tutoyer une vieille dame qu'on ne connaît pas bien.
7. Quand on rencontre une amie, on l'embrasse sur les joues.
8. Il est normal de resquiller quand il y a beaucoup de monde.
9. Il vaut mieux manger la bouche fermée.

ANSWERS TO Quel est le mot?

1
1. la main
2. le poignet
3. l'avant-bras
4. le coude
5. le doigt
6. le pouce
7. la joue
8. la bouche
9. la lèvre

2
1. Il est bien élevé.
2. Elle est mal élevée.
3. Elle est bien élevée.
4. Il est mal élevé.
5. Il est bien élevé.
6. Elle est mal élevée.
7. Il est bien élevé.
8. Elle est bien élevée.

3
1. C'est malpoli.
2. C'est malpoli.
3. C'est malpoli.
4. C'est malpoli.
5. C'est poli.
6. C'est malpoli.
7. C'est poli.
8. C'est malpoli.
9. C'est poli.

Définitions Quel est le mot?
1. donner la main pour dire bonjour
2. s'adresser à quelqu'un en utilisant «tu»
3. le contraire de «la bouche ouverte»
4. chaque main en a cinq
5. avoir rendez-vous
6. diviser les frais
7. ce qu'on utilise pour s'essuyer la bouche à table
8. caractéristique d'une personne ou d'une chose qui fait du bruit

Les deux copains se serrent la main.

 Bien élevé ou mal élevé? Travaillez avec un(e) camarade. Parlez de toutes les caractéristiques d'une personne bien élevée et celles d'une personne mal élevée.

Un café sur la place Plumereau à Tours

 Au café Parlez avec un groupe de copains. Décidez ce que vous allez prendre et comment vous allez partager les frais. Parlez aussi de vos projets pour le week-end.

Vocabulaire

4 After completing the activity, you may wish to have students use each word in an original sentence.

Geography Connection

Tours is a lovely city located in the beautiful Loire Valley. One can still visit the workshop on **rue Colbert** where **Jeanne d'Arc** bought her suit of armor before going to **Orléans** in April of 1429.

Learning from Photos

(page 409 top) The two boys shaking hands in this photo are **lycéens** at the lycée Montaigne in Paris.

Have students say as much about the photo as they can. Have them include a description of the boys, their clothing, where they are, and what they are doing.

Reteaching
Show Vocabulary Transparencies 13.2–13.3 and let students say as much as they can about them in their own words.

LEVELING
E: Activities 1, 2, 3, 5, 6
A: Activities 3, 4, 5, 6

ANSWERS TO *Quel est le mot?*

4
1. se serrer la main
2. tutoyer
3. la bouche fermée
4. les doigts
5. se retrouver
6. partager les frais (payer pour soi)
7. une serviette
8. bruyant(e)

5 Answers will vary but may include:

Une personne bien élevée…
mange la bouche fermée.
tutoie ses amis, mais vouvoie les adultes.
met ses poignets sur la table.
ne bouscule pas les gens.
fait la queue.

Une personne mal élevée…
mange la bouche ouverte.
tutoie tout le monde.
met ses coudes sur la table.
bouscule les gens.
resquille.

Vocabulaire Mots 2

1 Preparation

Resource Manager
Vocabulary Transparencies
   13.4–13.5
Audio Activities TE, pages 145–147
Audio CD 8
Workbook, page 148
Quiz 2, page 68
ExamView® Pro

Bellringer Review
Use BRR Transparency 13.2 or write the following on the board. Rewrite each sentence in the **passé composé**.
1. Les amis ont rendez-vous.
2. Les amis arrivent au café.
3. Ils trouvent une table libre.
4. Les garçons se serrent la main.
5. Les filles s'embrassent sur les joues.
6. Ils commencent à parler.
7. Le serveur leur sert.
8. Tout le monde partage les frais.

2 Presentation

Step 1 Show Vocabulary Transparencies 13.4–13.5. Have students close their books and repeat the words after you or Audio CD 8 as you point to the appropriate illustration on the transparency.

Step 2 Use facial expressions to convey the meaning of **avoir peur, être triste, être désolé, être surpris, être étonné, être content, être heureux, être furieux**.

Step 3 Have students repeat the sentences with as much expression as possible.

Step 4 Have students role-play the introductions.

410

Vocabulaire Mots 2

Les émotions

être étonné

Pierre a l'air étonné.
Il est étonné que tu ne saches pas son numéro de téléphone.

être contente

Marie a l'air contente.
Elle est contente que tu veuilles faire sa connaissance.

avoir peur

Jean a peur que tu dises quelque chose.

être furieux

Marc a l'air furieux.
Il est furieux que vous soyez en retard.

être triste
être désolée
regretter

Anne a l'air triste.
Anne est désolée que tu ne puisses pas venir.
Anne regrette que tu ne viennes pas.

410 ❧ *quatre cent dix*   CHAPITRE 13

Reaching All Students

Kinesthetic Learners
You may wish to have a student or several students mime the following:

Vous êtes content(e).	Vous êtes désolé(e).
Vous êtes furieux(se).	Vous êtes surpris(e).
Vous êtes heureux(se).	Vous avez l'air étonné(e).
Vous êtes triste.	Vous avez peur.

Les présentations

Note
Quand vous faites la connaissance de quelqu'un, vous pouvez dire:
(Je suis) enchanté(e) de faire votre connaissance.
(Je suis) très heureux(se) de vous connaître.

Ou vous pouvez dire tout simplement:
Enchanté(e).
Bonjour.
Salut.

LE SAVOIR-VIVRE

quatre cent onze 411

Vocabulaire Mots 2

Reaching All Students

Additional Practice Do the following activity with students who have mathematical intelligence and who can clearly see cause-effect relationships. Ask students how they would react to the following situations using **Je suis...**:
1. Il n'y a pas de cours demain.
2. Vous avez «A» à l'examen de français.
3. Vous avez raté tous vos examens.
4. Vous avez eu un petit accident de voiture.
5. Vous vous êtes cassé la jambe.
6. Quelqu'un vous telephone à trois heures du matin.

Dramatization Have students get up and introduce one another.

Assessment

As an informal assessment, you may wish to show Vocabulary Transparencies 13.4–13.5. Call on students to point to and identify various items at random.

Chapter Projects

 Salut! Have students prepare a list of formal and informal greetings and farewells in French.

 Savoir-vivre Have students write an article for a book entitled *Savoir-vivre*.

Chapter Projects

 À table Have students prepare in French a list of do's and don'ts concerning table manners in the United States.

 Des comparaisons Have students prepare a report that contrasts French and American table manners.

Bien élevé(e)? Have students make some simple drawings that depict good and bad manners. Have them write captions for their drawings. You may wish to use them for a bulletin board display.

411

Vocabulaire

3 Practice

Quel est le mot?

7 and 8 Have students practice these activities in pairs, then share their dialogues with the class.

9 Expansion: After completing the activity, have students imagine a reason the person is feeling the emotion. If the emotion is a negative one, have students say what the person can or should do.

 **Recycling**

Recycle clothing vocabulary. Have students describe the clothing of the people in the photographs on page 412.

Vocabulaire

Quel est le mot?

 7 **Un ami vous présente un copain.**
Complétez le dialogue.

—Paul, tu connais Henri?
—_____.
—Henri, Paul.
—_____.
—_____.

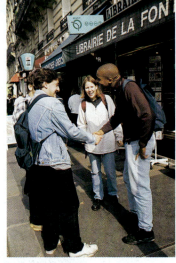
La rue Monge à Paris

Le quartier de la Villette à Paris

 8 **Votre mère vous présente un ami.**
Complétez le dialogue. Soyez très poli(e).
—Monsieur Bolduc, je vous présente ma fille Amélie (mon fils Cyril).
—Bonjour, Amélie (Cyril).
—_____.
—Je suis heureux de faire votre connaissance.
—_____.

 9 **Comment sont-ils?** Répondez d'après les photos.

1. Il a l'air content ou triste?

2. Elle a l'air contente ou pas contente?

3. Elle a l'air étonnée ou furieuse?

4. Il a l'air étonné ou triste?

Answers to Quel est le mot?

 7 Answers will vary but may include:
Non.
Salut.
Salut.

8 Answers will vary but may include:
Bonjour, monsieur.
Moi de même.

9
1. Il a l'air triste.
2. Elle a l'air contente.
3. Elle a l'air étonnée.
4. Il a l'air étonné.

Vocabulaire

10 **Comment réagissez-vous?** Choisissez et faites une phrase d'après le modèle.

Vous avez gagné un million de dollars. →
Je suis très étonné(e)!

1. Le Père Noël vous a apporté beaucoup de cadeaux.
2. Un ami vous présente le garçon/la fille de vos rêves.
3. Vous rencontrez dans la rue une amie que vous n'avez pas vue depuis longtemps.
4. Elle vous dit qu'elle a été très malade.
5. Votre copain ou copine vous dit qu'il/elle ne vous aime plus.
6. Vous faites la queue à la poste et quelqu'un essaie de resquiller.
7. Votre meilleur(e) ami(e) vous annonce son mariage.
8. Quelqu'un vous bouscule et vous fait tomber.

11 **Présentations** Travaillez par groupes de trois personnes. Préparez un sketch (skit) dans lequel vous présentez un(e) ami(e) à un(e) autre ami(e). Présentez ensuite deux adultes.

12   **Mime** Travaillez avec un(e) camarade. Mimez une émotion. Votre camarade doit deviner quelle émotion vous mimez. Changez ensuite de rôle.

 For more practice using words from *Mots 1* and *Mots 2*, do Activity 19 on page H20 at the end of this book.

LE SAVOIR-VIVRE

quatre cent treize ✤ 413

Structure

1 Preparation

Resource Manager
Audio Activities TE, pages 147–149
Audio CD 8
Workbook, pages 149–151
Quizzes 3–5, pages 69–71
ExamView® Pro

Bellringer Review

Use BRR Transparency 13.3 or write the following on the board. Complete the following statements.
1. Il faut que je…
2. Mes parents veulent que je…
3. La prof d'anglais préfère que nous…
4. Mon ami aimerait que je…

2 Presentation

 Le subjonctif après les expressions impersonnelles

Note: Once again, the concept we would like to emphasize is that even though an action is necessary (or important or good), it is not certain that it will take place. Since we do not know if it will take place, the subjunctive is used.

Step 1 Have students read the expressions and the model sentences aloud.

Structure

 ## Le subjonctif après les expressions impersonnelles
Expressing opinions

1. You have already seen that you use the subjunctive after the expression **il faut que.** You also use the subjunctive after the following expressions.

> Il est possible
> Il est impossible
> Il est important
> Il est nécessaire
> Il vaut mieux   } qu'elle écrive.
> Il est indispensable
> Il est bon
> Il est temps
> Il est rare

2. These expressions require the subjunctive because, as you have seen before, the action or situation being described in the clause introduced by **que** is not a fact; it may or may not take place.

> Il vaut mieux que tu le fasses tout de suite.
> Il est possible que tu n'aies pas le temps de finir.

Comment dit-on?

13 **Historiette** **Au café** Inventez une histoire.
1. Il est possible qu'ils aient rendez-vous au café?
2. Il est indispensable que Luc finisse son travail avant d'y aller?
3. Il vaut mieux que vous l'aidiez un peu?
4. Il n'est pas nécessaire que vous sortiez?
5. Il faut que vous restiez chez vous?

414 ❧ *quatre cent quatorze*   CHAPITRE 13

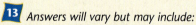
ANSWERS TO Comment dit-on?

13 *Answers will vary but may include:*
1. Oui, il est possible qu'ils aient rendez-vous au café.
2. Oui, il est indispensable que Luc finisse son travail avant d'y aller.
3. Oui, il vaut mieux que je l'aide un peu.
4. Non, il n'est pas nécessaire que je sorte.
5. Oui, il faut que je reste chez moi.

14 **Qu'en pensez-vous?** Répondez en utilisant **il est important que** ou **il n'est pas important que.**

1. Aidons les personnes âgées.
2. Disons toujours la vérité.
3. Parlons à table.
4. Ne parlons pas la bouche pleine.
5. Ne mettons pas les mains sur les genoux.
6. Écrivons des lettres à nos amis.

 15 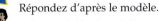 **Tu réussiras.**
Répondez d'après le modèle.

—Tu iras à l'université?
—Il est possible que j'aille à l'université.

1. Tu iras dans une bonne université?
2. Tu trouveras un bon travail?
3. Tu réussiras bien?
4. Tu te marieras?
5. Tu auras des enfants?
6. Tu seras professeur de français?

 16 **Ça dépend.** Travaillez avec un(e) camarade. Parlez des choses qu'il est bon que vous fassiez et des choses qu'il n'est pas absolument nécessaire que vous fassiez.

 17 **Possible ou impossible?**
Travaillez avec un(e) camarade. Dites-lui que vous ferez bientôt quelque chose ensemble. Il/Elle vous dira si c'est possible ou impossible. Par exemple:

—Nous irons à Paris le week-end prochain.
—Il est impossible que nous allions à Paris le week-end prochain. Nous n'avons pas d'argent.

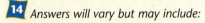

Le pont Royal à Paris

Structure

3 Practice

Comment dit-on?

13 to **15** These activities can be done with books closed or open. It is recommended that you go over each activity the first time with books closed. Then have students open their books and read the activities for additional reinforcement.

13 and **15** Have a student retell each activity in his or her own words.

Learning from Photos
(page 415 top) Have students imagine a dialogue between the two women.

(page 415 bottom) Le pont Royal was built in 1689.

LEVELING
E: Activities 13, 14, 15, 16
A: Activities 13, 15, 16, 17
C: Activity 17

ANSWERS TO Comment dit-on?

14 *Answers will vary but may include:*
1. Il est important que nous aidions les personnes âgées.
2. Il est important que nous disions toujours la vérité.
3. Il n'est pas important que nous parlions à table.
4. Il est important que nous ne parlions pas la bouche pleine.
5. Il est important que nous ne mettions pas les mains sur les genoux.
6. Il est important que nous écrivions des lettres à nos amis.

15
1. Il est possible que j'aille dans une bonne université.
2. Il est possible que je trouve un bon travail.
3. Il est possible que je réussisse bien.
4. Il est possible que je me marie.
5. Il est possible que j'aie des enfants.
6. Il est possible que je sois professeur de français.

16 *Answers will vary depending upon students' opinions. The verb in the clauses will be in the subjunctive.*

17 *Answers will vary depending upon the plans the students wish to make.*

Structure

1 Preparation

Bellringer Review

Use BRR Transparency 13.4 or write the following on the board.
Complete the following sentences with the present tense of the verbs in parentheses.
1. Ils _____ des chants de Noël. (apprendre)
2. Ils _____ des leçons de chant. (prendre)
3. Ils _____ leurs cartes de vœux. (envoyer)
4. Ils _____ avec nous à la messe de minuit. (venir)
5. Ils _____ encore au Père Noël. (croire)
6. Ils _____ beaucoup de cadeaux. (recevoir)

2 Presentation

D'autres verbes au présent du subjonctif

Step 1 Go over the Bellringer Review, which reviews the third person plural of the present indicative of many of these verbs.

Step 2 Have students repeat the verb forms in Items 1 and 2 after you.

Structure

D'autres verbes au présent du subjonctif
Talking about more things that may or may not happen

1. Certain verbs that have two stems in the present indicative have the same stems in the present subjunctive. Study the following forms.

Infinitive	Two stems	Subjunctive
prendre	ils **prenn** -ent nous **pren** -ons	que je prenne, tu prennes, il prenne, ils prennent que nous prenions, vous preniez
venir	ils **vienn** -ent nous **ven** -ons	que je vienne, tu viennes, il vienne, ils viennent que nous venions, vous veniez
recevoir	ils **reçoiv** -ent nous **recev** -ons	que je reçoive, tu reçoives, il reçoive, ils reçoivent que nous recevions, vous receviez
boire	ils **boiv** -ent nous **buv** -ons	que je boive, tu boives, il boive, ils boivent que nous buvions, vous buviez

2. The verbs **savoir**, **pouvoir**, and **vouloir** are irregular in the present subjunctive.

SAVOIR	POUVOIR	VOULOIR
que je sache	que je puisse	que je veuille
que tu saches	que tu puisses	que tu veuilles
qu'il/elle/on sache	qu'il/elle/on puisse	qu'il/elle/on veuille
que nous sachions	que nous puissions	que nous voulions
que vous sachiez	que vous puissiez	que vous vouliez
qu'ils/elles sachent	qu'ils/elles puissent	qu'ils/elles veuillent

Attention!

Verbs with a spelling change in the present indicative have the same spelling change in the subjunctive.

VOIR	que je voie	que nous voyions
PAYER	que je paie	que nous payions
APPELER	que j'appelle	que nous appelions
ACHETER	que j'achète	que nous achetions
PRÉFÉRER	que je préfère	que nous préférions

Comment dit-on?

18 **Elle fait du français.** Répondez d'après le modèle.

Elle voit le prof. (il faut que) →
Il faut qu'elle voie le prof.

1. Elle voit le prof tout de suite. (il est indispensable que)
2. Elle l'appelle. (il faut que)
3. Elle vient au cours de français avec nous. (il vaut mieux que)
4. Elle apprend le français. (je veux que)
5. Elle achète un bon dictionnaire. (il est important que)
6. Elle comprend tout. (il est impossible que)
7. Elle reçoit de bonnes notes. (ses parents veulent que)

19 **C'est nécessaire.** Complétez.

1. Elle veut que je ____ et que vous ____ aussi. (comprendre)
2. Il est important que je ____ et que vous ____ aussi. (venir)
3. Il faut que je le ____ et que vous le ____ aussi. (recevoir)
4. Elle veut que je l'____ et que vous l'____ aussi. (appeler)
5. Il voudrait que je le ____ et que vous le ____ aussi. (croire)

20 **Les bonnes manières.** Répondez d'après le modèle.

Ils savent se tenir à table. (il faut que) →
Il faut qu'ils sachent se tenir à table.

1. Tu sais faire des présentations. (il faut que)
2. Nous pouvons le voir. (il est possible que)
3. Ils peuvent faire ça. (il est impossible que)
4. Il veut bien nous serrer la main. (je souhaite que)
5. Elle veut te présenter son frère. (il est bon que)
6. Vous savez parler français. (il est indispensable que)
7. Je peux venir avec vous. (il est impossible que)

LE SAVOIR-VIVRE

Structure

1 Preparation

Bellringer Review

Use BRR Transparency 13.5 or write the following on the board. Complete the following to make statements about good table manners in France.
1. Il est indispensable que vous…
2. Il est important que tu…
3. Il vaut mieux que le garçon…

2 Presentation

Le subjonctif après les expressions d'émotion

Note: The use of the subjunctive after these expressions does not conform to the notion that the subjunctive is used when it is not certain that the action of the verb will take place. In these cases, the subjunctive is used because of the subjective nature of the statement. What makes one person happy could make another one sad, etc.

Step 1 Go over the information with the students.

3 Practice

Comment dit-on?

22 Expansion: Have students answer these questions, replacing **Françoise** with **vous**.

Structure

Le subjonctif après les expressions d'émotion
Expressing emotions

Verbs and expressions of emotion such as joy, anger, and fear require the subjunctive because they do not express facts, but subjective reactions. The following are common expressions that require the subjunctive.

> J'ai peur
> Je suis content(e)
> Je suis heureux(se)
> Je suis furieux(se) ⎫
> Je regrette   ⎬ qu'il ne **vienne** pas.
> Je suis triste
> Je suis étonné(e)
> Je suis désolé(e)

Comment dit-on?

21 **Content(e) ou désolé(e)**
Dites si vous êtes content(e) ou désolé(e)…
1. que Paul ne vienne pas.
2. qu'il connaisse votre sœur.
3. qu'il ait l'air triste.
4. qu'il ne sache pas votre numéro de téléphone.
5. qu'il veuille faire la connaissance de vos parents.
6. qu'il ne puisse pas vous fixer de rendez-vous.

22 **Françoise vient ou pas?** Répondez que oui.
1. Tu es triste que Françoise ne soit pas encore là?
2. Tu as peur qu'elle ne vienne pas?
3. Tu es content(e) qu'elle puisse venir?
4. Tu es étonné(e) qu'elle sache conduire?
5. Tu regrettes que son frère ne veuille pas l'accompagner?

Julie est contente que tu viennes à sa fête.

418 ✦ quatre cent dix-huit   CHAPITRE 13

ANSWERS TO Comment dit-on?

21 Answers will vary but may include:
1. Je suis désolé(e) que Paul ne vienne pas.
2. Je suis content(e) qu'il connaisse ma sœur.
3. Je suis désolé(e) qu'il ait l'air triste.
4. Je suis désolé(e) qu'il ne sache pas mon numéro de téléphone.
5. Je suis content(e) qu'il veuille faire la connaissance de mes parents.
6. Je suis désolé(e) qu'il ne puisse pas me fixer de rendez-vous.

22
1. Oui, je suis triste que Françoise ne soit pas encore là.
2. Oui, j'ai peur qu'elle ne vienne pas.
3. Oui, je suis content(e) qu'elle puisse venir.
4. Oui, je suis étonné(e) qu'elle sache conduire.
5. Oui, je regrette que son frère ne veuille pas l'accompagner.

23   **Je suis contente qu'il vienne!** Répétez la conversation.

Virginie: Laurent vient pour Noël?
Anne: Oui. Je suis contente qu'il puisse venir, mais je suis triste que Stéphane ne vienne pas.
Virginie: Moi, ça m'étonne que Stéphane ne veuille pas venir.

24 **Contente?** Répondez d'après la conversation.

1. Anne est contente que Laurent vienne pour Noël?
2. Elle est triste que Stéphane ne vienne pas?
3. Virginie est étonnée que Stéphane ne veuille pas venir?

25 **Opinions et émotions** Donnez des réponses personnelles.

1. Je regrette que vous…
2. Je suis très étonné(e) qu'il…
3. Je suis désolé(e) que tu…
4. J'ai bien peur qu'ils…
5. Je ne suis pas du tout content(e) que tu…
6. Je suis vraiment furieux(se) qu'elle…

26 **Mes émotions** Travaillez avec un(e) camarade. Parlez de ce qui vous a étonné(e), désolé(e), etc. Vous pouvez utiliser les expressions suivantes.

J'ai été content(e) que   J'ai été très étonné(e) que
J'ai été furieux(se) que   J'ai été désolé(e) que

Vous êtes sur le bon chemin. Allez-y!

Conversation

1 Preparation

Resource Manager
Audio Activities TE, pages 149–150
Audio CD 8
CD-ROM

Bellringer Review

Use BRR Transparency 13.6 or write the following on the board. Complete the following statements.
1. Il est important que les élèves...
2. Il est rare que le prof...
3. Il vaut mieux que je...
4. Il est indispensable que tu...

2 Presentation

Step 1 Have students close their books and listen as you read the conversation aloud or play Audio CD 8. Have students listen carefully to the recorded version and pay particular attention to the intonation.

Step 2 Have students open their books and read along with you or Audio CD 8.

Step 3 Call on a pair of volunteers to read the conversation to the class with as much expression as possible.

Glencoe Technology

CD-ROM
On the CD-ROM, students can watch a dramatization of this conversation. They can then play the role of either one of the characters and record themselves in the conversation.

Conversation

Il faut qu'on s'habille.

Chloé: Qu'est-ce que tu vas mettre samedi?
Adrien: Samedi? Qu'est-ce qu'il y a samedi?
Chloé: Tu as déjà oublié? On va au mariage de la sœur de Cédric.
Adrien: Oh là, là. Il faut qu'on s'habille?
Chloé: Tu vas tout de même pas y aller en jean.
Adrien: Pourquoi pas? Elle est cool, la sœur de Cédric.
Chloé: Je serais très, très étonnée que ses amis aillent à son mariage en jean!
Adrien: Ben, il vaut mieux que j'y aille en jean que pas du tout.
Chloé: Je sais pas. Je crois qu'elle serait contente que tu fasses un petit effort.
Adrien: Un petit effort! Un pantalon, une chemise et une cravate, moi, j'appelle ça un ÉNORME effort!!!

Vous avez compris?

Répondez.

1. Qu'est-ce qu'il y a samedi?
2. Qu'est-ce que Chloé demande à Adrien?
3. Comment Adrien veut-il s'habiller?
4. Comment est la sœur de Cédric?
5. D'après Chloé, comment vont s'habiller les amis de la sœur de Cédric?
6. Qu'est-ce qu'elle aimerait qu'Adrien fasse?
7. Qu'est-ce qui est un grand effort pour Adrien?

Learning from Photos

(page 420) The young people looking at the wedding invitation are in Saint-Cloud. Saint-Cloud is a pleasant town just west of Paris, perched above the river Seine.

Answers to Vous avez compris?

1. Il y a un mariage.
2. Elle lui demande s'il va s'habiller bien.
3. Il veut s'habiller en jean.
4. La sœur de Cédric est cool.
5. Ils ne vont pas aller au mariage en jean.
6. Elle aimerait qu'il fasse un petit effort.
7. Pour Adrien, mettre un pantalon, une chemise et une cravate est un grand effort.

Parlons un peu plus

A **Habillé ou pas habillé?** Travaillez avec un(e) camarade. Vous êtes invités à plusieurs fêtes—un mariage, une fête d'anniversaire chez un copain, un pique-nique avec des amis de vos parents. Parlez de ce que vous allez mettre à chaque occasion. Discutez si votre choix est approprié ou pas.

B **Une invitation de mariage** Vous êtes un(e) ami(e) d'Ida Solange Beugre et Jean-Luc Lamblin, un jeune couple d'Abidjan en Côte d'Ivoire. Vous avez reçu une invitation à leur mariage qui va avoir lieu le 18 décembre. Téléphonez à Ida ou Jean-Luc (votre camarade) pour lui dire si vous allez pouvoir assister à la cérémonie. Exprimez vos sentiments au sujet de son mariage. Ensuite posez-lui des questions sur les cérémonies civile et religieuse et la réception (ce que vous devez porter, qui va venir, etc.).

M. et Mme BEUGRE Richard
La famille BEUGRE-DIOKE
La famille KOKORA
Madame HEMERY Liliane
La famille LAMBLIN
La famille AHOGNY
La famille ASSEMIEN Paul
La famille AKE Etienne

ont la joie de vous faire part du mariage

de leur fille, petite-fille, nièce   de leur fils, petit-fils, neveu

Ida Solange & Jean-Luc

La cérémonie civile aura lieu le Samedi 18 Décembre, à 16 heures à l'Hôtel de Ville d'Abidjan suivie de la bénédiction nuptiale en l'église St Michel d'Adjamé

01 B.P. 3374 ABJ. 01
tel: 41 67 23

01 B.P. 6293 ABJ. 01
tel: 37 29 67

LE SAVOIR-VIVRE   quatre cent vingt et un ❖ 421

Lectures culturelles

Reading Strategy

Paraphrasing
After you read each section of the passage, try to restate the main idea in your own words. Paraphrasing will help you to better understand what you are reading.

Le savoir-vivre en France

Dans toutes les sociétés du monde, il existe des règles de politesse. Ces règles de politesse varient d'un pays à l'autre. Quand on se trouve dans un pays étranger, il faut faire attention de ne pas commettre de faux pas.

Les Français et les Américains

En général, on peut dire que les Français attachent plus d'importance aux convenances[1] que les Américains. Autrement dit, les Américains sont plus décontractés[2] que les Français.

Les salutations

Quand un Français rencontre qui que ce soit, un bon ami ou quelqu'un qu'il ne connaît pas très bien, ils se serrent la main. Les jeunes le font également quand ils se rencontrent. Il est assez rare que vous serriez la main à un bon ami, n'est-ce pas?

Les Français s'embrassent aussi pour se dire bonjour quand ils se connaissent bien. Ils s'embrassent sur les joues, pas sur les lèvres.

[1] convenances *social customs* [2] décontractés *informal*

Elles s'embrassent.

Ils se serrent la main.

Les noms et les titres

Quand on dit bonjour, au revoir ou merci à quelqu'un, on doit ajouter monsieur, madame ou mademoiselle.

Aux États-Unis, on appelle tout le monde par son prénom. En France, non. On peut appeler une personne par son prénom, uniquement si on la connaît bien ou si cette personne est très jeune.

À table

Il est important de bien se tenir à table. Il est poli, par exemple, de mettre les poignets sur la table et de les garder là pendant tout le repas.

En France, on boit du café après le repas. Pendant le repas, on boit du vin[3] et de l'eau minérale.

[3] vin *wine*

Deux amies se rencontrent.

Sur la terrasse de l'hôtel Crillon à Paris

Vous avez compris?

Poli ou malpoli Indiquez si c'est poli ou pas en France.
1. appeler tout le monde par son prénom
2. embrasser quelqu'un qu'on connaît sur les joues
3. serrer la main pour dire bonjour
4. dire bonjour sans ajouter monsieur, madame ou mademoiselle
5. mettre les poignets sur la table

Lecture supplémentaire 1

Le tutoiement

L'emploi du «tu» ou du «vous»—c'est-à-dire le tutoiement ou le vouvoiement—est très important en France. En général, on ne tutoie pas:

- un professeur
- un patron[1] ou une patronne
- une personne plus âgée
- un(e) commerçant(e)
- une personne qu'on ne connaît pas bien

Actuellement[2], les gens tutoient plus facilement. Les jeunes se tutoient toujours quand ils se parlent. D'une façon générale, il vaut mieux attendre qu'on vous tutoie avant de tutoyer quelqu'un. Sachez que les Français n'aiment pas qu'on les tutoie s'ils ne sont pas prêts à en faire autant[3].

Ils se tutoient ou se vouvoient?

[1] patron *boss*
[2] Actuellement *Nowadays*
[3] prêts à en faire autant *ready to do the same*

Madame vouvoie toujours ses clients?

Vous avez compris?

«Tu» ou «vous»? Expliquez en anglais le tutoiement et le vouvoiement. Cela existe-t-il en anglais?

Lecture supplémentaire 2

Les salutations en Afrique occidentale

Les salutations dans les pays africains sont très importantes. Au Sénégal, par exemple, quand on parle wolof, la salutation est un rite qui dure au moins trente secondes. On dit «Que la paix[1] soit avec vous», «Vous avez la paix?», «Tout va bien pour vous?», «Comment sont les gens de votre communauté?» On pose des questions sur la famille, la santé, le travail, le temps, etc. Et toutes les réponses indiquent que tout va bien, qu'il n'y a pas de problèmes, même s'[2]il y en a.

En ville, les salutations faites en français sont plus courtes. Pour ne pas commettre de faux pas, il faut suivre une règle importante: il ne faut jamais commencer à parler affaires[3] en premier. D'autre part, si vous êtes chez des gens, il faut saluer cordialement tous les adultes présents.

Les hommes se serrent toujours la main quand ils se rencontrent. La poignée de main[4] est moins forte qu'en France, et elle est rare entre hommes et femmes. Comme en France, on embrasse les ami(e)s et même les connaissances sur les deux joues.

[1] paix *peace*
[2] même s' *even if*
[3] affaires *business*
[4] poignée de main *handshake*

Deux amies à Dakar au Sénégal

Vous avez compris?

La politesse Vrai ou faux?
1. Les Africains de nombreux pays posent beaucoup de questions quand ils se saluent.
2. Les salutations dans les pays d'Afrique occidentale sont très courtes.
3. On pose des questions sur la famille et le travail, par exemple.
4. On peut commencer à discuter affaires immédiatement.
5. Les femmes serrent la main aux hommes quand ils se rencontrent.
6. On s'embrasse dans les pays africains comme en France.

LE SAVOIR-VIVRE

CONNEXIONS

National Standards

Connections
This reading about French etiquette establishes a connection with another discipline, allowing students to reinforce and further their knowledge of literature through the study of French.

Attention!

The readings in the **Connexions** section are optional. They focus on some of the major disciplines taught in schools and universities. The vocabulary is useful for discussing such topics as history, literature, art, economics, business, science, etc. You may choose any of the following ways to do the readings in the **Connexions** section.

Independent reading Have students read the selections and do the post-reading activities as homework, which you collect. This option is least intrusive on class time and requires a minimum of teacher involvement.

Homework with in-class follow-up Assign the readings and post-reading activities as homework. Review and discuss the material in class the next day.

Intensive in-class activity This option includes a pre-reading vocabulary presentation, in-class reading and discussion, assignment of the activities for homework, and a discussion of the assignment in class the next day.

CONNEXIONS

La littérature

Étiquette

Rules of politeness and etiquette vary greatly from one country to another. An interesting place to observe cultural differences related to customs and mores is on an elevator. In some countries, a person entering an elevator will stand near the person already on board. In other countries, the newcomer would step to the other side, leaving plenty of room between them. In some areas, people will greet a stranger in an elevator. In other areas, they say nothing. What would you do?

Pierre Daninos, a French humorist, wrote an essay entitled "Les Français dans l'ascenseur." Enjoy it!

L'auteur

Pierre Daninos est un humoriste français. Il est né à Paris en 1913. Pendant la Deuxième Guerre mondiale, il est officier de liaison dans l'armée britannique et voyage au Mexique et en Amérique du Sud. Il commence à publier en 1945. Mais c'est avec *Les carnets du Major Thompson* (1954) qu'il devient célèbre. Son héros est un Anglais, le Major Thompson qui observe les Français et ne cesse de s'étonner: ces Français sont vraiment très curieux. Le passage qui suit est un extrait du livre de Pierre Daninos intitulé *Les nouveaux carnets du Major Thompson*.

Les Français dans l'ascenseur

M. Chapoulot m'a dit à propos de ses rapports avec les locataires[1] de son immeuble: «C'est très simple: on ne s'adresse la parole dans l'ascenseur que[2] s'il tombe des cordes[3] «*Quel temps!*» ou si le soleil est radieux «*Quel temps!*»…

—Mais… le reste du temps… qu'est-ce qu'il se passe?
—Rien.»

Très impressionné par le coup de l'ascenseur, j'ai voulu, pour en avoir le cœur net[4], obtenir confirmation de M. Taupin. Il ne me l'a pas donnée, il est allé beaucoup plus loin:

[1] locataires *tenants*
[2] ne s'adresse la parole… que *only talk to each other*
[3] il tombe des cordes *it's pouring rain*
[4] en avoir le cœur net *to be sure*

LEVELING
C: Reading

«Vous ne le croirez pas, mon cher Major, mais moi qui vis depuis trente-deux ans dans le même immeuble, je mourrai[5], vous m'entendez, je mourrai, ou mon voisin de palier[6] le fera à ma place… sans que nous ne nous soyons jamais adressé la parole! On se salue, naturellement… Un petit coup de chapeau, et c'est fini. Chacun chez soi!

—Vous êtes fâchés?
—Absolument pas, c'est comme ça.
—Mais voyons… Vous habitez bien au cinquième?
—Oui.
—Alors, si vous prenez l'ascenseur en même temps?
—Eh bien! Nous montons… mais on ne se parle pas. S'il m'a fait entrer avant lui, je le laisserai sortir avant moi; en attendant, et on attend beaucoup car[7] cet ascenseur n'en finit pas de vous laisser en tête-à-tête, on joue avec ses clés. On regarde en l'air. On regarde par terre. On regarde sa montre. On fait semblant[8] de lire pour la dix-millième fois les *Instructions pour la manœuvre. Éloigner les enfants de la paroi lisse*[9]. On rêve de paroi lisse et d'enfance éloignée. On tripote[10] son chapeau. On le fait tourner. On soupire[11]. On regarde le bout de ses chaussures. On jette un coup d'œil[12] sur le journal—sans le lire, parce que ça, vraiment, ça ne serait pas poli. Mais on ne se parle pas.

—Mais le temps… M. Requillard m'a dit que tout de même s'il fait très, très mauvais…

—Eh bien… il a de la chance! Moi, j'ai dit une fois «Il fait une de ces chaleurs!» Mon voisin m'a répondu: «Pffh!» Un autre jour, j'ai dit: «Il fait un de ces froids!» Il m'a répondu «Ssss!» Depuis, je ne dis plus rien.»

Et c'est ainsi que, d'étage en étage, M. Taupin et son voisin monteront un jour au Ciel pour y goûter[13] la paix du silence éternel.

[5] je mourrai *I'll die*
[6] de palier *same floor*
[7] car *because*
[8] fait semblant *pretend*
[9] paroi lisse *shaft*
[10] tripote *fiddle with*
[11] soupire *sigh*
[12] coup d'œil *glance*
[13] goûter *taste, enjoy*

Vous avez compris?

A Dans l'ascenseur Répondez.

1. Quand est-ce qu'on adresse la parole à quelqu'un dans l'ascenseur en France?
2. Le reste du temps, qu'est-ce qu'on fait?
3. Depuis combien de temps M. Taupin habite-t-il dans le même immeuble?
4. Il parle à son voisin de palier dans l'ascenseur?
5. Son voisin lui a parlé quand M. Taupin a fait une remarque sur le temps?

B Et vous? Dites ce que vous faites quand vous prenez l'ascenseur avec d'autres personnes.

LE SAVOIR-VIVRE

C'est à vous

Use what you have learned

 Recycling

These activities allow students to use the vocabulary and structure from this chapter in completely open-ended, real-life situations.

Presentation

Encourage students to say as much as possible when they do these activities. Tell them not to be afraid to make mistakes, since the goal of these activities is real-life communication. If someone in the group makes an error, allow the others to politely correct him or her. Let students choose the activities they would like to do.

You may wish to separate students into pairs or groups. Encourage students to elaborate on the basic theme and to be creative. They may use props, pictures, or posters if they wish.

LEVELING

These activities encompass all three levels. All students will be able to do them at a sophistication level commensurate with their ability in French. Some students will be able to speak for several minutes, and others may be able to give just a few sentences. This is to be expected when students are functioning completely on their own generating their own language to the best of their ability.

C'est à vous

Use what you have learned

 Comparaisons
✔ Compare etiquette in France and the United States

Travaillez avec un(e) camarade. Comparez les règles de politesse françaises et les règles de politesse américaines.

 Le savoir-vivre aux États-Unis
✔ Talk about social etiquette

Vous parlez à Flore et Romain, deux amis français. Flore et Romain vont faire un voyage aux États-Unis. Ils vous demandent de leur dire ce qu'ils doivent savoir pour ne pas faire de faux pas quand ils seront aux États-Unis.

 Tenez-vous bien!
✔ Express opinions

Travaillez avec un(e) camarade. Faites une liste de ce qu'il est bon, important ou nécessaire que vous fassiez tous les jours. Faites un classement par ordre d'importance.

428 ✦ quatre cent vingt-huit   CHAPITRE 13

ANSWERS TO C'est à vous

 Answers will vary but students may discuss:
- handshake
- kissing on the cheek
- greetings
- table manners
- **tu** vs. **vous**
- use of titles with or without names

 Answers will vary but may include:
En France, on se serre la main plus souvent qu'aux États-Unis. Aux États-Unis, on ne s'embrasse pas sur les joues. Quand on dit *Mr.* ou *Mrs.* on donne aussi le nom de famille de la personne. Aux États-Unis on peut dire tout simplement *hi* à une personne du même âge.

 Answers will vary but the verb will be in the subjunctive.

CHAPITRE 13

4 Le savoir-vivre en France
✓ **Describe French customs**

Imaginez que vous écrivez un petit livre sur le savoir-vivre en France. Faites une liste de ce qu'on doit faire pour être poli. Ensuite faites une liste de ce qu'on ne doit pas faire.

Writing Strategy

Writing an anecdote An anecdote is a story about a lesson learned through experience. Good anecdotes are short, grab the reader's interest, and make a valid point about life. They include the following narrative elements: characters, setting, problem or conflict, and resolution.

5 À Rome il faut vivre comme les Romains.

Social customs vary from country to country. Sometimes while visiting another country you inadvertently do something humorous or embarrassing because you aren't familiar with the culture. Imagine that you are in a French-speaking country and such a situation occurs. Describe the characters and setting, what happened, and what you learned from the situation. Remember that anecdotes are short and interesting.

LE SAVOIR-VIVRE   quatre cent vingt-neuf ❖ 429

Assessment

Resource Manager

Communication Transparencies C 13
Quizzes, pages 67–71
Tests, pages 211–226
ExamView® Pro
Situation Cards
Performance Assessment, Task 13
Marathon mental Videoquiz

Assessment

This is a pre-test for students to take before you administer the chapter test. Answer sheets for students to do these pages are provided in your transparency binder. Note that each section is cross-referenced so students can easily find the material they have to review in case they made errors. You may wish to collect these assessments and correct them yourself or you may prefer to have the students correct themselves in class. You can go over the answers orally or project them on the overhead, using your Assessment Answers transparencies.

Assessment

##

1 Identifiez.

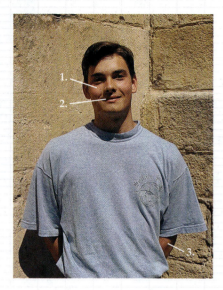

To review Mots 1, turn to pages 406–407.

2 Donnez un synonyme.

    4. poli
    5. dire «tu» à quelqu'un

To review Mots 2, turn to pages 410–411.

3 Donnez quatre émotions.

    6. être ____
    7. être ____
    8. être ____
    9. être ____

4 Complétez.

    10–11. —Je suis ____ de faire votre connaissance.
           —Moi ____.

430 quatre cent trente   CHAPITRE 13

ANSWERS TO Assessment

1
1. la joue
2. la lèvre (la bouche)
3. le coude

2
4. bien élevé
5. tutoyer

3 *Answers will vary but may include:*
6. triste
7. content
8. furieux
9. étonné

4
10. enchanté(e)
11. de même

Structure

5 **Complétez.**

12. Il est rare qu'elle _____ désagréable. (être)
13. Il vaut mieux que tu le _____ toi-même. (faire)
14. Il est important que vous leur _____. (écrire)
15. Il est possible qu'il te le _____. (dire)
16. Il est nécessaire que vous le _____. (trouver)
17. Il est impossible que nous _____ à l'heure. (arriver)

6 **Complétez.**

18. Je suis triste qu'ils ne _____ pas. (venir)
19. Il ne veut pas que vous le _____. (savoir)
20. J'ai peur qu'il ne _____ pas. (comprendre)
21. Ils regrettent que tu ne _____ pas y assister. (pouvoir)
22. Je suis content qu'il _____. (payer)

Culture

7 **C'est qui? Les Français ou les Américains?**

23. Ils s'embrassent souvent sur les joues pour se dire bonjour.
24. Les jeunes ne se serrent presque jamais la main quand ils se rencontrent.
25. On appelle une personne par son prénom uniquement si on connaît bien cette personne.

To review expressing opinions, turn to page 414.

To review these verbs in the subjunctive, turn to page 416.

To review this cultural information, turn to pages 422–423.

Ils se disent «au revoir».

LE SAVOIR-VIVRE

On parle super bien!

This unique page gives students the opportunity to speak freely and say whatever they can, using the vocabulary and structures they have learned in the chapter. The illustration serves to remind students of precisely what they know how to say in French. There are no activities that students do not have the ability to describe or talk about in French. The art not only depicts the vocabulary and content of this chapter, but also reinforces what they learned in previous chapters.

You may wish to use this page in many ways. Some possibilities are to have students do the following:

1. Look at the illustration and identify items by giving the correct French words.
2. Make up sentences about what they see in the illustration.
3. Make up questions about the illustration. They can call on another class member to respond if you do this as a class activity, or you may prefer to allow students to work in small groups. This activity is extremely beneficial because it enables students to actively use interrogative words.
4. Answer questions you ask them about the illustration.
5. Work in pairs and make up a conversation based on the illustration.
6. Look at the illustration and give a complete oral review of what they see.
7. Look at the illustration and write a paragraph (or essay) about it.

You can also use this page as an assessment or testing tool, taking into account individual differences by having students go from simple to quite complicated tasks. The assessment can be either oral or written. You may wish to use the rubrics provided on pages T20–T21 as you give students the following directions.

On parle super bien!

Tell all you can about this illustration.

1. Identify the topic or situation of the illustration.
2. Give the French words for as many items as you can.
3. Think of as many sentences as you can to describe the illustration.
4. Go over your sentences and put them in the best sequencing to give a coherent story based on the illustration.

Vocabulaire

Identifying more parts of the body

la joue	le doigt	le poignet
la bouche	le pouce	l'avant-bras (m.)
la lèvre	la main	le coude

Talking about polite and rude behavior

mal élevé(e),	bruyant(e)	bousculer
malpoli(e)	le bruit	resquiller
bien élevé(e), poli(e)		

Talking about table manners

la bouche	une serviette	s'essuyer
fermée	se tenir à table	faire du bruit
ouverte	manger	
pleine		

Talking about going out with friends

le tutoiement	se serrer la main
se tutoyer	s'embrasser
avoir rendez-vous	partager les frais
se retrouver	

Describing some emotions

une émotion	désolé(e)
étonné(e)	regretter
content(e)	avoir peur
furieux(se)	avoir l'air
triste	

Introducing people to each other

présenter	Je suis enchanté(e)
faire la connaissance de	Moi de même.

Other useful words and expressions

il vaut mieux

How well do you know your vocabulary?
Choose five emotions from the list. Write a sentence for each one, describing your reaction to an event or situation—for example, meeting someone new, an evening out with friends, or a situation where someone behaved rudely.

VIDÉOTOUR

Épisode 13
In this video episode, Manu and "Emmanuel" claim to be experts on etiquette. See page 512 for more information.

LE SAVOIR-VIVRE

Planning for Chapter 14

SCOPE AND SEQUENCE, PAGES 434–463

Topics
- Careers and professions
- Applying for a job

Functions
- How to express doubt
- How to express wishes about yourself and others
- How to express certainty and uncertainty

National Standards
- Communication Standard 1.1 pages 438, 439, 442, 443, 445, 446, 447, 448, 451, 458
- Communication Standard 1.2 pages 438, 439, 442, 443, 445, 446, 447, 448, 449, 450, 453, 454, 455, 457
- Communication Standard 1.3 pages 443, 446, 447, 448, 451, 458, 459
- Connections Standard 3.1 pages 456–457
- Communities Standard 5.1 pages 452–453, 454

Culture
- A young man named Bobby
- French and your career
- Job announcements
- **Reflets de l'Europe francophone**

Structure
- The subjunctive with expressions of doubt
- The infinitive or the subjunctive
- The subjunctive in relative clauses

PACING AND PRIORITIES

The chapter content is color coded below to assist you in planning.

■ required   ■ recommended   ■ optional

Vocabulaire *(required)* Days 1–4
- ■ Mots 1
  - Un lieu de travail
  - Des professions
  - Des métiers
- ■ Mots 2
  - Au bureau de placement
  - On travaille.

Structure *(required)* Days 5–7
- ■ Le subjonctif après les expressions de doute
- ■ L'infinitif ou le subjonctif
- ■ Le subjonctif dans les propositions relatives

Conversation *(required)*
- ■ Au bureau de placement

Lectures culturelles
- ■ Un jeune homme appelé Bobby *(recommended)*
- ■ Le français et votre carrière *(optional)*
- ■ Petites annonces *(optional)*

Connexions *(optional)*
- ■ L'économie

■ **C'est à vous** *(recommended)*

■ **Assessment** *(recommended)*

■ **On parle super bien!** *(optional)*

RESOURCE GUIDE

SECTION	PAGES	SECTION RESOURCES
Vocabulaire *Mots 1*		
Un lieu de travail	436	Vocabulary Transparencies 14.2–14.3
Des professions	436–437	Audio CD 8
Des métiers	437–439	Audio Activities TE, pages 154–156
		Workbook, pages 155–156
		Quiz 1, page 73
		ExamView® Pro
Vocabulaire *Mots 2*		
Au bureau de placement	440	Vocabulary Transparencies 14.4–14.5
On travaille.	441–443	Audio CD 8
		Audio Activities TE, pages 156–158
		Workbook, pages 156–157
		Quiz 2, page 74
		ExamView® Pro
Structure		
Le subjonctif après les expressions de doute	444–446	Audio CD 8
L'infinitif ou le subjonctif	447–448	Audio Activities TE, pages 158–159
Le subjonctif dans les propositions relatives	448–449	Workbook, pages 158–160
		Quizzes 3–5, pages 75–77
		ExamView® Pro
Conversation		
Au bureau de placement	450–451	Audio CD 8
		Audio Activities TE, pages 160–161
		Interactive CD-ROM
Lectures culturelles		
Un jeune homme appelé Bobby	452–453	Audio CD 8
Le français et votre carrière	454	Audio Activities TE, pages 161–162
Petites annonces	455	Tests, pages 229, 234
Connexions		
L'économie	456–457	Tests, page 235
C'est à vous		
	458–459	**Bon voyage!** Video, Episode 14
		Video Activities, Chapter 14
		French Online Activities
		french.glencoe.com
Assessment		
	460–461	Communication Transparency C 14
		Quizzes 1–5, pages 73–77
		Performance Assessment, Task 14
		Tests, pages 227–242
		ExamView® Pro
		Situation Cards, Chapter 14
		Marathon mental Videoquiz

Using Your Resources for Chapter 14

Transparencies

Bellringer 14.1–14.7

Vocabulary 14.1–14.5

Communication C 14

Workbook

Vocabulary, pages 155–157

Structure, pages 158–160

Enrichment, pages 161–164

Audio Activities

Vocabulary, pages 154–158

Structure, pages 158–159

Conversation, pages 160–161

Cultural Reading, pages 161–162

Additional Practice, pages 162–165

Assessment

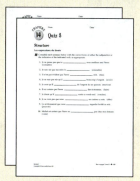
Vocabulary and Structure Quizzes, pages 73–77

Chapter Tests, pages 227–242

Situation Cards, Chapter 14

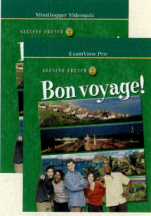
MindJogger Videoquiz, ExamView® Pro, Chapter 14

Timesaving Teacher Tools

TeacherWorks™

TeacherWorks™ is your all-in-one teacher resource center. Personalize lesson plans, access resources from the Teacher Wraparound Edition, connect to the Internet, or make a to-do list. These are only a few of the many features that can assist you in the planning and organizing of your lessons.

Includes:

- A calendar feature
- Access to all program blackline masters
- Standards correlations and more

ExamView® Pro

Test Bank software for Macintosh and Windows makes creating, editing, customizing, and printing tests quick and easy.

Technology Resources

In the Chapter 14 Internet activity, you will have a chance to learn more about the Francophone world. Visit **french.glencoe.com**.

On the Interactive Conversation CD-ROM, students can listen to and take part in a recorded version of the conversation in Chapter 14.

See the National Geographic Teacher's Corner on pages 138–139, 244–245, 372–373, 472–473 for reference to additional technology resources.

Bon voyage! Video and Video Activities, Chapter 14

Help your students prepare for the chapter test by playing the **Marathon mental** Videoquiz game show. Teams will compete against each other to review chapter vocabulary and structure and sharpen listening comprehension skills.

CHAPITRE 14

Preview

In this chapter, students will learn to talk about professions, occupations, and looking for work, including interviewing for a position. They will also learn to use the subjunctive after expressions of doubt and in relative clauses.

Communication
In Chapter 14, students will communicate in spoken and written French on the following topics:
- Professions and occupations
- Looking for work
- Interviewing for a job

Students will obtain and provide information about these topics, express doubt, and engage in conversations that would typically take place when discussing their future plans as they fulfill the chapter objectives listed on this page.

LEVELING

The activities, conversations, and readings within each chapter are marked according to level of difficulty. **E** indicates easy. **A** indicates average. **C** indicates challenging. Some activities cover a range of difficulty. The leveling indicators will help you individualize instruction to best meet your students' needs.

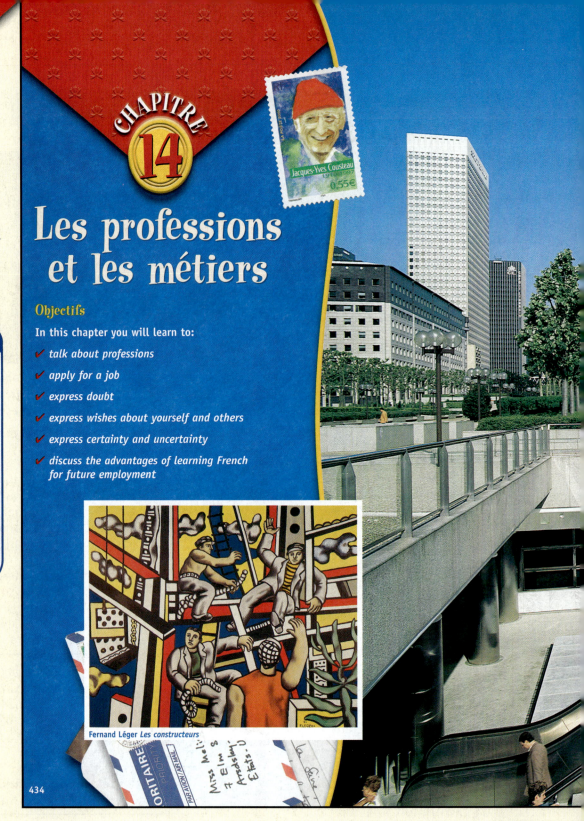

CHAPITRE 14

Les professions et les métiers

Objectifs
In this chapter you will learn to:
✓ talk about professions
✓ apply for a job
✓ express doubt
✓ express wishes about yourself and others
✓ express certainty and uncertainty
✓ discuss the advantages of learning French for future employment

Fernand Léger *Les constructeurs*

CHAPITRE 14

 Spotlight on Culture

Photograph This photo of the escalator from the **métro** was taken in the **quartier de La Défense**, the modern business district just west of Paris. The avenue leading to it is a continuation of the Champs-Élysées.

Painting Fernand Léger (1881–1955) worked as a draftsman in an architectural firm in Caen before dedicating himself to art. In the very early part of the twentieth century, he met Modigliani, Delaunay, Apollinaire, and Max Jacob, and he took part in the expositions of the Cubists. After World War I, he began to paint mechanical motifs. The Fernand-Léger museum was opened in 1960 in Biot, France. It is this museum that houses the painting seen here, **Les constructeurs**.

 Recycling

Have students describe the photo to recycle city and metro vocabulary.

 National Standards

Communities
Have students prepare their **curriculum vitæ** in French to pursue summer or future employment with an American company that does business in the French-speaking world. They might like to use the French C.V. on page 440 as a model.

Vocabulaire — Mots 1

1 Preparation

Resource Manager

Vocabulary Transparencies
  14.2–14.3
Audio Activities TE, pages 154–156
Audio CD 8
Workbook, pages 155–156
Quiz 1, page 73
ExamView® Pro

Bellringer Review

Use BRR Transparency 14.1 or write the following on the board.
Make a list of the trades and professions you have already learned in French.

2 Presentation

Step 1 Have students close their books. Use Vocabulary Transparencies 14.2–14.3 to present **Mots 1.** Have students repeat the words, phrases, and sentences after you or Audio CD 8.

Step 2 Have students open their books and read pages 436–437.

Step 3 Call on students to point to items on the transparencies and name the professions.

Note: To clarify the meaning of **cadre,** explain that it is a salaried employee at the managerial level—from lower management to upper management: **un cadre inférieur, un cadre moyen, un cadre supérieur.** A feminine form for the word does not exist: one would say **une femme cadre.**
   Chef de service also does not have a feminine form.

Vocabulaire — Mots 1

Un lieu de travail

une informaticienne

un bureau
une secrétaire = une assistante administrative
un chef de service

un comptable

Elle est cadre. Elle dirige des employés. C'est une femme d'affaires.

Des professions

un ingénieur

un cinéaste

un écrivain

une architecte

une journaliste

436 ✤ quatre cent trente-six   CHAPITRE 14

Reaching All Students

Kinesthetic Learners
Have students pantomime the following.
  Vous êtes informaticien(ne). Tapez sur votre ordinateur.
  Vous êtes cinéaste. Tournez un film.
  Vous êtes écrivain. Écrivez quelque chose.
  Vous êtes électricien(ne). Réparez une lampe.
  Vous êtes menuisier. Faites un placard.

LEVELING
A: Vocabulary

Vocabulaire
Mots 1

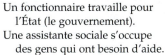

une assistante sociale — un fonctionnaire

un commerçant — un magasin

Un fonctionnaire travaille pour l'État (le gouvernement).
Une assistante sociale s'occupe des gens qui ont besoin d'aide.

un tribunal — un juge — une avocate

Des métiers

un électricien — un menuisier — un plombier — un peintre (en bâtiment)

Un électricien répare les lampes.
Un peintre peint des murs.
Un plombier répare les tuyaux.
Un menuisier fait des meubles et des placards.

LES PROFESSIONS ET LES MÉTIERS   quatre cent trente-sept ❧ 437

Vocabulaire

Quel est le mot?

1 **Les lieux de travail** Identifiez d'après les dessins.

1. C'est une école ou un bureau?

2. C'est un bureau ou une usine?

3. C'est une mairie ou une église?

4. C'est un hôpital ou une pharmacie?

5. C'est un supermarché ou un magasin?

6. C'est un tribunal ou une ferme?

2 **Qui fait ce travail?** Trouvez les mots qui correspondent.

1. aide un chirurgien
2. répare les lampes
3. fait le programme d'un ordinateur
4. défend les criminels au tribunal
5. vend des marchandises
6. tient les livres de comptes
7. répare les éviers, les lavabos, les toilettes
8. fait des placards, des tables, des chaises
9. dirige des employés
10. crée des routes, des bâtiments, etc.

a. un(e) comptable
b. un ingénieur
c. un(e) vendeur(se)
d. un cadre
e. un(e) avocat(e)
f. un(e) informaticien(ne)
g. un(e) infirmier(ère)
h. un(e) électricien(ne)
i. un plombier
j. un menuisier

438 *quatre cent trente-huit*

CHAPITRE 14

Vocabulaire

3 **Qui travaille où?** Répondez. Utilisez toutes les professions ou métiers que vous connaissez.

1. Qui écrit des livres?
2. Qui fait des films?
3. Qui écrit des articles pour un journal?
4. Qui dessine les bâtiments?
5. Qui peint les bâtiments?
6. Qui travaille dans une mairie?
7. Qui travaille dans un hôpital?
8. Qui travaille dans un bureau?
9. Qui travaille dans un tribunal?
10. Qui travaille dans une pharmacie?
11. Qui travaille dans un hôtel?
12. Qui travaille dans un théâtre?
13. Qui travaille dans un magasin?
14. Qui travaille dans une station-service?

Des architectes

4 **Une profession** Travaillez avec un(e) camarade. Parlez des métiers ou professions qui vous intéressent. Expliquez pourquoi.

Je pense à…

Pensez à une profession ou à un métier. Votre camarade doit vous poser au maximum cinq questions pour essayer de deviner la profession à laquelle vous pensez. Ensuite changez de rôle.

For more practice using words from *Mots 1*, do Activity 20 on page H21 at the end of this book.

Des avocats

LES PROFESSIONS ET LES MÉTIERS

quatre cent trente-neuf ❖ 439

Vocabulaire Mots 2

1 Preparation

Resource Manager

Vocabulary Transparencies
14.4–14.5
Audio Activities TE, pages 156–158
Audio CD 8
Workbook, pages 156–157
Quiz 2, page 74
ExamView® Pro

Bellringer Review

Use BRR Transparency 14.2 or write the following on the board. Complete the sentences about this past school year.
1. Je suis content(e) que…
2. Je regrette que…
3. Je suis triste que…
4. Je suis étonné(e) que…

2 Presentation

Step 1 Show Vocabulary Transparencies 14.4–14.5. Have students close their books and repeat the words after you or Audio CD 8 as you point to the appropriate illustration on the transparency.

Step 2 Ask questions such as: **La femme cherche du travail? Elle a donné son curriculum vitæ au D.R.H.? Elle a vu une petite annonce dans le journal? C'était pour quel poste?**, etc.

Vocabulaire Mots 2

Au bureau de placement

une carrière

une petite annonce

un curriculum vitæ (un C.V.)

un entretien

le directeur des ressources humaines (le D.R.H.)

une candidate

Mlle Leblanc est candidate à un poste.
Elle pose sa candidature.
Elle a un entretien avec le D.R.H.

Elle est libre immédiatement.
Elle peut commencer à travailler demain.

About the French Language

In the ad on this page, **déclarations sociales** refers to documents dealing with insurance, social security, pension, etc.

Vocabulaire
Mots 2

On travaille.

une entreprise
une multinationale
une grosse société

un employeur
un salaire
un stagiaire
une employée

Philippe fait un stage.
Un stagiaire est une personne qui travaille pour avoir de l'expérience.

Elle travaille à plein temps (35 heures par semaine).
Elle travaille pour une grosse société.
Une grosse société a beaucoup d'employés.

Il travaille à mi-temps (20 heures par semaine).

être à son compte

Elle ne travaille pas pour une entreprise.
Elle est à son compte.

Il est au chômage. Il est chômeur. Il n'a pas de travail.
Il y a chômage quand il n'y a pas d'emplois.

LES PROFESSIONS ET LES MÉTIERS

quatre cent quarante et un ❖ 441

Vocabulaire

3 Practice

Quel est le mot?

6 You may wish to have a student retell the story in his or her own words.

7 This activity is to be done with books open. **Expansion:** You may wish to have students use the words in the first column in original sentences.

Class Motivator

Jeu Use Activity 2, page 438, Activity 3, page 439, and Activity 7, page 442 to play a game. Divide the class into two teams. Read the definitions and have two players at a time compete to give the word first. Keep score and award a prize to the winning team!

Vocabulaire

Quel est le mot?

6 Historiette Elle cherche du travail.
Répondez d'après les indications.

1. Mme Robert cherche du travail? (oui)
2. Qu'est-ce qu'elle lit? (une annonce dans le journal)
3. Quelle compagnie cherche des candidats? (France Télécom)
4. C'est une grosse société ou une multinationale? (une grosse société)
5. Que fait Mme Robert? (poser sa candidature)
6. Qu'est-ce qu'elle donne à la directrice des ressources humaines? (son curriculum vitæ)
7. Elle a des références? (bien sûr)
8. Mme Robert est diplômée en quoi? (informatique)
9. Qu'est-ce qu'elle va avoir? (un entretien)
10. Quand est-ce qu'elle peut commencer à travailler? (tout de suite)

Une femme d'affaires

7 Définitions Trouvez les mots qui correspondent.

1. les petites annonces
2. un poste
3. être à son compte
4. être libre immédiatement
5. travailler à plein temps
6. être au chômage
7. travailler à mi-temps
8. un bureau de placement
9. une entreprise
10. un(e) employé(e)
11. une carrière

a. travailler environ 20 heures par semaine
b. un emploi
c. être sans travail
d. ce qu'on lit dans le journal quand on cherche du travail
e. une société
f. le lieu où on va quand on cherche du travail
g. pouvoir commencer à travailler tout de suite
h. travailler pour soi
i. quelqu'un qui travaille pour un employeur
j. travailler 35 heures par semaine
k. la profession qu'on choisit pour la vie

ANSWERS TO Quel est le mot?

6
1. Oui, elle cherche du travail.
2. Elle lit une annonce dans le journal.
3. France Télécom cherche des candidats.
4. C'est une grosse société.
5. Mme Robert pose sa candidature.
6. Elle lui donne son curriculum vitæ.
7. Bien sûr qu'elle a des références.
8. Mme Robert est diplômée en informatique.
9. Elle va avoir un entretien.
10. Elle peut commencer à travailler tout de suite.

7
1. d   7. a
2. b   8. f
3. h   9. e
4. g   10. i
5. j   11. k
6. c

8 Mon travail Donnez des réponses personnelles.
1. Tu travailles ou tu aimerais travailler? Où?
2. À plein temps ou à mi-temps?
3. Tu as ou tu aimerais avoir un bon salaire?
4. Qu'est-ce que tu fais ou ferais de ton argent?
5. Tu aimerais faire un stage pour avoir de l'expérience? Où?

 9 Un entretien Vous êtes le/la D.R.H. d'une grosse société. Votre camarade veut faire un stage dans votre société. Il/Elle vient pour un entretien. Vous lui posez des questions sur ses études, son expérience, ses intérêts, ses talents. Ensuite changez de rôle.

Au bureau

Un entretien

Structure

1 Preparation

Resource Manager
Audio Activities TE, pages 158–159
Audio CD 8
Workbook, pages 158–160
Quizzes 3–5, pages 75–77
ExamView® Pro

Bellringer Review
Use BRR Transparency 14.3 or write the following on the board.
Put the following conversation in logical order.
Mlle Chénier, je vous présente M. Ledoux.
Moi de même, mademoiselle.
M. Ledoux, vous connaissez Mlle Chénier?
Je suis heureuse de faire votre connaissance, monsieur.
Non, mais je voudrais bien faire sa connaissance.

2 Presentation

Le subjonctif après les expressions de doute

Step 1 Have students read the model sentences aloud.

Step 2 You may wish to explain to students that the future indicative is often used after expressions of belief or certainty.

Structure

Le subjonctif après les expressions de doute
Expressing doubt

1. In French, any verb or expression that implies doubt, uncertainty, or disbelief about present and future actions is followed by the present subjunctive.

   Je doute
   Je ne pense pas
   Je ne crois pas
   Je ne suis pas sûr(e)
   Je ne suis pas certain(e)   } qu'ils **soient** là.
   Ça m'étonnerait
   Il n'est pas évident
   Il n'est pas sûr
   Il n'est pas certain
   Il est peu probable

L'université McGill à Montréal

2. Note that many expressions of uncertainty or disbelief are actually expressions of certainty or belief in the negative. You use the indicative with expressions of certainty or belief. Compare the following pairs of sentences.

Certainty → Indicative	Uncertainty → Subjunctive
Elle est sûre qu'il **aura** un travail.	Elle n'est pas sûre qu'il **ait** un travail.
Elles croient qu'il **est** ingénieur.	Elles ne croient pas qu'il **soit** ingénieur.
Il est certain qu'il **fera** beau.	Il n'est pas certain qu'il **fasse** beau.

444   quatre cent quarante-quatre   CHAPITRE 14

Learning from Photos
(page 444) McGill University in Montreal is considered to be the finest English-language university in Canada. A wealthy Scottish fur trader named James McGill gave the money and the land to establish the university, which opened its doors in 1828. Today there are approximately 18,000 students in the undergraduate school.

Comment dit-on?

10 **Historiette Ça m'étonnerait.** Répondez selon le modèle.

— Il faut que Juliette lise les petites annonces.
— Ça m'étonnerait que Juliette lise les petites annonces.

1. Il faut que Juliette fasse un stage.
2. Il faut que Juliette envoie son C.V.
3. Il faut que Juliette écrive une lettre.
4. Il faut que Juliette ait un entretien.
5. Il faut que Juliette ait un travail.
6. Il faut que Juliette veuille travailler.

11 **Tu crois?** Suivez le modèle.

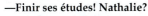

—Finir ses études! Nathalie?
—Oui, je crois qu'elle finira ses études. J'en suis certain(e).

1. Aller à l'université! Paul?
2. Recevoir un diplôme! Annette?
3. Travailler dans une grosse société! Julie?
4. Gagner beaucoup d'argent! Alexandre?
5. Bien réussir! Stéphane?
6. Voyager! Mélanie?

L'université de Yaoundé au Cameroun

Un amphithéâtre à la Sorbonne

LES PROFESSIONS ET LES MÉTIERS

Structure

3 Practice (continued)

Comment dit-on?

14 You may wish to use this activity as the basis for a classwide survey. Have students compile this sort of information about their classmates and share the results with the class.

♻ Recycling

Have students say everything they can about the marriage announcement on page 446.

LEVELING

E: Activities 14, 15
A: Activities 12, 13, 14, 16

Structure

```
mariages

M. et Mme
Romain KOSINSKI
M. et Mme
Hubert de LATAILLADE

sont heureux de vous faire part
du mariage de leurs enfants

Hélène et Jean

qui sera célébré le samedi
3 juin, à 16 h 30, en l'église de
Saint-Lons-les-Mines (Landes).
```

13 **Certain ou pas certain?**
Répondez d'après les indications.
1. Paul va aller à l'université? (Je crois)
2. Il finira ses études? (Il est probable)
3. Il aimera tous ses cours? (Je ne suis pas sûr)
4. Il sera avocat? (Ça m'étonnerait)
5. Il deviendra médecin? (Il est peu probable)
6. Il sera ingénieur? (Je crois)

14 **Mon avenir** Travaillez avec un(e) camarade. Parlez de ce qui vous arrivera probablement plus tard—votre profession, votre famille, etc. Parlez aussi de ce qui ne vous arrivera certainement pas. Vous pouvez utiliser les mots suivants.

| je crois que | il est probable que |
| je ne crois pas que | ça m'étonnerait que |

12 **Historiette** **Un mariage** Répondez en utilisant **Je crois que** ou **Je ne crois pas que**.
1. Ton meilleur ami ou ta meilleure amie va bientôt se marier?
2. Il/Elle aura deux cérémonies de mariage?
3. Tu seras son garçon d'honneur/sa demoiselle d'honneur?
4. La réception aura lieu dans un grand hôtel?
5. Tu lui feras un très beau cadeau?

Un ingénieur

446 quatre cent quarante-six

CHAPITRE 14

Answers to Comment dit-on?

12 Answers will vary but may include:
1. Je ne crois pas que mon meilleur ami se marie bientôt.
2. Je ne crois pas qu'il ait deux cérémonies de mariage.
3. Je ne crois pas que je sois son garçon d'honneur.
4. Je ne crois pas que la réception ait lieu dans un grand hôtel.
5. Je ne crois pas que je lui fasse un très beau cadeau.

If students answer with je crois que, the verb in the dependent clause will be in the future: Je crois que mon meilleur ami se mariera bientôt.

13
1. Je crois que Paul va aller à l'université.
2. Il est probable qu'il finira ses études.
3. Je ne suis pas sûr(e) qu'il aime tous ses cours.
4. Ça m'étonnerait qu'il soit avocat.
5. Il est peu probable qu'il devienne médecin.
6. Je crois qu'il sera ingénieur.

L'infinitif ou le subjonctif
Expressing wishes about oneself and others

You use the subjunctive when the subject of the second clause and the subject of the main clause are not the same. You use the infinitive when there is only one subject. Compare the following.

Different subjects	Same subject
J'aimerais que tu sois informaticien.	J'aimerais être informaticien.
Il voudrait que vous réussissiez dans la vie.	Il voudrait réussir dans la vie.

Comment dit-on?

15 **La même personne ou quelqu'un d'autre?**
Inventez des réponses.

1. Maman veut dormir un peu?
2. Elle veut que tu dormes?
3. Ton frère aime mieux sortir seul?
4. Ton frère aime mieux que tu sortes avec lui?
5. Thomas veut faire ses devoirs?
6. Il veut que tu lui fasses ses devoirs?
7. Florence veut acheter un dictionnaire ou elle veut que tu l'achètes?
8. Tu veux venir avec nous ou tu veux que Christine vienne à ta place?

Le rallye Paris-Dakar

16 **Ils le veulent.**
Répondez d'après le modèle.

—Ils veulent que tu y ailles.
—Oui, je sais. Et je veux y aller.

1. Ils veulent que tu fasses le voyage.
2. Ils veulent que tu viennes avec eux.
3. Ils veulent que tu conduises.
4. Ils veulent que tu prennes ta voiture.
5. Ils veulent que tu achètes une carte.
6. Ils veulent que tu partes immédiatement.

Structure

3 Practice (continued)

Comment dit-on?

 17 Expansion: Have students work in pairs and interview each other. Then have each partner choose what would be the best occupation for the other, based on the answers given.

 Recycling

Have students imagine the conversation between the men in the photo on page 448.

1 Preparation

Bellringer Review

Use BRR Transparency 14.5 or write the following on the board.
You are organizing a party for your French class. Complete the following sentences with instructions to your assistants.
1. Il est nécessaire que…
2. Il est important que…
3. Il vaut mieux que…
4. Il est possible que…

2 Presentation

Le subjonctif dans les propositions relatives

Step 1 Have students read the model sentences aloud.

Structure

 17 Vous préférez… ? Dites si vous préférez…
1. avoir un entretien ou envoyer votre C.V.
2. travailler pour une grosse société ou être à votre compte
3. travailler à mi-temps ou à plein temps
4. être stagiaire ou être employé(e)
5. être informaticien(ne) ou avocat(e)
6. travailler ou être au chômage
7. rester tout le temps au bureau ou faire des voyages d'affaires de temps en temps

 18 Mon week-end Travaillez avec un(e) camarade. Parlez de ce que vous voulez faire ce week-end. Ensuite, parlez de ce que vos parents respectifs veulent que vous fassiez.

Deux hommes d'affaires

Le subjonctif dans les propositions relatives
Expressing certainty and uncertainty

1. You know that clauses introduced by the relative pronouns **qui** and **que** describe people or things.

   > Nous avons un secrétaire qui parle très bien le français.
   > Nous avons un chef que nous aimons beaucoup.

2. You will sometimes use the subjunctive in a relative clause. The subjunctive indicates uncertainty—it is not certain that you will be able to find the person or thing in question. However, if there is no doubt, you use the indicative in the relative clause. Compare the following.

Certainty → Indicative	Uncertainty → Subjunctive
Elle a un ami qui **sait** conduire.	Elle cherche quelqu'un qui **sache** conduire.
J'ai un métier qui **est** intéressant.	Je voudrais un métier qui **soit** intéressant.

ANSWERS TO Comment dit-on?

 17 Answers will vary but may include:
1. Je préfère avoir un entretien.
2. Je préfère être à mon compte.
3. Je préfère travailler à mi-temps.
4. Je préfère être employé(e).
5. Je préfère être informaticien(ne).
6. Je préfère travailler.
7. Je préfère faire des voyages d'affaires de temps en temps.

18 Answers will vary depending upon what individual students want to do this weekend.

Comment dit-on?

19 **Historiette** **On cherche un représentant.** Répondez que oui.

1. La société Matras cherche un représentant?
2. Ils ont un poste qui paie bien?
3. Ils cherchent quelqu'un qui ait de l'expérience en marketing?
4. Ils veulent quelqu'un qui ait voyagé?
5. Ils ont besoin d'une personne qui connaisse des langues?
6. Ils cherchent un candidat qui soit libre immédiatement?

20 **Historiette** **Certaines qualifications** Complétez.

La société Calmant cherche quelqu'un qui __1__ (avoir) de l'expérience, qui __2__ (parler) bien le français et l'anglais et qui __3__ (pouvoir) voyager. Le directeur des ressources humaines m'a dit qu'ils avaient besoin de quelqu'un qui __4__ (être) libre immédiatement. Ils ont eu beaucoup de candidats. Finalement, ils ont trouvé une candidate qui __5__ (avoir) de l'expérience, qui __6__ (vouloir) et qui __7__ (pouvoir) commencer à travailler immédiatement. Malheureusement, elle parle seulement le français et la société continue à chercher quelqu'un qui __8__ (savoir) parler anglais et qui __9__ (connaître) le marché américain.

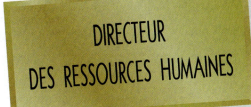

DIRECTEUR DES RESSOURCES HUMAINES

Vous êtes sur le bon chemin. Allez-y!

Conversation

1 Preparation

Resource Manager
Audio Activities TE, pages 160–161
Audio CD 8
CD-ROM

Bellringer Review

Use BRR Transparency 14.6 or write the following on the board. Complete the sentences with the indicative or subjunctive of the verbs in parentheses.

1. Je ne crois pas que nous _____ au Maghreb cette année. (aller)
2. Il est certain que vous y _____ l'année prochaine. (voyager)
3. Je suis sûr(e) que cette région _____ très belle. (être)
4. Ça m'étonnerait que mes parents ne _____ pas la visiter. (vouloir)
5. Mais il n'est pas certain qu'ils _____ assez d'argent. (avoir)

2 Presentation

Step 1 Have students close their books and listen as you read the conversation aloud or play Audio CD 8. Have students listen carefully to the recorded version and pay particular attention to the intonation.

Step 2 Have students open their books and read along with you or Audio CD 8.

Step 3 Call on a pair of volunteers to read the conversation to the class with as much expression as possible.

Conversation

Au bureau de placement

Conseillère: Je trouve votre C.V. très intéressant. Vous cherchez quel genre de travail?
Sandrine: J'aimerais travailler dans une grosse société. Mais… j'aimerais tout de même qu'il y ait des possibilités d'avancement.
Conseillère: Je crois que j'ai un poste qui pourrait vous intéresser. Mais il faut quelqu'un qui sache parler anglais.
Sandrine: Pas de problème. J'ai vécu deux ans à New York.
Conseillère: Parfait. C'est avec une société multinationale américaine, ici à Paris. Mais il faut pouvoir voyager.
Sandrine: Voyager? Pas de problème. J'aime beaucoup ça.
Conseillère: Alors, je vais leur faxer votre C.V. et arranger un entretien.
Sandrine: Merci beaucoup, madame.
Conseillère: Je vous en prie. Et ne vous en faites pas, je suis sûre que tout se passera très bien.

Vous avez compris?

Répondez d'après la conversation.

1. Où est Sandrine?
2. Qu'est-ce qu'elle aimerait faire?
3. Pourquoi Sandrine parle-t-elle anglais?
4. Quel genre de société cherche un(e) candidat(e)?
5. Est-ce qu'il faut voyager?
6. C'est un problème pour Sandrine?
7. Qu'est-ce que la conseillère va faire du C.V. de Sandrine?

Glencoe Technology

CD-ROM
On the CD-ROM, students can watch a dramatization of this conversation. They can then play the role of either one of the characters and record themselves in the conversation.

Answers to Vous avez compris?

1. Sandrine est au bureau de placement.
2. Elle aimerait travailler dans une grosse société.
3. Elle parle anglais parce qu'elle a vécu deux ans à New York.
4. Une société multinationale américaine cherche un(e) candidat(e).
5. Oui, il faut pouvoir voyager.
6. Non, elle aime beaucoup voyager.
7. Elle va le faxer à la société.

Parlons un peu plus

 Un poste idéal Travaillez avec un(e) camarade. Décrivez-lui ce qui serait pour vous un poste idéal. Ensuite changez de rôle.

Ils tournent un film.

 Possibilités de carrières Travaillez avec un(e) camarade. Préparez chacun une liste des choses qui vous intéressent et une liste des cours que vous aimez. Comparez vos listes et voyez si vous avez des intérêts communs. Parlez ensuite des carrières qui vous intéresseraient.

 Un entretien Lisez les petites annonces et choisissez-en une qui vous intéresse. Votre camarade vous accordera un entretien pour ce poste. Préparez ensemble votre conversation et présentez-la à la classe.

RESTAURANT, Nice, 120 couverts, cuisine locale et traditionnelle, recherche chef de cuisine à l'année, libre début août, références éxigées. Envoyer CV + prétentions : 38 Bd Victor Hugo, 06000 Nice.

ÉCOLE DE LANGUES recherche professeur anglais / américain, langue maternelle, large expérience adultes et anglais des affaires. CV : EUROSUD, 208 route de Grenoble, 06200 Nice, 00335799 qui transmettra.

LES PROFESSIONS ET LES MÉTIERS

quatre cent cinquante et un 451

Lectures culturelles

Resource Manager
Audio Activities TE, pages 161–162
Audio CD 8

Bellringer Review
Use BRR Transparency 14.7 or write the following on the board.
List the people you would find working in the following places.
une école, un tribunal, un hôpital, une mairie, une grosse société

National Standards
Cultures
This reading allows students to see how, by combining French with his college major, one young man was able to pursue a successful career in diplomacy.

Presentation

Pre-reading
Step 1 Ask students what they know about the Peace Corps.

Step 2 Go over the Reading Strategy on page 452.

Reading
Step 1 Have students first read the questions in the **Vous avez compris?** activity. Then have them read the selection once silently.

Step 2 Go over the **Lecture** again, having individuals read four or five sentences aloud.

Post-reading
Call on volunteers to summarize in their own words what they have learned about the young man named Bobby.

Lectures culturelles

Reading Strategy
Scanning for specific information
Before reading a passage, read the questions that follow it. Skim the text and look for the answers to the questions. This will help you focus on the important information in the selection.

Un jeune homme appelé Bobby

Cette histoire est une histoire vraie. Bobby, qu'on appelle aujourd'hui Robert, est américain. Il est allé dans une école publique américaine où il a fait quatre ans de français. Il a continué ses études de français à l'université où il s'est spécialisé en sciences politiques.

Après avoir été diplômé, Bobby est entré au service du Corps de la Paix[1]. Il a passé quelques mois de formation[2] dans le Vermont. Ensuite il est allé travailler au Sénégal, où il a appris aux paysans d'un village à construire des routes.

Après ses deux ans de bénévolat[3] au Corps de la Paix, il a passé un examen pour entrer au Ministère des Affaires Étrangères[4].

Bobby a réussi à son examen et il a commencé à travailler au Ministère des Affaires Étrangères. Comme il était intelligent et sérieux, il a très vite reçu de l'avancement[5]. Il a été nommé consul au Mali et attaché culturel en France. Et aujourd'hui, Bobby est ambassadeur.

[1] Corps de la Paix *Peace Corps*
[2] formation *training*
[3] bénévolat *volunteer work*
[4] Ministère des Affaires Étrangères *State Department*
[5] avancement *promotion*

L'ambassade des États-Unis à Bamako au Mali

Un jeune Américain du Corps de la Paix au Mali

LEVELING
E: Reading

Un bénévole du Corps de la Paix au Mali

Où a débuté l'illustre carrière diplomatique de Bobby? D'après lui, tout a commencé lorsqu'il était en neuvième et qu'il a choisi de faire du français!

Vous aimeriez faire une carrière comme celle de Bobby? Vous pourriez bien un jour être attaché culturel ou même ambassadeur dans un pays francophone. Qu'en pensez-vous? Avoir un poste qui paie bien et permet de voir le monde en même temps, ça vous intéresserait?

Vous avez compris?

Bobby est devenu Robert. Répondez.
1. Bobby est de quelle nationalité?
2. Il a étudié où?
3. Il a fait combien d'années de français?
4. Quelles études a-t-il faites à l'université?
5. Il a continué à faire du français?
6. Il a travaillé dans quelle organisation humanitaire?
7. Il est entré à quel ministère?
8. Quels postes a-t-il eus?
9. D'après lui, sa carrière a débuté où?
10. Aimeriez-vous faire la même carrière que Bobby?

Lecture supplémentaire 1

Le français et votre carrière

Vous ne savez pas si le français vous sera utile dans votre carrière parce qu'il est possible que vous n'ayez pas encore décidé ce que vous ferez ni où vous travaillerez quand vous aurez votre diplôme. Mais il n'y a pas de doute que la connaissance d'une langue étrangère comme le français sera un atout[1].

De nos jours, le commerce international est d'importance majeure. Ainsi, de nombreuses grosses sociétés américaines sont devenues multinationales. C'est-à-dire qu'elles se sont implantées à l'étranger[2]. Pour cette raison, il est possible que vous soyez engagé(e)[3] par une compagnie ou société américaine et que votre bureau se trouve dans un pays francophone.

Une agence immobilière à Auxerre

Souvenez-vous bien que le français en soi[4] n'est pas forcément une carrière. Mais le français avec une autre spécialisation peut vous être très utile. Si vous connaissez la médecine, la comptabilité, le commerce, l'informatique, etc. et qu'en plus vous parlez français, vous pourrez faire un travail intéressant, voyager à l'étranger et gagner beaucoup d'argent. Vive le français!

[1] atout *advantage*
[2] à l'étranger *abroad*
[3] engagé(e) *hired*
[4] en soi *in itself*

Une tour à la Défense

Vous avez compris?

Votre carrière Répondez.
1. Croyez-vous que le français vous sera utile dans votre carrière?
2. Vous avez choisi une carrière? Si oui, quelle carrière avez-vous choisie?
3. De nos jours qu'est-ce qui est très important?
4. Que sont devenues de nombreuses grosses sociétés américaines?
5. Qu'est-ce qui est un outil très utile?

Lecture supplémentaire 2

Petites annonces

Lisez les petites annonces suivantes:

→ GROUPE international de travail temporaire recrute son assistant(e) d'agence sur Paris, jeune, motivé(e), Bac à Bac + 2, 2 ans d'expérience minimum dans fonction similaire. Envoyer CV + lettre de motivation à Michelle Breton, 90 Bd Raspail, 75006 Paris.

Société de presse recherche 2 jeunes journalistes bilingues (fr./ang.) connaissant le secteur des technologies avec cinq ans d'expérience dans la profession. Adresser lettre de motivation et CV, sous réf. 103 à : Le Monde Publicité, 21 bis, rue Claude-Bernard, BP 218, 75226 Paris Cedex 05.

Vous avez compris?

A Groupe international Répondez.
1. C'est un groupe de quoi?
2. Qu'est-ce qu'il recrute?
3. Où est l'agence?
4. Il faut avoir combien d'années d'expérience?
5. Qu'est-ce qu'il faut envoyer? À quelle adresse?

B Société de presse Répondez.
1. Qu'est-ce que la société recherche?
2. Il faut parler quelles langues?
3. Il faut combien d'années d'expérience?
4. Où faut-il envoyer la lettre de motivation?

LES PROFESSIONS ET LES MÉTIERS

CONNEXIONS

National Standards

Connections
This reading about basic concepts in economics, such as opportunity cost, establishes a connection with another discipline, allowing students to reinforce and further their knowledge of the social sciences through the study of French.

Attention!

The readings in the **Connexions** section are optional. They focus on some of the major disciplines taught in schools and universities. The vocabulary is useful for discussing such topics as history, literature, art, economics, business, science, etc. You may choose any of the following ways to do the readings in the **Connexions** section.

Independent reading Have students read the selections and do the post-reading activities as homework, which you collect. This option is least intrusive on class time and requires a minimum of teacher involvement.

Homework with in-class follow-up Assign the readings and post-reading activities as homework. Review and discuss the material in class the next day.

Intensive in-class activity This option includes a pre-reading vocabulary presentation, in-class reading and discussion, assignment of the activities for homework, and a discussion of the assignment in class the next day.

CONNEXIONS

Les sciences sociales

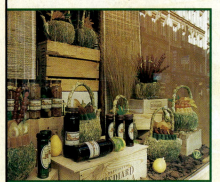

Hédiard, une épicerie fine à Paris

L'économie

Economics is the science that deals with the production, distribution, and consumption of goods and services for the welfare of humankind. It is an interesting and complex science because people need or desire all kinds of goods and services. However, we do not have at our disposal the resources we need to produce all that society would like to have. For this reason, economists provide the information necessary to those who must make decisions as to what will and will not be produced.

Qu'est-ce que l'économie?

Qu'est-ce que l'économie? On peut définir l'économie de plusieurs manières. L'économie, c'est l'étude des décisions que l'on prend en matière de production, de distribution et de consommation de biens[1] et services. C'est l'étude des décisions que prend la société quand elle détermine ce qui va être produit et pour qui. L'économie traite aussi de l'utilisation et du contrôle des ressources pour satisfaire les nécessités et les désirs des êtres humains. C'est un aspect important de l'économie parce que nos ressources sont limitées mais les besoins et les désirs des êtres humains n'ont pas de limite.

Les besoins des êtres humains peuvent être de première nécessité comme la nourriture, le logement et les vêtements. Il y a d'autres besoins qui ne sont pas de première nécessité, comme les voyages ou les châteaux, mais ces besoins sont importants pour certains individus. Les besoins et les désirs humains n'ont pas de limite, mais les ressources, elles, sont limitées. En réalité, il y a une rareté[2] de ressources.

[1] biens *goods* [2] rareté *scarcity*

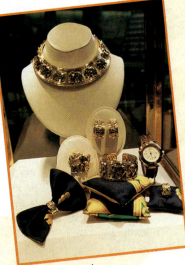

Une bijouterie à Paris

Critical Thinking Activity

Have pairs of students work together to consider other examples of **manque à gagner** either from their own lives or on a wider scale. They may present their examples to the class.

Les sciences sociales
L'économie

Une usine de camions à Anger

Les ressources économiques

Les ressources économiques représentent l'ensemble des ressources naturelles, des ressources financières (le capital), des ressources humaines (la main-d'œuvre[3]) et des ressources manufacturées (fabriquées) qu'on utilise pour la production de biens et la création et la distribution de services. Les ressources naturelles sont les matières premières[4], ce qui vient de la terre. Les ressources manufacturées ou fabriquées incluent les usines, les édifices commerciaux et tout l'équipement mécanique et technique. Les ressources humaines sont la main-d'œuvre—professionnelle, technique, administrative et ouvrière. Les ressources financières, c'est-à-dire le capital, c'est tout simplement l'argent disponible[5].

Le manque à gagner[6]

Puisque[7] toutes les ressources sont limitées, il est impossible de donner à la société tous les biens et services qu'elle désire. La rareté de matériels et de ressources nous oblige à choisir ce qu'on va produire. Si on décide de produire un bien avec les ressources disponibles, on perd l'occasion de produire un autre bien. Cette occasion manquée[8] s'appelle «le manque à gagner». Par exemple, si toute une usine produit des téléviseurs, cette usine ne peut pas fabriquer de réfrigérateurs. C'est le manque à gagner. Il faut toujours considérer le manque à gagner quand on prend une décision économique.

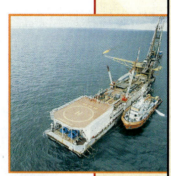

Une plate-forme pétrolière

[3] main-d'œuvre *workforce*
[4] matières premières *raw materials*
[5] disponible *available*
[6] manque à gagner *opportunity cost*
[7] Puisque *Since*
[8] occasion manquée *missed opportunity*

Vous avez compris?

A L'économie Donnez des exemples:
1. des besoins essentiels
2. des besoins pas essentiels
3. des ressources économiques
4. de la main-d'œuvre

B Le manque à gagner Expliquez ce qu'est le manque à gagner.

C'est à vous

Use what you have learned

1 Career Day
✔ Talk about the advantages of learning French for your future employment

C'est *Career Day* dans votre école. Votre professeur vous a demandé de préparer un petit discours sur l'importance des langues étrangères. Dans votre discours, dites pourquoi le français peut vous être utile plus tard. Présentez votre discours à une autre classe de français.

2 Voulez-vous travailler à l'étranger?
✔ Talk about professions

Travaillez avec un(e) camarade. Demandez-lui s'il/si elle aimerait travailler pour une société multinationale et pourquoi. Si votre camarade dit oui, demandez-lui s'il/si elle aimerait travailler à l'étranger ou aux États-Unis et pour quelles raisons. Ensuite changez de rôle.

La tour Elf à la Défense

CHAPITRE 14

3 Mon C.V.
✔ **Apply for a job**

Préparez votre C.V. en français. Il faut donner les détails suivants: nom, adresse, scolarité, talents, intérêts, une petite description du genre de travail qui vous intéresse, ce que vous aimeriez comme travail.

4 Quels sont les intérêts de tous?

It is likely that your classmates have varied opinions about their plans for the future. Prepare a survey to administer to your classmates, asking what they would like to do. After you have gathered the data, prepare a visual that gives an overview of the possible careers and job interests your class has. You may wish to use a computer to create a visual similar to the one above.

Writing Strategy

Using visuals Well-organized writing that conveys information clearly is the key to good communication. In addition, you can use visuals to organize, clarify, and summarize many different kinds of data. A visual can illustrate an important concept for your audience. Good visuals can portray at a glance an idea that might take several paragraphs to explain.

LES PROFESSIONS ET LES MÉTIERS

quatre cent cinquante-neuf 459

Assessment

Resource Manager

Communication Transparencies C 14
Quizzes, pages 73–77
Tests, pages 227–242
ExamView® Pro
Situation Cards
Performance Assessment, Task 14
Marathon mental Videoquiz

Assessment

Vocabulaire

1 Identifiez.

To review Mots 1, turn to pages 436–437.

2 Choisissez.

5. un tribunal	a. un cinéaste
6. un film	b. une commerçante
7. une mairie	c. un juge
8. un magasin	d. une fonctionnaire

To review Mots 2, turn to pages 440–441.

3 Donnez le mot.

9. pas occupé
10. une grosse société avec des bureaux dans plusieurs pays
11. une personne qui n'a pas de travail
12. une personne qui travaille pour avoir de l'expérience

460 quatre cent soixante CHAPITRE 14

ANSWERS TO Assessment

1
1. un chef de service
2. un secrétaire (un assistant administratif)
3. une informaticienne
4. un comptable

2
5. c
6. a
7. d
8. b

3
9. libre
10. une multinationale
11. un chômeur
12. un stagiaire

Structure

4 Complétez chaque phrase.

13. Je suis sûr(e) que tu…
14. Il ne croit pas que je…
15. Ça m'étonnerait qu'ils…
16. Elle est certaine que vous…

To review expressing doubt, turn to page 444.

5 Répondez.

17. Qu'est-ce que tu voudrais être un jour?
18. Qu'est-ce que tes parents voudraient que tu fasses?

To review expressing wishes, turn to page 447.

6 Complétez.

19. J'ai un très bon sécrétaire qui ___ bilingue. (être)
20. On cherche un candidat qui ___ voyager. (pouvoir)

To review expressing certainty and uncertainty, turn to page 448.

LES PROFESSIONS ET LES MÉTIERS

On parle super bien!

Tell all you can about this illustration.

1. Identify the topic or situation of the illustration.
2. Give the French words for as many items as you can.
3. Think of as many sentences as you can to describe the illustration.
4. Go over your sentences and put them in the best sequencing to give a coherent story based on the illustration.

Vocabulaire

Talking about offices and office personnel

un lieu de travail	une multinationale	un chef (de service)	un(e) assistant(e)
un bureau	un(e) employé(e)	un cadre	administratif(ve)
une entreprise	un employeur,	un(e) secrétaire	
une grosse société	une employeuse		

Discussing some legal professions

un tribunal
un(e) juge
un(e) avocat(e)

Talking about government jobs

une mairie
une assistante sociale
un(e) fonctionnaire

Identifying other professions

une profession	un(e) architecte	un écrivain	une femme d'affaires
un(e) informaticien(ne)	un(e) comptable	un(e) cinéaste	
un ingénieur	un(e) journaliste	un homme d'affaires	

Identifying some trades

un métier	un(e) électricien(ne)
un plombier	un peintre (en bâtiment)
un menuisier	un(e) commerçant(e)

Talking about jobs and job opportunities

une carrière	le directeur des	un(e) stagiaire	être
un poste	ressources humaines	un chômeur,	à son compte
une petite annonce	(le D.R.H.)	une chômeuse	au chômage
un bureau de	la directrice	poser sa candidature	faire un stage
placement	un(e) candidat(e)	travailler	
un curriculum vitæ	un entretien	à plein temps	
(un C.V.)	un salaire	à mi-temps	

Other useful words and expressions

libre
immédiatement

How well do you know your vocabulary?

Choose an occupation from the list. Write a few sentences about the job, describing the place of work, the hours per week, and how you would apply for the position.

VIDÉOTOUR

Épisode 14

In this video episode, Vincent interviews for a summer job. See page 513 for more information.

LES PROFESSIONS ET LES MÉTIERS

quatre cent soixante-trois 463

Révision

Preview

This section reviews the salient points from Chapters 12–14. In the **Conversation,** students will review career and job interview vocabulary as well as the subjunctive. The **Structure** section will review the formation and uses of the subjunctive.

Resource Manager
Workbook, Check-Up, pages 165–170
Tests, pages 243–253

Presentation

Conversation

Step 1 Call on two students to read the conversation aloud as the class listens with books closed.

Step 2 Read the conversation again as students follow along in their books.

Step 3 Go over the activity in the **Vous avez compris?** section.

Vocabulary Expansion
Explain to students that the word **abonnés** in the advertisement on page 464 means "subscribers." A subscription to anything is **un abonnement.** To subscribe to something is **s'abonner à.**

Révision

Conversation

Un peu de courage!

Marie: Ça va pas? Tu as une drôle de tête.
Hervé: Ben, ça pourrait aller mieux. J'ai un entretien demain pour un job.
Marie: Il ne faut pas que tu t'en fasses pour si peu.
Hervé: Tu es rigolotte, toi! Je suis très nerveux aux entretiens.
Marie: Écoute. D'abord, il faut que tu t'habilles bien: chemise et cravate. Pas de jean.
Hervé: Oh, je ne crois pas que les gens fassent attention à ce que tu portes.
Marie: Erreur! C'est très important. Aussi, il faut que tu fasses un petit effort pour une fois et que tu sois à l'heure.
Hervé: Ça, ça va être plus difficile.
Marie: Rappelle-toi. Il vaut mieux être en avance qu'en retard.
Hervé: Oui, mais il ne faut pas que j'aie l'air d'être désespéré.
Marie: Mais non. Autre chose: il est très important que tu écoutes bien les questions qu'on te pose et que tu répondes clairement et brièvement. Pas de longs discours.
Hervé: Oui, je sais. Mais il faut quand même que je leur dise ce que je sais faire!
Marie: Crois-moi. Il faut que tu apprennes à ne pas trop parler!

Vous avez compris?

Des conseils Répondez.

1. Comment va Hervé?
2. Qu'est-ce qu'il a demain?
3. Il aime les entretiens?
4. Quel est le premier conseil *(piece of advice)* de Marie?
5. Et le deuxième?
6. Et le troisième?
7. Et le quatrième?
8. Pourquoi Hervé veut-il parler?

Answers to Vous avez compris?

1. Hervé est nerveux.
2. Il a un entretien demain.
3. Il n'aime pas les entretiens.
4. Il faut s'habiller bien.
5. Il faut être à l'heure.
6. Il faut bien écouter les questions.
7. Il faut répondre clairement et brièvement.
8. Il veut leur dire ce qu'il sait faire.

Structure

Le subjonctif

1. Review the formation of the subjunctive.

	PARLER	FINIR	ATTENDRE
Present	ils parlent	ils finissent	ils attendent
Stem	parl-	finiss-	attend-
	que je parle	que je finisse	que j' attende
	que tu parles	que tu finisses	que tu attendes
	qu'il/elle/on parle	qu'il/elle/on finisse	qu'il/elle/on attende
	que nous parlions	que nous finissions	que nous attendions
	que vous parliez	que vous finissiez	que vous attendiez
	qu'ils/elles parlent	qu'ils/elles finissent	qu'ils/elles attendent

2. The subjunctive of most verbs is formed the same way.

PARTIR ils partent que je parte   que nous partions
                    que tu partes   que vous partiez
                    qu'il parte   qu'ils partent

Il faut qu'elle finisse son travail.

Révision

Presentation (continued)

Step 3 Have students go over these verb forms quickly. It will take quite a bit of practice and time exposure before students will be able to manipulate all verb forms with complete accuracy.

Révision

3. Remember that certain verbs that have two stems in the present indicative have the same stems in the present subjunctive.

Infinitive	Two stems	Subjunctive
prendre	ils **prenn** -ent nous **pren** -ons	que je prenne, tu prennes, il prenne, ils prennent que nous prenions, vous preniez
venir	ils **vienn** -ent nous **ven** -ons	que je vienne, tu viennes, il vienne, ils viennent que nous venions, vous veniez
recevoir	ils **reçoiv** -ent nous **recev** -ons	que je reçoive, tu reçoives, il reçoive, ils reçoivent que nous recevions, vous receviez
boire	ils **boiv** -ent nous **buv** -ons	que je boive, tu boives, il boive, ils boivent que nous buvions, vous buviez

4. The following verbs have an irregular subjunctive.

 ÊTRE que je sois, que tu sois, qu'il soit,
    que nous soyons, que vous soyez, qu'ils soient
 AVOIR que j'aie, que tu aies, qu'il ait,
    que nous ayons, que vous ayez, qu'ils aient
 FAIRE que je fasse, que tu fasses, qu'il fasse,
    que nous fassions, que vous fassiez, qu'ils fassent
 ALLER que j'aille, que tu ailles, qu'il aille,
    que nous allions, que vous alliez, qu'ils aillent
 SAVOIR que je sache, que tu saches, qu'il sache,
    que nous sachions, que vous sachiez, qu'ils sachent
 VOULOIR que je veuille, que tu veuilles, qu'il veuille,
    que nous voulions, que vous vouliez, qu'ils veuillent
 POUVOIR que je puisse, que tu puisses, qu'il puisse,
    que nous puissions, que vous puissiez, qu'ils puissent

5. You use the subjunctive in a dependent clause to talk about actions, events, or situations that may or may not happen.

 Il faut qu'il le **fasse**.
 Il est important que tu **saches** tous les détails.
 Il est possible qu'ils **soient** déjà là.
 Je veux que tu **viennes**.
 Elle préfère qu'on ne **fasse** pas ça.

6. You use the subjunctive after many expressions that convey an emotion.

> Je suis content qu'ils **se marient**.
> Moi, ça m'étonne qu'il n'**attende** pas un peu.
> Il a peur que je **dise** ce que je sais.
> Nous regrettons que vous **partiez** déjà.

7. You use the subjunctive after an expression of doubt, uncertainty, or disbelief. You use the indicative if there is no doubt or uncertainty.

> Je doute que tu **sois** fauché.
> Je ne doute pas que tu **es (seras)** fauché.
> Je ne crois pas qu'il **soit** au chômage.
> Je crois qu'il **est** au chômage.

La Sorbonne à Paris

 Toi Donnez des réponses personnelles.

1. Tes parents veulent que tu ailles à l'université?
2. Ils aimeraient que tu choisisses une université près de chez vous?
3. Il est important pour eux que tu reçoives de bonnes notes?
4. Il faut que tu fasses bien tes devoirs tous les jours?
5. Il est indispensable que tu aies un entretien avec le directeur des ressources humaines?

Révision

2 **Trois choses** Répondez.
1. Indique trois choses que tes parents veulent que tu fasses.
2. Indique trois choses que tu veux que tes amis fassent.
3. Indique trois choses que tu ne crois pas que ton frère ou ta sœur fasse.
4. Indique trois choses que tes profs aimeraient que toi et les autres élèves fassiez.
5. Indique trois choses que tu es content(e) que tes parents fassent.

3 **Peut-être** Complétez.
1. Il faut que tout le monde ___ poli. (être)
2. Il est important qu'on ___ l'air bien élevé. (avoir)
3. Je veux que tu ___ une cravate et que ta sœur ___ une jupe pour aller chez les Duroc. (mettre)
4. Ça m'étonnerait que personne ne te ___. (reconnaître)
5. Je ne suis pas contente que vous deux, vous ___ en retard. (arriver)
6. Je crois que mes autres amis ___ arriver à l'heure. (aller)
7. Les Duroc ne doutent pas que leurs cousins ___ venir. (pouvoir)

En famille

468 quatre cent soixante-huit   CHAPITRES 12–14

4 Chez le conseiller d'orientation Vous parlez au conseiller/à la conseillère d'orientation *(guidance counselor)* de votre école (votre camarade). Vous lui dites ce que vous voulez faire plus tard. Il/Elle vous donne des conseils. Changez ensuite de rôle. Par exemple:

5 Le rose et le noir Votre camarade est toujours pessimiste: il voit tout en noir. Vous, vous êtes toujours optimiste: vous voyez tout en rose. Avec votre camarade, vous préparez un pique-nique pour le week-end. Votre camarade exprime ses inquiétudes, mais vous restez optimiste. Par exemple:

 LITERARY COMPANION *You may wish to read the excerpt from* **Le Malade imaginaire,** *a play by Molière. You will find this literary selection on pages 492–497.*

Preview

This section, **Reflets de l'Europe francophone,** was prepared by the National Geographic Society. Its purpose is to give students greater insight, through these visual images, into the culture and people of French-speaking Europe. Have students look at the photographs on pages 470–473 for enjoyment. If they would like to talk about them, let them say anything they can, using the vocabulary they have learned to this point.

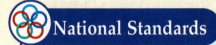

Cultures
The **Reflets de l'Europe francophone** photos and the accompanying captions allow students to gain insights into the people and culture of French-speaking Europe.

About the Photos

1. À Bruxelles, en Belgique, l'Atomium, symbole du progrès scientifique au 20ᵉ siècle Brussels, the capital of Belgium, is located in the center of the country. Flemish and French are the two official languages of this bilingual city. The EU (European Union) has its headquarters in Brussels. The monument seen here, commemorating scientific progress in the twentieth century, was built for the Universal Exposition held in Brussels in 1958.

2. Chefs cuisiniers récoltant herbes et salades près de Bouillon, en Belgique Many European chefs like to select their own produce and herbs as these Belgian chefs are doing in the small town of Bouillon, in the Wallonia, or French-speaking area of Belgium. Belgium, however, is not an agricultural country. It is one of the world's most industrialized countries. Only 5% of the population work in agriculture.

1. À Bruxelles, en Belgique, l'Atomium, symbole du progrès scientifique au 20ᵉ siècle
2. Chefs cuisiniers récoltant herbes et salades près de Bouillon, en Belgique
3. Le port de Monte-Carlo, à Monaco
4. Appartements donnant sur l'Alzette, au Luxembourg
5. La cueillette des abricots dans le Valais, en Suisse
6. Fenêtre de châlet fleurie, en Suisse
7. Péniche sur la Moselle, au Luxembourg

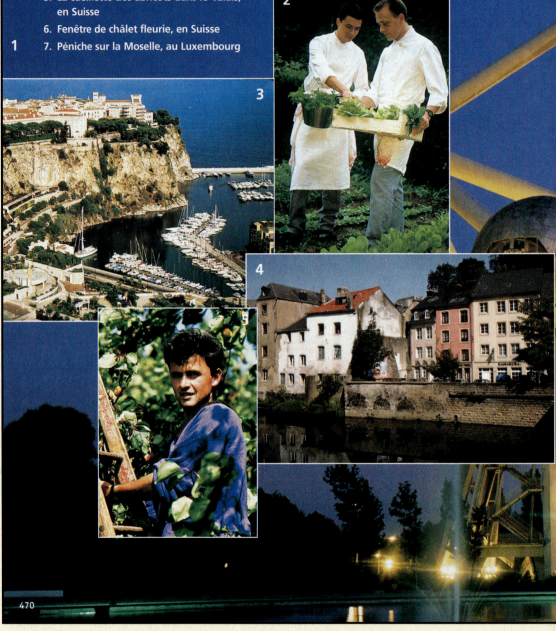

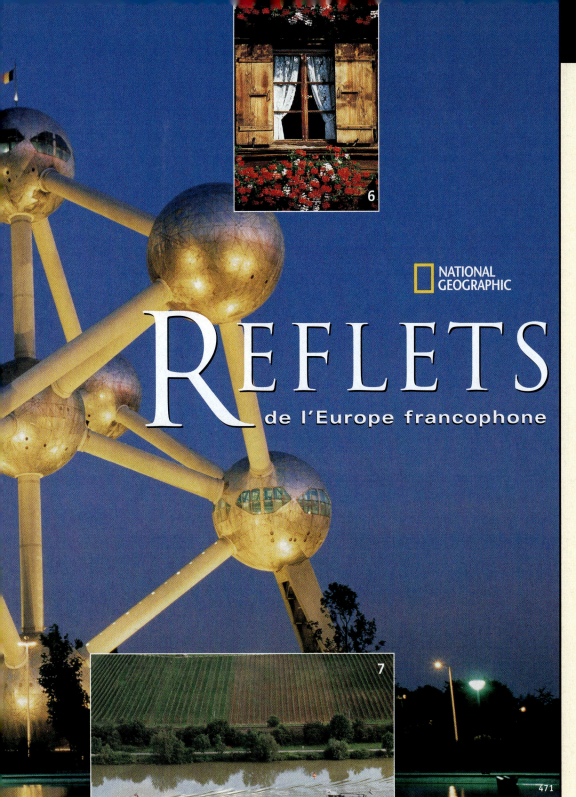

REFLETS
de l'Europe francophone

3. Le port de Monte-Carlo, à Monaco The principality of Monaco is one of the smallest countries in the world. It has the shape of a horseshoe, with the Mediterranean Sea on one side and the beginning of the Maritime Alps on the other. The principality has been ruled by members of the Grimaldi family since the Middle Ages. The natives of Monaco are called **Monégasques,** but actual citizens number only about 20% of the population. There are five immigrant residents for every citizen.

4. Appartements donnant sur l'Alzette, au Luxembourg Luxembourg is another small country, smaller than Rhode Island. Luxembourg rivals Switzerland as the capital of international banking. The Alzette River flows south to north through the middle of the country.

5. La cueillette des abricots dans le Valais, en Suisse Le Valais is a canton in the southwest of Switzerland. Two-thirds of its population is French-speaking, one-third speaks German. A fair portion of the economy in the area is based on agriculture, particularly the cultivation of peaches and apricots, as well as grains and tobacco. Agriculture, however, has been surpassed by industry. Hydroelectric plants in Le Valais provide 25% of the energy for the country.

6. Fenêtre de châlet fleurie, en Suisse This photo shows a window of a charming Swiss **châlet.** The white curtain and the geraniums are quite typical.

7. Péniche sur la Moselle, au Luxembourg The barge seen here on the Moselle is typical of many barges that ply the rivers of Europe, transporting goods from one place to another.

8. Les Alpes dans le Valais, en Suisse For information on Le Valais see #5, page 471.

9. Caves de l'Etivaz, fromage des Alpes Vaudoises, en Suisse Etivaz is a town in Switzerland that is well-known for its production of cheese.

10. Le jet d'eau de Genève, en Suisse Geneva is one of the most cosmopolitan cities of Switzerland. It is situated at the foot of the Jura Mountains and the Alps, on the West Bank of beautiful Lake Geneva **(le lac Léman).** It is a very short distance from the French border. The **jet d'eau** seen in this photo is the highest fountain in Europe, sending the water 145 meters, or 475 feet, into the air.

11. Ballons à air chaud à Château-d'Œx, en Suisse Hot air ballooning is popular in many areas of both France and Switzerland.

12. Horloger suisse The Swiss have long been known for their production of precision instruments, particularly clocks and watches.

8. Les Alpes dans le Valais, en Suisse
9. Caves de l'Etivaz, fromage des Alpes Vaudoises, en Suisse
10. Le jet d'eau de Genève, en Suisse
11. Ballons à air chaud à Château-d'Œx, en Suisse
12. Horloger suisse
13. Le Centre Européen du Kirchberg, à Luxembourg
14. La Grand-Place à Bruxelles, en Belgique

Teacher's Corner

Index to the NATIONAL GEOGRAPHIC MAGAZINE

The following related articles may be of interest:
- "Monaco," by Richard Conniff, May 1996.
- "Are the Swiss Forests in Peril?" by Christian Mehr, May 1989.
- "Switzerland: The Clockwork Country," by John J. Putman, January 1986.
- "Chocolate: Food of the Gods," by Gordon Young, November 1984.

REFLETS
de l'Europe francophone

13. Le Centre Européen du Kirchberg, à Luxembourg Luxembourg is the seat of all judicial and financial institutions of the European Union, many of which are housed in the **Centre Européen du Kirchberg,** as well as the secretariat of the European Parliament.

14. La Grand-Place à Bruxelles, en Belgique The Grand-Place in Brussels is a very ornate market square. There is a daily flower market, and on Sunday mornings there is even a bird market. The Grand-Place is also the venue for many local pageants.

Products available from GLENCOE/MCGRAW-HILL

To order the following products, call Glencoe/McGraw-Hill at 1-800-334-7344.
CD-ROM
- Picture Atlas of the World

Transparency Set
- NGS MapPack: Geography of Europe

Products available from NATIONAL GEOGRAPHIC SOCIETY

To order the following products, call National Geographic Society at 1-800-368-2728.
Books
- National Geographic World Atlas for Young Explorers
- National Geographic Satellite Atlas of the World

Software
- ZingoLingo: French Diskette

Video
- Europe

Literary Companion

Preview

All literary selections are optional. You may wish to skip them or present them very thoroughly. In some cases you may have students read the selection quickly just to get a general idea of the selection.

Attention!

The exposure to literature early in one's study of a foreign language should be a pleasant experience. As students read these selections, it is not necessary for them to understand every word. Explain to them that they should try to enjoy the experience of reading literature in a new language. As they read they should look for the following:
- Who the main characters are
- What they are like
- What they are doing—the plot
- What happens to them—the outcome of the story

Literary Companion

quatre cent soixante-quatorze

 Literary Companion

These literary selections develop reading and cultural skills and introduce students to French literature.

Le Livre de mon père 476
Émile Henriot

Deux poèmes africains 480
«À ma mère»
  Camara Laye
«L'homme qui te ressemble»
  René Philombe

Vol de nuit 486
Antoine de Saint-Exupéry

Le Malade imaginaire 492
Molière

Learning from Photos

(pages 474–475) Victor Schœlcher was a French politician who served as Undersecretary of State for the provisional government after the Revolution of February 1848. He had fought since 1840 for the abolition of slavery in the French colonies, and through his efforts, a decree was signed to abolish slavery. He served as deputy to Guadeloupe and Martinique from 1848–1851. During the Second Empire, he lived in exile in England, and in 1871, after the abdication of Napoleon III (1870), he was re-elected deputy from Martinique to the National Assembly. In 1875 he was named senator for life.

Today the town of Schœlcher, a residential beach area near Fort-de-France, carries his name. The campus of the **Université des Antilles** is in Schœlcher.

Littérature 1

Le Livre de mon père — Émile Henriot

Vocabulaire

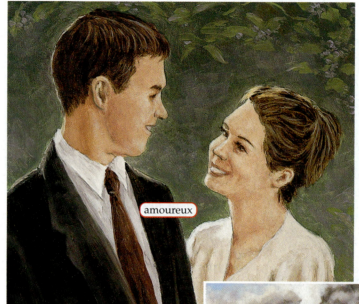

Le jeune homme est amoureux de la jeune fille.
Et elle est amoureuse de lui.

Le train a sifflé.
Le train a dépassé la gare à toute allure.

Littérature 1

une montre

un roman

L'homme règle sa montre.

L'auteur d'un roman est un romancier.
Un romancier écrit un roman.

saluer dire bonjour

Activités

A **Le train** Répondez d'après les indications.

1. Est-ce que le train siffle avant d'arriver à la gare? (oui)
2. Le train a fait un arrêt à la gare? (non)
3. Le train a dépassé la gare à toute allure? (oui)
4. Dans le train, qui salue les voyageurs? (le contrôleur)
5. Un voyageur lit le journal? (oui)
6. Il lit *le Temps,* un journal français? (oui)
7. Qu'est-ce que le voyageur regarde? (sa montre)
8. Sa montre indique l'heure exacte? (non)
9. Qu'est-ce que l'homme fait? (régler sa montre)

B **Un couple amoureux** Dites d'une autre façon.

1. Le jeune homme *dit bonjour à* sa fiancée.
2. La jeune fille *dit bonjour à* son fiancé.
3. La jeune fille *aime* son fiancé.
4. Et le jeune homme *aime* sa fiancée.
5. Le jeune homme a dépassé la maison *très, très vite.*
6. *L'auteur de ce roman* est très connu.

Un train français vers 1900

LITTÉRATURE 1

quatre cent soixante-dix-sept ✦ 477

Note: The following teaching suggestions are for a thorough presentation of *Le Livre de mon père.*

Teaching Vocabulary

Step 1 Have students look at the illustrations as they repeat the new vocabulary. As they repeat the vocabulary, you may wish to ask the following questions:

Est-ce que Roméo était amoureux de Juliette?
Et Juliette était amoureuse de lui?
Le train s'est arrêté ou il a dépassé la gare?
Le train a sifflé avant de dépasser la gare?
Qui écrit un roman?
Nommez deux romanciers américains.
Vous avez lu leurs romans en cours d'anglais?

Step 2 Quickly go over Activities A and B with the class.

ANSWERS TO Activités

A

1. Oui, le train siffle avant d'arriver à la gare.
2. Non, le train n'a pas fait d'arrêt à la gare.
3. Oui, le train a dépassé la gare à toute allure.
4. Dans le train le contrôleur salue les voyageurs.
5. Oui, un voyageur lit le journal.
6. Oui, il lit *le Temps,* un journal français.
7. Le voyageur regarde sa montre.
8. Non, sa montre n'indique pas l'heure exacte.
9. L'homme règle sa montre.

B

1. Le jeune homme salue sa fiancée.
2. La jeune fille salue son fiancé.
3. La jeune fille est amoureuse de son fiancé.
4. Et le jeune homme est amoureux de sa fiancée.
5. Le jeune homme a dépassé la maison à toute allure.
6. Le romancier est très connu.

Littérature 1

Discussing Literature

Introduction

Step 1 You may go over the Introduction with students or you may omit it and just have students read the story.

Step 2 You can ask the following questions about the Introduction:
Qu'est-ce que l'Académie Française?
Combien de membres y a-t-il?
On les appelle comment?

Step 3 Ask students the following questions in English: Is there an equivalent in America to the **Académie Française?** Do you think there should be? What are the advantages or disadvantages of such a regulatory body?

Le Livre de mon père

Le petit train

Step 1 Have students read several paragraphs silently. Then ask several general questions to ascertain if students got the main idea. Sample questions are:
Qu'est-ce qui indiquait l'arrivée du soir à Nesles?
Le jeune garçon allait où à bicyclette?
Il allait à la gare parce qu'il attendait quelqu'un?
Il attendait un colis-postal?
Les voyageurs venaient d'où?

Step 2 If students can answer the questions, move on to the next section. If they cannot, you may want to have them read selections or parts thereof aloud.

INTRODUCTION Émile Henriot (1889–1961) a d'abord été poète, puis romancier et critique littéraire. En 1945, il a été élu membre de la prestigieuse Académie Française.

L'Académie Française a été créée par Richelieu, ministre de Louis XIV, en 1634. Elle est composée de quarante membres, les «immortels». Ce sont en majorité des écrivains, mais aussi des diplomates, des avocats[1] et des médecins. Les «immortels» sont chargés de la rédaction[2] d'un «Dictionnaire de la langue française». Leur mission est essentiellement de «travailler à épurer et fixer la langue française».

L'extrait qui suit est tiré du *Livre de mon père*, publié en 1938. Dans ce roman Henriot évoque des souvenirs de son enfance et décrit comment la vie a changé depuis son enfance.

[1] avocats *lawyers*
[2] rédaction *editing*

Le petit train

Autrefois°, nous connaissions l'heure en écoutant siffler le petit train qui va de Valmondois à Marines et vice versa,
pour transporter les betteraves° et quelquefois aussi les gens.
C'était un événement que l'arrivée du soir à la gare de Nesles.
Même quand je n'attendais personne, et pas le moindre° colis-postal,
j'allais à bicyclette assister au débarquement des voyageurs qui venaient de Paris,
le notaire, ou Mademoiselle Durand, la fille du pharmacien, qui donne à Pontoise des leçons de musique,
Monsieur de Vigneron qui était allé à la Bourse°
et le jeune Henri Delarue qui rapportait *le Temps* à mon père.
Quelquefois encore, je voyais, ô bonheur, descendre du train
une jolie fille, ma voisine, dont j'étais éperdument amoureux.
Je la saluais d'un air indifférent et je rougissais°,
et pour me faire bien venir d'elle°,
je la dépassais à toute allure sur ma bicyclette,
et le soir, au lieu de dormir, j'exhalais° mon amour en vers désespérés et détestables.
Maintenant, les temps ont changé, il n'y a plus de jolie voisine
et, d'ailleurs°, je n'écris plus de vers.
Le petit train passe toujours aux mêmes heures,
mais ce n'est plus à lui que nous faisons attention.

Autrefois *In the past*

betteraves *sugar beets*

pas le moindre *not the littlest*

Bourse *Stock Exchange*

je rougissais *I blushed*
me faire bien venir d'elle *make her like me*

j'exhalais *I expressed*

d'ailleurs *besides*

Ce n'est plus lui qui nous fait dire: «Le petit train a passé depuis un moment, on va déjeuner.»
Maintenant, c'est sur l'avion de Londres que nous réglons nos montres.
Il passe quatre fois par jour, juste au-dessus de mon jardin,
tantôt° comme un pigeon noir, tantôt comme un beau navire d'argent°,
suspendu à rien dans le ciel où il glisse°.
Chaque fois, je lève la tête et le regarde. Et Jean-Claude, que plus rien n'étonne°,
Lui aussi, cependant°, lève la tête et dit, à peu près comme moi autrefois:
—«Voilà l'avion de Londres. On va déjeuner»— ou «on va dîner.»

tantôt *sometimes*
navire d'argent *silver ship*
glisse *glides*
étonne *surprises*
cependant *nevertheless*

Vous avez compris?

A **Autrefois** Répondez.
1. Autrefois, comment savait-on l'heure?
2. Qu'est-ce que le train transportait?
3. Il arrivait à quelle gare? À quel moment de la journée?
4. Le narrateur allait à la gare comment?
5. Il y allait pour attendre quelqu'un?
6. D'où venaient les voyageurs?
7. Qui donnait des leçons de musique? Dans quelle ville?
8. Qui rapportait le journal pour le père du narrateur?
9. Qui descendait du train quelquefois?
10. Le narrateur était amoureux d'elle?
11. Il la saluait comment?
12. Le soir, qu'est-ce qu'il écrivait?

B **Les temps ont changé.** Vrai ou faux?
1. La jolie voisine descend toujours du train.
2. Le narrateur continue à écrire des vers.
3. Le train passe toujours aux mêmes heures.
4. Maintenant quand le train passe, on va déjeuner.
5. Maintenant on règle sa montre d'après le passage du train.
6. On règle sa montre sur l'avion de Londres.
7. L'avion passe deux fois par jour.
8. L'avion atterrit dans le jardin.

C **La vie change.** Décrivez comment l'auteur indique que la vie a changé.

Littérature 2

National Standards

Cultures
Students experience, discuss, and analyze an expressive product of the culture: the poems, «À ma mère», by Camara Laye and «L'homme qui te ressemble», by René Philombe.

Attention!

This reading is optional. You may wish to present it after students have completed Chapters 5–7, as they will have acquired the vocabulary and structures necessary to read the selection by this point.

You may present the poems thoroughly as a class activity or you may have some or all students merely read them on their own. If you present them as a class activity, you may wish to vary presentation procedures from section to section. Some options are:
- Students read silently.
- Students read after you in unison.
- Call on individuals to read aloud.
- When dialogue appears in the story, call on students to take parts.

With any of the above procedures, intersperse some comprehension questions. Call on a student or students to give a brief synopsis of a section in French.

Littérature 2

Deux poèmes africains

«À ma mère» **Camara Laye**
«L'homme qui te ressemble» **René Philombe**

Vocabulaire

La mère porte son enfant sur le dos.

Elle essuie ses larmes.

LEVELING
E: Reading

Littérature 2

Le bébé a fait un pas.
C'est son premier pas.

Activités

 Une famille Répondez que oui.

1. Est-ce que la famille est dans les champs?
2. Il y a une rivière près des champs?
3. Il y a une enceinte de résidences?
4. Une mère porte son bébé sur le dos?
5. Le petit bébé a fait un pas? C'est son premier pas?
6. Il a commencé à pleurer?
7. Sa mère essuie ses larmes?
8. Le père est forgeron?

 Quel est le mot? Complétez.

1. On dort dans un _____.
2. Quand on va chez quelqu'un, on _____ à la porte avant d'entrer.
3. En hiver quand il fait froid, il y a souvent un _____ dans la cheminée.

Note: The following teaching suggestions are for a thorough presentation of «À ma mère» and «L'homme qui te ressemble».

Teaching Vocabulary

Step 1 The vocabulary from these two poems is quite easy, so you may wish to have students look at the illustrations and read the new words.

Step 2 Go over the activities. Activity A can be done orally.

ANSWERS TO Activités

A
1. Oui, la famille est dans les champs.
2. Oui, il y a une rivière près des champs.
3. Oui, il y a une enceinte de résidences.
4. Oui, une mère porte son bébé sur le dos.
5. Oui, le bébé a fait son premier pas.
6. Oui, il a commencé à pleurer.
7. Oui, sa mère essuie ses larmes.
8. Oui, le père est forgeron.

B
1. lit
2. frappe
3. feu

Littérature 2

Discussing Literature

Introduction

Step 1 You may wish to ask the following questions about the life of Camara Laye.

    Camara Laye est né où? Quand?
    Il est allé dans quel genre d'école?
    Camara Laye était un très bon élève?
    Pourquoi est-il allé en France pour étudier?
    De quoi souffrait-il en France?
    À quoi pensait-il?
    Quel est le titre de son premier roman?

Note: It is recommended that you let students look at the **passé composé** forms of each verb and just familiarize themselves with the **passé simple** forms. It is not suggested that you teach the **passé simple**. The **passé simple** is taught in **Bon voyage! Level 3**.

Learning from Photos

(page 482) Although houses vary from region to region throughout the rural areas of the West African countries, round houses with walls made from mud and thatched roofs such as we see here are quite common in many different areas.

INTRODUCTION Camara Laye est né à Kouroussa en Guinée en 1928. Il est allé dans une école technique à Conakry, la capitale. Il a toujours excellé dans ses études et il a reçu une bourse[1] pour étudier en France. En France, il souffrait beaucoup du mal du pays[2] et pensait souvent à l'enceinte familiale dans son petit village de Kouroussa.

Pendant ses moments de nostalgie, il a décidé d'écrire un roman—*L'Enfant noir*. C'était son premier roman. Le poème qui suit est la préface à ce roman autobiographique qui a eu un très grand succès dès sa publication.

[1] bourse *scholarship*
[2] mal du pays *homesickness*

Dans ce joli poème tendre, certains verbes sont au passé simple. Le passé simple est un temps littéraire qui décrit des actions passées. Dans la conversation, on utilise le passé composé. Voici les verbes qui sont au passé simple dans le poème «À ma mère».

portas as porté   **ouvris** as ouvert
m'allaitas m'as allaité   **fis** as fait
gouvernas as gouverné

Un village de la brousse en Guinée

«À ma mère»

Femme noire, femme africaine, ô toi, ma mère, je pense à toi…

Ô Dâman, ô ma mère, toi qui me portas sur le dos, toi qui m'allaitas°, toi qui gouvernas mes premiers pas, toi qui la première m'ouvris les yeux aux prodiges° de la terre, je pense à toi…

Femme des champs, femme des rivières, femme du grand fleuve, ô toi, ma mère, je pense à toi…

Ô toi Dâman, ô ma mère, toi qui essuyais mes larmes, toi qui me réjouissais le cœur°, toi qui, patiemment, supportais mes caprices°, comme j'aimerais encore être près de toi, être enfant près de toi!

Femme simple, femme de la résignation, ô toi, ma mère, je pense à toi…

Ô Dâman, Dâman de la grande famille des forgerons, ma pensée toujours se tourne vers toi, la tienne° à chaque pas m'accompagne, ô Dâman, ma mère, comme j'aimerais encore être dans ta chaleur°, être enfant près de toi…

Femme noire, femme africaine, ô toi, ma mère, merci; merci pour tout ce que tu fis pour moi, ton fils, si loin, si près de toi!

m'allaitas nursed me

prodiges wonders

me réjouissais le cœur brought me joy
caprices whims

la tienne yours
chaleur warmth

Une mère avec son enfant au Niger

Vous avez compris?

A **Ô Dâman** Répondez.

1. À qui pense l'auteur?
2. Quand il était petit, sa mère le portait sur le dos?
3. Elle l'allaitait?
4. Elle l'a aidé à faire ses premiers pas?
5. Elle essuyait ses larmes quand il pleurait?
6. Qu'est-ce qu'elle supportait?
7. Quels sont les désirs de l'auteur?
8. L'auteur dit merci à sa mère. Pourquoi?

B **Description** Discutez.

1. Quels sont les adjectifs que l'auteur utilise pour décrire sa mère?
2. Comment sait-on que l'auteur habitait à la campagne, c'est-à-dire dans une région rurale?

Littérature 2

Discussing Literature

Introduction

Step 1 You may wish to ask the following questions about the Introduction:

Il est né où, René Philombe?
Qu'est-ce qu'il a eu à l'âge de vingt-sept ans?
Quel mouvement l'a influencé?
Quel est son désir?

«L'homme qui te ressemble»

Step 1 This beautiful poem is quite easy. It is suggested that you have students listen to you read it as they follow along in their books.

Step 2 Then have the entire class recite the poem aloud in unison with as much expression as possible.

Un tissu du Cameroun

INTRODUCTION René Philombe est né au Cameroun en 1930. À l'âge de vingt-sept ans, il a eu la poliomyélite, mais il a continué sa carrière d'écrivain. Il est poète, romancier[1], journaliste et dramaturge[2].

Philombe a été influencé par le mouvement de la négritude. Sa poésie exprime son désir de voir un monde libre d'oppression. Pour lui, tous les hommes ont les mêmes droits[3]. Dans son poème, «L'homme qui te ressemble», René Philombe parle d'une fraternité entre les êtres humains qui transcende tout.

[1] romancier *novelist*
[2] dramaturge *playwright*
[3] droits *rights*

«L'homme qui te ressemble»

J'ai frappé à ta porte
J'ai frappé à ton cœur°
pour avoir bon lit
pour avoir bon feu
pourquoi me repousser°?
Ouvre-moi mon frère…!

Pourquoi me demander
si je suis d'Afrique
si je suis d'Amérique
si je suis d'Asie
si je suis d'Europe?
Ouvre-moi mon frère…!

cœur *heart*

repousser *reject*

Pourquoi me demander
la longueur de mon nez
l'épaisseur° de ma bouche
la couleur de ma peau°
et le nom de mes dieux°?
Ouvre-moi mon frère… !

épaisseur *thickness*
peau *skin*
dieux *gods*

Je ne suis pas un noir
Je ne suis pas un rouge
Je ne suis pas un jaune
Je ne suis pas un blanc
mais je ne suis qu'°un homme
Ouvre-moi mon frère… !

ne… qu' *only*

Ouvre-moi ta porte
Ouvre-moi ton cœur
Car° je suis un homme
l'homme de tous les temps
l'homme de tous les cieux°
l'homme qui te ressemble… !

Car *Because*

cieux *heavens*

Anna Belle Lee Washington *Le passé*

Vous avez compris?

A **Discussion** D'après l'auteur de ce poème, quelles sont les questions qu'on ne doit poser à personne? Pourquoi?

B **Résumé** Dites en anglais ce que ce poème vous suggère.

Art Connection

The American artist, Anna Belle Lee Washington, grew up in Detroit where she worked in social services, aiding the poor for more than thirty-eight years. When she retired from social services, she retired to St. Simons Island, Georgia. She volunteered to work at the Coastal Center for the Arts, where she began to take drawing and painting lessons. She quickly became a prominent figure among regional artists. Ms. Washington first started painting landscapes and seascapes using pure colors. An art teacher at the center, Bill Hendrix, suggested that she add human figures to her landscapes. She began to do so, and her human forms come from her imagination, not from models. Her forms spring naturally from her mind to the canvas.

Ms. Washington often draws on black rural life of the post–Civil War era for her paintings.

Littérature 3

Vol de nuit — Antoine de Saint-Exupéry

Vocabulaire

La femme parle au téléphone.
La conversation se prolonge.
Le secrétaire se trouble.
Il sait quelque chose qu'il ne veut pas lui dire.

Il donne l'écouteur à quelqu'un d'autre.

Littérature 3

L'avion vole dans le ciel.

des nouvelles des informations sur ce qui se passe

Activités

A Un coup de téléphone Répondez.
1. La femme téléphone?
2. Elle parle au secrétaire?
3. Elle veut avoir des nouvelles?
4. La conversation se prolonge?
5. Le secrétaire se trouble?
6. Le secrétaire veut dire quelque chose à la femme?
7. Il passe l'écouteur à quelqu'un d'autre?
8. L'avion vole dans le ciel?

B Encore une fois Exprimez d'une autre façon.
1. Le secrétaire *devient agité*.
2. La conversation *devient très longue*.
3. Il donne l'écouteur *à une autre personne*.

Teaching Vocabulary

Note: The following teaching suggestions are for a thorough presentation of *Vol de nuit*.

Step 1 You may wish to ask the following questions as you present the new vocabulary.
   La femme parle au téléphone avec qui?
   La conversation se prolonge?
   Le secrétaire sait quelque chose?
   Il ne veut pas dire ce qu'il sait à la femme?
   Qu'est-ce qu'il donne à quelqu'un d'autre?
   Il a peut-être de mauvaises nouvelles?

Step 2 Students merely need to be familiar with the vocabulary to help them understand the story. This vocabulary does not have to be a part of their active, productive vocabulary.

ANSWERS TO Activités

A
1. Oui, elle téléphone.
2. Oui, elle parle au secrétaire.
3. Oui, elle veut avoir des nouvelles.
4. Oui, la conversation se prolonge.
5. Oui, le secrétaire se trouble.
6. Non, le secrétaire ne veut pas dire quelque chose à la femme.
7. Oui, il passe l'écouteur à quelqu'un d'autre.
8. Oui, l'avion vole dans le ciel.

B
1. Le secrétaire se trouble.
2. La conversation se prolonge.
3. Il donne l'écouteur à quelqu'un d'autre.

Littérature 3

Discussing Literature

Introduction

Step 1 It is recommended that you go over the Introduction with the class, since it will help them understand the reading selection.

Step 2 As you read the Introduction, ask comprehension questions of the students.

Note: Before reading the selection, let students familiarize themselves with the **passé simple** verb forms.

Geography Connection

 Have students find the following places on a map.
Toulouse
Dakar
Buenos Aires
Commodoro
Trelew

INTRODUCTION Antoine de Saint-Exupéry est né à Lyon en 1900. Il a fait ses études à l'École Navale et aussi à l'École des Beaux-Arts. Il a commencé à piloter des avions pendant son service militaire. En 1927, il est devenu pilote de ligne entre Toulouse et Dakar. Ensuite, il est allé à Buenos-Aires en Argentine. Il a vécu les débuts de la liaison aérienne entre la France et l'Amérique du Sud. Il a disparu en 1944 au-dessus de la mer Méditerranée.

Saint-Exupéry était aussi écrivain et journaliste. Comme les œuvres d'André Malraux et de l'Américain Ernest Hemingway, l'œuvre de Saint-Exupéry est tirée des expériences qu'il a vécues. Par exemple, dans son roman *Courrier Sud* (1930), il décrit ses vols entre Toulouse et Dakar.

L'extrait qui suit est tiré de son roman *Vol de nuit* (1931). Un aviateur, Fabien, fait le vol Commodoro–Buenos Aires avec une escale à Trelew. Il n'est pas encore arrivé à Buenos Aires et on a perdu tout contact avec lui. Il fait très mauvais temps. La femme de Fabien téléphone à l'aéroport. Elle veut avoir des nouvelles de son mari. Elle veut savoir s'il a atterri.

Dans cet extrait, certains verbes sont au passé simple. Le passé simple est un temps littéraire qui exprime des actions passées. Dans la conversation, on utilise le passé composé. Voici les verbes qui sont au passé simple dans cet extrait.

téléphona a téléphoné
passa a passé
eut a eu
dut a dû
répondit a répondu
se décida s'est décidé
se rappela s'est rappelé

L'attente

La femme de Fabien téléphona […]. « Fabien a-t-il atterri? »
Le secrétaire qui l'écoutait se troubla un peu:
« Qui parle? »
—Simone Fabien.
—Ah! une minute… »
Le secrétaire, n'osant° rien dire, passa l'écouteur au chef de bureau: osant *daring*
« Qui est là? »
—Simone Fabien.
—Ah!… que désirez-vous, madame?
—Mon mari a-t-il atterri? »
Il y eut un silence qui dut paraître° inexplicable, puis on répondit   paraître *seemed*
simplement:
« Non.
—Il a du retard?
—Oui… »
Il y eut un nouveau silence.
« Oui… du retard.
—Ah!… »
C'était un « Ah! » de chair blessée°. Un retard ce n'est rien… ce n'est   chair blessée
rien… mais quand il se prolonge…   *wounded flesh*
« Ah!… Et à quelle heure sera-t-il ici?
—À quelle heure il sera ici? Nous… Nous ne savons pas. »

Littérature 3

Learning from Photos

(page 490) This photo shows a scene from the 1995 film *Wings of Courage,* directed by Jean-Jacques Annaud. The film tells the story of Henri Guillaumet, whose mail plane crashes in the Andes. The young pilot makes his way through the mountains while his wife and friends at home fear the worst.

Elle se heurtait maintenant à un mur°. Elle n'obtenait que l'écho même de ses questions.

« Je vous en prie, répondez-moi! Où se trouve-t-il?…

—Où il se trouve? Attendez… »

Cette inertie lui faisait mal. Il se passait quelque chose, là, derrière ce mur.

On se décida:

« Il a décollé de Commodoro à dix-neuf heures trente.

—Et depuis?

—Depuis?… Très retardé… Très retardé par le mauvais temps…

—Ah! le mauvais temps… »

[…] La jeune femme se rappela soudain qu'il fallait deux heures à peine° pour se rendre de Commodoro à Trelew.

« Et il vole depuis six heures vers Trelew! Mais il vous envoie des messages! Mais que dit-il?…

—Ce qu'il nous dit? Naturellement par un temps pareil°… vous comprenez bien… ses messages ne s'entendent pas.

—Un temps pareil!

—Alors, c'est convenu°, madame, nous vous téléphonons dès que° nous savons quelque chose.

—Ah! vous ne savez rien…

—Au revoir, madame…

—Non! non! Je veux parler au directeur!

—Monsieur le directeur est très occupé, madame, il est en conférence… »

se... mur *hit a brick wall*

à peine *just under, barely*

pareil *such*

convenu *agreed*
dès que *as soon as*

Littérature 3

Vous avez compris?

A **Au téléphone** Répondez.
1. Qui téléphone à l'aéroport?
2. Qu'est-ce qu'elle veut savoir?
3. Qui répond au téléphone?
4. Qu'est-ce qu'il dit à la femme de Fabien?
5. À qui est-ce qu'il passe l'écouteur?
6. Qu'est-ce qu'il dit à la femme de Fabien?
7. D'après vous, est-ce que le chef de bureau sait à quelle heure l'avion de Fabien va atterrir?

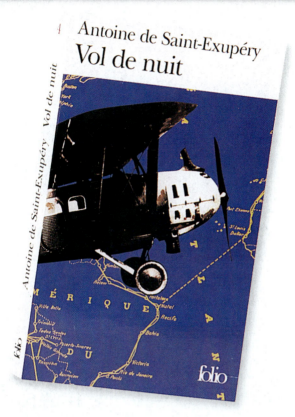

B **Un vol retardé** Complétez.
1. Fabien a décollé de Commodoro pour aller à _____.
2. Il est retardé par _____.
3. Normalement il faut deux heures pour aller de _____ à _____.
4. Et il vole depuis _____.
5. On ne peut pas entendre les messages à cause du _____.
6. Le chef de bureau ne sait _____.
7. La femme de Fabien veut parler au _____.
8. Le directeur est en _____.

C **Discussion** Pourquoi le secrétaire et le chef de bureau ne veulent-ils pas répondre aux questions de la femme de Fabien?

FRENCH Online
For more information about Saint-Exupéry and other French authors, go to the Glencoe French Web site:
french.glencoe.com

Littérature 4

National Standards

Cultures
Students experience, discuss, and analyze an expressive product of the culture: an excerpt from the play, *Le Malade imaginaire*, by Molière.

Attention!

This reading is optional. You may wish to present it after students have completed Chapters 12–14, as they will have acquired the vocabulary and structures necessary to read the selection by this point.

You may present the piece thoroughly as a class activity or you may have some or all students merely read it on their own. If you present it as a class activity, you may wish to vary presentation procedures from section to section. Some options are:
- Students read silently.
- Students read after you in unison.
- Call on individuals to read aloud.
- When dialogue appears in the story, call on students to take parts.

With any of the above procedures, intersperse some comprehension questions. Call on a student or students to give a brief synopsis of a section in French.

Littérature 4

Le Malade imaginaire Molière

Vocabulaire

Le médecin soigne le malade.
Il prend soin du malade.
Le médecin veut guérir sa maladie.

une marque un signe
le soin l'attention
un siècle une période de cent ans
un apothicaire un pharmacien
guérir rendre la santé à quelqu'un

se porter bien être en bonne santé
se servir de utiliser, employer
crever mourir
demeurer d'accord être d'accord

LEVELING
A: Reading

Activités

La médecine Vrai ou faux?

1. Quand on a de la fièvre, on est malade.
2. Un médecin soigne ses patients.
3. Au temps de Molière, on appelait un pharmacien «un apothicaire».
4. Les malades se portent bien.
5. Les médecins se servent des médicaments pour soigner et guérir les malades.
6. Les soins médicaux coûtent cher aux États-Unis.
7. Nous vivons au dix-huitième siècle.
8. «Crever» veut dire «guérir».

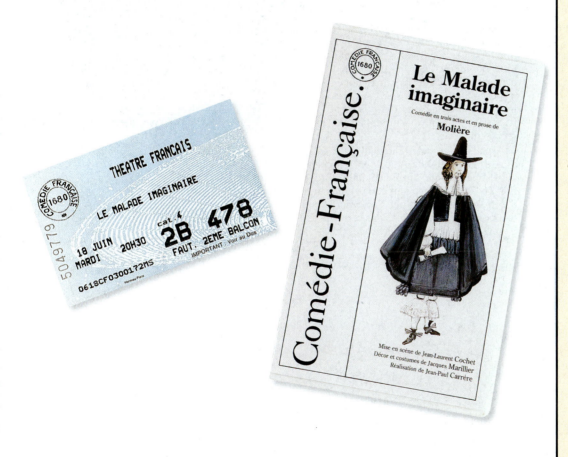

Littérature 4

Discussing Literature

Introduction

Step 1 It is recommended that you go over the Introduction with the class, since it will help them understand the reading selection.

Step 2 You may wish to ask the following questions about Molière.

- Quel est le vrai nom de Molière?
- Il est né où?
- Comment était son enfance?
- Il a reçu quel genre d'éducation?
- Quelle était sa vocation?
- Il a écrit quels genres de pièces?
- Quelle est sa dernière pièce?
- Comment Molière meurt-il?

INTRODUCTION Jean-Baptiste Poquelin, dit Molière, est né à Paris en 1622. Il a passé sa jeunesse dans un milieu aisé. Il a reçu une très bonne éducation. Il a étudié les mathématiques, la physique, le latin, la philosophie et la danse. Mais il avait la vocation du théâtre et il a donc décidé de devenir acteur. Il a commencé par écrire des farces. Puis très vite, il a écrit des comédies de mœurs[1]. Molière est un des auteurs français les plus connus. Ses comédies sont jouées dans le monde entier.

Dans *Le Malade imaginaire,* Molière exprime son scepticisme envers la médecine. Comme on le verra dans l'extrait qui suit, Molière n'aimait pas les médecins. *Le Malade imaginaire* est la dernière pièce de Molière. Il présente cette pièce-ballet pour la première fois le 10 février 1673. Molière est malade déjà depuis plusieurs années, mais il joue tout de même le rôle principal d'Argan. Pendant la quatrième représentation, Molière se sent très mal, mais il refuse de quitter la scène. Il meurt quelques heures après la représentation.

Argan est un malade imaginaire, c'est-à-dire, un hypochondriaque. Il est tellement obsédé par sa santé qu'il veut à tout prix marier sa fille au fils d'un médecin alors qu'elle aime quelqu'un d'autre. Il n'hésiterait pas à sacrifier le bonheur[2] de sa fille pour avoir un médecin dans la famille. Dans cette scène Béralde reproche à son frère Argan d'être obsédé par les médecins.

[1] comédies de mœurs *comedy of manners*
[2] bonheur *happiness*

Acte III, Scène 3

BÉRALDE: Est-il possible que vous serez toujours embéguiné° de vos apothicaires et de vos médecins, et que vous vouliez être malade en dépit° des gens et de la nature!

ARGAN: Comment l'entendez-vous°, mon frère?

BÉRALDE: J'entends, mon frère, que je ne vois point° d'homme qui soit moins malade que vous, et que je ne demanderais point une meilleure constitution que la vôtre. Une grande marque que vous vous portez bien, et que vous avez un corps parfaitement composé, c'est qu'avec tous les soins que vous avez pris, vous n'avez pu parvenir encore à gâter la bonté° de votre tempérament, et que vous n'êtes point crevé de toutes les médecines qu'on vous a fait prendre.

ARGAN: Mais savez-vous, mon frère, que c'est cela qui me conserve; et que monsieur Purgon dit que je succomberais, s'il était seulement trois jours sans prendre soin de moi?

BÉRALDE: Si vous n'y prenez garde°, il prendra tant de soin de vous, qu'il vous enverra en l'autre monde.

embéguiné *infatuated*

en dépit *in spite*
Comment l'entendez-vous? *What do you mean by that?*
ne… point *not*

parvenir à gâter la bonté *succeed in spoiling the goodness*

Si vous n'y prenez garde *If you don't watch out*

quatre cent quatre-vingt-quinze ✦ 495

Littérature 4

ARGAN: Mais raisonnons un peu, mon frère. Vous ne croyez donc point à la médecine?

BÉRALDE: Non, mon frère, et je ne vois pas que, pour son salut°, il soit nécessaire d'y croire.

salut salvation

ARGAN: Quoi! vous ne tenez° pas véritable une chose établie° par tout le monde, et que tous les siècles ont révérée?

tenez consider
établie taken for granted

BÉRALDE: Bien loin de la tenir véritable, je la trouve, entre nous, une des grandes folies qui soit parmi les hommes; et, à regarder les choses en philosophe, je ne vois point de plus plaisante momerie°, je ne vois rien de plus ridicule qu'un homme qui se veut mêler° d'en guérir un autre.

plaisante momerie masquerade
se veut mêler wants to get mixed up

ARGAN: Pourquoi ne voulez-vous pas, mon frère, qu'un homme en puisse guérir un autre?

BÉRALDE: Par la raison, mon frère, que les ressorts de notre machine° sont des mystères, jusques ici, où les hommes ne voient goutte°; et que la nature nous a mis au-devant des yeux des voiles trop épais° pour y connaître quelque chose.

ressorts de notre machine our body's mechanisms
ne… goutte nothing
voiles trop épais veils too thick

ARGAN: Les médecins ne savent donc rien, à votre compte?

BÉRALDE: Si fait°, mon frère. Ils savent la plupart de fort belles humanités, savent parler en beau latin, savent nommer en grec toutes les maladies, les définir et les diviser; mais pour ce qui est de les guérir, c'est ce qu'ils ne savent point du tout.

Si fait Of course

ARGAN: Mais toujours faut-il demeurer d'accord que, sur cette matière, les médecins en savent plus que les autres. […] Il faut bien que les médecins croient leur art véritable, puisqu'ils° s'en servent eux-mêmes.

puisqu'ils since they

496 quatre cent quatre-vingt-six

LITTÉRATURE 4

ANSWERS TO Vous avez compris?

A

1. Vous serez toujours embéguiné de vos apothicaires.
2. Comment l'entendez-vous, mon frère?
3. Je ne vois point d'homme…
4. Une grande marque que vous vous portez bien…
5. Vous n'avez pu parvenir encore à gâter la bonté de votre tempérament.
6. Si vous n'y prenez garde…
7. Il vous enverra en l'autre monde.
8. Vous ne tenez pas véritable une chose établie par tout le monde…
9. Je ne vois rien de plus ridicule qu'un homme qui se veut mêler d'en guérir un autre.
10. Les ressorts de notre machine sont des mystères, jusques ici, où les hommes ne voient goutte.
11. Les médecins ne savent donc rien à votre compte.
12. Si fait, mon frère.

Vous avez compris?

 A **D'une autre façon** Comment Molière exprime-t-il les phrases suivantes?

1. Vous serez toujours fasciné par vos pharmaciens.
2. Que voulez-vous dire, mon frère?
3. Je ne vois pas d'homme…
4. Une grande marque que vous allez bien…
5. Vous n'avez pas réussi à gâter la bonté de votre tempérament.
6. Si vous ne faites pas attention…
7. Il vous tuera.
8. Vous ne considérez pas véritable quelque chose que tout le monde accepte.
9. Je ne vois rien de plus stupide qu'un homme qui veut essayer de guérir un autre homme.
10. Les moyens de notre corps sont des mystères que les hommes ne comprennent pas.
11. Les médecins ne savent donc rien, à votre avis.
12. Bien sûr, mon frère.

 B **Pas du même avis** Répondez.

1. Est-ce que Béralde croit que son frère est vraiment malade?
2. Est-ce qu'il croit que le médecin donne trop de médicaments à son frère?
3. D'après Argan, qu'est-ce qui le conserve?
4. Comment s'appelle le médecin d'Argan?
5. D'après ce médecin, qu'est-ce qui se passerait s'il ne prenait pas soin d'Argan?
6. D'après Béralde, où le médecin va-t-il envoyer Argan?
7. D'après Béralde, qu'est-ce que la médecine?
8. Béralde croit qu'un homme peut guérir un autre homme?
9. Qui dit que notre corps est une machine mystérieuse?
10. D'après Béralde, que savent les médecins?

 C **Discussion** Vous êtes d'accord avec les idées de Béralde ou avec celles d'Argan? Expliquez pourquoi.

ANSWERS TO Vous avez compris?

 B

1. Béralde ne croit pas que son frère soit malade.
2. Oui, il croit que le médecin lui donne trop de médicaments.
3. Ce qui le conserve, c'est les médicaments.
4. Le médecin d'Argan s'appelle Purgon.
5. Argan mourrait.
6. Il va envoyer Argan en (dans) l'autre monde.
7. La médecine est une des grandes folies qui soit parmi les hommes.
8. Non, il ne croit pas qu'un homme puisse guérir un autre homme.
9. Béralde dit que notre corps est une machine mystérieuse.
10. Ils savent parler latin et grec. Ils savent nommer, définir et diviser les maladies.

C *Answers will vary.*

Video Companion

Using video in the classroom

The use of video in the classroom can be a wonderful asset to the World Languages teacher and a most beneficial learning tool for the language student. Video enables students to experience whatever it is they are learning in their textbook in a real-life setting. With each lesson, they are able to take a vicarious field trip. They see people interacting at home, at school, at the market, etc., in an authentic milieu. Students sitting in a classroom can see real people going about their real life in real places. They may experience the target culture in many countries. The cultural benefits are limitless.

Developing listening and viewing skills In addition to its tremendous cultural value, video, when properly used, gives students much needed practice in developing good listening and viewing skills. Video allows students to look for numerous clues that are evident in a tone of voice, facial expressions, and gestures. Through video students can see and hear the diversity of the target culture and, as discerning viewers and listeners, compare and contrast the French-speaking cultures to each other and to their own culture. Video introduces a dimension into classroom instruction that no other medium — teachers, overhead, text, Audio CDs—can provide.

Reinforcing learned language Video that is properly developed for classroom use has speakers reincorporate the language students have learned in a given lesson. In keeping with reality, however, speakers introduce some new words, expressions, and structures because students functioning in a real-life situation would not know every word native speakers use with them in a live conversation. The lively and interactive nature of video allows students to use their listening and viewing skills to comprehend new language in addition to seeing and hearing the language they have learned come to life.

Getting the most out of video The intrinsic benefit of video is often lost when students are allowed to read the scripted material before viewing. In many cases, students will have come to understand language used by the speakers in the video by means of reading comprehension, thus negating the inherent benefits of video as a tool to develop listening and viewing skills. Because today's students are so accustomed to the medium of video as a tool for entertainment and learning, a well-written and well-produced video program will help them develop real-life language skills and confidence in those skills in an enjoyable way.

Épisode 1 500	Épisode 8 507
Épisode 2 501	Épisode 9 508
Épisode 3 502	Épisode 10 509
Épisode 4 503	Épisode 11 510
Épisode 5 504	Épisode 12 511
Épisode 6 505	Épisode 13 512
Épisode 7 506	Épisode 14 513

On Location!

Vidéotour

Épisode 1

Video Synopsis

In this video episode, Chloé explores aspects of cultural life in Paris. As she wanders through the **musée d'Orsay**, we catch glimpses of famous Impressionist paintings. She also talks with some other French teens about the theater and the movies. Finally, the video introduces us to the lively street performers of Paris, demonstrating the wide variety of art forms on display throughout the city.

Vidéotour
Bon voyage!

Épisode 1: Les loisirs culturels

Chloé visite le musée d'Orsay. Elle trouve les tableaux fabuleux.

Chloé et Vincent sur la place Igor Stravinsky

Avant de regarder

Pouvez-vous les trouver?
1. une exposition
2. une danseuse
3. un tableau
4. une peinture
5. une statue

Après avoir regardé

Expansion Are you aware of your cultural heritage? Can you name some famous American painters, musicians, architects? Do some research on the Internet about the **musée d'Orsay**. Who are some of the artists whose art is shown there? Can you find out what special exhibitions there are currently?

VIDÉO VHS/DVD

The two photos show highlights from the Chapter 1 video episode. Discuss the photos with your students before having them view the episode.

Vidéotour

Bon voyage!

Épisode 2: La santé et la médecine

Le docteur Nguyen est très sympa.

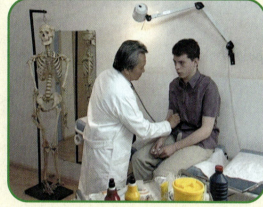

Vincent n'est pas en bonne santé.

Avant de regarder

Répondez aux questions.
1. Où est Vincent?
2. Pourquoi, d'après vous?
3. Vincent a un mouchoir dans la main. Pourquoi?
4. D'après vous, Vincent est très malade?
5. Que lui dit le médecin?

Après avoir regardé

Expansion Do you go to the doctor's everytime something is wrong with you? Why or why not? Does your doctor make house calls? Do some research online about medical achievements and famous doctors in France. You may want to begin with an online visit to **l'Institut Pasteur**.

Vidéotour

Épisode 2

Video Synopsis

In this video episode, Vincent has a bad dream about the famous Paris catacombs. The video flashes from these ancient skeletons to one in a doctor's office. Vincent explains his symptoms, and the doctor conducts a routine examination. Vincent is relieved to receive a diagnosis of the flu and not something more serious.

VIDÉO VHS/DVD

The two photos show highlights from the Chapter 2 video episode. Discuss the photos with your students before having them view the episode.

Vidéotour

Épisode 3

Video Synopsis

In this video episode, we see technology at work on a small and a large scale. Mme Séguin has just received new office equipment, including a computer and a fax machine. Christine guides her through the basic steps of using each one. Then, Christine introduces us to the technological wonders on display at **La Cité des Sciences**.

Vidéotour

Bon voyage!

Épisode 3: Les télécommunications

Mme Séguin apprend à utiliser un ordinateur.

Ensuite, elle envoie un fax.

Avant de regarder

Christine apprend à Mme Séguin à envoyer un fax. Elle lui dit:

1. comment mettre le document dans la machine
2. ce qu'il faut faire ensuite
3. comment transmettre finalement le document

Après avoir regardé

Expansion How often do you use a computer? What do you use it for most of the time? Do your older relatives use a computer? If so, do they have the same difficulties that Mme Séguin had?

VIDÉO VHS/DVD

The two photos show highlights from the Chapter 3 video episode. Discuss the photos with your students before having them view the episode.

Vidéotour

Bon voyage!

Épisode 4: Des voyages intéressants

Amadou arrive à Chartres. Il a pris le train de Paris.

Amadou filme la cathédrale de Chartres.

Avant de regarder

Justifiez les phrases suivantes à l'aide des photos.
1. Amadou arrive de Paris.
2. Il est dans la rue.
3. Il filme dans la rue.
4. Il est devant une cathédrale.

Après avoir regardé

Expansion In the video you view the famous **cathédrale de Chartres.** Can you compare that beautiful structure to anything near where you live? What famous buildings would you like to visit in your country or abroad?

Vidéotour

Épisode 4

Video Synopsis

In this video episode, Amadou sets off on a day-trip to Chartres to work on a report about the town's cathedral. He hurries to catch a train from the **gare Montparnasse**, nearly leaving some of his camera equipment behind. Fortunately, a fellow passenger finds it, and Amadou is able to film the cathedral. The video introduces us to some of the cathedral's architectural highlights, including the beautiful stained-glass windows.

 VIDÉO VHS/DVD

The two photos show highlights from the Chapter 4 video episode. Discuss the photos with your students before having them view the episode.

Vidéotour

Épisode 5

Video Synopsis

In this video episode, Amadou runs into Christine at the post office. She's mailing a package to Martinique and withdrawing money from her savings account. The two discuss their saving habits and realize that Manu owes both of them money. Amadou picks up a package from his native country; his cousin has sent him a traditional drum, and lively African drum music transports us to the harvest festival in a rural village in Mali.

Vidéotour

Bon voyage!

Épisode 5: La banque et la poste

Amadou et Christine se parlent à la poste.

Christine envoie un colis à la Martinique.

Avant de regarder

Pouvez-vous les trouver?
1. un bureau de poste parisien
2. une personne qui achète des timbres à un distributeur automatique
3. une personne qui envoie un colis
4. une employée des postes attentive

Après avoir regardé

Expansion The post office in France does more than deal with mail. Watch the video and go online (www.laposte.fr) to see the many services offered by the post office in France.

VIDÉO VHS/DVD

The two photos show highlights from the Chapter 5 video episode. Discuss the photos with your students before having them view the episode.

Vidéotour
Bon voyage!

Épisode 6: La gastronomie

Vincent et Manu parlent dans la cuisine.

Vincent croit qu'il va être malade.

Avant de regarder

Répondez aux questions.
1. Qui fait la cuisine?
2. Qu'est-ce qu'il y a comme aliments?
3. Dans quoi va-t-il faire cuire son repas?
4. D'après vous, pourquoi Vincent ne se sent-il pas bien?

Après avoir regardé

Expansion In the video you see the famous **école du Cordon Bleu.** Do some research online to find out more about this famous cooking school. Is there a similar school in your area. Are there any famous cooking shows or particular chefs on TV that you enjoy watching?

Vidéotour

Épisode 6

Video Synopsis

In this video episode, Manu has prepared a special dinner for Mme Chentouf's birthday. Vincent is impressed until Manu reveals some of his cooking shortcuts. Like many French people today, he prepares frozen and canned foods and relies on the microwave rather than the stove. For a look at more traditional French cooking, the video takes us to the **Cordon Bleu** cooking school.

VIDÉO VHS/DVD

The two photos show highlights from the Chapter 6 video episode. Discuss the photos with your students before having them view the episode.

Vidéotour

Épisode 7

Video Synopsis

In this video episode, Mme Séguin is behind the wheel as she and Christine drive to Fontainebleau for a picnic. Mme Séguin's haphazard driving style makes for an eventful trip: they miss the exit for the autoroute, nearly run out of gas, and finally Mme Séguin receives a speeding ticket! We then witness the speed of the Paris-Dakar road race as the video highlights some stages of this difficult course.

Vidéotour
Bon voyage!

Épisode 7: La voiture et la route

Mme Séguin fait le plein à la station-service.

Elle reçoit une contravention.

Avant de regarder

Continuez le dialogue entre Mme Séguin et le motard de la gendarmerie.

Le Motard: Bonjour, madame. Vos papiers, s'il vous plaît.

Mme Séguin: Mais pourquoi…

Après avoir regardé

Expansion Do some research on the Internet about driving in France. You may wish to visit www.preventionroutiere.asso.fr for some interesting information.

VIDÉO VHS/DVD

The two photos show highlights from the Chapter 7 video episode. Discuss the photos with your students before having them view the episode.

Vidéotour
Bon voyage!

Épisode 8: Un accident et l'hôpital

Vincent a eu un accident.

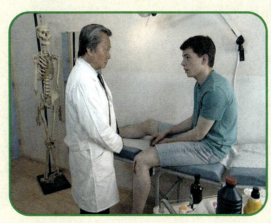

Le docteur Nguyen l'examine à l'hôpital.

Avant de regarder

Imaginez le dialogue entre Vincent et son docteur. Vincent raconte ce qui lui est arrivé.

Docteur: Alors, mon petit Vincent, qu'est-ce qui t'arrive?

Vincent: Eh bien voilà, Docteur…

Après avoir regardé

Expansion In the video you had a chance to view the famous **l'Institut Pasteur.** Do some research on the Internet to learn more about this place named after a famous doctor. Write a short paragraph explaining some of the major research that has been done there and the significance of this research.

Vidéotour

Épisode 8

Video Synopsis

In this video episode, Vincent is knocked down by a roller-blader on the streets of Paris. Christine takes him to the hospital where Doctor Nguyen examines him. The doctor prescribes some pain medication and reassures Vincent that the injury isn't serious. We then get a look at the Pasteur Institute, from the re-creation of Pasteur's laboratory to the modern facilities for scientific research.

VIDÉO VHS/DVD

The two photos show highlights from the Chapter 8 video episode. Discuss the photos with your students before having them view the episode.

Vidéotour

Épisode 9

Video Synopsis

In this video episode, Manu and Vincent have made plans to attend the **Fête de la Musique**, but Manu is disappointed that he has to work at the hotel reception desk that day. A journalist checks into the hotel, and when Manu learns that she is covering the festival, he insists on performing his rap song about hotels. The video later shows us real performers at the music festival and the crowds that gather to watch the entertainment.

Vidéotour

Bon voyage!

Épisode 9: L'hôtel

Manu s'occupe d'une cliente de l'hôtel.

Manu fait du rap.

Avant de regarder

Manu veut montrer son talent de musicien à une jeune journaliste.

Décrivez:

1. l'attitude de Manu
2. l'attitude de la jeune journaliste

Après avoir regardé

Expansion In the video, you saw a clip from the **Fête de la Musique.** Do some research online to find out more about this musical event in France.

VIDÉO VHS/DVD

The two photos show highlights from the Chapter 9 video episode. Discuss the photos with your students before having them view the episode.

Vidéotour
Bon voyage!

Épisode 10: Les transports en commun

Chloé prend son ticket au distributeur automatique.

Vincent passe par le tourniquet.

Avant de regarder

Répondez aux questions.
1. Où est Chloé?
2. Qu'est-ce qu'elle fait?
3. Vincent a déjà un billet?
4. Où va-t-il arriver?

Après avoir regardé

Expansion Do some research on the Internet to find out more about the Paris metropolitan transportation system: www.ratp.fr

---

Vidéotour

Épisode 10

Video Synopsis

In this video episode, we get an introduction to the Paris metro system. Chloé narrates a brief tour of some of the most interesting stations—many have Art Nouveau elements, while the **Louvre** station displays replicas from the museum. Then, Chloé and Vincent plan to take the metro to the **Grande Bibliothèque**. They are seasoned metro travellers but have great difficulty finding each other in the maze of the **Madeleine** station.

VIDÉO VHS/DVD

The two photos show highlights from the Chapter 10 video episode. Discuss the photos with your students before having them view the episode.

Vidéotour

Épisode 11

Video Synopsis

In this video episode, Vincent and Manu compete in a treasure hunt and hope to win the trophy. The clues lead them to various landmarks around the city of Paris: **la tour Montparnasse, le Bon Marché,** and the oldest church in Paris, **Saint-Germain-des-Prés.** Manu drives his scooter through the busy streets while Vincent gives directions. The final clue leads them to the small town of Senlis, just outside Paris, where we get a view of the town's beautiful cathedral and experience the slower pace of country life.

Vidéotour
Bon voyage!

Épisode 11: À la ville et à la campagne

Vincent et Manu ont fait la première étape du rallye.

Ils lisent les instructions devant l'église Saint-Germain-des-Prés.

Avant de regarder

Vrai ou faux?
1. Les deux garçons sont dans un village.
2. Ils stationnent dans la rue.
3. Ils portent des casques.
4. Ils sont devant une église.
5. Il y a beaucoup de circulation.

Après avoir regardé

Expansion In the video you see that the boys go to the town of Senlis. Do some research on the Internet to find out more about this lovely town. Then write a report about it. Tell why you might like to visit.

VIDÉO VHS/DVD

The two photos show highlights from the Chapter 11 video episode. Discuss the photos with your students before having them view the episode.

Vidéotour
Bon voyage!

Épisode 12: Les fêtes

Manu est habillé en Père Noël.

Manu et Chloé parlent de Noël et de Hanouka.

Avant de regarder

Le Père Noël arrive chez Chloé. Le reconnaissez-vous? Racontez comment le Père Noël est arrivé chez Chloé, si Chloé a été surprise et de quoi ils ont parlé.

Après avoir regardé

Expansion Ask your friends and neighbors what holidays they celebrate and how. Compare cultural and religious differences in your own community.

VIDEO COMPANION

cinq cent onze 511

Vidéotour
Épisode 12

Video Synopsis

In this video episode, Chloé enters her living room to find that Santa Claus has come down the chimney! It turns out to be Manu, dressed up in a Santa Claus costume. He is surprised that Chloé's family has no Christmas tree on display. Chloé explains that her family is Jewish and tells Manu some ways they celebrate Hanukkah. We then get a tour of celebrations in different parts of the Francophone world: Christmas in Paris, Carnaval in Martinique, and the winter carnival festivities in Quebec.

VIDÉO VHS/DVD

The two photos show highlights from the Chapter 12 video episode. Discuss the photos with your students before having them view the episode.

Vidéotour

Épisode 13

Video Synopsis

In this video episode, Manu and his counterpart, "Emmanuel," each demonstrate their version of good manners. They discuss greeting friends, being on time, eating quietly, and other table manners. Manu doesn't always follow his own guidelines, much to the annoyance of "Emmanuel," who takes the rules of etiquette to heart.

Vidéotour
Bon voyage!

Épisode 13: Les loisirs culturels

Est-ce que Manu est bien élevé?

«Emmanuel» sait comment se tenir à table.

Avant de regarder

Comparez les deux Manu.
1. Comment est-il habillé?
2. Comment se tient-il?
3. Comment est disposée sa table?

Après avoir regardé

Expansion Were your parents strict about good manners at home? And your grandparents? Give examples.

VIDÉO VHS/DVD

The two photos show highlights from the Chapter 13 video episode. Discuss the photos with your students before having them view the episode.

Vidéotour

Bon voyage!

Épisode 14: Les professions et les métiers

Mme Lauzon et Vincent se serrent la main.

Ils parlent dans le bureau de Mme Lauzon.

Avant de regarder

Vincent veut un job pour l'été. Commentez:
1. comment il est habillé
2. la façon de saluer Mme Lauzon
3. comment il se tient

Après avoir regardé

Expansion Do you work during the summer? What do you do? Do you think it is important to have a summer job? Why?

Vidéotour

Épisode 14

Video Synopsis

In this video episode, Vincent is ready to pursue his career goal of becoming an architect. He interviews for a summer job at an architectural firm where he hopes to gain experience. Despite being nervous, Vincent carries off the interview professionally, remembering to give his résumé and references to the director of Human Resources. At the end, the video takes us into the future where Vincent, Christine, Amadou, Chloé, and Manu are all professionals in different fields.

VIDÉO VHS/DVD

The two photos show highlights from the Chapter 14 video episode. Discuss the photos with your students before having them view the episode.

Handbook

InfoGap Activities H2
These communicative activities review and reinforce the vocabulary and structure just learned.

Study Tips H22
These helpful hints provide parents and guardians with an opportunity to help their children learn new material.

Verb Charts H38
French-English Dictionary H49
English-French Dictionary H79
Index H109

Handbook ❖ H1

InfoGap

Activity 1

CHAPITRE 1, Mots 1, pages 2–3

Élève A Ask your partner the following questions. Correct answers are in parentheses.

1. Qu'est-ce que tu aimes comme film?
   (J'aime les documentaires.)
2. Qu'est-ce qu'on monte?
   (On monte Roméo et Juliette.)
3. Tu aimes mieux aller au cinéma ou louer des vidéos ou DVD?
   (J'aime mieux louer des vidéos ou DVD.)

Élève A Answer your partner's questions according to the illustrations.

1.

2.

3.

Élève B Ask your partner the following questions. Correct answers are in parentheses.

1. Qu'est-ce que tu aimes comme film?
   (J'aime les dessins animés.)
2. Tu as déjà vu le chanteur?
   (Non, mais j'ai déjà vu la danseuse.)
3. Tu vas voir une pièce de théâtre?
   (Non, je vais voir un film au cinéma.)

Élève B Answer your partner's questions according to the illustrations.

1.

2. Roméo et Juliette
   ballet en trois actes
   d'après William Shakespeare
   musique
   Sergueï Prokofiev
   chorégraphie et mise en scène
   Rudolf Noureev
   réglées par
   Patricia Ruanne
   Frederick Jahn
   chorélogue
   Kristin Johnson
   décors
   Ezio Frigerio
   avec la collaboration de
   Alexandre Beliaev
   costumes
   Ezio Frigerio et Mauro Pagano
   lumières
   Vinicio Cheli
   production créée pour le Ballet
   de l'Opéra en 1984
   Orchestre de l'Opéra National de Paris
   direction
   Vello Pähn
   fin du spectacle vers 22 h 40

3. PONETTE / JACQUOT

Handbook

Activity 2

CHAPITRE 1, Mots 2, pages 6–7

Élève A Ask your partner the following questions. Correct answers are in parentheses.

1. C'est un musée ou un théâtre?
   (C'est un musée.)
2. Le musée est ouvert ou fermé?
   (Le musée est ouvert.)
3. Il y a beaucoup de tableaux ou de statues au musée?
   (Il y a beaucoup de tableaux.)

Élève A Answer your partner's questions according to the illustration.

Élève B Ask your partner the following questions. Correct answers are in parentheses.

1. Elle est peintre ou sculpteur?
   (Elle est peintre.)
2. Il est peintre ou sculpteur?
   (Il est sculpteur.)
3. Qu'est-ce qu'il y a au musée?
   (Il y a une exposition de peinture et sculpture au musée.)

Élève B Answer your partner's questions according to the photograph.

InfoGap

Activity 3
CHAPITRE 1, Structure, pages 10–11

Élève A You are familiar with some people, places, and things, but your partner knows some facts or information he or she wants to share with you about them. Make your statement and your partner will respond. Correct responses are in parentheses.

1. Je connais Nathalie.
   (Je sais qu'elle habite à Grenoble.)
2. Je connais Hamlet.
   (Je sais que c'est une pièce de Shakespeare.)
3. Je connais Paris.
   (Je sais que c'est la capitale de la France.)
4. Je connais l'œuvre de Degas.
   (Je sais que Degas est un peintre français.)
5. Je connais Paul.
   (Je sais quel est son numéro de téléphone.)

Élève A Your partner and some of his or her friends are familiar with certain people, places, and things, but you and your friends have some facts or information to share. Add your comment according to the cues. Begin your statements with **Nous savons…**

1. …qu'ils sont très beaux.
2. …quelle pièce on joue en ce moment.
3. …où se trouve le théâtre.
4. …qu'elles savent danser le tango.
5. …qu'elles sont célèbres.

Élève B You are familiar with some people, places, and things, but your partner knows some facts or information he or she wants to share with you about them. Make your statement and your partner will respond. Correct responses are in parentheses.

1. Nous connaissons les tableaux de Monet, Manet et Renoir.
   (Nous savons qu'ils sont très beaux.)
2. Nous connaissons les pièces de Molière.
   (Nous savons quelle pièce on joue en ce moment.)
3. Nous connaissons la Comédie-Française.
   (Nous savons où se trouve le théâtre.)
4. Nous connaissons des danseuses.
   (Nous savons qu'elles savent danser le tango.)
5. Nous connaissons les sculptures de Rodin.
   (Nous savons qu'elles sont célèbres.)

Élève B Your partner and some of his or her friends are familiar with certain people, places, and things, but you and your friends have some facts or information to share. Add your comment according to the cues. Begin your statements with **Je sais…**

1. …qu'elle habite à Grenoble.
2. …que c'est une pièce de Shakespeare.
3. …que c'est la capitale de la France.
4. …que Degas est un peintre français.
5. …quel est son numéro de téléphone.

Activity 4

CHAPITRE 1, Structure, pages 12–17

Élève A Ask your partner the following questions. Correct answers are in parentheses.

1. Tu connais les tableaux de Monet?
   (Oui, je les connais.)
2. Tu vois la sculpture moderne?
   (Non, je ne la vois pas.)
3. Tu sais le nom du film?
   (Oui, je le sais.)
4. Tu lis les sous-titres?
   (Non, je ne les lis pas.)
5. Tu veux voir la pièce?
   (Oui, je veux la voir.)

Élève A Your partner will ask a question. Respond according to the cues, using the correct object pronoun.

1. Oui…
2. Non…
3. Oui…
4. Oui…
5. Oui…

Élève B Ask your partner the following questions. Correct answers are in parentheses.

1. Tu m'invites au cinéma?
   (Oui, je t'invite.)
2. Ce film te plaît?
   (Non, ce film ne me plaît pas.)
3. Je te parle au téléphone avant le film?
   (Oui, tu me parles au téléphone avant le film.)
4. Le prof nous donne beaucoup de devoirs?
   (Oui, le prof nous donne beaucoup de devoirs.)
   or
   (Oui, le prof vous donne beaucoup de devoirs.)
5. Julie vous dit quand le musée est fermé?
   (Oui, Julie nous dit quand le musée est fermé.)
   or
   (Oui, Julie me dit quand le musée est fermé.)

Élève B Your partner will ask a question. Respond according to the cues, using the correct object pronoun.

1. Oui…
2. Non…
3. Oui…
4. Non…
5. Oui…

InfoGap

Activity 5
CHAPITRE 2, Mots 1, pages 34–35

Élève A Read your partner the following statements. He or she will tell you each person's symptoms. Possible responses are in parentheses.

1. Miriam n'est pas en bonne santé.
   (*Elle a mal aux oreilles.*)
2. Elle a besoin d'un mouchoir.
   (*Elle a le nez qui coule.*) or (*Elle a un rhume.*)
3. Anne est très malade, la pauvre.
   (*Elle a des frissons.*) or (*Elle a de la fièvre.*)
4. David ne se sent pas bien.
   (*Il tousse.*)

Élève A Use the pictures below to tell your partner about each person's symptoms.

1.
2.
3.
4.

Élève B Use the pictures below to tell your partner about each person's symptoms.

1.
2.
3.
4.

Élève B Read your partner the following statements. He or she will tell you each person's symptoms. Possible responses are in parentheses.

1. Pauline est malade.
   (*Elle est enrhumée.*) or (*Elle éternue.*)
2. Martine est en mauvaise santé.
   (*Elle a un rhume.*) or (*Elle tousse.*)
3. Juliette ne se sent pas bien.
   (*Elle a mal à la tête.*)
4. Jeanne est très malade, la pauvre.
   (*Elle a mal au ventre.*)

Activity 6

CHAPITRE 2, Mots 2, pages 38–39

Élève A You are the doctor and your partner, the patient, needs help. Ask him or her the following questions.

1. Où avez-vous mal?
   (J'ai mal au ventre.)
2. Qu'est-ce que vous avez?
   (J'ai une angine.)
3. Qu'est-ce que vous avez?
   (J'ai une sinusite aiguë.)
4. Qu'est-ce que vous avez?
   (J'ai un chat dans la gorge.)
5. Où avez-vous mal?
   (J'ai mal à la tête.)

Élève A Answer your partner's questions according to the cues below.

1. des frissons
2. aux oreilles
3. une allergie
4. une fièvre de cheval
5. une infection

Élève B Answer your partner's questions according to the cues below.

1. au ventre
2. une angine
3. une sinusite aiguë
4. un chat dans la gorge
5. à la tête

Élève B You are the doctor and your partner, the patient, needs help. Ask him or her the following questions.

1. Qu'est-ce que vous avez?
   (J'ai des frissons.)
2. Où avez-vous mal?
   (J'ai mal aux oreilles.)
3. Qu'est-ce que vous avez?
   (J'ai une allergie.)
4. Qu'est-ce que vous avez?
   (J'ai une fièvre de cheval.)
5. Qu'est-ce que vous avez?
   (J'ai une infection.)

Activity 7

CHAPITRE 2, Structure, pages 42–43

Élève A Ask your partner the following questions. Correct answers are in parentheses.

1. Tu parles souvent à ta copine?
   (Oui, je lui parle souvent.)
2. Les joueurs lancent le ballon à l'arbitre?
   (Oui, ils lui lancent le ballon.)
3. Le médecin prescrit des antibiotiques aux malades?
   (Oui, il leur prescrit des antibiotiques.)
4. Tu vas acheter un cadeau à ton frère?
   (Oui, je vais lui acheter un cadeau.)
5. Le pharmacien donne des médicaments à ta mère?
   (Oui, il lui donne des médicaments.)

Élève A Answer your partner's questions using **lui** or **leur.**

1. Oui, je _____ dis bonjour.
2. Oui, il _____ vend des billets.
3. Oui, il _____ fait une ordonnance.
4. Oui, ils _____ téléphonent.
5. Oui, elle _____ dit qu'il a de la fièvre.

Élève B Answer your partner's questions using **lui** or **leur.**

1. Oui, je _____ parle souvent.
2. Oui, ils _____ lancent le ballon.
3. Oui, il _____ prescrit des antibiotiques.
4. Oui, je vais _____ acheter un cadeau.
5. Oui, il _____ donne des médicaments.

Élève B Ask your partner the following questions. Correct answers are in parentheses.

1. Tu dis bonjour à tes amis?
   (Oui, je leur dis bonjour.)
2. L'employé vend des billets à ton père?
   (Oui, il lui vend des billets.)
3. Le médecin fait une ordonnance à Marie?
   (Oui, il lui fait une ordonnance.)
4. Les malades téléphonent au professeur?
   (Oui, ils lui téléphonent.)
5. Sa mère dit à Paul qu'il a de la fièvre?
   (Oui, elle lui dit qu'il a de la fièvre.)

Handbook

Activity 8

CHAPITRE 2, Structure, pages 45–47

Élève A Ask your partner the following questions. Correct answers are in parentheses.

1. Finir les devoirs?
   (Finis tes devoirs!)
2. Préparer le dîner?
   (Prépare le dîner!)
3. Choisir un film?
   (Choisissons un film!)
4. Travailler plus?
   (Travaille plus!)
5. Dîner au restaurant?
   (Dînons au restaurant!)

Élève A Use the imperative to answer your partner's questions based on the information in the chart below.

Personne(s)	Activité
tu	prendre le métro
vous	attendre devant la porte
tu	faire du ski
tu	sortir ce soir
vous	regarder le film

Élève B Ask your partner the following questions. Correct answers are in parentheses.

1. Prendre le métro?
   (Prends le métro!)
2. Attendre devant la porte?
   (Attendez devant la porte!)
3. Faire du ski?
   (Fais du ski!)
4. Sortir ce soir?
   (Sors ce soir!)
5. Regardez le film?
   (Regardez le film!)

Élève B Use the imperative to answer your partner's questions based on the information in the chart below.

Personne(s)	Activité
tu	finir les devoirs
tu	préparer le dîner
nous	choisir un film
tu	travailler plus
nous	dîner au restaurant

InfoGap

Activity 9

CHAPITRE 3, Mots 1, pages 66–67

Élève A Ask your partner the following questions. Correct answers are in parentheses.

1. Tu mets le document face écrite non visible?
   (Oui, je mets le document face écrite non visible.)

2. Quand tu tapes ton texte, tu regardes l'écran ou le clavier?
   (Je regarde l'écran.)

3. Qu'est-ce que tu mets dans le lecteur?
   (Je mets une disquette.)

Élève A Answer your partner's questions based on the pictures below.

1.

2.

3.

Élève B Ask your partner the following questions. Correct answers are in parentheses.

1. Tu as un dictionnaire sur CD-ROM?
   (Oui, j'ai un dictionnaire sur CD-ROM.)

2. Tu cliques sur l'icône du logiciel avec quoi?
   (Je clique sur l'icône du logiciel avec la souris.)

3. Tu tapes tes devoirs sur quoi?
   (Je tape mes devoirs sur le clavier.)

Élève B Answer your partner's questions based on the pictures below.

1.

2.

3.

Activity 10

CHAPITRE 4, Mots 1, pages 98–99

Élève A Ask your partner the following questions. Correct answers are in parentheses.

1. Quelles lignes desservent Mitry-Claye et Les Noues?
   (Les Lignes de Banlieue)
2. Quelle lignes desservent Londres et Lille?
   (Les Grandes Lignes)
3. La voiture du train a un couloir central?
   (Oui, la voiture du train a un couloir central.)
4. Il y a deux sièges de chaque côté?
   (Oui, il y a deux sièges de chaque côté.)

Élève A Answer your partner's questions based on the picture below.

M. et Mme Dubois   Madame Delacroix

Élève B Ask your partner the following questions. Correct answers are in parentheses.

1. Madame Delacroix est assise?
   (Oui, elle est assise.)
2. M. et Mme Dubois sont dans un compartiment?
   (Non, ils sont dans le couloir.)
3. Le compartiment est complet?
   (Oui, le compartiment est complet.)
4. M. et Mme Dubois sont assis?
   (Non, ils sont debout.)

Élève B Answer your partner's questions based on the pictures below.

1–2.

3–4.

InfoGap

Activity 11
CHAPITRE 5, Mots 1, pages 142–143

Élève A Ask your partner the following questions. Correct answers are in parentheses.

1. Marie a de l'argent liquide?
   (Oui, elle a de l'argent liquide.)
2. Elle dépense tout son argent?
   (Non, elle met de l'argent de côté.)
3. Sophie est au bureau de change?
   (Non, elle est au distributeur automatique.)
4. Elle retire de l'argent?
   (Oui, elle retire de l'argent.)

Élève A Answer your partner's questions based on the pictures below.

1–3.

4.

Élève B Answer your partner's questions based on the pictures below.

1–2.

3–4.

Élève B Ask your partner the following questions. Correct answers are in parentheses.

1. La touriste est allée au bureau de change?
   (Oui, elle est allée au bureau de change.)
2. Elle a changé des dollars?
   (Oui, elle a changé des dollars.)
3. Le caissier lui a donné des euros?
   (Oui, il lui a donné des euros.)
4. Elle a mis les pièces où?
   (Elle a mis les pièces dans son porte-monnaie.)

Activity 12

CHAPITRE 6, Mots 1, pages 174–175

Élève A Read your partner the following true and false statements. Correct responses are in parentheses.

1. C'est une cuisine moderne.
   (Oui, c'est une cuisine moderne.)
2. Le réfrigérateur a trois portes.
   (Non, le réfrigérateur a deux portes.)
3. Il y a un congélateur dans le réfrigérateur.
   (Oui, il y a un congélateur dans le réfrigérateur.)
4. Il y a des bananes dans la cuisine.
   (Oui, il y a des bananes dans la cuisine.)

Élève A Give your partner the correct information based on the picture below.

Élève B Read your partner the following true and false statements. Correct responses are in parentheses.

1. Une pomme de terre, c'est un fruit.
   (Non, c'est un légume.)
2. Les champignons sont des fines herbes.
   (Non, les champignons sont des légumes.)
3. Un oignon, c'est un légume.
   (Oui, c'est un légume.)
4. On met des haricots verts dans une salade de fruits.
   (Non, on ne met pas d'haricots verts dans une salade de fruits.)

Élève B Give your partner the correct information based on the picture below.

Activity 13

CHAPITRE 7, Mots 1, pages 206–207

Élève A Ask your partner the following questions. Correct answers are in parentheses.

1. Claire prend des leçons de conduite?
   (Oui, elle prend des leçons de conduite.)
2. Elle a mis sa ceinture de sécurité?
   (Oui, elle a mis sa ceinture de sécurité.)
3. Elle va avoir son permis de conduire?
   (Oui, elle va avoir son permis de conduire.)
4. Elle conduit un camion?
   (Non, elle conduit une voiture.)

Élève A Answer your partner's questions based on the picture below.

Élève B Ask your partner the following questions. Correct answers are in parentheses.

1. On fait le plein?
   (Oui, on fait le plein.)
2. On met de l'essence où?
   (On met de l'essence dans le réservoir.)
3. Qu'est-ce qu'on vérifie?
   (On vérifie les niveaux d'huile et d'eau.)
4. On lave le pare-brise?
   (Non, on ne lave pas le pare-brise.)

Élève B Answer your partner's questions based on the pictures below.

Activity 14

CHAPITRE 8, Mots 1, pages 248–249, and Mots 2, pages 252–253

Élève A Ask your partner the following questions. Correct answers are in parentheses.

1. L'infirmière lui fait une radio?
   (Non, l'infirmière lui prend la tension.)
2. Elle lui prend le pouls?
   (Oui, elle lui prend le pouls.)
3. Le médecin lui fait une piqûre?
   (Oui, le médecin lui fait une piqûre.)

Élève A Answer your partner's questions based on the picture below.

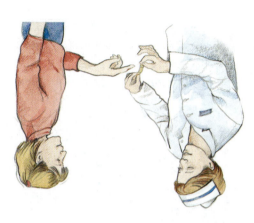

Élève B Ask your partner the following questions. Correct answers are in parentheses.

1. Jeanne s'est coupé le doigt ou le doigt de pied?
   (Elle s'est coupé le doigt.)
2. L'infirmière la soigne?
   (Oui, l'infirmière la soigne.)
3. L'infirmière lui fait un pansement?
   (Oui, elle lui fait un pansement.)

Élève B Answer your partner's questions based on the pictures below.

1.  2.

3.

InfoGap

Activity 15
CHAPITRE 9, Mots 1, pages 280–281, and Mots 2, pages 284–285

Élève A Ask your partner the following questions. Correct answers are in parentheses.

1. C'est la réception ou une chambre?
   (C'est la réception.)
2. Sandrine remplit la fiche de police?
   (Oui, elle remplit la fiche de police.)
3. La réceptionniste lui a donné une clé ou une serviette?
   (Elle lui a donné une clé.)
4. Sandrine ouvre la porte de sa chambre?
   (Oui, elle ouvre la porte de sa chambre.)
5. C'est une chambre avec salle de bains?
   (Oui, c'est une chambre avec salle de bains.)

Élève A Answer your partner's questions based on the picture below.

Élève B Ask your partner the following questions. Correct answers are in parentheses.

1. Mme Dubois a libéré sa chambre?
   (Oui, elle a libéré sa chambre.)
2. Elle parle à la femme de chambre ou à la réceptionniste?
   (Elle parle à la réceptionniste.)
3. Mme Dubois a demandé la note?
   (Oui, elle a demandé la note.)
4. Elle a vérifié les frais?
   (Oui, elle a vérifié les frais.)
5. Elle a payé en espèces ou avec une carte de crédit?
   (Elle a payé avec une carte de crédit.)

Élève B Answer your partner's questions based on the pictures below.

1–3.

4–5.

Handbook

Activity 16

CHAPITRE 10, Mots 2, pages 314–315

Élève A Ask your partner the following questions. Correct answers are in parentheses.

1. L'autobus a combien de portes?
   (L'autobus a trois portes.)
2. Les voyageurs montent par l'arrière de l'autobus?
   (Non, ils descendent par l'arrière.)
3. La descente est interdite par l'avant?
   (Oui, la descente est interdite par l'avant.)
4. Quelques voyageurs descendent par le milieu?
   (Oui, ils descendent par le milieu.)

Élève A Answer your partner's questions based on the picture below.

Élève B Ask your partner the following questions. Correct answers are in parentheses.

1. Marc veut descendre de l'autobus?
   (Non, il ne veut pas descendre.)
2. Il appuie sur le bouton?
   (Non, il n'appuie pas sur le bouton.)
3. Le conducteur prend son ticket?
   (Non, le conducteur ne prend pas son ticket.)
4. Il y a un appareil pour valider son ticket?
   (Oui, il y a un appareil pour valider son ticket.)

Élève B Answer your partner's questions based on the picture below.

Activity 17

CHAPITRE 11, Mots 2, pages 344–345

Élève A Ask your partner the following questions. Correct answers are in parentheses.

1. Quel animal donne des œufs?
   (Une poule donne des œufs.)
2. Quel animal mange des carottes et de la salade?
   (Un lapin mange des carottes et de la salade.)
3. C'est quel animal?
   (C'est un cochon.)
4. Quel animal donne du lait?
   (Une vache donne du lait.)

Élève A Answer your partner's questions based on the picture below.

Élève B Ask your partner the following questions. Correct answers are in parentheses.

1. Qui cultive la terre?
   (L'agriculteur cultive la terre.)
2. Il utilise des chevaux pour travailler la terre?
   (Non, il utilise un tracteur.)
3. C'est un champ ou un vignoble?
   (C'est un champ.)
4. Il cultive du raisin ou des céréales?
   (Il cultive des céréales.)

Élève B Answer your partner's questions based on the pictures below.

1.
2.
3.
4.

H18 ❦ Handbook

Activity 18

CHAPITRE 12, Mots 1, pages 376–377

Élève A Ask your partner the following questions. Correct answers are in parentheses.

1. Les soldats défilent?
   (Oui, les soldats défilent.)
2. Ils passent devant les tribunes?
   (Oui, ils passent devant les tribunes.)
3. Les tribunes sont pleines de spectateurs?
   (Oui, elles sont pleines de spectateurs.)
4. Il y a une fanfare?
   (Non, il n'y a pas de fanfare.)
5. Il y a des feux d'artifice?
   (Non, il n'y a pas de feux d'artifice.)

Élève A Answer your partner's questions based on the picture below.

Élève B Ask your partner the following questions. Correct answers are in parentheses.

1. C'est la fête nationale française ou le carnaval?
   (C'est la fête nationale française.)
2. La fête a lieu le 4 juillet?
   (Non, la fête a lieu le 14 juillet.)
3. Il y a des chars dans la rue?
   (Non, il n'y a pas de chars dans la rue.)
4. Il y a une fanfare?
   (Oui, il y une fanfare.)
5. Le défilé traverse la ville?
   (Oui, le défilé traverse la ville.)

Élève B Answer your partner's questions based on the picture below.

InfoGap

Activity 19
CHAPITRE 13, Mots 1, pages 406–407, and Mots 2, pages 410–411

Élève A Ask your partner the following questions. Correct answers are in parentheses.

1. Christine fait une présentation?
   (Oui, elle fait une présentation.)
2. Elle a l'air contente ou triste?
   (Elle a l'air contente.)
3. Les deux garçons s'embrassent sur les deux joues?
   (Non, ils se serrent la main.)
4. Ils sont bien ou mal élevés?
   (Ils sont bien élevés.)

Élève A Answer your partner's questions based on the pictures below.

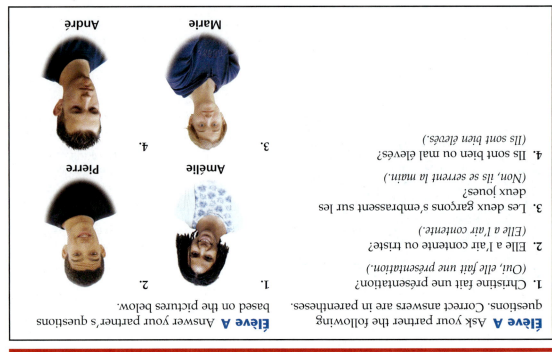

Élève B Ask your partner the following questions. Correct answers are in parentheses.

1. Amélie est désolée que tu viennes?
   (Non, elle est contente que je vienne.)
2. Pierre a l'air étonné ou furieux?
   (Il a l'air étonné.)
3. Marie est étonnée que tu ne saches pas son adresse?
   (Oui, elle est étonnée que je ne sache pas son adresse.)
4. André a l'air content ou triste?
   (Il a l'air triste.)

Élève B Answer your partner's questions based on the picture below.

H20 ❦ Handbook

Activity 20

CHAPITRE 14, Mots 1, pages 436–437

Élève A Ask your partner the following questions. Correct answers are in parentheses.

1. Que fait l'informaticienne?
   (Elle fait le programme d'un ordinateur.)
2. Que fait le comptable?
   (Il tient les livres de comptes.)
3. Que fait l'ingénieur?
   (Il crée des routes ou des bâtiments.)
4. Que fait le cinéaste?
   (Il fait des films.)
5. Que fait la journaliste?
   (Elle écrit des articles pour le journal.)

Élève A Choose the correct information from the chart below to answer your partner's questions.

…répare les éviers, les lavabos, les toilettes.
…fait des placards, des tables, des chaises.
…défend les criminels au tribunal.
…vend des marchandises.
…répare les lampes.

Élève B Choose the correct information from the chart below to answer your partner's questions.

…fait des films.
…tient les livres de comptes.
…fait le programme d'un ordinateur.
…écrit des articles pour le journal.
…crée des routes ou des bâtiments.

Élève B Ask your partner the following questions. Correct answers are in parentheses.

1. Que fait l'avocate?
   (Elle défend les criminels au tribunal.)
2. Que fait l'électricienne?
   (Elle répare les lampes.)
3. Que fait le plombier?
   (Il répare les éviers, les lavabos, les toilettes.)
4. Que fait la commerçante?
   (Elle vend des marchandises.)
5. Que fait le menuisier?
   (Il fait des placards, des tables, des chaises.)

Study Tips

For students and parents/guardians

This guide is designed to help you as students achieve success as you embark on the adventure of learning another language and to enable your parents or guardians to help you on this exciting journey. There are many ways to learn new information. You may find some of these suggestions more useful than others, depending upon which style of learning works best for you. Before you begin, it is important to understand how we acquire language.

Receptive Skills

Each day of your life you receive a great deal of information through the use of language. In order to get this information, it is necessary to understand the language being used. It is necessary to understand the language in two different ways. First you must be able to understand what people are saying when they speak to you. This is referred to as oral or listening comprehension. Oral comprehension or listening comprehension is the ability to understand the spoken language.

You must also be able to understand what you read. This is referred to as reading comprehension. Reading comprehension is the ability to understand the written language.

Listening comprehension and reading comprehension are called the *receptive skills*. They are receptive skills because as you listen to what someone else says or read what someone else has written, you receive information without having to produce any language yourself.

It is usually very easy to understand your native language. It is a bit more problematic to understand a second language that is new to you. As a beginner you are still learning the sounds of the new language, and you recognize only a few words. Throughout **Bon voyage!** we will give you hints or suggestions to help you understand when people are speaking to you in French or when you are reading in French.

HINTS FOR LISTENING COMPREHENSION
When you are listening to a person speaking French, don't try to understand every word. It is not necessary to understand everything to get the idea of what someone is saying. Listen for the general message. If some details escape you, it doesn't matter. Also, never try to translate what people are saying in French into English. It takes a great deal of experience and expertise to be a translator. Trying to translate will hinder your ability to understand.

HINTS FOR READING COMPREHENSION
Just as you will not always understand every word you hear in a conversation, you will not necessarily understand every word you encounter in a reading selection, either. In **Bon voyage!**, we have used only words you know or can easily figure out in the reading selections. This will make reading comprehension much easier for you. However, if at some time you wish to read a newspaper or magazine article in French, you will most certainly come across some unfamiliar words. Do not stop reading. Continue to read to get the "gist" of the selection. Try to guess the meanings of words you do not know.

Study Tips

Productive Skills

There are two productive skills in language. These two skills are speaking and writing. They are called productive skills because it is you who has to produce the language when you say or write something. When you speak or write, you have control over the language and which words you use. If you don't know how to say something, you don't have to say it. With the receptive skills, on the other hand, someone else produces the language that you listen to or read, and you have no control over the words they use.

There's no doubt that you can easily speak your native language. You can write, too, even though you may sometimes make errors in spelling or punctuation. In French, there's not a lot you can say or write as a beginner. You can only talk or write about those topics you have learned in French class.

HINTS FOR SPEAKING Try to be as accurate as possible when speaking. Try not to make mistakes. However, if you do, it's not the end of the world. French speakers will understand you. You're not expected to speak a language perfectly after a limited time. You have probably spoken with people from other countries who do not speak English perfectly, but you can understand them. Remember:

- Keep talking! Don't become inhibited for fear of making a mistake.
- Say what you know how to say. Don't try to branch out in the early stages and attempt to talk about topics or situations you have not yet learned in French.

HINTS FOR WRITING There are many activities throughout each chapter of **Bon voyage!** that will help you to speak and write in French. When you have to write something on your own, however, without the guidance or assistance of an activity in your book, be sure to choose a topic for which you know the vocabulary in French. Never attempt to write about a topic you have not yet studied in French. Write down the topic you are going to write about. Then think of the words you know that are related to the topic. Be sure to include some action words (verbs) that you will need.

From your list of words, write as many sentences as you can. Read them and organize them into a logical order. Fill in any gaps. Then proof your paragraph(s) to see if you made any errors. Correct any that you find.

When writing on your own, be careful not to rely heavily, if at all, on a bilingual dictionary. It's not that bilingual dictionaries are bad, but when you look up a word you will very often find that there are several translations for the same word. As a beginning language student, you do not know which translation to choose; the chances are great that you will pick the wrong one.

As a final hint, never prepare your paragraph(s) in English and attempt to translate word for word. Always write from scratch in French.

*In each chapter of **Bon voyage!** you will learn how to say and write new words. In Chapter 1, you learn how to discuss movies, plays, and museums. It won't be long before you'll be able to talk about many things in French. **Bon voyage!***

Study Tips

CHAPITRE 1

Vocabulaire

Mots 1 & 2 *(pages 2–9)*

1. Remember to listen to the words and repeat them orally before reading them.
2. After you have gone over the new vocabulary, see how many words you remember. Think of seven words about a movie. Think of five words about a play.
3. Go over each activity orally before you write the answers.

Structure

Les verbes **savoir** *et* **connaître** *(pages 10–11)*

1. Simplify the grammatical rule: just remember that **savoir** means to know something simple, and **connaître** means to know or be familiar with something complex.
2. When doing these activities, pay particular attention to the object of each verb to determine the use of **savoir** or **connaitre**.

Les pronoms **me, te, nous, vous** *(pages 12–13)*

Remember that the pronouns **me, te, nous,** and **vous** are part of the "filling in the sandwich." **Ne…pas** is the bread that goes around the filling.

	me parle	
Il ne	te parle	pas.
	nous parle	
	vous parle	

Les pronoms **le, la, les** *(pages 14–17)*

As you do these activities, determine which word is the direct object before trying to replace it with **le, la,** or **les.** Do each activity orally before you write it.

Conversation
(page 18)

1. An important skill in understanding a foreign language is to guess the meaning of words from the context in which they occur. In this conversation, you will hear and use the expression **travailler notre espagnol.** This is new to you, but you can figure it out from the context.

   In this conversation, **travailler** means which of the following?
   a. parler
   b. comprendre
   c. pratiquer

2. Note how Léa says **ça me dit** in response to the question **ça t'interesse?** Do you think **ça me dit** has the same meaning as the phrase **ça m'interesse?**

Lectures culturelles

Les loisirs culturels en France *(pages 20–21)*

Identifying the main idea is an important comprehension skill. Read the title and subtitles. What do you think is the main idea of this reading?

a. Il ya des musées et des théâtres en France.
b. Les Français apprécient les loisirs culturels.
c. L'entrée des musées est gratuite le premier dimanche du mois.

VOCABULAIRE *(page 31)*

Read the list of words and determine how many you know. Many of these words are easy to remember because they are cognates.

Chapitre 2

Vocabulaire

Mots 1 & 2 *(pages 34–41)*

1. Whenever you have the chance to review, do so. As you do **Mots 1**, think of all the parts of the body you have learned in French.
2. To determine if you know your new vocabulary from **Mots 2**, see whether you can do the following:
   - Tell three things a patient may do in a doctor's office.
   - Tell three things the doctor may do.
   - Tell three things a doctor may say to a patient.

Structure

Les pronoms lui, leur *(pages 42–43)*

Here's an easy way to tell the difference between a direct object and an indirect object. A direct object answers the question *whom* or *what*.

Whom did you see?   I saw **the doctor**.
What did you take?   I took **the medicine**.

An indirect object answers the question *to (for) whom* or *to (for) what*.

Les verbes souffrir et ouvrir *(page 44)*

Review the forms of a regular **-er** verb. Compare them to the verb **ouvrir**.

j'écoute	j'ouvre
tu écoutes	tu ouvres
il écoute	il ouvre
nous écoutons	nous ouvrons
vous écoutez	vous ouvrez
ils écoutent	ils ouvrent

L'impératif *(pages 45–47)*

Remember, you use the command (imperative) to tell someone what to do. You merely use the **tu** or **vous** form of the verb to form the command. Just remember that you drop the final **s** from the **tu** form of regular **-er** verbs.

Le pronom en *(pages 48–49)*

You will hear and use the word **en** quite frequently in French. Pay careful attention to the explanation of the use of this word.

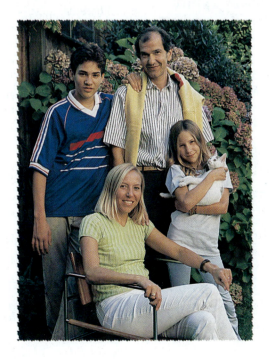

Study Tips   H25

Study Tips

CHAPITRE 3

Vocabulaire

 *(pages 66–73)*

1. As you study your vocabulary at home, remember to read it aloud.
2. If you learn better by writing down new information, copy each new word two or three times.
3. As you finish studying the vocabulary, cover up the sentences, look at the illustration or photo and say as much as you can about it.
4. After going over the vocabulary thoroughly, write the answers to the activities as the teacher assigns them.

HINT Do your French homework diligently and study for a short period of time each day. Do not skip some days and then try to cram. It doesn't work when studying a foreign language.

In each lesson of **Bon voyage!** you will learn a very manageable amount of new material. Since French is a romance language, much of the new material will involve word endings. Study each small set of new endings on a daily basis, and you'll have no problem. Don't wait until you have lots of them and try to cram them in all at once.

Structure

L'imparfait *(pages 74–81)*

1. Note that as is the case with many French verbs the **je, tu, il, ils** forms are pronounced the same in the imperfect. **Nous** is **–ions,** rather than **–ons** and **vous** is **–iez,** rather than **–ez.** The imperfect verb forms should be quite easy for you to learn. Pay particular attention to the spelling of the endings that are all pronounced the same:

   je/tu –ais   il/elle –ait   ils/elles –aient

2. Read aloud 5 on the top of page 75 in a very relaxed manner as if you were reminiscing about your own days in middle school (**collège**). One of the most important uses of the imperfect tense is to reminisce about things in the past. The exact time those things took place is not important.
3. Go over all the activities once aloud before you write them as the teacher assigns them.

Lectures culturelles

Le téléphone d'hier et d'aujourd'hui *(pages 84–85)*

1. Scan the reading and find all the verbs in the imperfect tense.
2. Read the questions in activity A and look for the answers as you read the selection.
3. Write out the answers to Activity A.
4. To ascertain if you know the content of the story well, see if you can answer the questions in Activity A without looking up the information.

Study Tips

CHAPITRE 4

Vocabulaire

Mots 1 & 2 *(pages 98–105)*

1. Read the sentences aloud as you look at each illustration or photo.
2. As the teacher assigns each Vocabulary Activity, do it first aloud. Then write the answers. Go over your written answers checking for accuracy.
3. After doing an Activity with the head **Historiette**, retell all the information in your own words.

Structure

L'imparfait et le passé compose
(pages 106–108)

HINT Always remember—If you know exactly when something happened, you use the **passé composé**. If the precise time at which it happened is not important, you use the imperfect.

1. Read the model sentences on page 106, keeping in mind the above **Hint**. Relate the **Hint** to each of the sentences.
2. Activities 11, 12, 13, 14, and 15, on pages 106–108, will help you zero in on this important time concept.

Raconter une histoire au passé
(pages 109–111)

HINT When trying to determine whether to use the imperfect or **passé composé**, pretend you are at the theater watching a play or that you are watching a movie. All the scenery or activity that is going on in the background is expressed by the **passé composé**. What the actors or actresses did is in the preterite. Just remember—background imperfect; action—**passé composé**.

1. Read the sentences on page 109 keeping in mind the above **Hint**.
2. Do all the activities orally and in written form as the teacher assigns them.

Les prépositions avec les noms géographiques *(pages 113–115)*

1. The prepositions with geographical names can be tricky. To try to simplify, remember: Almost all countries that end in silent **e** are feminine. You use the preposition **en** or **de** (**d'**) with all feminine countries AND all countries that begin with a vowel. You use **au** or **du** with masculine countries that begin with a consonant.

HINT Do these activities several times. Give your ear practice in hearing the correct preposition. The more you hear it, the more familiar you become with it and the easier it is to handle. There is no substitute for ear practice in acquiring a foreign language. Practice until it sounds right.

Lectures culturelles

(pages 118–121)

These reading selections provide you a great deal of reinforcement for the use of the **imparfait** and **passé composé**.

Even if your teacher does not assign these readings, you may wish to read them quickly. In addition to reintroducing French you already know, they contain some interesting cultural information.

Remember, the more you expose yourself to material in French, the easier the language will become.

Study Tips

CHAPITRE 5

Vocabulaire

Mots 1 & 2 *(pages 142–149)*

1. The sentences in these vocabulary sections will reintroduce the **passé composé** many times. As you study the vocabulary, identify the verbs in the **passé composé.**
2. After studying the vocabulary, cover up each photo or illustration and say as much as you can about it.
3. As you look at the sentences in the vocabulary section and the accompanying activities, observe whenever an **e** or **s** is added to the past participle of a verb in the **passé composé.**

Structure

L'accord du participe passé *(pages 153–154)*
It is not necessary to do the activities in this section orally at home since this point of agreement is basically a written problem. After you write the exercises, play copy editor.
  a. Read each sentence.
  b. Look for a direct object that precedes the verb.
  c. Be sure you added an –e ending if the preceding direct object is feminine, –es if it's feminine plural, and –s if it's masculine plural.

Les actions réciproques *(pages 155–156)*
Remember the difference between a direct and indirect object.

The direct object is the direct receiver of the action of the verb. It answers the question who or what.

  John threw the ball.
  What did he throw? The ball.

The indirect object is the indirect receiver of the action of the verb.

  John threw the ball…
  …to his friend.

His friend is the indirect object.

Personne ne… et rien ne… *(page 157)*
HINT Memorizing the following will help you use personne ne… and rien ne… correctly.

  Personne n'est là.
  Personne n'est au téléphone.
  Personne ne l'a dit.
  Personne n'est arrivé.
  Personne ne m'écoute.
  Personne ne l'a fait.

  Rien ne se passe.
  Rien n'est arrivé.
  Rien ne change.

H28 Handbook

Study Tips

CHAPITRE 6

Vocabulaire

Mots 1 & 2 *(pages 174–181)*

REVIEW Make a list of all the foods you already know in French.

HINT If you learn better by writing something down, copy each new word two or three times.

Do the activities that accompany these vocabulary sections both orally and in writing.

Structure

Le futur simple *(pages 182–184)*

NOTE Note the similarity between the future endings and the verb **avoir**.

j'ai	je parlerai	nous avons	nous parlerons
tu as	tu parleras	vous avez	vous parlerez
il a	il parlera	ils ont	ils parleront

Deux pronoms dans la même phrase *(pages 185–186)*

HINT When learning another language it is often necessary to repeat the same thing many times before you can use it quickly and easily. The object pronouns you are learning in this lesson are a point in case.

When you are carrying on a normal conversation, it is impossible to ask yourself the gender of the object, the pronoun that replaces it, and its place in the sentence—before or after the other pronouns. So, what's the solution? It's simple: practice makes perfect. Go over the activities as often as you can. Read the question aloud and then answer it. The more you hear **me, te, nous, vous, le, la,** and **les,** the easier it will be to use them.

1. Read the model sentences on page 185 several times.
2. Do the three activities on page 186 several times. The more you hear the pronouns together, the easier it will be for you to use them. This is one case where practice is absolutely essential.

Faire + *infinitif* *(pages 187–189)*

This **faire** construction is used a great deal in French. Just remember that the verb **faire** is followed by an infinitive when you have someone do something for you.

Note, too, the use of **faire** in many cooking expressions. You do not really cook the meat. The oven or the fire cooks the meat. You merely make it cook.

Je fais cuire la viande.

Read all the activities on page 188 aloud.

Conversation
(page 190)

This conversation uses some very informal expressions. Listen carefully to the intonation and expression of the speakers on the CD.

Lectures Culturelles

Lecture supplémentaire *(pages 194–195)*
Even if your teacher does not assign the reading on page 194, you may want to read it to learn about some dishes that are prepared in North Africa.

Study Tips

CHAPITRE 7

Vocabulaire

Mots 1 & 2 *(pages 206–213)*

1. If you learn better by writing down new information, copy each new word two or three times.
2. Read each sentence aloud as you look at the photo or illustration.
3. Go over the vocabulary activities orally first; then write them down.
4. When you complete your study of the vocabulary, write two lists—(1) car parts and (2) road expressions. See how many words and expressions you can come up with. Then check them out with the **Reference Vocabulary** list on page 235.

Structure

Le conditionnel *(pages 214–215)*

1. You should have no trouble learning the conditional. Remember:
   a. the root is the same as the future
   b. the endings are the same as the imperfect endings: **ais, ais, ait, ions, iez, aient**
   c. **ais, ait, aient** are pronounced the same
   d. the conditional is used the same in French as it is in English
2. After completing each **Historiette** activity, retell the information in your own words.

Les propositions introduites par **si** *(pages 218–219)*

1. The sequence of tenses for si clauses is very fixed.

Main clause	*Si* clause
Future	Present
Conditional	Imperfect

2. Before going over the activities on page 219, complete each of the following with as many options as you can.
   a. Si je reçois beaucoup d'argent…
   b. Si j'avais du temps libre…
   c. Je ferais un voyage en France si…
   d. Je regarderai la télé si…

Deux pronoms dans la même phrase *(pages 220–221)*

As you already read in previous Study Tips sections, the more you hear and use the object pronouns, the more comfortable you will be with them. For this reason, it is suggested that you go over each activity.

Lectures Culturelles

La conduite en France *(pages 224–225)*

Make comparisons as you read. Think about driving customs in the U.S. as you read this section.

Lecture supplémentaire *(pages 226–227)*

Even if your teacher does not assign this supplementary selection, you may want to read it quickly to learn about a very interesting motor trip in North Africa.

Study Tips

CHAPITRE 8

Vocabulaire

Mots 1 & 2 *(pages 248–255)*

1. Look at each new vocabulary word. Say it aloud two or three times. Cover it up and see if you can give the word on your own.
2. Review—Make a list of all the parts of the body you know in French.
3. Go over the vocabulary activities as your teacher assigns them. Do them orally first, and then write them out.

REMINDER Do your French homework diligently. A short period of time daily is much more beneficial than one long cram session.

Structure

Les pronoms interrogatifs et relatifs *(pages 256–257)*

Synopsis
Remember
- qui relates to a person or thing
- qui is the subject
- que relates to a thing
- que is the object

Les pronoms et l'impératif *(pages 258–260)*
This is another one of those points that takes a great deal of practice.

1. Read the model sentences on page 258 several times.
2. Go over each exercise at least twice orally.

Le superlatif des adjectifs *(pages 261–263)*
A great way to reinforce the superlative is to complete the following statements with as many adjectives as you can.

Marie est la plus___de toutes mes amies.
Paul est le plus___de notre classe.

Study Tips

CHAPITRE 9

Vocabulaire

Mots 1 & 2 *(pages 280–287)*

1. As you go over this vocabulary section, review the many forms of the **passé composé** in the sentences.
2. Copy the new words two or three times to help you retain them.
3. After studying the vocabulary, pretend you are at a hotel. Write what you do in the proper time and sequence.

Structure

Le passé composé: **être** *ou* **avoir**
(pages 288–289)
Rule simplification—if a verb has a direct object, it is communicated with **avoir**.

1. After writing the exercises, play copy editor. Double check to be sure you made the past participles agree when necessary.

Y *et* **en** *(pages 289–292)*
Rule simplification
Y can replace any expression of location. **En** can replace any expression with **de**. When both pronouns are used, **y** comes before **en**.

Conversation
(page 294)
Pay particular attention to the intonation as you listen to the voices on the CD. Unlike many of the **Conversations,** this one has a much more formal tone.

Lectures culturelles

L' Hôtel de la Gare (pages 296–297)
As you read this section, observe the many examples of the **passé composé** with **être** and **avoir**, as well as agreement of the past participle.

Handbook

Study Tips

CHAPITRE 10

Vocabulaire

Mots 1 & 2 *(pages 310–317)*

1. If you don't live in or near a very metropolitan area, the use of a subway or metro station will be new to you. As you study this vocabulary, familiarize yourself with the use of the subway.
2. Write out the answers, particularly to Activities 2, 3, 7, and 8 as your teacher assigns them. Be sure to read all answers aloud, too.
3. As you study your new vocabulary, a very good strategy is to ask yourself questions about the illustrations and answer them.

Quel est le numéro de la ligne de l'autobus?	48
Qu'est-ce qu'on fait pour demander un arrêt?	On appuie sur le bouton.
Quel est le dernier arrêt de l'autobus?	le terminus

Structure

Les questions *(pages 318–321)*

1. You have already encountered all the ways in which questions are made in French. Note that the variations have to do with the level of formality, not correctness.
2. Since you will more often ask questions orally than in written form, it is important to go over these exercises aloud.

Venir de + *infinitif* *(pages 321–322)*
This point is very easy. First however, review the forms of **venir**.

je viens	nous venons
tu viens	vous venez
il vient	ils viennent

Les expressions de temps *(page 323)*
Note that because the activity is still going on, you use the present tense. English speakers do not use the present for the same construction. For this reason, it is important to eliminate translation because it can lead to unnecessary confusion.

Conversation
(page 324)
Listen to the expression and intonation pattern used by people who do not know one another.

Lecture supplémentaire
(pages 328–329)
Even if your teacher does not assign this selection, you may want to read it on your own. It has some interesting information about how people get around some other areas of the French-speaking world.

Study Tips

CHAPITRE 11

Vocabulaire

Mots 1 & 2 *(pages 340–347)*

1. Remember you may want to copy each new word two or three times.
2. After you have studied each illustration and the accompanying vocabulary, cover up the French and say as much about the photo or illustration as you can.
3. Write out the answers to the accompanying activities as your teacher assigns them. Read your written answers to check for spelling, ending, accuracy, etc.

Structure

Lequel *et* celui-là *(pages 348–349)*
Remember:

Question	Answer
Lequel	Celui-là
Laquelle	Celle-là
Lesquels	Ceux-là
Lesquelles	Celles-là

Les verbes **suivre, conduire, vivre**
(page 350)
It has been some time since you learned the present tense of verbs. Remember that you can often drop the final sound of the **ils** form to get the sound for **je, tu, il**.

Sui~~vent~~	sui(s)	sui(s)	sui(t)
Condui~~sent~~	condui(s)	condui(s)	condui(t)
Vi~~vre~~	vi(s)	vi(s)	vi(t)

Study Tips

CHAPITRE 12

Vocabulaire

Mots 1 & 2 *(pages 376–383)*

1. Recite the new words aloud.
2. Read the sentences.
3. Copy the new words if necessary.
4. Write out the answers to the vocabulary activities as your teacher assigns them.
5. After writing out the activities, play copy editor. Go over them to check for accuracy.
6. Upon completion of any **Historiette** activity, retell the story in your own words.

Structure

Le subjonctif *(pages 384–389)*

1. Many students learning French consider the subjunctive to be very difficult. The subjunctive is traditionally presented as the verb form that is used following many different types of expressions such as: desire, volition, necessity, possibility, doubt, etc. It is difficult to keep all these categories in mind when speaking.

   The subjunctive is almost always introduced by **que**. If what follows **que** may or may not take place, if it is not a reality, you will then use the subjunctive. Always ask yourself "really or maybe." If the answer is maybe, you will almost always have to use the subjunctive.

2. To contrast the indicative, which you have already learned, and the subjunctive, which you are about to learn, take into account the following regarding the meaning of these words.
   * **Indicative—Indicates something, points something out, is objective, can stand alone, is independent**
   * **Subjunctive—Subjective, does not indicate anything concrete, is not objective, is the opposite of objective, cannot stand alone, is dependent upon something else.**

3. Once again, practice makes "perfect" in acquiring the subjunctive. Do each activity orally, then write it and after writing it, read your answers aloud.

Note that unlike many of the indicative verb forms, the final sounds of the subjunctive forms are pronounced.

Chapitre 13

Vocabulaire

Mots 1 & 2 *(pages 406–413)*

REVIEW Make a list of all the parts of the body you know in French.

1. As you look at the vocabulary photos, take note of the body language of the people. You will be learning about some French customs that involve body language in this lesson.

Structure

D'autres verbes au présent du subjonctif *(pages 416–417)*

HINT Pay particular attention to the following verbs that change in the **nous** and **vous** forms.

recevoir	que je reçoive que nous recevions que vous receviez
boire	que je boive que nous buvions que vous buviez
vouloir	que je veuille que nous voulions que vous vouliez

Le subjonctif après les expressions d'émotion *(pages 418–419)*

These expressions of emotion are followed by the subjunctive because they are dependent upon the subjective emotion that introduces them. They do not, however, adhere to the "may or may not" occur. The following will help to clarify their subjective connotation.

One could say (even if the person is in reality there)
Je suis content qu'il soit là.

This person is happy that he would be there, but someone else could say…
Pas moi. Je ne suis pas content qu'il soit là.
Franchement, je regrette qu'il soit là.

HINT Be sure to go over all the activities orally, as practice makes perfect when using the subjunctive.

Handbook

Study Tips

CHAPITRE 14

Vocabulaire

Mots 1 & 2 *(pages 436–443)*

REVIEW Make a list of all the jobs and professions you know in French.

Remember to copy the new words a few times if that will help you remember them.

Structure

Le subjonctif après les expressions de doûte *(pages 444–446)*
You may question the use of the indicative after **croire, il est certain,** etc. since there is still some "may or may not" involved in the information in the dependent clause. The only explanation is that more emphasis is placed on the belief or certainty that what follows **croire** will indeed take place.

L'infinitif ou le subjonctif *(pages 447–448)*
Make up additional sentences with

> Je voudrais que tu…
> Il préfère que…
> Il préfère que vous…
> J'aimerais être…

Verb Charts

VERBES RÉGULIERS			
INFINITIF	parler *to talk*	finir *to finish*	répondre *to answer*
PRÉSENT	je parle tu parles il parle nous parlons vous parlez ils parlent	je finis tu finis il finit nous finissons vous finissez ils finissent	je réponds tu réponds il répond nous répondons vous répondez ils répondent
IMPÉRATIF	parle parlons parlez	finis finissons finissez	réponds répondons répondez
PASSÉ COMPOSÉ	j'ai parlé tu as parlé il a parlé nous avons parlé vous avez parlé ils ont parlé	j'ai fini tu as fini il a fini nous avons fini vous avez fini ils ont fini	j'ai répondu tu as répondu il a répondu nous avons répondu vous avez répondu ils ont répondu
IMPARFAIT	je parlais tu parlais il parlait nous parlions vous parliez ils parlaient	je finissais tu finissais il finissait nous finissions vous finissiez ils finissaient	je répondais tu répondais il répondait nous répondions vous répondiez ils répondaient
FUTUR	je parlerai tu parleras il parlera nous parlerons vous parlerez ils parleront	je finirai tu finiras il finira nous finirons vous finirez ils finiront	je répondrai tu répondras il répondra nous répondrons vous répondrez ils répondront
CONDITIONNEL	je parlerais tu parlerais il parlerait nous parlerions vous parleriez ils parleraient	je finirais tu finirais il finirait nous finirions vous finiriez ils finiraient	je répondrais tu répondrais il répondrait nous répondrions vous répondriez ils répondraient
SUBJONCTIF PRÉSENT	que je parle que tu parles qu'il parle que nous parlions que vous parliez qu'ils parlent	que je finisse que tu finisses qu'il finisse que nous finissions que vous finissiez qu'ils finissent	que je réponde que tu répondes qu'il réponde que nous répondions que vous répondiez qu'ils répondent

Verb Charts

	VERBES RÉFLÉCHIS	VERBES AVEC CHANGEMENTS D'ORTHOGRAPHE	
INFINITIF	se laver *to wash oneself*	acheter[1] *to buy*	appeler *to call*
PRÉSENT	je me lave tu te laves il se lave nous nous lavons vous vous lavez ils se lavent	j'achète tu achètes il achète nous achetons vous achetez ils achètent	j'appelle tu appelles il appelle nous appelons vous appelez ils appellent
IMPÉRATIF	lave-toi lavons-nous lavez-vous	achète achetons achetez	appelle appelons appelez
PASSÉ COMPOSÉ	je me suis lavé(e) tu t'es lavé(e) il s'est lavé nous nous sommes lavé(e)s vous vous êtes lavé(e)(s) ils se sont lavés	j'ai acheté tu as acheté il a acheté nous avons acheté vous avez acheté ils ont acheté	j'ai appelé tu as appelé il a appelé nous avons appelé vous avez appelé ils ont appelé
IMPARFAIT	je me lavais tu te lavais il se lavait nous nous lavions vous vous laviez ils se lavaient	j'achetais tu achetais il achetait nous achetions vous achetiez ils achetaient	j'appelais tu appelais il appelait nous appelions vous appeliez ils appelaient
FUTUR	je me laverai tu te laveras il se lavera nous nous laverons vous vous laverez ils se laveront	j'achèterai tu achèteras il achètera nous achèterons vous achèterez ils achèteront	j'appellerai tu appelleras il appellera nous appellerons vous appellerez ils appelleront
CONDITIONNEL	je me laverais tu te laverais il se laverait nous nous laverions vous vous laveriez ils se laveraient	j'achèterais tu achèterais il achèterait nous achèterions vous achèteriez ils achèteraient	j'appellerais tu appellerais il appellerait nous appellerions vous appelleriez ils appelleraient
SUBJONCTIF PRÉSENT	que je me lave que tu te laves qu'il se lave que nous nous lavions que vous vous laviez qu'ils se lavent	que j'achète que tu achètes qu'il achète que nous achetions que vous achetiez qu'ils achètent	que j'appelle que tu appelles qu'il appelle que nous appelions que vous appeliez qu'ils appellent

---

[1] *Verbes similaires:* **emmener, se lever, peser, se promener, soulever**

Verb Charts

VERBES AVEC CHANGEMENTS D'ORTHOGRAPHE

INFINITIF	commencer[2] to begin	manger[3] to eat	payer[4] to pay	préférer[5] to prefer
PRÉSENT	je commence tu commences il commence nous commençons vous commencez ils commencent	je mange tu manges il mange nous mangeons vous mangez ils mangent	je paie tu paies il paie nous payons vous payez ils paient	je préfère tu préfères il préfère nous préférons vous préférez ils préfèrent
IMPÉRATIF	commence commençons commencez	mange mangeons mangez	paie payons payez	préfère préférons préférez
PASSÉ COMPOSÉ	j'ai commencé tu as commencé il a commencé nous avons commencé vous avez commencé ils ont commencé	j'ai mangé tu as mangé il a mangé nous avons mangé vous avez mangé ils ont mangé	j'ai payé tu as payé il a payé nous avons payé vous avez payé ils ont payé	j'ai préféré tu as préféré il a préféré nous avons préféré vous avez préféré ils ont préféré
IMPARFAIT	je commençais tu commençais il commençait nous commencions vous commenciez ils commençaient	je mangeais tu mangeais il mangeait nous mangions vous mangiez ils mangeaient	je payais tu payais il payait nous payions vous payiez ils payaient	je préférais tu préférais il préférait nous préférions vous préfériez ils préféraient
FUTUR	je commencerai tu commenceras il commencera nous commencerons vous commencerez ils commenceront	je mangerai tu mangeras il mangera nous mangerons vous mangerez ils mangeront	je paierai tu paieras il paiera nous paierons vous paierez ils paieront	je préférerai tu préféreras il préférera nous préférerons vous préférerez ils préféreront
CONDITIONNEL	je commencerais tu commencerais il commencerait nous commencerions vous commenceriez ils commenceraient	je mangerais tu mangerais il mangerait nous mangerions vous mangeriez ils mangeraient	je paierais tu paierais il paierait nous paierions vous paieriez ils paieraient	je préférerais tu préférerais il préférerait nous préférerions vous préféreriez ils préféreraient
SUBJONCTIF PRÉSENT	que je commence que tu commences qu'il commence que nous commencions que vous commenciez qu'ils commencent	que je mange que tu manges qu'il mange que nous mangions que vous mangiez qu'ils mangent	que je paie que tu paies qu'il paie que nous payions que vous payiez qu'ils paient	que je préfère que tu préfères qu'il préfère que nous préférions que vous préfériez qu'ils préfèrent

[2] *Verbe similaire:* **effacer**
[3] *Verbes similaires:* **changer, exiger, nager, voyager**
[4] *Verbes similaires:* **appuyer, employer, essayer, essuyer, nettoyer, tutoyer**
[5] *Verbes similaires:* **accélérer, célébrer, espérer, oblitérer, récupérer, sécher, suggérer**

Verb Charts

VERBES IRRÉGULIERS				
INFINITIF	aller *to go*	avoir *to have*	boire *to drink*	conduire *to drive*
PRÉSENT	je vais tu vas il va nous allons vous allez ils vont	j'ai tu as il a nous avons vous avez ils ont	je bois tu bois il boit nous buvons vous buvez ils boivent	je conduis tu conduis il conduit nous conduisons vous conduisez ils conduisent
IMPÉRATIF	va allons allez	aie ayons ayez	bois buvons buvez	conduis conduisons conduisez
PASSÉ COMPOSÉ	je suis allé(e) tu es allé(e) il est allé nous sommes allé(e)s vous êtes allé(e)(s) ils sont allés	j'ai eu tu as eu il a eu nous avons eu vous avez eu ils ont eu	j'ai bu tu as bu il a bu nous avons bu vous avez bu ils ont bu	j'ai conduit tu as conduit il a conduit nous avons conduit vous avez conduit ils ont conduit
IMPARFAIT	j'allais tu allais il allait nous allions vous alliez ils allaient	j'avais tu avais il avait nous avions vous aviez ils avaient	je buvais tu buvais il buvait nous buvions vous buviez ils buvaient	je conduisais tu conduisais il conduisait nous conduisions vous conduisiez ils conduisaient
FUTUR	j'irai tu iras il ira nous irons vous irez ils iront	j'aurai tu auras il aura nous aurons vous aurez ils auront	je boirai tu boiras il boira nous boirons vous boirez ils boiront	je conduirai tu conduiras il conduira nous conduirons vous conduirez ils conduiront
CONDITIONNEL	j'irais tu irais il irait nous irions vous iriez ils iraient	j'aurais tu aurais il aurait nous aurions vous auriez ils auraient	je boirais tu boirais il boirait nous boirions vous boiriez ils boiraient	je conduirais tu conduirais il conduirait nous conduirions vous conduiriez ils conduiraient
SUBJONCTIF PRÉSENT	que j'aille que tu ailles qu'il aille que nous allions que vous alliez qu'ils aillent	que j'aie que tu aies qu'il ait que nous ayons que vous ayez qu'ils aient	que je boive que tu boives qu'il boive que nous buvions que vous buviez qu'ils boivent	que je conduise que tu conduises qu'il conduise que nous conduisions que vous conduisiez qu'ils conduisent

Verb Charts

VERBES IRRÉGULIERS

INFINITIF	connaître *to know*	croire *to believe*	dire *to say*	dormir *to sleep*
PRÉSENT	je connais tu connais il connaît nous connaissons vous connaissez ils connaissent	je crois tu crois il croit nous croyons vous croyez ils croient	je dis tu dis il dit nous disons vous dites ils disent	je dors tu dors il dort nous dormons vous dormez ils dorment
IMPÉRATIF	connais connaissons connaissez	crois croyons croyez	dis disons dites	dors dormons dormez
PASSÉ COMPOSÉ	j'ai connu tu as connu il a connu nous avons connu vous avez connu ils ont connu	j'ai cru tu as cru il a cru nous avons cru vous avez cru ils ont cru	j'ai dit tu as dit il a dit nous avons dit vous avez dit ils ont dit	j'ai dormi tu as dormi il a dormi nous avons dormi vous avez dormi ils ont dormi
IMPARFAIT	je connaissais tu connaissais il connaissait nous connaissions vous connaissiez ils connaissaient	je croyais tu croyais il croyait nous croyions vous croyiez ils croyaient	je disais tu disais il disait nous disions vous disiez ils disaient	je dormais tu dormais il dormait nous dormions vous dormiez ils dormaient
FUTUR	je connaîtrai tu connaîtras il connaîtra nous connaîtrons vous connaîtrez ils connaîtront	je croirai tu croiras il croira nous croirons vous croirez ils croiront	je dirai tu diras il dira nous dirons vous direz ils diront	je dormirai tu dormiras il dormira nous dormirons vous dormirez ils dormiront
CONDITIONNEL	je connaîtrais tu connaîtrais il connaîtrait nous connaîtrions vous connaîtriez ils connaîtraient	je croirais tu croirais il croirait nous croirions vous croiriez ils croiraient	je dirais tu dirais il dirait nous dirions vous diriez ils diraient	je dormirais tu dormirais il dormirait nous dormirions vous dormiriez ils dormiraient
SUBJONCTIF PRÉSENT	que je connaisse que tu connaisses qu'il connaisse que nous connaissions que vous connaissiez qu'ils connaissent	que je croie que tu croies qu'il croie que nous croyions que vous croyiez qu'ils croient	que je dise que tu dises qu'il dise que nous disions que vous disiez qu'ils disent	que je dorme que tu dormes qu'il dorme que nous dormions que vous dormiez qu'ils dorment

Handbook

Verb Charts

VERBES IRRÉGULIERS				
INFINITIF	écrire to write	envoyer to send	être to be	faire to do, to make
PRÉSENT	j'écris tu écris il écrit nous écrivons vous écrivez ils écrivent	j'envoie tu envoies il envoie nous envoyons vous envoyez ils envoient	je suis tu es il est nous sommes vous êtes ils sont	je fais tu fais il fait nous faisons vous faites ils font
IMPÉRATIF	écris écrivons écrivez	envoie envoyons envoyez	sois soyons soyez	fais faisons faites
PASSÉ COMPOSÉ	j'ai écrit tu as écrit il a écrit nous avons écrit vous avez écrit ils ont écrit	j'ai envoyé tu as envoyé il a envoyé nous avons envoyé vous avez envoyé ils ont envoyé	j'ai été tu as été il a été nous avons été vous avez été ils ont été	j'ai fait tu as fait il a fait nous avons fait vous avez fait ils ont fait
IMPARFAIT	j'écrivais tu écrivais il écrivait nous écrivions vous écriviez ils écrivaient	j'envoyais tu envoyais il envoyait nous envoyions vous envoyiez ils envoyaient	j'étais tu étais il était nous étions vous étiez ils étaient	je faisais tu faisais il faisait nous faisions vous faisiez ils faisaient
FUTUR	j'écrirai tu écriras il écrira nous écrirons vous écrirez ils écriront	j'enverrai tu enverras il enverra nous enverrons vous enverrez ils enverront	je serai tu seras il sera nous serons vous serez ils seront	je ferai tu feras il fera nous ferons vous ferez ils feront
CONDITIONNEL	j'écrirais tu écrirais il écrirait nous écririons vous écririez ils écriraient	j'enverrais tu enverrais il enverrait nous enverrions vous enverriez ils enverraient	je serais tu serais il serait nous serions vous seriez ils seraient	je ferais tu ferais il ferait nous ferions vous feriez ils feraient
SUBJONCTIF PRÉSENT	que j'écrive que tu écrives qu'il écrive que nous écrivions que vous écriviez qu'ils écrivent	que j'envoie que tu envoies qu'il envoie que nous envoyions que vous envoyiez qu'ils envoient	que je sois que tu sois qu'il soit que nous soyons que vous soyez qu'ils soient	que je fasse que tu fasses qu'il fasse que nous fassions que vous fassiez qu'ils fassent

Verb Charts

VERBES IRRÉGULIERS

INFINITIF	lire *to read*	mettre[1] *to put*	ouvrir[2] *to open*	partir[3] *to leave*
PRÉSENT	je lis tu lis il lit nous lisons vous lisez ils lisent	je mets tu mets il met nous mettons vous mettez ils mettent	j'ouvre tu ouvres il ouvre nous ouvrons vous ouvrez ils ouvrent	je pars tu pars il part nous partons vous partez ils partent
IMPÉRATIF	lis lisons lisez	mets mettons mettez	ouvre ouvrons ouvrez	pars partons partez
PASSÉ COMPOSÉ	j'ai lu tu as lu il a lu nous avons lu vous avez lu ils ont lu	j'ai mis tu as mis il a mis nous avons mis vous avez mis ils ont mis	j'ai ouvert tu as ouvert il a ouvert nous avons ouvert vous avez ouvert ils ont ouvert	je suis parti(e) tu es parti(e) il est parti nous sommes parti(e)s vous êtes parti(e)(s) ils sont partis
IMPARFAIT	je lisais tu lisais il lisait nous lisions vous lisiez ils lisaient	je mettais tu mettais il mettait nous mettions vous mettiez ils mettaient	j'ouvrais tu ouvrais il ouvrait nous ouvrions vous ouvriez ils ouvraient	je partais tu partais il partait nous partions vous partiez ils partaient
FUTUR	je lirai tu liras il lira nous lirons vous lirez ils liront	je mettrai tu mettras il mettra nous mettrons vous mettrez ils mettront	j'ouvrirai tu ouvriras il ouvrira nous ouvrirons vous ouvrirez ils ouvriront	je partirai tu partiras il partira nous partirons vous partirez ils partiront
CONDITIONNEL	je lirais tu lirais il lirait nous lirions vous liriez ils liraient	je mettrais tu mettrais il mettrait nous mettrions vous mettriez ils mettraient	j'ouvrirais tu ouvrirais il ouvrirait nous ouvririons vous ouvririez ils ouvriraient	je partirais tu partirais il partirait nous partirions vous partiriez ils partiraient
SUBJONCTIF PRÉSENT	que je lise que tu lises qu'il lise que nous lisions que vous lisiez qu'ils lisent	que je mette qu tu mettes qu'il mette que nous mettions que vous mettiez qu'ils mettent	que j'ouvre que tu ouvres qu'il ouvre que nous ouvrions que vous ouvriez qu'ils ouvrent	que je parte que tu partes qu'il parte que nous partions que vous partiez qu'ils partent

[1] *Verbes similaires:* **permettre, remettre**
[2] *Verbes similaires:* **couvrir, découvrir, offrir, souffrir**
[3] *Verbe similaire:* **sortir**

Verb Charts

VERBES IRRÉGULIERS				
INFINITIF	pouvoir *to be able to*	prendre[4] *to take*	recevoir *to receive*	savoir *to know*
PRÉSENT	je peux tu peux il peut nous pouvons vous pouvez ils peuvent	je prends tu prends il prend nous prenons vous prenez ils prennent	je reçois tu reçois il reçoit nous recevons vous recevez ils reçoivent	je sais tu sais il sait nous savons vous savez ils savent
IMPÉRATIF	(pas d'impératif)	prends prenons prenez	reçois recevons recevez	sache sachons sachez
PASSÉ COMPOSÉ	j'ai pu tu as pu il a pu nous avons pu vous avez pu ils ont pu	j'ai pris tu as pris il a pris nous avons pris vous avez pris ils ont pris	j'ai reçu tu as reçu il a reçu nous avons reçu vous avez reçu ils ont reçu	j'ai su tu as su il a su nous avons su vous avez su ils ont su
IMPARFAIT	je pouvais tu pouvais il pouvait nous pouvions vous pouviez ils pouvaient	je prenais tu prenais il prenait nous prenions vous preniez ils prenaient	je recevais tu recevais il recevait nous recevions vous receviez ils recevaient	je savais tu savais il savait nous savions vous saviez ils savaient
FUTUR	je pourrai tu pourras il pourra nous pourrons vous pourrez ils pourront	je prendrai tu prendras il prendra nous prendrons vous prendrez ils prendront	je recevrai tu recevras il recevra nous recevrons vous recevrez ils recevront	je saurai tu sauras il saura nous saurons vous saurez ils sauront
CONDITIONNEL	je pourrais tu pourrais il pourrait nous pourrions vous pourriez ils pourraient	je prendrais tu prendrais il prendrait nous prendrions vous prendriez ils prendraient	je recevrais tu recevrais il recevrait nous recevrions vous recevriez ils recevraient	je saurais tu saurais il saurait nous saurions vous sauriez ils sauraient
SUBJONCTIF PRÉSENT	que je puisse que tu puisses qu'il puisse que nous puissions que vous puissiez qu'ils puissent	que je prenne que tu prennes qu'il prenne que nous prenions que vous preniez qu'ils prennent	que je reçoive que tu reçoives qu'il reçoive que nous recevions que vous receviez qu'ils reçoivent	que je sache que tu saches qu'il sache que nous sachions que vous sachiez qu'ils sachent

[4] *Verbes similaires:* **apprendre, comprendre**

Verb Charts

VERBES IRRÉGULIERS

INFINITIF	servir[5] *to serve*	suivre *to follow*	venir[6] *to come*	vivre *to live*
PRÉSENT	je sers tu sers il sert nous servons vous servez ils servent	je suis tu suis il suit nous suivons vous suivez ils suivent	je viens tu viens il vient nous venons vous venez ils viennent	je vis tu vis il vit nous vivons vous vivez ils vivent
IMPÉRATIF	sers servons servez	suis suivons suivez	viens venons venez	vis vivons vivez
PASSÉ COMPOSÉ	j'ai servi tu as servi il a servi nous avons servi vous avez servi ils ont servi	j'ai suivi tu as suivi il a suivi nous avons suivi vous avez suivi ils ont suivi	je suis venu(e) tu es venu(e) il est venu nous sommes venu(e)s vous êtes venu(e)(s) ils sont venus	j'ai vécu tu as vécu il a vécu nous avons vécu vous avez vécu ils ont vécu
IMPARFAIT	je servais tu servais il servait nous servions vous serviez ils servaient	je suivais tu suivais il suivait nous suivions vous suiviez ils suivaient	je venais tu venais il venait nous venions vous veniez ils venaient	je vivais tu vivais il vivait nous vivions vous viviez ils vivaient
FUTUR	je servirai tu serviras il servira nous servirons vous servirez ils serviront	je suivrai tu suivras il suivra nous suivrons vous suivrez ils suivront	je viendrai tu viendras il viendra nous viendrons vous viendrez ils viendront	je vivrai tu vivras il vivra nous vivrons vous vivrez ils vivront
CONDITIONNEL	je servirais tu servirais il servirait nous servirions vous serviriez ils serviraient	je suivrais tu suivrais il suivrait nous suivrions vous suivriez ils suivraient	je viendrais tu viendrais il viendrait nous viendrions vous viendriez ils viendraient	je vivrais tu vivrais il vivrait nous vivrions vous vivriez ils vivraient
SUBJONCTIF PRÉSENT	que je serve que tu serves qu'il serve que nous servions que vous serviez qu'ils servent	que je suive que tu suives qu'il suive que nous suivions que vous suiviez qu'ils suivent	que je vienne que tu viennes qu'il vienne que nous venions que vous veniez qu'ils viennent	que je vive que tu vives qu'il vive que nous vivions que vous viviez qu'ils vivent

[5] *Verbe similaire:* **desservir**
[6] *Verbes similaires:* **devenir, revenir, se souvenir**

Verb Charts

	VERBES IRRÉGULIERS		VERBES IMPERSONNELS	
INFINITIF	voir *to see*	vouloir *to want*	falloir *to be necessary*	pleuvoir *to rain*
PRÉSENT	je vois tu vois il voit nous voyons vous voyez ils voient	je veux tu veux il veut nous voulons vous voulez ils veulent	il faut	il pleut
IMPÉRATIF	vois voyons voyez	veuille veuillons veuillez		
PASSÉ COMPOSÉ	j'ai vu tu as vu il a vu nous avons vu vous avez vu ils ont vu	j'ai voulu tu as voulu il a voulu nous avons voulu vous avez voulu ils ont voulu	il a fallu	il a plu
IMPARFAIT	je voyais tu voyais il voyait nous voyions vous voyiez ils voyaient	je voulais tu voulais il voulait nous voulions vous vouliez ils voulaient	il fallait	il pleuvait
FUTUR	je verrai tu verras il verra nous verrons vous verrez ils verront	je voudrai tu voudras il voudra nous voudrons vous voudrez ils voudront	il faudra	il pleuvra
CONDITIONNEL	je verrais tu verrais il verrait nous verrions vous verriez ils verraient	je voudrais tu voudrais il voudrait nous voudrions vous voudriez ils voudraient	il faudrait	il pleuvrait
SUBJONCTIF PRÉSENT	que je voie que tu voies qu'il voie que nous voyions que vous voyiez qu'ils voient	que je veuille que tu veuilles qu'il veuille que nous voulions que vous vouliez qu'ils veuillent	qu'il faille	qu'il pleuve

Verb Charts

VERBES AVEC ÊTRE AU PASSÉ COMPOSÉ

aller *(to go)*	je suis allé(e)
arriver *(to arrive)*	je suis arrivé(e)
descendre *(to go down, to get off)*	je suis descendu(e)
entrer *(to enter)*	je suis entré(e)
monter *(to go up)*	je suis monté(e)
mourir *(to die)*	je suis mort(e)
naître *(to be born)*	je suis né(e)
partir *(to leave)*	je suis parti(e)
passer *(to go by)*	je suis passé(e)
rentrer *(to go home)*	je suis rentré(e)
rester *(to stay)*	je suis resté(e)
retourner *(to return)*	je suis retourné(e)
revenir *(to come back)*	je suis revenu(e)
sortir *(to go out)*	je suis sorti(e)
tomber *(to fall)*	je suis tombé(e)
venir *(to come)*	je suis venu(e)

Handbook

French-English Dictionary

This French-English Dictionary contains all productive and receptive vocabulary from Levels I and II. The numbers following each productive entry indicate the chapter and vocabulary section in which the word is introduced. For example, **2.2** in dark print means that the word first appeared in this textbook, **Chapitre 2, Mots 2**. A light print number means that the word first appeared in the Level 1 textbook. **BV** refers to the introductory **Bienvenue** lessons in Level 1. **L** refers to the optional literary readings. If there is no number or letter following an entry, the word or expression is there for receptive purposes only.

A

à at, in, to, 3.1
  à l'avance ahead of time; in advance, 9.1
  À bientôt! See you soon!, BV
  à bord (de) on board, 8.2
  à cause de because of
  à côté de next to, 11.1
  À demain. See you tomorrow., BV
  à destination de to (destination), 8.1
  à domicile to the home
  à l'extérieur outside, outside the home
  à l'heure on time, 8.1
  à mon avis in my opinion, 7.2
  à nouveau again
  à peu près about, approximately
  à pied on foot, 4.2
  à point medium-rare (meat), 5.2
  À tout à l'heure. See you later., BV
l' **abbé** (m.) priest
abondant(e) plentiful
absolument absolutely, 9.1
accéder to access
accélérer to accelerate
l' **accès** (m.) access; admission
l' **accessoire** (m.) accessory
accompagner to accompany, to go with
l' **achat** (m.) purchase
  faire des achats to shop
acheter to buy, 3.2
  acheter à crédit to buy on credit
l' **acteur** (m.) actor, 1.1
actif, active active
l' **actrice** (f.) actress, 1.1
actuel(le) of today
actuellement nowadays
l' **addition** (f.) check, bill, 5.2
l' **administration publique** (f.) public office
adorer to love
l' **adresse** (f.) address, 5.2
s' **adresser à** to speak to
l' **adversaire** (m. et f.) adversary, opponent
adverse opposing, 10.1
aérien(ne) air, flight (adj.)
l' **aérogare** (f.) airport terminal, 8.1
l' **aéroport** (m.) airport, 8.1
les **affaires** (f. pl.) business, 11.1
l' **affiche** (f.) poster
l' **âge** (m.) age, 4.1
  Tu as quel âge? How old are you?, 4.1
âgé(e) old
l' **agent** (m.) **de police** police officer, 11.1
l' **agglomération** (f.) urban area, 7.2
agité(e) choppy, rough (sea)
l' **agneau** (m.) lamb, 6.1, 6.2, 11.2
agréable pleasant
agricole agricultural, farm (adj.), 11.2
l' **agriculteur, l'agricultrice** farmer, 11.2
l' **aide** (f.) aid, help
  à l'aide de with the help of
aider to help, 3.2
aigu(ë) acute, severe, 2.2
l' **ail** (m.) garlic, 6.1
ailleurs elsewhere
aimer to like, love, 3.1
  aimer mieux to prefer, 7.2
l' **aîné(e)** older, L1
ainsi thus, so
  ainsi que as well as
l' **air** (m.) air, 7.1; melody
  l'air climatisé air conditioning, 9.2
  avoir l'air to look, 13.2
aisé(e) well-to-do
ajouter to add, 6.2
l' **aliment** (m.) food, 6.1

French-English Dictionary

l' **alimentation** *(f.)* nutrition; diet
l' **Allemagne** *(f.)* Germany
l' **allemand** *(m.)* German *(language)*, 2.2
aller to go, 5.1
  aller chercher to go (and) get, 6.1
  aller mieux to feel better, 2.2
l' **aller (simple)** *(m.)* one-way ticket, 9.1
l' **alliance** *(f.)* wedding ring, **12.2**
allô hello *(telephone)*
allonger to stretch out
allumer to turn on *(appliance)*, 12.2, **3.1**; to light, **12.2**
l' **allure** *(f.)*: **à toute allure** at full speed, **L1**
alors so, then, well then, BV
ambitieux (ambitieuse) ambitious
s' **améliorer** to get better; to improve
l' **amende** *(f.)* fine
l' **Amérique** *(f.)* **du Sud** South America
l' **amerrissage** *(m.)* landing at sea
l' **ami(e)** friend, 1.2
l' **amour** *(m.)* love, L4
amoureux, amoureuse in love, **L1**
ample large, full
amusant(e) funny; fun, 1.1
s' **amuser** to have fun, 12.2
l' **an** *(m.)* year, 4.1
  avoir... ans to be ... years old, 4.1
ancien(ne) old, ancient; former
l' **âne** *(m.)* donkey
l' **anesthésie** *(f.)* anesthesia, **8.2**
  faire une anesthésie to anesthetize, **8.2**

l' **angine** *(f.)* throat infection, tonsillitis, **2.1**
l' **anglais** *(m.)* English *(language)*, 2.2
anglais(e) English
l' **Angleterre** *(f.)* England
l' **année** *(f.)* year
  l'année dernière last year
l' **anniversaire** *(m.)* birthday, 4.1
  Bon anniversaire! Happy birthday!
l' **annonce** *(f.)* announcement, 8.2
  la petite annonce classified ad, **14.2**
annoncer to announce, 9.1
l' **annuaire** *(m.)* telephone directory, 3.2
annuler to cancel, **4.2**
l' **anorak** *(m.)* ski jacket, 7.1
Antilles: la mer des Antilles Caribbean Sea
l' **apothicaire** *(m.)* apothecary, **L4**
l' **appareil** *(m.)* apparatus; machine, **10.2**; appliance
l' **appartement** *(m.)* apartment, 4.2
l' **appel** *(m.)* (phone) call, **3.2**
  l'appel interurbain toll call
  l'appel téléphonique phone call, **3.2**
  l'appel urbain local call
appeler to call
s' **appeler** to be called, be named, 12.1
applaudir to applaud
appliquer to apply
apporter to bring, 11.1
apprécier to appreciate
apprendre (à) to learn (to), 5; to teach
appuyer sur to press, push, 3.1
  s'appuyer contre to lean against, **10.2**

après after, 3.2
  d'après according to
l' **après-midi** *(m.)* afternoon, 3.2
l' **aqueduc** *(m.)* aquaduct
l' **arabe** *(m.)* Arabic *(language)*
l' **arbitre** *(m.)* referee, 10.1
l' **arbre** *(m.)* tree, L3
  l'arbre de Noël Christmas tree, **12.2**
les **arènes** *(f. pl.)* amphitheater
l' **argent** *(m.)* money, 5.2
  l'argent liquide cash, **5.1**
  l'argent de poche pocket money
l' **argument** *(m.)* plot
l' **arme** *(f.)* weapon
l' **armée** *(f.)* army, L3
arranger to fix, set right
l' **arrêt** *(m.)* stop, 9.2, **10.2**
  l'arrêt d'autobus bus stop, **10.2**
arrêter to stop; to arrest
s'arrêter to stop, 10
les **arrhes** *(f. pl.)* deposit, 9.1
l' **arrière** *(m.)* rear, back, 8.2, **10.2**
l' **arrière-garde** *(f.)* rear guard
l' **arrivée** *(f.)* arrival, 8.1
arriver to arrive, 3.1; to happen, **8.1**
  arriver à (+ *inf.*) to manage to, to succeed in, 9.1
l' **arrobase** *(f.)* "at" symbol
l' **arrondissement** *(m.)* district (in Paris)
artistique artistic
l' **ascenseur** *(m.)* elevator, 4.2
asiatique Asian
l' **aspirine** *(f.)* aspirin, **2.1**
assez fairly, quite; enough, 1.1
l' **assiette** *(f.)* plate, 5.2
  ne pas être dans son assiette to be feeling out of sorts, **2.1**

French-English Dictionary

assis(e) seated, 9.2
l' **assistante sociale** *(f.)* social worker, **14.1**
assister à to attend
assurer to ensure; to carry out
l' **atelier** *(m.)* studio *(artist's)*
l' **athlétisme** *(m.)* track and field, 10.2
atroce atrocious
attacher to fasten, 8.2
attaquer to attack
attendre to wait (for), 9.1
Attention! Careful! Watch out!, 4.2
atterrir to land, 8.1
l' **atterrissage** *(m.)* landing, **4.2**
attraper to catch
 attraper un coup de soleil to get a sunburn, 11.1
au bord de la mer by the ocean, seaside, 11.1
au contraire on the contrary
au fond in the background
au revoir good-bye, BV
l' **auberge** *(f.)* **de jeunesse** youth hostel
aucun(e) no, not any, **4.2**
au-dessous (de) below, 7.2
au-dessus (de) above, 7.2
 la taille au-dessus the next larger size, 7.2
aujourd'hui today, BV
auprès de with
ausculter to listen with a stethoscope, **2.2**
aussi also, too, 1.1; as *(comparisons)*, 7; so
autant de as many
l' **auteur** *(m.)* author *(m. and f.)*, **L1**
 l'auteur dramatique playwright
l' **autobus** *(m.)* bus, **10.2**
l' **autocar** *(m.)* bus, coach
l' **auto-école** *(f.)* driving school, **7.1**

l' **automne** *(m.)* autumn, 11.2
l' **automobiliste** *(m. et f.)* driver, **7.1**
l' **autoroute** *(f.)* highway, **7.2**
autour de around, 4.2
autre other, L1
 autre chose something else, 6.2
 d'autres some other, 2.2
 l'un... l'autre one . . . the other
autrement dit in other words
avaler to swallow, **2.2**
avance: à l'avance ahead of time; in advance, 9.1
 en avance early, ahead of time, 9.1
l' **avancement** *(m.)* advancement; promotion
avant before
 avant de (+ *inf.*) before (+ *verb*)
 avant J.-C. (Jésus-Christ) B.C.
l' **avant** *(m.)* front, 8.2, **10.2**
l' **avantage** *(m.)* advantage
l' **avant-bras** forearm, **13.1**
avant-hier the day before yesterday, 10.2
avec with, 3.2
 Avec ça? What else? *(shopping)*, 6.1
l' **avenir** *(m.)* future, L2
l' **aventure** *(f.)* adventure
aveugle blind
l' **aviateur, l'aviatrice** aviator
l' **avion** *(m.)* plane, 8.1, **L3**
 en avion by plane
l' **avis** *(m.)* opinion, 7.2
 à mon avis in my opinion, 7.2
avoir to have, 4.1
 avoir l'air to look, **13.2**
 avoir... ans to be . . . years old, 4.1
 avoir besoin de to need, 10.1

 avoir de la chance to be lucky, to be in luck
 avoir envie de to want (to), to feel like
 avoir faim to be hungry, 5.1
 avoir une faim de loup to be very hungry
 avoir lieu to take place, **12.1**
 avoir mal à to have a(n) . . . -ache, to hurt, **2.1**
 avoir peur to be afraid, L1, **13.2**
 avoir du retard to be late *(plane, train, etc.)*, 8.1
 avoir soif to be thirsty, 5.1
l' **avocat(e)** lawyer, **14.1**

le **baccalauréat** French high school exam
la **bactérie** bacterium
 bactérien(ne) bacterial, **2.1**
les **bagages** *(m. pl.)* luggage, 8.1
 le bagage à main carry-on bag, 8.1
 le coffre à bagages baggage compartment, 8.2
la **baguette** loaf of French bread, 6.1
le **baigneur, la baigneuse** bather
le **bain** bath, 12.1
la **balance** scale, **5.2**
le **ballon** ball *(soccer, etc.)*, 10.1
la **banlieue** suburbs, **4.1**, **11.1**
la **banque** bank, 5.1
bas(se) low
la **base** base; basis
 à base de based on
le **basilic** basil
la **basilique** basilica

French-English Dictionary

la **basket** sneaker; running shoe, 7.1
le **basket(-ball)** basketball, 10.2
la **bataille** battle, L3
   le champ de bataille battlefield, L3
le **bateau** boat, L4
le **bâtiment** building, **11.1**
le **bâton** ski pole, 11.2
battre to beat; to defeat
bavarder to chat
beau (bel), belle beautiful, handsome, 4.2
beaucoup de a lot of, 3.1
le **beau-père** stepfather; father-in-law, 4.1
la **beauté** beauty
   de toute beauté of great beauty
le **bébé** baby, **L2**
belge Belgian
la **Belgique** Belgium
la **belle-mère** stepmother; mother-in-law, 4.1
ben (slang) well
ben oui yeah
le/la **bénévole** volunteer
la **béquille** crutch, **8.1**
berbère Berber
le **berger, la bergère** shepherd, shepherdess
le **besoin** need
   avoir besoin de to need, 10.1
la **bêtise** stupid thing, nonsense
le **beurre** butter, 6.1
le **bicentenaire** bicentennial
la **bicyclette** bicycle, 10.2
bien fine, well, good, BV
   bien cuit(e) well-done (meat), 5.2
   bien élevé(e) well-behaved, well-mannered, **13.1**
   bien sûr of course
bientôt soon

À bientôt! See you soon! BV
le/la **bienvenu(e)** welcome
bigarré(e) mottled
le **billet** ticket, 8.1; bill, **5.1**
   le billet aller (et) retour round-trip ticket, 9.1
blanc, blanche white, 7.2
le **blé** wheat, **11.2**
blessé(e) wounded, L3
se **blesser** to hurt oneself, **8.1**
la **blessure** wound, injury, **8.1**
bleu(e) blue, 7.2
   bleu marine (inv.) navy blue, 7.2
le **bloc-notes** notepad, 3.2
blond(e) blond, 1.1
bloquer to block, 10.1
le **blouson** (waist-length) jacket, 7.1
le **blue-jean** (pair of) jeans
le **bœuf** beef, 6.1, **6.2**
le **bogue** (computer) bug
bohème bohemian
boire to drink, 10.2
le **bois** wood
la **boisson** beverage, drink, 5.1
la **boîte: la boîte de conserve** can of food, 6.2
   la boîte crânienne skull
   la boîte aux lettres mailbox, **5.2**
boiteux, boiteuse lame
le **bol** bowl
bon(ne) correct; good, 6.2
   bon marché (inv.) inexpensive
   Bonne Année! Happy New Year!, **12.2**
   Bonne santé! Good health!, **12.2**
   de bonne heure early
bondé(e) packed, **10.1**
le **bonheur** happiness, joy
le **bonhomme de neige** snowman
bonjour hello, BV
le **bonnet** ski cap, hat, 11.2

la **bonté** goodness
le **bord: à bord (de)** aboard (plane, etc.), 8.2
   au bord de la mer by the ocean, seaside, 11.1
border to border
la **bosse** mogul (ski), 11.2
la **botanique** botany
le **boubou** boubou (long, flowing garment)
la **bouche** mouth, **2.1, 13.1**
le **boucher, la bouchère** butcher
la **boucherie** butcher shop, 6.1
le **bouchon** traffic jam, **7.2**
la **bougie** candle, 4.1, **12.2**
bouillant(e) boiling, **6.2**
bouillir to boil, **6.2**
la **boulangerie-pâtisserie** bakery, 6.1
bourguignon(ne) of or from Burgundy
bousculer to push and shove, **13.1**
le **bout** end, tip
la **bouteille** bottle, 6.2
la **boutique** shop, boutique, 7.1
le **bouton** button, 10.2
le **brancard** stretcher, **8.1**
la **branche** branch, **12.2**
le **bras** arm, **8.1**
le **break** station wagon, **7.1**
la **brebis** ewe
le **Brésil** Brazil
le/la **Brésilien(ne)** Brazilian (person)
la **Bretagne** Brittany
breton(ne) Breton, from Brittany
briller to shine
la **brioche** sweet roll
la **brique** brick
briser to break, L3
se **briser** to break
britannique British
la **bronche** bronchial tube
bronzer to tan, 11.1

H52 Handbook

la **brosse** brush, **12.1**
    la brosse à dents toothbrush, **12.1**
se **brosser** to brush, **12.1**
la **brousse** bush *(wilderness)*
le **bruit** noise, **L3**, **13.1**
brûler to burn
    brûler un feu rouge to run a red light, **7.2**
brun(e) brunette; dark-haired, **1.1**
bruyant(e) noisy, **13.1**
la **bûche de Noël** cake in the shape of a log
le **buffet** train station restaurant, **9.1**
le **bungalow** bungalow
le **bureau** office, **11.1, 14.1**
    le bureau de change foreign exchange office, **5.1**
    le bureau de placement employment office, **14.2**
    le bureau de poste post office, **5.1**
    le bureau de tabac tobacco shop
    le bureau de (du) tourisme tourist office
le **bus** bus, **5.2**
le **but** goal, **10.1**
    marquer un but to score a goal, **10.1**
le **buveur**, la **buveuse** drinker

ça that, **BV**
    Ça fait… euros. It's (That's) . . . euros., **6.2**
    Ça fait mal. It (That) hurts., **2.1**
    Ça va. Fine., Okay., **BV**
    Ça va? How's it going?, How are you? *(inform.)*, **BV**; How does it look?, **7.2**

    C'est ça. That's right., That's it.
la **cabine** cabin *(plane)*, **8.1**
    la cabine d'essayage fitting room
    la cabine téléphonique telephone booth, **3.2**
cacher to hide, **L3**
le **cadeau** gift, present, **4.1**
le **cadet**, la **cadette** younger, **L1**
le **cadre** manager, executive, **14.1**
le **café** café, **BV**; coffee, **5.1**
le **cahier** notebook, **3.2**
la **caisse** cash register, checkout counter, **3.2**
le **caissier**, la **caissière** cashier, **5.1**
le **calcul** arithmetic, **2.2**
    le calcul différentiel differential calculus
    le calcul intégral integral calculus
la **calculatrice** calculator, **3.2**
le **calendrier** calendar; schedule
le **calligramme** picture-poem
le **camembert** Camembert cheese
le **camion** truck, **7.1**
la **camionnette** small truck, van
le **camp** side *(in a sport or game)*, **10.1**
    le camp adverse opponents, other side, **10.1**
la **campagne** country(side), **11.2**; campaign
le **canard** duck
le/la **candidat(e) à un poste** job applicant, **14.2**
la **candidature: poser sa candidature** to apply for a job, **14.2**
la **canne à sucre** sugar cane
la **canneberge** cranberry
le **canoë** canoe

le **canot** *(open)* boat
la **cantine** school dining hall, **3.1**
le **canton** canton (Swiss state)
capable able
le **car** bus *(coach)*
Caraïbes: la mer des Caraïbes Caribbean Sea
la **carbonnade** charcoal-grilled meat
le **carnaval** carnival *(season)*, **12.1**
le **carnet** booklet; book of ten subway tickets, **10.1**
la **carotte** carrot, **6.2**
le **carrefour** intersection, **11.1**
la **carrière** career; *(employment)* field, **14.2**
la **carte** menu, **5.1**; map; card
    la carte d'adhésion membership card
    la carte de crédit credit card, **9.2**
    la carte de débarquement landing card, **8.2**
    la carte d'embarquement boarding pass, **8.1**
    la carte postale postcard, **9.1, 5.2**
    la carte (routière) road map, **7.2**
    la carte de vœux greeting card, **12.2**
le **carton** cardboard
le **cas** case
    en cas de in case of
le **casque** helmet, **7.1**
la **casquette** cap, baseball cap, **7.1**
casse-pieds pain in the neck *(slang)*
se **casser** to break (one's leg, etc.), **8.1**
la **casserole** pot, **6.2**
la **cassette** cassette, tape **3.1**
    la cassette vidéo videocassette, **12.2**

French-English Dictionary

cause: à cause de because of
causer to cause
la **cave** cellar
ce (cet), cette this, that, 9
  ce soir tonight
céder la place to give way
la **ceinture** belt, L3
  la **ceinture de sécurité** seat belt, 8.2, **7.1**
cela this, that
célèbre famous
célébrer to celebrate, L4
la **cellule** cell, L4
celte Celtic
celui-là, celle-là this/that one, **11.2**
cent hundred, 2.2
  pour cent percent
les **centaines** (f. pl.) hundreds
le **centre** center; downtown
  le **centre commercial** shopping center, mall, 7.1
le **centre-ville** downtown, **11.1**
le **cercle** circle
les **céréales** (f. pl.) cereal, grain(s), **11.2**
certainement certainly
certains (pron.) some
le **cerveau** brain
cesser to stop, cease
c'est it is, it's, BV
  C'est combien? How much is it?, 3.2
  C'est quel jour? What day is it?, BV
  C'est tout. That's all., 6.1
  c'est-à-dire that is
chacun(e) each (one), 5.2
la **chaîne** chain; TV channel, 12.2
la **chaise** chair
la **chaleur** heat
la **chambre** room (hotel), 9.1
  la **chambre à coucher** bedroom, 4.2
le **champ** field, L1, **11.2, L2**

le **champ de bataille** battlefield, L3
champêtre pastoral
le **champignon** mushroom, **6.1**
le/la **champion(ne)** champion
la **chance** luck
le **chandelier** candelabra, **12.2**
le **changement** change
  changer to exchange, **5.1**
  changer (de) to change, 9.2
la **chanson** song
le **chant de Noël** Christmas carol, **12.2**
chanter to sing, **1.1**
le **chanteur, la chanteuse** singer, **1.1**
chaque each, every, **4.1**
le **char** float, **12.1**
la **charcuterie** deli(catessen), 6.1
chargé(e) de in charge of
charger to load
  se charger de to be in charge of
le **chariot** shopping cart, 6.2; baggage cart, 9.1
charmant(e) charming
le **charpentier** carpenter
chasser to chase away, blow away
le **chasseur, la chasseuse** hunter
le **chat** cat, 4.1
le **château** castle, mansion
chaud(e) warm, hot
le **chauffeur** driver
la **chaussette** sock, 7.1
la **chaussure** shoe, 7.1
  les **chaussures de ski** ski boots, 11.2
le **chef** head, boss
  le **chef de service** department head, **14.1**
le **chemin** route; road; path
  le **chemin de fer** railroad
la **cheminée** chimney, **12.2**
la **chemise** shirt, 7.1

le **chemisier** blouse, 7.1
le **chèque** check, **5.1**
  le **chèque de voyage** traveler's check
cher, chère dear; expensive, 7.1
chercher to look for, seek
  aller chercher to go (and) get, 6.1
le **cheval** horse, **11.2**
  faire du cheval to go horseback riding, **11.2**
le **chevalier** knight
les **cheveux** (m. pl.) hair, 12.1
la **cheville** ankle, **8.1**
chez at (to) the home (business) of, 3.2
le **chien** dog, 4.1
la **chimie** chemistry, 2.2
chimique chemical
chinois(e) Chinese
le **chirurgien** surgeon (m. and f.), **8.2**
le **chirurgien-orthopédiste** orthopedic surgeon, **8.2**
le **chœur** choir
choisir to choose, 8.1
le **choix** choice
le **chômage** unemployment, **14.2**
  être au chômage to be unemployed, **14.2**
le **chômeur, la chômeuse** unemployed person, **14.2**
la **chose** thing
la **choucroute** sauerkraut, **6.1**
ciao good-bye (inform.), BV
ci-dessous below
le **ciel** sky, 11.1, **L3**
  le **Ciel** heaven
la **cigale** cicada
le/la **cinéaste** filmmaker, **14.1**
le **cinéma** movie theater, movies, **1.1**
le **cintre** hanger, 9.2
la **circulation** circulation; traffic, **7.2**

French-English Dictionary

circuler to move about, get around; to make its rounds, **11.1**
le **cirque** circus
citer to cite, mention
le **citron** lemon, **6.1**
   le citron pressé lemonade, **5.1**
clair(e) light *(color)*
clairement clearly
la **classe** class, **2.1**
   la classe économique coach class *(plane)*
le **classement** ranking
le **classeur** loose-leaf binder, **3.2**
classifier to classify
le **clavier** keyboard, **3.1**
la **clé** key, **7.1**
le **clignotant** turn signal, **7.2**
le **climat** climate
climatique climatic
climatisé(e) air conditioned, **9.2**
la **clinique** clinic
cliquer to click, **3.1**
le **club d'art dramatique** drama club
le **coca** cola, **5.1**
le **cochon** pig, **11.2**
le **code** code, **4.2**
   le code postal zip code, **5.2**
   le code de la route the rules of the road, **11.1**
le **coéquipier, la coéquipière** teammate
le **cœur** heart
le **coffre** chest, **L4**; trunk, **7.1**
   le coffre à bagages (overhead) baggage compartment, **8.2**
le **coin** corner, **10.1, 11.1**
   du coin neighborhood *(adj.)*
le **colis** package, **5.2**
la **collation** snack, **4.2**
le **collège** junior high, middle school, **1.2**

le/la **collégien(ne)** middle school/junior high student
le **combat** fight, battle, **L3**
combien (de) how much, how many, **3.2**
   C'est combien? How much is it (that)?, **3.2**
comble packed *(stadium)*, **10.1**
la **comédie** comedy, **1.1**
comique comic; funny, **1.1**
   le film comique comedy, **1.1**
commander to order, **5.1**
comme like, as; for; since
   comme ci, comme ça so-so
commémorer to commemorate
commencer to begin, **9.2**
comment how, what, **1.1**
   Comment ça? How is that?
le/la **commerçant(e)** shopkeeper, **14.1**
le **commerce** trade
commettre to commit
commun(e) common
   en commun in common
   les transports en commun mass transit
la **communauté** community
communiquer to communicate
la **compagnie aérienne** airline, **8.1**
la **comparaison** comparison
le **compartiment** compartment, **4.1**
la **compétition** contest
le **complet** suit *(man's)*, **7.1**
complet, complète full; complete, **4.1**
complètement completely, totally
compléter to complete
compliqué(e) complicated
comploter to conspire

comporter to call for; to behave
composer to dial *(phone number)*, **3.2**
composter to stamp, validate *(a ticket)*, **9.1**
comprendre to understand, **5**
le **comprimé** pill, **2.2**
compris(e) included, **5.2, 9.1**
   tout compris all included, **9.1**
la **comptabilité** accounting
le/la **comptable** accountant, **14.1**
le **compte** account
   le compte courant checking account, **5.1**
   le compte d'épargne savings account, **5.1**
   être à son compte to be self-employed, **14.2**
compter to count, **5.1**
le **comptoir** counter, **8.1**
le **comte** count, **L4**
le/la **concierge** doorkeeper
le **concombre** cucumber
le **concours** competition, contest
le **conducteur, la conductrice** driver, **7.1**
conduire to drive, **7.1, 11.1**
confier to entrust
la **confiture** jam, **6.2**
confortable comfortable
le **congé(lateur)** freezer, **6.1**
la **connaissance** acquaintance
   faire la connaissance de to meet, **13.2**
connaître to know, **1.2**; to meet, **13.2**
   se connaître to be acquainted, to know one another, **13.2**
connu(e) well-known; famous, **1.1**
conquérir to conquer
se **consacrer** to devote oneself
le **conseiller, la conseillère** counselor, adviser

French-English Dictionary

la **conserve: la boîte de conserve** can of food, **6.2**
conserver to preserve, save
la **consommation** drink, beverage, **5.1**
conspirer to plot
construire to build
la **consultation** medical visit
   donner des consultations to have office hours *(doctor)*
consulter to consult
le **contact** contact
   être en contact avec to be in touch with
contenir to contain
content(e) happy, glad, **13.2**
continuer to continue
le **contraire** opposite
la **contravention** traffic ticket, **7.2**
contre against, **10.1**
   par contre on the other hand, however
le **contremaître,** la **contremaîtresse** foreman, forewoman
le **contrôle** check; control
   le contrôle des passeports passport check, **4.2**
   le contrôle de sécurité security *(airport)*, **8.1**
contrôler to check; to control, **4.1**
le **contrôleur** conductor *(train)*, **9.2**
le **copain** friend, pal *(m.)*, **2.1**
la **copine** friend, pal *(f.)*, **2.1**
le **coq** rooster
le **cor** horn, **L3**
   sonner du cor to blow a horn, **L3**
la **cornemuse** bagpipes
le **corps** body, **8.1**
   le corps médical the medical profession

la **correspondance** correspondence; connection *(between trains)*, **9.2, 10.1**
corriger to correct
cosmopolite cosmopolitan
la **côte** coast
   la Côte d'Azur French Riviera
   la Côte d'Ivoire Ivory Coast
le **côté** side, **4.1**
   à côté de next to, **11.1**
   côté couloir aisle *(seat)*, **8.1**
   côté fenêtre window *(seat)*, **8.1**
la **côtelette de porc** pork chop, **6.2**
se **coucher** to go to bed, **12.1**
la **couchette** berth *(on a train)*
le **coude** elbow, **13.1**
couler to flow
   avoir le nez qui coule to have a runny nose, **2.1**
la **couleur** color, **7.2**
le **couloir** aisle, corridor, **8.2**
le **coup (de pied, de tête, etc.)** a hit, a kick, **10.1**
le **coup de chapeau** tip of the hat
le **coup de fil** phone call, **3.2**
le **coup de soleil** sunburn, **11.1**
le **coup de téléphone** telephone call, **3.2**
la **coupe** winner's cup, **10.2**
couper to cut, **6.2**
   se couper to cut (one's finger, etc.), **8.1**
la **cour** courtyard, **3.2**; court
courageux, courageuse courageous, brave
courant(e) fluent; common; current
le **coureur, la coureuse** runner, **10.2**

le **coureur (la coureuse) cycliste** racing cyclist, **10.2**
le **courrier** mail, **5.2**
le **cours** course, class, **2.1**
   en cours de (français, etc.) in (French, etc.) class
   le cours du change exchange rate, **5.1**
la **course** race, **10.2**
   la course cycliste bicycle race, **10.2**
les **courses** *(f. pl.)*: **faire des courses** to go shopping, **6.1**
court(e) short, **7.1**
le **couscous** couscous
le **couteau** knife, **5.2**
coûter to cost, **3.2**
   Ça coûte combien? How much does this cost?, **3.1**
   coûter cher to be expensive
le **couturier** designer *(of clothes)*
le **couvent** convent
le **couvercle** lid, **6.2**
couvert(e) covered
le **couvert** table setting; silverware, **5.2**
la **couverture** blanket, **4.2**
couvrir to cover
la **cravate** tie, **7.1**
le **crayon** pencil, **3.2**
créer to create
la **crème** cream
   la crème solaire suntan lotion, **11.1**
le **crème** coffee with cream *(in a café)*, **5.1**
la **crémerie** dairy store, **6.1**
le **créole** Creole *(language)*
la **crêpe** crepe, pancake, **BV**
creuser to dig, **L4**
crevé(e) exhausted
crever to die, **L4**
la **crevette** shrimp, **6.1**
crier to shout, **L4**

French-English Dictionary

la **critique** review
croire to believe, think, 7.2
le **croisement** intersection, 7.2
se **croiser** to cross, intersect, 10.1
la **croissance** growth
le **croissant** croissant, crescent roll, 5.1
le **croque-monsieur** grilled ham and cheese sandwich, 5.1
la **crosse** hockey stick
la **cuillère** spoon, 5.2
cuire to cook, 6.2
la **cuisine** kitchen, 4.2; cuisine *(food)*
   faire la cuisine to cook, 6
le **cuisinier**, la **cuisinière** cook, 6.2
la **cuisinière** stove, 6.1
cuit(e) cooked
   bien cuit(e) well-done *(meat)*, 5.2
le **cuivre** copper
cultiver to cultivate; to grow; to farm (land), 11.2
la **culture** culture, growing
culturel(le) cultural
curieux, curieuse odd
le **curriculum vitae (C.V.)** résumé, 14.2
le **cyclisme** cycling, bicycle riding, 10.2
cycliste bicycle, cycling *(adj.)*, 10.2
le/la **cycliste** cyclist, bicycle rider
les **cymbales** *(f. pl.)* cymbals, 12.1

d'abord first, 12.1
d'accord okay, all right *(agreement)*
   être d'accord to agree, 2.1
la **dame** lady
   les dames checkers

dangereux, dangereuse dangerous
dans in, 1.2
la **danse** dance
danser to dance, 1.1
le **danseur**, la **danseuse** dancer, 1.1
   la **danseuse** ballerina, 1.1
d'après according to
dater de to date from
la **datte** date
le **dattier** date palm
d'autres some other, 2.2
de from, 1.1; of, belonging to, 1.2; about
   de bonne heure early
   de près close, 11.1
   de temps en temps from time to time, occasionally
le **débarquement** landing, deplaning
débarquer to get off *(plane)*, 4.2
débarrasser la table to clear the table, 12.2
debout standing, 9.2
le **début** beginning
   au début in the beginning
le/la **débutant(e)** beginner, 11.2
débuter to begin
le **décalage horaire** time difference
la **décapotable** convertible, 7.1
le **déchet** waste
décider (de) to decide (to)
déclarer to declare, call
le **décollage** takeoff *(plane)*, 4.2
décoller to take off *(plane)*, 8.1
décorer to decorate
la **découverte** discovery
découvrir to discover
décrire to describe
décrocher (le téléphone) to pick up the (telephone) receiver, 3.2
dedans into it

dédié(e) dedicated
défaire to unpack, 9.1
le **défilé** parade, 12.1
défiler to march, 12.1
définir to define
déformer to distort
se **dégager** to be given off
dehors outdoors
   au dehors de outside
déjà already; ever; yet, BV
déjeuner to eat lunch, 3.1
le **déjeuner** lunch, 5.2
   le petit déjeuner breakfast, 5.2
délicieux, délicieuse delicious
demain tomorrow, BV
   À demain. See you tomorrow., BV
demander to ask, to ask for, 3.2
demeurer d'accord to agree, L4
demi(e) half
   et demie half past *(time)*, BV
le **demi-cercle** semi-circle; top of the key *(on a basketball court)*, 10.2
le **demi-frère** half brother, 4.1
la **demi-heure** half hour
la **demi-sœur** half sister, 4.1
le **demi-tarif** half price
le **demi-tour** about-face
   faire demi-tour to turn around, 11.1
la **demoiselle d'honneur** maid of honor, 12.2
le **dénouement** ending
la **dent** tooth, 12.1
le **dentifrice** toothpaste, 12.1
le **départ** departure, 8.1
le **département d'outre-mer** French overseas department
dépasser to pass, L1
se **dépêcher** to hurry, 12.1
dépendre (de) to depend (on)

French-English Dictionary

dépenser to spend *(money)*, **5.1**
depuis since, for, 9.2, **10.2**
le **dérangement** disturbance
dernier, dernière last, **10.2**
derrière behind, **11.1**
désagréable disagreeable, unpleasant
descendre to get off *(train, bus, etc.)*, 9.2; to take down, 9; to go down, 9; to take downstairs, **9**; to stay at *(hotel)*
  descendre à la prochaine to get off at the next station, **10.1**
la **descente** getting off, **10.2**
désert(e) deserted
le **désert** desert
désespéré(e) desperate, L4
le **désir** desire; wish
désirer to want, 5.1
désolé(e) sorry, 3.2, **13.2**
désormais from then on
le **dessert** dessert
desservir to serve, go to *(transp.)*, **4.1**
le **dessin** drawing, illustration; design
  le **dessin animé** cartoon, **1.1**
dessiner to design, draw
dessus on it
le/la **destinataire** addressee
la **destination** destination
  à destination de to *(destination)*, 8.1
destiné(e) à intended for
la **destinée** destiny
déterrer to unearth
détester to hate, 3.1
deux: tous (toutes) les deux both
deuxième second, 4.2
devant in front of, 8.2, **11.1**
développer to develop
devenir to become, **4**
déverser to spill

deviner to guess
la **devinette** riddle
la **devise** currency
devoir to owe, 10; must, to have to *(+ verb)*, 10.2
le **devoir** homework *(assignment)*
  faire ses devoirs to do homework, 6
dévoué(e) devoted
d'habitude usually, 12.2
le **diagnostic** diagnosis, **2.2**
le **diamant** diamond
dicter to dictate
le **dictionnaire** dictionary
difficile difficult, 2.1
la **difficulté** problem, difficulty
  être en difficulté to be in trouble
diffuser to spread, to propagate
la **dinde** turkey
le **dindon** turkey
dîner to eat dinner, 5.2
le **dîner** dinner, 5.2
le **diplôme** diploma
diplômé(e): être diplômé(e) to graduate
dire to say, tell, 9.2
  Ça me dit! I'd like that!
le **directeur (la directrice) des ressources humaines (D.R.H.)** director of human resources, **14.2**
diriger to manage, **14.1**
le **discours** speech
discuter to discuss
disparaître to disappear
disparu(e) disappeared, lost
disponible available, **4.1**
la **disquette** diskette, 3.1
distinguer to distinguish, to tell apart
distribuer to distribute, **5.2**

le **distributeur automatique** ATM, **5.1**; stamp machine, **5.2**; ticket machine, **10.1**
divers(e) various
diviser to divide
la **djellaba** djellaba *(long, loose garment)*
le **doigt** finger, 8.1, **13.1**
  le **doigt de pied** toe, **8.1**
le **dolmen** dolmen
le **domaine** domain, field
le **domicile: à domicile** to the home
dominer to overlook
donc so, therefore
les **données** *(f. pl.)* data, **3.1**
donner to give, 4.1
  donner à manger à to feed
  donner un coup de fil to call on the phone, **3.2**
  donner un coup de pied to kick, 10.1
  donner une fête to throw a party, 4.1
  donner sur to face, overlook, 4.2
dont of which, whose
doré(e) golden
dormir to sleep, 8.2
le **dortoir** dormitory
le **dos** back, L2
le **dossier du siège** seat back, **4.2**
la **douane** customs, **4.2**
doublé(e) dubbed *(movies)*, **1.1**
doubler to pass, **7.2**
la **douche** shower, 12.1
douloureux, douloureuse painful
le **doute** doubt
douter to doubt, **14**
la **douzaine** dozen, 6.2
le **drame** drama, 1.1
le **drap** sheet, 9.2
le **drapeau** flag, **12.1**

French-English Dictionary

dribbler to dribble *(basketball)*, **10.2**
le **droit** right
droite: à droite right, **7.2**
la **drôle de tête** strange expression
du coin neighborhood *(adj.)*
dur(e) hard
la **durée** duration
durer to last

l' **eau** *(f.)* water, **6.2**
   l'eau minérale mineral water, **6.2**
l' **échange** *(m.)* exchange
échanger to exchange
s' **échapper** to escape
l' **écharpe** *(f.)* scarf, **11.2**
éclaté(e) burst
l' **école** *(f.)* school, **1.2**
   l'école primaire elementary school
   l'école secondaire secondary school, **1.2**
écologique ecological
l' **économie** *(f.)* economics, **2.2**
   faire des économies to save money, **5.1**
économiser to save money
écouter to listen (to), **3.1**
l' **écouteur** *(m.)* earphone, headphone, **L3**
l' **écran** *(m.)* screen, **8.1, 3.1**
écrasé(e) crushed
écrire to write, **9.2**
l' **écriture** *(f.)* writing
l' **écrivain** *(m.)* writer *(m. and f.)*, **L2, 14.1**
l' **édifice** *(m.)* building
efficace efficient
égal(e): Ça m'est égal. I don't care.; It's all the same to me., **1.1**
également as well, also

égaliser to tie *(score)*
l' **église** *(f.)* church, **11.1, 12.2**
égoïste egotistical, **1.2**
égyptien(ne) Egyptian
l' **électricien(ne)** electrician, **14.1**
l' **électroménager** *(m.)* home appliances
l' **élevage** *(m.)*: **faire de l'élevage de chevaux** to raise horses
l' **élève** *(m. et f.)* student, **1.2**
élevé(e) high
   bien élevé(e) well-behaved, **13.1**
   mal élevé(e) impolite, **13.1**
éliminer to eliminate
éloigné(e) distant, remote
éloigner to distance
l' **embarquement** *(m.)* boarding, leaving
embarquer to board *(plane, etc.)*, **4.2**
s' **embrasser** to kiss (each other), **12.2, 13.1**
l' **émission** *(f.)* program, show *(TV)*, **12.2**
emmagasiner to store
emmener to send, **L4**; to take, **8.1**
l' **emploi** *(m.)* use; job, **14.2**
   l'emploi du temps schedule
l' **employé(e)** employee, **14.1**
   l'employé(e) des postes postal employee, **5.2**
l' **employeur, l'employeuse** employer, **14.2**
emprisonné(e) imprisoned
l' **emprunt** *(m.)* loan
emprunter to borrow, **5.1**
en in, **3.2**; by, **5.2**; as; on
   en avance early, ahead of time, **9.1**
   en avion plane *(adj.)*, by plane, **8**
   en ce moment right now
   en classe in class

   en face de across from, **11.1**
   en fait in fact
   en général in general
   en l'honneur de in honor of
   en particulier in particular
   en plein air outdoors
   en plus (de) besides, in addition
   en première (seconde) in first (second) class, **9.1**
   en provenance de arriving from *(flight, train)*, **8.1**
   en retard late, **9.1**
   en solde on sale, **7.1**
   en vain in vain
   en voiture by car, **5.2**
encaisser to cash
l' **enceinte de résidences** *(f.)* compound, **L2**
enchanté(e) delighted, **13.2**
encore still, **11**; another; again
s' **endetter** to go into debt
s' **endormir** to fall asleep
l' **endroit** *(m.)* place
énervé(e) irritable
l' **enfance** *(f.)* childhood
l' **enfant** *(m. et f.)* child, **4.1**
enfermer to shut up
enfin finally, at last, **12.1**
l' **ennemi(e)** enemy
ennuyeux, ennuyeuse boring
l' **enquête** *(f.)* inquiry, survey
enragé(e) rabid
enregistrer to tape, **12.2**
   (faire) enregistrer to check *(baggage)*, **8.1**
enrhumé(e): être enrhumé(e) to have a cold, **2.1**
ensemble together, **5.1**
l' **ensemble** *(m.)* outfit; whole, entirety
ensuite then *(adv.)*, **12.1**

French-English Dictionary

entendre to hear, 9.1
enthousiaste enthusiastic, 1.2
entier, entière entire, whole
l' **entracte** (*m.*) intermission, 1.1
entre between, among, 3.2
l' **entrée** (*f.*) entrance, 4.2; admission
entreposer to store, 11.2
l' **entreprise** (*f.*) firm, company, 14.2
entrer to enter, 7.1
l' **entretien** (*m.*) interview, 14.2
l' **enveloppe** (*f.*) envelope, 5.2
environ about
envoyer to send, 10.1, 3.1
l' **épée** (*f.*) sword, L3
épeler to spell
éperdument madly
l' **épice** (*f.*) spice
épicé(e) spicy
l' **épicerie** (*f.*) grocery store, 6.1
les **épinards** (*m. pl.*) spinach, 6.2
éplucher to peel, 6.2
l' **époque** (*f.*) period, times
épuisé(e) exhausted
épurer to purify
l' **équateur** (*m.*) equator
l' **équilibre** (*m.*) balance
équilibré(e) balanced
l' **équipe** (*f.*) team, 10.1
l' **équipement** (*m.*) equipment
l' **erreur** (*f.*) error; wrong number (phone), 3.2
l' **escale** (*f.*) stopover, 4.2
l' **escalier** (*m.*) staircase, 4.2
  l'escalier mécanique escalator, 10.1
l' **escalope** (*f.*) **de veau** veal cutlet, 6.2
l' **espace** (*m.*) space
  les grands espaces open spaces

l' **espagnol** (*m.*) Spanish (*language*), 2.2
les **espèces** (*f. pl.*): **payer en espèces** to pay cash, 9.2
espérer to hope, 6.2
l' **esprit** (*m.*) spirit; mind
essayer to try on, 7.2; to try
l' **essence** (*f.*) gas(oline), 7.1
essuyer to wipe, L2
  s'essuyer la bouche to wipe one's mouth, 13.1
et and, BV
l' **étable** (*f.*) cow shed, 11.2
établir to establish
l' **établissement** (*m.*) establishment
l' **étage** (*m.*) floor (*of a building*), 4.2
l' **étal** (*m.*) stand, stall
l' **étape** (*f.*) stage, lap
l' **état** (*m.*) state
les **États-Unis** (*m. pl.*) United States
l' **été** (*m.*) summer, 11.1
  en été in summer, 11.1
éteindre to turn off (*appliance*), 12.2, 3.1
éternuer to sneeze, 2.1
étonné(e) surprised, 13.2
étonner to surprise
  s'étonner to be surprised
étranger, étrangère foreign, 1.1
être to be, 1.1
  être d'accord to agree, 2.1
  être enrhumé(e) to have a cold, 2.1
  ne pas être dans son assiette to be feeling out of sorts, 2.1
l' **être** (*m.*) being
  l'être humain human being
l' **étude** (*f.*) study
l' **étudiant(e)** (*university*) student
étudier to study, 3.1
l' **euro** (*m.*) euro, 6.2
s' **évader** to escape, L4

l' **événement** (*m.*) event
évidemment evidently
évident(e) obvious, 14
l' **évier** (*m.*) kitchen sink, 12.2
éviter to avoid, 12.2
évoquer to evoke
exagérer to exaggerate
l' **examen** (*m.*) test, exam, 3.1
  passer un examen to take a test, 3.1
  réussir à un examen to pass a test
examiner to examine, 2.2
l' **excursion** (*f.*) excursion, outing
excuser to excuse
exécuter to execute, carry out
l' **exemple** (*m.*): **par exemple** for example
l' **exercice** (*m.*) exercise
exigeant(e) demanding
exister to exist, to be
l' **expéditeur, l'expéditrice** sender
expliquer to explain
exposer to exhibit
l' **exposition** (*f.*) exhibit, show, 1.2
l' **express** (*m.*) espresso, black coffee, 5.1
exprimer to express
expulser to expel, banish
exquis(e) exquisite
l' **extrait** (*m.*) excerpt

F

la **fable** fable
la **fabrication** manufacture
fabriquer to build
fabuleux, fabuleuse fabulous
la **face** side (*of paper*), 3.1
  face écrite non visible face down (*paper*), 3.1
  face écrite visible face up (*paper*), 3.1

French-English Dictionary

se **fâcher** to quarrel
facile easy, **2.1**
facilement easily
faciliter to facilitate
la **façon** way, manner
   d'une façon générale generally speaking
le **facteur**, la **factrice** mail carrier, **5.2**
la **facture** bill
facultatif, facultative optional
faible weak, **L1**
faim: avoir faim to be hungry, **5.1**
faire to do, make, **6.1**
   s'en faire to worry, **8.1**
   Ça fait mal. It (That) hurts., **2.1**
   faire du (+ nombre) to take size (+ number), **7.2**
   faire des achats to shop
   faire un appel to make a (phone) call, **3.2**
   faire attention to pay attention, **6**; to be careful, **11.1**
   faire du cheval to go horseback riding, **11.2**
   faire des courses to go shopping, **7.2**
   faire les courses to do the grocery shopping, **6.1**
   faire la cuisine to cook, **6**
   faire ses devoirs to do homework, **6**
   faire des économies to save money, **5.1**
   faire enregistrer to check (luggage), **8.1**
   faire escale to stop (plane), **4.2**
   faire des études to study
   faire du français (des maths, etc.) to study French (math, etc.), **6**
   faire du jogging to jog
   se faire mal to hurt oneself, **8.1**
   faire la monnaie de to make change for (bill), **5.1**
   faire la navette to go back and forth, make the run
   faire le numéro to dial the number, **3.2**
   faire une ordonnance to write a prescription, **2.2**
   faire un pansement to bandage, **8.1**
   faire partie de to be a part of
   faire un pas to take a step, **L2**
   faire de la planche à voile to go windsurfing, **11.1**
   faire le plein to fill up the gas tank, **7.1**
   faire une promenade to take a walk, **11.1**
   faire la queue to wait in line, **9.1**
   faire du ski nautique to water-ski, **11.1**
   faire un stage to intern, **14.2**
   faire du surf to go surfing, **11.1**
   faire la vaisselle to do the dishes, **12.2**
   faire les valises to pack (suitcases), **8.1**
   faire un voyage to take a trip, **8.1**
   Il fait quel temps? What's the weather like?, **11.1**
Vous faites quelle pointure? What size shoe do you take?, **7.2**
Vous faites quelle taille? What size do you take (wear)?, **7.2**
fait(e) à la main handmade
la **famille** family, **4.1**
   le nom de famille last name
le/la **fana** fan
la **fanfare** brass band, **12.1**
la **farce** stuffing
la **farine de sorgo** sorghum flour
fatigué(e) tired
fauché(e) (slang) broke, **5.1**
faut: il faut (+ inf.) one must, it is necessary to, **8.2**
   il faut que one must, it is necessary to, **12.2**
la **faute** fault, mistake
le **fauteuil roulant** wheelchair, **8.1**
faux, fausse false
   le faux pas social blunder
favori(te) favorite, **7.2**
le **fax** fax; fax machine, **3.1**
la **femelle** female
la **femme** woman, **7.1**; wife, **4.1**
   la femme de chambre maid (hotel), **9.2**
la **fenêtre** window
   côté fenêtre window (seat) (adj.), **8.1**
la **fente** slot, **3.2**
la **ferme** farm, **11.2**
   fermer to close, **9.1**
   fermer à clé to lock, **9.1**
le **fermier**, la **fermière** farmer, **11.2**
la **fête** party, **4.1**; holiday, **12.1**
   de fête festive
   la fête des Lumières Festival of Lights, Chanouka, **12.2**
le **feu** heat, **6.2**; traffic light, **7.2, 11.1**; fire, **L2**
   le feu d'artifice fireworks, **12.1**
   le feu doux low heat, **6.2**
   le feu vif high heat, **6.2**
la **feuille de papier** sheet of paper, **3.2**
le **feutre** felt-tip pen, **3.2**
les **fiançailles** (f. pl.) engagement, **L4**

French-English Dictionary

la **fiche** registration card, **9.1**
le **fichier** file *(computer)*
fictif, fictive fictional
fier, fière proud
la **fièvre** fever, **2.1**
    avoir de la fièvre to have a fever, **2.1**
la **figue** fig
la **figure** face, 12.1
la **file de voitures** line of cars, **7.2**
le **filet** net *(tennis, etc.)*, **10.2**; string bag
    le filet de sole fillet of sole, **6.2**
la **fille** girl, 1.1; daughter, 4.1
le **film** film, movie, **1.1**
    le film d'amour love story, **1.1**
    le film d'aventures adventure movie, **1.1**
    le film comique comedy, **1.1**
    le film étranger foreign film, **1.1**
    le film d'horreur horror film, **1.1**
    le film policier detective movie, **1.1**
    le film de science-fiction science-fiction movie, **1.1**
    le film en vidéo movie video, **1.1**
le **fils** son, 4.1
la **fin** end
financier, financière financial
la **fine herbe** herb, **6.1**
finir to finish, 8.2
fixe fixed
fixement: regarder fixement to stare at
fixer un rendez-vous to make an appointment
la **flèche** arrow, **7.2**
la **fleur** flower, 4.2
fleuri(e) in bloom, L2; decorated with flowers
fleurir to bloom

le **fleuve** river
la **flûte** flute
le **foie** liver
    avoir mal au foie to have indigestion
la **fois** time *(in a series)*, 10.2
    à la fois at the same time
    deux fois twice
la **fonction** function
le/la **fonctionnaire** civil servant, **14.1**
le **fonctionnement** functioning
fond: au fond in the background
    au fond de at the bottom of
    respirer à fond to breathe deeply, **2.2**
fonder to found
le **foot(ball)** soccer, 10.1
    le football américain football
la **force** strength
forcément necessarily
le **forgeron** blacksmith, **L2**
former to form; to train
le **formulaire** form, **8.2**
la **formule** phrase
fort hard *(adv.)*; very
fort(e) strong, 2.2
    fort(e) en maths good in math, 2.2
fou, folle crazy; insane
la **fouille** dig *(archaeol.)*
se **fouler** to sprain, **8.1**
le **four** oven, **6.1**
    le four à micro-ondes microwave oven, **6.1**
la **fourchette** fork, 5.2
la **fourmi** ant
la **fourniture** supply
    les fournitures scolaires school supplies, 3.2
la **fracture** fracture *(of bone)*, **8.2**
    la fracture compliquée compound fracture, **8.2**

frais: Il fait frais. It's cool. *(weather)*, 11.2
les **frais** *(m. pl.)* expenses; charges, **9.2, 13.1**
la **fraise** strawberry, 6.2
le **français** French *(language)*, 2.2
francophone French-speaking
frapper to hit, L3; to knock, L4, **L2**
freiner to break *(slow down)*, **7.1**
fréquemment frequently
fréquenter to frequent, patronize
le **frère** brother, 1.2
la **fresque** fresco
le **fric** *(slang)* money, **5.1**
le **frigidaire** refrigerator, 12.2, **6.1**
le **frigo** "fridge," **6.1**
les **frissons** *(m. pl.)* chills, **2.1**
les **frites** *(f. pl.)* French fries, 5.1
froid(e) cold
    Il fait froid. It's cold. *(weather)*, 11.2
le **fromage** cheese, 5.1
la **frontière** border
frugal(e) light, simple
le **fruit** fruit, 6.2, **6.1**
    les fruits de mer seafood, **6.2**
la **fumée** smoke
fumer to smoke, 4.2
le **funiculaire** funicular
furieux, furieuse furious, **13.2**
le **futur** future, L2

le/la **gagnant(e)** winner, 10.2
gagner to earn; to win, 10.1
la **gamme** range
le **gant** glove, 11.2
    le gant de toilette washcloth, 12.1, **9.2**

le **garage** garage, **4.2**
le **garçon** boy, **1.1**
   le garçon d'honneur best man, **12.2**
  garder to guard, watch; to keep
le **gardien** guard, **L4**
   le gardien de but goalie, **10.1**
la **gare** train station, **9.1**
   la gare routière bus terminal (Africa)
se **garer** to park, **7.1**
  gastronomique gastronomic, gourmet
le **gâteau** cake, **4.1**
  gâter to spoil
  gauche: à gauche left, **7.2**
le **gaz** gas
  le gaz carbonique carbon dioxide
  le gaz GPL liquefied petroleum gas
le/la **géant(e)** giant
  geler to freeze
  Il gèle. It's freezing. (weather), **11.2**
le **genou** knee, **8.1**
le **genre** type, kind, **1.1**; genre
les **gens** (m. pl.) people
  gentil(le) nice (person), **6.2**
  gérer to manage
le **gigot d'agneau** leg of lamb, **6.2**
le **gilet de sauvetage** life vest, **4.2**
la **glace** ice cream, **5.1**; ice, **11.2**; mirror, **12.1**
  glisser to slip, **8.1**
la **gomme** eraser, **3.2**
le **gommier** Caribbean flat-bottomed fishing boat
la **gorge** throat, **2.1**
  avoir mal à la gorge to have a sore throat, **2.1**
la **gousse d'ail** clove of garlic, **6.1**

le **goût** taste
le **gouvernement** government
  gouverner to govern
  grâce à thanks to
le **gradin** bleacher (stadium), **10.1**
la **graisse** fat
le **gramme** gram, **6.2**
  grand(e) tall, big, **1.1**; great
  le grand magasin department store, **7.1**
  de grand standing luxury (adj.)
  la grande surface large department store; large supermarket
  grandir to grow (up) (children)
la **grand-mère** grandmother, **4.1**
le **grand-père** grandfather, **4.1**
les **grands-parents** (m. pl.) grandparents, **4.1**
la **grange** barn, **11.2**
  gratter to scratch, **2.1**
  gratuit(e) free
  grave serious, **3.2**
  Ce n'est pas grave. It's not serious., **3.2**
le **grec** Greek (language)
la **Grèce** Greece
la **griffe** label
le **griot** griot (African musician-entertainer)
la **grippe** flu, **2.1**
  gris(e) gray, **7.2**
  gros(se) big, large, **14.2**
la **grotte** cave, **L4**
  guérir to cure, **L4**
la **guerre** war, **L3**
le **guerrier** warrior, **L3**
le **guichet** ticket window, **9.1**, **10.1**; box office, **1.1**; counter window (post office), **5.2**
le **guide** guidebook; guide

  guillotiné(e) guillotined
le **gymnase** gymnasium
la **gymnastique** gymnastics, **2.2**

  habillé(e) dressy, **7.1**
s' **habiller** to get dressed, **12.1**
l' **habitant(e)** inhabitant
  habiter to live (in a city, house, etc.), **3.1**
  hacher to grind, **6.2**
le **hall** lobby, **8.1**, **9.1**
le **hameau** hamlet
  handicapé(e) handicapped
le **hangar** shed, **11.2**
  Hanouka Hanukkah, **12.2**
les **haricots** (m. pl.) **verts** green beans, **6.2**, **6.1**
la **harpe** harp
  haut(e) high, **11.1**
  en haut de at the top of
  haut de gamme state of the art
le **hautbois** oboe
l' **herbe** (f.) grass, **11.2**
  la fine herbe herb, **6.1**
le **héros** hero
l' **heure** (f.) time (of day), BV; hour, **3.2**
  à l'heure on time, **8.1**
  à quelle heure? at what time?, **2**
  À tout à l'heure. See you later., BV
  de bonne heure early
  les heures de pointe rush hour, **10.1**
  heureusement fortunately
  heureux, heureuse happy, **13.2**
  hier yesterday, **10.1**
  avant-hier the day before yesterday, **10.2**

French-English Dictionary

hier matin yesterday morning, 10.2
hier soir last night, 10.2
l' **histoire** (f.) history, 2.2; story
l' **hiver** (m.) winter, 11.2
le/la **H.L.M.** low-income housing
le **homard** lobster, 6.2
l' **homme** (m.) man, 7.1
honnête honest
les **honoraires** (m. pl.) fees (doctor)
l' **hôpital** (m.) hospital, 8.1
l' **horaire** (m.) schedule, timetable, 9.1
l' **horloger, l'horlogère** clockmaker
l' **horodateur** (m.) time-stamp machine, 11.1
l' **horreur** (f.) horror
l' **hôtel** (m.) hotel, 9.1
l'**hôtel de ville** city hall
l' **Hôtel-Dieu** hospital
l' **hôtesse** (f.) **de l'air** flight attendant, 8.2
l' **huile** (f.) oil, 6.1
l'**huile d'olive** olive oil, 6.1
l' **huître** (f.) oyster, 6.2
humain(e) human
la **hutte** hut
l' **hydrate** (m.) **de carbone** carbohydrate
l' **hymne** (m.) anthem, 12.1
hyper: J'ai hyper faim. I'm super hungry.
l' **hypermarché** (m.) large department store, supermarket
l' **hypothèque** (f.) mortgage

l' **icône** (f.) icon
idéal(e) ideal
l' **idée** (f.) idea
idée fixe fixed idea; obsession

identifier to identify
il: il y a there is, there are, 4.1
il y a dix ans ten years ago
l' **île** (f.) island, L4
illisible illegible
l' **immeuble** (m.) apartment building, 4.2
s' **implanter** to be established
impoli(e) impolite
impressionné(e) impressed
les **impressionnistes** (m. pl.) Impressionists (painters)
l' **imprimante** (f.) printer, 3.1
imprimer to print
inaugurer to inaugurate
inconnu(e) unknown
l' **inconvénient** (m.) disadvantage
incroyable incredible
l' **indicatif** (m.): l'**indicatif du pays** country code, 3.2
l'**indicatif régional** area code, 3.2
l' **indication** (f.) cue
indiquer to indicate, to show
l' **individu** (m.) individual
inférieur(e) lower
infini(e) infinite
l' **infirmier, l'infirmière** nurse, 8.1
l' **informaticien(ne)** computer expert, 14.1
l' **information** (f.) information; data
les **informations** (f. pl.) news (TV)
l' **informatique** (f.) computer science, 2.2
l' **ingénieur** (m.) engineer (m. and f.), 14.1
innombrable countless
l' **inquiétude** (f.) worry
s' **installer** to settle
l' **instant** (m.) moment, 3.2
l' **institut** (m.) institute
l' **instrument** (m.) **à clavier** keyboard instrument

l' **instrument à cordes** string instrument
l' **instrument à vent** wind instrument
interdit(e) forbidden, 4.2
intéressant(e) interesting, 1.1
intéresser to interest
s'intéresser à to be interested in
l' **intérêt** (m.) interest
intérieur(e) domestic (flight), 8.1
interne internal
l' **interprète** (m. et f.) interpreter
l' **interro(gation)** (f.) quiz
interurbain(e): appel interurbain toll call
intervenir to step in
l' **intervention chirurgicale** (f.) operation
intime intimate
intitulé(e) entitled
introduire to insert
inventer to make up; to invent
l' **invité(e)** guest
inviter to invite, 4.1
isoler to isolate
l' **issue** (f.) **de secours** emergency exit
l' **italien** (m.) Italian (language), 2.2
l' **Ivoirien(ne)** Ivorian (inhabitant of Côte d'Ivoire)

jaloux, jalouse jealous
jamais ever
ne... jamais never, 11.2
la **jambe** leg, 8.1
le **jambon** ham, 5.1
janvier (m.) January, BV
japonais(e) Japanese
le **jardin** garden, 4.2

Handbook

French-English Dictionary

jaune yellow, 7.2
Je vous en prie. You're welcome. (form.), BV
le **jean** jeans, 7.1
jeter to throw, L4
le **jeu** game
jeune young
les **jeunes** (m. pl.) young people
la **jeunesse** youth
le **jogging: faire du jogging** to jog
la **joie** joy
joli(e) pretty, 4.2
la **joue** cheek, 13.1
jouer to play, 3.2; to show (movie); to perform, **1.1**
jouer à to play a sport, 10.1
jouer de to play a musical instrument
le **jouet** toy
le **joueur, la joueuse** player, 10.1
le **jour** day, BV
huit jours a week
le jour de l'An New Year's Day, **12.2**
de nos jours today, nowadays
quinze jours two weeks
tous les jours every day, **1.2**
le **journal** newspaper, 9.1
le journal télévisé TV news, **6.1**
le/la **journaliste** reporter, **14.1**
la **journée** day, 3.1
Belle journée! What a nice day!, 4.2
joyeux, joyeuse joyous
Joyeux anniversaire! Happy birthday!
Joyeux Noël! Merry Christmas!
le/la **juge** judge, **14.1**
juif, juive Jewish, **12.2**
le **jumeau, la jumelle** twin, L1

la **jupe** skirt, 7.1
le **jus** juice, 5.1
jusqu'à (up) to, until, 10.2
jusqu'ici up to now
jusqu'où? how far?
juste just, 2.1
juste à sa taille fitting (him/her) just right
juste là right there
tout juste just barely
justement exactly

le **kilo(gramme)** kilogram, 6.2
le **kilomètre** kilometer
le **kiosque** newsstand, 9.1
le **kleenex** tissue, **2.1**

là there; here, 3.2
là-bas over there, 10.1
là-haut up there
le **lac** lake
la **lagune** lagoon
laisser to leave (something behind), 5.2; to let, allow
le **lait** milk, 6.1
la **laitue** lettuce
lancer to throw, to shoot (ball), 10.2, **12.1**
le **langage: en langage courant** commonly known as
la **langue** language, 2.2
le **lapin** rabbit, **11.2**
large loose, wide, 7.2
la **larme** tear, L2
le **laurier** bay leaf, **6.1**
le **lavabo** (bathroom) sink
la **lavande** lavender
laver to wash, 12

se **laver** to wash oneself, 12.1
le **lave-vaisselle** dishwasher, 12.2
la **leçon** lesson, 11.1
la leçon de conduite driving lesson, **7.1**
le **lecteur, la lectrice** reader
le lecteur de disquettes diskette drive, **3.1**
la **lecture** reading
le **légume** vegetable, 6.2, **6.1**
lever to raise, 3.1
lever la main to raise one's hand, 3.1
se lever to get up, 12.1
la **lèvre** lip, 13.1
libérer to free; to vacate, **9.2**
la **liberté** freedom
libre free, 5.1; available, **14.2**
le **lieu** place; setting, **14.1**
au lieu de instead of
avoir lieu to take place, **12.1**
le lieu de travail workplace, **14.1**
la **ligne** line, 4.1
les grandes lignes main lines (train), **4.1**
les lignes de banlieue commuter trains, **4.1**
la **limitation de vitesse** speed limit, **7.2**
la **limite** limit
la **limonade** lemon-lime drink, BV
le **lipide** fat
le **liquide** liquid
l'argent liquide cash, **5.1**
en liquide in cash, **9.2**
lire to read, 9.2
le **lit** bed, **9.1, L2**
le **litre** liter, 6.2
la **livre** pound, 6.2
le **livre** book, 3.2
le **livret de caisse d'épargne** savings passbook

French-English Dictionary H65

French-English Dictionary

le **logement** housing
loger to house
le **logiciel** software, **3.1**
loin far (away)
  loin de far from, **4.2**
  plus loin farther
le **long: le long de** along
long(ue) long, **7.1**
longtemps (for) a long time, **11.1**
  trop longtemps (for) too long, **11.1**
la **longueur** length
le **look** style
louer to rent, **1.1;** to reserve
les **lunettes** (f. pl.) **de soleil** sunglasses, **11.1**
la **lutte** fight, battle, **L3**
lutter to fight, **L3**
luxueux, luxueuse luxurious
le **lycée** high school, **2.1**
le/la **lycéen(ne)** high school student

la **machine** machine, **10.2**
Madame (Mme) Mrs., Ms., **BV**
Mademoiselle (Mlle) Miss, Ms., **BV**
le **magasin** store, **3.2, 14.1**
  le **grand magasin** department store, **7.1**
le **magazine** magazine, **9.1**
le **Maghreb** Maghreb
le **magnétoscope** VCR, **12.2**
magnifique magnificent
le **mail** e-mail, **3.1**
le **maillot** jersey
  le **maillot de bain** bathing suit, **11.1**
la **main** hand, **3.1, 13.1**
  fait(e) à la main handmade
maintenant now, **2.2**
le **maire** mayor, **12.1**

la **mairie** town hall, **12.2, 14.1**
mais but, **2.1**
  Mais oui (non)! Of course (not)!
la **maison** house, **3.1**
  la maison d'édition publishing house
la **maisonnette** cottage
le **maître, la maîtresse** elementary school teacher
la **majorité** majority
mal badly, **2.1**
  avoir mal à to have a(n) . . . -ache, to hurt, **2.1**
  Ça fait mal. It (That) hurts., **2.1**
  Pas mal. Not bad., **BV**
malade ill, sick, **L1, 2.1**
le/la **malade** sick person, patient, **2.2**
la **maladie** illness, disease
le **mâle** male
malheureusement unfortunately
malheureux, malheureuse unhappy
malin, maligne: C'est malin! Very clever! (ironic)
la **maman** mom
la **mamie** grandma
la **Manche** English Channel
la **manche** sleeve, **7.1**
  à manches longues (courtes) long- (short-) sleeved, **7.1**
le **mandat** money order
manger to eat, **5.1**
la **manifestation culturelle** cultural event
la **manœuvre: instructions pour la manœuvre** operating instructions
le **manteau** coat, **7.1**
se **maquiller** to put on makeup, **12.1**
le/la **marchand(e) (de fruits et légumes)** (produce) seller, merchant, **6.2**

la **marchandise** merchandise
le **marché** market, **6.2**
  bon marché inexpensive
  le marché aux puces flea market
marcher to walk, **8.1**
le **mari** husband, **4.1**
le **mariage** marriage; wedding, **12.2**
le **marié** groom, **12.2**
la **mariée** bride, **12.2**
se **marier** to get married, **L4, 12.2**
le **marin** sailor, **L4**
le **Maroc** Morocco
marocain(e) Moroccan
la **marque** brand, **7.1;** sign, **L4**
  marquer un but to score a goal, **10.1**
marron (inv.) brown, **7.2**
marseillais(e) from Marseille
martiniquais(e) from or of Martinique
le **masque à oxygène** oxygen mask, **4.2**
masqué(e) masked, 1 **2.1**
  un groupe masqué group of masqueraders, **12.1**
le **mat** (fam.) morning
le **match** game, **10.1**
le **matériel** equipment, **11.2**
la **matière** subject (school), **2.2;** matter
le **matin** morning, **BV**
  du matin A.M. (time), **BV**
mauvais(e) bad; wrong, **2.2**
  Il fait mauvais. It's bad weather., **11.1**
le **médecin** doctor (m. and f.), **2.2**
  chez le médecin at (to) the doctor's office, **2.2**
le **médicament** medicine, **2.1**
meilleur(e) better, **8**
le **mélange** mixture
même (adj.) same; very, **2.1;** (adv.) even

H66 Handbook

French-English Dictionary

tout de même all the same, **5.2**
mener to lead
mensuel(le) monthly
le **menuisier** carpenter, **14.1**
la **mer** sea, **11.1**
    la **mer des Antilles** Caribbean Sea
    la **mer des Caraïbes** Caribbean Sea
    la **mer Méditerranée** Mediterranean Sea
merci thank you, thanks, BV
la **mère** mother, **4.1**
la **merveille** marvel, wonder
merveilleux, merveilleuse marvelous
le **messager,** la **messagère** messenger
la **messe de minuit** midnight mass, **12.2**
la **mesure** measurement
mesurer to measure
le **métier** trade, profession, **14.1**
le **mètre** meter
le **métro** subway, **4.2**, **10.1**
    la **station de métro** subway station, **4.2**, **10.1**
mettre to put (on), to place, **7.1**; to turn on (appliance), **7**
    mettre le contact to start the car, **7.1**
    mettre de côté to save, to put aside, **5.1**
    mettre une lettre à la poste to mail a letter, **5.2**
    mettre la table to set the table, **7**
les **meubles** (m. pl.) furniture
le **microbe** microbe, germ
la **micropuce** microchip
midi (m.) noon, BV
le **miel** honey
mieux better, **7.2**
    aimer mieux to prefer, **7.2**

aller mieux to feel better, **2.2**; to be better, **8.1**
il vaut mieux it is better, **13.2**
le **milieu** middle, **10.2**
mille (one) thousand, **3.2**
le **million** million
mimer to mime
le **ministère** ministry
minuit (m.) midnight, BV
la **minute** minute, **9.2**
la **mi-temps** halftime (sporting event)
la **mode: à la mode** in style
le **mode** means
la **moelle épinière** spinal cord
moi de même the same with me, **13.2**
moi-même myself
moins less, fewer, **7.1**; minus
le **mois** month, BV
le **monde** world
    beaucoup de monde a lot of people, **10.1**
    tout le monde everyone, everybody, **1.2**
le **moniteur** (computer) monitor
le **moniteur,** la **monitrice** instructor, **11.1**
la **monnaie** change (money); currency, **5.1**
    la **pièce de monnaie** coin
Monsieur (m.) Mr., sir, BV
le **mont** mount, mountain
la **montagne** mountain, **11.2**
monter to go up, **4.2**; to get on, get in, **9.2**; to take (something) upstairs, **9.1**
    monter une pièce to put on a play, **1.1**
la **montre** watch, **L1**
montrer to show
le **morceau** piece, **6.2**
le **morse** Morse code
la **mort** death
la **mosquée** mosque

le **mot** word
    le **mot apparenté** cognate
le **motard** motorcycle cop, **7.2**
la **moto** motorcycle, **7.1**
le **mouchoir** handkerchief, **2.1**
la **moule** mussel, **6.2**
mourir to die, **11**
la **moutarde** mustard, **6.2**
le **mouton** mutton; sheep, **11.2**
moyen(ne) average, intermediate
le **moyen de transport** mode of transportation
multicolore multicolored
la **multinationale** multinational corporation, **14.2**
multiplier to multiply
muni(e) de with
la **municipalité** city government
les **munitions** (f. pl.) ammunition
le **mur** wall, **L4**
le **musée** museum, **1.2**
la **musique** music, **2.2**
musulman(e) Moslem
mystérieux, mystérieuse mysterious

nager to swim, **11.1**
le **nageur,** la **nageuse** swimmer
naître to be born, **11**
la **nappe** tablecloth, **5.2**
la **natation** swimming, **11.1**
nature plain (adj.), **5.1**
naturel(le) natural
le **navarin** mutton stew
la **navette: faire la navette** to go back and forth, make the run
naviguer sur Internet to surf the Net

French-English Dictionary

ne: ne... jamais never, **11.2**
ne... pas not, **1.2**
ne... personne no one, nobody, **11**
ne... plus no longer, no more, **6.1**
ne... que only
ne... rien nothing, **11**
né(e): elle est née she was born
la **nécessité** necessity
　de première nécessité essential
la **négritude** black pride
la **neige** snow, **11.2**
　Il neige. It's snowing., **11.2**
nerveux, nerveuse nervous
n'est-ce pas? isn't it?, doesn't it (he, she, etc.)?, **2.2**
le **neveu** nephew, **4.1**
le **nez** nose, **2.1**
　avoir le nez qui coule to have a runny nose, **2.1**
ni... ni neither . . . nor
niçois(e) of or from Nice
la **nièce** niece, **4.1**
le **niveau** level, **7.1**
Noël Christmas, **12.2**
noir(e) black, **7.2**
le **nom** name; noun
　le nom de famille last name
le **nombre** number
nombreux, nombreuse numerous, many
　peu nombreux few
nommer to name, mention
non no; not
　non plus either, neither
　non-fumeurs non-smoking (section), **8.1**
le **nord** north
　nord-africain(e) North African
les **notables** (m. pl.) dignitaries, **12.1**

la **note** note; grade; bill (hotel), **9.2**
nourrir to feed
la **nourriture** food, nutrition
nouveau (nouvel), nouvelle new, **4.2**
　à nouveau again
la **nouvelle** short story
　les nouvelles news, **L3**
la **Nouvelle-Angleterre** New England
la **Nouvelle-Orléans** New Orleans
le **nuage** cloud, **11.1**
la **nuit** night
nul(le) (slang) bad
le **numéro** number, **5.2**
　le bon numéro right number, **3.2**
　composer/faire le numéro to dial the number, **3.2**
　le mauvais numéro wrong number, **3.2**
numéroté(e) numbered

ô oh
l' **objet** (m.) object
obligatoire mandatory
obtenir to obtain, get
l' **occasion** (f.) opportunity
occidental(e) western
occupé(e) occupied, taken, **5.1**; busy
　Ça sonne occupé. The line's busy., **3.2**
occuper to occupy, take up
　s'occuper de to take care of
l' **œil** (m.) eye, **2.1**
l' **œuf** (m.) egg, **6.1**
　l'œuf à la coque poached egg
　l'œuf brouillé scrambled egg

　l'œuf sur le plat fried egg
l' **œuvre** (f.) work(s) (of art or literature), **1.1**
offrir to offer
l' **oignon** (m.) onion, **5.1**, **6.1**
l' **oiseau** (m.) bird
l' **omelette** (f.) omelette, **5.1**
　l'omelette aux fines herbes omelette with herbs, **5.1**
　l'omelette nature plain omelette, **5.1**
on we, they, people, **3.2**
　On y va? Let's go.; Shall we go?
l' **oncle** (m.) uncle, **4.1**
opérer to operate
l' **or** (m.) gold, **L4**
l' **oranger** (m.) orange tree, **L2**
l' **ordinateur** (m.) computer, **3.1**
l' **ordonnance** (f.) prescription, **2.2**
　faire une ordonnance to write a prescription, **2.2**
l' **ordre** (m.) order
l' **oreille** (f.) ear, **2.1**
　avoir mal aux oreilles to have an earache, **2.1**
l' **oreiller** (m.) pillow, **4.2**
organiser to organize
l' **orgue** (m.) organ (musical instrument)
oriental(e) eastern
originaire de native of
l' **origine** (f.): **d'origine américaine (française, etc.)** from the U.S. (France, etc.)
orner to decorate
l' **os** (m.) bone, **8.2**
ou or, **1.1**
où where, **1.1**
　d'où from where, **1.1**
oublier to forget, **7.2**
l' **ouest** (m.) west
oui yes, **BV**
l' **outil** (m.) tool
ouvert(e) open, **1.2**

l' **ouvrage** (m.) work
l' **ouvrier, l'ouvrière** worker, **11.1**
ouvrir to open, **2.2**

le **paiement** payment
le **pain** bread, 6.1
    le **pain complet** whole-wheat bread
    le **pain grillé** toast
    la **tartine de pain beurré** slice of bread and butter
la **paire** pair, **7.1**
la **paix** peace
le **palais** palace
le **palet** puck
le **palmier** palm tree
le **pamplemousse** grapefruit, **6.1**
le **panier** basket, **10.2**
    réussir un panier to make a basket, **10.2**
la **panne** breakdown, **7.1**
le **panneau** road sign, **7.2**
le **pansement** bandage, **8.1**
le **pantalon** pants, **7.1**
la **papeterie** stationery store, 3.2
le **papier** paper, 3.2
    la **feuille de papier** sheet of paper, 3.2
    le **papier hygiénique** toilet paper, **9.2**
Pâques Easter
le **paquet** package, **6.2**
par by, through
    par conséquent as a result
    par exemple for example
    par semaine a (per) week, 3.2
le **parc** park
parce que because
le **parcmètre** parking meter, **11.1**
par-dessus over (prep.), **10.2**

le **pare-brise** windshield, **7.1**
paresseux, paresseuse lazy
parfait(e) perfect
le **parfum** flavor
le **parking** parking lot, **11.1**
    parler to speak, talk, 3.1
    parler au téléphone to talk on the phone, 3.2, **L3**
parmi among
les **paroles** (f. pl.) words, lyrics
la **part**:
    C'est de la part de qui? Who's calling?, 3.2
    d'autre part on the other hand
    de part et d'autre on each side
    de sa part on his (her) part
partager to share, **13.1**
particulier, particulière private (room, house, etc.)
la **partie** part
    faire partie de to be a part of
partir to leave, 8.1
partout everywhere
pas not, 2.1
    pas du tout not at all, 3.1
    Pas mal. Not bad., BV
    Pas question! Out of the question! Not a chance!
le **pas** step, **L2**
    faire un pas to take a step, **L2**
le **passage pour piétons** crosswalk, **11.1**
le **passager, la passagère** passenger, 8.1
la **passe** pass
le **passeport** passport, 8.1
passer to spend (time), 3.1; to go (through), 8.1; to pass, 10.1
    passer à la douane to go through customs, **4.2**
    passer un examen to take an exam, 3.1

se passer to happen
se passionner to become enthusiastic
la **patate douce** sweet potato
les **pâtes** (f. pl.) pasta, **6.1**
le **patin** skate; skating, **11.2**
    faire du patin à glace to ice-skate, **11.1**
la **patinoire** skating rink, **11.2**
le/la **patron(ne)** boss
le **pâturage** pasture
pauvre poor, L1, **2.1**
le **pavillon** small house, bungalow
payer to pay, 3.2
le **pays** country, 8.1
le **paysage** landscape, **4.1**
le/la **paysan(ne)** peasant, L1
le **péage** toll, **7.2**
la **pêche** fishing
le **pêcheur, la pêcheuse** fisherman (-woman)
le **peigne** comb, **12.1**
se peigner to comb one's hair, **12.1**
peindre to paint
le **peintre** painter, artist (m. and f.), **1.2**
    le **peintre (en bâtiment)** (house) painter, **14.1**
la **peinture** painting, **1.2**
pendant during, for (time), 3.2
la **péniche** barge
penser to think
la **pente** slope
perdre to lose, 9.2
le **père** father, 4.1
    le **Père Noël** Santa Claus, **12.2**
perfectionner to perfect
la **période** period
la **périphérie** outskirts
la **perle** pearl
permettre to permit, allow, let
le **permis de conduire** driver's license, **7.1**

French-English Dictionary

le **persil** parsley, **6.1**
le **personnage** character (in a story)
la **personne** person
  ne… personne no one, nobody, 11
le **personnel de bord** flight crew, 8.2
peser to weigh, **5.2**
petit(e) short, small, 1.1
  le **petit ami** boyfriend
  la **petite amie** girlfriend
  le **petit déjeuner** breakfast, 5.2
  les **petits pois** (m.) peas, 6.2
la **petite-fille** granddaughter, 4.1
le **petit-fils** grandson, 4.1
les **petits-enfants** (m. pl.) grandchildren, 4.1
le **pétrole** oil
le **pétrolier** oil tanker
peu (de) few, little
  à peu près about, approximately
  un peu a little, 2.1
  en très peu de temps in a short time
  très peu seldom, 5.2
peur: avoir peur to be afraid, L1, **13.2**
peut-être perhaps, maybe
le/la **pharmacien(ne)** pharmacist, **2.2**
la **phrase** sentence
le/la **physicien(ne)** physicist
physique physical
la **physique** physics, 2.2
la **pie** magpie
la **pièce** room, 4.2; play, **1.1;** coin, **5.1**
le **pied** foot, 10.1, **8.1**
  à pied on foot, 4.2
  donner un coup de pied to kick, 10.1
  être vite sur pied to be better soon, **2.1**

la **pierre** stone
  la **pierre précieuse** gem, L4
le **piéton, la piétonne** pedestrian, **11.1**
le/la **pilote** pilot, 8.2
piloter to pilot, to fly
le **pilotis** piling
piquer to sting, **2.1**
la **piqûre** injection, **8.2**
la **pirogue** pirogue (dugout canoe)
la **piscine** pool, 11.1
la **piste** runway, 8.1; track, 10.2; ski trail, 11.2
pittoresque picturesque
le **placard** closet, 9.2
la **place** seat (plane, train, movie, etc.), 8.1; place; square
  à ta place if I were you, **7.1**
la **plage** beach, 11.1
la **plaine** plain
le **plaisir** pleasure
le **plan** street map, **7.2**
  le **plan du métro** subway map, **10.1**
la **planche à voile: faire de la planche à voile** to windsurf, 11.1
le **plat** dish (food); serving dish, **6.1**
le **plateau** tray, 8.2
le **plâtre** cast, **8.2**
plâtrer to put in a cast, **8.2**
plein(e) full, 10.1, **13.1**
  avoir plein d'argent (slang) to have a lot of money, 5.1
pleurer to cry, L1
pleut (inf. **pleuvoir**): **Il pleut.** It's raining., 11.1
plissé(e) pleated, 7.1
le **plombier** plumber, **14.1**
le **plongeon** dive
plonger to dive, 11.1
la **pluie** rain
la **plupart (des)** most (of), 9.2

plus plus; more, 7.1
  de plus en plus more and more
  en plus de in addition to
  ne… plus no longer, no more, 6.1
  plus ou moins more or less
  plus tard later
plusieurs several
plutôt rather
le **pneu** tire, **7.1**
  le **pneu à plat** flat tire, **7.1**
la **poêle** frying pan, **6.2**
la **poésie** poetry
le **poids** weight
le **poignet** wrist, **13.1**
le **point** period; dot
  le **point de suture** stitch, **8.2**
  à point medium-rare (meat), 5.2
la **pointure** size (shoes), 7.2
  Vous faites quelle pointure? What (shoe) size do you take?, 7.2
la **poire** pear, 6.2
le **poisson** fish, 6.1, **6.2**
la **poissonnerie** fish store, 6.1
la **poitrine** chest (body)
le **poivre** pepper, 6.1
le **poivron rouge** red pepper, **6.1**
poli(e) polite, **13.1**
  malpoli(e) impolite, **13.1**
la **police** police
  appeler police secours to call 911, **8.1**
poliment politely, 9.2
la **politesse** courtesy, politeness, BV
polluant(e) polluting
pollué(e) polluted
le **polo** polo shirt, 7.1
la **pomme** apple, 6.2
  la **tarte aux pommes** apple tart, 6.1
la **pomme de terre** potato, 6.2, **6.1**

Handbook

French-English Dictionary

le/la **pompiste** gas station attendant, **7.1**
le **pont** bridge
le **porc** pork, 6.1, **6.2**
le **portable** mobile phone, laptop computer, **3.2**
la **porte** gate *(airport)*, **8.1**; door, L4, **9.1, L2**
le **porte-monnaie** change purse, **5.1**
porter to wear, 7.1; to bear, carry, **L2**
porter un toast à to toast
se porter bien to be in good health, **L4**
portugais(e) Portuguese
poser sa candidature to apply for a job, **14.2**
poser une question to ask a question, 3.1
posséder to possess, own
la **poste** mail; post office, **5.2**
  le bureau de poste post office, **5.2**
  mettre une lettre à la poste to mail a letter, **5.2**
  la poste par avion airmail
le **poste** job, **14.2**
le **pot** jar, 6.2; drink
le **pouce** thumb, **13.1**
la **poule** hen, **11.2**
le **poulet** chicken, 6.1
le **pouls** pulse, **8.2**
le **poumon** lung
pour for, 2.1; in order to
  pour cent percent
le **pourboire** tip *(restaurant)*, 5.2
pourquoi why, 6.2
  pourquoi pas? why not?
pousser to push, **10.2**
pouvoir to be able to, can, 6.1
pratique practical
la **pratique** practice
pratiquer to practice
le **pré** meadow, **11.2**
précaire precarious
précis(e) specific

préféré(e) favorite
préférer to prefer, 6
premier, première first, 4.2
  en première in first class, 9.1
prendre to have *(to eat or drink)*, 5.1; to take, 5.2; to buy
  prendre un bain (une douche) to take a bath (shower), 12.1
  prendre un bain de soleil to sunbathe, 11.1
  prendre des kilos to gain a few pounds
  prendre le métro to take the subway, 5.2
  prendre le petit déjeuner to eat breakfast, 5.2
  prendre possession de to take possession of
  prendre rendez-vous to make an appointment
le **prénom** first name
près: de près close, **11.1**
  près de near, 4.2
prescrire to prescribe, **2.2**
la **présentation** introduction, **13.2**
présenter to present; to introduce, **13.2**
  se présenter to occur
presque almost
la **pression** pressure, **7.1**
prestigieux, prestigieuse prestigious
prêt(e) ready
prêter to lend, **5.1**
prie: Je vous en prie. You're welcome., BV
primaire: l'école *(f.)* **primaire** elementary school
le **printemps** spring, 11.1
  au printemps in the spring
le **prisonnier, la prisonnière** prisoner, L4
privé(e) private
le **prix** price, cost, 7.1

le **prix forfaitaire** flat fee
le **processus** process
prochain(e) next, 9.2
  descendre à la prochaine to get off at the next station, **10.1**
proche close
procurer to provide
  se procurer to obtain, get
le **produit** product
le/la **prof** teacher *(inform.)*, 2.1
le **professeur** teacher *(m. and f.)*, 2.1
profiter de to take advantage of
la **programmation** programming
le **progrès** progress; improvement
le **projet** plan
se prolonger to be prolonged, **L3**
la **promenade: faire une promenade** to take a walk, 11.1
la **promesse** promise
promotion: en promotion on special, on sale
prononcer to pronounce
propos: à propos de on the subject of
proposer to suggest
propre clean, 9.2
le/la **propriétaire** owner
la **propriété** property
protéger to protect
provenance: en provenance de arriving from *(train, plane, etc.)*, 8.1
provençal(e) of or from Provence
la **province** province
  en province outside Paris
les **provisions** *(f. pl.)* food
prudemment carefully, **7.2**
la **publicité** commercial *(TV)*, 12.2; advertisement
publier to publish
les **puces** *(f. pl.)*: **le marché aux puces** flea market

French-English Dictionary

le **pull** sweater, 7.1
punir to punish
purifié(e) purified

le **quai** platform *(railroad)*, 9.1, **10.1**
quand when, 4.1
la **quantité** amount, number
le **quart: et quart** a quarter past *(time)*, BV
moins le quart a quarter to *(time)*, BV
le **quartier** neighborhood, district, 4.2, **11.1**
le quartier d'affaires business district, **11.1**
quatrième fourth
québécois(e) from or of Quebec
quel(le) which, what
Quel(le)…! What a . . . !
quelque some *(sing.)*
quelque chose something, 11
quelque chose à manger something to eat, 5.1
quelque chose de spécial something special
quelque part somewhere
quelquefois sometimes, 5.2
quelques some, a few *(pl.)*, 9.2
quelqu'un somebody, someone, 10.1
quelqu'un d'autre someone else, L3
qu'est-ce que what, 8
qu'est-ce qui what, 8
la **question** question, 3.1
Pas question! Out of the question! Not a chance!
poser une question to ask a question, 3.1
la **queue** line, 9.1
faire la queue to wait in line, 9.1

qui who, 1.1; whom, 10; which, that
qui que ce soit anyone at all
quitter to leave *(a room, etc.)*, 3.1
Ne quittez pas. Please hold. *(telephone)*, 3.2
quoi what *(after prep.)*
quotidien(ne) daily, everyday

raccrocher to hang up *(telephone)*, 3.2
raconter to tell (about)
radieux, radieuse dazzling
la **radio** radio, 3.2; X-ray, **8.2**
la **radiographie** X-ray, **8.2**
le **raisin** grape(s), 6.1
le raisin sec raisin
la **raison** reason
ralentir to slow down, 7.1
ramasser to pick up, 8.2
le **randonneur**, la **randonneuse** hiker
le **rang** row, **12.1**
le **rap** rap *(music)*
râper to grate, **6.2**
rapide quick, fast
rapidement rapidly, quickly
rappeler to call back; to call again, 3.2
se rappeler to remember
le **rapport** relationship; report
rapporter to bring back
se **raser** to shave, 12.1
le **rasoir** razor, shaver, 12.1
se **rassembler** to gather
rassurer to reassure
rater to miss *(train, etc.)*, 9.2
ravager to devastate
le **rayon** department *(in a store)*, 7.1

le **rayon des manteaux** coat department, 7.1
réaliser to achieve; to create
récemment recently
la **réception** front desk, **9.1**
le/la **réceptionniste** desk clerk, **9.1**
la **recette** recipe, **6.1**
recevoir to receive, 10.2
la **recherche** research
à la recherche de in search of
la **récolte** harvest, **11.2**
recommander to recommend
reconnaître to recognize
la **récré** recess, 3.2
la **récréation** recess, 3.2
recueillir to pick up
récupérer to claim *(luggage)*, **4.2**
le **recyclage** recycling
la **rédaction** composition
la **réduction** discount
réfléchir to think
le **réfrigérateur** refrigerator, 12.2, **6.1**
le/la **réfugié(e)** refugee
regarder to look at, 3.1
regarder fixement to stare at
le **régime** diet
faire un régime to follow a diet
réglable adjustable, **4.1**
la **règle** ruler, 3.2; rule
régler to order, plan; to set, L1
régler la circulation to direct traffic, **11.1**
regretter to be sorry, 6.1, **13.2**
la **reine** queen
la **relation** relationship
le **relevé** statement *(bank)*
se **relever** to get up (again)
relier to connect
religieux, religieuse religious, **12.2**
remarquer to notice

French-English Dictionary

rembourser to pay back, reimburse
remercier to thank
remettre un os en place to set a bone, **8.2**
le **rempart** rampart
remplacer to replace
remplir to fill out, 8.2, **8.2**
remuer to stir, **6.2**
rencontrer to meet
le **rendez-vous** meeting, appointment, **10.2**
   prendre rendez-vous to make an appointment
rendre to give back, **5.1**
   rendre bien service to be a big help
   rendre visite à to visit
renommé(e) renowned
rénover to renovate
les **renseignements** *(m. pl.)* information
rentrer to go home; to return, 3.2
renvoyer to return *(a ball)*, 10.2
réparer to repair
le **repas** meal, 5.2
répéter to repeat
le **répondeur automatique** answering machine, **3.2**
répondre (à) to answer, 9.2
la **réponse** answer
le **reportage** news article
reposer to lie
réputé(e) reputed
le **réseau** network
la **réserve: mettre en réserve** to store
réservé(e) reserved
réserver to reserve, 9.1; to have in store
le **réservoir** gas tank, **7.1**
respecter to abide by, **7.2, 11.1**
la **respiration** breathing; respiration
respirer to breathe, **2.2**

respirer à fond to take a deep breath, **2.2**
resquiller to cut in line, **13.1**
ressembler à to resemble
ressortir to leave
le **restaurant** restaurant, 5.2
la **restauration** food service
   la restauration rapide fast food
rester to stay, remain, 11.1
   il reste there remains
   rester en contact to keep in touch
les **restes** *(m. pl.)* leftovers
le **restoroute** roadside restaurant
le **résultat** result(s)
le **retard** delay
   avec une heure de retard one hour late, **4.2**
   avoir du retard to be late *(plane, train, etc.)*, 8.1
   en retard late, 9.1
retirer to remove, to take out, 3.1; to withdraw, **5.1**
le **retour** return
la **retraite** retreat, retirement
se **retrouver** to get together, **13.1**
réuni(e) reunited
réussir to succeed, 10.2
   réussir à un examen to pass an exam
   réussir un panier to make a basket, 10.2
le **rêve** dream
réveillé(e) awake
se **réveiller** to wake up, 12.1
le **réveillon** Christmas Eve or New Year's Eve dinner, **12.2**
réveillonner to celebrate Christmas Eve or New Year's Eve, **12.2**
revenir to come back, 4
la **revue** magazine, L2
le **rez-de-chaussée** ground floor, 4.2

le **rhume** cold *(illness)*, **2.1**
rien nothing
   ne… rien nothing
   rien à voir avec nothing to do with
rigoler to joke around, 3.2
   Tu rigoles! You're kidding!, 3.2
rigolo(tte) funny, 4.2
la **rigueur** harshness
la **rime** rhyme
rincer to rinse
risquer to risk
la **rivière** river, **L2**
le **riz** rice
la **robe** dress, 7.1
le **rocher** rock, boulder, L3
le **roi** king, L3
le **rôle** role
romain(e) Roman
le **roman** novel, **L1**
   le roman policier mystery
le **romanche** Romansh
le **romancier,** la **romancière** novelist, **L1**
le **romarin** rosemary
rond(e) round
la **rondelle** round, slice *(piece)*, **6.2**
le **rond-point** traffic circle, **7.2, 11.1**
rose pink, 7.2
le **rôti de bœuf** roast beef, **6.2**
la **roue de secours** spare tire, **7.1**
rouge red, 7.2
le **rouleau de papier hygiénique** roll of toilet paper, **9.2**
rouler (vite) to go, drive, ride (fast), 10.2, **7.2**
la **route** road, **7.2**
le **rubis** ruby
la **rue** street, 3.1, **5.2, 11.1**
   la rue à sens unique one-way street, **11.1**
russe Russian

French-English Dictionary

S

le **sable** sand
le **sac** bag, 6.1
    le sac à dos backpack, 3.2
sage wise; well-behaved, **12.2**
saignant(e) rare *(meat)*, 5.2
la **saison** season
la **salade** salad, 5.1; lettuce, 6.2
le **salaire** salary, **14.2**
sale dirty, **9.2**
la **salle** room
    la salle à manger dining room, 4.2
    la salle d'attente waiting room, 9.1
    la salle de bains bathroom, 4.2
    la salle de cinéma movie theater, **1.1**
    la salle de classe classroom, 2.1
    la salle d'opération operating room, **8.2**
    la salle de séjour living room, 4.2
saluer to greet, **L1**
Salut. Hi.; Bye., BV
la **salutation** greeting
les **sandales** *(f. pl.)* sandals, 7.1
le **sandwich** sandwich, BV
le **sang** blood
sans without
    sans escale nonstop *(flight)*, **4.2**
    sans que without
la **santé** health, **2.1**
le **sapin** fir tree, **12.2**
satisfaire to satisfy
la **saucisse** sausage, **6.1**
    la saucisse de Francfort hot dog, BV
le **saucisson** salami, 6.1
sauf except (for), **1.2**
le **saumon** salmon, 6.2

sauvegarder to safeguard; to save, **3.1**
sauver to save
le **savant** scientist
savoir to know *(information)*, **1.2**
le **savoir-vivre** good manners
le **savon** soap, 12.1, **9.2**
scintiller to sparkle
scolaire school *(adj.)*, 3.2
la **scolarité** schooling, education
le **sculpteur** sculptor *(m. and f.)*, **1.2**
la **séance** show(ing) *(movie)*, **1.1**
sec, sèche dry
sécher to dry
    se sécher to dry oneself, **9.2**
le/la **secouriste** paramedic, **8.1**
le **secours** help, aid, **8.1**
le **séjour** stay, 9.1
le **sel** salt, 6.1
selon according to
la **semaine** week, 3.2; allowance
    la semaine dernière last week, 10.2
    la semaine prochaine next week
    par semaine a (per) week, 3.2
semblable similar, L1
le/la **Sénégalais(e)** Senegalese *(person)*
le **sens** direction, **7.2**; meaning
    dans le bon (mauvais) sens in the right (wrong) direction, **11.1**
le **sentiment** feeling
se sentir to feel *(well, etc.)*, **2.1**
séparer to separate
sérieux, sérieuse serious, 7
le **serpentin** streamer, **12.1**
serré(e) tight, 7.2
se serrer la main to shake hands, **13.1**

le **serveur, la serveuse** waiter, waitress, 5.1
le **service** service, 5.2
    Le service est compris. The tip is included., 5.2
    le service radio radiology department
    le service des urgences emergency room, **8.1**
la **serviette** napkin, 5.2, **13.1**; towel, 11.1, **9.2**
servir to serve, 8.2; 10.2
    se servir de to use, 3.2, **L4**
seul(e) alone, 5.2; single; only *(adj.)*
    tout(e) seul(e) all alone, by himself/herself, 5.2
seulement only *(adv.)*
le **shampooing** shampoo, 12.1
le **shopping** shopping, 7.2
le **short** shorts, 7.1
si if; yes *(after neg. question)*, 7.2; so *(adv.)*
le **sida** (syndrome immuno-déficitaire acquis) AIDS
le **siècle** century, **L4**
le **siège** seat, 8.2
siffler to (blow a) whistle, 10.1, **L1**
le **sifsari** type of veil worn by Tunisian women
la **signification** meaning, significance
signifier to mean
simplement simply
sinon or else, otherwise, 9.2
la **sinusite** sinus infection, **2.2**
le **sirop** syrup, **2.1**
le **site** site; Web site
situé(e) located
le **ski** ski, skiing, 11.2
    faire du ski to ski, 11.2
    faire du ski nautique to water-ski, 11.1
    le ski alpin downhill skiing, 11.2
    le ski de fond cross-country skiing, 11.2

French-English Dictionary

le skieur, la skieuse skier, 11.2
le snack-bar snack bar, 9.2
sociable sociable, outgoing, 1.2
la société company; corporation, **14.2**
   la grosse société large corporation, **14.2**
la sœur sister, 1.2
soi oneself, himself, herself
soif: avoir soif to be thirsty, 5.1
soigner to take care of, **8.1, L4**
soigneusement carefully, **9.1**
le soin care
   de soins polyvalents general care *(adj.)*
   prendre soin de to take care of, **L4**
le soir evening, BV
   ce soir tonight
   du soir in the evening, P.M. *(time)*, BV
   le soir in the evening, 5.2
le sol ground, 10.2
le soldat soldier, L3, **12.1**
le solde balance
les soldes sale *(in a store)*, 7.1
la sole sole, **6.2**
le soleil sun, 11.1
   au soleil in the sun, 11.1
   Il fait du soleil. It's sunny., 11.1
sombre dark
la somme sum
le sommet summit, mountaintop, 11.2
le son sound, L3
le sondage survey, opinion poll
sonner to ring *(telephone)*, **3.2**
   Ça sonne occupé. The line's busy, **3.2**

sonner du cor to blow a horn, L3
la sonnerie ringing
la sorte sort, kind, type
la sortie exit, **7.2**
sortir to go out; to take out, 8.2
   sortir victorieux (victorieuse) to win (the battle)
la souche tree stump
   dormir comme une souche to sleep like a log
soudain suddenly
souffrir to suffer; to be hurt, to be in pain, 2.2
souhaiter to wish, 9.1, 12.2
le souk North African market
soulever to lift up
le soulier shoe, 12.2
la soupe soup, 5.1
   la soupe à l'oignon onion soup, 5.1
la source source; spring
la souris mouse, 3.1
sous under, 8.2
les sous-titres *(m. pl.)* subtitles, **1.1**
soustraire to subtract
souterrain(e) underground
le souvenir memory
souvent often, 5.2
sport *(inv.)* casual *(clothes)*, 7.1
le sport sport, 10.2
   le sport collectif team sport
   le sport d'équipe team sport, 10.2
sportif, sportive athletic
le squelette skeleton
le stade stadium, 10.1
le stage internship, **14.2**
   faire un stage to intern, **14.2**
le/la stagiaire intern, **14.2**

standing: de grand standing luxury
la station station, 4.2, **10.1**; resort
   la station balnéaire seaside resort, 11.1
   la station de métro subway station, 4.2
   la station de sports d'hiver ski resort, 11.2
   la station thermale spa
stationner to park, 11.1
la station-service gas station, **7.1**
la statue statue, **1.2**
le steak frites steak and French fries, 5.2
le steward flight attendant *(m.)*, 8.2
stimuler to stimulate
stocker to store
le studio studio (apartment)
le stylo-bille ballpoint pen, 3.2
le sucre sugar
le sud south
   suffisant(e) enough
   suggérer to suggest
   suivant(e) following
   suivre to follow, **11.1**
   suivre une voiture de trop près to tailgate, **11.1**
le sujet subject
   au sujet de about
   super terrific, super
   supérieur(e) higher
le supermarché supermarket, 6.2
le supplément additional charge
supporter to tolerate
sur on, 4.2
sûr(e) sure, certain
le surf: faire du surf to go surfing, 11.1
le surfeur, la surfeuse surfer, 11.1
surgelé(e) frozen, 6.2
surtout especially, above all; mostly

French-English Dictionary

surveiller to watch, keep an eye on, **7.2**
le **survêtement** warmup suit, 7.1
la **survie** survival
survoler to fly over
le **sweat-shirt** sweatshirt, 7.1
sympa (inv.) nice (abbrev. for **sympathique**), 1.2
sympathique nice (person), 1.2
le **symptôme** symptom
le **syndicat d'initiative** tourist office

le **tabac: le bureau de tabac** tobacco shop
la **table** table, 5.1
  à table at the table, **13.1**
le **tableau** painting, **1.2**; chart; arrival/departure board (train), **4.1**
  le tableau noir blackboard
la **taille** size (clothes), 7.2
  juste à sa taille fitting (him/her) just right
  la taille au-dessous next smaller size, 7.2
  la taille au-dessus next larger size, 7.2
  Vous faites quelle taille? What size do you take/wear?, 7.2
le **tailleur** suit (woman's), 7.1
le **tambour** drum, **12.1**
la **tante** aunt, 4.1
taper to type; to keyboard, **3.1**
tard late, 12.1
  plus tard later
le **tarif** fare
la **tarte** pie, tart, 6.1
  la tarte aux pommes apple tart, 6.1
la **tartine** slice of bread with butter or jam

la **tasse** cup, 5.2
le **taux** level
  le taux d'intérêt interest rate
la **techno** techno (music)
la **télécarte** phone card, **3.2**
télécharger to download
la **télécommande** remote control, 12.2
la **télécopie** fax, **3.1**
le **télécopieur** fax machine, **3.1**
le **téléphone** telephone, 3.2, **3.1**
  le numéro de téléphone telephone number
  le téléphone à cadran rotary phone
  le téléphone à touches touch-tone telephone, **3.2**
téléphoner to call (on the telephone)
le **télésiège** chairlift, 11.2
la **tempe** temple
tempéré(e) temperate
temporaire temporary
le **temps** weather, 11.1; time; tense
  de temps en temps from time to time, 11.1
  l'emploi (m.) **du temps** schedule
  en très peu de temps in a short time
  Il fait quel temps? What's the weather like?, 11.1
se **tenir** to behave, **13.1**
la **tension** blood pressure, **8.2**
le **terme** term
le **terminus** last stop, **10.2**
le **terrain de football** soccer field, 10.1
la **terrasse** terrace, patio, 4.2
  la terrasse d'un café sidewalk café, 5.1
la **terre** earth, land, **11.2**
  à terre on the ground
tester to test

la **tête** head, 10.1
  avoir mal à la tête to have a headache, **2.1**
le **TGV (train à grande vitesse)** high-speed train, **4.1**
thaïlandais(e) Thai
le **thé** tea
le **théâtre** theater, **1.1**
le **thon** tuna
le **thym** thyme, **6.1**
le **ticket** bus or subway ticket, **10.1**
tiens! hey!
le **timbre** stamp, **5.2**
timide shy, timid, 1.2
tirer to take, to draw
la **toilette: faire sa toilette** to wash
  les toilettes (f. pl.) bathroom, toilet, 4.2
le **toit** roof
  le toit de chaume thatched roof
tomber to fall, 11.2, **8.1**
  tomber malade to get sick, L1
  tomber en panne to break down, **7.1**
la **tonalité** dial tone, **3.2**
se **tordre** to twist (one's knee, etc.), **8.1**
tôt early, 12.1
totalement totally
la **touche** button, key, **3.1**
toucher to touch, 10.2; to cash, **5.1**
toujours always, 4.2; still, **10.2**
la **tour** tower, 11.1
le **tour: à son tour** in turn
  À votre tour. (It's) your turn.
tourner to turn, 7.2
  tourner en rond to go around in a circle
le **tourniquet** turnstile, **10.1**
tous, toutes (adj.) all, every, 2.1, 8

tous (toutes) les deux both
tous les jours every day, **1.2**
tousser to cough, **2.1**
tout *(pron.)* all, everything
  C'est tout. That's all., **6.1**
  en tout in all
  pas du tout not at all, **3.1**
  tout le monde everyone, everybody, **1.2**
  toutes les cinq minutes every five minutes, **10.1**
tout *(adv.)* very, completely, all, **4.2**
  À tout à l'heure. See you later., **BV**
  tout autour de all around *(prep.)*
  tout compris all inclusive, **9.1**
  tout droit straight ahead, **7.2**
  tout de même all the same, **5.2**
  tout près de very near, **4.2**
  tout(e) seul(e) all alone, all by himself/herself, **5.2**
  tout de suite right away
toxique toxic
la **tradition** tradition
  traditionnel(le) traditional
la **tragédie** tragedy, **13.1**
  tragique tragic
le **train** train, **9.1**
le **trait** characteristic
la **traite** monthly payment
le **traitement** treatment
  traiter to treat
le **trajet** trip, **10.2**
la **tranche** slice, **6.2**
  tranquillement peacefully
  transmettre to transmit, **3.1**
  transporter to transport
les **transports en commun** mass transit
le **travail** work

travailler to work, **3.1, 14.2**; to practice
travailler à mi-temps to work part-time, **14.2**
travailler à plein temps to work full-time, **14.2**
traverser to cross, **11.1**
très very, **BV**
le **trésor** treasure, **L4**
le **tribunal** court, **14.1**
la **tribune** grandstand, **12.1**
triste sad, **L1, 13.2**
troisième third, **4.2**
le **tronc cérébral** brain stem
le **trône** throne
trop too *(excessive)*, **2.1**
  trop de too many, too much
le **trottoir** sidewalk, **11.1**
le **trou** hole, **L4**
le **trouble digestif** indigestion, upset stomach
se **troubler** to become flustered, **L3**
le **troupeau** flock, herd, **11.2**
trouver to find, **5.1**; to think *(opinion)*, **7.2**
  se **trouver** to be located
le **t-shirt** T-shirt, **7.1**
tuer to kill
le **tutoiement** the use of *tu*, **13.1**
tutoyer to call someone *tu*, **13.1**
le **type** type; guy *(inform.)*
typique typical

l' **un(e)... l'autre** one ... the other
un(e) à un(e) one by one
unique single, only one
uniquement solely, only
l' **unité** *(f.)* unit
l' **université** *(f.)* university

urbain(e): appel urbain local call
l' **urgence** *(f.)* emergency
l' **usine** *(f.)* factory, **11.1**
utile useful
utiliser to use, **3.1**

les **vacances** *(f. pl.)* vacation
  en vacances on vacation
  les grandes vacances summer vacation
la **vache** cow, **11.2**
la **vague** wave, **11.1**
le **vaisseau sanguin** blood vessel
la **vaisselle** dishes, **12.2**
  faire la vaisselle to do the dishes, **12.2**
valable valid
la **valeur** value
  valider to validate, **10.1**
la **valise** suitcase, **8.1**
  faire les valises to pack, **8.1**
la **vallée** valley
la **vanille: à la vanille** vanilla *(adj.)*, **5.1**
  vaut: il vaut mieux it is better, **13.2**
le **veau** veal, **6.2**; calf, **11.2**
la **veille** eve, **12.2**
la **veine** vein
le **vélo** bicycle, bike, **10.2**
le **vélomoteur** lightweight motorcycle, **7.1**
la **vendange** grape harvest
le **vendeur,** la **vendeuse** salesperson, **7.1**
vendre to sell, **9.1**
vengé(e) avenged
la **vengeance** vengence
se **venger** to get revenge
venir to come, **4.2**
  venir chercher (quelqu'un) to meet; to pick up, **4.2**

French-English Dictionary

venir de to have just (done something), **10**
le **vent** wind, 11.1
 Il y a du vent. It's windy., 11.1
le **ventre** abdomen, stomach, **2.1**
 avoir mal au ventre to have a stomachache, **2.1**
vérifier to check, verify, 8.1
 vérifier les niveaux to check under the hood, **7.1**
véritable real
la **vérité** truth
le **verre** glass, 5.2
vers toward
le **vers** verse
 verser to deposit, **5.1**; to pour, **6.2**
 verser des arrhes to pay a deposit, **9.1**
le **verso** back (of a paper)
vert(e) green, 5.1
la **veste** (sport) jacket, 7.1
les **vestiges** (m. pl.) remains
les **vêtements** (m. pl.) clothes, 7.1
la **viande** meat, 6.1, **6.2**
vide empty, **7.1**
la **vidéo** video, 3.1
 la cassette vidéo videocassette, 12.2
 le film en vidéo movie video, **1.1**
la **vie** life
 en vie alive
vieux (vieil) vieille old, 4.2
 mon vieux buddy
le **vignoble** vineyard, 11.2
la **villa** house
le **village** village, small town
la **ville** city, town, 8.1, **5.2**, **11.1**

en ville in town, in the city, **11.1**
le **vin** wine
le **vinaigre** vinegar, 6.1
la **virgule** comma
visionner to view
visiter to visit (a place), **1.2**
vite fast (adv.), 10.2
la **vitesse** speed, 4.1
 à grande vitesse high-speed, **4.1**
la **vitrine** (store) window, 7.1
vivant(e) living
Vive... ! Long live . . . !, Hooray for . . . !
vivre to live, 11
voici here is, here are, 4.1
la **voie** track (railroad), 9.1; lane (highway), 7.2
voilà there is, there are; here is, here are (emphatic), 1.2
le **voile** veil
voir to see, 7.1
 rien à voir avec nothing to do with
 voir en rose to look on the bright side
le/la **voisin(e)** neighbor, 4.2
la **voiture** car, 4.2
 en voiture by car, 5.2; "All aboard!"
la **voix** voice
le **vol** flight, 8.1
 le vol intérieur domestic flight, 8.1
 le vol international international flight, 8.1
 le vol sans escale nonstop flight, **4.2**
voler to fly, L3
le **volley(-ball)** volleyball, 10.2
le/la **volontaire** volunteer
la **volonté** willpower

vouloir to want, 6.1
le **vouvoiement** the use of vous
le **voyage** trip, 8.1; voyage
 faire un voyage to take a trip, 8.1
voyager to travel, 8.1
le **voyageur, la voyageuse** traveler, passenger, 9.1
vrai(e) true, real, 2.2
vraiment really, 1.1
la **vue** view

le **wagon** (railroad) car, 9.2
le **wagon-restaurant** dining car
le **week-end** weekend
le **western** Western movie
le **wolof** Wolof (West African language)

le **yaourt** yogurt, 6.1
les **yeux** (m. pl; sing. œil) eyes, L1, **2.1**
 avoir les yeux qui piquent to have itchy eyes, **2.1**

zapper to zap, to channel surf, 12.2
la **zone** zone
 la zone de conflit war zone
Zut! Darn!, BV

English-French Dictionary

This English-French Dictionary contains all productive vocabulary from the text. The numbers following each entry indicate the chapter and vocabulary section in which the word is introduced. For example, **2.2** in dark print means that the word first appeared in this textbook, **Chapitre 2, Mots 2.** A number in light print means that the word first appeared in the Level 1 textbook. **BV** refers to the introductory **Bienvenue** lessons in Level 1. **L** refers to the optional literary readings. If there is no number or letter following an entry, the word or expression is there for receptive purposes only.

a lot beaucoup, 3.1
able capable
  to be able to pouvoir, 6.1
aboard à bord (de), 8.2
about *(on the subject of)* de, au sujet de;
  (approximately) à peu près
about-face le demi-tour
above au-dessus (de)
  above all surtout
absolutely absolument, 9.1
access l'accès *(m.)*
to **access** accéder
accident l'accident *(m.)*, 8.1
to **accompany** accompagner
according to d'après; selon
account le compte
  checking account le compte courant, 5.1
  savings account le compte d'épargne, 5.1
accountant le/la comptable, 14.1
accounting la comptabilité
to **accuse** accuser
to **achieve** réaliser
acquaintance la connaissance
acquainted: to be acquainted (se) connaître, 13.2
across from en face de, 11.1
act l'acte, *(m.)*, 1.1
action l'action *(f.)*

active actif, active
activity l'activité *(f.)*
actor l'acteur *(m.)*, 1.1
actress l'actrice *(f.)*, 1.1
acute aigu(ë), 2.2
to **add** additionner; ajouter, 6.2
address l'adresse *(f.)*
addressee le/la destinataire
adjustable réglable, 4.1
administrative assistant l'assistant administratif, l'assistante administrative, 14.1
to **admire** admirer
admission l'entrée *(f.)*; l'accès *(m.)*
adolescent l'adolescent(e)
adult l'adulte *(m. et f.)*
advance: in advance à l'avance, 9.1
advancement l'avancement *(m.)*
advantage l'avantage *(m.)*
  to take advantage of profiter de
adventure l'aventure *(f.)*
adversary l'adversaire *(m. et f.)*
advertisement la publicité
afraid: to be afraid avoir peur, L1, 13.2
Africa l'Afrique *(f.)*
African africain(e)
African-American afro-américain(e)

after après, 3.2
afternoon l'après-midi *(m.)*, 3.2
again encore; à nouveau
against contre, 10.1
age l'âge *(m.)*, 4.1
agent *(m. and f.)* l'agent *(m.)*, 8.1
ago: ten years ago il y a dix ans
to **agree** être d'accord, 2.1
agricultural agricole, 11.2
ahead of time à l'avance, 9.1
aid l'aide *(f.)*; le secours, 8.1
AIDS le sida
air l'air *(m.)*, 7.1; *(adj.)* aérien(ne)
  air conditioning l'air climatisé; la climatisation, 9.2
airline la compagnie aérienne, 8.1
airplane l'avion *(m.)*, 8.1, L3
airport l'aéroport *(m.)*, 8.1
  airport terminal l'aérogare *(f.)*, 8.1
aisle le couloir, 8.2
  aisle seat (une place) côté couloir, 8.1
album l'album *(m.)*
algebra l'algèbre *(f.)*, 2.2
Algeria l'Algérie *(f.)*
Algerian algérien(ne)
alive en vie
all tout(e), tous, toutes, 2.1

English-French Dictionary ❖ H79

English-French Dictionary

All aboard! En voiture!
all alone tout(e) seul(e), 5.2
all around tout autour de
all inclusive tout compris, **9.1**
all right (*agreement*) d'accord, 2.1
all the same tout de même, 5.2
in all en tout
not at all pas du tout
That's all. C'est tout., 6.1
allergic allergique, **2.1**
allergy l'allergie (*f.*), **2.1**
to **allow** laisser; permettre
almost presque
alone seul(e), 5.2
   all alone tout(e) seul(e), 5.2
along le long de
already déjà, BV
also aussi, 1.1; également
always toujours, 4.2
A.M. du matin, BV
ambitious ambitieux, ambitieuse
ambulance l'ambulance (*f.*), **8.1**
American (*adj.*) américain(e), 1.1
ammunition les munitions (*f. pl.*)
among entre, 3.2; parmi
amount la quantité
to **analyse** analyser
analysis l'analyse (*f.*)
and et, BV
anesthetist l'anesthésiste (*m. et f.*)
to **anesthetize** faire une anesthésie, **8.2**
animal l'animal (*m.*), **11.2**
ankle la cheville, **8.1**
to **announce** annoncer, 9.1
announcement l'annonce, (*f.*), 8.2
anonymous anonyme
another un(e) autre; encore
to **answer** répondre (à), 9.2

answering machine le répondeur automatique, **3.2**
anthem l'hymne (*f.*), **12.1**
antibiotic l'antibiotique (*m.*), **2.1**
Anything else? Avec ça?, 6.1; Autre chose?, 6.2
apartment l'appartement (*m.*), 4.2
   apartment building l'immeuble (*m.*), 4.2
apothecary l'apothicaire (*m.*), L4
apparatus l'appareil (*m.*)
to **applaud** applaudir
apple la pomme, 6.2
   apple tart la tarte aux pommes, 6.1
appliance l'appareil (*m.*)
   home appliances l'électroménager (*m.*)
to **apply for a job** poser sa candidature, **14.2**
appointment le rendez-vous
   to make an appointment prendre rendez-vous; fixer un rendez-vous
to **appreciate** apprécier
April avril (*m.*), BV
Arab arabe
Arabic (*language*) l'arabe (*m.*)
archaeologist l'archéologue (*m. et f.*)
archaeology l'archéologie (*f.*)
architect l'architecte (*m. et f.*), **14.1**
area code l'indicatif régional, **3.2**
arithmetic le calcul
arm le bras, **8.1**
army l'armée (*f.*), L3
around autour de, 4.2
to **arrest** arrêter
arrival l'arrivée (*f.*), 8.1
arrival/departure board le tableau, **4.1**
to **arrive** arriver, 3.1

arriving from (*flight*) en provenance de, 8.1
arrow la flèche, **7.2**
art l'art (*m.*), 2.2
artery l'artère (*f.*)
article l'article (*m.*)
artist l'artiste (*m. et f.*); le/la peintre (*painter*)
artistic artistique
as aussi (*comparisons*), 7; comme
   as ... as aussi... que, 7
   as many autant de
   as well également
   as well as ainsi que
   the same ... as le (la, les) même(s)... que
Asian asiatique
to **ask (for)** demander, 3.2
aspirin l'aspirine (*f.*), **2.1**
at à, 3.1; chez, 3.2
   at the home (business) of chez, 3.2
   at last enfin, 12.1
   "at" symbol l'arrobase (*f.*)
athletic sportif, sportive
Atlantic Ocean l'océan Atlantique
ATM le distributeur automatique (de billets), **5.1**
atrocious atroce
to **attach** attacher
to **attack** attaquer
to **attend** assister à
attention l'attention (*f.*)
attitude l'attitude (*f.*)
August août, (*m.*), BV
aunt la tante, 4.1
author l'auteur (*m.*), L1
automatic automatique
autumn l'automne (*m.*), 11.2
available disponible, **4.1;** libre, **14.2**
avenged vengé(e)
avenue l'avenue (*f.*), **11.1**
average moyen(ne)
aviator l'aviateur (*m.*), l'aviatrice (*f.*)
to **avoid** éviter, 12.2

English-French Dictionary

baby le bébé, **L2**
back l'arrière (m.), 8.2, **10.2**; le dos, **L2**
  seat back le dossier du siège, **4.2**
background le fond
backpack le sac à dos, 3.2
bacon le bacon
bacterial bactérien(ne), **2.1**
bad mauvais(e), 2.2; nul(le) (slang)
  Not bad. Pas mal., BV
badly mal, **2.1**
bag le sac, 6.1
baggage les bagages (m. pl.), 8.1
  baggage cart le chariot, 9.1
  baggage compartment le coffre à bagages, 8.2
bagpipes la cornemuse
bakery la boulangerie-pâtisserie, 6.1
balance l'équilibre (m.); le solde
balcony le balcon, 4.2
ball (soccer, etc.) le ballon, 10.1
ballerina la danseuse, **1.1**
ballet le ballet
ballpoint pen le stylo-bille, 3.2
banana la banane, 6.2
band (brass) la fanfare, **12.1**
bandage le pansement, 8.1
to **bandage** faire un pansement, **8.1**
bank la banque, **5.1**
barn la grange, **11.2**
base la base
baseball le base-ball, **10.2**
baseball cap la casquette, 7.1
based on à base de
basil le basilic
basilica la basilique
basis la base
basket le panier, 10.2
basketball le basket(-ball), 10.2
bath le bain, 12.1
  to take a bath prendre un bain, 12.1
bather le baigneur, la baigneuse
bathing suit le maillot (de bain), 11.1
bathroom la salle de bains, les toilettes (f. pl.), 4.2
battle la bataille, L3
battlefield le champ de bataille, L3
bay (leaves) le laurier, **6.1**
B.C. avant J.-C. (Jésus-Christ)
to **be** être, 1.1
  to be able to pouvoir, 6.1
  to be afraid avoir peur, L1, **13.2**
  to be better soon être vite sur pied, **2.1**
  to be born naître, 11
  to be called s'appeler, 12.1
  to be careful faire attention, 11.1
  to be early être en avance, 9.1
  to be hungry avoir faim, 5.1
  to be in luck avoir de la chance
  to be late être en retard, 9.1; avoir du retard (plane, train, etc.), 8.1
  to be lucky avoir de la chance
  to be on time être à l'heure, 8.1
  to be part of faire partie de
  to be sorry regretter, 6.1, **13.2**
  to be thirsty avoir soif, 5.1
  to be … years old avoir… ans, 4.1
beach la plage, 11.1
bean: green beans les haricots verts (m. pl.), 6.2
to **beat** battre
beautiful beau (bel), belle, 4.2
beauty la beauté
because parce que
  because of à cause de
to **become** devenir, 4
bed le lit, 9.1, **L2**
  to go to bed se coucher, 12.1
bedroom la chambre à coucher, 4.2
beef le bœuf, 6.1, **6.2**
  roast beef le rôti de bœuf, **6.2**
beet la betterave, **L1**
before avant; avant de
to **begin** commencer, 9.2; débuter
beginner le/la débutant(e), 11.2
beginning le début
  in the beginning au début
to **behave** se tenir, **13.1**
beige beige (inv.), 7.2
being l'être (m.)
  human being l'être humain (m.)
Belgian belge
Belgium la Belgique
to **believe** croire, 7.2
below au-dessous (de); ci-dessous
belt la ceinture, L3
  seat belt la ceinture de sécurité, 8.2, **7.1**
best (adj.) le (la, les) meilleur(e)(s), **8**; (adv.) le mieux, **8**
  best man le garçon d'honneur, **12.2**
better (adv.) mieux, 7.2; (adj.) meilleur(e), **8**
  it is better il vaut mieux, **13.2**
  to feel better aller mieux, **2.2**
between entre, 3.2

English-French Dictionary ❖ H81

English-French Dictionary

beverage la boisson; la consommation, **5.1**
bicycle la bicyclette, **10.2**; le vélo, **10.2**
  bicycle race la course cycliste, **10.2**
  bicycle racer le coureur cycliste, **10.2**
big grand(e), **1.1**; gros(se), **14.2**
bike le vélo, **10.2**
  to go for a bike ride faire une promenade à vélo
bill *(money)* le billet, **5.1**; *(invoice)* la facture; *(hotel)* la note, **9.2**
biological biologique
biologist le/la biologiste
biology la biologie, **2.2**
bird l'oiseau *(m.)*
birthday l'anniversaire *(m.)*, **4.1**
  Happy birthday! Bon (Joyeux) anniversaire!
black noir(e), **7.2**
  black pride la négritude
blacksmith le forgeron, **L2**
blanket la couverture, **4.2**
bleacher le gradin, **10.1**
blind aveugle
to **block** bloquer, **10.1**
blond blond(e), **1.1**
blood le sang
  blood pressure la tension, **8.2**
  blood vessel le vaisseau sanguin
bloom: in bloom fleuri(e), **L2**
blouse le chemisier, **7.1**
to **blow a horn** sonner du cor, **L3**
to **blow a whistle** siffler, **10.1**
blue bleu(e), **7.2**
  navy blue bleu marine *(inv.)*, **7.2**
to **board** *(plane)* embarquer, **4.2**
  boarding l'embarquement *(m.)*
  boarding pass la carte d'embarquement, **8.1**
boat le bateau, **L4**
body le corps, **8.1**
to **boil** bouillir, **6.2**
boiling bouillant(e), **6.2**
bone l'os *(m.)*, **8.2**
book le livre, **3.2**
booklet le carnet
border la frontière
to **border** border
boring ennuyeux, ennuyeuse
to **borrow** emprunter, **5.1**
boss le chef; le/la patron(ne)
botany la botanique
both tous (toutes) les deux
bottle la bouteille, **6.2**
boulevard le boulevard, **11.1**
boutique la boutique, **7.1**
bowl le bol
box office le guichet, **1.1**
boy le garçon, **1.1**
boyfriend le petit ami
brain le cerveau
branch la branche, **12.2**
brand la marque, **7.1**
brass band la fanfare, **12.1**
brave courageux, courageuse; brave
Brazil le Brésil
Brazilian (person) le/la Brésilien(ne)
bread le pain, **6.1**
  loaf of French bread la baguette, **6.1**
  slice of bread and butter la tartine de pain beurré
  whole-wheat bread le pain complet
to **break** briser; casser, **8.1**; *(slow down)* freiner, **7.1**
to **break down** tomber en panne, **7.1**
breakdown la panne, **7.1**
breakfast le petit déjeuner, **5.2**
to **breathe** respirer, **2.2**
  to breathe deeply respirer à fond, **2.2**
Breton breton(ne)
brick la brique
bride la mariée, **12.2**
  bride and groom les mariés, **12.2**
bridge le pont
to **bring** apporter, **11.1**
British britannique
Brittany la Bretagne
broke fauché(e) *(slang)*, **5.1**
brother le frère, **1.2**
brown brun(e), marron *(inv.)*, **7.2**
brunette brun(e), **1.1**
brush la brosse, **12.1**
to **brush (one's teeth, hair, etc.)** se brosser (les dents, les cheveux, etc.), **12.1**
bug *(computer)* le bogue
to **build** construire; fabriquer
building le bâtiment, **11.1**; l'édifice *(m.)*
built up area l'agglomération *(f.)*, **7.2**
bungalow le bungalow
to **burn** brûler
burst éclaté(e)
bus le bus; l'autocar *(m.)*; l'autobus *(m.)*, **10.2**
  bus stop l'arrêt *(m.)* d'autobus, **10.2**
  bus terminal la gare routière (Africa)
  by bus en bus
bush *(wilderness)* la brousse
business les affaires *(f. pl.)*, **11.1**
busy occupé(e)
  I'm getting a busy signal. Ça sonne occupé., **3.2**
but mais, **2.1**
butcher le boucher, la bouchère
butcher shop la boucherie, **6.1**
butter le beurre, **6.1**
button le bouton, **10.2**; la touche, **3.1**
to **buy** acheter, **3.2**
  to buy on credit acheter à crédit
by par
Bye. Salut., **BV**

English-French Dictionary

cabaret le cabaret
cabin *(plane)* la cabine, **8.1**
café le café, **BV**
cafeteria la cafétéria
cake le gâteau, **4.1**
calcium le calcium
calculator la calculatrice, **3.2**
calendar le calendrier
calf le veau, **11.2**
call *(telephone)* l'appel *(m.)*, **3.2**
   local call l'appel urbain
   toll call l'appel interurbain
to call appeler; *(on the telephone)* téléphoner; donner un coup de fil, **3.2**
   to call a penalty déclarer un penalty
   to call back rappeler, **3.2**
   to call 911 appeler police secours, **8.1**
calm calme
calorie la calorie
Camembert cheese le camembert
campaign la campagne
can pouvoir, **6.1**
can of food la boîte de conserve, **6.2**
Canadian *(adj.)* canadien(ne), **6**
to cancel annuler, **4.2**
candelabra le chandelier, **12.2**
candle la bougie, **4.1, 12.2**
cap la casquette, **7.1**
capital la capitale
car la voiture, **4.2**; *(railroad)* le wagon
   by car en voiture, **5.2**
   dining car le wagon-restaurant
   sleeping car le wagon-couchettes (lits)
carbohydrate la glucide; l'hydrate *(m.)* de carbone

carbon dioxide le gaz carbonique
card la carte
   credit card la carte de crédit, **9.2**
   greeting card la carte de vœux, **12.2**
cardboard le carton
cardiac cardiaque
care le soin
to care: I don't care. Ça m'est égal., **1.1**
career la carrière, **14.2**
Careful! Attention!, **4.2**
carefully prudemment, **7.2;** soigneusement
Caribbean Sea la mer des Caraïbes, la mer des Antilles
carnival *(season)* le carnaval, **12.1**
carpenter le charpentier; le menuisier, **14.1**
carrot la carotte, **6.2**
to carry porter, **L2**
carry-on luggage les bagages *(m. pl.)* à main, **8.1**
to carry out exécuter; assurer
cartoon le dessin animé, **1.1**
case le cas
   in case of en cas de
cash l'argent liquide, **5.1**
   cash register la caisse, **3.2**
   in cash en liquide, **9.2**
   to pay cash payer en espèces, **9.2**
to cash toucher, **5.1**
cashier le caissier, la caissière, **5.1**
cassette la cassette, **3.1**
cast le plâtre, **8.2**
   to put in a cast plâtrer, **8.2**
castle le château
casual *(clothes)* sport, **7.1**
cat le chat, **4.1**
catalog le catalogue
to catch attraper
to cause causer
cave la grotte, **L4**
CD le CD, **3.1**

CD-ROM le CD-ROM, **3.1**
to celebrate célébrer, **L4**
   to celebrate Christmas Eve or New Year's Eve réveillonner, **12.2**
cell la cellule, **L4**
Celtic celte, celtique
center le centre
century le siècle, **L4**
cereal les céréales *(f. pl.)*
ceremony la cérémonie, **12.2**
certainly certainement
chairlift le télésiège, **11.2**
champion le/la champion(ne)
change *(money)* la monnaie, **5.1**
   change purse le porte-monnaie, **5.1**
   to make change for faire la monnaie de, **5.1**
to change changer (de), **9.2**
channel *(TV)* la chaîne, **12.2**
   to channel surf zapper, **12.2**
character *(in a story)* le personnage
characteristic la caractéristique; le trait
charge: in charge of chargé(e) de
charges les frais *(m. pl.)*, **9.2, 13.1**
charm le charme
charming charmant(e)
to chat bavarder
check le chèque, **5.1;** *(in restaurant)* l'addition *(f.)*, **5.2**
   traveler's check le chèque de voyage
to check vérifier, **8.1;** contrôler, **4.1**
   to check *(luggage)* (faire) enregistrer, **8.1**
   to check under the hood vérifier les niveaux, **7.1**
cheek la joue, **13.1**
cheese le fromage, **5.1**

English-French Dictionary

chemical chimique
chemist le/la chimiste
chemistry la chimie, **2.2**
chest la poitrine; le coffre, **L4**
chewing gum le chewing-gum
chic chic *(inv.)*
chicken le poulet, **6.1**
child l'enfant *(m. et f.)*, **4.1**
childhood l'enfance *(f.)*
chills les frissons *(m. pl.)*, **2.1**
chimney la cheminée, **12.2**
Chinese chinois(e)
chocolate le chocolat; *(adj.)* au chocolat, **5.1**
choir le chœur
to **choose** choisir, **8.1**
choppy *(sea)* agité(e)
Christmas le Noël, **12.2**
  Christmas carol le chant de Noël, **12.2**
  Christmas Eve dinner le réveillon, **12.2**
  Christmas gift le cadeau de Noël, **12.2**
  Christmas tree l'arbre *(m.)* de Noël, **12.2**
church l'église *(f.)*, **11.1, 12.2**
circle le cercle
  traffic circle le rond-point, **7.2, 11.1**
circuit le circuit
circus le cirque
to **cite** citer
city la ville, **8.1, 5.2, 11.1**
  city hall l'hôtel *(m.)* de ville
  in the city en ville, **11.1**
civil civil(e)
  civil servant le/la fonctionnaire, **14.1**
civilization la civilisation
civilized civilisé(e)
to **claim** *(luggage)* récupérer, **4.2**
clarinet la clarinette
class *(people)* la classe, **2.1**; *(course)* le cours, **2.1**
  in class en classe
  in (French, etc.) class en cours de (français, etc.)
classical classique
classified ad la petite annonce, **14.2**
classroom la salle de classe, **2.1**
clean propre, **9.2**
to **clear the table** débarrasser la table, **12.2**
clearly clairement
clever: Very clever! *(ironic)* C'est malin!
to **click** cliquer, **3.1**
climate le climat
clinic la clinique
close *(adv.)* de près, **11.1**; *(adj.)* proche
to **close** fermer, **9.1**
closet le placard, **9.2**
clothes les vêtements *(m. pl.)*, **7.1**
cloud le nuage, **11.1**
clove of garlic la gousse d'ail, **6.1**
clown le clown
coach l'autocar *(m.)*
coast la côte
coat le manteau, **7.1**
code le code, **4.2**
coffee le café, **5.1**
  black coffee l'express *(m.)*, **5.1**
  coffee with cream *(in a café)* le crème, **5.1**
coin la pièce, **5.1**
cola le coca, **5.1**
cold froid(e) *(adj.)*; *(illness)* le rhume, **2.1**
  to have a cold être enrhumé(e), **2.1**
collection la collection
color la couleur, **7.2**
  What color is . . . ? De quelle couleur est… ?, **7.2**
comb le peigne, **12.1**
to **comb one's hair** se peigner, **12.1**
to **come** venir, **4.2**
  to come back revenir, **4**
  Come on! Allez!, **9.2**
comedy la comédie, **1.1**; le film comique, **1.1**
  musical comedy la comédie musicale, **1.1**
comfortable confortable
comic comique, **1.1**
commercial *(TV)* la publicité, **12.2**
to **commit** commettre
common commun(e); courant(e)
  in common en commun
to **communicate** communiquer
communication la communication
community la communauté
commuter trains les lignes de banlieue, **4.1**
company la société, **14.2**; l'entreprise, **14.2**
  in the company of en compagnie de
to **compare** comparer
compartment le compartiment, **4.1**
complete complet, complète
to **complete** compléter
completely complètement
complicated compliqué(e)
composed of composé(e) de
composer le compositeur, la compositrice
composition la composition; la rédaction
compound enceinte de résidences, **L2**
compound fracture la fracture compliquée, **8.2**
computer l'ordinateur *(m.)*, **3.1**
  computer expert l'informaticien(ne), **14.1**
  computer science l'informatique *(f.)*, **2.2**
concept le concept
concert le concert

English-French Dictionary

concisely brièvement
condition la condition
conductor (train) le contrôleur, **9.2**
to **connect** connecter; relier
connection (between trains) la correspondance, **9.2**, **10.1**
to **conspire** comploter
to **consult** consulter
to **contain** contenir
contamination la contamination
contest la compétition, le concours
continent le continent
to **continue** continuer
contrary: on the contrary au contraire
to **control** contrôler, **4.1**
convent le couvent
conversation la conversation, **L3**
to **converse** converser
convertible la décapotable, **7.1**
cook le cuisinier, la cuisinière, **6.2**
to **cook** faire la cuisine, **6**; cuire, **6.2**
cooked cuit(e)
cool frais, fraîche **11.2**
copper le cuivre
corner le coin, **10.1**, **11.1**
  on the corner au coin, **11.1**
corporation la société, **14.2**
  large corporation la grosse société, **14.2**
correspondence la correspondance
corridor le couloir, **8.2**
cosmopolitan cosmopolite
cost le prix, **7.1**
to **cost** coûter, **3.2**
to **cough** tousser, **2.1**
counselor le conseiller, la conseillère
count le comte, **L4**
to **count** compter, **5.1**
counter le comptoir, **8.1**

counter window (post office) le guichet, **5.2**
country le pays, **8.1**
  country code (tel.) l'indicatif (m.) du pays, **3.2**
country(side) la campagne, **11.2**
courage le courage
courageous courageux, courageuse
course le cours, **2.1**
  of course bien sûr; mais oui
  of course not mais non
court la cour; le tribunal, **14.1**
courtesy la politesse, BV
courtyard la cour, **3.2**
cousin le/la cousin(e), **4.1**
to **cover** couvrir
covered couvert(e)
cow la vache, **11.2**
crab le crabe, **6.1**, **6.2**
crazy fou, folle
cream la crème
  coffee with cream (in a café) le crème, **5.1**
to **create** créer; réaliser
credit card la carte de crédit, **9.2**
Creole (language) le créole
crepe la crêpe, BV
criminal le/la criminel(le), **L4**
critic le/la critique
croissant le croissant, **5.1**
to **cross** traverser, **11.1**; se croiser, **10.1**
crosswalk le passage pour piétons, **11.1**
crushed écrasé(e)
crutch la béquille, **8.1**
to **cry** pleurer, **L1**
cucumber le concombre
to **cultivate** cultiver, **11.2**
cultural culturel(le)
  cultural event la manifestation culturelle
culture la culture
cup la tasse, **5.2**

winner's cup la coupe, **10.2**
to **cure** guérir, **L4**
currency la devise; la monnaie, **5.1**
current courant(e)
customer le/la client(e)
customs la douane, **4.2**
  to go through customs passer à la douane, **4.2**
to **cut** couper, **6.2**
  to cut (one's finger, etc.) se couper, **8.1**
  to cut in line resquiller, **13.1**
cycling le cyclisme, **10.2**; (adj.) cycliste
cyclist (in race) le coureur (la coureuse) cycliste, **10.2**
cymbals les cymbales (f. pl.), **12.1**

dad papa
daily quotidien(ne)
dairy store la crémerie, **6.1**
dance la danse
to **dance** danser, **1.1**
dancer le danseur, la danseuse, **1.1**
dangerous dangereux, dangereuse
dangerously dangereusement, **7.2**
dark sombre
dark haired brun(e), **1.1**
Darn! Zut!, BV
data les données (f. pl.), **3.1**
date la date; (fruit) la datte
  date palm le dattier
  What is today's date? Quelle est la date aujourd'hui?, BV
to **date from** dater de
daughter la fille, **4.1**
day le jour, BV; la journée, **3.1**
  the day before yesterday avant-hier, **10.2**

English-French Dictionary

every day tous les jours
What a nice day! Belle journée!, **4.2**
dear cher, chère
death la mort
debt: to go into debt s'endetter
December décembre *(m.)*, BV
to decide (to) décider de
decision la décision
  the decision is made la décision est prise
to declare déclarer
to decorate orner; décorer
dedicated dédié(e)
to defeat battre
delay le retard
delicatessen la charcuterie, **6.1**
delicious délicieux, délicieuse
delighted enchanté(e), **13.2**
demanding exigeant(e)
dentist le/la dentiste
deodorant le déodorant
department *(in a store)* le rayon, **7.1**; *(in a company)* le service
  coat department le rayon des manteaux, **7.1**
  department head le chef de service, **14.1**
  department store le grand magasin, **7.1**
departure le départ, **8.1**
to depend (on) dépendre (de)
deplaning le débarquement
deposit les arrhes *(f. pl.)*, **9.1**
  to pay a deposit verser des arrhes, **9.1**
to deposit verser, **5.1**
descendant le/la descendant(e)
to describe décrire
description la description
desert le désert
deserted désert(e)
to design dessiner

designer *(clothes)* le couturier
to desire désirer, **3.2**
desk clerk le/la réceptionniste, **9.1**
desparate désespéré(e), **L4**
dessert le dessert
destination la destination
destiny la destinée
detail le détail
to devastate ravager
to develop développer
devoted dévoué(e)
diagnosis le diagnostic, **2.2**
to dial *(phone number)* composer, **3.2**; faire le numéro, **3.2**
dial tone la tonalité, **3.2**
dialect le dialecte
diamond le diamant
dictionary le dictionnaire
to die mourir, **11**; crever, **L4**
diet l'alimentation *(f.)*; le régime
  to follow a diet faire un régime
difference la différence
different différent(e), **8.1**
difficult difficile, **2.1**
difficulty la difficulté
  with difficulty difficilement
dig *(archaeol.)* la fouille
to dig creuser, **L4**
dignitaries les notables *(m. pl.)*, **12.1**
dining car la voiture-restaurant
dining hall *(school)* la cantine, **3.1**
dining room la salle à manger, **4.2**
dinner le dîner, **5.2**
  to eat dinner dîner, **5.2**
diploma le diplôme
direction la direction, **10.1**; le sens, **7.2**
  in the right (wrong) direction dans le bon (mauvais) sens, **11.1**
directly directement

director of human resources le directeur (la directrice) des ressources humaines (D.R.H.), **14.2**
to direct traffic régler la circulation, **11.1**
dirty sale, **9.2**
disadvantage l'inconvénient *(m.)*
disagreeable désagréable
to disappear disparaître
discount la réduction
to discover découvrir
discovery la découverte
to discuss discuter
disease la maladie
dish *(food)* le plat
dishes la vaisselle, **12.2**
  to do the dishes faire la vaisselle, **12.2**
dishwasher le lave-vaisselle, **12.2**
diskette la disquette, **3.1**
diskette drive le lecteur de disquettes, **3.1**
to distinguish distinguer
to distribute distribuer, **5.2**
district le quartier, **4.2**, **11.1**; *(Paris)* l'arrondissement *(m.)*
  business district le quartier d'affaires, **11.1**
dive le plongeon
to dive plonger, **11.1**
to divide diviser
to do faire, **6.1**
  to do the grocery shopping faire les courses, **6.1**
doctor le médecin *(m. et f.)*, **2.2**
  at (to) the doctor's office chez le médecin, **2.2**
document le document, **3.1**
documentary le documentaire, **1.1**
dog le chien, **4.1**
domain le domaine
domestic *(flight)* intérieur(e), **8.1**
donkey l'âne *(m.)*

English-French Dictionary

door la porte, L4, **9.1, L2**
dormitory le dortoir
to **doubt** douter, **14**
to **download** télécharger
downtown le centre-ville, **11.1**
dozen la douzaine, 6.2
drama le drame, **1.1**
  drama club le club d'art dramatique
drawing le dessin
dream le rêve
dress la robe, 7.1
dressed: to get dressed s'habiller, 12.1
dressy habillé(e), 7.1
to **dribble** (basketball) dribbler, 10.2
drink la boisson; la consommation, 5.1; le pot
to **drink** boire, 10.2
to **drive** conduire, **7.1, 11.1**
  driver l'automobiliste (m. et f.), **7.1**; le conducteur, la conductrice, **7.1**; le chauffeur
  driver's license le permis de conduire, **7.1**
  driving lesson la leçon de conduite, **7.1**
  driving school l'auto-école (f.), **7.1**
drugstore la pharmacie, **2.2**
druid le druide
drum le tambour, **12.1**
dry sec, sèche
to **dry** sécher
dubbed (movie) doublé(e), **1.1**
duck le canard
duration la durée
during pendant, 3.2
dynamic dynamique, 1.2

each (adj.) chaque, **4.1**
each (one) chacun(e), 5.2
ear l'oreille (f.), **2.1**

earache: to have an earache avoir mal aux oreilles, **2.1**
early en avance, 9.1; de bonne heure; tôt, 12.1
to **earn** gagner
earphone l'écouteur (m.), **L3**
earth la terre, **11.2**
easily facilement
Easter Pâques
eastern oriental(e)
easy facile, 2.1
to **eat** manger, 5.1
  ecological écologique
  ecology l'écologie (f.)
  economics l'économie (f.), 2.2
  egg l'œuf (m.), 6.1
    fried egg l'œuf sur le plat
    poached egg l'œuf à la coque
    scrambled egg l'œuf brouillé
egotistical égoïste, 1.2
Egyptian égyptien(ne)
elbow le coude, 13.1
electric électrique
electrician l'électricien(ne), **14.1**
electronic électronique
element l'élément (m.)
elevator l'ascenseur (m.), 4.2
to **eliminate** éliminer
elsewhere ailleurs
e-mail l'e-mail (m.), le mail, 3.1
emergency l'urgence (f.)
  emergency exit l'issue (f.) de secours
  emergency medical technician le/la secouriste, **8.1**
  emergency room le service des urgences, **8.1**
emission l'émission (f.)
emotion l'émotion (f.), 13.2
employee l'employé(e), **14.1**

employer l'employeur, l'employeuse, **14.2**
employment office le bureau de placement, **14.2**
empty vide, **7.1**
encyclopedia l'encyclopédie (f.)
end la fin; le bout
ending le dénouement
enemy l'ennemi(e)
energetic énergique, 1.2
energy l'énergie (f.)
engagement les fiançailles (f. pl.), L4
engineer l'ingénieur (m.), **14.1**
England l'Angleterre (f.)
English anglais(e)
English (language) l'anglais (m.), 2.2
English Channel la Manche
enormous énorme
enough assez, 1.1
enriched enrichi(e)
to **ensure** assurer
to **enter** entrer, 7.1
  enthusiastic enthousiaste, 1.2
entire entier, entière
entitled intitulé(e)
entrance l'entrée (f.), 4.2
envelope l'enveloppe (f.)
equipment l'équipement (m.); le matériel, **11.2**
equivalent l'équivalent (m.)
eraser la gomme, 3.2
escalator l'escalier mécanique, **10.1**
to **escape** s'échapper; s'évader, L4
especially surtout
espresso l'express (m.), 5.1
essential essentiel(le); de première nécessité, indispensable
to **establish** établir
establishment l'établissement (m.)
euro l'euro (m.)
Europe l'Europe (f.)

English-French Dictionary

European *(adj.)* européen(ne)
eve la veille, **12.2**
evening le soir, BV
event l'événement *(m.)*
ever jamais
every tous, toutes, 2.1, 8; chaque, **4.1**
  every day tous les jours, **1.2**
  every five minutes toutes les cinq minutes, **10.1**
everybody tout le monde, 1.2
everyday *(adj.)* quotidien(ne)
everyone tout le monde, 1.2
everything tout
everywhere partout
evidently évidemment
exact exact(e)
exactly exactement; justement
to **exaggerate** exagérer
exam l'examen *(m.)*, 3.1
  to pass an exam réussir à un examen
  to take an exam passer un examen, 3.1
to **examine** examiner, 2.2
example: for example par exemple
excellent excellent(e)
except excepté(e); sauf, **1.2**
exception l'exception *(f.)*
exceptional exceptionnel(le)
exchange l'échange *(m.)*
  exchange rate le cours du change, **5.1**
to **exchange** échanger; changer, **5.1**
exclusively exclusivement
excursion l'excursion *(f.)*
to **excuse** excuser
  excuse me pardon
to **execute** exécuter
exercise l'exercice *(m.)*
exhausted crevé(e); épuisé(e)
exhibit l'exposition *(f.)*, **1.2**

to **exist** exister
existence l'existence *(f.)*
exit la sortie, **7.2**
to **expel** expulser
expenses les frais *(m. pl.)*, **9.2, 13.1**
expensive cher, chère, **7.1**
experience l'expérience *(f.)*
expert *(adj.)* expert(e)
to **explain** expliquer
explanation l'explication *(f.)*
explosion l'explosion *(f.)*
to **express** exprimer
expression l'expression *(f.)*
exquisite exquis(e)
exterior l'extérieur *(m.)*
extraordinary extraordinaire
extreme extrême
extremely extrêmement
eye l'œil *(m., pl.* yeux*)*, **2.1**
  to have itchy eyes avoir les yeux qui piquent, **2.1**
eyes les yeux *(m. pl.)*, L1

fable la fable
fabulous fabuleux, fabuleuse
face la figure, 12.1
  face down *(paper)* face écrite non visible, **3.1**
  face up *(paper)* face écrite visible, **3.1**
to **face** donner sur, 4.2
to **facilitate** faciliter
factory l'usine *(f.)*, **11.1**
fairly assez, 1.1
fall *(season)* l'automne *(m.)*, 11.2
to **fall** tomber 11.2, **8.1**
  to fall asleep s'endormir
false faux, fausse
to **falsify** falsifier
family la famille, 4.1
famous célèbre; connu(e), **1.1**

fan le/la fana
fantastic fantastique
far (away) loin
  far from loin de, 4.2
  farther plus loin
fare le tarif
farm la ferme, **11.2**; *(adj.)* agricole, **11.2**
to **farm** *(land)* cultiver, **11.2**
farmer l'agriculteur, l'agricultrice, **11.2**; le fermier, la fermière, **11.2**
fast *(adj.)* rapide; *(adv.)* vite 10.2
to **fasten** attacher, 8.2
fast-food *(adj.)* de restauration rapide
  fast-food restaurant le fast-food
fat la graisse; le lipide
father le père, 4.1
fault la faute
favorite favori(te); préféré(e)
fax le fax; la télécopie, **3.1**
  fax machine le fax; le télécopieur, **3.1**
February février *(m.)*, BV
to **feed** nourrir; donner à manger
to **feel (well, etc.)** se sentir, **2.1**
  to feel better aller mieux, **2.2**
  to feel like avoir envie de
  to feel out of sorts ne pas être dans son assiette, **2.1**
feeling le sentiment; la sensation
fees *(doctor)* les honoraires *(m. pl.)*
felt-tip pen le feutre, 3.2
female la femelle
festival le festival
  Festival of Lights la fête des Lumières, **12.2**
festive de fête
festivity la festivité
fever la fièvre, **2.1**
  to have a fever avoir de la fièvre, **2.1**

English-French Dictionary

few peu (de); peu nombreux
  a few quelques, **9.2**
fiancé(e) le/la fiancé(e), **L4**
fictional fictif, fictive
field le champ, **L1**, **11.2**, **L2**; le domaine; *(employment)* la carrière, **14.2**
fig la figue
fight le combat, **L3**; la lutte, **L3**
to **fight** lutter, **L3**
file le fichier *(computer)*
to **fill out** remplir, **8.2**, **8.2**
to **fill up the gas tank** faire le plein, **7.1**
fillet of sole le filet de sole, **6.2**
film le film, **1.1**
  adventure film le film d'aventures, **1.1**
  detective film le film policier, **1.1**
  foreign film le film étranger, **1.1**
  horror film le film d'horreur, **1.1**
  science fiction film le film de science-fiction, **1.1**
filmmaker le/la cinéaste, **14.1**
finally enfin, **12.1**; finalement
financial financier, financière
to **find** trouver, **5.1**
fine ça va, bien, **BV**
fine l'amende *(f.)*
finger le doigt, **8.1**, **13.1**
to **finish** finir, **8.2**
fir (tree) le sapin, **12.2**
fire le feu, **L2**
fireworks le feu d'artifice, **12.1**
firm l'entreprise *(f.)*, **14.2**
first premier, première *(adj.)*, **4.2**; d'abord *(adv.)*, **12.1**
  in first class en première, **9.1**
fish le poisson, **6.1**, **6.2**
  fish store la poissonnerie, **6.1**

fishing la pêche
fitting room la cabine d'essayage
to **fix** réparer; arranger
flag le drapeau, **12.1**
flat tire le pneu à plat, **7.1**
flavor le parfum
flea market le marché aux puces
flight le vol, **8.1**
  domestic flight le vol intérieur, **8.1**
  flight attendant l'hôtesse *(f.)* de l'air, le steward, **8.2**
  flight crew le personnel de bord, **8.2**
  international flight le vol international, **8.1**
float le char, **12.1**
flock *(sheep)* le troupeau, **11.2**
floor (of a building) l'étage *(m.)*, **4.2**
  ground floor le rez-de-chaussée, **4.2**
flower la fleur, **4.2**
flu la grippe, **2.1**
fluent courant(e)
flute la flûte
to **fly** *(plane)* piloter; voler, **L3**
  to fly over survoler
to **follow** suivre, **11.1**
  following suivant(e)
food la nourriture; l'aliment *(m.)*; les provisions *(f. pl.)*
  food service la restauration
foot le pied, **10.1**, **8.1**
  on foot à pied, **4.2**
football le football américain
for pour; *(time)* pendant, **3.2**; depuis, **9.2**
  for example par exemple
forbidden interdit(e), **4.2**
forearm l'avant-bras *(m.)*, **13.1**
foreign étranger, étrangère, **1.1**

foreign exchange office le bureau de change, **5.1**
foreman, forewoman le contremaître, la contremaîtresse
to **forget** oublier, **7.2**
fork la fourchette, **5.2**
form la forme; le formulaire, **8.2**
to **form** former
formality la formalité
format le format
former ancien(ne)
fortunately heureusement
fortune la fortune
to **found** fonder
fracture la fracture, **8.2**
  compound fracture la fracture compliquée, **8.2**
free libre, **5.1**; gratuit(e)
to **free** libérer
freedom la liberté
freezer le congé(lateur), **6.1**
French français(e) *(adj.)*, **1.1**; *(language)* le français, **2.2**
  French fries les frites *(f. pl.)*, **5.1**
  French-speaking francophone
to **frequent** fréquenter
frequently fréquemment
Friday vendredi *(m.)*, **BV**
friend l'ami(e), **1.2**; *(pal)* le copain, la copine, **2.1**; le/la camarade
from de, **1.1**
  from then on désormais
front l'avant *(m.)*, **8.2**, **10.2**
  front desk la réception, **9.1**
  in front of devant, **8.2**, **11.1**
frozen surgelé(e), **6.2**
fruit le fruit, **6.2**, **6.1**
frying pan la poêle, **6.2**
full plein(e), **10.1**, **13.1**; complet, complète, **4.1**
  at full speed à toute allure, **L1**
fun amusant(e), **1.1**

English-French Dictionary

to have fun s'amuser, 12.2
function la fonction
funny amusant(e), 1.1; rigolo, 4.2; comique, 1.1
furious furieux, furieuse, 13.2
furniture les meubles (*m. pl.*)
future l'avenir (*m.*), le futur, L2

to **gain a few pounds** prendre des kilos
game le match, 10.1; le jeu
garage le garage, 4.2
garden le jardin, 4.2
garlic l'ail (*m.*), 6.1
gas station la station-service
gas station attendant le/la pompiste, 7.1
gas tank le réservoir, 7.1
gasoline l'essence (*f.*), 7.1
gate (*airport*) la porte, 8.1
to **gather** se rassembler
gem la pierre précieuse, L4
general le général
generally généralement
   generally speaking d'une façon générale
generosity la générosité
genre le genre
geography la géographie, 2.2
geometry la géométrie, 2.2
germ le microbe
German (*language*) l'allemand (*m.*), 2.2
Germany l'Allemagne (*f.*)
to **get** recevoir, 10.2; obtenir; se procurer
   to get dressed s'habiller, 12.1
   to get married se marier, L4, 12.2
   to get off (*bus, train, etc.*) descendre, 9.2; (*plane*) débarquer, 4.2
   to get off at the next station descendre à la prochaine, 10.1
   to get on (board) monter, 9.2
   to get sick tomber malade, L1
   to get a sunburn attraper un coup de soleil, 11.1
   to get together se retrouver, 13.1
   to get up se lever, 12.1
getting off la descente, 10.2
gift le cadeau, 4.1
gigantic gigantesque
girl la fille, 1.1
girlfriend la petite amie
to **give** donner, 4.1
   to give back rendre, 5.1
   to give change for faire la monnaie de, 5.1
   to give way céder la place
glad content(e), 13.2
glass le verre, 5.2
glove le gant, 11.2
to **go** aller, 5.1
   to go down descendre, 9
   to go fast rouler vite, 10.2, 7.2
   to go (and) get aller chercher, 6.1
   to go home rentrer, 3.2
   to go out sortir, 8.2
   to go surfing faire du surf, 11.1
   to go to (*transp.*) desservir, 4.1
   to go to bed se coucher, 12.1
   to go up monter, 4.2
   to go windsurfing faire de la planche à voile, 11.1
   to go with accompagner
   Should we go? On y va?
goal le but, 10.1
   to score a goal marquer un but, 10.1
goalie le gardien de but, 10.1
God bless you! À tes souhaits!, 2.1
gold l'or (*m.*), L4
golden doré(e)
good bon(ne), 6.2
   Good health! Bonne santé!, 12.2
   good manners le savoir-vivre
   good in math fort(e) en maths, 2.2
good-bye au revoir; ciao (*inform.*), BV
goodness la bonté
goods les produits
gourmet le gourmet
government le gouvernement
grade la note
to **graduate** être diplômé(e)
grain(s) les céréales (*f. pl.*), 11.2
gram le gramme, 6.2
grammar la grammaire
granddaughter la petite-fille, 4.1
grandfather le grand-père, 4.1
grandmother la grand-mère, 4.1
grandparents les grands-parents (*m. pl.*), 4.1
grandson le petit-fils, 4.1
grandstand la tribune, 12.1
grape(s) le raisin, 6.1
grapefruit le pamplemousse, 6.1
grass l'herbe (*f.*), 11.2
to **grate** râper, 6.2
gray gris(e), 7.2
great grand(e)
Greece la Grèce
green vert(e), 5.1
   green beans les haricots (*m. pl.*) verts, 6.2
to **greet** saluer, L1
   greeting card la carte de vœux, 12.2
   grilled ham and cheese sandwich le croque-monsieur, 5.1

English-French Dictionary

to **grind** hacher, **6.2**
grocery store l'épicerie (f.), **6.1**
groom le marié, **12.2**
ground le sol, 10.2
  ground floor le rez-de-chaussée, **4.2**
  on the ground à terre
group le groupe
to **grow** (crop) cultiver, **11.2**
  to grow (up) grandir
growth la croissance
guard le gardien, L4
to **guard** garder
to **guess** deviner
guest l'invité(e)
guide le guide
guidebook le guide
guillotined guillotiné(e)
guitar la guitare
guitarist le/la guitariste
guy le type
gymnasium le gymnase
gymnastics la gymnastique, **2.2**

habitual habituel(le)
hair les cheveux (m. pl.), **12.1**
Haitian haïtien(ne)
half demi(e)
  half brother le demi-frère, **4.1**
  half hour la demi-heure
  half past (time) et demie, BV
  half price le demi-tarif
  half sister la demi-sœur, **4.1**
halftime (sporting event) le mi-temps
ham le jambon, **5.1**
hamburger le hamburger
hamlet le hameau
hand la main, **3.1**, **13.1**
handicapped handicapé(e)
handkerchief le mouchoir, **2.1**

handmade fait(e) à la main
handsome beau (bel), **4.2**
to **hang up** raccrocher, **3.2**
  hanger le cintre, **9.2**
Hanukkah la Hanouka, **12.2**
to **happen** arriver, **8.1**; se passer
happiness le bonheur
happy content(e), **13.2**; heureux, heureuse, **13.2**
  Happy birthday! Bon (Joyeux) anniversaire!
  Happy New Year! Bonne Année!, **12.2**
harbor le port
hard dur(e); (adv.) fort
hardware (computer) le hardware
harp la harpe
harshness la rigueur
harvest la récolte, **11.2**
hat (ski) le bonnet, 11.2
to **hate** détester, **3.1**
to **have** avoir, **4.1**; (to eat or drink, in café or restaurant) prendre, **5.1**
  to have a(n) . . . -ache avoir mal à (aux)… , **2.1**
  to have just (done something) venir de, 10
head la tête, 10.1; (of department or company) le chef
headphones les écouteurs (m. pl.), **4.2**
health la santé, **2.1**
to **hear** entendre, 9.1
heart le cœur
heat: high heat le feu vif, **6.2**
  low heat le feu doux, **6.2**
heaven le ciel
hello bonjour, BV; (telephone) allô
helmet le casque, **7.1**
help l'aide (f.); le secours, **8.1**
  to be a big help rendre bien service
  with the help of à l'aide de

to **help** aider, **3.2**
hemisphere l'hémisphère (m.)
hen la poule, 11.2
herb la fine herbe, **6.1**
herd le troupeau, **11.2**
here is, here are voici, **4.1**; (emphatic) voilà, **1.2**
hero le héros
hey! tiens!
hi salut, BV
to **hide** cacher, L3
high élevé(e); haut(e), **11.1**
  high school le lycée, **2.1**
higher supérieur
high-speed train le TGV, **4.1**
highway l'autoroute (f.), **7.2**
hiker le randonneur, la randonneuse
history l'histoire (f.), **2.2**
to **hit** frapper, L3; donner un coup (de pied, de tête, etc.), 10.1
hockey le hockey
  hockey stick la crosse
hold: Please hold. (telephone) Ne quittez pas., **3.2**
hole le trou, L4
holiday la fête, **12.1**
home: at (to) the home of chez, **3.2**
  to go home rentrer, **3.2**
homework (assignment) le devoir
  to do homework faire ses devoirs, 6
honest honnête
honey le miel
to **hope** espérer, **6.2**
horn le cor, L3
horrible horrible
horror l'horreur (f.)
horse le cheval, **11.2**
horseback: to go horseback riding faire du cheval, **11.2**

English-French Dictionary

hospital l'hôpital (m.), **8.1**; (adj.) hospitalier, hospitalière
hot chaud(e)
hot dog la saucisse de Francfort, BV
hotel l'hôtel (m.), **9.1**
house la maison, 3.1; la villa
  publishing house la maison d'édition
  small house le pavillon
to **house** loger
housing le logement
how comment, 1.1
  how far? jusqu'où?
  How's it going? Ça va?, BV
  How is that? Comment ça?
  how many, how much combien (de), 3.2
human humain(e)
  human being l'être humain (m.)
hundred cent, 2.2
hungry: to be hungry avoir faim, 5.1
hunter le chasseur, la chasseuse
to **hurry** se dépêcher, 12.1
to **hurt** avoir mal à, **2.1**
  to hurt oneself se faire mal, **8.1**; se blesser, **8.1**
  It (That) hurts. Ça fait mal., **2.1**
husband le mari, 4.1

ice la glace, 11.2
  ice cream la glace, 5.1
icon l'icône (f.)
idea l'idée (f.)
ideal idéal(e)
identify identifier
if si
  if I were you à ta place, **7.1**
ill malade, L1, **2.1**

illegible illisible
illness la maladie
illustration le dessin
to **imagine** imaginer
immediate immédiat(e)
immediately immédiatement, **14.2**
immense immense
impolite mal élevé(e), **13.1**; malpoli(e), **13.1**
important important(e), 13
impossible impossible, 13
impressed impressionné(e)
Impressionists les impressionnistes (m. pl.)
imprisoned emprisonné(e)
to **improve** s'améliorer
improvement le progrès
in dans, 1.2; à, 3.1; en, 3.2
  in addition to en plus de
  in fact en fait
  in first (second) class en première (seconde), 9.1
  in front of devant, 8.2, 11.1
  in general en général
  in particular en particulier
  in search of à la recherche de
  in vain en vain
  In what month? En quel mois?, BV
included compris(e), 5.2, **9.1**
  The tip is included. Le service est compris., 5.2
incredible incroyable
to **indicate** indiquer
indigestion le trouble digestif
  to have indigestion avoir mal au foie
indiscreet indiscret, indiscrète
indispensable indispensable
individual l'individu (m.); (adj.) individuel(le)
industrial industriel(le)
inexpensive bon marché (inv.)

infection l'infection (f.), **2.1**
influence l'influence (f.)
information l'information (f.); les renseignements (m. pl.)
ingredient l'ingrédient (m.)
inhabitant l'habitant(e)
injection la piqûre, **8.2**
  to give an injection faire une piqûre, **8.1**
injury la blessure, **8.1**
innocent innocent(e)
insane fou, folle
to **insist** insister
instead of au lieu de
institute l'institut (m.)
instructions les instructions (f. pl.)
instructor le moniteur, la monitrice, 11.1
instrument l'instrument (m.)
  keyboard instrument l'instrument à clavier
  percussion instrument l'instrument à percussion
  string instrument l'instrument à cordes
  wind instrument l'instrument à vent
intellectual intellectuel(le)
intelligent intelligent(e), 1.1
intended for destiné(e) à
interest l'intérêt (m.)
  interest rate le taux d'intérêt
interested: to be interested in s'intéresser à
interesting intéressant(e), 1.1
intermediate moyen(ne)
intermission l'entracte (m.), **1.1**
intern le/la stagiaire, **14.2**
to **intern** faire un stage, **14.2**
internal interne
international international(e), 8.1
Internet Internet, 3.1

H92 Handbook

English-French Dictionary

internship le stage, **14.2**
interpreter l'interprète *(m. et f.)*
to **intersect** se croiser, **10.1**
intersection le croisement, **7.2**; le carrefour, **11.1**
intimate intime
to **introduce** présenter, **13.2**
introduction la présentation, **13.2**
to **invent** inventer
invitation l'invitation *(f.)*
to **invite** inviter, **4.1**
irritable énervé(e)
to **irritate** irriter
island l'île *(f.)*, L4
Italian *(adj.)* italien(ne)
Italian *(language)* l'italien *(m.)*, 2.2
to **itch** piquer, **2.1**
Ivory Coast la Côte d'Ivoire

jacket le blouson, 7.1
  (sport) jacket la veste, 7.1
  ski jacket l'anorak *(m.)*, 7.1
jam la confiture, 6.2
January janvier *(m.)*, BV
Japanese japonais(e)
jar le pot, 6.2
jazz le jazz
jealous jaloux, jalouse
jeans le jean, 7.1; le blue-jean
jersey le maillot
Jewish juif, juive, **12.2**
job l'emploi *(m.)*, **14.2**; le poste, **14.2**
job applicant le/la candidat(e) à un poste, **14.2**
to **jog** faire du jogging
to **joke around** rigoler, 3.2
joy la joie, le bonheur
judge le/la juge, **14.1**
juice le jus, 5.1
July juillet *(m.)*, BV
June juin *(m.)*, BV

junior high student le/la collégien(ne)
just juste, 2.1
  fitting (him/her) just right juste à sa taille
  just barely tout juste

to **keep** garder
  to keep an eye on surveiller, **7.2**
  to keep in touch rester en contact
key la clé, **7.1**; le demi-cercle *(basketball)*, 10.2; *(button)* la touche, **3.1**
keyboard le clavier, **3.1**
to **keyboard** taper, **3.1**
to **kick** donner un coup de pied, 10.1
to **kid: You're kidding!** Tu rigoles!, 3.2
to **kill** tuer
kilo(gram) le kilo(gramme), 6.2
kilometer le kilomètre
kind la sorte; le genre, **1.1**
king le roi, L3
to **kiss (each other)** s'embrasser, **12.2, 13.1**
kitchen la cuisine, 4.2
  kitchen sink l'évier *(m.)*, 12.2
knee le genou, **8.1**
knife le couteau, 5.2
knight le chevalier
to **knock** frapper, L4, **L2**
to **know** connaître *(be acquainted with)*; savoir *(information)*, **1.2**

label la griffe
laboratory le laboratoire
lagoon la lagune
lake le lac

lamb l'agneau *(m.)*, 6.1
lame boiteux, boiteuse
land la terre, **11.2**
to **land** atterrir, 8.1
landing l'atterrissage *(m.)* 4.2
landing card la carte de débarquement, 8.2
landscape le paysage, **4.1**
lane la voie, **7.2**
language la langue, 2.2
lap *(race)* l'étape *(f.)*
large grand(e); ample; gros(se), **14.2**
last dernier, dernière, 10.2
  last name le nom de famille
  last night hier soir, 10.2
  last stop le terminus, **10.2**
  last week la semaine dernière, 10.2
  last year l'année *(f.)* dernière
to **last** durer
late en retard, 9.1; *(adv.)* tard, 12.1
  to be late être en retard, 9.1; avoir du retard *(plane, train, etc.)*, 8.1
  one hour late avoir une heure de retard, **4.2**
later plus tard
  See you later. À tout à l'heure., BV
Latin le latin, 2.2
  Latin American latino-américain(e)
lavender la lavande
lawyer l'avocat(e), **14.1**
lazy paresseux, paresseuse
to **lead** mener
to **lean against** s'appuyer contre, **10.2**
to **learn (to)** apprendre (à), 5
to **leave** partir, 8.1
  to leave (a room, etc.) quitter, 3.1
  to leave (something behind) laisser, 5.2
left à gauche, **7.2**
leftovers les restes *(m. pl.)*

English-French Dictionary

leg la jambe, **8.1**
  leg of lamb le gigot d'agneau, **6.2**
legend la légende
lemon le citron, **6.1**
lemonade le citron pressé, 5.1
lemon-lime drink la limonade, BV
to **lend** prêter, **5.1**
length la longueur
less moins, **7.1**
  less than moins de
lesson la leçon, **11.1**
to **let** laisser; permettre
letter la lettre, **5.2**
lettuce la salade, 6.2; la laitue
level le taux; le niveau, **7.1**
liaison la liaison
lid le couvercle, **6.2**
life la vie
  life vest le gilet de sauvetage, **4.2**
to **lift up** soulever
light (color) clair(e)
light (traffic) le feu, **7.2, 11.1**
to **light** allumer, **12.2**
like comme
to **like** aimer, 3.1
  I'd like that! Ça me dit!
  I would like je voudrais, 5.1
  What would you like? (café, restaurant) Vous désirez?, 5.1
limit la limite
line la ligne, **4.1**; (of people) la queue, 9.1
  line of cars la file de voitures, **7.2**
  main lines (trains) les grandes lignes, **4.1**
  to wait in line faire la queue, 9.1
lip la lèvre, **13.1**
liquid le liquide
to **listen (to)** écouter, 3.1
  to listen with a stethoscope ausculter, **2.2**

literature la littérature, 2.2
little: a little un peu, 2.1; un peu de
to **live** vivre, **11**; (in a city, house, etc.) habiter, 3.1
liver le foie
living vivant(e)
  living room la salle de séjour, **4.2**
to **load** charger
loan l'emprunt (m.)
lobby le hall, 8.1, **9.1**
lobster le homard, **6.2**
local local(e)
  local call l'appel urbain
located situé(e)
  to be located se trouver
to **lock** fermer à clé, **9.1**
lonely solitaire
long long(ue), 7.1
  (for) a long time longtemps, 11.1
  (for) too long trop longtemps, 11.1
  Long live...! Vive...!
longer: no longer ne... plus, 6.1
to **look** (seem) avoir l'air, **13.2**
to **look at** regarder, 3.1
to **look for** chercher
loose (clothing) large, 7.2
loose-leaf binder le classeur, 3.2
to **lose** perdre, 9.2
  to lose patience perdre patience, 9.2
lot:
  a lot of beaucoup de, 3.2
  a lot of people beaucoup de monde, 10.1
love l'amour (m.), L4
  in love amoureux, amoureuse, **L1**
to **love** aimer, 3.1; adorer
low bas(se)
lower inférieur(e)
low-income housing le/la H.L.M.
luck la chance
  to be in luck avoir de la chance

luggage les bagages (m. pl.), 8.1
lunch le déjeuner, 5.2
lung le poumon
luxurious luxueux, luxueuse
luxury (adj.) de grand standing
lyrics les paroles (f. pl.)

ma'am madame, BV
machine la machine, **10.2**; l'appareil (m.), **10.2**
magazine le magazine, L2, 9.1; la revue, L2
Maghreb le Maghreb
magnificent magnifique
maid (hotel) la femme de chambre, **9.2**
  maid of honor la demoiselle d'honneur, **12.2**
mail la poste; le courrier, **5.2**
  mail carrier le facteur, la factrice, **5.2**
to **mail** mettre à la poste, **5.2**
mailbox la boîte aux lettres, **5.2**
main principal(e)
majority la majorité
to **make** faire, 6.1; fabriquer
  to make a basket réussir un panier (basketball), 10.2
  to make its rounds circuler, **11.1**
  to make up inventer
male le mâle
mall le centre commercial, 7.1
man l'homme (m.), 7.1
to **manage** diriger, **14.1**
  to manage to arriver à, 9.1
manager le cadre, **14.1**
mandatory obligatoire
manner la façon

English-French Dictionary

good manners le savoir-vivre
manufacture la fabrication
many beaucoup de, **3.2**
map la carte
  road map la carte routière, **7.2**
  street map le plan, **7.2**
  subway map le plan du métro, **10.1**
to **march** défiler, **12.1**
March mars *(m.)*, BV
market le marché, **6.2**
  flea market le marché aux puces
marriage le mariage, **12.2**
married marié(e)
  to get married se marier, L4, **12.2**
marvelous merveilleux, merveilleuse
masculine masculin(e)
masked masqué(e), **12.1**
mass transit les transports *(m. pl.)* en commun
math les maths *(f. pl.)*, **2.2**
mathematics les mathématiques *(f. pl.)*, **2.2**
matter: What's the matter with you? Qu'est-ce que tu as?, **10**
May mai *(m.)*, BV
maybe peut-être
mayor le maire, **12.1**
meadow le pré, **11.2**
meal le repas, **5.2**
to **mean** signifier
meaning la signification; le sens
means le mode
to **measure** mesurer
measurement la mesure
meat la viande, **6.1**, **6.2**
medical médical(e), **2.1**
  the medical profession le corps médical
medicine *(medical profession)* la médecine; *(remedy)* le médicament, **2.1**
medina la médina

Mediterranean Sea la mer Méditerranée
medium-rare *(meat)* à point, **5.2**
to **meet** rencontrer; retrouver *(get together with)*; faire la connaissance de, **13.2**; connaître, **13.2**; venir chercher (quelqu'un), **4.2**
melody l'air *(m.)*
melon le melon, **6.2**
member le membre
membership card la carte d'adhésion
memory le souvenir; la mémoire
menorah la menorah, **12.2**
to **mention** citer; mentionner
menu la carte, **5.1**
merchandise la marchandise
merchant le/la marchand(e), **6.2**
  produce merchant le/la marchand(e) de fruits et légumes, **6.2**
message le message, **3.1**
messenger le messager, la messagère
metal le métal
meter le mètre
metric system le système métrique
microbe le microbe
microchip la micropuce
microprocessor le microprocesseur
microscope le microscope
microwave oven le four à micro-ondes, **6.1**
middle le milieu
  middle school student le/la collégien(ne)
midnight minuit *(m.)*, BV
  midnight mass la messe de minuit, **12.2**
military militaire
milk le lait, **6.1**
mineral le minéral
mineral water l'eau *(f.)* minérale, **6.2**

minus moins
minute la minute, **9.2**
miracle le miracle
mirror la glace, **12.1**
Miss (Ms.) Mademoiselle (Mlle), BV
to **miss** *(train, etc.)* rater, **9.2**
mistake la faute
mixture le mélange
mobile phone le portable, **3.2**
model le modèle
modem le modem
modern moderne
modest modeste
mogul la bosse, **11.2**
mom la maman
moment le moment; l'instant *(m.)*
Monday lundi *(m.)*, BV
money l'argent *(m.)*, **5.2**; le fric *(slang)*, **5.1**
  to have a lot of money avoir plein d'argent *(slang)*, **5.1**
  money order le mandat
  pocket money l'argent *(m.)* de poche
monitor *(computer)* le moniteur
monster le monstre
month le mois, BV
monthly mensuel(le)
  monthly payment la traite
monument le monument
more *(comparative)* plus, **7.1**
  more or less plus ou moins
  more and more de plus en plus
  more ... than plus... que, **7**
  no more ne... plus, **6.1**
morning le matin, BV; le mat *(fam.)*
  in the morning le matin
Moroccan marocain(e)
Morocco le Maroc
mortgage l'hypothèque *(f.)*
Moslem musulman(e)

English-French Dictionary

mosque la mosquée
most (of) la plupart (des), **9.2**
mother la mère, **4.1**
motorcycle la moto, **7.1**
　lightweight motorcycle le vélomoteur, **7.1**
　motorcycle cop le motard, **7.2**
mountain le mont; la montagne, **11.2**
mountaintop le sommet, **11.2**
mouse la souris, **3.1**
mouth la bouche, **2.1, 13.1**
movement le mouvement
movie le film, **1.1**
　detective movie le film policier, **1.1**
　movies le cinéma, **1.1**
　movie theater le cinéma, la salle de cinéma, **1.1**
　movie video le film en vidéo, **1.1**
　science-fiction movie le film de science-fiction, **1.1**
Mr. Monsieur (M.), BV
Mrs. (Ms.) Madame (Mme), BV
multicolored multicolore
multinational corporation la multinationale, **14.2**
to **multiply** multiplier
municipal municipal(e)
muscle le muscle
muscular musculaire
museum le musée, **1.2**
mushroom le champignon, **6.1**
music la musique, **2.2**
musical comedy la comédie musicale, **1.1**
musician le/la musicien(ne)
mussel la moule, **6.2**
must devoir, **10.2**
　one must il faut, **8.2**
mustard la moutarde, **6.2**
myself moi-même
mysterious mystérieux, mystérieuse

mystery (novel) le roman policier
myth le mythe

name le nom
　first name le prénom
　last name le nom de famille
　My name is . . . Je m'appelle… , BV
napkin la serviette, **5.2, 13.1**
nationality la nationalité
native of originaire de
natural naturel(le)
　natural sciences les sciences naturelles (f. pl.), **2.1**
nature la nature
navy blue bleu marine (inv.), **7.2**
near près de, **4.2**
　very near tout près, **4.2**
necessarily nécessairement; forcément
necessary nécessaire
　it is necessary il faut, **8.2**; il faut que, **12.2**; il est nécessaire que, **13**
need le besoin
to **need** avoir besoin de, **10.1**
neighbor le/la voisin(e), **4.2**
neighborhood le quartier, **4.2, 11.1**; (adj.) du coin
nephew le neveu, **4.1**
nervous nerveux, nerveuse
net le filet, **10.2**
network le réseau
never ne… jamais, **11.2**
new nouveau (nouvel), nouvelle, **4.2**
　New England la Nouvelle-Angleterre
　New Orleans la Nouvelle-Orléans
　New Year's Day le jour de l'An, **12.2**

New Year's Eve dinner le réveillon, **12.2**
news les nouvelles (f. pl.), **L3**
　news article le reportage
　TV news les informations (f. pl.); le journal télévisé, **6.1**
newspaper le journal, **9.1**
newsstand le kiosque, **9.1**
next prochain(e), **9.2**
　next to à côté de, **11.1**
nice (person) sympa, **1.2**; aimable; sympathique; gentil(le), **6.2**
niece la nièce, **4.1**
night la nuit
　last night hier soir, **10.2**
no non; aucun(e), **4.2**
　no longer ne… plus, **6.1**
　no more ne… plus, **6.1**
　no one ne… personne, **11**; personne ne… , **5**
　no smoking (section) (la zone) non-fumeurs, **8.1**
nobody ne… personne, **11**; personne ne… , **5**
noise le bruit, **L3, 13.1**
noisy bruyant(e), **13.1**
non-smoking (section) non-fumeurs, **8.1**
nonstop (flight) sans escale, **4.2**
noon midi (m.), BV
north le nord
North African nord-africain(e), maghrébin(e)
nose le nez, **2.1**
　to have a runny nose avoir le nez qui coule, **2.1**
not any aucun(e), **4.2**
not at all pas du tout, **3.1**
not bad pas mal, BV
note la note
notebook le cahier, **3.2**
notepad le bloc-notes, **3.2**
nothing ne… rien, **11**; rien ne… , **5**

English-French Dictionary

nothing to do with rien à voir avec
to **notice** remarquer
novel le roman, **L1**
novelist le romancier, la romancière, **L1**
November novembre (m.), BV
now maintenant, 2.2
  right now en ce moment
nowadays de nos jours; actuellement
number le nombre; le numéro, **5.2**
  right number le bon numéro, **3.2**
  telephone number le numéro de téléphone
  wrong number l'erreur (f.); le mauvais numéro, **3.2**
numbered numéroté(e)
numerous nombreux, nombreuse
nurse l'infirmier, l'infirmière, **8.1**

object l'objet (m.)
to **oblige** obliger
oboe le hautbois
to **observe** observer
obsession l'idée (f.) fixe
to **obtain** obtenir; se procurer
obvious évident(e), **14**
occupied occupé(e)
to **occupy** occuper
ocean l'océan (m.)
o'clock: It's ... o'clock. Il est... heure(s)., BV
October octobre (m.), BV
odd curieux, curieuse
of (belonging to) de, 1.2
  of course bien sûr
  Of course (not)! Mais oui (non)!
to **offer** offrir
office le bureau, **11.1, 14.1**
official officiel(le)

often souvent, 5.2
oil l'huile (f.), **6.1**; le pétrole
  oil tanker le pétrolier
okay (health) Ça va.; (agreement) d'accord, BV
  Okay! Bon!, **6.1**
old vieux (vieil), vieille, 4.2; âgé(e); ancien(ne)
  How old are you? Tu as quel âge? (fam.), 4.1
older (child) l'aîné(e), L1
olive oil l'huile (f.) d'olive, **6.1**
omelette (with herbs/plain) l'omelette (f.) (aux fines herbes/nature), 5.1
on sur, 4.2
  on board à bord de, 8.2
  on foot à pied, 4.2
  on sale en solde, 7.1
  on time à l'heure, 8.1
  on Tuesdays le mardi, **1.2**
one by one un(e) à un(e)
oneself soi
one-way street la rue à sens unique, **11.1**
one-way ticket l'aller simple (m.), 9.1
onion l'oignon (m.), 5.1, **6.1**
only seulement; uniquement; (adj.) seul(e)
open ouvert(e), **1.2**
to **open** ouvrir, **2.2, 13.2**
opera l'opéra (m.)
  comic light opera l'opéra bouffe
  light opera l'opéra comique
to **operate** opérer
operating room la salle d'opération, **8.2**
operation l'opération (f.); l'intervention (f.) chirurgicale
opinion l'avis (m.), 7.2
  in my opinion à mon avis, 7.2
opponent l'adversaire (m. et f.)
  opponents le camp adverse, 10.1

opportunity l'occasion (f.)
to **oppose** opposer, 10.1
opposing adverse, 10.1
opposite le contraire
optional facultatif, facultative
or ou, 1.1
  or else sinon, 9.2
orange (fruit) l'orange (f.), 6.2, **6.1**; (color) orange (inv.), 7.2
  orange tree l'oranger (m.), L2
orchestra l'orchestre (m.)
  symphony orchestra l'orchestre symphonique
order: in order to pour
to **order** commander, 5.1
ordinary ordinaire
organ (of the body) l'organe (m.); (musical instrument) l'orgue (m.)
to **organize** organiser
orthopedic surgeon le chirurgien-orthopédiste, **8.2**
other autre
  in other words autrement dit
  on the other hand par contre; d'autre part
  some others d'autres, 2.2
otherwise sinon, 9.2
outdoors en plein air; dehors
outfit l'ensemble (m.)
outgoing sociable, 1.2
outing l'excursion (f.)
outside (n.) l'extérieur (m.); (adv.) à l'extérieur, dehors; (prep.) au dehors de
  to work outside the home travailler à l'extérieur
outskirts la périphérie
oven le four, **6.1**
  microwave oven le four à micro-ondes, **6.1**
over (prep.) par-dessus, 10.2
  over there là-bas, **10.1**
to **overlook** donner sur, 4.2; dominer

English-French Dictionary

overseas *(adj.)* d'outre-mer
to **owe** devoir, 10
to **own** posséder
owner le/la propriétaire
ox le bœuf, 11.2
oxygen l'oxygène *(m.)*
  oxygen mask le masque à oxygène, 4.2
oyster l'huître *(f.)*, 6.2

to **pack** *(suitcases)* faire les valises, 8.1
package le paquet, 6.2; le colis, 5.2
packed *(stadium)* comble, 10.1; *(train)* bondé(e), 10.1
pain in the neck *(slang)* casse-pieds
painful douloureux, douloureuse
to **paint** peindre
painter l'artiste peintre *(m. et f.)*, le/la peintre, 1.2
  house painter le peintre en bâtiment, 14.1
painting la peinture, 1.2; le tableau, 1.2
pair la paire, 7.1
pal le copain, la copine, 2.1
palace le palais
palm tree le palmier
pancake la crêpe, BV
pants le pantalon, 7.1
paper le papier, 3.2
  sheet of paper la feuille de papier, 3.2
parade le défilé, 12.1
paragraph le paragraphe
parents les parents *(m. pl.)*, 4.1
Parisian *(adj.)* parisien(ne)
park le parc
to **park** se garer, 7.1; stationner, 11.1
parking lot le parking, 11.1
parking meter le parcmètre, 11.1
parsley le persil, 6.1

part la partie
  to be part of faire partie de
to **participate (in)** participer (à)
party la fête, 4.1
  to throw a party donner une fête, 4.1
pass la passe
to **pass** passer, 10.1; doubler, 7.2
  to pass an exam réussir à un examen
passage le passage
passageway le passage
passbook *(bank)* le livret de caisse d'épargne
passenger le passager, la passagère, 8.1
passport le passeport, 8.1
  passport check le contrôle des passeports, 4.2
past passé(e)
pasta les pâtes *(f. pl.)*, 6.1
pasture le pâturage
pâté le pâté
patience la patience, 9.2
  to lose patience perdre patience, 9.2
patient le/la malade, 2.2; *(adj.)* patient(e), 1.1
patio la terrasse, 4.2
to **pay** payer, 3.2
  to pay attention faire attention
  to pay back rembourser
  to pay cash payer en espèces, 9.2
  to pay a deposit verser des arrhes, 9.1
payment le paiement
peace la paix
pear la poire, 6.2
peas les petits pois *(m. pl.)*, 6.2
peasant le/la paysan(ne), L1
pedestrian le piéton, la piétonne, 11.1
to **peel** éplucher, 6.2
pen: ballpoint pen le stylo-bille, 3.2

felt-tip pen le feutre, 3.2
penalty *(soccer)* le penalty
pencil le crayon, 3.2
penicillin la pénicilline, 2.1
people les gens *(m. pl.)*
pepper le poivre, 6.1
percent pour cent
perfect parfait(e)
to **perfect** perfectionner
perfectly parfaitement
to **perform** jouer, 1.1
perhaps peut-être
period l'époque *(f.)*; la période; le point
to **permit** permettre
person la personne
personal personnel(le)
personality la personnalité
personally personnellement, 1.2
pharmacist le/la pharmacien(ne), 2.2
pharmacy la pharmacie, 2.2
phenomenon le phénomène
phone card la télécarte, 3.2
photograph la photo
physical physique
physicist le/la physicien(ne)
physics la physique, 2.2
to **pick up** ramasser, 8.2; recueillir; venir chercher (quelqu'un), 4.2
  to pick up the (telephone) receiver décrocher (le téléphone), 3.2
pickup truck le pick-up
picnic le pique-nique
picturesque pittoresque
pie la tarte, 6.1
piece le morceau, 6.2
pig le cochon, 11.2
pill le comprimé, 2.2
pillow l'oreiller *(m.)*, 4.2
pilot le/la pilote, 8.2
pink rose, 7.1
pizza la pizza, BV
place l'endroit *(m.)*; la place, le lieu

H98 Handbook

English-French Dictionary

to take place avoir lieu, **12.1**
to **place** mettre, 7.1
plain la plaine
plan le projet
plane l'avion *(m.)*, 8.1, **L3**
  by plane en avion
plant la plante
plastic le plastique
plate l'assiette *(f.)*, 5.2
platform *(railroad)* le quai, 9.1, **10.1**
play la pièce (de théâtre), **1.1**
  to put on a play monter une pièce, **1.1**
to **play** jouer, 3.2
  to play *(a sport)* jouer à, 10.1; *(an instrument)* jouer de, **12.1**
player le joueur, la joueuse, 10.1
playwright l'auteur *(m.)* dramatique
pleasant agréable
please s'il vous plaît *(form.)*, s'il te plaît *(fam.)*, BV
pleasure le plaisir
pleated plissé(e), 7.1
plot l'argument *(m.)*
plumber le plombier, **14.1**
plus plus
p.m. de l'après-midi; du soir, BV
pocket money l'argent *(m.)* de poche
poem le poème
poet *(m. and f.)* le poète
police la police
  police officer l'agent *(m.)* de police, **11.1**
polite poli(e), **13.1**
politely poliment
politeness la politesse, BV
political politique
polluted pollué(e)
pollution la pollution
polo shirt le polo, 7.1
pool la piscine, 11.1
poor pauvre, L1, **2.1**
pop *(music)* pop

popular populaire, 1.2
pork le porc, 6.1, **6.2**
  pork chop la côtelette de porc, **6.2**
port le port
Portuguese portugais(e)
position la position
to **possess** posséder
possession la possession
possibility la possibilité
possible possible
post office la poste, 5.2; le bureau de poste, **5.2**
postal postal(e)
  postal employee l'employé(e) des postes, **5.2**
postcard la carte postale, 9.1, **5.2**
poster l'affiche *(f.)*
pot la casserole, **6.2**
potato la pomme de terre, 6.2, **6.1**
pound la livre, 6.2
practical pratique
to **practice** pratiquer; travailler
to **prefer** préférer, 6
prehistoric préhistorique
to **prepare** préparer
to **prescribe** prescrire, **2.2**
prescription l'ordonnance *(f.)*, **2.2**
  to write a prescription faire une ordonnance, **2.2**
present le cadeau, 4.1
to **present** présenter
to **press** appuyer sur, **3.1**
pressure la pression, **7.1**
prestigious prestigieux, prestigieuse
pretty joli(e), 4.2
price le prix, 7.1
priest l'abbé *(m.)*
principal principal(e)
to **print** imprimer
printer l'imprimante *(f.)*, **3.1**
prison la prison, L4

prisoner le prisonnier, la prisonnière, L4
private individuel(le); privé(e)
problem le problème; la difficulté
product le produit
profession la profession
professional professionnel(le)
program le programme; *(TV)* l'émission *(f.)*, 12.2; *(computer)* le logiciel
programming la programmation
progress le progrès
promise la promesse
promotion l'avancement *(m.)*
to **pronounce** prononcer
property la propriété
protein la protéine
proud fier, fière
public public, publique
to **publish** publier
pulse le pouls, 8.2
to **punish** punir
purchase l'achat *(m.)*
to **push** pousser, 10.2; *(button, etc.)* appuyer sur, **3.1**
  to push and shove bousculer, 13.1
to **put (on)** mettre, 7.1
  to put on makeup se maquiller, 12.1
  to put on a play monter une pièce, **1.1**

quality la qualité
to **quarrel** se fâcher
Quebec: from or of Quebec québécois
queen la reine
question la question, 3.1
  to ask a question poser une question, 3.1
quick rapide
quickly rapidement

English-French Dictionary

quite assez, 1.1
quiz l'interro(gation) (f.)

rabbit le lapin, **11.2**
race (human population) la race; (competition) la course, 10.2
  bicycle race la course cycliste, 10.2
radio la radio, 3.2
railroad le chemin de fer
rain la pluie
to rain: It's raining. Il pleut., 11.1
to raise lever
  to raise one's hand lever la main, 3.1
raisin le raisin sec
rap (music) le rap
rapidly rapidement
rare (meat) saignant(e), 5.2; rare
rather plutôt
razor le rasoir, 12.1
to read lire, 9.2
reading la lecture
ready prêt(e)
real vrai(e), 2.2; véritable
reality la réalité
really vraiment, 1.1
rear l'arrière (m.), 8.2, **10.2**
  rear guard l'arrière-garde (f.)
reason la raison
to reassure rassurer
to receive recevoir, 10.2
recently récemment
recess la récré(ation), 3.2
recipe la recette, **6.1**
to recognize reconnaître
to recommend recommander
recycling le recyclage
red rouge, 7.1
referee l'arbitre (m.), 10.1
refrigerator le frigidaire, 12.2; le réfrigérateur, 12.2, **6.1**; le frigo (slang), **6.1**

region la région
registration card la fiche, **9.1**
  police registration card la fiche de police, **9.1**
regular régulier, régulière
to reimburse rembourser
religious religieux, religieuse, **12.2**
to remain rester, 11.1
remains les vestiges (m. pl.)
to remember se rappeler
remote éloigné(e)
  remote control la télécommande, 12.2
to renovate rénover
renowned renommé(e)
to rent louer, 1.1
to repair réparer
to replace remplacer
reporter le/la journaliste, **14.1**
to represent représenter
research la recherche
to resemble ressembler à
to reserve réserver, **9.1**
respective respectif, respective
respiratory respiratoire
responsible responsable
restaurant le restaurant, 5.2; le resto (inform.)
result le résultat
  as a result par conséquent
résumé le curriculum vitae (C.V.), **14.2**
return le retour
to return rentrer, 3.2; (volleyball) renvoyer, 10.2
reunited réuni(e)
revolution la révolution
revolutionary révolutionnaire
rhyme la rime
rhythm le rythme
rice le riz
rich riche
ridiculous ridicule
right le droit; (adv.) à droite, **11.1**
  right away tout de suite

right there juste là
to ring (telephone) sonner, **3.2**
ringing la sonnerie
to rinse rincer
river le fleuve; la rivière, **L2**
Riviera (French) la Côte d'Azur
road la route, **7.2**; le chemin
  road map la carte (routière), **7.2**
  road sign le panneau, **7.2**
roast beef le rôti de bœuf, **6.2**
rock le rocher, **L3**; (music) le rock
role le rôle
roll of toilet paper le rouleau de papier hygiénique, **9.2**
Roman romain(e)
romantic romantique
roof le toit
  thatched roof le toit de chaume
room (in house) la pièce, 4.2; la salle; (in hotel) la chambre, **9.1**
  dining room la salle à manger, 4.2
  living room la salle de séjour, 4.2
rooster le coq
rosemary le romarin
round rond(e)
  round (piece) la rondelle, **6.2**
round-trip ticket le billet aller-retour, 9.1
route le chemin
routine la routine, 12.1
row le rang, **12.1**
royal royal(e)
ruin la ruine
to ruin ruiner
rule la règle
  rules of the road le code de la route, **11.1**
ruler la règle, 3.2
to run a red light brûler un feu rouge, **7.2**
runner le coureur, 10.2

English-French Dictionary

running shoe la basket, 7.1
runway la piste, 8.1
rural rural(e)
rush hour les heures (f.) de pointe, **10.1**
Russian (language) le russe

sad triste, L1, **13.2**
sailor le marin, L4
salad la salade, 5.1
salami le saucisson, 6.1
salary le salaire, **14.2**
sale: on sale en solde, 7.1; en promotion
salesperson le vendeur, la vendeuse, 7.1
salmon le saumon, **6.2**
salt le sel, 6.1
same même, 2.1
  all the same tout de même, 5.2
  It's all the same to me. Ça m'est égal., **1.1**
  the same goes for me moi de même, **13.2**
sand le sable
sandals les sandales (f. pl.), 7.1
sandwich le sandwich, BV
Santa Claus le Père Noël, **12.2**
sardine la sardine
to **satisfy** satisfaire
Saturday samedi (m.), BV
sauce la sauce, **6.2**
sauerkraut la choucroute, **6.1**
sausage la saucisse, **6.1**
to **save** sauver; sauvegarder, **3.1**; (money) faire des économies, **5.1**; économiser; mettre de côté, **5.1**
saxophone le saxophone
to **say** dire, 9.2
scale la balance, 5.2
scarf l'écharpe (f.), 11.2
scene la scène, **1.1**

schedule l'emploi (m.) du temps; l'horaire (m.), 9.1
school l'école (f.), 1.2; (adj.) scolaire, 3.2
  elementary school l'école primaire
  high school le lycée, 2.1
  junior high/high school l'école secondaire, 1.2
  junior high/middle school le collège, 1.2
  school supplies les fournitures scolaires, 3.2
schooling la scolarité
science les sciences (f. pl.), 2.1
  natural sciences les sciences naturelles, 2.1
  social sciences les sciences sociales, 2.1
scientific scientifique
scientist le savant (m. et f.)
to **score a goal** marquer un but, 10.1
to **scratch** gratter, **2.1**
screen l'écran (m.), 8.1, **3.1**
sculptor le sculpteur (m. et f.), **1.2**
sculpture la sculpture, **1.2**
sea la mer, 11.1
  by the sea au bord de la mer, 11.1
seafood les fruits de mer, **6.2**
seashore le bord de la mer, 11.1
seaside resort la station balnéaire, 11.1
season la saison
seat le siège, 8.2; la place (plane, train, movie, etc.), 8.1
  seat back le dossier du siège, **4.2**
  seat belt la ceinture de sécurité, 8.2, **7.1**
seated assis(e), 9.2
second (adj.) deuxième, 4.2; second(e)
  in second class en seconde, 9.1
secret (adj.) secret, secrète; (noun) le secret

secretary le/la secrétaire, **14.1, L3**
security (airport) le contrôle de sécurité, 8.1
to **see** voir, 7.1
  See you later. À tout à l'heure., BV
  See you soon! À bientôt!, BV
  See you tomorrow. À demain., BV
seldom très peu
self-employed: to be self-employed être à son compte, **14.2**
to **sell** vendre, 9.1
to **send** envoyer, 10.1, **3.1**; emmener, L4
sender l'expéditeur, l'expéditrice
separate séparer
September septembre (m.), BV
serious sérieux, sérieuse, 7; grave, **3.2**
to **serve** servir, 8.2; 10.2; (go to) desservir, **4.1**
service le service, 5.2
serving dish le plat, **6.1**
to **set** régler, L1
  to set a bone remettre un os en place, **8.2**
  to set the table mettre la table, 7; mettre le couvert
to **settle** s'installer
several plusieurs
to **shake hands** se serrer la main, **13.1**
Shall we go? On y va?
shampoo le shampooing, 12.1
shape la forme
to **share** partager, **13.1**
to **shave** se raser, 12.1
shaver le rasoir, 12.1
shed le hangar, **11.2**
sheep le mouton, **11.2**
sheet le drap, 9.2
  sheet of paper la feuille de papier, 3.2
shepherd le berger
to **shine** briller
shirt la chemise, 7.1

English-French Dictionary

shoe la chaussure, 7.1; le soulier, **12.2**
to **shoot** (ball) lancer, 10.2
shop la boutique, 7.1
to **shop** faire des achats
shopkeeper le/la commerçant(e), **14.1**
shopping le shopping, 7.2
  to do the grocery shopping faire les courses, 6.1
  to go shopping faire des courses, 7.2
  shopping cart le chariot, 6.2
  shopping center le centre commercial, 7.1
short petit(e), 1.1; court(e), 7.1
  in a short time en très peu de temps
  short story la nouvelle
shorts le short, 7.1
to **shout** crier, L4
show (TV) l'émission (f.), 12.2
show(ing) (movies) la séance, **1.1**
to **show** montrer; (movie) jouer
shower la douche, 12.1
  to take a shower prendre une douche, 12.1
shrimp la crevette, 6.1
shy timide, 1.2
sick malade, **2.1**, L1
  to get sick tomber malade, L1
  sick person le/la malade, **2.2**
side le côté, **4.1**; (in a sporting event) le camp, 10.1
sidewalk le trottoir, **11.1**
  sidewalk café la terrasse (d'un café), 5.1
sign le signal; la marque, L4
to **sign** signer
signal le signal
similar semblable, L1
simply simplement

since (time) depuis, 9.2, **10.2**
to **sing** chanter, **1.2**
  singer le chanteur, la chanteuse, **1.1**
single unique; seul(e)
sink (kitchen) l'évier (m.), 12.2; (bathroom) le lavabo
sinus infection la sinusite, **2.2**
sir monsieur, BV
sister la sœur, 1.2
to **sit: Where would you like to sit?** Qu'est-ce que vous voulez comme place?, 8.1
site le site
size (clothes) la taille; (shoes) la pointure, 7.2
  the next larger size la taille au-dessus, 7.2
  the next smaller size la taille au-dessous, 7.2
  to wear size (number) faire du (nombre), 7.2
  What size do you wear? Vous faites quelle taille (pointure)?, 7.2
skate le patin, 11.2
to **skate** (ice) faire du patin (à glace), 11.1
  to go skating faire du patin, 11.1
  skating rink la patinoire, 11.2
skeleton le squelette
ski le ski, 11.2
  ski boot la chaussure de ski, 11.2
  ski cap le bonnet, 11.2
  ski jacket l'anorak (m.), 7.1
  ski pole le bâton, 11.2
  ski resort la station de sports d'hiver, 11.2
  ski trail la piste, 11.2
to **ski** faire du ski, 11.2
  skier le skieur, la skieuse, 11.2
  skiing le ski, 11.2
  cross-country skiing le ski de fond, 11.2

  downhill skiing le ski alpin, 11.2
skirt la jupe, 7.1
skull la boîte crânienne
sky le ciel, 11.1
to **sleep** dormir, 8.2
  sleeping car le wagon-couchette
sleeve la manche, 7.1
  long-(short-)sleeved à manches longues (courtes), 7.1
slice la tranche, 6.2
  slice of bread with butter or jam la tartine
to **slip** glisser, **8.1**
slope la pente
slot le fente, **3.2**
to **slow down** ralentir, **7.1**
small petit(e), 1.1
smoke la fumée
to **smoke** fumer, **4.2**
snack la collation, **4.2**
  snack bar (train) le snack-bar, 9.2
sneaker la basket, 7.1
to **sneeze** éternuer, **2.1**
snow la neige, 11.2
to **snow: It's snowing.** Il neige., 11.2
snowman le bonhomme de neige
so alors, BV; donc; si (adv.)
soap le savon, 12.1, **9.2**
soccer le foot(ball), 10.1
  soccer field le terrain de football, 10.1
sociable sociable, 1.2
social social(e)
  social blunder le faux pas
  social sciences les sciences sociales (f. pl.), 2.1
  social worker l'assistant(e) social(e), **14.1**
sock la chaussette, 7.1
software le software, **3.1**; le logiciel, **3.1**
soldier le soldat, L3, **12.1**
sole le sole, **6.2**
solely uniquement
solid solide

English-French Dictionary

solution la solution
some quelques, **9.2**; certains
  some other d'autres, **2.2**
somebody quelqu'un, **10.1**
someone quelqu'un, **10.1**
  someone else quelqu'un d'autre, **L3**
something quelque chose, **11**
  something else autre chose
  something special quelque chose de spécial
sometimes quelquefois, **5.2**
somewhere quelque part
son le fils, **4.1**
song la chanson
soon bientôt
  See you soon. À bientôt., **BV**
sore throat: to have a sore throat avoir mal à la gorge, **2.1**
sorry désolé(e), **3.2, 13.2**
  to be sorry regretter, **6.1, 13.2**
  I'm sorry. Désolé(e)., **3.2**
so-so comme ci, comme ça
sound le son, **L3**
soup la soupe, **5.1**
source la source
south le sud
South America l'Amérique (f.) du Sud
south-east le sud-est
space l'espace (m.)
  open spaces les grands espaces
spaghetti les spaghettis (m. pl.)
Spanish espagnol(e)
Spanish (language) l'espagnol (m.), **2.2**
spare tire la roue de secours, **7.1**
to **sparkle** scintiller
to **speak** parler, **3.1**
  to speak to s'adresser à
special spécial(e)
specialty la spécialité

specific précis(e)
spectator le spectateur, la spectatrice, **10.1**
speech le discours
speed la vitesse, **4.1**
  speed limit la limitation de vitesse, **7.2**
to **spell** épeler
to **spend** (time) passer, **3.1**; (money) dépenser, **5.1**
spice l'épice (f.)
spicy épicé(e)
to **spill** déverser
spinach les épinards (m. pl.), **6.2**
spinal cord la moelle épinière
spirit l'esprit (m.)
splendid splendide, **4.1**
to **spoil** gâter
spoon la cuillère, **5.2**
sport le sport, **10.2**
  sports car la voiture de sport, **7.1**
  team sport le sport collectif; le sport d'équipe, **10.2**
to **sprain one's ankle** se fouler la cheville, **8.1**
spring (season) le printemps, **11.1**; (water) la source
square la place
stable l'étable (f.), **11.2**
stadium le stade, **10.1**
stage (of a race) l'étape (f.)
staircase l'escalier (m.), **4.2**
stall (market) l'étal (m.)
stamp le timbre **5.2**
  stamp machine le distributeur automatique (de timbres), **5.2**
to **stamp (a ticket)** composter, **9.1**
stand l'étal (m.)
standing debout, **9.2**
to **stare at** regarder fixement
to **start** commencer, **9.2**
  to start the car mettre le contact, **7.1**
state l'état (m.)

state of the art haut de gamme
statement (bank) le relevé
station la station, **4.2, 10.1**
  gas station la station-service, **7.1**
  station wagon le break, **7.1**
  subway station la station de métro, **4.2**
  stationery store la papeterie, **3.2**
statue la statue, **1.2**
stay le séjour, **9.1**
to **stay** rester, **11.1**
steak and French fries le steak frites, **5.2**
step le pas, **L2**
  to take a step faire un pas, **L2**
to **step in** intervenir
stepfather le beau-père, **4.1**
stepmother la belle-mère, **4.1**
still toujours, **10.2**; encore, **11**
to **stir** remuer, **6.2**
stitch le point de suture, **8.2**
stomach le ventre, **2.1**
stone la pierre
stop l'arrêt (m.), **9.2, 10.2**
  bus stop l'arrêt d'autobus, **10.2**
to **stop** s'arrêter, **10.1**; cesser; (plane) faire escale, **4.2**
stopover l'escale (f.), **4.2**
store le magasin, **3.2, 14.1**
  department store le grand magasin, **7.1**
to **store** stocker; emmagasiner; entreposer, **11.2**; mettre en réserve
story l'histoire (f.)
  short story la nouvelle
stove la cuisinière, **6.1**
straight ahead tout droit, **7.2**
strategy la stratégie
strawberry la fraise, **6.2**
streamer le serpentin, **12.1**

English-French Dictionary

street la rue, 3.1, **5.2**, **11.1**
  one-way street la rue à sens unique, **11.1**
  street map le plan, **7.2**
strength la force
to **stretch out** allonger
stretcher le brancard, **8.1**
strict strict(e), 2.1
strong fort(e), 2.2
student l'élève (m. et f.), 1.2; (university) l'étudiant(e)
studio (apartment) le studio
studio (artist's) l'atelier (m.)
study l'étude (f.)
to **study** étudier, 3.1; faire des études
  to study French (math, etc.) faire du français (des maths, etc.), 6
stuffing la farce
stupid stupide
  stupid thing la bêtise
style le look
  in style à la mode
subject le sujet; (in school) la matière, 2.2
  on the subject of à propos de
subtitles les sous-titres (m. pl.), **1.1**
to **subtract** soustraire
suburbs la banlieue, **4.1**, **11.1**
subway le métro, 4.2, **10.1**
  subway map le plan du métro, **10.1**
  subway station la station de métro, 4.2, **10.1**
to **succeed in (doing)** arriver à (+ inf.), 9.1
success le succès
suddenly soudain
to **suffer** souffrir, **2.2**
sugar le sucre
to **suggest** proposer; suggérer
suit (men's) le complet; (women's) le tailleur, 7.1
suitcase la valise, 8.1

sum la somme
summer l'été (m.)
  in summer en été, 11.1
summit le sommet, 11.2
sun le soleil, 11.1
to **sunbathe** prendre un bain de soleil, 11.1
sunburn le coup de soleil, 11.1
Sunday dimanche (m.), BV
sunglasses les lunettes (f. pl.) de soleil, 11.1
sunny: It's sunny. Il fait du soleil., 11.1
suntan lotion la crème solaire, 11.1
super super
superbe superbe
supermarket le supermarché, 6.2
supply la fourniture
  school supplies les fournitures scolaires, 3.2
sure sûr(e)
to **surf the Net** naviguer sur Internet
surfer le surfeur, la surfeuse, 11.1
surfing le surf, 11.1
  to go surfing faire du surf, 11.1
surgeon le chirurgien, 8.2
  orthopedic surgeon le chirurgien-orthopédiste, 8.2
surprise la surprise
to **surprise** étonner
surprised étonné(e), 13.2
survey le sondage, l'enquête (f.)
survival la survie
to **swallow** avaler, 2.2
sweater le pull, 7.1
sweatshirt le sweat-shirt, 7.1
sweet potato la patate douce
to **swim** nager, 11.1
  swimmer le nageur, la nageuse
swimming la natation, 11.1

sword l'épée (f.), L3
symphony la symphonie
symptom le symptôme
syrup le sirop, **2.1**
system le système

table la table, 5.1
  table setting le couvert, 5.2
tablecloth la nappe, 5.2
to **tailgate** suivre une voiture de trop près, **11.1**
to **take** prendre, 5.2; (someone somewhere) emmener, **8.1**
  to take care of s'occuper de; soigner, **8.1**, **L4**; prendre soin de, **L4**
  to take down descendre, 9
  to take an exam passer un examen, 3.1
  to take the... line (subway) prendre la direction…, **10.1**
  to take off (airplane) décoller, 8.1
  to take out retirer, **3.1**
  to take place avoir lieu, **12.1**
  to take possession of prendre possession de
  to take size (number) faire du (nombre), 7.2
  to take the subway prendre le métro, 5.2
  to take a trip faire un voyage, 8.1
  to take up occuper
  to take (something) upstairs monter, **9.1**
  to take a walk faire une promenade, 11.1
  What size do you take? Vous faites quelle taille (pointure)?, 7.2
taken occupé(e)

English-French Dictionary

takeoff *(plane)* le décollage, **4.2**
to **talk** parler, 3.1
   to talk on the phone parler au téléphone, 3.2, **L3**
tall grand(e), 1.1
to **tan** bronzer, 11.1
tape la cassette, 7.1
to **tape** enregistrer
tart la tarte, 6.1
   apple tart la tarte aux pommes, 6.1
taste le goût
tea le thé
to **teach (someone to do something)** apprendre (à quelqu'un à faire quelque chose)
teacher le/la prof *(inform.)*, 2.1; le professeur, 2.1
   elementary school teacher le maître, la maîtresse
team l'équipe *(f.)*, 10.1
teammate le coéquipier, la coéquipière, 10.1
tear la larme, **L2**
techno (music) la techno
technology la technologie
teenager l'adolescent(e)
telephone le téléphone, 3.2, 3.1; *(adj.)* téléphonique, **3.2**
   telephone booth la cabine téléphonique, **3.2**
   telephone call l'appel (téléphonique), **3.2**; le coup de téléphone
   telephone card la télécarte, **3.2**
   telephone directory l'annuaire *(m.)*, **3.2**
   telephone number le numéro de téléphone
   touch-tone telephone le téléphone à touches, **3.2**
television (TV) la télé, 12.2
to **tell** dire, 9.2
   to tell (about) raconter
temperate tempéré(e)
temperature la température

temple la tempe
temporary temporaire
tendon le tendon
term le terme
terrace la terrasse, 4.2
terrible terrible
terrific super; terrible
test l'examen *(m.)*, 3.1
   to pass a test réussir à un examen
   to take a test passer un examen, 3.1
text le texte, **3.1**
Thai thaïlandais(e)
thank you merci, BV
thanks merci, BV
   thanks to grâce à
that ça; ce (cet), cette; cela
   that is (to say) c'est-à-dire
   that one celui-là, celle-là, **11.2**
   That's all. C'est tout., 6.1
   That's it., That's right. C'est ça.
thatched roof le toit de chaume
theater le théâtre, **1.1**
theme le thème
then alors, BV; ensuite, 12.1
there là, 3.2
   over there là-bas, **10.1**
   there are il y a, 4.1
   there is il y a, 4.1
therefore donc
thing la chose
to **think** penser; croire, 7.2; *(opinion)* trouver, 7.2; réfléchir
thousand mille, 3.2
throat la gorge, 2.1
   throat infection l'angine *(f.)*, **2.1**
through par
to **throw** lancer, 10.2, **12.1**
   to throw a party donner une fête, 4.1
thumb le pouce, **13.1**
Thursday jeudi *(m.)*, BV
thyme le thym, **6.1**
ticket le billet, 8.1

bus or subway ticket le ticket, **10.1**
one-way ticket l'aller *(m.)* (simple), 9.1
round-trip ticket le billet aller (et) retour, 9.1
ticket machine le distributeur automatique, **10.1**
ticket window le guichet, 9.1, **10.1**
traffic ticket la contravention, **7.2**
tie la cravate, 7.1
to **tie** *(score)* égaliser
tight serré(e), 7.2
time *(of day)* l'heure *(f.)*, BV; *(in a series)* la fois, 10.2; le temps
   (for) a long time longtemps, 11.1
   at the same time à la fois
   at what time? à quelle heure?, 2
   in a short time en très peu de temps
   it's time that il est temps que, 13
   on time à l'heure, 8.1
   time difference le décalage horaire
   times l'époque *(f.)*
   What time is it? Il est quelle heure?, BV
timetable l'horaire *(m.)*
tip le bout; *(restaurant)* le pourboire, 5.2
   to leave a tip laisser un pourboire, 5.2
   The tip is included. Le service est compris., 5.2
tire le pneu, 7.1
   flat tire le pneu à plat, **7.1**
   spare tire la roue de secours, **7.1**
tired fatigué(e)
tissue le kleenex, **2.1**
to **à**, 3.1; à destination de *(plane, train, etc.)*, 8.1; *(in order to)* pour
   (up) to jusqu'à

English-French Dictionary

toast le pain grillé
to **toast** porter un toast à
tobacco shop le bureau de tabac
today aujourd'hui, BV; de nos jours
toe le doigt de pied, **8.1**
together ensemble, **5.1**
  to get together with retrouver
toilet paper le papier hygiénique, **9.2**
toll le péage, **7.2**
toll call l'appel interurbain
tomato la tomate, **6.2**
tomorrow demain, BV
  See you tomorrow. À demain., BV
tonight ce soir
tonsillitis l'angine (f.), **2.1**
too (also) aussi, **1.1**; (excessive) trop, **2.1**
tool l'outil (m.)
tooth la dent
toothbrush la brosse à dents, **12.1**
toothpaste le dentifrice, **12.1**
totally complètement; totalement
to **touch** toucher, **10.2**
  to be in touch with être en contact avec
  touch-tone telephone le téléphone à touches, **3.2**
tourist le/la touriste
  tourist office le bureau de (du) tourisme; le syndicat d'initiative
toward vers
towel la serviette, **11.1**, **9.2**
tower la tour, **11.1**
town la ville, **8.1**, **5.2**, **11.1**; le village
  in town en ville, **11.1**
  small town le village
  town hall la mairie, **12.2**, **14.1**
toxic toxique
toy le jouet

track la piste, **10.2**; (railroad) la voie, **9.1**
track and field l'athlétisme (m.), **10.2**
trade le métier, **14.1**; le commerce
tradition la tradition
traditional traditionnel(le)
traffic la circulation
  traffic circle le rond-point, **7.2**, **11.1**
  traffic jam le bouchon, **7.2**
  traffic light le feu, **7.2**, **11.1**
  traffic ticket la contravention, **7.2**
tragedy la tragédie
tragic tragique
train le train, **9.1**
  train station la gare, **9.1**
  train station restaurant le buffet, **9.1**
traitor le traître, la traîtresse
to **transform** transformer
to **transmit** transmettre, **3.1**
to **transport** transporter
transportation le transport
traveler le voyageur, la voyageuse, **9.1**
tray le plateau, **8.2**
treasure le trésor, L4
to **treat** traiter
treatment le traitement
tree l'arbre (m.), L3
trigonometry la trigonométrie, **2.2**
trip le voyage, **8.1**; le trajet, **10.2**
  to take a trip faire un voyage, **8.1**
trombone le trombone, **12.1**
tropical tropical(e)
trouble: to be in trouble être en difficulté
truck le camion, **7.1**
  small truck la camionnette
true vrai(e), **2.2**
trumpet la trompette, **12.1**
truth la vérité

to **try on** essayer, **7.2**
T-shirt le t-shirt, **7.1**
Tuesday mardi (m.), BV
tuna le thon
tunic la tunique
Tunisian tunisien(ne)
tunnel le tunnel
turkey le dindon; la dinde
to **turn** tourner, **7.2**
  to turn around faire demi-tour, **11.1**
  to turn off (appliance) éteindre, **12.2**, **3.1**
  to turn on (appliance) mettre, **7**; allumer, **12.2**, **3.1**
  turn signal le clignotant, **7.2**
turnstile le tourniquet, **10.1**
TV la télé, **12.2**
  on TV à la télé, **12.2**
twin le jumeau, la jumelle, L1
to **twist** (one's knee, etc.) se tordre, **8.1**
type le type, la sorte, le genre, **1.1**
to **type** taper
typical typique
typically typiquement

uncle l'oncle (m.), **4.1**
under sous, **8.2**
underground souterrain(e)
to **understand** comprendre, **5**
to **unearth** déterrer
unemployed au chômage, **14.2**
  unemployed person le chômeur, la chômeuse, **14.2**
unemployment le chômage, **14.2**
unfortunately malheureusement
unhappy malheureux, malheureuse

English-French Dictionary

unit l'unité (f.)
United States les États-Unis (m. pl.)
university l'université (f.)
unknown inconnu(e)
to **unpack** défaire, **9.1**
until jusqu'à
up there là-haut
upset stomach le trouble digestif
use l'emploi (m.)
to **use** utiliser, **3.1**; se servir de, **3.2, L4**
useful utile
usually d'habitude, **12.2**

to **vacate** libérer, **9.2**
vacation les vacances (f. pl.)
  on vacation en vacances
  summer vacation les grandes vacances
valid valable
to **validate** valider, **10.1**
valley la vallée; le val
value la valeur
vanilla (adj.) à la vanille, **5.1**
varied varié(e)
variety la variété
various divers(e)
to **vary** varier
VCR le magnétoscope, **12.2**
veal le veau, **6.2**
  veal cutlet l'escalope (f.) de veau, **6.2**
vegetable le légume, **6.2, 6.1**
veil le voile
vein la veine
vengence la vengeance
to **verify** vérifier, **8.1**
very très, **BV**; tout
  very near tout près, **4.2**
  very well très bien, **BV**
victorious victorieux, victorieuse
victory la victoire

video la vidéo, **3.1**
  movie video le film en vidéo, **1.1**
videocassette la cassette vidéo, **12.2**
Vietnamese vietnamien(ne), **6**
view la vue
village le village
vinegar le vinaigre, **6.1**
vineyard le vignoble, **11.2**
violin le violon
viral viral(e)
virus le virus
visit la visite
to **visit** (a place) visiter, **1.2**; (a person) rendre visite à
vitamin la vitamine
voice la voix
volleyball le volley(-ball), **10.2**
volunteer le/la bénévole; le/la volontaire
voyage le voyage

to **wait (for)** attendre, **9.1**
  to wait in line faire la queue, **9.1**
waiter le serveur, **5.1**
waiting room la salle d'attente, **9.1**
waitress la serveuse, **5.1**
walk la promenade, **11.1**
  to take a walk faire une promenade, **11.1**
to **walk** marcher, **8.1**
walkway le passage piéton
wall le mur, **L4**
to **want** désirer, vouloir, avoir envie de
war la guerre, **L3**
  war zone la zone de conflit
warm chaud(e)
warmup suit le survêtement, **7.1**

warrior le guerrier, **L3**
to **wash** se laver, **12.1**; faire sa toilette
  to wash one's hair (face, etc.) se laver les cheveux (la figure, etc.), **12.1**
washcloth le gant de toilette, **12.1, 9.2**
waste le déchet
watch la montre, **L1**
to **watch** surveiller, **7.2**
  Watch out! Attention!, **4.2**
water l'eau (f.), **6.2**
to **water-ski** faire du ski nautique, **11.1**
way la façon
weak faible, **L1**
weapon l'arme (f.)
to **wear** porter, **7.1**
weather le temps, **11.1**
Web site le site
wedding le mariage, **12.2**
  wedding ring l'alliance (f.), **12.2**
Wednesday mercredi (m.), **BV**
week la semaine, **3.2**
  a week huit jours
  a (per) week par semaine, **3.2**
  last week la semaine dernière, **10.2**
  next week la semaine prochaine
  two weeks quinze jours
weekend le week-end
to **weigh** peser, **5.2**
weight le poids
welcome le/la bienvenu(e)
  Welcome! Bienvenue!
  You're welcome. Je t'en prie. (fam.), **BV**; Je vous en prie. (form.), **BV**
well bien, **BV**; eh bien; ben (slang)
  well then alors, **BV**
well-behaved bien élevé(e), **13.1**; sage, **12.2**

English-French Dictionary

well-done (meat) bien cuit(e), **5.2**
well-known connu(e), **1.1**
well-mannered bien élevé(e), **13.1**
well-to-do aisé(e)
west l'ouest (m.)
western occidental(e)
western (movie) le western
wheat le blé, **11.2**
wheelchair le fauteuil roulant, **8.1**
when quand, **4.1**
where où, **1.1**
  from where d'où, **1.1**
which quel(le), **6**
to **whistle** siffler, **10.1, L1**
white blanc, blanche, **7.2**
who qui, **1.1**
whole (adj.) entier, entière; (n.) l'ensemble (m.)
whole-wheat bread le pain complet, **6.1**
whom qui, **10**
why pourquoi, **6.2**
  why not? pourquoi pas?
wide large, **7.2**
wife la femme, **4.1**
to **win** gagner, **10.1**; sortir victorieux (victorieuse)
wind le vent, **11.1**
window (seat) (une place) côté fenêtre, **8.1**
window (store) la vitrine, **7.1**
windshield le pare-brise, **7.1**
windsurfing la planche à voile, **11.1**
  to go windsurfing faire de la planche à voile, **11.1**
windy: It's windy. Il y a du vent., **11.1**
wine le vin

winner le/la gagnant(e), **10.2**
winner's cup la coupe, **10.2**
winter l'hiver (m.), **11.2**
to **wipe** essuyer, **L2**
wise sage
wish le désir
to **wish** souhaiter, **9.1, 12.2**
with avec, **3.2**; auprès de; muni(e) de
to **withdraw** retirer, **5.1**
without sans; sans que
woman la femme, **7.1**
wood le bois
word le mot
  words (of song, etc.) les paroles (f. pl.)
work le travail; (of art or literature) l'œuvre (f.), **1.1**; l'ouvrage (m.)
to **work** travailler, **3.1, 14.2**
  to work full-time (part-time) travailler à plein temps (à mi-temps), **14.2**
worker l'ouvrier, l'ouvrière, **11.1**
workplace le lieu de travail, **14.1**
world le monde
worry l'inquiétude (f.)
to **worry** s'en faire, **8.1**
wound la blessure, **8.1**
wounded blessé(e)
wrist le poignet, **13.1**
to **write** écrire, **9.2**; rédiger
  to write a prescription faire une ordonnance, **2.2**
writer l'écrivain (m.), **L2, 14.1**
wrong mauvais(e), **2.2**
  What's wrong? Qu'est-ce qui ne va pas?

What's wrong with him? Qu'est-ce qu'il a?, **2.1**
wrong number l'erreur (f.); le mauvais numéro, **3.2**

x-ray la radio(graphie), **8.2**

year l'an (m.), **4.1**; l'année (f.)
yellow jaune, **7.2**
yes oui, BV; si (after neg. question), **7.2**
yesterday hier, **10.1**
  the day before yesterday avant-hier, **10.2**
yogurt la yaourt, **6.1**
young jeune
  young people les jeunes (m. pl.)
younger le cadet, la cadette, **L1**
youth la jeunesse
  youth hostel l'auberge (f.) de jeunesse

to **zap** zapper, **12.2**
zero zéro
zip code le code postal, **5.2**
zone la zone
zoology la zoologie

Index

adjectives superlative of, 261 (8); 262 (8)
adverbs formation of, 292 (9)
agreement direct object and past participle, 153 (5); 155 (5)
aller conditional of, 214 (7); future of, 182 (6); subjunctive of, 385 (12)
avoir conditional of, 214 (7); future of, 182 (6); subjunctive of, 385 (12); verbs conjugated with **être** or **avoir**, 288 (9)
bien comparison of, 262 (8)
boire subjunctive of, 416 (13)
bon(ne) comparison of, 262 (8)
ce que 256 (8)
ce qui 256 (8)
celui (celle) 348 (11)
commands (*see imperative*)
comparison of adjectives, 261 (8); 262 (8); of **bien**, 262 (8); of **bon(ne)**, 262 (8)
conditional tense of irregular verbs, 214 (7); 216 (7); of regular verbs, 214 (7); with **si** clauses, 218 (7); use of, 214 (7); 217 (7)
conduire present tense and **passé composé** of, 350 (11); subjunctive of, 385 (12)
connaître present tense and **passé composé** of, 10 (1); vs. **savoir**, 10 (1); subjunctive of, 385 (12)
depuis 323 (10)
descendre conjugated with **être** or **avoir** in the **passé composé**, 288 (9)
devenir 112 (4)
dire subjunctive of, 385 (12)
direct object pronouns agreement with past participle, 153 (5); 155 (5); with **faire** + infinitive, 187 (6); with imperative, 258 (8); **le, la, les,** 14 (1); **me, te, nous, vous,** 12 (1)
écrire subjunctive of, 385 (12)
en 48 (2); with another pronoun, 291 (9)
-er verbs (*see conditional tense; future tense; imperfect tense; subjunctive*)
être conditional of, 214 (7); imperfect of, 74 (3); future of, 182 (6); subjunctive of, 385 (12); verbs conjugated with **être** or **avoir**, 288 (9)
expressions of doubt followed by subjunctive, 444 (14)
expressions of emotion followed by subjunctive, 418 (13)
faire conditional of, 214 (7); future of, 182 (6); plus infinitive, 187 (6); subjunctive of, 395 (12)
future tense formation and use of, 182 (6); with **si** clauses, 218 (7)
geographical names prepositions with, 113 (4)
il y a with **en**, 291 (9)
imperative formation and use of, 45 (2); object pronouns with, 258 (8)
imperfect tense formation of, 74–75 (3); in **si** clauses, 218 (7); use of, 75 (3); 78 (3); 106 (4); 109 (4); vs. **passé composé**, 106 (4); 109 (4)
impersonal expressions followed by subjunctive, 414 (13)
indirect object pronouns with imperative, 258 (8); **lui, leur,** 42 (2); **me, te, nous, vous,** 12 (1)
infinitive after preposition, 351 (11); vs. subjunctive, 447 (14)
interrogatives with **est-ce que**, 318 (10); by intonation, 318 (10); by inversion, 318 (10); **lequel,** 348 (11); **qu'est-ce que,** 256 (8); **qu'est-ce qui,** 256 (8)
-ir verbs (*see conditional tense; future tense; imperfect tense; subjunctive*)
irregular verbs (*see individual verb entries*)
lequel 348 (11)
lire subjunctive of, 385 (12)
meilleur(e) 262 (8)
mettre subjunctive of, 385 (12)

mieux 262 (8)
monter conjugated with **être** or **avoir** in the **passé composé**, 288 (9)
negation personne ne..., 157 (5); **rien ne...**, 157 (5)
object pronouns with imperative, 258 (8); two object pronouns in same sentence, 185 (6); 220 (7); 291 (9); (*see also direct object pronouns; indirect object pronouns*)
ouvrir present tense and **passé composé** of, 44 (2)
partir subjunctive of, 385 (12)
passé composé verbs conjugated with **être** or **avoir**, 288 (9); vs. imperfect, 106 (4); 109 (4)
passer conjugated with **être** or **avoir** in the **passé composé**, 288 (9)
past participle agreement with direct object, 150 (5); 155 (5)
pouvoir subjunctive of, 416 (13)
prendre subjunctive of, 416 (13)
prepositions with geographic names, 113 (4); followed by infinitive, 351 (11)
present tense with **depuis**, 323 (10); in **si** clauses, 218 (7)
pronouns demonstrative pronouns, 348 (11); direct object pronouns, 12 (1); **en,** 48 (2); indirect object pronouns, 12 (1); 14 (1); interrogative pronoun **lequel,** 348 (11); relative pronouns, 150 (5); 256 (8); 348 (11); two object pronouns in same sentence, 185 (6); 220 (7); 291 (9); **y,** 289 (9)
quand future tense with, 182 (6)
que relative pronoun, 150 (5); 348 (11)
qu'est-ce que 256 (8)
qu'est-ce qui 256 (8); **question words** (*see interrogatives*)
qui relative pronoun, 150 (5); 348 (11)
-re verbs (*see conditional tense; future tense; imperfect tense; subjunctive*)
recevoir subjunctive of, 416 (13)
reciprocal verbs 155 (5)
relative pronouns que, 150 (5); 348 (11); **qui,** 150 (5); 348 (11); **ce que,** 256 (8); **ce qui,** 256 (8); subjunctive after, 448 (14)
rentrer conjugated with **être** or **avoir** in the **passé composé**, 288 (9)
revenir 112 (4)
savoir vs. **connaître**, 10 (1); present tense and **passé composé** of, 10 (1); subjunctive of, 416 (13)
si clauses 218 (7)
sortir conjugated with **être** or **avoir** in the **passé composé**, 288 (9)
souffrir present tense and **passé composé** of, 44 (2)
spelling changes verbs with, 216 (7); 416 (13)
subjunctive after expressions of doubt, 444 (14); after expressions of emotion, 418 (13); after impersonal expressions, 414 (13); vs. infinitive, 447 (14); of irregular verbs, 385 (12); 416 (13); of regular verbs, 384 (12); in relative clauses, 448 (14); uses of, 384 (12); 388 (12); 414 (13); 418 (13); 444 (14); 448 (14); with verbs expressing wishes or preferences, 388 (12); of verbs with spelling changes, 416 (13)
suivre present tense and **passé composé** of, 350 (11); subjunctive of, 385 (12)
superlative of adjectives, 261 (8); 262 (8)
tenses (*see names of individual tenses*)
venir present tense and **passé composé** of, 112 (4); subjunctive of, 416 (13); **venir de,** 321 (10)
verbs conjugated with both **avoir** and **être** in the **passé composé**, 288 (9); expressing wishes or preferences, subjunctive with, 388 (12); (*see also individual verb entries*)
vivre present tense and **passé composé** of, 350 (11)
vouloir subjunctive of, 416 (13)
y 289 (9)

Credits

Glencoe would like to acknowledge the artists and agencies who participated in illustrating this program: Paul Casale; Meg Aubrey represented by Cornell & McCarthy; Domenick D'Andrea; Len Ebert; Glencoe; Fanny Mellet Berry represented by Anita Grien Representing Artists; Joseph Hammond; Renate Lohmann; Ortelius Design Inc.; Karen Rhine; Shannon Stirnweis; Carol Strebel; Studio InkLink; Kathleen O'Malley represented by Christina A. Tugeau; Susan Jaekel; Jane McCreary and DJ Simison represented by Remen-Willis Design Group.

COVER (top to bottom)Bro Brannhage/Panoramic Images, (2)Mark Segal/Panoramic Images, (3)Sylvain Grandadam/Getty Images, (4)Gavriel Jecan/CORBIS, (students)Philippe Gontier; **i** (top to bottom)Bro Brannhage/Panoramic Images, (2)Mark Segal/Panoramic Images, (3)Sylvain Grandadam/Getty Images, (4)Gavriel Jecan/CORBIS, (students)Philippe Gontier; **iv** Jose Fuste Raga/The Stock Market; **v** (l)K. N'Dour/Liaison Agency, (r)AFP/CORBIS; **vi** (tl)Timothy Fuller, (tr)CH. Vioujard/Liaison Agency, (b)Curt Fischer; **vii** (l)A. Schroeder/Reporters-DIAF, (r)P. Dannic/DIAF; **viii** (l)Marge/Sunset, (r)Aaron Haupt; **ix** Larry Hamill; **x** (tl)Leyreloup/Wallis Phototheque, (tr)Larry Hamill, (b)J. D. Sudres/DIAF; **xi** Tom Craig/FPG; **xii** (l)Michael Krasowitz/FPG, (r)Winston Fraser; **xiii** (l)Macduff Everton/The Image Works, (r)Steven Ferry; **xiv** (tl)Mark Antman, (tr)Tony Savino/The Image Works; **xv** (t)Camille Moirenc/DIAF, (b)PhotoDisc; **xvi** (tl)Jacques Brinon/AP/Wide World Photos, (tr)A. Ramey/PhotoEdit, (b)Melissa Gerr; **xvii** (l)Stuart Cohen/The Image Works, (r)Timothy Fuller; **xviii** Coo Lwa-Dann Tardif/The Stock Market; **xix** (t)Massimo Listri/CORBIS, (b)Philippe Gontier; **R0–R1** Robert Fried; **R2** (tl br)Catherine et Bernard Desjeux; (tr)Aaron Haupt; (others) Curt Fischer; **R3** (tl)Wayne Rowe, (br)John Evans; **R4** (t)Jose Fuste Raga/The Stock Market, (b)Matt Meadows; **R5** (l)Everton/The Image Works, (r)Sylva Villerot/DIAF; **R6** The Purcell Team/CORBIS; **R7** (l)Robert Fried, (r)Beryl Goldberg; **R8** (t)Timothy Fuller, (b)Owen Franken/CORBIS; **R9** (t)Michael Yamashita/CORBIS, (b)Tim Courlas/Horizons; **R10–R11** Guy Durand/DIAF; **R12** (l)Stuart Cohen/The Image Works, (c)Jorge Ramirez/International Stock, (b)Michelle Chaplow; **R13** (t)Pictor, (cl)Curt Fischer, (cr b) Amanita Pictures; **R14** (l)Catherine et Bernard Desjeux, (tr)Morton Beebe, SF/CORBIS, (br)Matt Meadows; **R15** Duchene/Wallis Phototheque; **R16** Mark Antman; **R17** Steven Needham/Envision; **R18** Beryl Goldberg; **R20–R21** Michael Busselle/CORBIS; **R22** (l)Robert Fried, (r)Catherine et Bernard Desjeux; **R23** Robert Holmes/CORBIS; **R24** (t)Roberto Soncin Gerometta/Photo 20-20/PictureQuest, (b)Matt Meadows; **R25** Brooks Walker/Envision; **R26** O. Baumgartner/Sygma CORBIS; **R27** (l)Robert Fried, (r)Curt Fischer; **R28–R29** SuperStock; **R30** (bl)Icone/The Image Works, (others)Larry Hamill; **R31** (l)courtesy Air France, (r)D. Cordier/Sunset; **R32** (l)B.B.Holding/Sunset, (r)Larry Hamill; **R33** Courtesy Air France; **R34** Larry Hamill; **R35** Jose Nicolas/Hemispheres Images; **R36–R37** J. Langevin/Teamsport/Sygma CORBIS; **R38** (tl)Pawel Wysocki/Hemispheres Images, (tr inset)Garufi /Wallis Phototheque, (tl inset)Charlier/Wallis Phototheque, (tr)J. Christophe Pratt/DIAF, (b)Amwell/Stone; **R39** (tl)SuperStock, (tr)Patrick Somelet/DIAF, (b)Amwell/Stone; **R40** (l)Larry Hamill, (r)Stone; **R41** Creatas/PictureQuest; **R42** (t)Camille Moirenc/DIAF, (b)Tim Gibson/Envision; **R43** Chris Harvey /Stone; **R44** (l)Iconos/DIAF, (b)Ron Angle/Liaison Agency; **R45** J.Ch. Gerard/DIAF; **R46–R47** David Simson/Stock Boston/PictureQuest; **R48** (tl tr)Larry Hamill, (b)R. Sidney/The Image Works; **R49** (t)Stuart Cohen/The Image Works, (b)Larry Hamill; **R50** Larry Hamill; **R51** John Evans; **R54** J. Sierpinski/DIAF; **R56** (t)Rick Souders/Index Stock, (b)Larry Hamill; **0** British Museum, London/Bridgeman Art Library, London/SuperStock; **0–1** Mark Burnett; **2** Timothy Fuller; **3** (t)Timothy Fuller, (bl)SuperStock, (br)Pictor; **4** (t)Timothy Fuller, (b)Jackson Smith/ImageState/Picture Quest; **5** (l)Collections de la Comedie-Francaise, (r)Mark Burnett; **7** Timothy Fuller; **8** Giraudon/Art Resource, NY; **9** © Photo RMN - Hervé Lewandowski/Musee D'Orsay; **10** Jacques Sierpinski/DIAF; **11** Scala/Art Resource, NY; **12** Timothy Fuller; **13** (tl)file photo, (tr)Monika Graff/The Image Works; **14** Yann Arthus-Bertrand/CORBIS; **15** (l)Monika Graff/The Image Works, (r)Peter McCabe/The Image Works; **16** (t)J. MarcLallemand/Wallis Phototheque, (b)© Photo RMN - Hervé Lewandowski/Musee D'Orsay; **17** Vanni/Art Resource, NY; **18** Larry Hamill; **20** (l)Derek Croucher/The Stock Market, (r)Larry Hamill; **21** (t)AFP/CORBIS, (c)Ramsay/Wallis Phototheque, (b)Gérard Lacz/Sunset; **22** (t)Jason Laure, (b)Kavanah/Stone; **23** (tl)Neal Preston/CORBIS, (tr)Mark Burnett, (b)K. N'Dour/Liaison Agency; **24–25** (bkgd) Steve Cole/PhotoDisc; **25** (t)Robbie Jack/CORBIS, (c)Kevin Winter/Getty Images, (b)Stephane Cardinale/CORBIS/Sygma; **26** (t)Robert Fried Photography, (b)Larry Hamill; **27** Timothy Fuller; **29** Curt Fischer; **31** Mark Burnett; **32** Roger-Viollet, Paris/The Bridgeman Art Library; **32–33** Stefano Bianchetti/CORBIS; **34** (t)John Evans, (l cr bcr)Timothy Fuller, (br)Aaron Haupt; **35** Timothy Fuller; **36** Curt Fischer; **37** Mark Burnett; **38** Timothy Fuller; **39** (tl bl br) Timothy Fuller, (tr)Larry Hamill; **40** (t)John Evans, (b)Timothy Fuller; **42** (l r)Catherine et Bernard Desjeux, (c)Image Club Graphics; **44** (t)Timothy Fuller, (b)Larry Hamill; **47** Ken Karp; **49** (t)Thomas Marc, (bl)Monika Graff/The Image Works, (br)Ken Karp; **50** Timothy Fuller; **51** (l)Monika Graff/The Image Works, (r)Ken Karp; **52 54** Timothy Fuller; **55** (t)SuperStock, (b)CH. Vioujard/Liaison Agency; **56** (l)Curt Fischer, (r)Mark Burnett, (b)Clasen/Wallis Phototheque; **56–57** (bkgd) Mitch Hrdlicka/PhotoDisc; **57** (t)Owen Franken/CORBIS, (b)Larry Hamill; **59** (t)Larry Hamill, (b)P. Wysocki/Explorer; **60** Curt Fischer; **63** (l)John Evans, (r)Timothy Fuller; **64** Galerie Daniel Malingue, Paris, France/Bridgeman Art Library; **64–65** P. Savin/CORBIS Sygma; **66 67 68** Larry Hamill; **69** (t)Curt Fischer, (b)Larry Hamill; **70** (cell phones)PhotoDisc, (coins)Mathias Kulka/The Stock Market, (others)Larry Hamill; **71** Larry Hamill; **72** (t)Larry Hamill, (b)Mark Burnett; **73** A. Schroeder/Reporters-DIAF; **74** Ken Lax/Photo Researchers, Inc.; **76** Travelpix/FPG; **77** (t)C. Vaisse/Hoa Qui, (b)Patrick Somelat/DIAF; **78** Aaron Haupt; **79** (t)Roger-Viollet, (b)Larry Hamill; **81** Grant V. Faint/The Image Bank; **82 83** Larry Hamill; **84** (l)Sylva Villerot/DIAF, (c r)Larry Hamill; **85** Larry Hamill; **86** (t)Halle/Marco Polo, (c)Larry Hamill, (b)Suzanne Murphy-Larronde; **87** Larry Hamill; **88** file photo; **88–89** (bkgd) PhotoDisc; **89** (t)P. Dannic/DIAF, (b)Larry Hamill; **90** (l)A. Schroeder/DIAF, (c)P. Dannic/DIAF, (r)Larry Hamill; **91** Vincent Gauvreau; **92** (1 4)Curt Fischer, (2 3)Timothy Fuller, (5)Curt Fischer; **95** Larry Hamill; **96** Musee d'Orsay, Paris/AKG, Berlin/SuperStock; **96–97** Georgia Bowater/The Stock Market; **98** (t)Patrick Bedout, (c)Robert Fried, (b)Larry Hamill; **99** David Barnes/The Stock Market; **100** (t)Dave Bartruff/CORBIS, (b)Mark Burnett; **102** (t)Barret/Wallis Phototheque, (others)Larry Hamill; **103** Stephane Frances/Hemispheres Images; **104** Larry Hamill; **105** Tom Hussey/The Image Bank; **106** Patrick Ward/CORBIS; **107** (t)Manfred Mehlig/Stone, (b)Mark Antman/The Image Works; **108** Andre Jenny/Focus Group/PictureQuest; **110** Andrew Payti; **112** Petit/Wallis Phototheque; **114** (t)Michele Burgess/The Stock Market, (b)Alain Choisnet/The Image Bank; **115** Guido A. Rossi/The Image Bank; **116** (t)Peter Turnley/CORBIS, (b)Aaron Haupt; **117** Stephane Frances/Hemispheres Images; **118** Marge/Sunset; **119** (t)Paul Almasy/AKG London, (b)Marge/Sunset; **120** (t)Art Wolfe/Stone, (c)Cosmo Condina/Stone, (b)Hans Wolf/The Image Bank; **121** (l)Stephane Frances/Hemispheres Images, (r)Olivier Blaise/Liaison Agency; **122** D. Thierry/DIAF; **122–123** (bkgd) CORBIS; **123** (t)Jose F. Poblete/CORBIS, (bl)Roger Wood/CORBIS, (br)SuperStock; **124** (l)David Ball/Stone, (r)Larry Hamill; **127** Wayne Rowe; **129** (t)David Barnes/The Stock Market, (bl)Manfred Mehlig/Stone, (br)Alain Choisnet/The Image Bank; **130** Larry Hamill; **132** (l)Stuart Cohen/The Image Works, (r)Reunion des Musees Nationaux/Art Resource, NY; **135** Larry Hamill; **136–137** (1) Bruce Dale, National Geographic Image Collection;

H110 Handbook

Credits

136 (2)Todd Gipstein, National Geographic Image Collection, (3)Bruno De Hogues/Stone, (4)Francois Ducasse/Rapho/Photo Researchers, (5)Bob Handelman/Stone; **137** (6)Kelly/Moony Photography, (7)Michael Busselle/CORBIS; **138** (9)Michel Viard/Peter Arnold, Inc., (10)Michael Busselle/Stone, (11)Michael Boys/Stone, (12)Herve Donnezan; **138–139** (8)Pictor; **139** (13)Pictor, (14)Ric Ergenbright/Stone; **140** Kunsthaus, Zurich, Switzerland/Giraudon, Paris/SuperStock; **140–141** Matthieu Colin/Hemispheres Images; **142** (tl)Peter Weber/Stone, (tc tr bl)Larry Hamill, (br)Icone/The Image Works; **142** Larry Hamill; **143** (l)Larry Hamill, (r)Aaron Haupt; **144** Larry Hamill; **145** (t)Larry Hamill, (b)Stephane Frances/Hemispheres Images; **146** Larry Hamill; **147** (tl)Wayne Rowe, (tr bl br)Larry Hamill; **148** (1)Curt Fischer, (2 b)Larry Hamill, (3)Mark Burnett, (4)Catherine et Bernard Desjeux; **150 151** Larry Hamill; **152** (t)Sylvain Grandadam/Stone, (b)Monika Graf/The Image Works; **153** Robert Fried; **154** Aaron Haupt and Jeff Malony/PhotoDisc; **156** Richard Laird/FPG; **157 158** Larry Hamill; **159** Diagentur/Sunset; **160** Larry Hamill; **161** (t)Mark Burnett, (b)Larry Hamill; **162** (tl)Paul Thompson/International Stock, (tr)Larry Hamill, (bl)Aaron Haupt, (br)Gary Rhijnsburger/Masterfile; **163** (t)Stuart Cohen/The Image Works, (b)Larry Hamill; **164** (t)file photo, (b)Bernard Regent/DIAF; **164–165** (bkgd)file photo; **168** (1 2)Peter Weber/Stone, (7)Larry Hamill; **171** (l)Larry Hamill, (r)Aaron Haupt; **172** Hermitage Museum, St. Petersburg/SuperStock; **172–173** Jean-Claude Amiel/Saola/Liaison Agency; **174** (t)Stan Ries/International Stock, (b)Larry Hamill; **175** Larry Hamill; **176** (t)Larry Hamill, (b)Rita Maas/The Image Bank; **177 178 179** Larry Hamill; **180** (t)Tina Buckman/Index Stock, (b)Simeone Huber/Stone; **181** (t)Larry Hamill, (b)Simeone Huber/Stone; **183** (c)Victor Scocozza/FPG, (b)Judy Buie/Bruce Coleman, Inc; **184** J. D. Sudres/DIAF; **186** Larry Hamill; **188** Andrew Payti; **190** Catherine et Bernard Desjeux; **192** Larry Hamill; **193** (l)Larry Hamill, (r)J. D. Sudres/DIAF; **194** (t)Michael Boys/CORBIS, (b)Larry Hamill; **195** Larry Hamill; **196** (t)Hulton Archives/Stone, (b)Giraudon/Art Resource, NY; **196–197** (bkgd)file photo; **197** (t)Reunion des Musees Nationaux/Art Resource, NY, (b)H. Gyssels/DIAF; **198** Leyreloup/Wallis Phototheque; **199** Jeanetta Baker/Photobank/Sunset; **201** Rosine Mazin/DIAF; **203** Larry Hamill; **204** AKG London; **204–205** Edouard Berne/Stone; **206** (tl)IPA/The Image Works, (tr)Dean Siracusa/FPG, (cl)Stuart Cohen/The Image Works, (cr)Alain Gaveau, (b)Larry Hamill; **207** Steven Ferry; **208** (1 2 4)Larry Hamill, (3)J. M. Leligny/DIAF; **209** (t)T. H. Werbung/Sunset, (b)Mark Burnett; **211** Mark Burnett; **212** (1 2 4)Mark Burnett, (3)Hans Wolf/The Image Bank, (5)Gerard Gsell/DIAF; **213** Mark Burnett; **215** (t)Gail Mooney/CORBIS, (b)Max Hunn/FPG; **218** Andrew Payti; **219** Mark Burnett; **221** Ken Karp; **222** Patrick Bedout; **223** Curt Fischer; **224** Joachim Messerschmidt/FPG; **225** (t)Mark Burnett, (b)Pete Turner/The Image Bank; **226** (t)Holt Studios/Sunset, (b)T. H. Werbung/Sunset; **227** (t)Bertrand Rieger/Hemispheres Images, (b)Lorne Resnick/Stone; **228–229** (bkgd) Kent Knudson/PhotoLink/PhotoDisc; **229** Tom Craig/FPG; **230** (t)Daniel Perret/La Phototheque, SDP-DIAF, (b)Mark Burnett; **233** Wayne Rowe; **235** Larry Hamill; **236** (t)Steven Ferry, (b)Gilles Bassignac/Liaison Agency; **238** Joe Carini/The Image Works; **240** Arthur Beck/The Stock Market; **241** Xavier Yestelin/Liaison Agency; **242–243** (1)Wolfgang Kaehler/CORBIS; **242** (2)Hans Georg Roth/CORBIS, (3)Rohan/Stone, (4)Frances Linzee Gordon/Lonely Planet Images, (5)Lonely Planet Images; **243** (6)Paul Stepan-Vierow/Photo Researchers, (7)Sidi Brahim/Woodfin Camp & Assoc.; **244–245** (8)Nicholas DeVore/Stone; **244** (9 10) Nik Wheeler/CORBIS, (11)Sandro Vannini/CORBIS, (12)John Beatty/Stone; **245** (13)G. Boutin, Explorer, (14)Glen Allison/Stone; **246** Giraudon/Art Resource, NY; **246–247** P. Moulu/Sunset; **248** Steven Ferry; **249** (t)John Evans, (b)Aaron Haupt; **251** J. P. Porcher/Sunset; **252** (t)Steven Ferry, (b)Aaron Haupt; **253** (t)V. Audet/Sunset, (b)Yoav Levy/PhotoTake; **254** Michael Krasowitz/FPG; **255** B. Yarvin/Sunset; **257** Mark Burnett; **258** Curt Fischer; **259** (tr br)Ken Karp, (tl)file photo, (bl)Peter McCabe/The Image Works; **260** (l)Peter McCabe/The Image Works, (r)Ken Karp; **262** Larry Hamill; **263** Trip/P. Rauter; **264** Steven Ferry; **265** (t)Steven Ferry, (b)Infra/La Phototheque, SDP-DIAF; **266** (l)Ulrike Welsch, (r)Steven Ferry; **267** Mark Burnett; **268** Frank Fournier/Contact Press/PictureQuest; **270–271** (bkgd)PhotoLink/PhotoDisc; **270** (t)Mark Burnett, (b)The Image Works; **271** (t)Jean-Loup Charmet/Science Photo Library/Photo Researchers, (b)Christian Vioujard/Liaison Agency; **272** Winston Fraser; **277** (l)Curt Fischer, (r)B. Yarvin/Sunset; **278** Private collection/Portal Gallery Ltd/Bridgeman Art Library; **278–279** Wolfgang Kaehler/CORBIS; **280 281 282** Steven Ferry; **284** (t)Catherine et Bernard Desjeux, (bl)Photo FERNAND/Sunset, (br)Steven Ferry; **285** Steven Ferry; **286** Peter Vanderwarker/Stock Boston; **287** (t)Macduff Everton/The Image Works, (b)M. Ajuria/Sunset; **289** Gerald Buthaud/Woodfin Camp & Associates; **290** Steven Ferry; **292** Photo Gabrielle/Treal/Liaison Agency; **294** Steven Ferry; **296** (t)Bruno Bebert/Liaison Agency, (b)Nik Wheeler/CORBIS; **297** (t)Joachim Messerschmidt/FPG, (c b)SuperStock; **298** Bruno Bebert/Liaison Agency; **299** Robert Fried/Stock Boston; **300–301** (bkgd)CORBIS; **300** (l)Stuart Cohen/The Image Works, (r)Maurice Smith/La Phototheque, SDP-DIAF; **301** (t)Mark Burnett, (bl)Beryl Goldberg, (br)David Barnes/La Phototheque SDP; **302** Camille Moirenc/DIAF; **303** Larry Hamill; **305** Mark Antman; **308** Manu Sassoonian/Art Resource, NY; **308–309** Betty Press/Woodfin Camp & Associates/PictureQuest; **310** Steven Ferry; **311** (l)Robert Holmes/CORBIS, (r)Catherine et Bernard Desjeux; **312** (1)Franck Dunouau/SDP-DIAF, (2)Stephen Studd/Stone, (4 5)Larry Hamill; **314** Philippe Gontier/The Image Works; **315** (tl tr)Steven Ferry, (b)Catherine et Bernard Desjeux; **316** Larry Hamill; **317** (t)Larry Hamill, (bl)Rosine Mazin/DIAF, (bc)Tom Craig/FPG, (br)Marc Verin/DIAF; **319** (t)Larry Hamill, (b)Steven Ferry; **320** (l)G. Martin Raget/Wallis Phototheque, (r)Andrew Payti; **322** Larry Hamill; **323** SuperStock; **324** Curt Fischer; **325** (tl)Pierre Schwartz/Sunset, (tr)Gerard Gsell/DIAF, (bl)Toyohiro Yamada/FPG, (br)Jon Lawrence/Stone; **326** (l)Peter Gridley/FPG, (r)Jacques Kerebel/DIAF; **328** (t)Tony Savino/The Image Works, (b)Sandro Vannini/CORBIS; **329** Andrew Payti; **330** (t)F. Astier/Sygma CORBIS, (c)Doug Armand/Stone, (b)Larry Hamill; **331 332** Larry Hamill; **335** Mark Antman; **337** (l)Rosine Mazin/DIAF, (c)Philippe Gontier/The Image Works, (r)SuperStock; **338** Charles Lenars/CORBIS; **338–339** Joe Cornish/Stone; **340** (tl)P. Moulu/Sunset, (tr)S. Chatenay/Sunset, (c)D. Ermakoff/The Image Works, (b)Stuart Cohen/The Image Works; **341** (tl b)Timothy Fuller, (tr cl)Robert Fried, (cr)Paul Almasy/CORBIS; **342** Robert Fried; **343** (t)Telegraph Colour Library/FPG, (b)Gerard Lacz/Sunset; **344** (tl)B. Rowland/The Image Works, (tr)Serge Coupe/La Phototheque, SDP-DIAF, (bl)Ian Shaw/Stone, (br)Robert Fried; **345** (tl tr)Timothy Fuller, (others)PhotoDisc; **346** (t)Alain Marcay/La Phototheque, (b)S.T.F./Sunset; **347** Leroy H. Mantell/The Stock Market; **349** (t)Larry Hamill, (b)Esbin-Anderson/The Image Works; **350** Suzanne & Nick Geary/Stone; **351 352** Larry Hamill; **353** (t)Capel/Sunset, (bl)Camille Moirenc/DIAF, (br)Walter Bibikow/FPG; **354** (l)Larry Hamill, (r)John Elk III; **355** (t)Lanthiez/Wallis Phototheque, (b)Frances S/Photo Researchers; **356** (t)Gilles Rouget/La Phototheque, SDP-DIAF, (b)Michael Dwyer/Stock Boston; **357** (tl)Dave G. Houser, (tr)Phillippe Renault/Hemispheres Images, (b)SuperStock; **358–359** (bkgd)Roger K. Burnard; **358** Camille Moirenc/DIAF; **359** (t)David Turnley/CORBIS, (b)Larry Hamill; **360** Robert Fried; **361** (l)Earl Kogler/International Stock, (r)Farrell Grehan/CORBIS; **363** Curt Fischer; **365** (l)S.T.F./Sunset, (r)Leroy H. Mantell/The Stock Market; **366 367** Timothy Fuller; **368** (t)Charlie Waite/Panoramic Images, (b)Aaron Haupt; **369** (t)Nik Wheeler/CORBIS, (b)John Elk III; **370–371** (1)Andre Gallant/The Image Bank; **370** (2)Robin Hill/Southern Stock/PictureQuest, (3)Michael Yada, (4)Andre Jenny/Focus Group/PictureQuest, (5)Philip Gould/CORBIS; **371** (6 7) James P. Blair; **372–373** (8) Marc Garanger/CORBIS; **372** (9)Robert Fried/

Credits

Stock Boston/PictureQuest, (10)Philip Gould/CORBIS, (11)B. Stichelbaut/Masterfile, (12)Paul Thompson/Eye Ubiquitous/CORBIS; **373** (13)Bob Krist/CORBIS, (14)Christopher Morris/Black Star/PictureQuest; **374** Private collection/Bridgeman Art Library. Artists Rights Society(ARS), NY/ADAGP, Paris; **374–375** Kelly-Mooney Photography/CORBIS; **376** (tl)Remy de la Mauviniere/AP Photos, (tr)Vince Streano/CORBIS, (cl)Curt Fischer, (cr)AFP/CORBIS, (b)Ary Diesendruck/Stone; **377** (tl)Reuters/Eric Gaillard/Archive Photos, (tr)Trip/N. Ray, (b)Charles Lenars/CORBIS; **378** (tl)Phyllis Picardi/Stock Boston, (tc)Gail Mooney/CORBIS, (tr)Beryl Goldberg, (bl)PhotoDisc, (br)AFP/CORBIS; **379** (t)Rosine Mazin/DIAF, (b)Philip Gould/CORBIS; **380** (tl)Owen Franken/CORBIS, (tr)Patrick Somelet/DIAF, (c)Mark Antman, (b)M. Rougemont/Sygma CORBIS; **381** (rings)Bernsau/The Image Works, (others)Timothy Fuller; **382** (l)Gerard Lacz/Sunset, (r)E. Rossolin/Wallis Phototheque; **383** (t)Michael Shay/FPG, (b)Tom McCarthy/PhotoEdit; **386** (t)G.Guittot/DIAF, (b)Bernard Boutrit/Woodfin Camp & Associates; **387** Chris Duranti/Wallis Phototheque; **389** O. Nicolas/Sygma CORBIS; **390** (t)J. Sierpinski/DIAF, (b)Timothy Fuller; **391** Bob Daemmrich/The Image Works; **392** (t)Robert Fried, (b)Mark Antman/The Image Works; **393** (t)A. Ramey/PhotoEdit, (b)Timothy Fuller; **394** (t)J.Ch. Gerard/DIAF, (b)Melissa Gerr; **395** (t)Nathan Benn/CORBIS, (c)Mark Antman/The Image Works, (b)Melissa Gerr; **396–397** (bkgd)Aaron Haupt; **396** (t)FPG, (b)Dave G. Houser; **397** (t)North Wind Picture Archives, (b)John Elk III; **398** (l)J.Ch. Gerard/DIAF, (r)Dominique Cordier/Sunset; **399** Jean du Boisberranger/Hemispheres Images; **400** (3)Curt Fischer, (others)Mark Antman; **401** Jacques Brinon/AP/Wide World Photos; **403** Philip Gould/CORBIS; **404** AKG London; **404–405** Larry Hamill; **406 407** Timothy Fuller; **408** (t)Timothy Fuller, (b)Larry Hamill; **409** (t)Stuart Cohen/The Image Works, (b)Robert Fried; **411** Timothy Fuller; **412** (t)Stuart Cohen/The Image Works, (c)Timothy Fuller, (others)Mark Burnett; **413** Terry Sutherland; **415** (t)Timothy Fuller, (b)Thomas Jullien/DIAF; **417** Mark Burnett; **420** Timothy Fuller; **422** (l)Timothy Fuller, (r)Larry Hamill; **423** (t)Catherine et Bernard Desjeux, (b)Patrick Ward/Stock Boston/PictureQuest; **424** (t)David Hall/Masterfile, (b)Timothy Fuller; **425** Alex Wasinski/FPG; **426–427** (bkgd)CORBIS; **426** Mark Burnett; **429** (l)Larry Hamill, (r)Mark Burnett; **430 431** Wayne Rowe; **433** Timothy Fuller; **434** SuperStock; **434–435** P. Thompson/Sunset; **436** (director)PhotoFest, (journalist)Beryl Goldberg, (others)Timothy Fuller; **437** Timothy Fuller; **439** (t)L. Zylberman/DIAF, (b)H. Gyssels/DIAF; **440 441** Timothy Fuller; **442** Coo Lwa-Dann Tardif/The Stock Market; **443** (t)Arnaud Fevrier/DIAF, (b)Timothy Fuller; **444** PhotoDisc; **445** (t)Ken Karp, (bl)Victor Englebert, (br)Owen Franken/CORBIS; **446** SuperStock; **447** Pierre Goraz/DIAF; **448** Getty Images; **450** Timothy Fuller; **451** Sygma CORBIS; **452** (l)Beryl Goldberg, (r)photo courtesy The Peace Corps; **453** photo courtesy The Peace Corps; **454** (t)Margot Granitsas/The Image Works, (b)Vince Streano/CORBIS; **455** (t c)Aaron Haupt, (b)Mark Steinmetz; **456–457** (bkgd)John A. Rizzo/PhotoDisc; **456** (t)Timothy Fuller, (b)Alaine Le Bot/DIAF; **457** (l)Alaine Le Bot/DIAF, (r)L. Wiame/Sunset; **458** Trip/B. Turner; **461** Brigit Koch/DIAF; **463 464 465** Timothy Fuller; **467** Robert Fried; **468** Curt Fischer; **469** (t)Monika Graf/The Image Works, (b)Ken Karp; **470–471** (1)Tony Craddock/Stone; **470** (2)Macduff Everton (3)Gerard Del Vecchio/Stone, (4)Craig Aurness/CORBIS, (5)Rapa /Explorer; **471** (6)Antoine Lorgnier/Masterfile, (7)Farrell Grehan/CORBIS; **472–473** (8)Rapa/Explorer; **472** (9)Jodi Cobb, (10)Oliver Benn/Stone, (11)Alain Morovan/Liaison Agency, (12)Cotton Coulson; **473** (13)Wysocki/Explorer/Photo Researchers, (14)Hideo Kurihara/Stone; **474–475** Dave G. Houser; **477** Henry Guttmann Collection/Hulton Archive/Archive Photos; **478** file photo; **479** Timothy Fuller; **482** (t)file photo, (b)Marc & Evelyne Bernheim from Rapho-Guillumette/Woodfin Camp & Associates; **483** Chuck Cecil/Words & Pictures/PictureQuest; **484** Schomburg Center, The New York Public Library/Art Resource, NY, **484–485** Annabelle Lee Washington/SuperStock; **488** Hulton/Archive Photos; **489** Reuters New Media Inc./CORBIS; **490** Tom Hulce/PhotoFest; **491** Timothy Fuller; **493** Curt Fischer; **494** (detail) Bulloz/bibliotheque Nationale, Paris; **495 496** Roger-Viollet; **498–513** One Nation Films, LLC; **H2** (t)Timothy Fuller, (c)Pictor, (b)John Evans; **H3** Timothy Fuller; **H6** (tl tr)Timothy Fuller, (bl)John Evans, (br)Aaron Haupt; **H7** Timothy Fuller; **H10** (t)Timothy Fuller, (cl cr)Larry Hamill, (bl br)Curt Fischer; **H12** (t)Aaron Haupt, (c)Larry Hamill, (b)Icone/The Image Works; **H13** (t)Larry Hamill, (b)Stan Ries/International Stock; **H17** Larry Hamill; **H18** (t)Serge Coupe/La Phototheque, SDP-DIAF, (cr)Timothy Fuller, (others)PhotoDisc; **H19** Rosine Mazin/DIAF; **H20** (b)Timothy Fuller, (others)Mark Burnett; **H32** Sitki Tarlan/Panoramic Images.